The Charismatic Leader

Quaid-i-Azam Mohammad Ali Jinnah and
the Creation of Pakistan

The Charismatic Leader
Quaid-i-Azam Mohammad Ali Jinnah and
the Creation of Pakistan

S<small>IKANDAR</small> H<small>AYAT</small>

OXFORD
UNIVERSITY PRESS

954.
9
Max

OXFORD
UNIVERSITY PRESS

Great Clarendon Street, Oxford OX2 6DP

Oxford University Press is a department of the University of Oxford.
It furthers the University's objective of excellence in research, scholarship,
and education by publishing worldwide in

Oxford New York

Auckland Cape Town Dar es Salaam Hong Kong Karachi
Kuala Lumpur Madrid Melbourne Mexico City Nairobi
New Delhi Shanghai Taipei Toronto
with offices in
Argentina Austria Brazil Chile Czech Republic France Greece
Guatemala Hungary Italy Japan Poland Portugal Singapore
South Korea Switzerland Turkey Ukraine Vietnam

Oxford is a registered trade mark of Oxford University Press
in the UK and in certain other countries

ISBN 978-0-19-547475-6

Typeset in Bembo
Printed in Pakistan by
Print Vision, Karachi.
Published by
Ameena Saiyid, Oxford University Press
No. 38, Sector 15, Korangi Industrial Area, PO Box 8214
Karachi-74900, Pakistan.

For

Samina

Contents

Preface

1976, the birth centennial year of *Quaid-i-Azam* (Great Leader) Mohammad Ali Jinnah (1876-1948), celebrated in Pakistan with a host of activities, including an international conference in Islamabad, marked the beginning of a renewed interest in the study of Mohammad Ali Jinnah not only in Pakistan, but also in Britain, the United States of America, and indeed, in many parts of the world. Writers from different disciplines and persuasions came together to contribute to a greater understanding of the political life and career of Mohammad Ali Jinnah, his demand for Pakistan, and its ultimate creation in August 1947. Soon after, a number of doctoral dissertations also contributed in the process. One of them was my dissertation entitled, 'Quaid-i-Azam Mohammad Ali Jinnah and the Creation of Pakistan: A Study in Political Leadership', submitted in 1986 to the Department of History at the Quaid-i-Azam University (named after the Quaid-i-Azam in 1976), Islamabad. The dissertation revolved around the concept of charisma and the emergence of the charismatic leadership of Jinnah in 1937–47, the last decade of British rule in India. Research papers based upon sections of the dissertation were subsequently published in national and international journals from time to time and I am truly grateful to all these publishers. In particular, I would like to thank publishers of the *Journal of South Asian and Middle Eastern Studies*; *Asian Profile; Pakistan Journal of History and Culture* (Islamabad); *Journal of Pakistan Historical Society* (Karachi); *Journal of the Research Society of Pakistan* (Lahore); and *South Asian Studies* (Lahore). The dissertation, as a whole, however, remained unpublished and thus mostly inaccessible to interested scholars and informed readers.

Over this long period of time, I have not found much to change my assessment of the charismatic nature of Jinnah's political leadership. A number of subsequent studies have also described Jinnah as a charismatic leader of Muslim India and Pakistan. In most cases, it was mere appellation rather than an analytical usage of the concept of charisma to describe the political leadership. Still, encouraged by this development I thought I owed it to a larger community of readers to review and rework my dissertation into a book and share my ideas with them. In the process, of course, I have consulted and engaged with a number of renowned scholars on the subject. The result is this systematic, conceptual study of Jinnah's charisma and charismatic leadership.

In the course of research, writing, and publication of this book, I have incurred many more debts of gratitude that can be recounted here. First of all, I am indebted to my dissertation supervisors, Professors (late) Waheed-uz-Zaman and Muhammad Aslam Syed who supported me in pursuing a conceptual framework for the analysis of Jinnah's political leadership, a not very common historiographic approach amongst Pakistani scholars. Throughout the period of my dissertation research and ever since, till the completion of this book, I was helped and encouraged by Professor Sharif al Mujahid, a leading authority on Jinnah and the founder Director of the Quaid-i-Azam Academy, Karachi (1976–89). He readily shared with me his vast knowledge, expertise and insights on Jinnah. I am grateful to him. I am also grateful to Ilhan Niaz, my young colleague at the Quaid-i-Azam University's Department of History, for generously spending his time and energy for reading the whole manuscript, suggesting ways and means to improve the text both intellectually and technically, typing the manuscript, and indeed, being instrumental in bringing the dissertation and manuscript into a book form. I am most thankful to my friend and colleague, Professor Mohammad Waseem for his invaluable advice and comments on the manuscript which helped me reconsider some of my arguments. I benefited greatly from interaction with numerous students at the Quaid-i-Azam University who took courses with me on political leadership and politics of Pakistan. One of my students, Mohammad Naeem, helped me check the sources used in this book. I am thankful to him for his tireless efforts. I am also thankful to Muhammad Altaf for computerizing the original dissertation.

I owe a special debt of gratitude to a number of scholars who stimulated my interest in the subject and provided much of my knowledge. I am particularly grateful to Professors Ainslie Embree, Howard Wriggins, Stanley Wolpert, Lawrence Ziring, Craig Baxter, Charles Kennedy, David Gilmartin, Hafeez Malik, Afak Hayder, Anwar Syed, Ian Talbot, Z.H. Zaidi, Rafique Afzal, Naeem Qureshi, and Sayed

Wiqar Ali Shah. I also wish to thank my colleagues at the History Department, especially Riaz Ahmad, Iftikhar H. Malik, Waheed Ahmad, Dushka H. Saiyid, Razia Sultana, Masood Akhtar, (late) Aziz Ahmed, Javed Haider Syed, Rabia Umar Ali, Tanvir Anjum, and Farooq Ahmad Dar for all their support. I am indebted to many scholars and colleagues who have helped me in numerous ways, some of them having continually urged me to publish my work on Jinnah. In particular, I would like to thank Saeed Shafqat, Ahmad Hassan Dani, K.F. Yusuf, Fateh Mohammad Malik, Pervaiz Iqbal Cheema, Rifaat Hussain, Saeeduddin Ahmad Dar, Ijaz Hussain, Tahir Amin, Rasul Bakhsh Rais, Tariq Rahman, Ghulam Hyder Sindhi, Lal Baha, Hassan Askari-Rizvi, Qalb-i-Abid, Mussarat Abid, Iqbal Chawla, and Munir Ahmad Baloch. I would also like to thank Ameena Saiyid, Managing Director, Oxford University Press for her personal interest and help in the publication of the book. I am also thankful to my editor, Rehana Khandwalla, for all her efforts in making the book possible in its present form.

I am indebted to a number of institutions for invaluable help during the various phases of research. I am particularly indebted to the American Institute of Pakistan Studies which, through its Scholar-in-Residence programme, facilitated my stay in the United States in 1995–96, to seek relevant sources, and initiate sustained work on this study. I also gratefully acknowledge the support provided by the Quaid-i-Azam University in 2003–4 to pursue research in Pakistan. I am thankful to the staff of the National Archives of Pakistan, Islamabad, and the Archives of the Freedom Movement of the University of Karachi, as well as the libraries of the Quaid-i-Azam Academy, Karachi; National Assembly of Pakistan, Islamabad; National Institute of Historical and Cultural Research, Islamabad; National Institute of Pakistan Studies, Islamabad; and last, but not least, the Quaid-i-Azam University, Islamabad. Their help and cooperation was immensely useful. However, I must add that any mistakes or errors in facts or interpretations are solely mine. No individual or institution is responsible for them.

Finally, I wish to express my profound gratitude to my family, my wife, Samina, and my children, Tehnia (Tina), Umar and Ali, and my son-in-law, Nauman, for their patience, understanding and support through the various hazards of research and publication of the book.

Introduction

The basic theme of this book is that Quaid-i-Azam Mohammad Ali Jinnah[1] was a charismatic leader of Indian Muslims and the role he played in directing and determining events in the cataclysmic decade of 1937–47 led to the creation of Pakistan. His personality, matured by decades of experience as a prominent political leader, his abilities as a constitutionalist and lawyer, his deep commitment towards Muslim interests and demands, his knack for offering viable formulas to promote and protect Muslim interests, his capacity for organization, his strategic thinking and tactical skills, and above all, his absolute faith in himself and his cause, contributed to his emergence as the charismatic leader of Muslim India.

In this process Jinnah was, of course, helped by a host of situational factors including the persistence of the Hindu–Muslim problem, the inadequacy of the system of government introduced by the British in India, based as it was on the majority principle, the devolution of British authority in India, especially during the war years, and most importantly, the failure of the Muslim 'traditional' leadership to show a way out of the difficulties faced by the Muslims as India moved towards self-government and freedom. The result was that the Muslims faced a distressful situation. Indeed, it was because of this situation that they turned to Jinnah who had the necessary qualities and was willing and ready to lead them into a safe and secure future.

Although recognized by a significant number of Muslims in 1937 as the right man to address the distressful situation of Muslim India, and hence a charismatic leader, the validation of his charisma had to wait until Jinnah could offer a 'formula' that would galvanize the Muslims and precipitate a solution of the crises they were confronted with. In March 1940, Jinnah demanded a separate homeland for the Muslims—Pakistan—evoking an enthusiastic and emotional response from a vast majority of the Muslims throughout the length and breadth of India. This response, and the popular recognition of his leadership in the process, validated and enhanced his charisma. However, formulas alone do not overcome crises. Jinnah had to mobilize and organize the Muslims around his demand for Pakistan before he could force the British and the Indian National Congress (founded in 1885) to accept it. He had to reorganize the All-India Muslim League (founded in 1906), his own political party since 1913. The Muslim League was to represent him as 'the sole, representative body of Muslim India'. The League, of course, could not accommodate all of his charisma which, besides a host of Muslim social groups and classes, both traditional and modern, extended to the Muslim masses, and not all of them necessarily interested in the League or involved in party politics. The masses responded directly to his personal charisma and the demand for Pakistan.

In colonial societies, charismatic leaders were often up against powerful, authoritarian rulers. The charismatic leaders did not hold office or instruments of power. Thus, they treaded weary paths in compelling their rulers to concede the principle of their demands, and once they succeeded, negotiations began on matters of substance (territory, assets, obligations, etc.) Often, the actual substance conceded fell short of the demands. In this situation, the real test of the leaders' charisma was whether they had earned enough recognition, respect, and trust from their followers to enable them to adjust or compromise on their demands. Jinnah, as his response to the Cabinet Mission Plan of 1946 (within the Indian Union) and the 3 June Partition Plan of 1947 (with the Muslim-majority provinces of the Punjab and Bengal divided) showed, did possess that kind of trust which allowed him to 'compromise' on details without losing his charismatic authority.[2] Indeed, all the evidence suggests that with the creation of Pakistan in August 1947, his charisma was at its 'zenith'. The Muslims realized their ultimate goal of Pakistan under his charismatic political leadership.

Several prominent scholars have recognized Jinnah to be a charismatic leader including Waheed-uz-Zaman, Sharif al Mujahid, R.J. Moore, and Stanley Wolpert.[3] Others have denied charisma to Jinnah and offered alternative explanations for his rise and role as the undisputed leader of Indian Muslims from 1937–47. Some of the more important studies may be summarized under the following hypotheses:

1. 'Saviour' hypothesis—Z.A. Suleri, A.A. Ravoof, S.A. Lateef, M.H. Saiyid, Sharif al Mujahid, G. Allana, Mohammad Noman,

Khalid bin Sayeed, Saleem M.M. Qureshi, Abdul Hamid, Waheed-uz-Zaman, H.V. Hodson, Z.H. Zaidi, and Ian Talbot, tend to emphasize the redemptive nature of Jinnah's political leadership.[4]

2. 'Personal' power hypothesis—B.R. Ambedkar, William Metz, and Ayesha Jalal explore Jinnah's leadership in terms of power for himself.[5] He wanted to be 'the sole spokesman of all Muslims.'[6]

3. 'Vacuum' hypothesis—Saleem Qureshi, S.M. Ikram and Waheed-uz-Zaman suggest that Jinnah emerged as the undisputed leader of Muslim India only because there was no other leader of stature available to lead the Muslims at that point in time.[7]

4. 'Congruence' hypothesis—Sayeed, Hodson, Mujahid, and Moore explain the leadership of Jinnah in terms of congruence between his personal needs and those of the Muslims of India.[8]

5. 'Gandhi and Gandhi-dominated Congress' hypothesis—S.K. Majumdar, Suleri, Allana, Saiyid, Saleem Quershi, Waheed-uz-Zaman, Mujahid, and Wolpert, maintain that Jinnah's emergence in Muslim politics had much to do with the hostile, uncompromising attitude of Mohandas Karamchand Gandhi (1869–1948) and the Congress towards Jinnah, the Muslim League, and the Muslim community as a whole.[9]

All the above hypotheses create two problems in particular. First, few writers confine themselves to any one explanation. They offer several explanations and obviously not all of them are mutually compatible. Secondly, some explanations are untenable. For instance, one finds it very difficult to believe that a saviour leader could play the role of a saviour simply because of the acts of commission and omission of an adversary forcing it on him. It is equally hard to maintain that a leader called upon to lead a distressed people could be a product of vacuum conditions. It also seems unconvincing to suggest that a leader seeking power for its own sake may readily find congruity with the interests of the people he is scheming to control and dominate. On the other hand, it is difficult to conceive of a political leader who will not be interested in power, if not for its own sake, at least in the first place. But then, power does not come to a leader simply by his or her own seeking. It comes from the response of the people, community or nation he is trying to lead. Leadership is not a function of the leader acting alone, above and independent of the led. Leadership is a 'group' process. It involves both the leader and the led. More importantly, these hypotheses or explanations do not offer any conceptual framework. For instance, we do not know exactly how Jinnah emerged as a saviour leader, although all the proponents of this explanation stress his personal qualities and the difficult times. Nor do we know from these explanations how Jinnah was able to evoke the kind of response he received from his followers, or what sustained him in his leadership role, or how did he actually manage to lead his followers in the struggle for the creation of Pakistan. Indeed, we do not know about the leadership behaviour and processes at all. We do not really follow Jinnah's political leadership.

The present study is an effort to answer some of these questions by analyzing Jinnah's political leadership conceptually through the concept of charisma and charismatic leadership. Formulated by Max Weber,[10] and developed systematically by a host of writers on the subject including Edward A. Shils, David E. Apter, Ann and Dorothy Ruth Willners, Dankwart A. Rustow, and Robert C. Tucker,[11] the concept of charisma offers a useful framework for the analysis of political leaders in the developing societies in general and the colonial societies in particular. This framework has been applied to the case of Jinnah by organizing the study into the following chapters.

Chapter 1 builds the conceptual framework of charisma at some length after establishing the need for studying Jinnah as a charismatic leader and after identifying the conceptual difficulties and the resultant conflicting interpretations in the accounts of writers who attribute charisma to Jinnah as well as those who argue that he could not be described as a charismatic leader given their understanding of the concept. Weber's own formulations are discussed in detail to explain and clarify the concept. In this context, the ascetic-rational perspective emerging from his later writings, the 'Second Perspective', as it is called here, is carefully highlighted. This is reinforced by the contributions of Shils, Apter, the Willners, Rustow, and Tucker, who developed the concept more as an instrument of political modernization and change in the developing societies. Finally, in the light of the foregoing, a general framework emphasizing both 'personality' and 'situational' factors for a systematic analysis of charisma and charismatic leadership is outlined.

Chapter 2 analyzes Jinnah's early political career leading up to his emergence as the charismatic leader of Muslim India in the late 1930s, as Quaid-i-Azam. The idea is to trace the origins of his charisma long before the attainment of the charismatic status itself. In this context, all the relevant developments, particularly those related to his efforts to reconcile Muslim interests with all-India national interests and to promote Hindu–Muslim unity are discussed. His disappointments with the Congress and its leadership, especially during the Congress rule of the provinces in 1937–39, the system of government being inherently biased in favour of Hindu majority community, and the anxieties and despair of the Muslims in the changed circumstance of the Second World War, are dealt with here. In the end, his realization that Muslim interests could not be secured in a united India and as a 'minority' and that the Muslims were a 'nation' and thus entitled to self-rule and freedom is highlighted. Finally, an effort is made to stress the personality-related factors that made him an ideal charismatic leader of the Muslims.

Chapters 3 and 4 identify and discuss the distressful situation of Muslim India in the 1930s, affected by a number of crises, including systemic and leadership crises. In Chapter 3, the systemic crisis is discussed at length. This crisis covered the whole socio-political system and comprised communal, constitutional, and devolutionary dimensions. The three dimensions were interrelated and tended to reinforce each other. Hindu-Muslim communalism led to the constitutional problem and the two, together, exacerbated Muslim fears as the devolution of British authority in India, especially during the war years, hastened the prospect of Hindu-majority rule in the country. This systemic crisis, along with the leadership crisis, contributed to Jinnah's emergence as the charismatic leader of the Muslims.

Chapter 4 describes the role of Muslim traditional political leadership, comprising social elites, provincial leadership, and the *ulama*, and highlights their failure to show the Muslims a way out of the crises they were faced with as India advanced towards freedom. Their failures facilitated the emergence of Jinnah as the charismatic leader of Muslim India. Indeed, one important argument of this study is that Jinnah did not emerge as the charismatic leader simply because there was no one else available and willing to give the lead. In fact, there were too many leaders. The problem was that they lacked the capability to deliver the goods. They had little understanding of the distressful Muslim situation, let alone the capacity to suggest any clear-cut idea or 'formula' to alleviate their distress. A number of prominent Muslim leaders such as the Aga Khan, Sir Sultan Mohammad Shah (1877–1957), Sir Mian Fazl-i-Husain (1877–1936), Sir Sikandar Hayat Khan (1892–1942), Sir Malik Khizar Hayat Khan Tiwana (1900–1975), Maulana Abul Kalam Azad (1889–1958), and Maulana Hussain Ahmad Madani (1879–1957), are discussed in particular.

Chapter 5 concentrates upon Jinnah's 'formula' of a separate homeland for the Muslims to alleviate their distressful situation. As expressed in the Lahore Resolution of 1940, the formula promised them power, security, and a sense of purpose in their own homeland. An effort is made to explain both the content and context of this formula. In particular, the criticism of some writers that it was inspired by the British to counter the Congress demand for independence is carefully addressed. An effort is also made to highlight Muslim and Hindu responses to the Resolution, especially the Hindu opposition to the 'vivisection' of India. Finally, some of the ambiguities implied in the Resolution are clarified. Although the title of Quaid-i-Azam was conferred upon Jinnah as early as 1938, it was the Lahore Resolution, and the enthusiastic Muslim response to it, that validated Jinnah's charisma in the eyes of his followers and truly made him their *Quaid-i-Azam*.

Chapter 6 highlights the role Jinnah played in mobilizing and organizing the Muslims through the All-India Muslim League. This was not to be an easy task. The Muslim League was moribund and dominated by the old traditional groups. The modern groups, especially the educated, urban middle-classes, professionals, women and students had no part in it. Then, there were the provincial leaders of the Muslim-majority provinces who were keen to pursue their own narrow, provincial interests, and thus keep the League out of these provinces, the mainstay of the Lahore Resolution and the Pakistan demand. They were not prepared to yield to the central, unifying authority of the League. What did Jinnah do? What kind of strategy did he devise? How did he reorganize the League to accommodate both traditional and modern groups? How did he deal with the provincial leaders? What was the nature and scope of his charismatic appeal? How did it work? How did he succeed in mobilizing the Muslim masses and winning the 1945–46 elections? Who helped him and how? How did he deal with the war situation and to what effect? These and other related questions are addressed to explain the development of the League as 'the sole representative body' of the Muslims, ready at last to deal with its powerful adversaries, the British and the Congress.

Chapter 7 covers the intense political and constitutional struggle against the British rulers and the Congress leadership to create Pakistan. An attempt is made to explore and examine Jinnah's strategy for the purpose, particularly during the war years, when the British were most vulnerable and the Congress out of the contest for the most part. In fact, it was this war-time strategy, insisting on the Pakistan demand in particular, that made Pakistan the main issue in all negotiations between the League and the British, and the League and the Congress, and indeed, the three of them together. Even the Cabinet Mission Plan of 1946, which denied Jinnah his demand for a sovereign Pakistan comprising the Muslim-majority provinces of India, conceded the 'right to secession' from the Indian Union. But, still, Jinnah's acceptance of the Cabinet Mission Plan remained one of the most difficult and perplexing questions for historians and political scientists working on the politics of modern South Asia. An effort is made to explain and explicate it. Finally, developments related to the eventual rejection of the Cabinet Mission Plan, 'Direct Action Day', Interim Government, and the ultimate creation of Pakistan in August 1947 are discussed. In the process, of course, the issue of division of the Muslim-majority provinces of the Punjab and Bengal is also addressed. In the end, Pakistan of 1947 was a 'compromise' and not a 'settlement'. It was 'the only solution' of the Indian problem and the only way out for the Muslims in the prevalent distressful situation. The Muslims were elated, making Pakistan the crowning achievement of Jinnah's charisma and charismatic leadership.

Finally, the study evaluates Jinnah's role as a charismatic leader and reflects on the concept of charisma itself in a broad and comparative perspective. A number of charismatic leaders are identified for the purpose. The discussion suggests that charismatic leaders share several traits and thus are a type by themselves. They need to be distinguished from other types of leaders in any meaningful analysis of political leadership. They should be studied separately and for their own sake in the light of a conceptual framework of charisma and charismatic leadership.

Notes

1. Originally Jinnahbhai, the ending of the name, 'bhai', was dropped by Jinnah during his stay in London in 1896. See his letter to the Steward of Lincoln's Inn in this regard in Saleem Qureshi, comp., *Jinnah: The Founder of Pakistan* (Karachi: Oxford University Press, 1998), 59.

2. See Jinnah's speech on 3 June 1947 and the League Council's resolution of 10 June 1947, on the 3 June Partition Plan. Jamil-ud-Din Ahmad, ed., *Speeches and Writings of Mr Jinnah*, Vol. II (Lahore: Sh. Muhammad Ashraf, 1976), 394–95; and Syed Sharifuddin Pirzada, ed., *Foundations of Pakistan: All India Muslim League Documents, 1906–1947*, Vol. II (Karachi: National Publishing House, 1970), 568.

3. Waheed-uz-Zaman, *Quaid-i-Azam Mohammad Ali Jinnah: Myth and Reality* (Islamabad: National Institute of Historical and Cultural Research, 1985); Sharif al Mujahid, *Quaid-i-Azam Jinnah: Studies in Interpretation* (Karachi: Quaid-i-Azam Academy, 1981); R.J. Moore, 'Jinnah and the Pakistan Demand', *Modern South Asian Studies*, Vol. 17, No. 4 (1983); and Stanley Wolpert, *Jinnah of Pakistan* (New York: Oxford University Press, 1984).

4. Z.A. Suleri, *My Leader* (Lahore: Nawa-i-Waqt Press, 1973); A.A. Ravoof, *Meet Mr Jinnah* (Lahore: Sh. Muhammad Ashraf, 1955); S.A. Lateef, *The Great Leader* (Lahore: Lion Press, 1947); Matlubul Hasan Saiyid, *Mohammad Ali Jinnah: A Political Study* (Karachi: Elite Publishers, 1970); Mujahid, *Studies in Interpretation*; G. Allana, *Quaid-i-Azam Jinnah: The Story of a Nation* (Lahore: Ferozsons, 1967); Mohammad Noman, *Muslim India: Rise and Growth of the All-India Muslim League* (Allahabad: Kitabistan, 1942); Khalid bin Sayeed, *Pakistan: The Formative Phase, 1858–1947* (London: Oxford University Press, 1968) and 'The Personality of Jinnah and his Political Strategy', in C.H. Philips and Mary Doreen Wainwright, eds., *The Partition of India: Policies and Perspectives, 1935–1947* (London: George Allen & Unwin, 1970); Saleem M.M. Qureshi, *Jinnah and the Making of a Nation* (Karachi: Council for Pakistan Studies, 1969) and 'The Consolidation of Leadership in the Last Phase of the Politics of the All-India Muslim League', *Asian Profile*, 1:2 (October 1973); Abdul Hamid, *On Understanding the Quaid-i-Azam* (Lahore: National Committee for Birth Centenary Celebrations of Quaid-i-Azam Mohammad Ali Jinnah, 1977); Waheed-uz-Zaman, *Myth and Reality*; H.V. Hodson, *The Great Divide* (London: Hutchinson, 1969); Z.H. Zaidi, 'Introduction', in Z.H. Zaidi, ed., *Quaid-i-Azam Mohammad Ali Jinnah Papers: Prelude to Pakistan, 20 February–2 June 1947*, Vol. I, Part I (Islamabad: National Archives of Pakistan, 1993) and Z.H. Zaidi, 'Aspects of the Development of Muslim League Policy, 1937–47', in Philips, and Wainwright, *Partition of India;* and Ian Talbot, *India and Pakistan: Inventing the Nation* (London: Arnold, 2000).

5. B.R. Ambedkar, *Pakistan or the Partition of India* (Bombay: Thacker & Co., 1946); William Metz, 'The Political Career of Mohammad Ali Jinnah', Ph.D. Dissertation, University of Pennsylvania, 1952; and Ayesha Jalal, *The Sole Spokesman: Jinnah, the Muslim League and the Demand for Pakistan* (Cambridge: Cambridge University Press, 1985).

6. Jalal, *The Sole Spokesman,* 130.

7. Saleem Qureshi, *Jinnah and the Making of a Nation*; S.M. Ikram, *Modern Muslim India and the Birth of Pakistan* (Lahore: Sh. Muhammad Ashraf, 1970); and Waheed-uz-Zaman, *Myth and Reality*.

8. Sayeed, *Formative Phase;* Hodson, *Great Divide*; Mujahid, *Studies in Interpretation*; and Moore, 'Jinnah and the Pakistan Demand.'

9. S.K. Majumdar, *Jinnah and Gandhi: Their Role in India's Quest for Freedom* (Lahore: People's Publishing House, 1976); Suleri, *My Leader*; Allana, *The Story of a Nation*; Saiyid, *A Political Study*; Saleem Qureshi, *Jinnah and the Making of a Nation* and 'The Consolidation of Leadership in the Last Phase of the Politics of the All-India Muslim League'; Waheed-uz-Zaman, *Myth and Reality*; Mujahid, *Studies in Interpretation*; and Wolpert, *Jinnah of Pakistan*.

10. Max Weber, *The Theory of Social and Economic Organization*, trans. and eds. A.R. Henderson and Talcott Parsons (New York: Free Press, 1947) and *From Max Weber: Essays in Sociology*, trans, ed., and with and introduction by H.H. Gerth and C. Wright Mills (New York: Oxford University Press, 1958). For some criticism of the concept in the theoretical literature see, Carl J. Friderich, 'Political Leadership and the Problem of Charismatic power', *The Journal of Politics*, Vol. 23, No. 1 (1961); K.J. Ratnam, 'Charisma and Political Leadership', *Political Studies*, Vol. XII, No. 3 (1964); and D.L. Cohen, 'The Concept of Charisma and Analysis of Leadership', *Political Studies*, Vol. XX, No. 3 (1972).

11. Edward A. Shils, 'Charisma, Order, and Status,' *American Sociological Review*, Vol. 30, No. 2 (1965) and 'The Concentration and Dispersion of Charisma', *World Politics*, Vol. XI, No. 1 (1958); David E. Apter, 'Nkrumah, Charisma, and the Coup', *Daedalus*, Vol. 97, No. 3 (1968); Ann Ruth Willner and Dorothy Willner, 'The Rise and Role of Charismatic Leaders', *The Annals of the Academy of Political and Social Sciences*, Vol. 358 (1965); Ann Ruth Willner, 'Charismatic Political Leadership: A Theory,' Princeton University Center of International Studies (1968) and *The Spellbinders: Charismatic Political Leadership* (New Haven: Yale University Press, 1984); Dankwart A. Rustow, 'Ataturk as Founder of a State', *Daedalus*, Vol. 97, No. 3 (1968); and Robert C. Tucker, 'The Theory of Charismatic Political Leadership', *Daedalus*, Vol. 97, No. 3 (1968).

1 Towards a Conceptual Framework of Charisma

In the 1930s, Indian Muslims confronted a severe political crisis. A feeling of 'despondency and helplessness'[1] prevailed among them. The Congress, under the guidance and inspiration of Gandhi, had opted for 'pure and unadulterated Nationalism' devoid of 'any kind of communalism', implying Muslim 'communalism'.[2] The British parliamentary system of government introduced into India was based on numbers that further convinced the Muslims that they constituted a 'minority' and a permanent one at that,[3] and thus could not wield much power at the centre. The outbreak of the Second World War, and the initial setbacks to the British in the region added to 'the vacuum of authority and very ambiguous expectations'.[4] Although they wanted an end to the British Raj in India, the Muslims could not accept an imminent Hindu rule in its place. Thus, they were in a state of despair. The Muslim traditional political leadership, comprising social elites (nobility, titled gentry, landowning classes), provincial/regional leaders and the *ulama*, especially those associated with the Jamiat-ul-Ulama-i-Hind (founded in 1919), were preoccupied with the promotion of their narrow sectional interests. They could not clearly see what 'freedom' would mean for the Muslims as a whole, as a community, let alone suggest any positive way out of their difficulties.[5] In Jinnah's own words, the Indian Muslims were 'Like a No Man's Land'.[6]

From 1932 to 1934, Jinnah was in self-imposed exile in London, disappointed with the attitude of both the Muslim and the Hindu leaders at the Round Table Conference (1930–32).[7] However, he remained deeply concerned with the fate of Muslims, and given their worsening situation at home, could not stay aloof. Responding to their pleas, and realizing the gravity of the situation they were confronted with, he did not hesitate to return to India to save them from 'the great danger' they faced.[8] In 1935, he eventually returned and as its elected President, systematically launched a campaign to reorganize the

All-India Muslim League, hoping that a revived Muslim League could secure and promote Muslim interests in the ensuing struggle for power in India. He felt confident that once the Muslim League was able to represent the vast majority of the Muslims, the Congress would be compelled to recognize it as a 'party'—an equal party—in the political life of India,[9] and indeed, would act to allay Muslim fears and apprehensions about their future. However, the Congress felt that freedom was around the corner and they need not worry about the League or its demands. In fact, during its rule of the Hindu-majority provinces from 1937 to 1939, the Congress insisted that the Muslims had no special claims or interests. They had to follow and trust the Congress, the inevitable successor to the British Empire in India.

Thus, convinced that the Congress was not willing to accomodate the Muslims and their special interests, Jinnah made the most important decision of his political career. He abandoned his life-long passion and search for 'Hindu-Muslim Unity' in the common cause of self-government for India. Instead, in March 1940, he offered the Muslims a 'formula' to alleviate their distress through the demand for a separate Muslim homeland comprising Muslim-majority areas of India. He claimed that Hindus and Muslims were two distinct 'nations'. They could never 'evolve a common nationality' for the simple reason that the 'Hindus and Muslims belong to two different religious philosophies, social customs, and literatures.'[10] In fact, he warned: 'To yoke together two such nations under a single state, one as a numerical minority and the other as a majority must lead to growing discontent and final destruction of any fabric that may be so built up for the government of such a state'.[11]

This was a clarion call to which the Muslims readily responded. The idea of a separate state stirred them and aroused feelings and aspirations of a host of Muslim groups and classes. The educated, urban middle-classes, merchant-industrialists, traders, bankers, and professionals, in particular, saw great opportunities in a state where they would be a majority and in power, and where the bureaucracy, army, industries, banks and professions would belong to them.[12] They realized that the new state would also provide them opportunities to 'work for the regeneration of Islam so that its people may climb to new heights of grandeur and its values be re-expressed in new concrete achievement'.[13] The Muslim masses already saw the prospects of an Islamic order in the new state. In this sense, the idea of a separate Muslim state came to offer the Muslims the only way out of the difficulties and into a promising and purposeful future. It soon became the symbol of their nationalism, their hopes, and their ultimate goal.

The years following the demand for a separate Muslim state, named Pakistan, saw the steady rise of Jinnah as the charismatic leader of Muslim India. The response of the Muslims to the demand and Jinnah's charismatic authority grew together. In the end, Jinnah became a 'living symbol of Muslim unity, Muslim aspirations and Muslim pugnacity'.[14] The Muslims saw him as their saviour and 'man of the moment'.[15] They followed him enthusiastically and conferred upon him the honorific title of 'Quaid-i-Azam'.[16]

Jinnah, however, could not remain content merely with a popular response to his call. He had to mobilize the Muslims for the creation of Pakistan. But, more importantly, he had to organize them on the platform of the Muslim League. He, therefore, planned and pursued a strategy that involved several initiatives. He started with the 'expansion' of the Muslim League to accommodate newly mobilized social groups and classes. He reinforced it with the 'concentration' of powers in the office of the President of the League to ensure a well-knit, disciplined organization capable of disciplining the strong-minded leaders of Muslim-majority provinces.[17] He followed it up with a political mobilization campaign to secure mass support for the League and Pakistan. Finally, he made a skillful use of the opportunities offered by the Second World War, especially the political mistakes committed by the Congress during the war years to develop the League as the most representative body of Indian Muslims.

In fact, the Second World War provided an ideal setting for Jinnah's strategic goal of Pakistan. The British were hard pressed to woo the non-Congress parties in the wake of the Congress's refusal to cooperate with the war effort. On 8 August 1940, Jinnah prompted them to declare that the British Government 'could not contemplate the transfer of their present responsibilities for the peace and welfare of India to any system of government' which was not acceptable to 'large and powerful elements in India's national life'.[18] In 1942, in the wake of the Cripps Proposals, Jinnah forced the British to recognize the 'principle of partition', for the first time.[19] Remaining persistent, and taking full advantage of the precarious situation created by the 'Quit

India' movement launched by the Congress in August 1942, Jinnah made the British 'face up to the root problem which was the problem of Pakistan'.[20] Refusing to yield to the 'Wavell Plan' of June–July 1945, at the Simla Conference, he 'reiterated his conviction that Pakistan was eventually both necessary and desirable.'[21]

With an enormous electoral victory in the 1945–46 elections on the Pakistan issue,[22] and convinced that the British were on their way out of India, Jinnah decided to deal with the government with a strong hand. Thus, when the Congress did not agree to a compulsory 'grouping' clause under the 1946 Cabinet Mission Plan, Jinnah refused to attend the newly constituted Constituent Assembly, and thereby destroyed the British–Congress concept of a 'united India'.[23] Resorting to 'direct action',[24] he finally created a situation where the partition of India emerged as the 'inevitable' alternative to civil war and chaos.[25] He told Lord Mountbatten (1900–1979), the last Viceroy of India, in a meeting in April 1947, 'there was only one solution, a 'surgical operation' on India'.[26] On 3 June 1947, the British Government was constrained to announce the partition of India. On 14 August 1947, Pakistan appeared on the map of the world as a separate and independent Muslim state.

The new nation-state of Pakistan received Jinnah with 'adulation amounting almost to worship'.[27] On 11 August 1947, the Constituent Assembly of Pakistan elected him as its first President, with the 'official' title of 'Quaid-i-Azam'. On 15 August he was sworn in as the first Governor-General of Pakistan. This was indeed the pinnacle of Jinnah's political career as the charismatic leader of Muslim India. Never before in the history of Muslim India, wrote one of his ardent followers:

> …had any single person attained such a political stature or had commanded such implicit confidence and trust of his people as did the Quaid-i-Azam. He was a man who…[with] his singleness of purpose, his unbending will and complete faith in the righteousness of his cause, created a nation with life and vision out of an exhausted, disarrayed and frustrated people.[28]

Jinnah was a leader of Indian Muslims even before he advocated the cause of the Muslim 'nation' in 1940.[29] He had received his 'first mead of general recognition' from the Muslims of India in 1913 in recognition of his tireless efforts in successfully piloting the *Waqf-alal-*

Aulad Bill, a matter of special concern to the community.[30] He was the chief architect of the Lucknow Pact of 1916, the only time the Congress conceded to the Muslims some of their most fundamental demands, including separate electorates.[31] He was the main formulator of Muslim interests and demands in the form of his now famous 'Fourteen Points' of 1929,[32] which remained the Muslim creed during the Round Table Conference in London in 1930–32.[33] He was the most prominent leader of the Muslim League all these years.[34] He was recognized for his character, courage, integrity and honesty.[35] He was known for his perseverance, political sense, organizational skills, and an extraordinary ability for identifying problems and finding viable solutions to them.[36] Yet, paradoxical as it may appear, he was not *the* leader. He was one of the more prominent of a number of British India's Muslim leaders.

It was only when Indian Muslims found themselves trapped between a distressful present and an uncertain future that they began to look up to him as their deliverer and urged him to lead them out of their predicament. The difference between the Jinnah of the earlier and later years was not so much in terms of his 'personal' qualities of leadership, but in the 'situation'.

This interplay between personality and the situational factors affecting political leadership is addressed clearly and convincingly in the accounts of Weber,[37] Shils, Apter, Ann and Dorothy Willners, Rustow, and Tucker,[38] the most authoritative exponents of the concept of charisma and charismatic leadership. Indeed, these exponents suggest a useful basis for the development of a systematic framework for the evaluation of charismatic leadership which is utilized here, in this study, to delineate and discuss the nature of Jinnah's political leadership.

Although a number of prominent scholars described Jinnah's leadership as 'charismatic', including Waheed-uz-Zaman, Sharif al Mujahid, R.J. Moore, and Stanley Wolpert[39], equally prominent scholars such as Khalid bin Sayeed and Saleem M.M. Qureshi[40] refused to apply the concept of charisma to Jinnah's political leadership. They did not regard Jinnah as a charismatic leader. In the process, they made it extremely difficult to comprehend the true nature of Jinnah's leadership. It will be useful, therefore, to examine their interpretations first before we make an effort to analyse the nature of Jinnah's political leadership ourselves. We must ascertain, in particular, whether it is a problem of information, theory or a combination of the two, which leads to conflicting interpretations. This will also help demonstrate how this analysis differs in form and substance from other analyses of Jinnah's charismatic political leadership.

A Critique of Conflicting Interpretations

To begin with the proponents of Jinnah's charismatic leadership, Waheed-uz-Zaman[41] holds that Jinnah emerged as the leader of Muslim India in the late 1930s when the 'political horizon' had been darkened with the indifferent, if not hostile, policies of the Congress towards the Muslims. Maulana Mohammed Ali (1874–1931) and Sir Mian Mohammad Shafi (1869–1932) were no more. Fazl-i-Husain was in poor health. The Aga Khan was no longer involved in Indian politics. Moreover, the Muslims, by and large, were fragmented. The two major organizations, the Muslim League and the Muslim Conference, were 'in a deplorable state of indiscipline and chaos'.[42]

According to Waheed-uz-Zaman, Jinnah was the only Muslim leader of national standing and stature. He had lost faith in the Congress led by Gandhi. In his opinion, 'The surprising thing is not that Jinnah left the Congress in the 1920s but that he did not quit it earlier'.[43] Indeed, to expect Jinnah to have stayed in the Congress 'in spite of Gandhi's ascendancy with Hindu philosophy as the guiding star of his politics', was 'highly unlikely'.[44] Jinnah came as 'a Divine gift to the submerged Muslim masses' of India,[45] offering them the prospect of an independent Muslim state as the only way out of their difficulties. But Waheed-uz-Zaman does not agree that Pakistan came into being merely because Jinnah 'willed' it: 'No one person, however charismatic his personality and however his hold over his people could have single-handedly carved an independent country....'[46] He believes that the Muslims, having 'once adopted the ideal of an independent Muslim state...were not prepared to settle for anything less than a sovereign status for the areas in which they command majorities and but for this Pakistan would have always remained a mere dream'.[47]

On the other hand, Sharif al Mujahid,[48] argues that Pakistan's creation was the direct result of Jinnah's 'bold and enchanting promise to restore political power' to the Muslims of India.[49] In this sense,

Jinnah 'answered their psychic need for endowing and sanctifying their sense of community with a sense of power'.[50] Indeed, Mujahid feels that, by 1940, Jinnah had discovered the 'Muslim soul' and was thus ready to give 'coherence and direction to the Muslims' innermost, but as yet vague, urges and aspirations' in the form of 'a viable permanent platform' in Pakistan.[51]

Thus, Mujahid argues that Pakistan could not have come into being but for Jinnah's leadership. Jinnah alone could bring the ideal within the compass of 'popular comprehension' by spelling it out in clear, practical and realizable terms, and then stand by it steadfastly and firmly. Mujahid believes that the Muslim League, without Jinnah, might have 'compromised' on the demand for Pakistan at various stages of its development, in 1942 (the Cripps Mission), 1944 (the Gandhi–Jinnah talks), 1945 (the Simla Conference), or at least in 1946 (the Cabinet Mission). The League might have agreed to the idea of a 'coalition' with the Congress at the centre, and would have thus 'lost' the battle for Pakistan. All through the critical years of the Pakistan movement, he argues, Jinnah's 'strategy' was not to join any coalition at the centre lest it got 'crystallized and became permanent'. It was only because of this strategy that 'alternative paths of development' for Muslim politics could not take root.[52]

Mujahid criticizes the deterministic view that Pakistan was somehow 'in the womb of time',[53] and would have come into being anyhow, regardless of Jinnah's leadership. He concedes that 'separatist tendencies' among the Muslims of India had been at work long before the emergence of Jinnah. But then, he insists, Jinnah did not simply receive 'influences', 'legacies' and 'supports' from these tendencies, he also gave as much to the concept and cause of Pakistan through his 'personal talent, and political and intellectual leadership, and concrete achievements'.[54] Jinnah 'represents a watershed between the past and the present, and *the* bridge between them as well'.[55]

Mujahid observes that, until the late 1930s, Jinnah's political career was 'largely unproductive', despite his 'brilliant qualities' of character. But then, the 'circumstances' had not crystallized enough to create a 'desire' and 'determination' among the Muslims to chart their own course. It was only when the 'confluence and configuration' of 'circumstances' and 'character' came about that Jinnah's leadership could come into its own, and he could be identified in the Muslim mind with the concept of a 'charismatic community', the concept 'whose dethronement, in mundane terms, had haunted Muslims ever since they had lost power to the British.' Jinnah emerged as a charismatic leader in the Weberian sense of the term.[56]

Similarly, R.J. Moore, seeks to clarify the relationship between Jinnah's political leadership, and the creation of Pakistan between 1937 and 1947, 'in terms of both his charisma and his constitutional strategy....'[57] The main thrust of his argument is that Jinnah, by the late 1930s, had come to suffer an 'acute sense of persecution' at the hands of the Congress and Gandhi. The Congress, under Gandhi's leadership and driven by 'the forces of Hindu orthodoxy' was not willing to accommodate him in the political life and processes of India. In fact, the Congress had no place for Jinnah in its scheme of things. Moore also suggests that Jinnah's woes did not end there. He was not trusted even by many Muslim leaders of the day, as was reflected during the course of the Round Table Conference in London. To add to all these difficulties, there was the tragedy in his private life, the estrangement and premature death of his wife, leaving him 'bereaved'.[58]

Moore believes that Jinnah was not alone in suffering persecution. By 1937, Muslim India, under Congress 'totalitarianism', had also come to suffer this sense of persecution. Jinnah's 'personality and experience' disposed him to feel 'bitterly' about this Muslim predicament. He 'internalized' the Muslims' sense of 'suffering' and 'sacrifice' from the 'fire of persecution'. He expressed the interest of Muslim India with personal conviction: 'I have got as much right to share in the government of this country as any Hindu'; and 'I must have (an) equal, real and effective share in the power'.[59] Thus, an 'extraordinary match of man and movement followed'.[60]

In Moore's view, the widespread assumptions about 'vanity, pride, ambition and megalomania'[61] or generalization about 'political style' exaggerate 'the intellectual distance between the leader and his followers', and obscure 'the doctrinal cut and thrust' from which emerged the constitutional strategy of Jinnah. He observes that the main element of this strategy was to speak of the Muslim League as the sole representative body of the Muslim nation, and thus seek 'parity' with Congress in the future constitution of India.[62] This, he maintains, was the logical extension and corollary of his 'two-nation' theory. The Congress refusal to yield to this theory led Jinnah to finally seek refuge from the perceived persecution in the separate state of Pakistan. Thus, according to Moore, Jinnah articulated neither 'the Koran's promise of political power nor memories of the Mughals but the Muslim's sense of persecution at the sudden threat to all he had achieved in the twentieth century'.[63]

Stanley Wolpert argues in the same vein. He explains Jinnah's rise and role in terms of the acts of commission and omission of the Congress in general and Gandhi and Pandit Jawaharlal Nehru (1889–1964) in particular. In his opinion, the 'Congress insults, stupidity, negligence, venality, genuine and imagined anti-Muslim feeling, fatigue, frustration, fears, doubts, hopes, shattered dreams, passions turned to ashes, pride—all contributed to the change in Jinnah. He would not go softly, or silently, into that dark night'.[64]

Wolpert contends that Jinnah and Gandhi 'seemed always to be sparring even before they put on any gloves'. They saw each other as 'natural enemies', rivals for national power, popularity, and charismatic control of their audiences, however small or awesomely vast they might become'.[65] In his opinion, this 'tone of their relationship' led to the partition of India. If Jinnah and Gandhi could have come to some better understanding of each other, they 'might even have avoided partition'.[66]

Indeed, according to Wolpert, by adopting different approaches to political processes, 'suited to different constituencies, attuned to different languages and goals, fashioned by different worlds', both went their separate ways.[67] In the process, Jinnah suffered 'humiliation and personal rejection' at Nagpur and Calcutta. However, this did not put him off. He discovered the importance of his 'Islamic identity'. He began a 'new phase of his political life', a 'more cautious ascent, by another route'.[68] He delivered his 'swan song to Indian nationalism'[69] by identifying Muslims as a 'separate and equal nation.'[70] He thought it 'far better to die fighting at the head of his own smaller party-nation' rather than subsist under the 'shadow' of a derisive 'enigma'.[71]

Wolpert observes that Nehru's attitude was not different from that of Gandhi. His 'political errors of judgment' in 'prodding and challenging' Jinnah to leave elitist politics and reach down to the Muslim masses helped him charter a course which would 'stir' the Muslim masses, 'awaken' them, and 'lure' them 'to march behind *Muslim* leadership', with the 'cry of Islam-in-danger'.[72] The result was that, in

March 1940, Jinnah 'lowered the final curtain on any prospects for a single united independent India'.[73] Finally, there was 'no reconciliation, no solution to the problem of fundamental mistrust, suspicion, fear and hatred'.[74] All that remained to be done was for his party, the Muslim League, his 'inchoate nation', and the British to agree to 'the formula he had resolved upon'.[75] In the process, Wolpert concludes, Jinnah emerged as 'one of the recent history's most charismatic leaders', who not only altered 'the course of history' and 'modified the map of the world', but also created a 'nation-state', a unique achievement in the annals of history.[76]

Khalid bin Sayeed does not accept Jinnah as a charismatic leader of Indian Muslims.[77] He argues that 'the secret of Jinnah's mesmeric hold over the Muslim masses'[78] lay in the fact that, through Pakistan, Jinnah was 'answering one of the deepest urges of the Muslim community, namely the fulfillment of the promise of political power that the Qur'an offered to Muslims', from which their forbears had strayed.[79] That is why, he believes, the Muslims of India considered it their 'religious duty' to follow Jinnah, 'who was prepared to unite the community and bring earthly glory to Islam', rather than the prominent religious leaders, such as Maulana Abul Kalam Azad or Maulana Hussain Ahmad Madani.[80]

According to Sayeed, there was congruence between the 'personal needs' and 'ambitions' of Jinnah and the 'needs' of the Muslim community.[81] Jinnah had received a rebuff in the 1920s not only in his political life, with the ascent of Gandhi in the Congress and in Indian politics in general, but had also experienced a disappointment in his personal life. The 'traumatic experience' of separation from his wife and her tragic death soon after in 1929 deeply affected him. He, therefore, 'sought power as a means of compensation for the deprivations that he had suffered'.[82] The Muslims, too, needed Jinnah for there was no one else to lead them. The death of Maulana Mohammed Ali had robbed Muslim India of the only other leader of 'sufficient stature to lead them'.[83] The result was that the Muslims turned to Jinnah as 'a great saviour'.[84]

However, Sayeed insists that Jinnah could not be described as a 'charismatic' leader in the Weberian sense. According to him, charismatic leaders are 'crowd compellers', that is, 'men who can conceive a great idea, mould a crowd big enough to carry it into effect and force the crowd to do it'. Jinnah's leadership 'cannot be explained away only in such terms'.[85] One can understand 'the greatness of a Gandhi or Churchill for they possessed on an elevated plane the inherent qualities of their respective races'. But Jinnah was 'so different from his people. The Muslims of India by reputation and by nature are warm-hearted people. And it continues to be an enigma how these people followed a leader who was so austere and so remote from them'.[86]

Strangely enough, Sayeed still referred to Jinnah's 'charisma' or 'charismatic leadership' in his estimate. For instance, in calling the Muslim League 'a nationalist movement' rather than a political party in the ordinary sense of the term, he suggests that this type of movement is always 'led by charismatic leaders'.[87] He acknowledges that the 'charismatic leadership of Jinnah' gave the Muslims 'a sense of power'.[88] He even goes on to claim that 'more charisma' was bestowed on Jinnah than he 'actually had'.[89] He also suggests that the League 'was not the only party' in India 'which developed the cult of leadership'. The Congress 'had also built up the charismatic authority' of Gandhi.[90]

On the other hand, Saleem M.M. Qureshi [91] proceeds from the premise that politics in India had 'always been dominated by personalities'.[92] In 1937, Jinnah assumed the leadership of Muslim India. In 1940, he gave the Muslims 'a positive goal to work for, a party, a flag and a programme to support and fight for'.[93] The result was that Jinnah became the 'supreme oracle' of Muslim nationalism, indeed, their Quaid-i-Azam.

In Qureshi's estimate, in this ascent to the political leadership of Muslim India, two factors contributed the most. One was 'the entry of Gandhi in Indian politics,' with all his 'mysticism' and 'religiosity,' and more importantly, his 'un-constitutional or extra-constitutional, non-violent, non-cooperation' methods, which helped his cause but rendered the Congress an 'uncomfortable political habitat' for Jinnah.[94] Gandhi's entry in the political arena also showed to Jinnah that the Congress brand of nationalism was in fact 'Hindu nationalism' under the guise of 'secularism'.[95] The other factor was the absence of effective Muslim leadership at the national level. The Aga Khan was no longer active on the political scene. Hakim Ajmal Khan (1863–1927), Maulana Mohammed Ali, Sir Mian Mohammad Shafi, and Dr Mukhtar Ahmad

Ansari (1880–1936) were dead, and Maulana Azad had joined the Congress. There was a 'vacuum' in the ranks of Muslim leadership.[96] Jinnah was the 'only leader of a stature and reputation' who was 'not only available but also eager to provide leadership of the kind acceptable' to the Muslims.[97]

According to Qureshi, Jinnah adopted the 'separatist creed' after his bitter experience of dealing with the Congress, especially after its rule in 1937–39, and after realizing the grave implications of the working of the 1935 Act, which granted 'a real measure of self-government' to the Indians, upon the Muslims in particular.[98] Jinnah's separatist 'words fell on extremely receptive ears' and the Muslim enthusiasm for politics 'swelled up again and acquired greater vitality', putting Jinnah 'on top of the Muslim political totem pole'.[99] Indeed, Qureshi insists that 'during the decade of the last phase [i.e., 1937–47] there was no Muslim rival to Jinnah's leadership'.[100]

However, Qureshi, like Sayeed, and for almost the same reasons, refuses to call Jinnah 'a charismatic leader'. He believes that the 'essential element in charisma' is the 'emotional involvement of the leaders with the followers'.[101] Jinnah was 'too much a man of cool, calculated deliberation, and reasoned logic to show any emotion'. Indeed, he claims, Jinnah had practically 'no emotions and he never tried to appear what he was not'.[102]

But then, Qureshi, like Sayeed, alludes to Jinnah's charisma again and again. For instance, he argues that it was Jinnah's 'identification' with the specific Muslim cause, his steadfastness, and total commitment to Muslim India, which 'transferred the emotional, charismatic appeal of the cause to the man espousing it'.[103] He notes that Jinnah's 'personal charisma' was such that Muslim masses 'sat spell-bound even without understanding a word while he spoke in English.'[104]

Thus, the arguments advanced both by proponents and dissenters of Jinnah's charismatic political leadership, strangely enough, reveal an almost identical explanation of the rise and role of Jinnah in the political life of Muslim India. Both stress that Jinnah emerged under very difficult circumstances in the late 1930s, when the Muslims were frustrated and in a state of despair. The Congress was not willing to accommodate Muslim rights and interests as India advanced towards self-government and freedom. The Congress was also not willing to concede political power to the Muslims. Thus, Jinnah took it upon himself to save the Muslims from their predicament. He showed them a way out in the form of a separate Muslim state, and through his able and devoted leadership, helped create Pakistan.

But then, the question arises: why should some writers define Jinnah's political leadership as 'charismatic' while others would disagree, especially when the information given is more or less the same. The answer lies in the understanding of the concept of charisma itself. Both proponents and dissenters of Jinnah's charismatic political leadership fail to follow the concept carefully.[105]

To begin with, none of the proponents of Jinnah's charismatic political leadership systematically defines the concept of charisma and charismatic leadership. Waheed-uz-Zaman and Wolpert seem to use it in the sense of 'popularity', more significantly the great extent of popularity, and the intensity with which the followers support their leaders. Moore's whole discussion about the 'persecution' of Muslim India and of Jinnah at the hands of the Congress is subsumed under the heading, 'Sources of Charisma', but there is no attempt at explaining the concept. Mujahid does well to talk about the concept of a 'charismatic community' but he does not quite dwell upon the rise and role of charismatic leaders in general and Jinnah in particular. Thus, in the absence of any precise definition and discussion of charisma on the part of these scholars, it is very difficult to see how Jinnah can be described as a charismatic leader in the real sense of the term.

The dissenters do not fare any better. Both Sayeed and Qureshi do not define 'charisma' in an analytical manner. Sayeed does make an effort to delineate the concept but depends on secondary sources for the purpose. He is content to rely upon the inferences drawn by Harold Lasswell, Abraham Kaplan, and Reinhard Bendix. These scholars are undoubtedly recognized and respected in the field, but their analyses do not cover the whole range of Weber's ideas especially his later writings. Both Sayeed and Qureshi could have benefited greatly from these writings.[106]

To further complicate matters, both Sayeed and Qureshi depend upon a peculiar perspective of charisma and charismatic leadership in Weber's ideas that stemmed from his 'anti-ascetic' thought prior to the First World War which equated charisma with 'the emotional' in politics. Using this criterion, they are convinced that Jinnah could not be considered a charismatic leader of Muslim India. Here, of course, they are not entirely wrong. Max Weber, in his unfinished, posthumously published work, *Wirtschaft und Gesellschaft* (1925), translated into English as the *Theory of Social and Economic Organization* (1947), and carrying for the most part the 'anti-ascetic' perspective, did consider charisma to be 'based on an emotional form of communal relationship'.[107]

But, then, there was another perspective too, particularly in his later writings. In *Politik als Beruf* (*Politics as a Vocation*),[108] Weber reformulates the concept into an 'ascetic-rational' code. He rules out the possibility of any useful transformation of *Gesellschaft* through a charismatic leader who was not organized, sober and rational. Weber adapts charisma to rationality, everyday routine of life, *alltag*, suggesting any kind of specifically irrational and 'emotional' behaviour of political leaders as 'false charisma'. Indeed, Weber made the rationality and sobriety of the charismatic leadership the necessary condition of the 'calling for politics'.[109]

Weber did not integrate the two perspectives into a final statement. This difficulty was further compounded by the fact that the first perspective on charisma and charismatic leadership gripped the English-speaking public, and consequently the transformation of the concept in the second perspective failed to impress the already impressed. The concept had come to be largely associated with the first perspective.

The recognition of Weber's second and final perspective at this stage might be hard, even uncomfortable, for the conformist scholar. Still it is the 'rational', rather than the 'emotional', perspective on charisma that must prevail. This perspective is the creation of Weber's own mind and will, and thus cannot be ignored in any meaningful discussion of the concept. It outlines the necessary framework in which the concept of charisma should be understood and analysed by all scholars.

As the present study sets out to analyse the nature of Jinnah's political leadership in the light of this framework, taking into account the second perspective, it will not be inappropriate to explore the two perspectives at some length first.

Max Weber's Concept of Charisma: First Perspective

The first perspective on charisma and charismatic leadership represents Max Weber's anti-ascetic conception of the extraordinary, 'supernatural', and 'superhuman' charismatic leaders with specifically exceptional powers or qualities.[110] It is not only opposed to the rational everyday life, but also considers the very idea of modernity and rationality a 'cultural catastrophe'. It expresses Weber's brief interest in 'mysticism' at that time and the influence of the flamboyant leadership of Kaiser Wilhelm II in Germany, and remains in force until the start of the First World War. Weber defines charisma as:

> …a certain quality of an individual personality by virtue of which he is set apart from ordinary men and treated as endowed with supernatural, superhuman, or at least specifically exceptional powers or qualities. These are such as are not accessible to the ordinary person but are regarded as of divine origin or as exemplary and on the basis of them the individual concerned is treated as a leader.[111]

Thus, charisma depends on 'recognition' by disciples and followers. The followers recognize charisma because they are inspired by a 'sign' or 'proof', initially always a 'miracle', emanating from the person of the charismatic leader. Psychologically, this recognition is a matter of 'complete personal devotion' to the charismatic leader born out of 'enthusiasm, despair, and hope'.[112] The result of this recognition on the part of the followers is that the charismatic leader must manage to demonstrate charismatic power to his followers if he has to retain his following. Thus, if the proof of charismatic power fails him for long, for his 'magical or heroic powers have deserted him', or if he is unsuccessful for long, or, 'above all, if his leadership fails to benefit his followers, it is likely that his charismatic authority will disappear'. This, in fact, is the genuine meaning of '*gift of grace*'.[113]

The charismatic leader-follower relationship is essentially 'an emotional form of communal relationship'. The charismatic leader and his followers live in a relationship where there is no administrative hierarchy or a clear-cut sphere of authority and no appropriation of official powers and functions. There is but only a "call' at the instance of the leader....'[114]

The charismatic rule is not managed according to general norms, either traditional or rational, but in principle, revolves around 'judgements' originally perceived to be 'divine judgements and revelations'. The charismatic leader 'preaches, creates, or demands new obligations', and the followers tend to obey. It is their 'duty'. They subscribe to the proposition: 'It is written...but I say unto you'.[115] The charismatic authority is not bound to the existing order. It is specifically 'outside the realm of everyday routine and the profane sphere', and is thus 'irrational in the sense of being foreign to all rules'.[116] The only source of 'legitimacy' is 'personal charisma,' as long as it is 'proved', has 'recognition, and is able to satisfy the followers or disciples'.[117]

However, according to Weber, charisma is not only foreign to rules but also 'specifically foreign to economic considerations'. While it does not always renounce property or even its acquisition, it despises the 'traditional or rational every-day economizing, the attainment of a regular income by continuous economic activity devoted to this end'. In this sense, it is a 'a typical anti-economic force', and does not recognize appropriation of positions of power by virtue of the possession of the property, either on the part of the charismatic leader or of socially privileged groups under his authority.[118]

In the 'traditionally stereotyped periods' of history, charisma is 'the greatest revolutionary force'.[119] While the 'equally revolutionary' force of 'reason' influences from outside 'by altering the situation of action, and hence its problems', charisma works upon 'subjective' or 'internal reorientation' of the followers 'born out of suffering, conflicts, or enthusiasm'. It encourages men not only to alter their perceptions and 'attitudes', but also helps them acquire a 'completely new orientation of all attitudes towards the different problems and structures of the 'world'.[120]

The very fact that charisma has a 'character' specifically foreign to daily routine and economic considerations makes it, essentially, 'a purely transitory phenomenon'.[121] In order to take on the character of a 'permanent relationship forming a stable community of disciples or a band of followers or a party organization', it is therefore imperative for 'the character of charismatic authority' to become institutionalized through a process of 'routinization' of charisma. It becomes 'either traditionalized or rationalized', or evolves into 'a combination of both'. In this process, of course, it is helped by 'the ideal and also material interests' of the followers and disciples who seek the charismatic leadership for their own good.[122]

Weber's Second Perspective

The second perspective on charisma and charismatic leadership represents the transformation of the concept into an ascetic-rational construct. Distressed by the disaster inflicted upon imperial Germany by the irrational and irresponsible leadership of Wilhelm II during the First World War and subsequently encouraged by the rise of the so-called 'genuine' charismatic movements in the post-war Germany, Weber sees no necessary contradiction between charisma and rationalization.[123] He even suggests 'the adaptation of the charismatic spirit to the increasingly rationalized and organized mass politics of the modern age'.[124]

While Weber still defines charisma as the authority of the extraordinary and personal 'gift of grace', he rules out the development of a modern state through a charismatic leader who is not sober and rational and who does not work his politics, his 'vocation' through 'organized domination'.[125] He derides the earlier conditions in which the charismatic leader and his followers lived outside an organized economy and insists that the charismatic leader must be 'economically independent of the income politics can bring him'.[126] He 'must be wealthy or must have a personal position in life which yields a sufficient income'.[127] In fact, in his opinion, the significance of the economy was 'steadily rising', and with increasing emphasis on organized political activity, 'especially with increasing socialization', it may well be further augmented in future.[128]

The most significant aspect of this organized political activity is 'a relation of men' dominating men. There are men who dominate and there are men who obey. In general, the men obey out of 'highly robust motives of fear and hope'.[129] In the case of charismatic domination, 'the leader is personally recognized as the innerly "called" leader of men'.[130] But, then, men obey him not only because they believe in his person and his qualities but also because of 'material reward and social honour'.[131] However, Weber insists that the charismatic leader cannot become the decisive figure in political life unless he has at his disposal 'auxiliary means' to maintain and enforce his authority. He must have the means to force his followers to obey the authority he claims to represent. In other words, he must have 'control of the personal executive staff and the material implements of administration', an 'organization', essentially.[132]

The inevitable result of this 'organized domination' is that material means of control like political parties are required not only to encourage struggles for 'the patronage of office' and 'subjective goals' but also to retain the disciples and followers tied to the charismatic leader through specifically secure livelihoods in the form of 'spoils'.[133] In this sense, the political parties become, 'more and more a means of the end being provided for in this manner'.[134] The parties 'expect that the demagogic effect of the leader's *personality* during the election fight of the party will increase votes and mandates and thereby power, and, thereby, as far as possible, will extend opportunities to their followers to find the compensation for which they hope'.[135] Thus, the parties themselves prefer that 'the charismatic element of the leadership is at work in the party system'.[136]

However, Weber suggests that in spite of the fact that the charismatic leader is personally recognized by party members and followers, one of the conditions necessary for the 'success' of the charismatic leader is 'depersonalization' and 'routinization' of charisma, indeed in the interest of 'discipline'.[137] The discipline brings out the 'rational' transformation of the society and helps the charismatic leader in maintaining his alertness and superiority over his followers. The strongly conscious and rationally intended character of discipline may even help the charismatic leader to 'expand' his sphere of domination.[138] Indeed, Weber points out that many charismatic leaders created 'strict disciplinary' organizations, which helped build lasting dominions.[139]

Weber not only makes room for rational behaviour for charisma but also identifies certain rational qualities to be found in a charismatic leader. In particular, he demands, the qualities of 'responsibility' and 'a sense of proportion'.[140] Although he likes to retain the heroic quality of 'passion' (of the first perspective), he wants it tempered by reason. As he explains in some detail:

...passion in the sense of *matter of factness*, of passionate devotion to a 'cause'.... It is not passion in the sense of... 'sterile excitation' ...running into emptiness, devoid of all feeling of objective responsibility.

To be sure, mere passion, however, genuinely felt, is not enough. It does not make a politician, unless passion as devotion to a 'cause' also makes responsibility to this cause the guiding star of his action. And for this, a sense of proportion is needed. This is the decisive psychological quality of the politician: his ability to let realities work upon him with inner concentration and calmness. Hence his *distance* to things and men...that firm taming of the soul, which distinguishes the passionate politician and differentiates him from the 'sterilely excited' and mere political dilettante, is possible only through habituation to detachment in every sense of the word. The 'strength' of a political 'personality' means, in the first place, the possession of these qualities of passion, responsibility, and proportion.[141]

The rational ingredient in the code of the charismatic leader is so pervasive in Weber's account now that he does not hesitate to refer to him as a 'genuinely principled politician', a politician who, unlike a 'power politician', represents the ultimate ends of politics and a sense of responsibility and objectivity, and thus has the 'calling for politics' in the true sense of the word.[142] For politics, he contends:

...is a strong and slow boring of hard boards. It takes both passion and perspective. Certainly all historical experience confirms the truth—that man would not have attained the possible unless time and again he had reached out for the impossible. But to do that a man must be a leader, and not only a leader but a hero as well, in a very sober sense of the word.... Only he has the calling for politics who is sure that he shall not crumble when the world from his point of view is too stupid or too base for what he wants to offer. Only he who in the face of all this can say 'In spite of all!' has the calling for politics.[143]

The two perspectives, the first and the second, taken together, affirm that charisma, in essence, means a personal attribute of a charismatic leader, endowed with extraordinary qualities, and involves a relationship which is based on the recognition and validity of these qualities. Charisma is devotion of the disciples and followers born out of distress and enthusiasm. The charismatic leader not only conveys a sense of mission but also, indeed, helps followers to alleviate their distress through a completely new orientation of attitudes and goals.

However, while the first perspective suggests that charismatic leadership is not managed according to general rules and normal economic conditions, and is essentially 'irrational' and 'transitory' in nature, the second perspective leaves no doubt that charisma is fully compatible with normal economy and daily routine. The charismatic leader is reconciled to the economically and politically inevitable advance of modernity and is ready to give way to rational-legal forms of authority, forming an institutional and permanent relationship with his disciples and followers. He is a rational, sober leader, and is endowed with rational qualities of mind. He has a matter-of-fact approach to his 'cause', and thus he seeks 'distance' from others and pursues a policy of conscious 'detachment'. Indeed, Weber makes a clean break from the original spiritual substance of the concept. He sees charisma in the realm of rationality and a rational-legal order, and even suggests institutionalization through a process of routinization of charisma.

This process of institutionalization, however, is not as systematic as one would expect in the present discourse of social sciences,[144] and thus fails to provide an analytical guide for research. This problem is addressed by recent exponents of the concept, such as Shils, Apter, Willners, Rustow and Tucker who offer a number of propositions appropriate to the operability and systematization of the concept in the contemporary political world. They stress in particular the pattern in which charismatic leadership emerges and becomes institutionalized in the form of an alternative source of 'authority', especially in the societies undergoing crises of structural and behavioural ambiguity and uncertainty. They also show how charisma as a rational-ascetic force can lead these societies, quite realistically, into the world of 'modernization'. Broadly, they are scholars of political modernization and change, and thus, their contributions help us add a developmental dimension to the concept of charisma and charismatic leadership.

Charisma as an Instrument of Political Modernization and Change

Edward Shils employs the term 'charisma' and charismatic leadership to explain the role of political leaders in 'new' nations moving towards national integration and modernity.[145] He holds that the 'traditional' sector is rooted mainly in local, territorial and kinship groups, and is thus, for the most part, 'pre-political', and 'pre-national'. Political leaders who live in the 'modern' sector are 'often the creators of the new nation, and not merely of the new state', and are 'nationalized' and 'politicized'. Indeed, they are enraptured by 'the sacredness of the nation'.[146] This sacredness, which remained dormant for ages and is now alive in them, endows them with charismatic attributes. With the help of this sacred quality, they acquire the status and authority of charismatic leaders, and thus help move the ordinary people, peasants, and working men of their societies along the path of modernization and nationhood, incurring relatively little conflict in the process. The traditional leadership such as tribal chiefs, religious leaders, heads of kinship groups simply yield because they do not share the charisma of the nation and cannot compete with it.[147]

David Apter maintains that the conflict between traditional and modern values creates a moral and structural vacuum, which induces a 'heroic' leader to step in and bestow instant 'political grace' by forcing new standards and norms associated with his own behaviour.[148] But this behaviour, he insists, needs a structural variable. Charisma 'can only affect behaviour when it consolidates itself in a new structural system'.[149] In his opinion, Kwame Nkrumah failed in Ghana because he could not alter the structure of political interests and motivations of his followers. Ghana was at an early stage of development, and 'traditionalism' still flourished in the society. Apter, therefore, suggests that a charismatic leader can be 'part traditional and part modern'.[150]

Ann Ruth and Dorothy Willners[151] describe charisma as a leader's 'capacity to elicit from a following deference, devotion and awe toward himself as the source of authority'.[152] Concentrating upon the case of 'ex-colonial' societies of Asia, Africa, and Latin America, they argue that a charismatic leader arises at a time when the colonial order is breaking down and there are no longer clear-cut and generally acceptable norms for legitimacy of authority and the mode of its operation. The traditional order already stands discredited during the colonial rule. It is into this 'climate of uncertainty and unpredictability' that a charismatic leader moves in, to bridge the 'gap'. Indeed, he himself emerges as a new system of authority.[153]

The Willners suggest that the appeal of a charismatic leader lies at two levels. The first level relates to the 'special grievance and special interest of each group' in the society, operating in 'opposition to the rule of a colonial power.' The second and the deeper level, pertains to the assimilation of 'the thought and feelings' of a people in its 'sacred figures, divine beings, or heroes.' This, they insist, helps the charismatic leader devise an appropriate strategy of 'cultural management' to represent to his followers a 'sense of continuity between himself and his mission and their legendary heroes and their missions'.[154] Indeed, the Willners argue that a charismatic leader 'is charismatic because in the breakdown of other means of legitimate authority he is able to evoke and associate with himself the sacred symbols of his culture'.[155]

In a work devoted to the study of seven charismatic political leaders, that is, Ahmad Sukarno, Fidel Castro, Ayatollah Khomeini, Adolf Hitler, Benito Mussolini, Franklin D. Roosevelt, and M.K. Gandhi,[156] Ann Ruth Willner revises and expands her theoretical formulations. She argues that charisma arises out of 'a situation of extreme social stress or crisis, often one producing major deprivations'.[157] If the given rulers 'seem unwilling or unable to cope with or alleviate the crisis', people get 'alienated' from the political system and thus become 'susceptible to the political appeal of a strong leader who can be seen as the symbol and the means of rescue from distress'.[158]

However, Ann Willner reiterates that the 'roots of charismatic belief and emotion lie deeper than the levels of grievance a leader can exploit or of doctrine he can propound'.[159] The deeper source is culture that he shares with his followers, including 'myths' that prevail in that society. The charismatic leader, thus, is:

> ...the one who can inadvertently or deliberately tap the reservoir of relevant myths that are linked to its sacred figures, to its historical and legendary heroes, and its historical and legendary ordeals and triumphs. He evokes, invokes, and assimilates to himself the values and actions embodied in the myths by which that society has organized and recalls its past experience.[160]

Willner also dwells upon certain personal qualities that charismatic leaders generally share and which makes them 'extraordinary' or somehow 'supernatural' to their followers. Of particular importance are supreme 'self-confidence or self-assurance', exceedingly high 'energy or vitality', 'self-control,' 'powerful mind, with a unbelievable wide range of knowledge,' and, a keen 'sense of mission.'[161] However, Willner concedes that it is the 'perception' of the followers that determines 'the defining characteristics of the existence of a charismatic relationship'.[162] It may not necessarily be directly related to any of the above characteristics. Very often, the followers 'develop a generalized or an undifferentiated notion of the extraordinary power or capability of their leaders'.[163]

Dankwart Rustow argues that charismatic situations typically are those of 'a collapse of established authority or a profound but vague threat to the welfare of a human group'.[164] In a word, they are 'crisis' situations. The defeat of the Ottoman Empire in the First World War created a crisis facilitating the rise of Kemal Ataturk (1881–1938) as the charismatic leader of modern Turkey. Rustow, therefore, suggests that political study of charisma must begin not with the leader's 'personality, but with the vacuum that he fills'.[165] However, in his opinion, this vacuum 'is not the mere absence of leadership, institutions, or, legitimate authority, but rather the default of these at a time when they are intensely felt to be needed'.[166] In this sense, charismatic leadership is essentially 'a form of crisis leadership'.[167]

Robert Tucker assigns charisma to a leader who can convincingly offer himself to a group of people in 'distress' as the only one qualified to lead them out of their 'predicament'.[168] He should not only be able to diagnose the difficulties of his followers, but should also be capable of offering a 'formula or set of formulas' for their 'salvation'.[169] His authority should indeed grow as he comes to embody the promised salvation. Tucker, therefore, suggests that an analyst should 'always go back to the beginnings of the given leader-personality's emergence as a leader, rather than start with the status achieved at the zenith of his career'.[170] He should recognize 'indications of a charismatic following or movement…[sic] very early in the career and in any event before power is achieved'.[171] Although Tucker identifies two types of charismatic leaders, the 'prophet' type and the 'activist' type, he is convinced that these leaders possess many qualities in common.[172] In particular, they demonstrate 'a peculiar sense of mission, comprising a belief both in the movement and in themselves as the chosen instruments to lead the movement to its destination'.[173] Tucker also points out that 'what is probably a universal feature of the charismatic leader' is the 'capacity to inspire hatred as well as loyalty and love'.[174] That is why, he argues, the 'same leader who is charismatic in the eyes of people in distress, for whom salvation lies in change, will be counter-charismatic in the eyes of those who see in change not salvation but ruination'.[175]

A Framework for the Analysis of Charisma and Charismatic Leadership

In spite of the fact that each exponent of the concept of charisma has a particular emphasis, given his or her own interest and disciplinary focus, the essential argument remains in line with Weber's formulation of the concept of charisma and charismatic leadership. The only difference is that it is expressed in the modern parlance of social sciences. Thus, it is possible to propose a general framework of charisma, which will be capable of giving direction to the study of charisma in the contemporary world. Taken together with Weber's ideas, especially in his second perspective, the salient features of this framework will be as follows:

Charisma is a function of both 'personality' and 'situational' factors. Personality-related factors are a necessary requirement for charisma, but they are not sufficient by themselves. There *must* first be a crisis or a distressful situation. But then, a potential charismatic leader may *himself* contribute to the making of this situation through his pronouncements, or actions, or both. Therefore, it is important that the study of personality-related factors precedes the study of the situation, which the charismatic leader is called upon to deal with.

Personality-related factors include:

1) *extraordinary* personal qualities of leadership, at least that is how the leader is perceived by disciples and followers. Charisma rests upon the belief that the charismatic leader can alleviate the distress of his followers;
2) a capacity to offer to his followers a 'formula or set of formulas' for their salvation;
3) an ability to inspire his followers to respond to and work for the realization of the goal associated with his 'formula or set of formulas.' In fact, his stature would rise along with the increase in his following;

4) an absolute faith in himself and in his mission. He is confident of his abilities and the success of his mission, against all odds;

5) a sober, rational character. He has 'passions', but they are tempered by 'reason'. In fact, a charismatic leader possesses 'passion, responsibility, and proportion'. He has the ability to concentrate and contemplate even if it amounts to a conscious 'detachment' in his everyday routine of life; and

6) last, but not least, a genuinely charismatic leader is able to manifest his 'charisma' long before he attains power. Therefore, a systematic study of charisma should begin with the early political career of a potential charismatic leader rather than at the 'zenith' of power.

Situational factors include:

1) the absence or loss of traditional authority, more so often in the 'ex-colonial societies' where the traditional order gives way to colonial rule and its 'rational-legal' system of government;

2) the rational-legal institutions of authority, introduced by the colonial rulers, are weak or underdeveloped or inadequate, incapable, and ill-suited to respond to the needs and interests of the people; and

3) consequently, the people are confronted with a crisis or a set of crises of authority. They are lost, frustrated and in a state of distress. They want a way out of the distressful situation.

A combination of these factors, both personality-related and situational, constitutes a systematic framework on charisma and charismatic leadership. That is why, this framework is employed to explore the case of Jinnah here, beginning, in the next chapter, with personality-related factors in his early political career leading to his emergence as the *Quaid-i-Azam*. The succeeding two chapters, that is Chapters 3 and 4 deal with the situational factors. Chapter 5 concentrates upon the formula for salvation. Chapters 6 and 7 focus, again, upon the role of personality-related factors in the accomplishment of the mission of Pakistan as given in the formula. Indeed, all the discussion in the following chapters revolves around the personality-related and situational factors, identified above, as they explain and explicate the charismatic nature of Jinnah's political leadership.

Notes

1. Syed Shamsul Hasan, *Plain Mr Jinnah* (Karachi: Royal Book Co., 1976), 54. Almost all contemporary Muslim writers mentioned the desperate situation of Muslim India.

2. Pattabhi Sitaramyya, *The History of the Indian National Congress: 1885–1935* (Madras: The Working Committee of the Congress, 1935), 859.

3. The 1931census showed 67 million Muslims against 177.7 million Hindus in British India. The situation in the Princely States was even more daunting. There were only 10.7 million Muslims against 61.5 million Hindus. See Edward Thompson and G.T. Garratt, *Rise and Fulfillment of British Rule in India* (Allahabad: Central Book Depot, 1962), App. E, 663.

4. Wayne Wilcox, 'Wellsprings of Pakistan', in Lawrence Ziring, Ralph Braibanti, and Howard Wriggins, eds., *Pakistan: The Long View* (Durham: Duke University Press, 1977), 34. One sure indicator of this 'vacuum of authority and very ambiguous expectations' was the rapidity with which Muslim India was devising schemes to escape the imminent Hindu-dominated authority. There were, at least, six schemes in the air: 1) *The Confederacy of India* by 'A Punjabi' (Sir Muhammad Shah Nawaz Khan of Mamdot); 2) *The Aligarh Professors' Scheme*, by Professors Syed Zafrul Hasan and Mohammad Afzal Hussain Qadri of Aligarh; 3) Choudhry Rahmat Ali's Scheme—contained in his pamphlet, *The Millat of Islam and the Menace of 'Indianism'* (n.d. 1941?); 4) Dr S.A. Lateef's scheme, in his *Muslim Problem in India*; 5) Sir Sikandar Hayat Khan's scheme—*Outline of a Scheme of Indian Federation*; 6) Sir Abdullah Haroon Committee's scheme—under the instructions of the Muslim League. (Jinnah, however, considered this scheme as merely suggestions from individuals or groups). For details on these schemes see, *The Indian Annual Register* (Calcutta: Government Press, 1939); Maurice Gwyer and A. Appadorai, eds., *Speeches and Documents on the Indian Constitution, 1921–47*, Vol. II (Bombay: Oxford University Press, 1957), 456–62; Reginald Coupland, *Report on the Constitutional Problem in India, Part I, The Indian Problem, 1833–1935* (London: Oxford University Press, 1968), 203–4; Alhaj Mian Ahmad Shafi, *Haji Sir Abdullah Haroon: A Biography* (Karachi: Begum Daulat Anwar Hidayatullah, n.d.), 138–40; Syed Sharifuddin Pirzada, *Evolution of Pakistan* (Lahore: All-Pakistan Legal Decisions, 1963); and Y.B. Mathur, *Growth of Muslim Politics in India* (Lahore: Book Traders, 1980); App. II, 'Plans for Partition of India', 293–329. Chaudhary Khaliquzzaman also claims having proposed, in 1939, in his meeting with Lord Zetland, Secretary of State for India, the establishment of three or four federations of India, including 'a federation of Muslim Provinces and States in North-West India'. See Chaudhary Khaliquzzaman, *Pathway to Pakistan* (Lahore: Longman, 1961), 2.

5. The 'traditional' leadership of Muslim India comprised the nobility, titled gentry, landowning classes, provincial leaders, and the *ulama*. On their role in the politics of Muslim India at this juncture see, in particular, Mujahid, *Studies in Interpretation*, 25–8, 400; Abdul Hamid, *Muslim Separatism in India* (Lahore: Oxford University Press 1967), 233; Wolpert, *Jinnah of Pakistan*, 141-2; Ikram, *Modern Muslim India*, 226; Mushirul Hasan, *Nationalism and Communal Politics in India: 1916–1928*

(Delhi: Manohar, 1979), 79-80, 227-8; W.C. Smith, *Modern Islam in India: A Social Analysis* (London: Victor Gollacz, 1946) 231-51; Shila Sen, *Muslim Politics in Bengal, 1937–47* (New Delhi: Impex India, 1976), 91; Zia-ul-Hasan Faruqi, *The Deoband School and the Demand for Pakistan* (Bombay: Asia Publishing House, 1963); Mushirul Haq, *Muslim Politics in Modern India, 1857–1947* (Meerut: Meenkshi Parakashan, 1970), 94-5; Aziz Ahmad, *Islamic Modernism in India and Pakistan* (London: Oxford University Press, 1967), 93; Ishtiaq Hussain Qureshi, *Ulema in Politics* (Karachi: Ma'aref, 1977), 343; and Peter Hardy, *Partners in Freedom—and True Muslims: The Political Thought of some Muslim Scholars in British India, 1912–1947* (Lund: Student Literature Scandinavian Institute of Asian Studies, 1971) 35-7.

6. Jamil-ud-Din Ahmad, ed., *Speeches and Writings of Mr Jinnah*, Vol. I (Lahore: Sh. Muhammad Ashraf, 1968), 41.

7. Jinnah participated in the first two sessions of the Conference. He was not invited by the British Government to the third session.

8. Ahmad, *Speeches and Writings,* Vol. I, 41.

9. On 18 September 1936 and, again, on 10 January 1937, that is, before and during the 1937 elections, Nehru had claimed there were only '*two forces*'/'two parties' in India, the Congress, and the British. He refused to recognize the League. See S. Gopal, ed., *Selected Works of Jawaharlal Nehru*, Vols. VII and VIII (New Delhi: Orient Longman, 1976), 468 and 120-1, respectively.

10. Ahmad, *Speeches and Writings,* Vol. I, 169.

11. Ibid.

12. Khalid bin Sayeed, *The Political System of Pakistan* (Boston: Houghton Mifflin Company, 1967), 51-2.

13. W.C. Smith, *Modern Islam in India,* 275.

14. Saleem Qureshi, 'The Consolidation of Leadership in the Last Phase of the All-India Muslim League', 298. This was generally the feeling of the Muslims. See, for instance, Suleri, *My Leader,* 230; Ravoof, *Meet Mr Jinnah,* 225; Lateef, *Great Leader;* Saiyid, *A Political Study;* Allana, *Story of a Nation,* preface; M.A.H. Ispahani, *Quaid-i-Azam Jinnah as I knew Him* (Karachi: Forward Publications Trust, 1966), 243-4; Rais Ahmad Jafari, *Quaid-i-Azam aur unka Ehad* (Urdu) (Lahore: Maqbool Academy, 1962), 26; and Aga Khan, with a Foreword by W. Somerset Maugham, *The Memoirs of Aga Khan: World Enough and Time* (New York: Cassel and Co., 1954), 314.

15. Lateef, *Great Leader,* 181-4. By the same token, his opponents characterized him as 'a menace for both India and the Indian Mussalmans'. See Majumdar, *Jinnah and Gandhi,* 171. A typical instance of 'counter-charismatic' appeal of a charismatic leader.

16. There are two views on the subject. One suggested that it was Maulana Mazharuddin Ahmad, editor, Daily *Aman,* who proposed the title of Quaid-i-Azam. Mujahid believed that it was, in fact, proposed by Maulana Ahmad Saeed, Secretary of the Jamiat-ul-Ulama-i-Hind in his speech at Muradabad's Jamia Masjid on 7 December 1936. In this assessment, Mujahid, of course, followed the lead given by Muhammad Amin Zuberi. For a detailed discussion of the arguments on both sides see, in particular, Jamil-ud-Din Ahmad, *Glimpses of Quaid-i-Azam* (Karachi: Educational Press, 1960); Muhammad Amin Zuberi,

Siyasat-i-Milliayah (Urdu) (Agra: n.p., 1941); Syed Sharifuddin Pirzada, *Some Aspects of Quaid-i-Azam's Life* (Islamabad: National Commission on Historical and Cultural Research 1978); and Mujahid, *Studies in Interpretation*, App. I, 419-36. Whoever may be attributed the authorship of the title of Quaid-i-Azam, the fact of the matter was that it came to be so widely employed for Jinnah that, in the end, even a political adversary like Gandhi did not hesitate to use it, much to the annoyance of Maulana Abul Kalam Azad, a leading 'nationalist Muslim' in the Congress camp. See Maulana Azad's views on the subject in Maulana Abul Kalam Azad, *India Wins Freedom* (New Delhi: Orient Longman, 1988), 92. (This is an extended version of the original 1959 publication, and contains an additional thirty pages of material scattered all over the manuscript, and was released thirty years after Maulana Azad's death). However, there were some 'nationalist Muslims', who opposed Jinnah's 'two-nation' theory and the demand for Pakistan and still referred to Jinnah as Quaid-i-Azam. Dr Zakir Hussain, for instance, who was one of the staunch supporters of the Congress, and who later on rose to be the first Muslim President of India (1967–69), addressed Jinnah as 'Revered Quaid-i-Azam' as late as October 1946. *Syed Shamsul Hasan Collection*, Miscellaneous, Vol. I, National Archives of Pakistan, Islamabad.

17. Samuel P. Huntington, discussing the role of political leaders in the politics of modernization in the 'new nations' of Asia, Africa, and Latin America, wrote: 'Depending upon one's perspective, one can thus define political modernization to mean either the concentration of power, the expansion of power, or the dispersion of power....At one point or another in a country's history each does constitute 'modernization'.' Samuel P. Huntington, *Political Order in Changing Societies* (New Haven: Yale University Press, 1968), 145.

18. Nicholas Mansergh and E.W.R. Lumby, eds., *Constitutional Relations between Britain and India: The Transfer of Power, 1942–7*, Vol. I (London: HM's Stationery Office, 1970), App. I, 787. Ironically, Gandhi confessed in the *Harijan* of 6 April 1940, much before the August Declaration, that there was 'no non-violent method of compelling the obedience of eight crores of Muslims to the will of the rest of India, however powerful majority the rest may represent. The Muslims must have the same rights of self-determination that the rest of India has'. See B.R. Nanda, *Mahatma Gandhi: A Biography* (London: Unwin Books, 1965), 213-24; and V.P. Menon, *The Transfer of Power in India* (Princeton: Princeton University Press 1957), 92-5.

19. Ahmad, *Speeches and Writings*, Vol. I, 395. However, for all practical purposes, the 'option' clause in the Cripps proposals was more of a bait than a genuine acceptance of the political realities of Muslim India.

20. Nicholas Mansergh and Penderel Moon, eds., *Constitutional Relations between Britain and India: The Transfer of Power, 1942–7*, Vol. VI (London: HM's Stationery Office, 1976), 175.

21. Nicholas Mansergh and Penderel Moon, eds., *Constitutional Relations Between Britain and India, The Transfer of Power, 1942-7*, Vol. V (London: HM's Stationery Office, 1974), 281.

22. The League won 30 seats in the central legislative assembly, 'every single Muslim seat.' 86.6 per cent of the total Muslim votes. In all, the League secured 453 out of 524 central and provincial assembly seats, that is 86.45 per cent. In the process,

it bagged 4.70 million votes—that is about 75 per cent of the total Muslim vote. In this sense, Mujahid reckoned, 'the League's share during 1945–46 came to 24 per cent of the total vote cast in all the constituencies, and since the Muslims constituted some 26.9 per cent of the total population in British India, the League's voting record was termed brilliant.' See Sharif al Mujahid, 'Jinnah: the Role of the Individual in History', in M.R. Kazmi, ed., *M.A. Jinnah: Views and Reviews* (Karachi: Oxford University Press, 2005), 161. Also see, I.H. Qureshi, *The Struggle for Pakistan* (Karachi: University of Karachi, 1969), 237-8. For the election results see, Z.H. Zaidi, *Jinnah Papers*, Vol. I, App. XIII, 'Results of 1945-46 Elections....', 608-29.

23. Jinnah had accepted the Cabinet Mission Plan on the clear understanding that 'the Sections and Groups were an essential feature of the scheme....' See the text of Jinnah's meeting with the Mission on 25 June 1946 in Nicholas Mansergh and Penderel Moon, eds., *Constitutional Relations between Britain and India: The Transfer of Power, 1942–7*, Vol. VII (London: HM's Stationery Office, 1977), 1044-5. On 21 November 1946, Jinnah asked the Muslim League members of the Constituent Assembly not to attend the Assembly session on 9 December accusing the Viceroy and the British Government of playing into the hands of the Congress. *Dawn*, 21 November 1946.

24. In a press statement on 1 August, however, Jinnah clarified that the decision 'to resort to direct action is not a declaration of war against anybody....' It is 'a statement concerning the steps we propose to take for our own self-preservation and self-defence'. *Civil and Military Gazette*, 1 August 1946.

25. The result of the efforts to by-pass the League in the formation of the Interim Government was a fast deteriorating law and order situation. There were riots in Calcutta (Kolkata), Noakhali and several places in Bihar, indeed, dreadful riots in other parts of the country too. Disturbances were markedly communal. 'Jinnah', Lord Pethick Lawrence, Secretary of State for India, wrote, 'is not only angry with us, but is threatening open rebellion'. See Lord Pethick Lawrence to Wavell, 19 August 1946 in Nicholas Mansergh and Penderel Moon, eds., *Constitutional Relations between Britain and India: The Transfer of Power, 1942–7*, Vol. VIII (London: HM's Stationery Office, 1979), 263.

26. Nicholas Mansergh and Penderel Moon, eds., *Constitutional Relations between Britain and India: The Transfer of Power, 1942–7*, Vol. X (London: HM's Stationery Office, 1981), 138-9. By then, Sardar Patel and Jawaharlal Nehru had become supporters of the partition in spite of the fact that Maulana Azad had warned the latter 'that history would never forgive us if we agreed to partition. The verdict would be that India was divided not by the Muslim League but by Congress.' Azad, *India Wins Freedom*, 202.

27. Keith Callard, *Pakistan: A Political Study* (London: George Allen & Unwin, 1968), 19.

28. Raja Sahib of Mahmudabad, 'Foreword', in Ispahani, *As I knew Him*. Raja Muhammad Amir Ahmed Khan (1914–1973), known popularly as Raja Sahib of Mahmudabad was a devoted follower of Jinnah. He remained the Treasurer of the All-India Muslim League during the decade of 1937–47. He was the eldest son of Raja Muhammad Ali Muhammad Khan of Mahmudabad (1877–1931), a leading Muslim politician of his day.

29. This is not to say that Jinnah was not an all-India leader. He was a leading politician all along, prompting a man like V.P. Menon to state on record that Jinnah was 'the hero of my generation.' Menon, *Transfer of Power in India*, 437.

30. Sarojini Naidu, ed., *Mohammed Ali Jinnah: An Ambassador of Unity* (Lahore: Atishfishan Publications, 1989. rep.), 16. Incidentally, this was also the first instance of a bill passing into legislation on the motion of a private member.

31. Also see, Sayeed, *Formative Phase*, 42; and Abdul Lateef, 'From Community to Nation: The development of the Idea of Pakistan', Ph.D. Dissertation, Southern Illinois University, 1965, 88-9.

32. There were actually 'Fifteen Points', the fifteenth point being an elabouration of the fifth point. See 'M.A. Jinnah's Fifteen Points', *Quaid-i-Azam Papers*, F/1050, National Archives of Pakistan, Islamabad. Also see, Mujahid, *Studies in Interpretation*, App. 10, 'Jinnah's Fourteen Points', 1929', 479-81.

33. According to Jahan Ara Shahnawaz, a delegate to the Conference, Jinnah's 'Fourteen Points' were 'our goal' as far as the Muslims were concerned. Jahan Ara Shahnawaz, *Father and Daughter* (Karachi: Oxford University Press, 2002, first published Lahore: Nigarishat, 1971), 101. Gandhi already had a copy of the 'Fourteen Points' with him at London. It was presented to him by a delegation from the All-India Muslim Conference on 4 April before his departure from India. See Judith M. Brown, *Gandhi and Civil Disobedience: The Mahatma in Indian Politics, 1928–34* (Cambridge: Cambridge University Press, 1977), 221.

34. Elected President of the League first at the Lucknow Session of the League in 1916, he went on to head the organization for a number of years during the 1920s. In 1924, he was President of the Lahore session of the League. He was re-elected for a term of three years. In 1927, he was President of the Muslim Conference, comprising prominent Muslim leaders, wherein 'minimum' Muslim demands, popularly known as the Delhi Muslim Proposals, were finalized.

35. Almost all contemporaries of Jinnah agree on this point. They are unanimous in regarding him as 'a man of high integrity, principles, sincerity, honesty, incorruptibility and honour'. This was the finding of a study by Saleem M.M. Qureshi to seek a 'personality assessment' of Jinnah by his contemporaries, and was based on extensive interviews with British, Pakistani, Indian and family members. See Saleem M.M. Qureshi, 'Mohammad Ali Jinnah: A Personality Assessment by His Contemporaries', in A.H. Dani, ed., *Quaid-i-Azam and Pakistan* (Islamabad: Quaid-i-Azam University, 1981), 118. For details of interviews and analysis see, ibid., 109-26.

36. Mujahid, *Studies in Interpretation*, 401.

37. Weber, *The Theory of Social and Economic Organization* and *From Max Weber: Essays in Sociology*.

38. Shils, 'Charisma, Order, and Status', and 'The Concentration and Dispersion of Charisma'; Apter, 'Nkrumah, Charisma, and the Coup'; Ann Ruth and Dorothy Willner, 'The Rise and Role of Charismatic Leaders'; Ann Ruth Willner, *Charismatic Political Leadership: A Theory* and *The Spellbinders: Charismatic Political Leadership* (New Haven: Yale University Press, 1984); Rustow, 'Ataturk as Founder of a State'; and Tucker, 'The Theory of Charismatic Leadership'.

39. There are others too who called Jinnah 'charismatic' such as, Wayne Wilcox, Peter Hardy, and Mohammed Waseem, but for obvious reasons the discussion will be

confined to those writers who are involved with the study of Jinnah's political leadership as a primary field of specialization. See Wayne Wilcox, 'The Wellsprings of Pakistan', in Ziring, *Pakistan: The Long View*, 31; Peter Hardy, *The Muslims of British India* (Cambridge: Cambridge University Press, 1972), 254; and Mohammad Waseem, *Politics and the State in Pakistan* (Lahore: Progressive, 1989).

40. Saleem Qureshi, in a later article, concentrated primarily on the assessment of Jinnah's personality. He did, however, suggest that Jinnah could be regarded as a 'charismatic' leader. See Saleem Qureshi, 'Mohammad Ali Jinnah: A Personality Assessment', in Dani, *Quaid-i-Azam and Pakistan*, 109-10. But since it was not a detailed account of his leadership as such, there was no way of finding out how in fact Qureshi would have liked to apply this concept to Jinnah's political leadership. It has been decided, therefore, to restrict Qureshi's views on the nature of Jinnah's political leadership to his more developed and explicit writings. There are other dissenters too, but they are not included in this discussion, as their work does not fall into the category of primary contribution on Jinnah. See, for instance, Hugh Tinker, *Re-orientation* (London: Pall Mall, 1966), 71-2.

41. In general, Waheed-uz-Zaman's views have been taken from his detailed study of Jinnah's political leadership, *Myth and Reality*.

42. Ibid., 20-1.

43. Ibid., 13.

44. Ibid., 13-14.

45. Ibid., 145.

46. Ibid., 144-5.

47. Ibid.

48. This account is based primarily on Sharif al Mujahid's *Quaid-i-Azam Jinnah: Studies in Interpretation*, second revised edition, Nov. 1981. In the first edition, published in June 1981, Mujahid emphatically stated: 'Jinnah, it is true, may be credited with some of the attributes that characterize charisma as defined in political terms—attributes such as having a special grace or an extraordinary power to rule by the force of his personality alone' and such as having acquired the power to call forth, 'strengths that people would be reluctant to entrust to anyone else'. Yet, he was 'not a charismatic leader in the Max Weber sense'. 44. Also see Mujahid's 'Jinnah's Rise to Muslim Leadership', in A.H. Dani, ed., *World Scholars on Quaid-i-Azam Mohammad Ali Jinnah* (Islamabad: Quaid-i-Azam University, 1979), 395.

49. Mujahid, *Studies in Interpretation*, 44.

50. Ibid.

51. Ibid., 38.

52. Ibid., 403-411.

53. Ibid., 361.

54. Ibid., 413.

55. Ibid., 359

56. Ibid., 44.

57. Moore, 'Jinnah and the Pakistan Demand', 531.

58. Ibid., 532.

59. Ibid., 535.

60. Ibid., 559.

61. Moore was referring to Lord Mountbatten's assessment of Jinnah, in turn, influenced by Nehru and Gandhi, when Jinnah was 'hell bent' on the demand for Pakistan. See Mountbatten's *Personal Report to the Secretary of State for India*, in Nicholas Mansergh and Penderel Moon, eds., *Constitutional Relations between Britain and India: The Transfer of Power, 1942–7*, Vol. XI (London: HM's Stationery Office, 1982), 898. Also see the accounts of Alan-Campbell Johnson, *Mission with Mountbatten* (London: Robert Hale, 1951); Lord Ismay, *The Memoirs of General the Lord Ismay* (London: Heinemann, 1960); and Larry Collins and Dominque Lapierre, *Freedom at Midnight* (New York: Simon & Schuster, 1975).

62. Moore, 'Jinnah and the Pakistan Demand', 550.

63. Ibid., 559.

64. Wolpert, *Jinnah of Pakistan*, 162.

65. Ibid., 38.

66. Ibid., 55.

67. Ibid., 69.

68. Ibid., 79.

69. Ibid., 102.

70. Ibid., 175.

71. Ibid., 248.

72. Ibid., 148.

73. Ibid., 182.

74. Ibid., 294.

75. Ibid., 182.

76. Ibid., Preface.

77. Khalid bin Sayeed's views have been followed from a number of sources. Thus, each source is specifically cited here.

78. Sayeed, *Formative Phase*, 294.

79. Ibid.

80. Sayeed, 'The Personality of Jinnah', 282.

81. Sayeed, *Formative Phase*, 293.

82. Sayeed, 'The Personality of Jinnah', 279, 292-3. In the professional literature, there is little empirical evidence to suggest that kind of causal relationship. Thus, as Waheed-uz-Zaman explained, 'Change in Jinnah's political outlook' may better be 'searched in the quickly changing political developments rather than in his ruined family or political isolation'. Waheed-uz-Zaman, *Myth and Reality*, 18-19.

83. Sayeed, *Formative Phase*, 294.

84. Ibid.

85. Sayeed, 'The Personality of Jinnah', 293.

86. Ibid.

87. Sayeed, *Formative Phase*, 288.

88. Ibid., 9.

89. Sayeed, 'Political Leadership and Institution Building Under Jinnah, Ayub and Bhutto', in Ziring, *Pakistan: The Long View*, 244.

90. Sayeed, *Formative Phase*, 184.

91. Saleem Qureshi's main arguments have been taken from his principal works, *Jinnah and the Making of a Nation,* and 'The Consolidation of Leadership in the Last Phase of the Politics of the All-India Muslim League'.
92. Saleem Qureshi, *Jinnah and the Making of a Nation*, 28.
93. Ibid., 78-80.
94. Ibid., 76-7.
95. Ibid., 77.
96. Saleem Qureshi, 'The Consolidation of Leadership in the Last Phase of the Politics of the All-India Muslim League', 299.
97. Ibid., 305-23.
98. Ibid., 322-4.
99. Ibid., 324.
100. Ibid., 327.
101. Ibid., 325.
102. Ibid.
103. Ibid.
104. Saleem Qureshi, *Jinnah and the Making of a Nation*, 38.
105. For example see, Weber, *Theory of Social and Economic Organization* and *From Max Weber: Essays in Sociology.*
106. Subsequently, however, Qureshi suggested a very broad definition of the concept. He wrote: 'The stage of national liberation is a stage of struggle, clearly marked by "we" and "they". The bond, on the one side, among the "we", i.e. members of the community and on the other between the community and the leader, is one of common identification, essentially an ascriptive bond that helps establish a basis for consensus on the goals sought. By and large, the leader-follower bond has been an emotional bond, a commitment with destiny. That is why most national liberation leaders have been charismatic personages.' Saleem Qureshi, 'Mohammad Ali Jinnah: A Personality Assessment', in Dani, *Quaid-i-Azam and Pakistan*, 109. However, this makes it extremely difficult to distinguish charismatic leadership from other kinds of leadership. Indeed, the concept of charisma no longer remains connotatively specific. See, for instance, Ratnam's criticism on Willard A. Hanna's *Eight Nation Makers: Southeast Asia's Charismatic Statesmen* (New York: St. Martins, 1964), in Ratnam, 'Charisma and Political Leadership', 341-54.
107. Weber, *Theory of Social and Economic Organization*, 360.
108. 'Politics As a Vocation', in *From Max Weber: Essays in Sociology*, 77-128. In this line of inquiry and argument, I have benefited from an excellent cultural and psychoanalytical history of Max Weber written by Arthur Mitzman. See his *The Iron Cage: An Historical Interpretation of Max Weber* (New York: Alfred A. Knopf, 1970), especially Ch. 8, 'Aristocracy and Charisma in Weber's Political Thought (1911-1919)'.
109. Not to talk of encyclopedia articles, essays, and general writings on the subject of charisma and charismatic leadership, even scholars such as Bendix and Eisenstadt did not emphasize the second perspective in their specialized accounts. Bendix did not discuss it in his massive review of Weber's intellectual ideas, and Eisenstadt failed to include it in his meticulous collection of Weber's selected papers on charisma and institution building. Eisenstadt, however, discussed in

great depth the problem of the extension of 'substantive rationality' to the nature of the charismatic authority in general and of 'routinization' of charisma as a major aspect of institutionalization in particular in his 'Introduction' to the volume. See Reinhardt Bendix, *Max Weber: An Intellectual Portrait* (New York: Doubleday & Co., 1960); and S.M. Eisenstadt, *Max Weber: On Charisma and Institution Building* (Chicago: University of Chicago Press, 1980).

110. Weber, *Theory of Social and Economic Organization*, 358.
111. Ibid., 358-9.
112. Ibid., 359.
113. Ibid., 360. Although the distinction between charismatic leadership and charismatic authority was implied in Weber's analysis, it was not quite systematic. The constant shifts in emphasis from charismatic leadership to charismatic authority and back again created not only a good deal of confusion but also obscured the full significance of the two terms. It is easier to understand, however, if these terms are seen in reference to the relation with the followers. In a leadership relation, the person is basic. In an authority relation, the person is unacquainted with the person who issues it. See Robert Bierstedt, 'The problem of Authority', in Morroe Berger, eds., *Freedom and Control in Modern Society* (New York: D. Van Nostrand Company, 1954), 71-2.
114. Weber, *Theory of Social and Economic Organization*, 360.
115. Ibid., 361.
116. Ibid.
117. Ibid., 362.
118. Ibid.
119. Ibid., 363.
120. Ibid.
121. Ibid., 364.
122. Ibid.
123. Like he saw earlier, as evident in the first perspective here. Indeed, the war and Germany's defeat completely changed Weber's ideas on charisma. The earlier 'archaic irrationality' was gone. See Mitzman, *Iron Cage*, 246-55.
124. Ibid., 246.
125. Weber, 'Politics as a Vocation,' 80-7.
126. Ibid., 85.
127. Ibid.
128. Ibid., 88.
129. Ibid., 79.
130. Ibid.
131. Ibid., 80.
132. Ibid.
133. Ibid., 80-7.
134. Ibid., 87.
135. Ibid., 103.
136. Ibid.
137. Weber, 'The Meaning of Discipline,' 262. For details see Ibid., 253-64.
138. Ibid., 254.
139. Ibid.

140. Weber, 'Politics as a Vocation', 115.
141. Ibid., 115-16.
142. Ibid., 116-27.
143. Ibid., 128.
144. It should be remembered, however, that the concept of charisma was developed at a time when the tradition of modern analytical inquiry itself was beginning to take root, in the hands of a man no other than Weber himself, the chief proponent of positivist thought, who wanted to give his concept of charisma and charismatic leadership and the social science methodology associated with it the same matter-of-fact approach that characterized the natural sciences. However, as W.G. Runciman pointed out, the very fact that Weber conceded the necessary distinction between natural and social sciences made his claims for social science, 'better tenable, as well as more cautious' than anybody else's. See W.G. Runciman, *Social Science and Political Theory* (Cambridge: Cambridge University Press, 1967), 61.
145. Shils, 'The Concentration and Dispersion of Charisma', 1-19.
146. Ibid., 2-3.
147. Ibid., 2-5.
148. Apter, 'Nkrumah, Charisma, and the Coup', 764.
149. Ibid., 766.
150. Ibid., 765-71.
151. Willners, 'The Rise and Role of Charismatic Leaders'; and Ann Ruth Willner, *Charismatic Political Leadership*, 34-48, esp. 45-8.
152. Willners, 'The Rise and Role of Charismatic Leaders', 79.
153. Ibid., 81.
154. Ibid., 82-3.
155. Ibid., 84.
156. *The Spellbinders* was primarily a development of her earlier work of 1968 which she had to rush 'somewhat prematurely' to 'protect' her 'pioneer rights'. However, like her previous studies, Ann Willner remained committed to a 'cultural' rather than political explanation, largely, as she readily admitted to the influence of her cultural anthropologist sister, Dorothy Willner. As she put it: 'Since I cannot distinguish my own ideas from those of hers I have co-opted, I consider her my co-author of this book as well'. Ibid., x-xi.
157. Ibid., 43.
158. Ibid.
159. Ibid., 62.
160. Ibid.
161. Ibid., 130-47.
162. Ibid., 128.
163. Ibid., 128-9.
164. Rustow, 'Ataturk as Founder of a State', 794. Also see, Patrick Kinross, *Atatürk: The Rebirth of a Nation* (London: Weidenfeld and Nicolson, 1966).
165. Rustow, 'Ataturk as Founder of a State', 794.
166. Ibid.
167. Ibid.

CARDIFF
CAERDYDD

168. Tucker, 'The Theory of Charismatic Leadership', 742. Tucker, however, did not necessarily see charisma as a tool in the process of modernization, as other writers discussed above did. He was primarily concerned with 'movements for change' including 'charismatic' movement, in the communist states in general and the then Soviet Union in particular. However, he was convinced that his concept of charisma could be usefully applied to the case of the developing societies. As he himself described it: 'The outcome is a reformulation of the theory of charismatic leadership from a perspective other than that of political development and modernization, although there is nothing in the reformulated theory that would keep it from being applied to charismatic leadership of "new states".' Ibid., 732-5.
169. Ibid., 751.
170. Ibid., 739.
171. Ibid., 739-40.
172. Ibid., 748-52.
173. Ibid., 749.
174. Ibid., 746.
175. Ibid. In a similar vein, Willner also argued that 'the charismatic appeal of a leader is, by definition, limited to those who share the traditions of a given culture, that is, to those who understand and respond to the symbols expressed in the myths a charismatic leader evokes'. Willner, 'The Rise and Role of Charismatic Leaders', 84.

2 The Emergence of the Quaid-i-Azam

Mohammad Ali Jinnah, the first child of Jinnahbhai Poonjah, an Ismaili Khoja,[1] was born in Karachi on 25 December 1876.[2] Jinnah's ancestral home was in Kathiawar, in the princely state of Gondal and his mother tongue was Gujarati. His father had moved to Karachi in search of business opportunities, and of this quaint overgrown village, writes Fatima Jinnah (1893–1967), his sister, 'He had never seen a city as big'.[3] Jinnahbhai Poonjah came to know Sir Fredrick Croft, the General Manager of Douglas Graham and Company, who offered the young Jinnah an apprenticeship at the company's London office, 'near Threadneedle Street'.[4]

In January 1893, Jinnah left for London. He soon developed and pursued an interest in law, and left the apprenticeship for a legal career. He joined Lincoln's Inn. He was also inspired to play the lead role of Romeo at the Old Vic Theater, and visited Hyde Park, where he 'listened to the rash and incoherent utterances of these irresponsible speakers, who attacked their own government in the most scathing terms' and internalized 'the importance and necessity of freedom of speech'.[5] In 1895, he was called to the Bar. In May 1896, he returned to India.

While Jinnah was away in London, both his mother and young bride had passed away. His father's business had suffered losses. Realizing that he was responsible for his family, Jinnah decided to leave Karachi for Bombay (Mumbai), which offered better career prospects. In 1897, he was enrolled as an advocate at the Bombay High Court. Bombay 'tested' his 'faith in himself as he trudged briefless between the humble locality whe[re] he lived and the courts'.[6] He worked tirelessly at his cases, 'though with clarity', he 'drove his point home with cold logic and a slow merciless delivery'.[7] In 1900, the Advocate-General of Bombay, John Molesworth MacPherson, appointed him as Third Presidency Magistrate. Jinnah, whose reputation had steadily grown, turned down the offer of permanent employment as a magistrate and returned to his private practice, which 'soon proved his real mettle and started to lay the foundation of his notable legal success'.[8] This success enabled him to look after his siblings better (his father had passed away in 1902) and embark on a political career.

In December 1906, Jinnah formally joined active politics,[9] when he attended the Calcutta session of the Congress as a delegate and honorary personal secretary to President Dadabhai Naoroji (1825–1917), often called 'the Grand Old Man of India', known to him since his stay in London.[10] His choice of Congress platform was as significant as, in retrospect, the choice of the two issues he spoke on was suggestive. One was the issue of *Waqf-alal-Aulad*, which primarily affected the Muslim community. British interference with the Muslim Personal Law had hurt the Muslims' right to make *waqfs* to their families and descendants. The other issue was self-government for India. The Congress demanded that the system of representative government should be extended to India. But mindful of differential growth of the communities, it also suggested that 'there should be a reservation for the backwardly educated class'.[11] Jinnah did not approve the reservation part of the demand. 'I understand', he noted,

> that by backward class is meant the Mohammadan community. If the Mohammadan community is meant by it, I wish to draw your attention to the fact that the Mohammadan community should be treated in the same way as the Hindu community. The foundation upon which the Indian National Congress is based, is that we are all equal, that there should be no reservation for any class or community and…that the reservation should be deleted.[12]

Thus, Jinnah made it very clear at the outset of his political career that the Muslims were equal to the Hindus in the struggle for self-government. They did not need any special favours or treatment. They were as good as any other community. However, he was convinced that there must not be any conflict between Muslim interests and all-India national interests—that would not serve well the cause of self-government. Thus, in spite of the fact that, personally, he was opposed to the principle of separate electorates, he did not hesitate to urge the British to concede separate electorates to the Muslims after he learnt that the community 'felt keenly on the subject....'[13] He assured the

Hindus that 'the demand for separate electorates is not a matter of policy but a matter of necessity' to the Muslims who needed to be mobilized for political action.[14] He felt that there were many 'other questions of most vital and paramount importance' to both the communities, and thus methods of securing Muslim representation in the assemblies 'should not be allowed to create an *impasse*, and one side or the other must give in'.[15] The Muslims and the Hindus, he argued, should work out their differences and present a 'united demand' leading to the higher goal of 'transfer of power from the bureaucracy to democracy'.[16]

Jinnah was confident that the Congress could, through mutual accommodation and adjustments, lead the way. In supporting the Congress resolution on *Waqf-alal-Aulad* in 1906, he observed: 'This shows one thing, gentlemen, that we Muhammadans can equally stand on this common platform and pray for our grievances being remedied through the programme of the National Congress'.[17] Jinnah knew that 'there was a section which was dreaming in terms of the Hindu raj'.[18] Bepin Chandra Pal and his many supporters stood for 'Hindu nationalism'.[19] But, he maintained, 'hope sprang almost eternally in my heart and soul, derived from Dadabhoy Naoroji. I was not going to give it up, but nourish it'.[20]

Jinnah's choice of Congress party to give public expression to his political ideals was, in fact, typical of the prevalent educated, urban middle-class optimism about the emergence of 'Indian nationalism'. Indeed, Jinnah wondered: '…is it too much to ask and appeal to Hindus and Mohamedans, the two great communities in India to combine in one harmonious union for the common good, where we have to live together in every district, town and hamlet, where our daily life is interwoven with each other in every square mile of one common country'.[21] The liberal ideas that he had imbibed during his stay in London from 1893 to 1896, which 'thrilled' him very much,[22] and which were represented in India by Naoroji, Sir Pherozeshah Mehta (1845–1915) and Gopal Krishna Gokhale (1866–1915), made the Congress all the more comfortable habitat for him.[23] He could share with the Congress leaders 'the dawning hopes of enlightened India' in the pursuit of liberalism and self-government.[24]

Association with the Congress helped Jinnah move quickly to the centre of the political stage. The Congress, represented both Hindu and

Muslim educated, urban middle-classes, and was agitating for self-government and responsible rule. Jinnah decided to cultivate this growing sense of inter-communal identification among educated Indians of the day. In 1913, he went with Gokhale to London to meet Lord Islington, Under-Secretary of State for India, and spent eight months travelling with his mentor in Europe. In 1914, he left again for London as leader of a Congress delegation, which included prominent leaders such as Congress President-elect Bhupendranath Basu (1859–1924) and Lala Lajpat Rai (1865–1928) to apprise members of the Parliament and the Secretary of State for India, of their views on the Council of India Bill which was due for its first reading in the House of Lords on 15 May 1914. Though the Bill was rejected and his hopes for an early breakthrough on political reforms were not realized, Jinnah did not despair. He was convinced that India's freedom largely depended on 'the united will and effort of this generation'.[25]

In order to mobilize the support of Muslims for the All-India Muslim League, a Muslim political organization founded in 1906, Jinnah joined it in 1913 and helped it adopt the goal of 'self-government suitable to India'. Sarojini Naidu (1879–1949), and many subsequent writers on the subject have insisted that Jinnah joined the Muslim League after his 'two sponsors were required to make a solemn preliminary covenant that loyalty to the Muslim League and the Muslim interest would in no way and at no time imply even the shadow of disloyalty to the larger national cause to which his life was dedicated'.[26] However, there seems to have been little need or justification for this kind of assurance. As Jinnah told the League Council meeting of 31 December 1912, where he was specially invited to attend the session, the League, by adopting the goal of 'a self-government suitable to India' could 'well be congratulated for going ahead, even of the Congress, in the formation of the ideal'.[27] In his speech, Jinnah even chided Mazhar-ul-Haque (1866–1930), a prominent Muslim League leader, for his opposition to this ideal: 'If he knew the English language, he was sure it meant government of the people by the people'.[28] Though he himself was a 'Congressman',[29] Jinnah believed that the Congress was lagging behind. He indeed 'prophesied that very soon the Congress would adopt the same form as suggested by the League....'[30] Thus, the question of a conflict of interests between the League and the larger national cause or seeking any assurances on that account did not arise. Jinnah was convinced that the League itself represented 'the larger national cause'. This was further clear from his address to the Lucknow session of the All-India Muslim League in 1916. As he put it:

> The main principle on which the first All-India Muslim political organisation was based was the retention of Muslim communal individuality strong and unimpaired in any constitutional readjustment that might be made in India in the course of its political evolution. The creed has grown and broadened with the growth of political life and thought in the community. In its general outlook and ideals as regards the future, the All-India Muslim League stands abreast of the Indian National Congress and is ready to participate in any patriotic efforts for the advancement of the country as a whole.[31]

In November 1916, acting as the President of the Lucknow session of the League, barely two months after he had signed, along with some prominent Indian leaders, the Memorandum of the Nineteen, suggesting several constitutional reforms, Jinnah moved the League and the Congress to draft a scheme for Indian self-government to which both organizations agreed. Popularly known as the Lucknow Pact, the main gain for the Muslims was the acceptance of the principle of separate electorates by the Congress. The Muslims were particularly happy

> to remove the danger of Hindu and Congress opposition to separate Muslim electorates so that the government...would be convinced that on the issue of Muslim representation there was no opposition from anyone in India.[32]

In addition, the Muslims of the Muslim-minority provinces such as, United Provinces, Bombay, Bihar, etc., received a greater share of representation than merited by their numerical strength.[33] In fact, the Lucknow Pact showed that it was possible for Hindu and Muslim middle-classes to reach 'an amicable settlement of Hindu-Muslim constitutional and political problems'.[34] It also enhanced 'the strength of Indian nationalism'.[35] Jinnah was declared not only an 'ambassador', but 'an embodied symbol of Hindu-Muslim Unity'.[36] Sarojini Naidu hastened to publish a selection of his speeches and statements entitled, *Mohamed Ali Jinnah: An Ambassador of Unity*.

Although Jinnah was an acknowledged all-India leader, he continued to seek reconciliation between Muslim interests and all-India national interests. While he reprimanded critics of the League for 'the reproach of "separatism"'[37] he took special pains to assure the Muslims that self-government did not necessarily mean Hindu Government. The Muslims were a large community, and thus things could not be imposed upon them against their will. Indeed, he went on to ask, rather rhetorically, 'If 70 millions Musalmans do not approve of the measure, which is carried by a ballot box, do you think it could be enforced or administered in this country?'[38]

In 1916, Jinnah helped conciliate the Congress 'moderates' led by Gokhale and Mehta and 'extremists' led by Bal Gangadhar Tilak (1856–1920), whom Jinnah had defended at one of his trials over sedition and other charges. In October 1917, he joined the Home Rule League founded by Annie Besant (1847–1933) in September 1916, to further the common cause of attainment of self-government for India.[39] On 17 June 1918, after Besant's internment he was elected president of the Bombay Home Rule League. He used his position to organize public meetings throughout the Bombay Presidency, mobilized propaganda and publicity campaigns, and personally supervised the publication of the *Bombay Chronicle*, a paper edited by B.C. Horniman, a leading British journalist working in India. Although these activities helped promote the cause he was devoted to, the result was a serious clash with Lord Freeman-Thomas Willingdon (1866–1941), the Governor of Bombay who alleged that the Home Rule league was causing difficulties for the government during the war years. In June 1918, Willingdon publicly cast aspersions on the loyalty and commitment of the Home Rule League to the war effort. The worst happened on the eve of a farewell memorial, planned by some supporters of Willingdon in the Town Hall on 11 December 1918. In the company of hundreds of his supporters present on the occasion, Jinnah told Willingdon to his face that the people of Bombay were not party to 'commemorating or approving' his services as governor.[40] Though assaulted by the police, which caused the meeting to end in pandemonium, Jinnah made his point and was instantly recognized by the people as their hero. A one-rupee public fund was instituted to build the 'Jinnah Peoples Memorial Hall' in the compound of the Bombay office of the Congress, in recognition of his brave fight against the 'combined forces of bureaucracy and autocracy....'[41] The Hall was formally inaugurated in 1919 by Besant. Jinnah was not present on the occasion. He was in England with the Muslim League delegation on constitutional reforms and the Khilafat issue. He was telegraphed: 'A prophet is honoured in his own country in his own times'.[42]

It is obvious that, by this time, Jinnah had risen high in Indian politics. However, the situation began to change radically with the development of the Khilafat sentiment and the launching of the Khilafat–Non-cooperation movement. Jinnah was neither indifferent to the fate of the *Khilafat* (Caliphate) in Turkey nor unmindful of the Punjab situation born out of the Amritsar massacre of 1919. Addressing the Calcutta session of the League on 7 September 1920, for instance, he bitterly criticized the British Government for its 'Punjab atrocities' and 'the spoilation of the Ottoman Empire and the *Khilafat*'. In his own words: 'The one attacks our liberty, the other our faith'.[43] In March 1919, indeed, he resigned from the Imperial Legislative Council in protest against the passage of the Rowlatt Bill, which precipitated the troubles in the Punjab. He led a delegation to London to apprise the British Government of Muslim feelings on the *Khilafat*. On 19 January 1920, in an address presented to the Viceroy, he demanded that the British Government 'in concluding any settlement to which they attach any degree of finality...should take into the fullest consideration the most binding religious obligations and the most highly cherished sentiments of 70 millions of Indian Musalmans....'[44]

The problem was that Jinnah disagreed with the non-cooperation 'methods' promoted by Gandhi,[45] which, among other things, called for the triple boycott of law courts, schools and legislatures. Jinnah personally led the agitation against Lord Willingdon. He was not afraid of taking on the government. However, he believed that the struggles for *Khilafat* and self-government must be waged through a well-thought plan, after considered deliberation, rather than by expressing impulsive indignation. He explained to the Special Congress session at Calcutta on 8 September 1920: 'I am fully convinced of non-cooperation. I see no other way except the policy of non-cooperation. But before I put this policy into practice I want to take stock of the situation to find what are the materials and forces'.[46]

Thus, when Gandhi, at the head of the Khilafat–Non-cooperation movement, invited him 'to take share in the new life that has opened up before the country', Jinnah was not amused. If by 'new life', he charged,

> You mean your methods and programmes, I am afraid I cannot accept them; for I am fully convinced that it must lead to disaster…your extreme programme has for the moment captured the imagination mostly of the inexperienced youth and the ignorant and the illiterate. All this means complete disorganisation and chaos. What the consequences of this may be, I shudder to contemplate….[47]

In fact, as Ayesha Jalal has pointed out, 'Jinnah alone stuck to the methods of moderate constitutionalism',[48] and remained aloof from Indian politics during the years of the Khilafat–Non-cooperation movement, that is, from 1921 to 1924. He was convinced that the non-cooperation methods were impossible 'from the point of view of practical politics, and its complete lack of touch with the realities of modern politics'.[49] He had to wait until constitutional politics and methods made a comeback. He preferred to stay on the sidelines rather than fall in line with the government. In 1921, he spurned a tempting offer to enlist the support of those who had stayed out of the Non-cooperation movement. He was not interested. He recognized and understood the exigencies of the situation. As he explained at some length:

> The Non-cooperation movement is only an expression of general dissatisfaction, owing to the utter disregard of public opinion and of outstanding grievances. Every country has an extreme section of opinion but it will be impossible for that section to make any headway if the bulk of the people are satisfied. And my reading of the Indian situation is that, leave alone the bulk of the people, even the intellectual and reasonable section is far from satisfied with the present policy of the Government.[50]

Thus, as far as a way out of the difficulties could be found through negotiation with the government, Jinnah was willing to work for it. Indeed, he did his best to 'prevent a complete polarization' between the government and the Congress.[51] In January 1922, he made an effort through the All-Parties Conference to bring the government and the important leaders of the Non-cooperation movement together in a round table conference. But, before any positive outcome could be expected, the Chauri Chaura incident of 5 February claimed the lives of 22 policemen, and changed the entire situation. Gandhi hastened to call off the movement.[52] Fissures within the Khilafat–Non-cooperation leadership had developed as early as 1921, due in part to the Moplah uprising. Remarkably, both Maulana Hasrat Mohani (1877–1951) and Gandhi, 'though speaking from opposite sides at the annual Congress session at Ahmedabad in December 1921, admitted that Hindu–Muslim unity was not yet a fact of life'.[53]

The Khilafat–Non-cooperation movement received a major shock on 1 November 1922, when Turkish Parliament abolished the Ottoman Sultanate. On 24 July 1923, the Treaty of Lausanne that formally ended the fighting between the Allies and Turkish nationalists 'marked the beginning of the end of the Indian Muslim agitation against the British until the abolition of the caliphate by Ankara [Mustafa Kemal Ataturk] in March 1924 took the wind out of its sails'.[54]

The result of the Khilafat–Non-cooperation movement had become apparent long before its final collapse. Jinnah had sensed it much earlier than any other political leader, Muslim or Hindu. He was convinced from the beginning that this movement was bound to fail. However, this prognosis was 'much too practical to be popular at a time when his community was surcharged with religious zeal for the Khilafat' and the entire country seemed to believe that 'freedom was at hand and they had to make one final attempt to grasp it'.[55] Once, however, the religious passions of the Muslims and Hindus were aroused and used for the attainment of impractical political objectives, the inter-communal harmony that leaders like Jinnah sought to cultivate became ever more elusive. Though Jinnah's stand was vindicated by the turn of events, this could not help him regain his former status in Indian politics. 'The graph of Jinnah's career', as his biographer, Hector Bolitho, put it, 'showed a downward trend'.[56] The elevation of provincial politics under the reforms of 1919, and the growing Hindu–Muslim antagonism made his position all the more precarious. Jinnah did not have a power base at the provincial level. He was essentially an all-India leader, operating at the national level, and for a good reason. Self-government could only come with responsibility at the centre. The only provincial office Jinnah ever held was that of the Bombay Home

Rule League, and that too for a limited period of time, and as pointed out earlier, for all-India purposes.

The years of political inactivity and setback for Jinnah ended in November 1923. Jinnah was elected unopposed as an independent candidate to the Legislative Assembly.[57] On the opening of the Assembly in January 1924, he was also appointed, in recognition of his past parliamentary services,[58] on the panel of the Chairman to the Assembly. In May 1924, he was elected President of the Lahore session of the League, and re-elected unopposed as the League's President for a further term of three years. He was the only Muslim leader of an all-India standing who had remained outside the Khilafat–Non-cooperation movement. Therefore, he was not hurt by its eventual collapse. His standing as a Muslim leader, despite his low profile during the Khilafat movement, was unimpaired. His re-emergence also 'brought to the fore the fundamental differences between the two sections of Muslim opinion—one represented by Mohammed Ali Jinnah believing in a constitutional fight through the councils, and the other by Mohammed Ali Jauhar who preferred a policy of obstructionism'.[59] The balance of power, however, now favoured the former as evidenced by the 1924 Lahore session of the League, where, in spite of the imposing presence of the Khilafatists and non-cooperators, such as Maulana Mohammed Ali, Maulana Shaukat Ali (1873–1938), Dr Mukhtar Ansari, and Dr Saifuddin Kitchlew (1884–1963), Jinnah dominated the proceedings.[60] Jinnah indeed felt so sure of his position with the Muslims that he did not hesitate to declare publicly that 'the Triple Boycott was a failure....'[61] Although the Khilafatists, as Naeem Qureshi has pointed out, were 'indignant at the prospect of the leadership slipping out of their hands...they had no solution for the new situation. Jinnah at the head of the All-India Muslim League seemed to be more suited to take up the challenge'.[62]

Jinnah called for a radical revision of the Lucknow Pact of 1916. In the post-1919 reforms situation, with a devolution of power to the provinces, Jinnah wanted a greater share of power for the Muslims in the provincial governments. In particular, he demanded that statutory majorities should be restored in the Punjab and Bengal, the majorities which the Muslims had lost through the Lucknow Pact. Only a new pact between the Muslims and Hindus, represented by the League and

Congress, respectively, as in the past, he insisted, could satisfy the Muslims. By now Jinnah was also convinced that there was 'no escaping away from the fact that communalism did exist in the country' and that the Congress position was 'far from reassuring for the Muslims'.[63]

This realization led Jinnah to devise a two-pronged strategy. One was to identify, articulate, and express Muslim interests as best as he could and to secure their rights in the future constitution of India. In fact, he stressed, '…you cannot give any constitution to India of responsible government without making provisions for safeguarding the rights and interests of the Musalmans…you cannot separate one from the other if a constitution is to be completed'.[64] The second was to persuade the Congress to see the worth of those interests and accept them as a basis for cooperation between the Muslims and the Hindus in the common cause of self-government for India. 'I would…appeal to my Hindu brethren', he pleaded, 'that, in the present state of position, they should try to win the confidence and trust of the Mohammedans who are, after all, in the minority in the country'.[65] Indeed, he took it upon himself to help the Hindus produce a constitution acceptable both to the Muslims and the Hindus.

This was not to be an easy task in the changed circumstances of India. Jinnah had not only to contend with the Congress but, more problematically, also deal with the Hindu Mahasabha which emerged as the dominant Hindu force of the 1920s 'representing as it did Hindu nationalism' in Indian politics.[66] The Mahasabha was bitterly opposed to the principle of separate electorates for the Muslims.

Jinnah made a determined effort to assure the Congress and the Mahasabha that separate electorates were negotiable. The percentage, the ratio on the population, were only means for 'an adequate and effective representation', to 'be fixed by mutual good will and consent, in order to secure the success of any scheme that may come in force for representation to the municipalities and legislatures'.[67] Indeed, Jinnah convened and presided over a representative conference of the Muslim leaders[68] at Delhi in March 1927, and prevailed upon them to agree to the institution of 'joint electorates' for representation in the various legislatures in the future scheme of constitution, under certain conditions. These conditions, *inter alia*, included the separation of Sindh from the Bombay Presidency, political reforms in the North-West

Frontier Province and Balochistan on the same footing as in any other province in India, electoral representation in the Punjab and Bengal in accordance with population, and one-third representation in the central legislature.[69] Jinnah still was a 'nationalist', and even suggested that the Muslims had placed 'an exaggerated faith' in separate electorates. However, he recognized that joint electorates 'could not be forced on an embittered minority'.[70]

Initial reactions to Delhi Muslim Proposals were mixed. While the All-India Congress Committee, in its meetings of May 1927, and December 1927, reacted favourably to these proposals, the Hindu Mahasabha was furious. 'In what ways', the *Hindustan Times* asked, echoing Madan Mohan Malaviya (1861–1946) and Lajpat Rai, 'is the establishment of joint electorates connected with the separation of Sindh, and the introduction of reforms in North-West Frontier Province...? The object Muslims have in view is to obtain as much as they can while conceding as little as possible'.[71] To make things difficult for Jinnah, some prominent Muslim leaders such as Sir Mian Mohammad Shafi and Fazl-i-Husain, were not prepared to surrender separate electorates.[72] Jinnah's position was seriously undermined.

However, Jinnah was encouraged by the immediate Congress response to the proposals. He appointed a Muslim League Committee to discuss with the Congress, and convene an All-Parties Conference to negotiate a compromise. The Conference met at Delhi on 11 February 1928, but the Congress, led by Gandhi, failed to respond positively. Apparently, 'more anxious' about 'the pattern of government rather than its principles' the Congress backed out of its earlier stance.[73] On 11 March, the League was left with no option but to walk out of the Conference. On 19 May, the Conference formally rejected the Muslim proposals. However, the Conference agreed to constitute a special committee under the Chairmanship of Pandit Motilal Nehru (1861–1931) to 'consider and determine the principles of the constitution for India'.[74] Though this move meant the resumption of Hindu–Muslim talks on the future of India, it cannot be denied that Jinnah's 'bold and patriotic initiative which had interjected a ray of light into the encircling gloom',[75] as one writer put it, was squandered. This was the first time a prominent group of Muslim leaders had agreed to abandon separate electorates for the larger all-India cause.

Jinnah was dismayed. He had proposed an alternative to the Lucknow Pact of 1916, and incorporated some of the more salient demands of the two communities: joint electorates, as demanded by the Hindus, Muslim representation in the Punjab and Bengal according to their population and one-third Muslim representation at the centre as desired by the Muslims. This formula had cost him the popular support of the Muslim community, which was largely opposed to the surrendering of separate electorates.[76] In spite of all this, the Congress, ostensibly under pressure from the Mahasabha, let him down. Yet, compulsive nationalist that he was, and keen to advance the cause of Indian freedom, Jinnah decided to cooperate with the Congress rather than with the British Government, which had already announced the formation of the Simon Commission in November 1927. 'India cannot', Jinnah declared, 'participate in this policy and share in the work of the Commission in any form at any stage because it is a complete negation of India's status as partner'.[77]

It was only when the Nehru Report was published and his efforts to amend it to the satisfaction of the Muslims failed, that Jinnah realized that Muslim interests and Indian national interests as pursued by the Congress were not easily reconciliable. He felt that the so-called 'national interests' were largely an expression of Hindu interests. Still, at the All-Parties Conference at Calcutta on 22 December 1928, he tried hard to reach an amicable settlement with the Hindus. In an appeal, more as an Indian than a Muslim leader, he entreated,

> What we want is that Hindus and Muslims should march together until our object is attained. Therefore, it is essential that you must get not only the Muslim League but the Mussalmans of India and here I am not speaking as a Mussalman but as an Indian. And it is my desire to see that we get seven crores of Mussalmans to march along with us in the struggle for freedom.[78]

Jinnah reiterated the point in a speech in the Central Legislative Assembly on demands for budget grants and constitutional reforms in India on 12 March 1929. He explained that the Nehru Report 'is nothing more than a Hindu counter-proposal to the Muslim proposals which were made in 1927, as far as the communal question is concerned. It has not been accepted by the Mussalmans...and the sooner we realise that fact the better....'[79] But the Congress was not moved. Ignoring Jinnah and the hostile Muslim reaction it decided to present the British with an ultimatum to accept the Nehru Report within a year, or else face the Civil Disobedience Movement. It is very hard to explain Congress attitude at this point in time except to argue, with some justification, that the moderate leaders of the Congress found it difficult to deal 'with the tide of Hindu Nationalism or communalism, especially in view of the leadership provided to the latter by such towering leaders as Malaviya and Lajpat Rai, who, like the Ali brothers [Maulana Mohammed Ali and Maulana Shaukat Ali], also occupied an exalted position inside the Congress'.[80] The upsurge in communal violence further undermined moderates. Between April and September 1928 there were twenty-five riots, including ten in the United Provinces (UP), and some twenty-two riots during the Simon Commission's visit. Three hundred persons were killed and about 2000 injured by communal violence at this critical juncture.[81] Jinnah had gone out on a limb to offer the Congress a compromise that did away with separate electorates in exchange for some of the major Muslim demands. But, Motilal Nehru failed to demonstrate a similar level of statesmanship and refused to take on the communalists in his camp. On the contrary, he threatened to 'resign as President' if the Congress rejected his report and 'looked to Gandhi to concoct some formula of conciliation.' Gandhi obliged by reaffirming his support for the Nehru Report in an article in *Young India* in December 1928.[82]

In March 1929, Jinnah formulated and presented his 'Fourteen Points'[83] to the Muslim League Council which readily approved them. Besides insisting on separate electorates and other Muslim demands, these points sought to create five Muslim-majority provinces to balance six Hindu-majority provinces under a truly federal constitution with sufficient safeguards for all communities, but especially the Muslims. The idea was 'to ensure the "unity of India" at the top while providing the Muslims with a sense of participation and belonging'.[84] This was a position different, radically different, from the position taken in the Delhi Muslim Proposals. While in those proposals Jinnah had endeavoured to represent both Muslims and Hindus in the greater cause of Hindu–Muslim unity, the Fourteen Points clearly represented Muslim interests and aspirations. In fact, like the resolutions of the All-Parties Muslim Conference held in January 1929 at Delhi, it 'showed the trend of Muslim political opinion away from agreement with Congress, and its focus on common communal demand to safeguard Muslim interests in the face of constitutional change and threatened agitation'.[85] The Fourteen Points brought Jinnah essentially to the centre-stage of Muslim politics. Jinnah did not become a Muslim 'communalist', but he 'could no longer be called the Ambassador of Unity in the same sense as the title had been applied to him theretofore'.[86]

Jinnah was not the only leader who had been disappointed with the attitude of the Hindus in general and of the Congress in particular. Maulana Mohammed Ali, Allama Muhammad Iqbal (1877–1938) and a number of other important Muslim leaders felt the same way. Maulana Mohammed Ali even accused Gandhi of encouraging the communalism of the Hindu majority at the expense of the 'nationalist' cause promoted by the Congress in the past.[87] But while he had no further interest left in persuading the Congress to rectify the situation, Jinnah was still keen to carry on his efforts. He had not lost faith in Hindu–Muslim unity for the common cause of Indian self-government. Thus, on 19 June 1929, he wrote to the British Prime Minister, Ramsay MacDonald (1866–1937), to invite 'representatives of India, who would be in a position to deliver the goods' to sit in a conference with them to reach a solution that may have the 'willing assent of the political India'. As far as the Simon Commission was concerned, he told the Prime Minister that it was 'boycotted by political India', and when its report, 'whatever it may be, is published in due course, every effort will be made in India to damn it'.[88] Prophetically, the Report, published in May 1930, was dismissed in India as worthless. The British Government itself did not hesitate to shelve its recommendations and await the outcome of the Round Table Conference to be convened in November 1930 in London.

But Jinnah was in for another disappointment at the hands of the Congress. Armed with the Independence Declaration at Lahore in 1929, the Congress went ahead with the launching of the Civil Disobedience Movement in the country. It refused to come to the Round Table Conference unless certain prior conditions, which, in particular, included the major demand that India should first be given a dominion status, were accepted. 26 January 1930 was fixed as 'Independence Day' (*Purna Swaraj* Day, as Gandhi called it). Jinnah tried his best to persuade the Congress to be realistic and practical and make use of the opportunity in London for what it was worth. But led by Gandhi, who Jinnah now charged, was 'mentally and constitutionally incapable of learning things', the Congress preferred the Disobedience Movement to the Round Table Conference.[89] Jinnah, however, decided to take part in the Conference to make yet another effort to solve the Indian problem.

Though the Congress took part in the second Round Table Conference in 1931, after calling-off its Civil Disobedience Movement and entering into a 'pact' with the Viceroy, Lord Irwin, considerable damage had already been done to the interests of India. While Jinnah, at the first Conference, was able to persuade the Muslim delegation, in spite of Fazl-i-Husain's proposed 'strategy',[90] to accept joint electorates, contingent, of course, upon certain conditions, things had become far more difficult by the time the Congress joined the proceedings. Both Hindu and Muslim delegates had hardened their positions. The Hindus insisted on a federation with a strong centre. The Muslims desired a loose federation with autonomous provinces. They were also now determined to retain separate electorates, weightage, and statutory majorities in the Punjab and Bengal. To further complicate matters, Gandhi, through his public pronouncements and gestures, helped widen the gulf between the Muslims and the Hindus on a host of political issues. The result was, as Jinnah put it, 'we went round and round in London…without reaching the straight path that would lead us to freedom'.[91]

Jinnah stressed that the Muslims wanted self-government for India as much as the Hindus, but they desired 'that sense of security among the minorities, which will secure a willing cooperation and allegiance to the state….'[92] In fact, Jinnah was so deeply committed to the idea of self-government that he did not hesitate to introduce what the *Times* reported as 'the first suggestion of controversy' in his very first address at the Round Table Conference when he told Prime Minister MacDonald: 'I am glad, Mr President that you referred to the fact that "the declarations made by British sovereigns and statesmen from time to time that Great Britain's work in India was to prepare her for self-government have been plain"…But I must emphasize that India now expects translation and fulfillment of these declarations into action'.[93] While he conceded that the British 'have a great interest in India, both commercial and political…[he wanted them] equally to concede that we have a greater and far more vital interest than you have, because you have the financial or commercial interest, and the political interest, but to us it is all in all.'[94] He even warned the British that unless the Round Table Conference made a positive contribution to reach a 'settlement' to 'satisfy' the Indian demand for self-government the 70 million Muslims who had 'kept aloof' from the Civil Disobedience Movement might be tempted to 'join' it.[95]

The British Prime Minister tried to restrain Jinnah from his fierce advocacy of self-government. During a conversation, he even suggested that, in view of the constitutional changes in India the British Government would be looking for prominent Indians for appointment as Provincial Governors implying in no uncertain terms that 'Jinnah would have an excellent chance if he proved to be a good boy'. But Jinnah was offended. Indeed, he saw this remark as 'an attempt to bribe him'.[96] In the end, of course, Jinnah was not invited to participate in the future deliberations of the Conference when the British Government took upon itself the task of framing a federal scheme for India. The Aga Khan, leader of the Muslim delegation at the Conference, and at times, Jinnah's challenger for the leadership of Muslim India, could not help 'regret Mr Jinnah's absence' during this period. He lamented that: 'It was, I think, extremely unfortunate that we Muslims did not insist on having Mr Jinnah with us....' His presence could have been very helpful.[97] Jinnah believed that he was 'not invited to the later sittings of the Conference because I was the strongest opponent of the scheme that was being constructed...' by the British Government for India.[98] He was sure that this scheme 'would never materialise in a manner which would satisfy the legitimate aspirations of India'.[99]

However, what hurt Jinnah most during the proceedings of the Conference was not so much the attitude of the British Government as the attitude of the Indians themselves, the Muslims and the Hindus, who failed to rise to the occasion. Gandhi, as its sole representative, insisted that the Congress represented 'the whole of India, all interests',[100] and refused to recognize and concede Muslim interests and demands. Lord Zetland (1876–1961) suggested that it was 'possible' that Gandhi may have persuaded himself of 'the expediency' of agreeing to the Muslim demands but for Malaviya, leader of the Hindu Mahasabha, who sat 'at Mr Gandhi's elbow, alert to detect and to squash any sign of weakness on the part of his less orthodox fellow countrymen'.[101] However, Jinnah was convinced by now that the only difference between the Congress and the Hindu Mahasabha so far as the Muslims were concerned, was that while Congress 'masquerades under the name of nationalism...the Hindu Mahasabha does not mince words'.[102] Jinnah felt sorry that the Muslims had no idea of what was at stake and thus failed to act in concert and for the betterment of the community. Disillusioned and disappointed, Jinnah indeed withdrew from active politics, and settled in London. Years later, he recalled:

> I received the shock of my life at the meetings of the Round Table Conference. The Hindu sentiment, the Hindu mind, the Hindu attitude led me to the conclusion that there was no hope of unity. I felt very pessimistic about my country. The position was most unfortunate. The Musalmans were like the No-Man's land; they were led either by the flunkeys of the British Government or the camp-followers of the Congress. Whenever attempts were made to organise the Muslims, toadies and flunkeys on the one hand and traitors in the Congress camp on the other frustrated the efforts. I began to feel that neither could I help India, nor change the Hindu mentality, nor could I make the Musalmans realise their precarious position. I felt so disappointed and so depressed that I decided to settle down in London. Not that I did not love India; but I felt utterly helpless.[103]

Jinnah's self-imposed exile was not simply a turning point in his own political career. It was also, in a way, 'a turning point in the Indo-British history, for the failure of the Hindus and Muslims to reach a settlement marked the final parting of the ways which ended in the creation of Pakistan....'[104] However, Jinnah still kept 'in touch with India'.[105] He regularly wrote to Abdul Matin Choudhury (1895–1949), a former colleague and member of the Indian Legislative Assembly, and others to learn the details of developments and to give them advice and guidance. For, as he wrote to Matin Choudhury on 25 March 1931, even his stay in London was meant to help the cause of India: 'The centre of gravity is here and in next two or three years London will be the most important scene of Indian drama of Constitutional reforms'.[106] However, in a letter to Matin Choudhury on 2 March 1932, he stressed:

The Musalmans must stand united and I agree that there should be one organization… If the Muslim leaders know how to play their cards, I am sure the community will get what they want and after all it is not much. You cannot live on safeguards, but on your own merits and exertions. The community is very backward and has to make up a lot.[107]

The fact of the matter was that the Muslims lacked unity and a sense of purpose and direction at this point in time. In particular, they did not know how to respond to the crisis precipitated by Gandhi's insistence, after attending the Round Table Conference in London, that India proceed 'only on the basis of Indian nationalism untainted by any communal considerations'.[108] They were completely lost. Instinctively, they decided to appeal to Jinnah, an old, tried and tested leader, to return to India and take charge of the situation. They could not think of any other leader capable of leading them out of their difficulties. Sir Mohammad Yakub (1879–1942), member of the Legislative Assembly, Raja Mohammad Amir Ahmed Khan of Mahmudabad (1914–1973), popularly known as Raja Sahib of Mahmudabad, Sir Abdullah Haroon (1872–1942), and many leaders of public opinion sent personal letters to Jinnah to plead with him for his early return to India.[109] Most importantly, the Muslim League Council, in its meeting held on 12 March 1933, after deliberating upon the difficult situation, especially in the wake of the White Paper embodying the recommendations of the Round Table Conference published in March 1933, sent Jinnah an urgent telegram to return to India and lead the Muslims in this hour of crisis.[110] On 15 March 1933, the *Civil and Military Gazette* of Lahore, a paper hardly sympathetic to Jinnah, headlined 'Muslim "SOS" to Mr Jinnah' and succinctly summed up the whole situation in these words: '…in a community so prolific in leaders as the Muslims…a message to Mr Jinnah across the seas is a pathetic confession of failure of some of these leaders to visualize the dangers threatening their community at this critical juncture…[Indeed] an appeal to Caesar has been necessary'.[111]

There is no gainsaying that the Muslims were confronted with a grave situation: 'Chartless on the sea of India's most crucial years',[112] as one writer described it, they had no real leader to give them direction. They were divided into numerous groups motivated by narrow, parochial interests, and engaged in mutual acrimony and hostilities. By one estimate, there were at least five distinct groups asserting Muslim rights in different ways.[113] The League itself, ever since Jinnah relinquished its presidency in 1930, was stagnant. It was ridden with factions, each of them claiming to be the authentic Muslim League. In 1933, two insignificant sessions of the League were held. One group, led by Mian Abdul Aziz, convened on 21 October 1933 at Howrah. The other, led by Hafiz Hidayat Hussain, met on 25 and 26 November at Delhi.[114] Various internecine conflicts were exacerbated by the communal bitterness, rancour, insecurity, and uncertainty, generated by the Congress's declaration of 'independence' and the resultant Civil Disobedience Movement, which did not take the Muslims into confidence. In addition, the Muslims were upset with some provisions of the Communal Award, announced by the British Government in 1932. They were particularly disappointed with their majorities not being restored in the Punjab and Bengal. Indeed, as one Muslim leader wrote to Jinnah: 'The closing scene of the Round Table Conference has left the Muslims in the cold. We are unable to judge the real position, and there is no one else to give correct lead and take up the command'.[115]

In these difficult circumstances, in spite of the fact that he had started to practice at the Privy Council Bar in London, Jinnah could not long disassociate himself from the fate of the Muslims or Indian politics for that matter. In 1934, he decided to re-enter the political scene. In March 1934, he was elected Permanent President of the Muslim League. In October 1934, he was elected member of the Indian Legislative Assembly for Bombay Muslims. In 1935, after a couple of short visits, he finally returned to India to lead the Muslims out of their difficult situation. As he explained years later, 'I found that the Musalmans were in the greatest danger. I made up my mind to come back to India, as I could not do any good from London'.[116] Not surprisingly, when a law colleague expressed his desire to buy his very precious office furniture in London, which included some 'lovely mahogany pieces', Jinnah obliged: 'it is yours. I don't care about these chattels. I am on a grand mission to India'.[117]

But, this certainly did not mean that the 'grand mission' entailed a break with 'Indian nationalism' as such. Jinnah still stood for 'national self-government' for India. In fact, he insisted that the 'Muslims are in no way behind any other community in their demand for national self-government.'[118] The only thing he wanted to make sure for the Muslims was their 'proper and effective share' in the political system, which had been denied to them over the years. He was an ardent Indian nationalist, and was prepared 'to revive the entente of the Lucknow Pact period in the cause of nationalism'.[119] He strongly condemned the 1935 Act. He believed that this Act in no way satisfied nationalist aspirations. But then, he was realistic enough to accept it under the circumstances. As he saw it:

> The German nation, when it was forced to sign the Treaty of Versailles, signed it. If I have to deal with this constitution as the Germans dealt with the Versailles Treaty, I shall begin by tearing off as many pages as the Government of India Act has, and we shall not rest content until that constitution is replaced by a constitution which is acceptable to us.[120]

But what Jinnah was not prepared to do was to allow nationalist interests to develop at the expense of Muslim interests. He demanded that Muslim interests should be recognized as genuine interests of a community and secured in the future constitution of India. This was clearly reflected in his response to the report of the Joint Parliamentary Committee which was published in India in November 1934, and came up before the Legislative Assembly in February 1935 for consideration. While the Congress wanted that the recommendations of the Report on all its aspects, federal, and provincial, and the Communal Award, should be rejected outright, Jinnah tried to secure the measures benefitting the Muslims, no matter how little. With the help of his 'Independent Group' of 22, he voted against the Congress and defeated the motion by 72 to 61 votes. Subsequently, he moved an amendment, divided into three parts, for the purposes of separate voting. The first related to the acceptance of the Communal Award, the second to the scheme of provincial autonomy in the sense that it was an advance over the 'dyarchy' of the 1919 Act, and the third to the scheme of All-India Federation, which he condemned as 'fundamentally bad and totally unacceptable' to the people of India. He got the first part adopted by 68 votes to 15, the Congress remaining neutral, and the second and the third parts together being adopted by 74 votes to 58. The result was not only 'a personal triumph' for Jinnah but also a clear message to the Congress and the British that the Muslims 'would refuse to support any measure' that ignored their interests.[121]

To safeguard and promote Muslim interests, Jinnah devoted his attention to the reorganization of the Muslim League. His earlier experience in Indian politics had convinced him that Muslim interests would not receive recognition and respect unless these were backed by an organized political party. He was rebuffed at the Calcutta Convention in December 1928 and his amendments to the Nehru Report were rejected, in part, because he had not been able to show to the Congress (and the Mahasabha) the necessary strength of the League for the purpose. He did not want to suffer the same fate again. Therefore, he was very keen to organize the League for the benefit of the Muslims without any apology to the so-called votaries of Indian nationalism. 'Muslims', he told the Jamiat-ul-Ulama Conference in April 1936, 'must think of the interests of our [sic] community. Unless you make the best efforts, you will fail and will command no respect and nobody will bother to consult you. Organise yourself and play your part'. There was nothing wrong, he insisted, in working for one's own community: 'The Hindus and Muslims must be organized separately and once when they are both organised they will understand each other better and then we will not have to wait for years for an understanding'. Responding to the charge of his critics that he was encouraging Muslim communalism, Jinnah retorted: 'I am helping eighty million people and if they are more organized they will be all the more useful for the national struggle'.[122] Not surprisingly, he entered the 1937 elections emphasizing that, 'if Muslims would speak with one voice, a settlement between Hindus and Muslims would come quicker....'[123] The June 1936 manifesto had already declared the Lucknow Pact of 1916 as 'one of the greatest beacon lights in the constitutional history of India.'[124]

However, the League did not do well in the 1937 elections, and for a number of reasons. It had fought the elections on an all-India basis for the first time, and it had neither the provincial set-up nor adequate finances to spread its message across the length and breadth of the country. The Central Parliamentary Board and its provincial counterparts had to be established from the scratch. In addition, there was considerable opposition from leaders in the Muslim-majority provinces determined to promote their own particular interests. One problem with the Muslim-majority provinces was that, in general, 'with a Muslim always at the head of the administration' they 'felt less fearful of Hindu domination'.[125] In the Punjab, for instance, Sikandar Hayat Khan was not interested in the League or its election campaign. Indeed, except for some educated, urban middle class leaders like Allama Iqbal, Khalifa Shuja-ud-Din (1887–1955) and Malik Barkat Ali (1886–1946), there were hardly any takers for the League.[126] Most of the local leaders were tied to their *biradaris*, and remained committed to the Unionist Party. Sindh was likewise preoccupied with local and factional politics, and there was little interest in the League or its centrist cause now that Sindh was a separate province. In the NWFP, the League could not find a single candidate willing to stand from the League platform. Ethnicity and local politics dominated the scene. The only consolation was Bengal where the provincial United Muslim Party led by Sir Khwaja Nazimuddin (1894–1964) and Huseyn Shaheed Suhrawardy (1893–1963), for their own local considerations, merged with the Muslim League. However, the League was more successful in the Muslim-minority provinces, especially the United Provinces (UP). A number of prominent leaders agreed to support the League, although some of them, including Nawabzada Liaquat Ali Khan (1895–1951), Secretary of the Central Board, chose not to fight elections on the League ticket.[127] Above all, the League had barely six months to prepare for the elections.

Thus, it was no surprise that the League secured only 109 out of 482 seats reserved for Muslims.[128] It could not win a single seat in Sindh. In the Punjab, it secured only two seats. It was only in Bengal that the League fared well and bagged 39 seats, a few more than the rival Krishak Praja Party of Maulvi Abul Kasem Fazlul Haq (1873–1962). However, this did not mean that the Muslims had supported the Congress instead. While the Congress secured 711 out of 1,585 general seats, it could capture only 26 Muslim seats, 19 of them in the NWFP, in alliance with the Khudai Khidmatgars of Abdul Ghaffar Khan (1891–1988).[129] The Congress failed to return any Muslim candidate from the Punjab, Sindh, Bengal Assam, UP, Central Provinces (CP), Orissa and Bombay. Its 'claim to represent Muslim opinion had been badly tarnished'.[130] Thus, understandably, Jinnah was far from disappointed with the overall outcome. In fact, he sounded very optimistic. As he put it: 'In each and every province where the League

Parliamentary Board was established and the League parties were constituted we carried away about 60 and 70 per cent of the seats that were contested by the League candidates....'[131] Indeed, he advised the disillusioned supporters of the League 'to have courage and faith— *Delhi Durnest*'.[132]

More importantly, Jinnah, who had fought the elections on a conciliatory note, hoped that the Congress would treat the League with respect and understanding, and thus it would not be difficult to secure accord between the two parties for the greater cause of self-government for India. He believed that they had a common goal. 'There could not be any self-respecting Indian who favoured foreign domination or did not desire complete freedom and self-government for his country'.[133] But, the Congress buoyed by its success in the general elections, had different ideas. It felt confident of imminent freedom, and regarded the support of the League and its Muslim supporters as inconsequential. Indeed, according to one contemporary observer, the Congress simply wanted to make 'a good feast of all the loaves and fishes that are at present available....'[134] This was most evident in the UP, where, rather than form a coalition government with the League, which won 29 out of 64 Muslim seats, the Congress offered 'not partnership but absorption'.[135] Jawaharlal Nehru, who had recently assumed presidency of the Congress, could not resist 'the temptation of winding up the United Provinces Muslim League and absorbing it into the Congress' to 'free [the] field for our work without communal troubles'.[136] In the end, of course, this 'temptation' proved too costly for the Congress and for the cause of Indian unity. According to Rajmohan Gandhi, accommodative 'gestures from Congress to the League' in the Hindu-majority provinces 'would have made it more difficult for Jinnah to convince the *qaum* (the Muslim nation)' at a later stage 'that Congress was its enemy', but that 'opportunity' went begging.[137]

Still, Jinnah, who never tired of seeking Hindu–Muslim settlement took special pains to assure the Congress that he was 'not in the slightest degree affected by anything that has happened in the past, and nobody will welcome an honourable settlement between the Hindus and the Musalmans more than I and nobody will be so ready to help'.[138] He appealed to Gandhi in particular to 'take up the question of Hindu–Muslim settlement' earnestly. But Gandhi was not moved.

He wryly wrote: 'I wish I could do something but I am utterly helpless. My faith in unity is bright as ever; only I see no daylight out of the impenetrable darkness and in such distress I cry out to God for light'.[139]

Jinnah was now convinced, more than ever, that the Muslims had to stand on their own feet for the realization of their special interests and demands. They needed to come together, unite and reinforce the League as their truly representative organization. A representative League, he believed, would attract the attention of the Congress and indeed encourage it to negotiate a settlement of the Hindu–Muslim problem. In addition, a representative, re-organized League would contribute better to the attainment of the objective of self-government for India, which the Congress had so far pursued in a desultory manner. These ideas, which Jinnah was to reiterate and elabourate later in the 1937–40 period, found their first public expression in the Lucknow session of the Muslim League in October 1937, which in Jinnah's own words, was 'one of the most critical that has ever taken place during its existence for the last more than thirty years'.[140] Since this session was the first indication of a marked shift in Jinnah's political standing and stature, and eventually his emergence as the charismatic leader of Muslim India, a more detailed reference to his presidential address is required.[141]

Jinnah started with a scathing criticism of the Congress and its policies, especially in the formation and administration of provincial ministries, and held its leadership primarily 'responsible for alienating the Musalmans of India...by pursuing a policy which is exclusively Hindu....'[142] The end result, he warned, would be 'class bitterness, communal war and strengthening of the imperialistic hold as a consequence'.[143] He felt that the British would give the Congress 'a free hand in this direction', for 'it is all to the good, so long as their interests, imperial or otherwise, are not touched and the Defence remains intact....'[144] He charged that, the Congress had already compromised the struggle for Indian freedom through misdirected enthusiasm and unilateral acts. Various declarations, like 'Purna Swaraj', 'self-government', 'complete independence', 'responsible government', 'substance of independence', and 'dominion status' were mere 'slogans and shibboleths' which could not carry India forward.[145] 'What India requires', Jinnah suggested, 'is a complete united front and honesty of purpose and then by whatever name you may call your government is a matter of no consequence as long as it is a government of the people, by the people, and for the people'.[146]

Jinnah assured his enthusiastic audience that he was still prepared to work for 'full national democratic self-government for India' provided the Congress agreed 'to inspire confidence and to create a sense of security' among the Muslims.[147] In the meanwhile, he insisted, the Muslims had no choice but to organize themselves around 'one common platform and flag of the All-India Muslim League'.[148] In this context, he was particularly critical of the 'nationalist' Muslims who aligned themselves with the Congress. He thought they had 'lost faith in themselves', and thus were 'making a great mistake when they preach unconditional surrender' and throw themselves 'on the mercy and goodwill of others....'[149] He exhorted the Muslims to organize themselves to their full potential to the 'exclusion of every other consideration'.[150] There was no other way to secure a 'settlement' with the Hindus. 'Settlement', he explained, 'can only be achieved between equals, and unless the two parties learn to respect and fear each other, there is no solid ground for any settlement.... Politics means power and not relying only on cries of justice or fair play or good will'.[151]

The Lucknow session of the League not only saw 'the declaration of a new faith'[152] for the Muslims but also the ushering in of a new era in Jinnah's long, chequered political career. Indeed, according to Peter Hardy, it was 'the transformation of the arrogant, proud, cold-blooded logician and lawyer Jinnah, into the charismatic Muslim leader of the nineteen-forties....'[153] Jinnah had emerged as the charismatic leader of Muslim India. Three Chief Ministers of Muslim-majority provinces, of Bengal, Assam, and the Punjab, especially Sikandar Hayat Khan of the Punjab, whose Unionist Party had so far defied Jinnah, were there to acknowledge his leadership. One of the delegates at the session was so moved by the inspiring presence of Jinnah that he, in his speech, chose to call him the *Quaid-i-Azam*,[154] a title that was to stay with him for ever, as a symbol of his charismatic political leadership. The refusal of the Congress to accept the League offer of coalition in the provincial governments, and ignoring or rejecting Muslim grievances under the Congress rule in the provinces had created an 'hour of bleak despair and dark foreboding for the Muslims', bringing him to the fore, 'as if inspired by Divine Power....'[155] One of his disciples and followers, who was present at Lucknow Railway station on the evening of 13 October 1937 when Jinnah arrived in the city thus described the fervor of the crowd:

> So exuberant was their enthusiasm and so fiery their determination to resist Hindu aggression that Mr Jinnah, otherwise calm and imperturbable, was visibly moved.... His face wore a look of grim determination coupled with satisfaction that his people were aroused at last. He spoke a few soothing words to pacify their inflamed passions. Many Muslims, overcome by emotion, wept tears of joy to see their leader who, they felt sure, would deliver them from bondage.[156]

Jinnah came to Lucknow a completely changed man, not only in his political style and substance, but also in his physical appearance. He shed his lifelong famous Saville Row suits and arrived at the session attired in a black *sherwani* (long coat) *shalwar* (traditional trousers) and *Karakuli* cap, henceforth called the Jinnah Cap. This was to be Jinnah's dress of the future as the charismatic leader of Indian Muslims and the 'national dress' of Pakistan after its creation in 1947. Jinnah made a conscious 'show of his Muslim cultural identity'.[157] Hailed as the Quaid-i-Azam, Jinnah was now an unrelenting and fierce champion of Muslim interests, determined and ready to lead the Muslims out of their difficulties.

To begin with, Jinnah urged the Muslims to organize themselves and join the Muslim League *en masse*. As he put it: 'I entreat and implore that every man, woman and child should rally around one common platform and flag of the All-India Muslim League.'[158] The Muslims, he insisted, had no other option but to 'concentrate and devote their energies to self-organization and full development of their power to the exclusion of every other consideration'.[159] Being an organization man all his life, there was hardly anything surprising or new about this emphasis on organization. Indeed, as the theoretical literature suggests, it is a common trait among successful charismatic leaders.

Disappointed and distressed with the Congress rule in the procinces, the Muslims responded positively to Jinnah's call for 'self-organization'. Slowly but surely, they started joining the Muslim League and lending it strength. First proof of the League's increasing strength came in the by-elections of 1938 in the UP in which it captured 4 out of 5 seats reserved for the Muslims. Muslim grievances against the Congress government helped the matters. The Pirpur, Shareef, and Fazlul Huq reports, the provocative Congress Muslim Mass-Contact Campaign, the Wardha scheme of education, and *Bande Mataram* were combined to encourage the Muslims to rally 'around the League by playing on their fears'.[160] Indeed, as Yunus Samad pointed out, 'the League–Congress controversy polarized Hindu-Muslim relations, making it difficult for Muslim elites to remain outside the League'.[161] However, the League's success was not confined to the relatively receptive Muslim-minority provinces like the UP. Even in the NWFP, the League secured 2 out of 5 Muslim seats. A public testimony to the popularity of the League was provided by the enthusiastic response of the Muslims to Jinnah's call to commemorate 22 December 1939, the day the Congress resigned its ministries, as the 'Day of Deliverance', which, in the estimate of *Amrita Bazar Patrika* and the *Times of India*, appeared as if 'the Muslims were really celebrating some festival....'[162] The League's membership in 1940 was well over half a million. This was no small number given the fact that this membership in 1937 was a mere few thousand. The result was that between 1937 and 1943, in 61 by-elections for Muslim constituencies, the League won 47 seats against Congress's 4.[163] Clearly, the Muslims had supported the League over the Congress.

Jinnah felt confident that the increased strength of the League would help dispel doubts and misgivings about Muslim interests and demands and make the Congress better appreciate its point of view. Thus, he approached Congress leaders for yet another attempt at Hindu–Muslim settlement. He entered into negotiations and correspondence with Subhas Chandra Bose (1897–1945), then Congress President and Jawaharlal Nehru demanding that the Congress recognize the League as 'the authoritative and representative organization of the Indian Muslims'.[164] In the light of Nehru's statement about 'two parties', in 1937, this was but a natural concern and priority with Jinnah. However, the Congress refused to oblige. Indeed, Bose, in his letter of 25 July 1938, told Jinnah that it was an 'improper' demand. The Congress Working Committee, he wrote,

has received warnings against recognising the exclusive status of the League. There are Muslim organisations which have been functioning independently of the Muslim League. Moreover, there are individual Muslims who are Congressmen, some of whom exercise no inconsiderable influence in the country. Then there is the Frontier Province which is overwhelming [sic] Muslim and which is solidly with the Congress. You will see that in the face of these known facts it is not only impossible, but improper for the Congress to make the admission which the…League…apparently desires the Congress to make.[165]

On 6 April 1938, Nehru added that although the League was 'an important communal organisation' it did not merit consideration as the sole representative body of the Muslims. In fact, he tried to ridicule Jinnah and the League by suggesting: 'We do not determine the measure of importance or distinction…inevitably, the more important the organization, the more the attention paid to it, but this importance does not come from outside recognition but from inherent strength'.[166] Jinnah was most upset. In a letter to Nehru, on 12 April he not only blasted him for his inability to 'interpret my letter' but also conveyed to him in clear and categorical terms that,

…unless the Congress recognises the Muslim League on a footing of complete equality and is prepared as such to negotiate for a Hindu–Muslim settlement, we shall have to wait and depend upon our 'inherent strength' which will 'determine the measure of importance or distinction' it possessed.[167]

Jinnah's correspondence with Gandhi was no help either. On 5 November 1937, Gandhi accused Jinnah of making a 'declaration of war' in his speech at Lucknow.[168] In his letter of 3 February 1938, he even went further and claimed: 'In your speeches I miss the old nationalist…. Are you still the same Mr Jinnah? If you are, in spite of your speeches, I shall accept your word'.[169] Obviously, Jinnah was not amused. In his reply on 5 February 1938, he retorted: 'Nationalism is not the monopoly of any single individual, and in these days it is very difficult to define it; but I don't wish to pursue this line of controversy any further'.[170] Jinnah and Gandhi carried on an acrimonious correspondence for some time till, on 3 March 1938, Jinnah insisted:

We have reached a stage where no doubt should be left that you recognise the All-India Muslim League as the one authoritative and representative organisation of the Muslims of India and, on the other hand, you represent the Congress and other Hindus throughout the country. It is only on that basis that we can proceed further and devise a machinery of approach.[171]

As the correspondence served no useful purpose, Jinnah proposed that they must sit for talks instead. Gandhi hesitated and, eventually, suggested that he open talks 'in the first instance' with Maulana Abul Kalam Azad.[172] But Jinnah refused to see Maulana Azad, a Muslim leader of the Congress. He did not mind seeing Jawaharlal Nehru or Bose. But then, he contended, 'The matter, as you know, will not be clinched without reference again to you by either of them. Therefore, I will prefer to see you first'.[173] The two leaders met at Bombay on 28 April 1938, where they were closeted for more than three and a half hours, but failed to reach any agreement or understanding on the Hindu-Muslim problem. Jinnah was left with no choice but to continue to develop his 'inherent strength', so obtusely suggested by Nehru in his letter of 6 April.

Indeed, Jinnah told Karachi Conference of the League in October 1938 that the Muslims must 'stand on our own inherent strength and build up our own power and forge sanctions behind our decisions'. They must get united. In fact, he warned: 'If the Musalmans are going to be defeated in their national goal and aspirations it will only be by the betrayal of the Musalmans amongst us, as it has happened in the past'.[174] Though it was Jinnah's first public reference to the concept of 'national goal', it was by no means an idle or stray comment. In several speeches since 1936, Jinnah had already 'referred to the Muslims as a "nation".'[175] In large part, it was due to the influence of Allama Iqbal, who had been in touch with him between the crucial years of 1936 and 1937, emphasizing that 'the Muslims of India are the only Indian people who can fitly be described as a nation in the modern sense of the word'.[176] Jinnah agreed, and thus accorded approval of a resolution adopted at the conference which 'in the interest of an abiding peace of the vast Indian continent and in the interests of unhampered cultural development, the economic and social betterment and political self-determination of the two nations, known as Hindus and Muslims', recommended to the Muslim League 'to review and revise the entire conception of what should be the suitable constitution for India which will secure honourable and legitimate status to them'. Interestingly, the original resolution recommending to the League 'to devise a scheme of constitution under which Muslim-majority provinces, Muslim Indian States and areas inhabited by a majority of Muslims may attain full independence in the form of a federation of their own with permission to admit any other Muslim State beyond the Indian frontiers to join the Federation....'[177] was more radical and more revealing of the Muslim mind at that time. But, although he attacked the Congress for having 'killed every hope of Hindu–Muslim settlement in the right royal fashion of Fascism,'[178] and proclaimed that 'it is Mr Gandhi who is destroying the ideal with which the Congress was started',[179] Jinnah was not willing to go that far in his espousal of Muslim interests for several reasons.

First, Jinnah was convinced that the Muslims were still not supporting the League to the extent that he would have liked them to. They were not that forthcoming. Dwelling upon the comparative strength of the League and the Congress, he had noted in his speech in February 1938:

> If Wardha makes any decision and issues orders tomorrow, millions of Hindus will follow and obey. I ask you, suppose the Muslim League were to issue any order, what will happen to it? We are not sufficiently equipped and trained and therefore it will be difficult to produce lakhs of Muslims to carry out orders.[180]

Secondly, Jinnah felt that the Muslims had yet to acquire 'national' consciousness. 'That is the force', he emphasized, 'I want the Muslims to acquire. When you have acquired that, believe me, I have no doubt in my mind, you will realise what you want'.[181] Finally, Jinnah still believed in the possibility of a Hindu–Muslim settlement if it amounted to a 'pact' along the lines agreed between two sovereign nations. 'One does not see much light at present', he told the Old Boys Association of the Osmania University on 28 September 1939, 'but you can never say when the two communities would unite. We have a recent example of the German–Soviet Pact between two nations which were the bitterest of enemies'.[182]

Jinnah welcomed the resignation of Congress ministries in October–November 1939 over the British declaration of India being at war. He called upon the Muslim League to observe a 'Day of Deliverance' as a mark of relief that the Congress ministries had at last ceased to function. However, he still chose to write to Gandhi, once again, a lengthy letter on 1 January 1940, highlighting the need for a just solution of the Hindu–Muslim problem. 'More than anyone else', he pleaded, 'you happen to be the man today who commands the confidence of Hindu India and are in a position to deliver the goods on their behalf'.[183] But Gandhi's response was most patronizing and perplexing. He wrote:

> I do not mind your opposition to the Congress. But your plan to amalgamate all the parties opposed to the Congress at once gives your movement a national character. If you succeed you will free the country from communal incubus, and, in my humble opinion, give a lead to the Muslims and others for which you will deserve the gratitude not only of the Muslims but of all the other communities.[184]

This was indeed the end of correspondence between Jinnah and Gandhi for the purpose of the settlement of the vexatious Hindu–Muslim problem within the framework of a federal India.

On 19 January 1940, in an article he wrote for *Time and Tide* of London, Jinnah took a momentous step forward and proposed a solution of the problem which, among other things, stressed:

1. That the British Government should review and revise the entire problem of India's future constitution *de novo* in the light of the experience gained by the working of the present provincial constitution, and developments that have taken place since 1935 or which may take place hereafter.
2. While the Muslim League stands for a free India, it is irrevocably opposed to any federal objective which must necessarily result in a majority community rule, under the guise of democracy and parliamentary system of government.
3. No declaration regarding the question of constitutional advance for India should be made without the consent and approval of the All-India Muslim League, nor any constitution framed and finally adopted by His Majesty's Government and the British Parliament without such consent and approval.
4. To conclude, a constitution must be evolved that recognizes that there are in India two nations who both must share the

governance of their common motherland. In evolving such a constitution, the Muslims are ready to cooperate with the British Government, the Congress or any party so that the present enmities may cease and India may take its place amongst the great nations of the world.[185]

The main burden of these demands clearly was the need to recognize 'two nations' in India.[186] The Muslims were a separate nation, a nation by themselves. They were not part of one Indian nation any more. This was a fundamental change in the situation.

Jinnah had come a long way from his position at the Calcutta session of the Congress in 1906. He had started his political career as an Indian nationalist with the firm belief that Indian national interests and the particular Muslim interests could be reconciled to facilitate the struggle for self-government. Though the stresses and strains of the 1920s and late 1930s, especially because of the Congress indifference and insensitivity to the Muslim interests, forced him to revise his ideas from time to time, Jinnah continued to hold on to his essential creed. He wanted freedom for India, but wanted to ensure that this freedom was meaningful for the Muslims as well. He believed that the cause of Indian freedom could not be separated from the cause of the Indian Muslims who, being a minority in India, were justified in seeking necessary safeguards and security in a free India.

At no stage was Jinnah willing to surrender the Muslim cause. Whether he opposed the granting of separate electorates or supported the principle of separate electorates, whether he joined or left the Congress, whether he organized the League in aid of the Congress or separately for its own sake, whether he formulated the Lucknow Pact of 1916 or the 'Lucknow Pact' of 1937 (exclusively for the Muslim community), whether he propounded Delhi Muslim Proposals or offered his Fourteen Points, or whether he criticized and castigated the Congress between 1937 and 1940 or entered into protracted negotiations with its leadership to settle the Hindu–Muslim problem, the primary objective was to secure and promote Muslim interests in India.

By January 1940, Jinnah no longer had any faith left in the idea that Muslim interests and Indian nationalism were reconcilable. There were no longer any illusions in his mind as to the 'nationalist' pretensions of the Congress or the possible fate of the Muslims in their scheme of things. He also came to doubt the relevance and usefulness of the parliamentary system of government in India. In 1935, he was prepared to consider the provincial part of the Act of 1935 for whatever it was 'worth', but now he condemned it outright for its failure to safeguard Muslim interests. He was convinced that the parliamentary system, 'based on the majority principle must inevitably mean the rule of the majority nation. Experience has proved that, whatever the economic and political programme of any political party, the Hindu, as a general rule, will vote for his caste-fellow and the Muslims for his co-religionist'.[187] One reason, he reckoned, why the Hindu–Muslim problem could not be solved was that 'the Congress (which is mainly a Hindu body) had long foreseen that in the Western form of democracy lay the fulfillment of their hopes of permanent all-India dominance. All their efforts and energies had, therefore, been bent towards securing for India a completely democratic form of government....'[188] That also explained Congress demand on 14 September 1939, for immediate independence and the right to frame the Indian constitution through a Constituent Assembly. Once the British were out of the way, the Muslims could be dealt with more conveniently.

In Jinnah's estimate, the Second World War provided the Congress 'a heaven-sent means' of extending its rule from some provinces to the whole of India, states and provinces.[189] Indeed, one very important factor that encouraged him to break away from the old pattern of thinking, always hopeful that the Congress would help work out a Hindu–Muslim settlement, was the evolving war situation. The war intensified the Congress pressure on the British, thereby raising Jinnah's fears:

> If the British Government are stampeded and fall into the trap under the stress of the critical situation created by the War, India will face a crisis the result of which no man could prophesy, and I feel certain that Muslim India will never submit to such a position and will be forced to resist it with every means in their power.[190]

The problem, Jinnah explained at a meeting of the League Council on 25 February 1940, is 'very simple. Great Britain wants to rule India.

Mr Gandhi and the Congress want to rule India and the Musalmans. We say that we will not let either the British or Mr Gandhi to rule the Musalmans. We want to be free'.[191]

This was a point of no return in Jinnah's political life and career. Henceforth, he was to devote himself to building a political future for the Muslims, independent of the Hindus and the British. He abandoned his past practices and preferences. He wanted the Muslims to stand independently, develop their own 'inherent' strength, and refuse to submit to the Congress or the British:

> Let me tell you and I tell both of you that you alone or…both combined will never succeed in destroying our souls. You will never be able to destroy that culture which we have inherited…you may overpower us; you may oppress us; and you can do your worst. But we have come to the conclusion and we have now made a grim resolve that we shall go down, if we have to go down, fighting.[192]

The Muslims saw in this resolve, grim resolve, a true reflection of their hopes, aspirations, fears, and their claim as a political community in their own right. They rallied behind Jinnah. Although they had begun to look up to him for help and guidance since 1933, the year the League formally and urgently requested Jinnah to return to India and save the Muslims from their present difficulties, the state of 'despondency and frustration' developed by the end of 1930s, had made them recognize and seek Jinnah like never before, as the only man who could 'launch them on a new path of hope and action'.[193] They saw him as their saviour, their deliverer, their charismatic leader.

Charisma, which had started to manifest itself in the perception and attitudes of the Muslims since his return to India in 1935, and received recognition at the Lucknow session of the League in 1937, was now finally vested in the person of Jinnah. Confluence of circumstances to which he himself had contributed in a very significant manner and his own personal qualities of leadership cultivated over decades of service to the Muslim cause made him an ideal choice for a charismatic leader. But what made him increasingly charismatic was the belief among the Muslims that *he,* and not anybody else, could lead them out of their difficult situation. They saw in him extraordinary qualities of leadership which specifically equipped him for the kind of situation they faced, and in this sense, 'his greatness resembled that of a surgeon or lawyer who possessed the brilliant skill to prevail against all odds'.[194] These qualities had already helped him survive and withstand the political vicissitudes in his early political career but now they were to be his main assets as a charismatic leader. The new and difficult situation of Muslim India gave them a new meaning, significance, and purpose, enabling him to enjoy the trust and confidence of the Muslims in a way in which he had never enjoyed before. Some of these qualities need to be identified and understood.

First, Jinnah was a man absolutely sure of himself and his cause. Indeed, according to one contemporary observer, it never occurred to him 'that he might be wrong'.[195] He had incredible faith in himself and 'never courted popularity'.[196] As he told one of his political rivals: 'You try to find what will please people and then you act accordingly. My way of action is quite different. I first decide what is right and I do it. The people come around me and the opposition vanishes'.[197] It was precisely because of this conviction that nothing could detract him from his mission, and he could 'neither be bought nor cajoled, neither be influenced nor trapped into any position that he had not himself decided upon'.[198] Having once decided to unite the Muslims 'behind a demand for recognition as a nation, nothing deterred him, least of all the practical difficulties of separation, which he declined to discuss....'[199] Thus, as Ayesha Jalal aptly put it: 'One clue to Jinnah's extraordinary resilience in the face of grave political setbacks, overwhelming odds, and unremitting squeeze play, was his extraordinary capacity to fight when all would have appeared lost to lesser men'.[200] His opponents failed to grasp 'his drive and singleminded dedication to the cause he made his own'.[201] One result of this dedication to his cause, of course, was that he appeared to his followers as having an attitude of 'detachment'. This detachment not only saved him from 'involvement in ignoble strife' between different individuals and groups of the Muslim society,[202] but also contributed to 'the power of his national leadership'.[203] In addition, it added to his 'magnetic presence'.[204] Max Weber, as argued earlier, saw this attitude of 'detachment' as an essential attribute of a charismatic leader for it gives him time and energy to concentrate on the problems facing his community.

Secondly, Jinnah not only responded to Muslim aspirations but was also the only Muslim leader of his time who 'knew how to express the stirrings of their minds in the form of concrete propositions'.[205] Indeed, his great strength 'lay in orchestrating the common anxieties of desperately divided groups and parties hitherto engaged in parochial and local politics, and to give them an overriding sense of direction'.[206] This also explains why the traditional leaders in their opposition to the demand for Pakistan in 1940 were 'hard put to presenting an alternative programme', and some of them had no choice but 'to swear by [the] Pakistan goal' in public, at least.[207] Even the so-called 'nationalist' Muslims who were pro-Congress were forced to water down 'their opposition to the Lahore Resolution and qualified their support for the Congress by demanding protection from Hindu domination'. Indeed, steadily, 'the siren call of the Pakistan slogan drew the pro-Congress Muslims closer to the League until there was very little to differentiate them'.[208] The idea of a separate homeland for the Muslims or for that matter the very idea of 'two nations' was of course not new when it was formulated by Jinnah. As one prominent Indian historian readily conceded:

> Almost all the leaders of the movement for Muslim awakening and solidarity from the second half of the nineteenth century onwards believed in Muslims being a nation by themselves and actively propagated it through their writings and speeches. Similarly, almost all the leaders of Hindu awakening and solidarity believed in the concept of Hindu nationhood and gave enthusiastic expression to their views.[209]

Of course, for the Muslims, the concept of Muslim nationhood had already been stated clearly and convincingly by Allama Iqbal. But what distinguished Jinnah's formulation of the demand as more striking, tangible, and concrete was his insistence on the division of India, complete and full. He saw clearly the 'inherent inevitabilities' in the regional solutions, and thus offered a solution which would make the Muslim destiny far more 'safe and inalienable'.[210]

Thirdly, Jinnah, as a constitutionalist endowed with an exceptional legal mind was ideally suited to the conduct of negotiations with the Congress and the British to secure the interests of Muslims in the future constitution of India. He seemed qualified for a constitutional role from the start, had faithfully imbibed the constitutionalism of his political mentors, such as Naoroji, Gokhale, and Mehta, and was genuinely convinced that this was the only way to attain self-government. His political experience also suggested to him that 'Armed revolution was an impossibility, while non-cooperation had been tried and found a failure'.[211] He was a 'political craftsman' and regarded politics as 'the art of the possible'.[212] In following the constitutional path, he was, of course, helped by his immense knowledge of law and constitution. As early as 1917, the Secretary of State for India, Edwin Samuel Montague (1879–1924), had noted: 'Jinnah is [a] very clever man, and it is of course an outrage that such a man should have no chance of running the affairs of his own country'.[213] Unlike Gandhi, who, in spite of being a barrister himself, had no penchant for constitutional issues [in 1942, he confessed to a bewildered Viceroy, Lord Linlithgow (1887–1952), that he had not read the 1935 Act],[214] and who was never a member of any Indian legislature, Jinnah was a part of nearly all constitutional deliberations and discussions in India whether held inside the assembly or outside, or whether between the League and the Congress or between the League, Congress and the British. The only two occasions when he was not directly involved in the formulation of any constitutional proposal was in 1928, when the Nehru Committee was working on its constitutional formula, and in 1932, during the Third Round Table Conference in London. Both the Nehru Report and the 1935 Act failed to carry Indian public opinion. Except for brief interludes when he purposefully chose to stay away from the legislatures between 1913 and 1916 and 1919 and 1923 (he was elected in November 1923) in protest against the passage of the Rowlatt Bill and the Khilafat–Non-cooperation movement, and between 1931 and 1934 when he went into self-exile in London, Jinnah was a member of the Indian legislative assembly right from the year 1910, when he was first elected to the Imperial Legislative Council by non-official members of Bombay on a seat reserved for Muslims, till the very end—the partition of India in 1947. His forceful speeches, 'debating and dialectical capabilities, power of reasoning, qualities of dignified eloquence, and his terrible repartee', made him a parliamentarian of very outstanding ability.[215] He was elected by the Bombay Muslims each and every time elections to the assemblies were held, often unopposed, and even when absent from the country in 1934.

In addition, Jinnah was a very able lawyer. Even Gandhi admitted that Jinnah— along with Sir Tej Bahadur Sapru (1875–1949)—was the most distinguished lawyer of India. His masterful grasp of the intricacies of law was evident from the fact that Jinnah, according to one observer, pointed out in a constitutional document prepared by the eminent lawyers comprising Muslim delegation to the Round Table Conference, 'the flaw where none seemed to exist—a flaw that would have meant the annulment of most of what had been conceded'.[216] This knack for legal-constitutional details made Jinnah 'a hard and shrewd negotiator' with the British leaders.[217] Indeed, as Ian Talbot noted: 'His lengthy and successful legal career suited him for this task, as did his dogged determination which so exasperated British officials from Lord Mountbatten downwards'.[218] He was demanding and fastidious in all his negotiations, 'never to give in, never to retreat, always to attack the opponent at his weakest point, and constantly repeat his own position'.[219] These forensic qualities came very naturally to him. As he himself revealed in a rare moment: 'I am a very peculiarly constituted person. I am guided by cold-blooded reason, logic and judicial inquiry'.[220] People who happened to come into personal contact with Jinnah, one way or the other, agreed. As Saleem Qureshi, on the basis of his extensive interviews conducted in Britain, India and Pakistan over a period of several years put it: 'a logical and methodical mind, the ability to see things through, realism and pragmatism to be able to [sic] see things as they are qualities of Jinnah that struck interviewees of every category'.[221] In fact, there is ample evidence to suggest that he was one of the most rational leaders of India. He 'was never the demagogue', was 'averse to the politics of symbolism', and always 'avoided the display of emotion in public'.[222] Indeed, it was claimed that, 'what distinguished Jinnah from his great contemporaries is that he was, quite self-consciously, a modern man—one who above all valued reason, discipline, organization and economy'.[223] This did not mean, however, that Jinnah was devoid of 'passions'. He believed passionately in his 'cause', and in the words of his biographer, Bolitho, 'in the end, he was to hasten his own death in a cause to which he gave his will and logic, as passionately as Gandhi led his disciples, with his zeal and intuition'.[224] In this sense, Jinnah was an ideal charismatic leader in the Weberian sense of the term, possessing both reason and passion (tempered by reason).

Fourthly, Jinnah was a keen organizer in both private and public life. Strong evidence on the way his life was organized and disciplined has been provided by a number of contemporary observers, acquaintances, friends, and colleagues, and need not be recounted here. As Z.H. Zaidi described it: 'In private as well as public matters, his character was all of a piece. He was consistent in his methodical, business-like handling of affairs, in his legal sense of what was just and due in the leader's constant concern for all the countless individuals who followed him'.[225] In politics, nothing was to be taken for granted or left to chance. All moves had to be carefully planned and executed. As he himself explained: '…in politics one has to play one's game as on the chessboard'.[226] He was a thorough organization man. He never operated outside 'party' routine and discipline. His entire political life revolved around party activity whether as member of the Congress, Muslim League or, briefly, the Home Rule League. In particular, in his efforts to mobilize the Muslim masses around the League, 'he emerged as a legendary organization-man keeping communications open between Muslim minority and majority provinces, between feudal lords, commercial interests and urban middle classes, and between constitutional debates and ideological standpoints'.[227] It was only because of his organizational skills and charisma that the League was transformed into 'a new kind of party with one foot in the countryside and the other in the town'.[228] In this sense, the League owed all its success to him.

Still Jinnah insisted, against the wishes of his ardent followers, on standing for the office of the president on a routine yearly basis rather than become its life-president. In the meetings of the various organs of the League, too, he listened to, and respected, every member's opinion and saw to it that decisions of the League were made through consensus of all the members present. Indeed, it would be no exaggeration to say that all decisions made by Jinnah during his charismatic period had either the prior blessing of the League or the League subsequently ratified it. This knack for self-discipline and organization was equally evident in his relations with his followers and disciples. As soon as Indian Muslims validated his charisma in 1940, he instituted the office of Private Secretary to help him stay in touch with his followers on a regular, systematic basis. Indeed, thousands of elabourate, detailed letters (now available in the *Quaid-i-Azam Papers*, Islamabad) were sent by him to rather 'unimportant' persons dealing with various issues and concerns of the League. This correspondence, thus, conveyed,

...with fresh clarity Jinnah's command of the essentials of leadership and brings out once again the way in which Jinnah's life was based upon a strict self-discipline, upon adherence to certain rules which he did not abandon or relax even when he seemed engrossed in his profession or in politics.[229]

Finally, Jinnah was a keen strategist who knew fully well 'when to take 'the tide' and when to make suitable mends in the furnace of reality and expediency'.[230] He always knew what were his limitations and what were the weak points of his opponents, and thus through his 'unrivaled tactical skill' was able 'to take advantage of every situation, however unpromising'.[231] In this context, he was also helped by the mistakes of his opponents. The mistakes of the Congress, for instance, enabled him 'to convince the vast majority of Muslims that Congress rule meant Hindu domination....'[232] In addition, the Congress, by resigning its provincial governments in 1939, in protest against the war, pushed itself into the political wilderness and provided Jinnah a singular opportunity to organize and strengthen his League even in the Congress-dominated provinces, such as the NWFP, the only Muslim-majority province allied to the Congress. In fact, the Congress resignation was a 'major miscalculation' leaving 'the field open for Jinnah'.[233] The mistakes of the British rulers, who underrated him and his cause by insisting that his Pakistan demand was 'a deliberate over-bid'[234] cost them dearly. In the end, they were constrained to concede Pakistan in spite of their vehement opposition to the idea of partition. Jinnah was able to make the most of difficult and demanding circumstances of the Second World War.

These extraordinary qualities of leadership, which crystallized with the years and which he demonstrated in abundant measure in the charismatic decade of 1937–1947, were buttressed by the widespread belief shared equally by those Muslims who did not approve of his future demand for Pakistan that he had no personal axe to grind. Dr Syed Hussain, a nationalist Muslim, for instance, swore publicly:

Though I am opposed to Pakistan, I must say that Mr Jinnah is the only man in the public life whose public record is most incorruptible. You cannot buy him by money or by offer of post. He has not gained anything from the British. He is not that kind of man. His character is as high as that of any leader in India. He had not accepted from the British benefit or title although Mr Gandhi did accept one from Britain after the Boer war. The Muslim masses know that Mr Jinnah is the only man who is not in need of money and who has no lust for power.[235]

As for his need for money, there is no gainsaying that he was one of the most wealthy political leaders of India. His primary source of income, of course, was 'his enormous legal practice; he charged a fee of Rs. 1,500 per day in 1936'.[236] But then he had also invested heavily 'in stocks and shares'.[237] In addition, he had a number of residential properties, including his residence in Delhi and a 'palatial residence' at Mount Pleasant Road, Bombay, occupying an area of 15,476 square yards.[238] Thus, Jinnah's 'enormous riches' and 'financial independence'[239] made sure that, as a truly charismatic leader, he was 'economically independent of the income politics can bring him'.[240] In fact, his vast income enabled him to donate money 'quite liberally for charity causes'.[241]

The very fact that Jinnah in 1937, past 60 years in age, undertook the task of leading the Muslims even at the risk of his own health[242] could only be explained in terms of the crisis-ridden, distressful situation of Muslim India, a situation necessitating the rise of a charismatic leader, rather than to any personal agenda. In this sense, it is necessary 'to define the charismatic role of Jinnah not only on the basis of comparatively objective views about his personality' as already done here, but also 'in relation to the political system of British India', which caused this distressful situation to develop in the first place.[243] Indeed, a detailed and systematic analysis of the Muslim situation will help us better understand the rise and role of Jinnah as a charismatic leader of the Muslims.

Notes

1. Jinnah left the Ismaili faith and reportedly became a Shia (*Ithna Ashari*) in 1897. See Riaz Ahmed, *Quaid-i-Azam Mohammad Ali Jinnah: The Formative Years, 1892–1920* (Islamabad: National Institute of Historical and Cultural Research, 1986), 25, 52. But Jinnah was not a sectarian. He 'did not like to be associated with any particular sect'. When pointedly asked, 'whether he was a Shia or a Sunni', he inquired: 'What was the Prophet?' To this the questioner's reply was that he was neither, and the Quaid-i-Azam said that his reply was that he followed the Prophet (PBUH), and that he was a Mussalman'. Portion from the

Judgment of Abul Kadir Sheikh of the High Court of Sindh, reported in *Pakistan Legal Decisions*, 1970. Cited in Liaquat H. Merchant, comp. and ed., *The Jinnah Anthology* (Karachi: Oxford University Press, 1999), 86, 88.

2. While Jinnah insisted that this was his date of birth, also supported by his sister, Fatima Jinnah, there is evidence to suggest that other dates appeared too. For instance, school records of Karachi and Bombay show the date of birth to be 20 October 1875. Riaz Ahmed argued that this was mainly due to the reason that when Jinnah was sent to Bombay and admitted into the Anjuman-i-Islam school, his birth date was wrongly entered in the school register by his uncle who did not know the exact date. It was based on this school-leaving certificate that Jinnah's birth date of 20 October 1875 was also recorded in the school in Karachi. See Ibid., 24. Also see, Fatima Jinnah, *My Brother* (Karachi: Quaid-i-Azam Academy, 1987), 50; G. Allana, *The Story of a Nation*, 4; Hector Bolitho, *Jinnah: Creator of Pakistan* (Karachi: Oxford University Press, 1964), 3; and Rizwan Ahmad, *Quaid-i-Azam: Ibtidai Tees Saal* (Urdu) (Karachi: n.p., 1977), 10-15.

3. Fatima Jinnah, *My Brother*, 47.

4. Ibid., 71.

5. Ibid., 77.

6. Rajmohan Gandhi, *Eight Lives: A Study of the Hindu Muslim Encounter* (Albany: State University of New York Press, 1986), 124.

7. Ibid., 125.

8. Naidu, *Ambassador of Unity*, 15.

9. Jinnah had, of course, started taking part in politics much earlier, through Sir Pherozshah Mehta's Bombay Presidency Association which voted in early May 1905 'to send him, along with Gokhale, on a Congress deputation to England to plead for self-government for India during the impending British elections.' Sharif al Mujahid, 'Jinnah and the Congress Party', in D.A. Low, ed., *The Indian National Congress: Centenary Hindsights* (Delhi: Oxford University Press, 1988), 209.

10. Naoroji's faith in constitutional methods and liberalism left a lasting impression on his mind. For Jinnah's attachment to liberalism see, in particular, Bolitho, *Creator of Pakistan*, 9; and S. Qudratullah Fatimi, 'Quaid-i-Azam and Lord Morely', in Dani, *World Scholars*, 75-83.

11. Syed Sharifuddin Pirzada, ed., *The Collected Works of Quaid-i-Azam Mohammad Ali Jinnah* (Karachi: East and West Publishing Co., 1984), 4. This was with reference to a resolution on competitive examinations and reforms, to which Jinnah moved an amendment.

12. Ibid.

13. Ibid., 13. Although the separate electorates helped contribute to Muslim solidarity in the years ahead, they were not 'the sole cause of the evolution of a separate Muslim nationalism' in India. They were an 'independent demand' of a people 'apprehensive of its political future' in the British system of government. They were not 'discreetly created by the British for their own purposes' of rule. Indeed, the 'habit of Indian nationalists to view the history of the last one hundred years in the light of the divide and rule policy of the British, had led them to a blind alley, where frustration abounds and issues of Hindu–Muslim relations are further obfuscated'. Hafeez Malik, *Sir Sayyid Ahmed Khan and Muslim*

Modernization in India and Pakistan (Karachi: Royal Book Co., 1988), 252. For a detailed discussion of Jinnah's understanding of separate electorates and its relevance for the Muslims see, Sharif al Mujahid, 'Jinnah and Separate Electorates', *Pakistan Perspectives*, Vol. 6, No. 2 (July–December 2001).

14. Pirzada, *Collected Works of Quaid-i-Azam*, 159.

15. Ibid.

16. Ibid., 159–60. In fact, Jinnah 'fervently believed that the commitment to freedom and unity among India's teeming millions was strong enough to dilute and transcend the communal, social, economic, and regional cleavages over time', leading the way to 'an all-inclusive pan-Indian nationalism' in due course of time. Mujahid, 'Jinnah and Separate Electorates', 13.

17. Pirzada, *Collected Works of Quaid-i-Azam*, 2.

18. Ahmad, *Speeches and Writings*, Vol. I, 497. Also see, C.A. Bayly, *The Birth of the Modern World: 1780-1914* (Oxford: Blackwell Publishing, 2004), 240-1.

19. Ahmad, *Speeches and Writings*, Vol. I, 498.

20. Ibid.

21. Pirzada, *Collected Works of Quaid-i-Azam*, 15. Also see Sir Ibrahim Rahimtullah's presidential address at the Agra Session of the League, December 1913. Syed Sharifuddin Pirzada, ed., *Foundations of Pakistan: All-India Muslim League Documents, 1906–1947*, Vol. I (Karachi: National Publishing House, 1969), 284-311.

22. Bolitho, *Creator of Pakistan*, 9.

23. After Badruddin Tyabji (1844–1906), who presided its third annual session in 1887, Jinnah was the most prominent Bombay Muslim to join the Congress.

24. Metz, 'The Political Career of Mohammad Ali Jinnah', Preface.

25. Pirzada, *Collected Works of Quaid-i-Azam*, 189.

26. Naidu, *Ambassador of Unity*, 19. Mujahid was of the opinion that this 'solemn preliminary covenant' assertion 'seems a figment of Sarojini Naidu's fertile imagination. The young poetess might well have concocted it to sell her hero as a 'nationalist'; it has no foundation in fact.' Sharif al Mujahid, 'Jinnah's Entry into Mainstream Muslim Politics: A Reappraisal', in Riaz Ahmad, ed., *Pakistani Scholars on Quaid-i-Azam Mohammad Ali Jinnah* (Islamabad: National Institute of Historical and Cultural Research, 1999), 39.

27. Pirzada, *Collected Works of Quaid-i-Azam*, 48.

28. Ibid.

29. Ibid. So far, there was no bar on members of the Congress or the Muslim League, for that matter, joining other political organizations, and thus holding dual memberships. In 1938, the Muslim League, vide its Council resolution No. 12 of 4 December, 'Resolved that any member of the Muslim League who is associated with any party whose general policy is opposed to the Muslim League should not be allowed to become or remain a member of the Muslim League'. See *Quaid-i-Azam Papers*, F/228, 4. Also see Jinnah's letter to a leader of the League from Lyallpur (Faisalabad) on this subject. *Quaid-i-Azam Papers*, F/195, 2.

30. Ibid.

31. M. Rafique Afzal, ed., *Selected Speeches and Statements of the Quaid-i-Azam Mohammad Ali Jinnah, 1911–34 and 1947–48* (Lahore: Research Society of

Pakistan, 1976), 56. His joining of the League 'brought him to the centre of mainstream Muslim politics'. Mujahid, 'Jinnah and Separate Electorates', 15.

32. Mohammad Saleem Ahmad, *The All-India Muslim League: A History of the Growth and Consolidation of Political Organization* (Bhawalpur: Ilham Publishers, 1988), 229.

33. See Mujahid, *Studies in Interpretation*, App. 7, 'The Congress-League Scheme of Reform, 1916', 462-5.

34. Sayeed, *Formative Phase*, 42. However, the Pact reduced representation in the Muslim-majority provinces of the Punjab and Bengal, something that the leaders of these two provinces went on to resent subsequently, and indeed led to the demand for restoration of their statutory majorities in the following years.

35. Coupland, *Indian Problem*, 52.

36. Naidu, *Ambassador of Unity*, 24.

37. Afzal, *Selected Speeches and Statements*, 56.

38. Pirzada, *Collected Works of Quaid-i-Azam*, 252.

39. See his speech in ibid., 241.

40. Saiyid, *A Political Study*, 200-2.

41. Ibid., 217. However, Jinnah was convinced that 'India's major battles would have to be fought on the floor of the Assembly rather than in the streets'. Mujahid, *Studies in Interpretation*, 86.

42. Cited in Allana, *Story of a Nation*, 119.

43. Pirzada, *Collected Works of Quaid-i-Azam*, 388.

44. Ibid., 375.

45. For more on Gandhi see, Yogesh Chada, *Rediscovering Gandhi* (London: Century, 1997); and Stanley Wolpert, *Gandhi's Passion: The Life and Legacy of Mahatma Gandhi* (New York: Oxford University Press, 2001). For Gandhi's own version see, M.K. Gandhi, *An Autobiography or the Story of my Experiment with Truth* (Ahmedabad: Navajivan Publishing House, 1945, rep.).

46. Pirzada, *The Collected Works of Quaid-i-Azam*, 396.

47. Saiyid, *A Political Study*, 91. In fact, Jinnah's 'respect for institutions prompted him to leave the Congress in 1920', for good. Christophe Jafferlot, 'Islamic Identity and Ethnic Tensions' in Christophe Jafferlot, ed., *A History of Pakistan and its Origins* (London: Anthem Press, 2002), 11. According to Jinnah, Gandhi had already ruined the Home Rule League with these methods after becoming its president in 1920. This was in spite of the fact that Gandhi had explicitly assured Home Rule League leaders at the time of his joining the League that 'you need have no apprehension' that your League will be called upon to accept my 'theories'. M.R. Jayakar, *The Story of My Life 1873–1922* (Bombay: Asia Publishing House, 1958), 318. For Jinnah's association with the Home Rule League and his criticism of the role played by Gandhi see, Rafique Afzal, 'Quaid-i-Azam Mohammad Ali Jinnah and the Home Rule Movement', *The Journal of the Research Society of Pakistan*, Vol. XX, No.1 (1983), esp., 17-21.

48. Ayesha Jalal, *Self and Sovereignty: Individual and Community in South Asian Islam since 1850* (Lahore: Sang-e-Meel, 2001), 197.

49. Metz, 'The Political Career of Mohammad Ali Jinnah', 60.

50. Saiyid, *A Political Study,* 95.

51. David Taylor, 'Jinnah's Political Apprenticeship 1906–24', in Dani, *World Scholars*, 118.

52. The movement was called off on 12 February. Gandhi was arrested on 10 March. He was released in 1924. In early 1944, Jinnah told Kanji Dwarkadas 'that he was mainly responsible for getting Gandhiji released in 1924'. Dwarkadas added: 'that he was also responsible for the release from internment of Mrs Besant in September 1917', Kanji Dwarkadas, *Ten Years to Freedom* (Bombay: Popular Prakashan 1968), 86.

53. Bimal Prasad, *Pathway to India's Partition*, Vol. II, *A Nation Within a Nation: 1877-1937* (New Delhi: Manohar Publishers, 2000), 168.

54. M. Naeem Qureshi, *Pan-Islam in British Indian Politics: A Study of the Khilafat Movement, 1918–1924* (Boston: Brill, 1999), 364.

55. Sayeed, *Formative Phase*, 49-50.

56. Bolitho, *Creator of Pakistan*, 78. It was a measure of Jinnah's 'integrity' that he preferred to go down rather than seek favours from the government which, 'almost certainly', would have got him a 'High Court Judgeship'. David Taylor, 'Jinnah's Political Apprenticeship 1906-24', in Dani, *World Scholars*, 118.

57. Jinnah's decision to capture the councils rather than boycott them was vindicated in September 1925 when an amendment to the Muddiman Committee Report stressing the immediate setting up of a fully responsible government was carried in the house by 72 votes to 45 amidst wild scenes of jubilation. Allana, *Story of a Nation*, 186.

58. In Wolpert's estimate: 'Just as Gokhale had been for the Central Legislative Council of Calcutta, Jinnah emerged in this interlude (1924) as the gadfly of Delhi's assembly, speaking on most resolutions, pursuing every document and report with the precision of a lawyer, and expressing himself without fear or hope of favour'. Wolpert, *Jinnah of Pakistan*, 81. Bombay Muslims elected him to the Council of the Governor-General (Imperial Legislative Council) in 1910, 1916, 1923 (unopposed),1926 (unopposed) 1934 (in spite of his absence from the country) and 1946. Bombay Muslims, in fact, continuously elected Jinnah to the Indian legislature till the partition of India in 1947.

59. Naeem Qureshi, *Pan-Islam in British Indian Politics*, 399.

60. Of course, Jinnah, was helped by the large contingent from the Punjab, under the influence of Fazl-i-Husain, who was neither supportive of the non-cooperation movement nor its leadership. See Azim Husain, *Fazl-i-Husain*, 243-4.

61. Afzal, *Selected Speeches and Statements*, 131.

62. M. Naeem Qureshi, 'Jinnah and the Khilafat Movement (1918–1924), *Journal of South Asia and Middle Eastern Studies*, Vol.1, No. 2, Iqbal Centennial Issue (December 1977), 107.

63. *The Indian Quarterly Register* (Calcutta), 1926, Vol. 2, 376.

64. Afzal, *Selected Speeches and Statements*, 345.

65. Pirzada, *Collected Works of Quaid-i-Azam*, 159.

66. Jawaharlal Nehru, *An Autobiography* (London: Bodley Head, 1958), 159. According to Nehru, 'The aggressive activities of the Mahasbha acted on and stimulated… Muslim communalism, and so action and reaction went on, and in the process the communal temperature of the country went up.' *Ibid*.

67. Saiyid, *A Political Study*, 102.
68. Some of the prominent leaders attending the Conference were Maulana Mohammed Ali, Raja Sahib of Mahmudabad, Sir Mian Mohammad Shafi, Mohammad Yakub, Dr Mukhtar Ansari, Nawab Mohammad Ismail Khan, Raja Ghazanfar Ali Khan, Sir Abdul Qaiyum, Abdul Matin Choudhuri, Abdul Aziz, and Mohammed Shafee Daoodi. For the names of all the participants see, Mujahid, *Studies in Interpretation*, App. 8, 'Delhi Muslim Proposals, 1927', 467.
69. Ibid., 466-7.
70. Hamid, *On Understanding the Quaid-i-Azam*, 13.
71. *The Indian Quarterly Register*, Vol. I (1927), 34-5. Also see, Tara Chand, *History of the Freedom Movement in India*, Vol. IV (Lahore: Book Traders, 1972), 107.
72. See, for instance, the views of the Punjab Muslims in the letter sent by Mian Fazl-i-Husain to Sir Malcolm Hailey on 22 September 1928. Waheed Ahmad, ed., *Letters of Mian Fazl-i-Husain* (Lahore: Research Society of Pakistan, 1976), 56-7.
73. Saiyid, *A Political Study*, 120.
74. Ibid. 128.
75. Tara Chand, *History of the Freedom Movement in India*, Vol. IV, 107.
76. Almost all the prominent signatories to the Delhi Muslim Proposals went on to repudiate not only Jinnah's leadership but also to join the Aga Khan at the All-Parties Muslim Conference in 1929. More prominent being Maulana Mohammed Ali, Sir Mian Mohammad Shafi, Nawab Mohammad Ismail Khan, Shafee Daoodi, Sir Abdul Qaiyum and Mohammad Yakub.
77. Waheed Ahmad, ed., *Jinnah–Irwin Correspondence, 1927–30* (Lahore: Research Society of Pakistan, 1969), 6. In fact, Jinnah's cooperation with the Congress led to the break-up of the Muslim League into Jinnah and Shafi factions, with Shafi faction supporting the Commission.
78. Cited in S.M. Burke and Salim Al-Din Quraishi, *The British Raj in India: A Historical Review* (Karachi: Oxford University Press, 1995), 267.
79. Afzal, *Selected Speeches and Statements*, 297.
80. Prasad, *A Nation within a Nation*, 241. Ayesha Jalal's opinion is that 'Unfortunately, neither Jinnah nor the Congress had the support of all those belonging to the categories "Muslim" and "Hindu".' Ayesha Jalal, *Self and Sovereignty*, 301.
81. Ibid., 258-9.
82. Brown, *Gandhi and Civil Disobedience*, 36.
83. See Mujahid, *Studies in Interpretation*, App. 10, 'Jinnah's 'Fourteen Points', 1929', 479-81. Not only Jinnah, but the Muslim Conference under the presidency of the Aga Khan had also 'repudiated' the Nehru Report. As Judith Brown put it, 'In such circumstances the report was a feebler instrument for affecting unity than Gandhi had earlier thought'. Brown, *Gandhi and Civil Disobedience*, 36.
84. Hamid, *On Understanding the Quaid-i-Azam*, 13. Also see, Mujahid, *Studies in Interpretation*, 19.
85. Brown, *Gandhi and Civil Disobedience*, 47.
86. Metz, 'The Political Career of Mohammad Ali Jinnah', 93. Earlier, in February 1929, Jinnah's wife, Ruttie (Rattanbai), had passed away after a protracted illness. Daughter of Sir Dinshaw Petit, a successful Parsi businessman of Bombay, she had married Jinnah after conversion to Islam. She was buried with solemn

Muslim rituals. Jinnah insisted on it, asserting his growing Muslim consciousness and identity in life. This was clearly reflected in his changed political outlook, in the Fourteen Points and his subsequent moves in Indian politics.

87. Rais Ahmad Jafari, *Nigarishat-Mohammad Ali* (Urdu) (Hyderabad-Deccan: Razzaqui Machine Press 1944), 248-54.

88. Afzal, *Selected Speeches and Statements*, 306-7, 310.

89. Saiyid, *A Political Study*, 149-50. Gandhi had already 'proved unable through civil disobedience to convince either Muslim politicians or the Muslim masses that he was a leader worth following'. Brown, *Gandhi and Civil Disobedience*, 149.

90. See, for instance, his note on 'Suggested Muslim Strategy at the [R.T.] Conference, 1930, in Waheed Ahmad, *Diary and Notes of Mian Fazl-i-Husain*, 211-33.

91. For an informative discussion of Gandhi's activities outside the deliberations of the Round Table Conference see, in particular, Majumdar, *Jinnah and Gandhi*, 140-1.

92. *Proceedings of the Indian Round Table Conference, First Session, 12 November 1930–19 January 1931* (London: HM's Stationery Office, 1931), 148.

93. *The Times* (London), 13 November 1930, 14. Quoted in Wolpert, *Jinnah of Pakistan*, 119.

94. Ibid., 121.

95. Ibid.

96. Cited in Kanji Dwarkadas, *India's Fight for Freedom, 1913-1937* (Bombay: Popular Prakashan, 1966), 385.

97. Aga Khan, *Memoirs*, 232.

98. Ahmad, *Speeches and Writings*, Vol. I, 3.

99. Ibid., 2.

100. Christine Dobbin, ed., *Basic Documents in the Development of Modern India and Pakistan* (London: Van Nostrand Reinhold Co., 1970), 110. According to the Aga Khan, the problem was that Gandhi 'sought to impose a first and fundamental condition: that the Muslims should, before they asked for any guarantees for themselves, accept Congress's interpretation of *swaraj*—self-government as their goal'. Jinnah, he maintains, 'very rightly answered' that since Gandhi 'was not imposing this condition on the other Hindu members of the various delegations attending the Round Table, why should he impose it on the Muslims?' Aga Khan, *Memoirs*, 229.

101. Cited in Hamid, *Muslim Separatism in India*, 211.

102. Ahmad, *Speeches and Writings*, Vol. I, 30.

103. Ibid., 41-2.

104. Frank Moraes, *Witness to an Era: India 1920 to the Present Day* (London: Weidenfeld & Nicolson, 1973), 31.

105. Ahmad, *Speeches and Writings*, Vol. I, 42.

106. Syed Sharifuddin Pirzada, ed., *Quaid-i-Azam Jinnah's Correspondence* (Karachi: East and West Publishing Co., 1977), 21. In fact, 'opting to live in London's Hampstead Heath, he showed his understanding of where the political pendulum had momentarily come to rest'. Ayesha Jalal, *Self and Sovereignty*, 319. However, there were some who argued that the years 1930 to 1935 were 'one of isolation for Jinnah. Although he participated in the two Round Table Conferences, and

formulated the Muslim demands in the form of the Fourteen Points, his was a solitary figure, respected but without a following and he settled down in London.' Saad R. Khairi, *Jinnah Reinterpreted* (Karachi: Oxford University Press, 1996), 441.

107. Pirzada, *Quaid-i-Azam Jinnah's Correspondence,* 21.

108. Sitaramayya, *History of the Indian National Congress,* 859.

109. See, for instance, *Quaid-i-Azam Papers*, F/15, 83-4, 87-9, 116. In July 1933, Liaquat Ali Khan visited Jinnah at his Hampstead residence and appealed to him to return to India to lead the Muslim League and save the Muslims. Muhammad Reza Kazimi, *Liaquat Ali Khan: His Life and Work* (Karachi: Oxford University Press, 2003), 28.

110. Shamsul Hasan, *Plain Mr Jinnah*, 55.

111. *Civil and Military Gazette*, 15 March 1933.

112. Suleri, *My Leader*, 58-9.

113. Saleem Qureshi, *Jinnah and the Making of a Nation*, 38-9. All of them, including the League, All-India Muslim Conference of the Aga Khan and the Jamiat-ul-Ulama-i-Hind, were not quite organized or active. Their activities were mostly confined to their annual sessions.

114. A combined meeting of the two groups was held on 4 March 1934, electing Jinnah as president of the unified Muslim League.

115. *Quaid-i-Azam Papers*, F/15, 84.

116. Ahmad, *Speeches and Writings*, Vol. I, 42.

117. Bolitho, *Creator of Pakistan*, 106.

118. Pirzada, *Foundations of Pakistan,* Vol. II, 223.

119. Reginald Coupland, *India: A Re-statement* (London: Oxford University Press, 1945), 150.

120. Allana, *Story of a Nation*, 255-6.

121. Saiyid, *A Political Study*, 162.

122. Ibid., 173.

123. *Civil and Military Gazette*, 28 April 1936. Indeed, many leaders wrote to Jinnah imploring him to unite the Muslims and reorganize the Muslim League. See, for instance, *Quaid-i-Azam Papers,* F/25.

124. Cited in S.M. Burke, *Landmarks of the Pakistan Movement* (Lahore: Research Society of Pakistan, 2001), 273.

125. Burke and Quraishi, *British Raj in India*, 313.

126. However, Iqbal's support was more intellectual than political. He provided the intellectual basis for the Muslim struggle in India, influencing Jinnah in particular at a very critical stage in his political career

127. For an interesting discussion on the regional groups and their attitudes and constraints at this point in time see, Yunus Samad, *A Nation in Turmoil: Nationalism and Ethnicity in Pakistan, 1937–1958* (New Delhi: Sage Publications, 1995), 27-46.

128. It did not contest all the seats. Pirzada, *Foundations of Pakistan,* Vol. I, lxviii; and Z.H. Zaidi, 'Aspects of the Development of Muslim League Policy, 1937–47', in Philips and Wainwright, *Partition of India*, 253. According to Sayeed, however, the League captured 104 out of 489 seats reserved for the Muslims. Sayeed, *Formative Phase*, 83.

129. The Congress was a force in the Hindu constituencies. Of course, it took advantage of the popularity of the Khudai Khidmatgars 'to justify its boast that it was a genuinely national and secular organization. This was a myth'. Hardy, *Muslims of British India*, 217.

130. Ian Talbot, *Freedom's Cry: The Popular Dimension in the Pakistan Movement and Partition Experience in North-West India* (Karachi: Oxford University Press, 1996), 10. *Freedom's Cry* highlights the role of 'popular participation' in the Pakistan movement.

131. Ahmad, *Speeches and Writings*, Vol. I, 27.

132. *Civil and Military Gazette,* 28 July 1937. The turn of events proved Jinnah right. The League's 'defeat set the scene for future victories'. Jaffrelot, 'Islamic Identity and Ethnic Tensions', 12.

133. *Star of India,* 4 January 1937. Cited in Sayeed, *Formative Phase*, 82.

134. *Civil and Military Gazette,* 28 July 1937.

135. Penderel Moon, *Divide and Quit* (London: Chatoo & Windus, 1961), 15. Maulana Azad called it 'a most unfortunate development', and felt that it gave the 'League in the UP a new lease of life'. In fact, he then went on to argue: 'All students of Indian politics know that it was from the UP that the League was reorganized. Mr Jinnah took full advantage of the situation and started an offensive which ultimately led to Pakistan'. Azad, *India Wins Freedom*, 171.

136. Samad, *A Nation in Turmoil, 54*. Earlier, during the election campaign in January 1937, Nehru had publicly declared that there were 'only two parties' in India, the Congress and the government. Jinnah disagreed: 'There is a third party in this country and that is the Muslims.... Were not going to be camp followers of any party'. Bolitho, *Jinnah: Creator of Pakistan*, 113-4.

137. Rajmohan Gandhi, *Eight Lives*, 146-7. But then the Congress refused 'to share power with *all* minorities, not just Muslims, and with the Muslim League....' Thus, a Muslim member of the Congress government in Bihar, Syed Mahmud, complained to Nehru that: 'The Congress is full of provincialism, caste prejudices and [Hindu] revivalism....' Benjamin Zachariah, *Nehru* (London: Routledge, 2004), 93.

138. Ahmad, *Speeches and Writings*, Vol. I, 24.

139. Ibid., 25.

140. Ibid., 25-6.

141. For the complete address see ibid., 25-39. Relevant passages are indicated in the subsequent discussion.

142. Ibid., 29.

143. Ibid., 30.

144. Ibid.

145. Ibid., 28.

146. Ibid., 28-9.

147. Ibid., 28-34.

148. Ibid., 38.

149. Ibid., 30.

150. Ibid., 31.

151. Ibid., 32.

152. Saiyid, *A Political Study*, 188.

153. Hardy, *Muslims of British India*, 223.
154. That delegate was Maulana Zafar Ali Khan, a prominent Muslim politician and editor of the *Zamindar*. See Mujahid, *Studies in Interpretation*, 433.
155. Jamil-ud-Din Ahmad, *Creation of Pakistan* (Lahore: Publishers United, 1976), 2.
156. Jamil-ud-Din Ahmad, *Glimpses of Quaid-i-Azam*, 11.
157. Jalal, *Self and Sovereignty*, 441.
158. Ahmad, *Speeches and Writings*, Vol. 1, 38.
159. Ibid., 31.
160. Samad, *A Nation in Turmoil*, 57.
161. Ibid.
162. Cited in Deepak Pandey, 'Congress–Muslim League Relations 1937–39', *Modern Asian Studies*, 12, 4 (1978), 652.
163. Mushirul Hasan, ed., *India Partitioned: The Other Face of Freedom*, Vol. I (New Delhi: Roli Books, 1997), 15.
164. Pirzada, *Quaid-i-Azam Jinnah's Correspondence*, 46.
165. Ibid., 48-49.
166. Ibid., 264.
167. Ibid., 267.
168. Ibid., 89.
169. Ibid., 90.
170. Ibid., 91.
171. Ibid., 93
172. Ibid., 92.
173. Ibid., 93.
174. A.M. Zaidi, ed., *Evolution of Muslim Political Thought*, Vol. V (Delhi: S. Chand & Co, 1979), 121.
175. Sharif al Mujahid, *Ideology of Pakistan* (Islamabad: International Islamic University, 2001), 73.
176. Latif Ahmad Sherwani, ed., *Speeches, Writings and Statements of Iqbal* (Lahore: Iqbal Academy, 1977), 23.
177. See Allen H. Jones, 'Mr Jinnah's Leadership and the Evolution of the Pakistan Idea: The Case of the Sind Provincial Muslim Conference, 1938' in Dani, *World Scholars*, 191-203. For the text of the resolution adopted by the League see, G. Allana, ed., *Pakistan Movement: Historic Documents* (Lahore: Islamic Book Service, 1977), 196. However, Muhammad Aslam Malik was of the opinion that 'by dropping the word "federation", the resolution "gave the Muslims [a] free hand to choose the form of government warranted by the circumstances representing rather a more pragmatic approach".' Muhammad Aslam Malik, *The Making of the Pakistan Resolution* (Karachi: Oxford University Press, 2001), 25.
178. Ahmad, *Speeches and Writings*, Vol. I, 74.
179. Ibid., 77.
180. Ibid., 47. Lakhs mean hundreds of thousands.
181. Ibid., 79.
182. Ibid., 92.
183. Ibid., 133. 'Together', Wolpert argued, 'they [Jinnah and Gandhi] might not have persuaded the British to grant Indian freedom overnight, but they could certainly

have accelerated the transfer of power timetable. They might even have avoided partition.' Wolpert, *Jinnah of Pakistan,* 55.

184. Pirzada, *Quaid-i-Azam Jinnah's Correspondence,* 95-6.
185. Ahmad, *Speeches and Writings,* Vol. I, 130-1.
186. According to one writer, this 'did not imply Partition at all but sharing of power in a united India'. A.G. Noorani, 'Muslim Identity: Self-Image and Political Aspirations,' in Mushirul Hasan, ed., *Islam, Communities and the Nation* (Delhi: Manohar, 1998), 124.
187. Ahmad, *Speeches and Writings,* Vol. I, 124.
188. Ibid., 125.
189. Ibid., 129.
190. Ibid.
191. Ibid. 145.
192. Ibid., 90.
193. Jamil-ud-Din Ahmad, *Glimpses of Quaid-i-Azam,* 33.
194. Burke and Quraishi, *British Raj in India,* 136.
195. R.G. Casey, Governor of Bengal, 1944-46. Cited in Sayeed, 'The Personality of Jinnah and his Political Strategy', in Philips and Wainwright, *Partition of India,* 277.
196. Burke and Quraishi, *British Raj in India,* 136.
197. Bolitho, *Jinnah: Creator of Pakistan,* 87.
198. Saleem Qureshi, 'The Consolidation of Leadership in the Last Phase of the Politics of the All-India Muslim League', 325.
199. Hodson, *Great Divide,* 42.
200. Jalal, *Sole Spokesman,* 220-1.
201. Stanley Wolpert, *India* (Englewood Cliffs: Prentice Hall, 1965), 140.
202. Jamil-ud-Din Ahmad, *Glimpses of Quaid-i-Azam,* 27-8. Indeed, as Jinnah told a very prominent leader of the Muslim League in October 1941: 'I am not interested in quarrels between individuals. I am concerned with League, our political organization....' *Quaid-i-Azam Papers,* F/458, 29.
203. According to Hodson, 'His aloofness, his detachment from detail and the infighting of parliamentary politics, even his lack of Muslim roots which might have labeled him a Shia or Sunni or partisan of this or that Mahomedan tradition, such as Punjabi aristocracy, all contributed to the power of his national leadership'. Hodson, *Great Divide,* 42. In addition, Jinnah 'did not want to tarnish the All-India Muslim League's reputation by becoming too closely involved with the day-to-day squabbles of the provincial politicians'. Ian Talbot, *Provincial Politics and the Pakistan Movement* (Karachi: Oxford University Press, 1990), 111.
204. Ravoof, *Meet Mr Jinnah,* 221.
205. Jamil-ud-Din Ahmad, 'A Disciple Remembers', in Jamil-ud-Din Ahmad, ed., *Quaid-i-Azam as Seen by His Contemporaries* (Lahore: Publishers United, 1976), 211.
206. Z.H. Zaidi, *Jinnah Papers,* Vol. I, Part I, xxvi.
207. Mujahid, *Studies in Interpretation,* 398.
208. Samad, *A Nation in Turmoil,* 67.
209. Prasad, *A Nation within a Nation,* 7.

210. Kenneth Cragg, *Counsels in Contemporary Islam: Islamic Surveys* (Edinburgh: University Press, 1965), 21.

211. Syed Sharifuddin Pirzada, ed., *Foundations of Pakistan: All-India Muslim League Documents, 1906–1947*, Vol. II (Karachi: National Publishing House, 1970), 261.

212. Sayeed, *Formative Phase*, 285.

213. Edwin S. Montague, *An Indian Diary* (London: William Heinemann, 1930), 58.

214. And added that, if only he had studied that Act carefully when it was first proposed, the course of Indian history might well have been different. C.H. Philips, *The Partition of India* (London: George Allen & Unwin, 1970), 1.

215. Sharif al Mujahid, *Founder of Pakistan Quaid-i-Azam Mohammad Ali Jinnah, 1876–1948* (Islamabad: National Committee for the Birth Centenary Celebrations of the Quaid-i-Azam Mohammad Ali Jinnah, 1976), 4.

216. Jahan Ara Shahnawaz, *Father and Daughter*, 112.

217. Sayeed, *Formative Phase*, 63.

218. Talbot, *Freedom's Cry*, 10.

219. Saleem Qureshi, 'The Consolidation of Leadership in the Last Phase of the Politics of the All-India Muslim League', 311.

220. Cited in Ravoof, *Meet Mr Jinnah*, 232.

221. Saleem M.M. Qureshi, 'Mohammad Ali Jinnah: A Personality Assessment by His Contemporaries', in Dani, *Quaid-i-Azam and Pakistan*, 115. The accommodating qualities of 'adaptiveness and compromise', in the end, helped him accept 'a Pakistan which fell short of his demands'. Waseem, *Politics and the State in Pakistan*, 84.

222. Z.H. Zaidi, *Jinnah Papers*, Vol. I, Part I, xxvi.

223. Ibid.

224. Bolitho, *Jinnah: Creator of Pakistan*, 69. Percival Spear described it as a 'certain icy passion'. The result, he maintained, was that unlike most people in 'anger', being 'heated and confused', Jinnah was 'colder and clearer than ever'. Percival Spear, *India: A Modern History* (Ann Arbor: University of Michigan, 1961), 410.

225. Z.H. Zaidi, *Jinnah Papers*, Vol. I, Part I, xxxviii.

226. Ahmad, *Speeches and Writings*, Vol. I, 83.

227. Waseem, *Politics and the State in Pakistan*, 84.

228. Ibid., 85.

229. Z.H. Zaidi, 'M.A. Jinnah: The Man, His Glimpses through Personal Correspondence', in Dani, *World Scholars*, 83.

230. Mujahid, *Studies in Interpretation*, 181.

231. Hodson, *Great Divide*, 42.

232. Moraes, *Witness to an Era*, 60.

233. Samad, *A Nation in Turmoil*, 52.

234. Hugh Tinker, *Experiment with Freedom: India and Pakistan, 1947* (London: Oxford University Press, 1967), 24.

235. Cited in Ravoof, *Meet Mr Jinnah*, 228.

236. Z.H. Zaidi, ed., *Quaid-i-Azam Mohammad Ali Jinnah Papers*, Vol. II, *3 June–30 June, 1947* (Islamabad: National Archives, 1994), xxxix.

237. Ibid.

238. Ibid., xi.

239. Ibid., xxix.

240. Which is what Max Weber suggested in his Second Perspective discussed earlier.

241. For instance, Rs. 1,03,00,000 each was paid to Sind Madressah-tul-Islam Karachi, Islamia College Peshawer, and Aligarh Scholarship Trust. In addition, his will stipulated that another '7 crore rupees would be given to those institutions after the sale of Mohatta Palace'. Z.H. Zaidi, *Jinnah Papers*, Vol. II, liii. Interestingly, as Hector Bolitho noted, the 'proof of his devotion to Aligarh lies in two or three short pages of his will, written on some sheets of Legislative Assembly paper, on 30 May 1939 eight years before the Partition of India.' But, more importantly, he 'never revised his will, even after Partition. Although Aligarh was then in an alien territory, he did not withdraw his gesture.' Bolitho, *Jinnah: Creator of Pakistan*, 43.

242. Indeed, as recent revelations have shown, Jinnah was suffering from a lung fatally affected by tuberculosis. He himself had come to know of this only during 1945–46. According to Miss Fatima Jinnah, his sister, who was closer to him than anybody else in his life, recalled in an interview to Hector Bolitho, his biographer: 'For several years before his death there was a constant tug of war between his physicians and the Quaid-i-Azam. They warned him to take long intervals of rest and short hours of hard work....' Jinnah himself told Lt. Col. Ilahi Baksh, his physician during his last days at Ziarat, in 1948: 'For the last few years I had annual attacks of fever and cough. My doctors in Bombay regarded these attacks as bronchitis...for the last year or two, however, they have increased, both in frequency and severity, and they are much more exhausting'. Bolitho, *Jinnah: Creator of Pakistan*, 219. Also see, Ilahi Baksh, *With the Quaid-i-Azam: During his Last Days* (Karachi: Quaid-i-Azam Academy, 1978), 53-61; Collins and Lapierre, *Freedom at Midnight*, 124-6; and Aziz Beg, *Jinnah and his Times* (Islamabad: Babur and Amer Publishers, 1986), 851-66. Also see, Suleri, *My Leader*, LII-LVI, for some details on treatment provided at Ziarat in particular. For an additional account of Jinnah's political activities at Ziarat see, Wolpert, *Jinnah of Pakistan*, 362-9. Mountbatten, years after the creation of Pakistan, wondered: 'If Mr Jinnah had died of this illness [tuberculosis] about two years earlier [than 1948], I think we would have kept the country united. He was the one man who really made it possible. He had completely made up his mind. Nothing would move him.' Larry Collins and Dominique Lapierre, *Mountbatten and the Partition of India*, Vol. I (Delhi: Vikas, 1982), 42.

243. Waseem, *Politics and the State in Pakistan*, 83.

3 The Muslim Situation: Systemic Crisis

By the late 1930s, Indian Muslims were confronted with a set of worsening crises that ranged from systemic to leadership crises. They were in a state of anxiety, despair and helplessness. They felt that their fate was sealed, as India advanced towards freedom in the wake of the Second World War. The prospect of British withdrawal from India heralded the arrival of Hindu rule in the country. The Muslims saw it as the worst crisis they had faced since the beginning of British rule in India in 1858.

In this chapter, we will concentrate upon the systemic crisis, highlighting both its social and political dimensions. We will discuss in particular the communal, constitutional, and devolutionary aspects of the crisis. The leadership crisis will be discussed in the next chapter. However, in all this discussion about the crises affecting the Muslim situation, an effort will be made to analyse these crises for their own sake. The idea is to highlight the situation that facilitated the emergence of Jinnah as the charismatic leader of Muslim India. Jinnah's role will be discussed to the extent that he himself is involved with the situation or contributes to it one way or the other as a potential charismatic leader. The main emphasis will remain on the situation itself.

The Hindu-Muslim Communalism

Most analyses of communalism in India emphasized religion and asserted that it was probably 'the most effective force' in the political life of India.[1] It would be difficult to name, they argued, 'two creeds, two attitudes to life so violently opposed' as Hinduism and Islam.[2] Indeed, as a 'religio-cultural force', they saw Hinduism and Islam as the very 'antithesis' of each other.[3]

While it cannot be denied that Hindu–Muslim communalism was derived from deeply ingrained religio-cultural differences, the argument suffers from two serious limitations. First, it leaves little room for comment on the magnitude and change in Hindu–Muslim relations in the different periods of British rule until the partition of the Indian subcontinent in 1947. Secondly, it tends to put the whole perspective in a 'predetermined course', precluding any discussion of the role of events and personalities affecting these relations. Indeed, as Paul Brass pointed out, 'what stands in the history of Muslim separatism is not the ineluctable movement of events on a historically predetermined course, but the process of conscious choice by which men decide, because it suits their interests to do so.'[4] Unless we understand this clearly, we are bound to reify Hindu–Muslim communalism into something that existed outside the role of men influencing the course of history in modern India.

This is not to suggest that religio-cultural differences did not matter. These differences had an objective existence. They were present, and had an unmistakable influence on the turn of events and outcomes. For instance, the Muslims found it hard to comprehend the sanctity given to the cow under the Hindu law. For them, it is a legitimate sacrificial animal. The Muslim slaughter of cows 'for both dietary and ritual purposes, became a major cultural marker.'[5] The result was that any overt or covert indiscretion on the part of one community quickly inflamed the feelings of the other, resulting in frequent Hindu–Muslim riots. Thus, these riots represented a clash of the two religio-cultural values. They were a manifestation of the opposing sentiments between the Muslims and the Hindus rather than being the cause of it.[6]

Indeed, a wide 'gulf' between the Muslims and Hindus persisted all along,[7] in spite of all the efforts made in the past, particularly by many Muslim rulers, including Emperor Akbar whose concept of political, economic, and religious 'synthesis' failed in bridging the communal chasm between the two communities. The communal units remained isolated, and indeed, became hostile to each other especially as the Muslim authority at the centre began to collapse. Communal sentiment remained a source of conflict during the British rule. The 'injection' of the British as 'a third factor', in fact, 'worked as a catalyst on the extant strands in India's politics'.[8] The religio-cultural differences in the situation came to be further reinforced by economic and political factors.

Economic development in India clearly favoured the Hindus. Most of the gainers were high-caste Hindus though the Parsis and Sikhs also did fairly well. The Muslims, who had formed the major part of the Mughal nobility, officer corps, lawyers, and artisans in luxury handicrafts suffered a great deal.[9] The British not only dispossessed them from positions of power and pelf but also singled them out for 'deliberate repression'[10] for attempting to rehabilitate the Mughal Empire during the revolt of 1857–58. To add to their miseries, the Muslims resisted what they regarded as the imposition of the British system of education. By the time they began to be reconciled to the system of education and the British rule, mainly due to the tireless efforts of Sir Syed Ahmad Khan (1817–1898), they lagged generations behind the Hindus in terms of education, literacy, government employment, and professional experience. Indeed, by the time educated Muslims began to seek gainful positions, the Hindus were well entrenched in the new set-up.[11]

The situation was no different for the Muslims in the private sector. The Hindus started earlier, and soon were able to dominate (along with the Parsis and the Sikhs) industry, commerce and the professions. By 1946, the Hindu capitalist group had developed to a point where it was 'ready to dominate the entire country'.[12] Some like the Birlas and Dalmias were already big industrialists, lending their financial support and patronage to Hindu interests in general and the Congress in particular.[13] Muslim industrialists were very few and far between. For the most part, the Muslims were traders belonging to a few communities like Memons, Bohras and Ismailis operating from their Bombay base.[14] Muslim-majority regions were not favoured by the British for industrial purposes.[15] Muslim areas in general, apart from Bengal, were agrarian, and the Punjab, the land of the five rivers, was developed as the granary of India essentially through a paternalistic approach to agriculture.[16] The result was, as Gustov F. Papenek described the state of Pakistan's economy at independence in 1947: 'The country was among the poorest in the world and had no industries to speak of, almost no industrial raw materials, no significant industrial or commercial groups. It was difficult to see how Pakistan's economy could grow....'[17]

To add to the economic plight of the Muslims was the British system of government based on the 'majority' principle, which necessarily placed the Hindu majority community in a predominant position and thus encouraged 'communalism'. This was evident with the extension of the elective principle in local self-government in the wake of Lord Ripon's reforms of 1882–83, followed by the devolution of authority initiated in the 1909 and 1919 reforms. The communal divisions at the provincial level brought about by the working of these reforms not only strained relations in politics but also in the social spheres, resulting in riots and attempts to reconvert the communal rivals, as reflected in Hindu *Shuddhi* and *Sangathan* and Muslim *Tabligh* and *Tanzim* campaigns. Communalism emerged as a dominant force of Indian politics, reinforcing Muslim fear of Hindu domination.[18]

To make the complex of communal relations more intricate was the demographic factor in its most telling form. Hindus, the majority community in India, were principally concentrated in the centre and south. Muslims were concentrated in the north-west and east along the central latitudes of India, and constituted more than 50 per cent of the populations of the Punjab and Bengal. This peculiar demographic pattern of distribution of the Hindu and Muslim populations, like their total numbers, was to become a major factor in Hindu–Muslim relations as India advanced towards self-government and freedom.[19]

In spite of these inherent difficulties, both Muslim and Hindu leaders in British India made conscious, and at times, forceful efforts to promote Hindu–Muslim unity. Jinnah, in particular, tried hard to promote unity and for a good reason: 'If I can achieve this unity, believe me, half the battle of the country's freedom is won....'[20] Jinnah continued with his efforts until it became absolutely clear to him that the Hindus and Congress leaders were not prepared for any kind of 'understanding' with the Muslims.[21] They would neither allow a system of government to evolve where the Muslims could have 'a sense of security' nor would they agree to share tangible 'power' with them.[22] The result was that Jinnah was left with no option but to offer a new 'formula' to save the Muslims from their predicament that ultimately led to the partition of India and the creation of a separate Muslim state of Pakistan.

Hindu–Muslim communalism was, thus, far from a settled fact of Indian politics, let alone a deterministic historical constant. It was a political process, involving concrete choices and preferences. It manifested itself, between 1858, the year the British Crown directly took over the administration of India, and 1940, the year Jinnah gave up in helplessness and frustration his efforts at communal unity, in at least seven distinct phases in Hindu–Muslim relations. In the following pages, an effort shall be made to delineate and discuss some of the essential features of these phases for a better understanding of the communal problem.

The first phase (1858–1905) was one of Hindu–Muslim separateness. Syed Ahmad Khan, in his efforts to help the Muslims reconcile to the British rule exhorted them to stay away from the recently formed Indian National Congress. He felt that the Congress was inclined towards subversive activity, something that the Muslims could hardly afford in the difficult circumstances, and that its demands, particularly the extension of representative principle in India, were geared to Hindu interests, and would result in Hindu domination over the Muslims. In fact, Syed Ahmad Khan launched organizations such as, the United Indian Patriotic Association (1888) and the Mohammadan Anglo-Oriental Defence Association (1893) to convince the British that the Congress was not a representative body of India and they should not pay any heed to its demands.[23] The obvious implication of 'explicit denial of the Congress' faith in one nation'[24] was to suggest that the Muslims were a separate 'nation', and thus they must not be subjected to Hindu-majority rule. Syed Ahmad Khan argued that they were a 'minority', they were separate from the Hindus, their interests were separate from those of the Hindus, and that their interests could be secured and promoted only through a separate group life and activity. The Muslims and Hindus thus remained estranged and distant towards each other during this phase.

The second phase (1905–12), dominated by the thought and activities of Bal Gangadhar Tilak and other Hindu revivalists, and the convulsions caused by the partition of Bengal in October 1905, was one of open hostility in Hindu–Muslim relations. Tilak revived militant traditions of Sivaji, prompting an era of religious antagonism and alienation of the Muslims. Swami Dayanand and Lajpat Rai had founded the Arya Samaj, with emphasis on 'Back to the Vedas', in deference to one of the most sacred Hindu texts. The Punjab was the main centre of their activities.[25] Similarly, Bankim Chandra Chatterjee influenced and promoted the use of Hindu symbols and lore, identified in Bengal with the Kali cult. These strands, which in course of time also travelled into Congress politics, could hardly be expected to attract Muslims to the Congress platform even if there had been no Syed Ahmad Khan to urge them to stay away from it.[26] Indeed, the Congress 'embodied strands of both a secular, territorial nationalism and a cultural Hindu-tinged nationalism.'[27] In particular, Gandhi used the Hindu religion politically in such a way that eventually many Muslims became convinced that the so-called 'national' movement was linked with a revivalism of Hinduism in India. As R.P. Dutt put it, this 'emphasis on Hinduism must bear a share of the responsibility for the alienation of wide sections of Moslem opinion from the national movement'.[28]

The partition of Bengal created the province of Eastern Bengal and Assam with a Muslim majority and gave further impetus to Hindu revivalism. The movement, which began in opposition to an allegedly 'unpopular measure' soon acquired the force of a religious cause and was marked by a violent campaign against the Muslims.[29] Public meetings addressed by Muslim leaders were broken up, some were assaulted, and those who refused to participate in the agitation were harassed.[30] The Hindus viewed the partition as an exemplification of 'Divide and Rule' and a ploy to arrest the growth of 'Indian nationalism'.[31] But there was hardly any evidence to support this line of argument. First, the partition had not intended to divide the Muslims and Hindus, only the Bengal province. As Lord Curzon (1859–1925), the so-called author of the partition stated in the House of Lords in February 1912, the partition scheme was discussed for a long time and was intended to be no more than 'an administrative device to tackle the administrative problem of a province which had become far too unwieldy'.[32] The new province of East Bengal with a population of 31 million still carried two Hindus to three Muslims. The remainder of Bengal with some 50 million population was a Hindu-dominated province. Secondly, there was no definite sense of solidarity between the Muslims and the Hindus in the first place. The Muslims in Bengal were 'too disorganized and backward' to take an active part in political life, which was predominantly Hindu in form and substance.[33] This was proved by the fact that even after the announcement of the partition, which was clearly to their advantage, the Muslim community was divided on the issue. It was the partition rather than the prospect of partition, which later on formulated and developed 'Muslim opinion against the anti–partition agitation'.[34] After all, the partition 'proved to be a great boon to many Muslims in East Bengal'.[35] However, the British Government yielded to Hindu pressure and propaganda, and at the Delhi coronation ceremony on 12 December 1911, King George V personally announced the annulment of the partition. This shocked the Muslims and made them aware that they could no longer trust the British to safeguard their interests. They had to find a way to relate to the Hindus and work with them. This marked the beginning of the third phase in Hindu–Muslim relations (1912–16).

Although the Muslims were by no means happy with the Hindus for their violent opposition to the partition of Bengal, their grievances against the British government at this stage were compelling. Coupled with their disappointment at the annulment of the partition, events such as, the Cawnpore mosque affair, the British refusal to raise Aligarh College to university status, and above all, the hostile British policy towards the Ottoman Empire persuaded the Muslims to think in terms of cooperation with the Hindus and the Congress. In order to pressurize the British to grant self-government to India at an early date, the Congress readily welcomed them. In return for support on self-government, the Congress even agreed to make a few concessions to them. These concessions were made in the Congress–League Pact of 1916 (Lucknow Pact), which conceded to the Muslims the principle of separate electorates, weightage at the centre and in various Hindu-majority provinces and a provision that any resolution affecting either community, that is the Muslims or Hindus, could be passed only if a three-fourth majority of that community in the provincial or central legislature agreed. The Pact further stipulated that one-third of Indian members in the Central Council must be Muslims.[36] These concessions, which, according to Reginald Coupland, were far weightier than those given by the British under the Act of 1909,[37] proved a great source of satisfaction to the Muslims.[38] Jinnah, who was instrumental in bringing about this Pact, was particularly happy to 'conciliate' Hindu opinion on issues of vital concern to the Muslims. One sure proof of this conciliation was the fact that even Hindu revivalists like Tilak came to support the Pact. Jinnah was declared the 'Ambassador of Unity'.

Hindu–Muslim relations moved into its fourth phase (1916–24) on this encouraging manifestation of an Hindu–Muslim accord. The policy pursued by the British towards the Ottomans on the one hand and repression in the Punjab, especially the Jallianwalla Bagh tragedy of 13 April 1919, on the other hand brought the two communities closer. The bonds were further cemented by their opposition to the 1919 constitutional reforms and the Rowlatt Act. The Act, which allowed the internment of persons without a due process, added to the growing frustration of the political leaders, Muslims as well as Hindus. Indeed, as Khalid bin Sayeed pointed out, the British 'did everything possible to force the Hindus and Muslims to unite' against the administration.[39] The result was a formidable alliance between the Muslims and the Hindus as expressed in the Khilafat–Non-cooperation movement.[40]

The alliance, however, did not last long. It failed to shake the foundations of British rule in India or foster Hindu–Muslim unity as its leaders expected. The clash of 'primary loyalties' was too strong to auger well for the success of proclaimed unity.[41] Maulana Mohammed Ali and Gandhi joined hands to forge a common front against the British. The cause of Indian freedom appeared to coincide with the cause of Islam and the Muslim world situation. Beyond that, the two leaders had little in common, and in fact, very few knew what would happen if the British, whom they clearly knew they were fighting against, were removed from the scene. The petering out of the movement marked the end of the most enthusiastic chapter in Hindu–Muslim relations and compromised hopes for the growth of Indian nationalism. Indeed, by bringing the element of religion 'into political questions', the leaders of the movement 'prepared the path for further Hindu–Muslim antagonism in a fiercer form'.[42] There were several Hindu–Muslim riots during the next few years, resulting in the loss of many lives on both sides. In fact, the alarming increase in the number of riots encouraged both Muslim and Hindu partisans to organize more systematic attacks against each other. Gandhi refused to get involved: 'The regulation of cow-slaughter and playing of music must be left to the goodwill of the respective communities.'[43] The fifth phase in Hindu–Muslim relations (1924–29) was but one manifestation of this indifferent and apathetic trend, though not without desperate efforts on the part of Jinnah to arrest the course of events many a time.

Although Jinnah largely remained in the background during the Khilafat–Non-cooperation period, he still sought a settlement, between the Muslims and the Hindus. But this was not an easy undertaking in the difficult circumstances. The Muslim trust 'in all-India political deals with the Congress' was badly shaken.[44] The Muslims felt the need to develop their own position to be able to gain the cooperation of the Hindus. The growth of provincial politics under the Act of 1919 had also suggested to them that it was desirable to build a Muslim political base in the Muslim-majority provinces than to depend on the Congress for the protection of their particular interests. In 1924, therefore, Jinnah proposed to the Congress a revision of the Lucknow Pact, emphasizing that the Muslims should be given statutory majorities in the Punjab and Bengal and full provincial autonomy and a federal set-up must be guaranteed. The idea was not to prejudice but to further the 'national' cause.[45] As he explained:

> The domination by the Bureaucracy will continue as long as the Hindus and Muhammadans do not come to a settlement. I am almost inclined to say that India will get Dominion Responsible Government the day the Hindus and the Muhammadans are united. Swaraj is an almost interchangeable term with Hindu-Muslim unity.[46]

However, the Congress, sensing the ultimate prospect of a Hindu-majority government in the first signs of the transfer of power to the Indians, as reflected in the 1919 Act, saw things differently. Not only did it claim the position of a majority, but also relied upon numbers to confine its attention primarily to Hindu claims and interests. The result was that, while before the coming of the Act, the Hindu–Muslim conflict was essentially religio-cultural, the immediate causes being playing music before mosques or cow-slaughter, the prospect of 'self government' for India raised political stakes. In the early days of the Khilafat struggle, Gandhi claimed that 'so far as the vast mass of Hindus are concerned, they are interested only in the Cow and Music resolution'.[47] Now Gandhi admitted that the Hindu–Muslim question also involved 'a division of political power—spoils of office' between the two communities.[48] Nothing illustrated this attitude more forcefully than the Nehru Report of 1928.

The Nehru Report was the work of a committee headed by Motilal Nehru and supported by various political organizations of the country, including the Congress and the Jinnah faction of the Muslim League. Jinnah was opposed to the all-British Simon Commission on constitutional reforms announced in 1927. 'Unless a Commission on which British and Indian statesmen are invited to sit on equal terms is set up', he declared along with other prominent leaders of India, 'we cannot conscientiously take any part or share in the work of the Commission as at present constituted'.[49]

To the utter dismay of Jinnah and other Muslim leaders, what the Nehru Report produced was 'the charter of the Hindu intelligentsia'.[50] The Report opposed most of the Muslim demands, conceding only the demand for the formation of separate provinces of the North-West Frontier and Sindh, and that too at the expense of a compensatory concession to Hindus in the creation of a new Canarese-speaking province. The Report recommended a system of government that was all but in name a unitary form of government. To upset the Muslims further, it rejected separate electorates as well as the principle of weightage for minorities. 'If communal protection was necessary for any group in India', the Report concluded, 'it was not for the two major communities—the Hindus and the Muslims'.[51] It might have been useful 'for the smaller communities which together form 10 per cent of the total'.[52] The Report, thus, far from uniting the Muslims and Hindus, went on to alienate and separate them.

Jinnah, however, was not one to give up easily. He went to the All-Parties Convention held in Calcutta in the last week of December 1928 to help modify the Report and make it acceptable to the Muslims. He demanded, in particular, that the Muslims should be allowed one-third of seats in the Central Legislature, residuary powers should be vested in the provinces and not in the centre, and that Muslims in the Punjab and Bengal should be allowed to have seats on the basis of their respective populations at least for ten years, if not more. He pleaded for 'statesmanship', and stressed:

Believe me that there is no progress for India until the Mussalmans and Hindus are united and let no logic, philosophy or squabble stand in the way of our coming to a compromise and nothing will make me more happy than to see the Hindu–Muslim union.[53]

The Hindu leaders, however, were in no mood to respond to Jinnah's impassioned pleas. M.R. Jayakar (1873–1959), speaking for the Hindu Mahasabha, questioned Jinnah's credentials as the Muslim spokesman.[54] He refused to support any amendment to the Report. The result was a foregone conclusion. Jinnah's amendments were rejected. Jinnah was thoroughly disappointed. He, reportedly, called it 'the parting of the ways'.[55]

Jinnah moved to draft his own proposals in the form of the 'Fourteen Points', insisting that 'no scheme for the future constitution of the government of India' will be acceptable to the Muslims until and unless provisions were made 'to safeguard their rights and interests'.[56] Thus, the main thrust of these Points was to secure a maximum number of Muslim-majority provinces in a federal system with adequate representation of the Muslims in the centre. Although, by now, Jinnah seemed reluctant 'to trust his erstwhile Congress colleagues',[57] he was still prepared to work for a Hindu–Muslim settlement. He was willing to do his part. This was the making of the sixth phase of Hindu–Muslim relations (1929–37).

Jinnah attended the Round Table Conference in London in 1930 in the hope that it could lead to Hindu–Muslim settlement for the greater cause of India. An agreement between the Muslims and the Hindus was the key to self-government. But, Gandhi, the sole representative of the Congress, failed to deliver. Indeed, according to Judith Brown, he proved 'incapable of leading Indian delegates into a compromise agreement' and forging 'inter-communal unity'.[58] The result was that Jinnah saw 'no hope of unity' and, indeed, felt so 'pessimistic' about the whole situation that he decided not to return to India.[59] However, urged by the Muslims, when he did finally return to India in 1935, he was still ready to come to an understanding with the Hindus and the Congress. He saw no other way out for India in its struggle for self-government and freedom. Thus, the election manifesto issued by the Muslim League in 1937 was conciliatory towards the Congress. In fact, it recalled the spirit of the Lucknow Pact implying in no small way that he was keen to revive the spirit of 1916.[60]

The Congress, however, after winning 'mainly in Hindu constituencies',[61] asserted that it was the only national political party in India. It did not include any Muslim Leaguer in the Congress ministries it eventually formed in eight out of eleven provinces. In a circular to Provincial Congress Committees on 3 March 1937, the Congress President, Jawaharlal Nehru, declared: 'You may also be approached by other groups in the legislature. It is highly desirable that the response to all such requests should be clear and definite and uniform all over India. With other groups, we can form no alliances'.[62] The Muslim leadership and the masses in general saw it as an attempt at 'Hindu domination'. Further attempts, with Gandhi's blessings, to force Sanskritized Hindi and to remould the educational system, particularly at the primary level, as represented by the *Vidyamandir* scheme, made matters worse. The Muslims perceived these measures to be an attack on Muslim culture in India. In their estimate, the purpose was to prepare 'a generation which would cease to be Muslim in thought, character and action'.[63] Muslim apprehensions, in fact, went as far as they could go. The 'fear of the future that weighed heavily on the Muslim mind' since the introduction of parliamentary institutions in India[64] further convinced Jinnah and many Muslim leaders that Gandhi, Congress, and the Hindu community in general sought Hindu 'Raj' in India. Of course, Gandhi and other Congress leaders insisted that the Hindu–Muslim question is 'a bogy', indeed 'the direct product of the British rule'.[65] But then, as B.R. Tomlinson observed, it showed how 'little they understood nationalism' and how 'little they knew each other'.[66] This was the main feature of the last, fateful, phase in Hindu–Muslim relations (1937–40).

Indeed, for most writers, the Congress's failure to accommodate Jinnah and the Muslim League at this crucial phase in the political history of India had the ultimate effect of making either the partition of India, or a vicious communal war between the Muslims and the Hindus, the principal alternatives. The demand for Pakistan, or for that matter the creation of the state of Pakistan, they argue, was the direct result of the policy adopted by the Congress government from 1937 to 1939. Sharif al Mujahid, for instance, found it almost 'inexplicable, unless explained in terms of terrible lack of political prescience and foresight'.[67] Hindu–Muslim unity, though elusive, was theoretically possible. Now, the Muslim faith in Congress policies and programmes was exhausted. Jinnah, who, in spite of all the difficulties and disappointments, had for decades tried to achieve Hindu–Muslim unity, was convinced that the time had come to 'revise our notions of settlement in the light of experience and lessons we have learnt during the past 25 years'.[68] He had come to realize the power of religio-cultural factors in Hindu–Muslim relations. In his article for *Time and Tide*, he boldly stated:

> The British people, being Christians, sometimes forget the religious wars of their own history and today consider religion as a private and a personal matter between man and God. This can never be the case in Hinduism and Islam, for both these religions are definite social codes, which govern not so much man's relations with his God, as man's relations with his neighbour. They govern not only his law and culture but every aspect of his social life, and such religions, essentially exclusive, completely preclude that merging of identity and unity of thought on which western democracy is based.[69]

By 1940, the Hindu–Muslim relations had, in fact, reached a point where Jinnah could claim that it was futile to expect that the two communities would be transformed into 'one nation merely by means of subjecting them to a democratic constitution and holding them forcibly together by unnatural and artificial method of British Parliamentary Statute'.[70] The differences between the Muslims and the Hindus were 'fundamental' and 'deep-rooted'. He, therefore, warned that the Muslims

> ...cannot accept any constitution, which must necessarily result in a Hindu majority government. Hindus and Muslims brought together under a democratic system forced upon the minorities can only mean Hindu raj. Democracy of the kind with which the Congress High Command is enamoured would mean the complete destruction of what is most precious in Islam. We have had ample experience of the working of the provincial constitutions during the last two and a half years and any repetition of such a government must lead to civil war....[71]

The prospect of a Hindu-majority government agitated the Muslims and reinforced their fear of being overwhelmed by the system. They could not contemplate their fate in a system of government 'democratic' in theory but Hindu in practice. They had reached a dead end. They saw no way out of the constitutional problem in India.

The Constitutional Problem

In order to understand the constitutional problem better, particularly as it affected the Muslims and alienated them from the system of government, it will be useful to trace the history of constitutional advance in India first. This history influenced and shaped the system in becoming what it eventually was, a system inherently biased in favour of the Hindu-majority community.

The British initiated the growth of representative institutions in India with much reluctance. They never really wanted to promote them. This was abundantly clear from the Charter Act of 1833. The Act stipulated that the Government of India was to be a 'purely official government'. Executive authority was vested in the Governor-General and his Council of officials and in the Governors of the Presidencies and their Councils. Legislative authority was vested in the Governor-General in Council alone. Members of the Council were supposed to be British. The only thing 'representative' about the Act was a clause in the Bill that suggested that some day Indians might hold office, however high, in the government.

There were many British officials who were 'alarmed' at even the thought of a representative system of government in India. John Malcolm, for instance, did not mince words:

> I am most alarmed at the effects of the active zeal and desire to enact laws of a permanent legislative council. A long period must elapse before we have sufficient correct materials for such a Council to work upon; for every man of knowledge and experience of India must confess that we are as yet much in the dark on those points on which legislation should be grounded. Every new inquiry that descends minutely into the conditions of a town or district in India, or into the habits and history of a community, brings along with it proofs of our ignorance.[72]

In 1853, after two decades of the establishment of the Legislative Council, the Indians did not have seats in the Council and their consultative role was severely limited. The only way they were consulted was 'by selecting persons who to their knowledge are well informed, and talking to them in their own way and at their own times'.[73] While men like Lord Ellenborough and Elphinstone were willing to recommend that Indians 'should be members of a consultative council, which might be in attendance on the Governor-General, to whom he might refer to ascertain the wishes and feelings of the natives on several points' they, too, were reluctant to allow the Indians to have representation in the Legislative Council.[74] Sir Charles Wood thought that it was 'impossible to do so without creating the greatest jealousy among the numerous [sic] sects which would necessarily remain unrepresented'.[75]

It was only after the revolt of 1857, which revealed to the British 'the gap of ignorance and misunderstanding' that separated them from their subjects, that they sought closer contact with the Indians. As Sir Bartle Frere explained: '...the addition of the native element has, I think, become necessary owing to our diminished opportunities of learning through indirect channels what natives think of our measures and how the native community will be affected by them'.[76] But, this did not mean the creation of 'an Indian Parliament'.[77] Thus, when Surendranath Banerjee (1848–1925) in a speech on 30 December 1886, echoing Congress demands for political reforms, proclaimed that 'self-government is the ordering of the nature, the will of Divine Providence',[78] the British were not moved. Lord Dufferin not only felt that the demand was not simply 'a further step in advance, but a very big jump into the unknown—by the application to India of democratic methods of government, and the adoption of a parliamentary system, which England herself has only reached by slow degrees and through the discipline of many centuries of preparation'. Indeed, he claimed that the demand was 'eminently unconstitutional; for the essence of constitutional government is that responsibility and power should be committed to the same hands'.[79] Lord Curzon, taking part in a debate on the Indian Councils Bill, 1892, went one step further:

The people of India were voiceless millions, who could neither read or write their native tongue, who had no knowledge whatever of English.... [They] were ryots and peasants.... The Government assumed the responsibility of stating that, in their opinion, the time had not come when representative institution, as we understood the term, could be extended to India. The idea of representation was alien to the Indian mind....[80]

Apart from the fact that the British felt that the Indians were not fit for parliamentary representation, there were other considerations[81] as well that led them to conclude that the system, as understood and practiced in England, was not meant for India. One was their estimate of the political traditions in India. As the Secretary of State for India, Lord Morley (1838–1923), who played a leading role in the formulation of 1909 reforms, succinctly put it:

> From time immemorial in India the power of the state has rested in the hands of absolute rulers. Neither under Hindu kings nor Mohammedan Emperors had the people any voice in the affairs of the state.... [Thus] The Government of India must remain autocratic; the sovereignty must be vested in British hands and cannot be delegated to any kind of representative assembly.[82]

The other important and perhaps more critical factor was the sharp communal division of India between the adherents of Islam and Hinduism. The British understood that the difference between Islam and Hinduism was 'not a mere difference of articles of religious faith. It is a difference in life, in tradition, in history, in all the social things as well as articles of belief that constitute a community'.[83] Thus, the British Prime Minister, Lord Asquith, did not hesitate to defend the granting of separate electorates to the Muslims in the 1909 Act in these words:

> To us here in this country at first sight it looks an objectionable thing, because it discriminates between people, segregating them into classes, on the basis of religious creed...the distinction between Mohammedan and Hindu is not merely religious, it cuts deep down not only into the traditions and historic past, but into the habits and social customs of the people.[84]

The rules made under the 1909 Act not only granted special representation to the Muslims but also to other minority communities of India such as the Anglo-Indians, Indian Christians, Sikhs, Europeans, besides landlords, university graduates, commercial and industrial classes. This mode of representation clearly 'accorded with Indian "conceptions" and "conditions" rather than British'.[85] No wonder, Lord Morley asserted: 'If it could be said that this chapter of reforms led directly or necessarily to the establishment of a parliamentary system in India, I for one, would have nothing at all to do with it'.[86]

But while the British politicians insisted that parliamentary process was neither intended nor desirable, the very existence of legislative councils and its working, no matter how haltingly, stimulated the 'appetite' for more.[87] In the end, it was but a foregone conclusion that these councils assumed the character of 'parliaments.' As Coupland, the leading British constitutional expert explained the paradox:

> One after another, British statesmen had repudiated a particular method of advance towards a self-governing India, but none of them had suggested an alternative. If they had any conception of the direction in which the sequence of Reforms was moving, it was towards what Minto called 'Constitutional autocracy'. But they seem never to have considered at what point the paradoxical process of making autocracy constitutional would stop, nor how in the end a British autocracy could be converted into an Indian one. It might almost be said that they were still 'walking in darkness', as in Macaulay's day, without seeing where they were going.[88]

Whatever the case may be, the fact of the matter was that India was made to receive the parliamentary system of government sooner than expected. The 'seeds the fruit of which is Parliamentary government' had been planted.[89] The Act of 1919 not only adopted the British parliamentary system in the provinces under the famous scheme of 'dyarchy', the brainchild of the Indian Study of the Round Table, reformulated by Lionel Curtis,[90] but also created a central legislature for British India, elected through a system of franchise consisting of an electorate of 5 million voters.[91] This was a considerable advance over the Act of 1909 where the electorate comprised 500,000 voters on the principle of indirect elections through municipal or local bodies. The 1919 Act also crossed the line between legislative and executive authority. Now Indians were 'to govern, so to speak on their own.'[92] They were to take control of many departments of provincial administration, not as official nominees, as had been the case in previous measures, but as leaders of the elected majorities in their legislatures and responsible only to them. Provinces became the major centres of political responsibility and government. Although the Act divided responsibilities for government between the provincial governors and elected ministers, it committed the British to 'some form of parliamentary institutions'.[93] This was reinforced by the

Government of India Act of 1935, the last in the long series of constitutional advances in India.

The Act of 1935 was an attempt to recognize the increasing Indian demand for self-government. The framers intended to capture the form of a federal constitution, establishing a 'Federation of India' and a new set of powers for the provinces of British India. It invested the provinces, for the first time, with a separate legal personality, exercising executive and legislative powers in their fields in their own right, in concert with the federal authority. But the Act did not establish a federation by itself. The birth of the federation required the accession of half the Princely States, which occupied 52 of the 104 seats allotted to the States in the upper house of the Federal Legislature, and the approval of the British Parliament.[94] Although it did not happen in actual fact due to the inconsistent attitude of the princes, the Act transformed the 'grammar and syntax' of Indian politics by lowering the franchise qualifications and thus increasing the electorate to over 30 million.[95] The increase in the number of general seats in the legislative assemblies helped the Indians claim a larger share of responsibility in government. India had eventually acquired a constitution modelled on Westminster, though it was not free of the control of the British Parliament.

However, the British efforts to apply the parliamentary principles upon Indian conditions placed severe 'stress and strain' on its body politic.[96] While the Hindus, the majority community, had reasons to be dissatisfied with the meagre advance under the Act,[97] the Muslims confronted the fundamental issue of 'majority rule' sanctioned by the representative principle. Their old fear and mistrust of the British parliamentary system of government, biased heavily in favour of the majority community, had come to life. Though the Act provided the Muslims, like all other minorities, specific safeguards, it did not alter the basic fact that they were a 'minority', and 'in democracies, majorities rule'.[98]

The Muslims were wary and critical of parliamentary system of government in India since their inception. Syed Ahmad Khan was convinced that representative institutions in India would result in the domination of the Hindus over the Muslims. The Hindus would obtain four times as many votes as the Muslims because their population was four times as large: 'It would be like a game of dice in which one man had four dice and the other only one'.[99] Electoral qualifications, like income, and education,[100] he was convinced, would hurt rather than help.[101]

However, while at first, under the influence of Syed Ahmad Khan, the Muslims opposed the system of government vehemently, in the subsequent years, they were reconciled to it in the hope of securing their interests with some safeguards. The immediate safeguard they insisted upon was, of course, the right to elect their representatives by separate electorates. The Muslim leaders were convinced that the Act of 1892 had introduced the concept of 'election', and that more constitutional reforms were likely to extend the application of elective principle.[102] Thus, they felt that they had no option but to demand separate representation to secure their particular interests. The British, too, based on their experience of the working of the legislative councils in 1893, realized that 'territorial representation' had not made possible the participation of all the important classes and groups of India, especially the Muslims.[103] Though the Act of 1909 granted separate electorates,[104] the Muslims still failed to receive 'adequate' representation in various councils. Their weak position was clearly reflected in the elections of 1912. In the Bengal Legislative Council, they managed to elect only 5 Muslim members out of 28. In the Punjab, where they were not conceded separate electorates as they were considered strong enough to protect their interests, they could send only one Muslim out of the eight elected members in the Legislative Council.[105] Already, the Muslims had suffered heavily in the municipal elections. In Calcutta, for instance, where the Muslims were not less than one-third of the entire population, they could capture only five out of the 48 seats of the Municipality.[106] Indeed, due to electoral qualifications, such as proprietorship, payment of income tax, and graduation from a university, the Muslim position remained precarious. No wonder, they did not hesitate to join hands with the Congress in 1916 in order to secure better terms in the proposed 1919 reforms.

The Act of 1919 took very little from the Congress–League Pact except, of course, the principle of separate electorates, which was reaffirmed. It rejected the Muslim demand for adequate representation in the legislatures. To add to their difficulties, the Muslims lost their legitimate share in the Muslim-majority provinces. In the Punjab, for instance, with its 55.2 per cent (1921 census) Muslim majority in the province, they were offered thirty-four Muslim seats, equal to the member of seats given to the Hindus and Sikhs together. In Bengal, another Muslim-majority province, with its 54.6 per cent Muslim population, they formed only 45.1 per cent of the electorate for reasons of economic and educational backwardness. The result was that, in the provincial legislature, they got only 39 of 114 seats. Muslims, as such, were 'a political minority both in those areas where they were in a population minority and in those where in a population majority'.[107] The Act of 1919 thus set the stage for a keen Muslim campaign for statutory majorities in the Muslim-majority provinces of Bengal and the Punjab, and the creation of a federation of self-governed provinces, with a weak centre. This was the only way the Muslims thought they could reasonably expect to secure their position in the emerging system of government. In fact, with no advance at the centre, the whole focus of politics had shifted to the provinces. The Muslims wanted control of their Muslim-majority provinces. Indeed, the most significant impact of the 1919 reforms was also to shift 'power and influence from the Muslim minority provinces to the Muslim majority provinces'.[108]

This concern with the provinces was most clearly reflected in the Lahore session of the League in December 1924, over which Jinnah presided, and wherein it was resolved, *inter alia* that:

a. The existing provinces of India shall all be united under a common Government on a federal basis so that each province shall have full and complete provincial autonomy, the functions of the central government being confined to such matters only as are of general and common concern.
b. Any territorial redistribution that might at any time became necessary shall not in any way affect the Muslim majority of population in the Punjab, Bengal and NWF Province.[109]

The Aligarh session of the League in December 1925 reiterated the demand for federation, provincial autonomy, and statutory majorities in the Punjab and Bengal at a meeting which was representative of almost all shades of opinion in the Muslim camp, led by Jinnah, Mian Mohammad Shafi, Maulana Mohammed Ali, Maulana Shaukat Ali and Abdur Rahim of Bengal (1867–1948). The substance of the resolution adopted and Sir Abdur Rahim's presidential speech was that further constitutional advance was not helpful unless these essential Muslim demands were met.[110] On 20 March 1927, Jinnah and a number of prominent Muslim leaders who met at Delhi were willing to renounce separate electorates if the number of Muslim-majority provinces could be raised to five by separating Sindh from Bombay and giving NWFP and Balochistan full provincial status.[111] Though the idea of abandoning separate electorates was soon disavowed by the Muslim leadership in the wake of Hindu failure, in the Nehru Report, to respond to the proposal, the move clearly illustrated the extent of the growing Muslim faith in the provincial alternative. In the Muslim-majority provinces of the Punjab and Bengal, the Muslims formed their own ministries, enjoyed the fruits of power, and sought to increase the number of Muslim-majority provinces with maximum provincial autonomy.

The appointment of a Royal Commission on constitutional reforms announced in November 1927, popularly known as the Simon Commission, primarily to look into the failings of the 1919 Act,[112] raised hopes only to dash them to the ground. The leaders of the Muslim-majority provinces, particularly in the Punjab, went all the way to welcome and support the Commission in spite of an appeal for general boycott by most political parties including the Jinnah faction of the League. While the Simon Commission Report, submitted in May–June 1930, conceded in principle the Muslim demand for provincial autonomy and a federal constitution, it rejected the specific Muslim demand for majorities in the Punjab and Bengal. As one member of the Commission remarked: '…It was only by conceding the Punjab and Bengal point against the Moslems that we got them [Hindus] to agree to communal electorates and weightage for Muslims elsewhere'.[113] This rejection of the Muslim demand for statutory majorities in the Punjab and Bengal evoked bitter reaction against the report not only among the erstwhile supporters of the Commission but also its opponents. Indeed, Jinnah claimed, 'So far as India is concerned we have done with it….'[114] The British also realized the futility of constitutional advance through this report, shelved it and held consultations with Indian leaders at a Round Table Conference in London.

The Memorandum submitted by the Muslim delegates at the Round Table Conference on 27 December 1932 demanded a federal constitution and provincial autonomy and linked statutory majorities with a guarantee that the Muslims should form governments in those areas of north-west and north-east India where they had such majorities.[115] However, the Conference was not moved. The Hindus joined the British to oppose what they termed the 'imposition' of Muslim statutory majorities in the Punjab and Bengal. They also opposed the maintenance of separate electorates, weightage, and provincial autonomy. All that Gandhi could promise on behalf of the Hindu-dominated Congress was that: 'The residuary powers shall vest in the federating units, unless [sic] on further examinations, it is found to be against the best interests of India'.[116] The result was tedious and inconclusive negotiations that ultimately compelled the British to impose their own solution, and on 16 August 1932, the British Prime Minister, MacDonald, announced the Communal Award.

Although the Award, like previous reforms, conceded the Muslim demand for separate electorates, it failed to oblige the Muslims on other points. The seats allotted to them in the Punjab and Bengal were fewer than what their population warranted and fell short of the number of seats required for majorities in either of these two provinces. Indeed, the Award rejected the Muslim demand for statutory majorities in the Punjab and Bengal. Besides, the Award took no concrete decision on the distribution of powers between the centre and the provinces. The Muslim demand that residuary powers be vested in the provinces was also turned down.[117]

Not surprisingly, the constitutional advance in the Act of 1935 failed to carry Muslim support and approval as it did not meet the federal objectives stressed by the Muslim leadership since the early 1920s. Instead, the Act promoted a federation with a strong unitary bias. The centre was empowered to legislate the 'Federal' and 'Concurrent' lists of subjects. The ministerial responsibility in the provinces was restricted by 'safeguards' placed in the hands of the governors. To further restrict the scope of the ministerial responsibility, the Act placed the Governor under the 'superintendence' and 'general control' of the Governor-General in all those respects in which he could exercise his 'discretion' or 'individual judgment', thereby reinforcing central authority over Indian legislatures.[118] Jinnah described the Act as: '...totally unacceptable ...devoid of all the basic and essential elements and fundamental requirements which are necessary to form any federation'.[119]

If the Act of 1935 proposed a system of government with a strong unitary bias, the Congress, during its two and a half years of rule in the provinces (1937–39) left no doubt about it in anyone's mind. It insisted on the formation of one-party ministries in the provinces, taking upon itself the mantle of 'national' authority 'in order to prove its claim to be the successor to the British raj'.[120] It rejected the Muslim League's proposals for a coalition in the UP and elsewhere,[121] openly flouted the reservations and safeguards written into provincial constitutions,[122] and thus, showed the Muslims that the majority-rule meant 'Congress rule, exerted from a centre dominated by the Hindu majority through an organization which brooked no opposition and refused to share its power'.[123] It can hardly be overemphasized that the Congress, like the British, had always an inclination towards unitary government. This was clearly shown by the Nehru Report as well as by the stand taken by the Congress at the Round Table Conference. In both cases, the Congress recommended a unitary form of government, with powers vested in the centre. The problem with the Congress was that it always claimed to be doing no more than 'expressing the will of the nation'[124] without realizing the force of Muslim opinion opposed to it.[125]

The Muslims were certainly not prepared to submit to 'a central government with the Hindu majority and Hindu rule throughout the country'.[126] They had a difficult and frustrating experience, based on the results of available evidence, of the working of the representative system of government in India. The 'hegemonic tendencies' of the Congress had already 'made it difficult for the 'difference' of the minority to be accepted on anything other than the majority's terms.'[127] The Muslims realized that they were a permanent minority, and indeed, saw no hope in a system of government dominated by the centre. The more they saw the powers vested in the centre, the more they feared it must, in practice, favour the Hindus, who formed the majority community. They were no doubt somewhat protected by the principle of separate electorates, but, then, the working of the Act of 1935 confirmed the frightful inadequacy of this electoral device in the face of an overwhelming Hindu majority determined to pursue its own interests. In the end, the British, too, were convinced that the parliamentary system of government was not the best system for India.[128] In fact, the Secretary of State for India, Leopold S. Amery

(1873–1955), more than once, pressed for the introduction of the Swiss system to help resolve the constitutional problem. On 15 July 1943, he explained the system in a letter to the Viceroy, Lord Linlithgow,

> The essence of that system is that the Executive is elected by the Legislature as a whole, by secret ballot on proportional representation, and is thus permanently enthroned for the lifetime of Parliament. That makes it necessarily a coalition government, and being relatively free from party pressure in the chamber, more inclined to get down to business and to work together. Moreover, the secret ballot is a further protection against the mischievous power of the party caucuses in Indian affairs. I have sometimes wondered whether the system might not be conceivably introduced in the case of any deadlock without any change either in legislation or even in the Letters of Instructions to the Governors, provided always that the Legislature itself was prepared to play.[129]

Again, writing to Linlithgow's successor and the new Viceroy, Lord Wavell (1883–1950), on 21 October 1943, in the context of troubles in Bengal Ministry, Amery reiterated his point: 'The more I hear of the working of the Bengal Government, both under Fazlul Haq and of all the intrigues and recrimination since, the more I am convinced...that the Swiss constitutional system might have a better chance of succeeding in an Indian province than the British'.[130]

Although nothing came out of this suggestion, it is very difficult to believe that the Swiss system could have helped overcome the majority-minority conflict rooted in religion, culture, and history. The idea merely exposed the weakness of parliamentary system of government in the eyes of policy-makers. In exasperation, Amery even suggested the American system. In a strongly worded Memo on the political situation of India in September 1943, he wrote:

> The one type of government to which there is not the slightest hope of ever reaching agreement in a united India is the British type in which the executive is directly and continuously dependent on a parliamentary majority. For under Indian conditions that means that the executive will be a puppet of a Congress, or at any rate Hindu party caucus of Gandhi or whoever may succeed him. Only an executive representative of all communities and enjoying tenure of office independent of parliamentary vote can hold India together. The idea is unfamiliar to us, but it is the basis of the whole American constitutional system. In a somewhat different form

it is also the basis of the Swiss system…we should jettison the idea that… a government can be established on convention[al] British parliamentary lines.[131]

Whether the British at this point in time could seriously 'jettison' the idea that a government in India can be established on conventional 'British parliamentary lines' or not, the Muslims had made up their mind. They were not interested. They were convinced that the system was, by definition, biased against them. The Hindus had an unassailable power as a majority community, and nothing could be done about it. The representative form of government in India, Jinnah claimed,

> has definitely resulted in a permanent communal majority government ruling over minorities, exercising its powers and functions and utilising the machinery of Government to establish the domination and supremacy of the majority communal rule over the minorities.[132]

This realization became all the more intense and profound with the feelings, in the war years, that the British were on their way out and the majority community would inherit the mantle of power. The process of devolution of British authority and the threat of imminent Hindu rule in India heightened Muslim anxieties and fears about their fate in united India.

The Devolution of British Authority

The devolution of British authority in India happened at two levels. The first level was that of the declining ability of the British to use coercive power and the increasing erosion of their legitimacy to rule India over the years. The second, and perhaps the more significant level, reflected the Muslim desire to be free as much from the British rule as from the Hindu domination. The Muslims were not willing to exchange the British rule with the Hindu rule. As Jinnah described it, this would confront India 'with [the] worst disaster that had ever taken place….'[133]

The British rule in India rested on their physical strength and resources to continue to hold their possession. Although the revolt of 1857 was successfully put down with substantial help from 'loyal' Indian troops including the recently recruited Sikhs, the main burden of the task was carried out by the regular British soldiers and officers.[134] This experience encouraged the British to develop an 'irresistible force of British troops' along with a strong bureaucracy to maintain law and order in the country.[135] To help produce 'immediate and most salutary results', the bureaucracy was armed with additional Acts and Regulations.[136] Thus, various coercive measures were resorted to as early as 1908 to stop, what the government called, 'the saturnalia of lawlessness'[137] of the terrorists in Bengal and the Punjab. Regulation III of 1818, which empowered the government to intern a person without trial for any length of time, was used in the Punjab to check the 'rebellious' activities of the people. But the clearest manifestation of the British intent to put down challenge to their authority by the use of force was reflected in the Defence of India Act of 1915, followed by the Rowlatt Act of 1919, which armed the government with special powers to deal with all kinds of situations.[138]

That these regulations were meant for use was soon demonstrated at Jalianwala Bagh in Amritsar in 1919. Not only was terror let loose on a peaceful public meeting but martial law was brought into force— for the first time after 1857—to prevent the so-called 'boiling wrath' of the local people from spreading to other areas of the Punjab.[139] India was 'mad with pity, grief and horror'.[140] But the British had provided ample proof of their 'love of arbitrary power' being exercised.[141] Again, in the wake of the disturbances in the Muslim areas of Malabar, the British responded brutally by equipping military authorities with 'power to impose the death sentence on rebels after conviction by a drumhead court martial.'[142] In these disturbances, according to one estimate, 2,339 Mappillas were killed, 1,652 wounded, 5,955 captured and 39,348 surrendered to the military or to the police. In April 1923, the number of prisoners in jails, excluding a very large number which had been transported to the island of Andamans, was 7,900. In addition, fines worth over a million rupees were imposed which, in majority of cases, were beyond the resources of the Mappillas because of their abject poverty.[143]

Though the British pursued a policy of patient restraint in the Khilafat–Non-cooperation movement of 1920–22,[144] they could not continue their cautious policy for long. During the Civil Disobedience Movement of 1930 they did not hesitate to take repressive measures, including arrests, and 'violence, physical outrage, shooting and beating up, punitive expeditions, collective fines on villages and seizure of lands.'[145] With the issuance from time to time of such measures as special ordinances, the use of military and local application of martial law orders, the British rule was nothing short of a 'civil marital law'.[146] The 'Quit India' movement of 1942 was suppressed even more severely. Though martial law was not declared, the actions taken by civilian officers were 'no less severe than would have been taken under martial law....'[147] Not only did the British allow officials to exercise their extraordinary authority, they also protected them through special ordinances and indemnity acts when they exceeded that authority.[148]

It was this open resort to arbitrary power which prompted some politicians to describe the British conception of ruling India as 'the police conception of the State.'[149] They did not approve of violence, and were indeed happy to know that, in the end, 'the belief in terrorism was dying down',[150] but they were shocked at the stark contradiction between the values of the British professed in Britain and practiced in India.[151] Jinnah, for instance, could not understand the need for the Rowlatt Bill, with all the 'draconian measures' included in it.[152] In his letter of resignation from the membership of the Imperial Legislative Council as a mark of protest against the 'passage' of the Bill, he told the Viceroy:

The passage of the Rowlatt Bill by the government of India, and the assent given to it by your Excellency as Governor-General against the will of the people, has severely shaken the trust reposed by them in the British Justice.... Neither the unanimous opinion of the non-official Indian members nor the entire public opinion and feeling outside has met with the least respect. The government of India and your Excellency, however, have thought it fit to place on the statute-book a measure admittedly abnoxious and decidedly coercive at a time of peace, thereby substituting the executive for the judicial.... The fundamental principles of justice have been uprooted, and the constitutional rights of the people have been violated at a time when there is no real danger to the State by an overfretful and incompetent bureaucracy which is neither responsible to the people nor in touch with the real public opinion and their sole plea is that the powers when they are assumed will not be abused.... In my opinion, a Government that passes or sanctions such a law in a time of peace forfeits its claim to be called a civilized government....[153]

Ironically enough, the Rowlatt Bill was passed in an era characterized by some analysts as a 'new angle of vision' reflecting British appreciation of India's contribution to the war efforts.[154] Years later, during the Second World War when Indian support was suspect in British eyes, and with the Hindu majority community led by the Congress not supporting the war effort, British outrage was beyond bounds. A Revolutionary Movement Ordinance was enacted to 'crush' the Indian challenge. Even though the British Government pledged that after the war they would help India 'devise the framework of the new constitution,'[155] there were doubts all around. As Ernest Bevin, Minister of Labour and National Service in the War Cabinet, confided to the Secretary of State for India, Amery:

> I must confess that leaving the settlement of the Indian problem until after the war fills me with alarm.... We made certain definite promises in the last war and practically a quarter of a century has gone, and though there has been an extension of self-government, we have not, in my view, 'delivered the goods' in a broad and generous way. It is quite understandable that neither Muslim nor Hindu places much confidence in our 'after war promises.' It seems to me that the time to take action to establish Dominion status is now—to develop or improvise the form of Government to carry us through the war but to remove from all doubt the question of Indian freedom at the end of war.[156]

However, the war changed the whole situation. Though the British emerged victorious, they were exhausted and drained. Their economy, faced as it was with numerous problems of post-war reconstruction, also put severe strain on their dispensation in India. In fact, the difficulty was apparent even in the war years. As John Gallagher and Anil Seal described it at some length:

> Nodding plumes and gleaning lances were no longer enough. Once the world-wide scale of British commitments in the face of international pressures had become plain, then it would have to be the Indian army which provided much of the imperial mobile reserve. That meant that this army had to be dragged out of the Old Curiosity Shop, modernized and mechanized. This had political implications. The better the Indian army, higher the cost. Who was going to pay for them? Even the obsolescent army was costing more than half the budget of the Government of India. Now the Generals wanted more...so this is what it came to. In the interest

of imperial defence and security the Indian army was to cost more. But in the interest of Indian political security, most of the additional cost was to fall on Britain…for the first time since the eighteenth century, it was the British taxpayer who would have to pay for it. Here, then, would be a way of testing his will for empire.[157]

Understandably, the British were keen 'to pull resources out of India, not to put them into it.' They could not agree to make India 'a burden' on the British taxpayer.[158] To further complicate matters, the bureaucracy in India began to disintegrate with each passing day. The British found it increasingly difficult to run the administrative machinery.[159] As Lord Mountbatten told Larry Collins and Dominique Lapierre during interviews in 1971–73:

> We had stopped recruiting for the Indian Civil Services in 1939. We'd stopped recruiting for the Indian Police. The people carrying on included a lot of people who were past retirement age. They were running it extremely competently—but supposing Churchill had come back, and given a decision that we were not going to discuss anything for 25 years, *I don't know if we could have restored that machine that we had. It had run completely down.*[160]

The extent to which British rule in India had come to suffer during the war years could also be gauged from the fact that the British were now willing to envisage a 'national government' in association with the Indians. This government would deal with all matters (except Defence) and a declaration of Dominion Status immediately after the war, carrying with it, if desired, the right to 'secede.'[161] Of course, this was British Prime Minister, Winston Churchill's (1874–1965) response not only to the situation in India but also to the demands of the Allied powers, particularly the United States.[162] By 1945, Britain was willing to terminate its rule in India. In September 1946, the Viceroy, Wavell even proposed a 'Breakdown Plan' to meet any 'dangerous and disadvantageous situation out of the final act'.[163] The British indeed were left with little choice but to devise a scheme of calculated withdrawal. Military and Police, the ultimate guarantee of British rule in India, could no longer be trusted. In Wavell's own words: 'I consider that on administrative grounds we could not govern the whole of India for more than a year and a half now…[the] withdrawal should be completed not later than the spring of 1948.'[164] In 1929, Lord Birkenhead had claimed in Parliament: 'what man in this house can say that he can see in a generation, in two generations, in a hundred years, any prospect that the people of India will be in a position to assume control of the Army, the Navy, the Civil Services, and to have a Governor-General who will be responsible to the Indian Government and not to any authority in this country?'[165] In November 1942, Churchill had publicly boasted: 'We intend to remain the effective rulers of India for a long and indefinite period.... I have not become king's First Minister in order to preside over the liquidation of the British Empire....'[166] The stark reality in 1947 was that the British could no longer hold India. The power and the will to perpetuate their rule through coercion had been lost. As an outspoken official put it: 'The steel frame was now more like lath and plaster, and more plaster than lath.'[167]

But the Second World War alone did not terminate the British rule. The increasing loss of legitimacy added to their woes. This was in spite of the fact that the British, from 1858 to 1935, had come up with a number of constitutional reforms, essentially to associate the Indians in their system of government in order to legitimize their rule. But by the war years these measures had been exhausted. The British were not willing to go beyond what they had given in the 1935 Act. The result was that the Indians found the political system hopelessly ineffective, lacking even a semblance of responsible self-government. While Jinnah insisted that 'the will of the legislature which is responsible to the electorates, must prevail over the Executive...',[168] the Act suggested just the opposite. First, it established a 'dyarchy' at the centre. Foreign affairs and defence were to be the exclusive preserve of the Governor-General responsible to the Secretary of State. Secondly, all the 'safeguards' in the constitution—and there were quite a few of them—were placed in the hands of the Governor-General. This was 'a novel constitutional device,' to remind the Indians that 'India would not attain Dominion Status by the Act of 1935'. And finally, the federation, if it came into being, would be subservient to the British Parliament. It would be subject to a refusal of assent or to reservation by the Governor-General, acting under the control of the Secretary of the State, responsible only to the British Parliament.[169] Thus, under the 1935 Act, the ultimate goal of self-government by Indians was a far cry. The only worthwhile measure that came out of it was 'provincial autonomy'. But to the Indians, as Brailsford correctly put it, 'the key to their problem lay at the centre and not in the provinces.'[170] Without responsibility at the centre, they knew fully well that India could never be self-governing. The 1935 Act had thus no appeal for the Indians. Jinnah, in a speech on the report of the Joint Parliamentary Committee on Indian Constitutional Reforms in February 1935, denounced the absence of responsibility in these words:

> Here there are 98 per cent of the safeguards and two per cent of responsibility! ...Now, next what we find about the safeguards? I am not going into the various clauses of the Statue. I will give only a short summary to the House.... Reserve Bank, Currency, Exchange—nothing doing. Railway Board—nothing doing, mortgaged to the hilt. What is left? Fiscal Autonomy Convention (Laughter). Next, what is left? Defence, External Affairs—reserved; Finance—it is already mortgaged to the hilt, our Budget, and the little that may be here, what do we find? Special responsibility of the Governor-General! His powers as to the budget and the estimates, his powers as to the interference in legislation, his extraordinary powers, his special responsibility. Sir, what do they leave us? What will this legislature do? ...I say, I do not like this Constitution, it is humiliating, it is intolerable....[171]

But the British could not agree to compromise their ulimate right to rule India. They could not offer a constitution which would provide responsibility to the Indians, and thus lead to the loss of their colony. They were determined to keep it. The Secretary of State for India, Lord Zetland, made it abundantly clear when he stated:

> But there is also our own position in India to be taken into account. After all we framed the constitution as it stands in the Act of 1935, because we thought that was the best way—given the political position of both countries—of maintaining British influence in India. It is no part of our policy, I take it, to expedite in India constitutional changes for their own sake, or gratuitously to hurry over the handing over of control to Indian hands at any pace faster than we regard at best calculated on a longer view, to hold India to the Empire.[172]

And yet, paradoxically enough, each constitutional reform proved to be a major step towards the devolution of British authority in India.

With the introduction of these reforms 'a chink appeared in the armour of autocracy; for however restricted the franchise, electoral institutions offered to the opponents of the imperial system an opportunity to secure by organization what they could not achieve by deputation and petition.'[173] Thus, the British provided the Indians an opportunity to govern themselves in the provinces. The executive was made responsible to the legislatures. This responsibility was a significant factor in the process of devolution of authority in India. The British had to concede the transfer of power eventually. The only question was how best it could be transferred to the people of India. As the Secretary of State for India, Amery, observed on 28 January 1942:

> The political deadlock in India today is concerned ostensibly with the transfer of power from British to Indian hands. In reality it is mainly concerned with the far more difficult issue of what Indian hands, what Indian Government or Governments, are capable of taking over without bringing about general anarchy or even civil war.[174]

Indeed, the process of devolution of authority brought to the fore the issue of devolution of power among the Muslims and the Hindus, the two major communities in India's political life and processes. There was no way one could have avoided this issue. But then, there was hardly anything surprising about it. The roots of the problem could easily be traced to the very system of government introduced by the British in India. As David Page put it:

> The working of the electoral system forced the Raj to the wall. Imperialism and democracy were incompatible bedfellows.... In the days of autocracy this was their strength. In the days of electoral politics, it became their undoing. With each stage of devolution, Indian was set against Indian, caste against caste, community against community.[175]

Thus, the devolution of British authority in India strained Hindu–Muslim relations steadily but surely. As Valentine Chirol wrote:

> The fact is the more we delegate our authority in India to the natives of India on the principles which we associate with self-government, the more we must necessarily in practise delegate it to the Hindus, who form the

majority, however much we may try to protect the rights and interests of the Mohammedan minority.[176]

The more the process of this devolution of authority proceeded and the prospects of British withdrawal became imminent, the more the conflict of interests between the Muslims and the Hindus increased. Unlike the Act of 1909, when the absence of devolution of authority acted as a spur to Hindu–Muslim unity, as exemplified by the 1916 Lucknow Pact between the League and the Congress, the working of the Act of 1919 strained relations between the two communities. There arose the issues of the distribution of seats in the legislative councils and municipal bodies, and the proportion of representation in government jobs. Thus, the 1920s saw a series of bloody Hindu–Muslim riots and increased polarization of their interests. The Muslims and Hindus vied with each other for scarce 'loaves and fishes'. Those who watched these developments could not fail to see that a struggle for power had begun. As the Indian Statutory Commission of 1930 perceptively recorded:

So long as authority was firmly established in British hands, and self-government was not thought of, Hindu–Muslim rivalry was confined within a narrower field…. But [the] coming of the Reforms and the anticipation of what may follow them have given new point to Hindu–Muslim competition…. The true cause is the struggle for political power and for the opportunity which political power confers.[177]

As the point of devolution came closer under the Act of 1935, and the prospects of Hindu power at the centre became apparent, the Hindu–Muslim struggle intensified. The anticipated freedom not only moved the Muslims to a greater realization of their special interests and demands, it also fanned their fear of Hindu dominance. They were not prepared to submit to a Hindu-dominated polity. As Wayne Wilcox explained:

Although the Muslims hated the British for offenses past and present, they had little desire to trade British for Hindu rule. The implications of a unified democratic India included majority rule, dooming the Muslims, therefore, as a permanent three-to-one minority.[178]

The experience of Congress rule in the provinces from 1937 to 1939, despite the British presence, had already convinced the Muslims that the majority community would promote and pursue its own agenda without any regard to their interests. Indeed, in many ways, the Congress rule was an eye-opener for them. It exposed them to the impact of Hindu communalism in politics. It showed to them the implications of the Congress brand of 'Indian nationalism'. Most importantly, it

> ...demonstrated the unworkability of parliamentary rule, the constitutional safeguards for minorities being fragile. The Muslims felt that the remedy of minority troubles did not lie within a federal framework, because the advantages offered by provincial autonomy would be negative if the central government was placed, as it was bound to be under Hindu domination.[179]

This was the herald of a crisis in which the Muslims having lost 'power' to the British were now confronted with the possibility of losing it 'permanently' to the Hindus in a free India.[180] There was no way they could deal with a situation which permitted political and constitutional power to a community which they felt was 'inspired by ideals, religious and political, diametrically opposed to its own',[181] and which, for all practical purposes, had turned the Congress into 'an instrument for the revival of Hinduism' in the country.[182]

The major stress of politics so far had been on self-government and freedom for India. Once the devolution of British authority in India brought freedom in sight, the complex of Indian unity was torn asunder. The 'dualities' of 'advancing towards national freedom and unity'[183] had exhausted themselves. While the prospects of freedom satisfied the Muslims, the idea of being left at the mercy of the Hindu majority agitated their minds and stoked their fears for the future. With the British gone, they reckoned, nothing would stand between the absolute authority of the Hindus and their own subjugation. Indeed, in the words of Jinnah, they were caught 'between the devil and the deep sea'. However, Jinnah was convinced that,

> I do not think that the devil or the deep sea is going to get away with it.... We stand unequivocally for the freedom of India. But it must be

freedom for all India and not freedom of one section or, worse still, of the Congress caucus and slavery of Musalmans and other minorities.[184]

While this espousal of the Muslim cause bought Jinnah to the forefront of Muslim politics as a charismatic leader, Muslim traditional political leadership remained hardly aware or prepared for the impending crisis. They were preoccupied with the present. They were keen to save their present privileges and positions. They failed to offer any solution to deal with the situation confronting the Muslims. Their failure aptly fits the hypothesis that the rise of charismatic leaders is also helped by the 'absence' or 'default' of leadership at a time when it is 'intensely felt to be needed'.[185] It is therefore necessary to evaluate and assess the role of traditional leadership at some length. It will help us understand and appreciate fully the Muslim situation.

Notes

1. Norman Brown, *The United States and India, Pakistan, Bangladesh* (Cambridge, Massachusetts: Harvard University Press, 1972), 30. Even Jawaharlal Nehru, in spite of all his rhetoric about it, admitted that communalism was widespread in the country. See Jawaharlal Nehru, *An Autobiography,* Chapter XIX, 'Communalism Rampant', 134-41.
2. H.N. Brailsford, *Subject India* (Bombay: Vohra & Co., 1946), 97.
3. Aziz Ahmad, *Studies in Islamic Culture in the Indian Environment* (Oxford: Clarendan Press, 1964), 73. Also see, Ainslie Embree, *India's Search for National Identity* (New York: Alfred Knopf, 1972), 102; Sayeed, *Formative Phase*, 24; Brown, *United States and India, Pakistan, Bangladesh*, 38, 131-7; and Percival Spear, *India, Pakistan and the West* (New York: Oxford University Press, 1967), 46-56. More recently, according to one writer, 'One fact that proved to be a determining factor in the genesis of Pakistan was the irreducibility of the two religions in the subcontinent vis-à-vis each other, i.e. Islam and Hinduism'. Pierre Lafrance, 'And Yet Pakistan Exists', in Christophe Jaffrelot, ed., *Pakistan: Nationalism without a Nation* (London: Zed Books, 2002), 342.
4. Paul R. Brass, *Language, Religion and Politics in North India* (Cambridge: Cambridge University Press, 1974), 179.
5. Talbot, *India and Pakistan*, 47.
6. For some of the discussion on this aspect of Hindu–Muslim communal life see, Coupland, *Indian Problem*, 29-33; M. Mujeeb, *The Indian Muslims* (London: George Allen & Unwin, 1967), 437, W.C. Smith, *Modern Islam in India,* 175-89, Brown, *United States and India, Pakistan, Bangladesh*, 130-41; Hamid, *On Understanding the Quaid-i-Azam*, 79; and K. L Gauba, *Passive Voice: A Penetrating Study of Muslims in India* (Lahore: Student Services, 1975), 23. For a narrative of

a typical communal riot see, Penderel Moon, *Strangers in India* (London: Faber & Faber 1944), 86–98.

7. Al-Beruni, a Muslim traveller and scholar who visited India as early as AD 1030 noted this 'gulf'. Edward C. Sachau, ed., *Alberuni's India,* Vol. I (London: Kegan-Paul & Co., 1914), 19–20.

8. Mujahid, *Ideology of Pakistan*, 34.

9. Angus Maddison, *Class Structure and Economic Growth: India and Pakistan Since the Moghuls* (New York: W.W. Norton, 1971), Chapters 3 & 4.

10. Smith, *Modern Islam in India,* 162. Also see for a historical backdrop to the British feelings about the Muslims, Percival Spear, *Twilight of the Mughuls: Studies in Late Mughul Delhi* (Karachi: Oxford University Press, 1980); Thomas Metcalf, *The Aftermath of Revolt* (Princeton: Princeton University Press, 1964); and W.W. Hunter, *The Indian Musalmans* (Calcutta: Comrade Publishers, 1945).

11. See, for instance, a survey of the Muslim condition in Bengal in the 1920s, in 'Past and Present condition of Muslims—Presidential Address by Haji A.K. Ghazanavi', cited in Y.B. Mathur, *Growth of Muslim Politics in India*, 72.

12. Smith, *Modern Islam in India*, 189.

13. See G.D. Birla, *In the Shadow of the Mahatma: A Personal Memoir* (Bombay: Orient Longmans, 1955). In a letter to Birla on 1 October 1927 Gandhi wrote: 'My thirst for money is simply unquenchable. I need at least Rs. 200,000/- for Khadi, Untouchability and Education. The dairy work makes another Rs. 50,000. Then there is the Ashram expenditure. No work remains unfinished for want of funds, but god gives after severe trials. This also satisfies me. You can give me as much as you like for whatever work you have faith in'. Ibid., 32

14. Gustav. F. Papanek, *Pakistan's Development: Social Goal and Private Incentives* (Cambridge, Massachusetts: Harvard University Press, 1967), 40-2.

15. While 80 per cent of the jute was grown in predominately Muslim Bengal (now Bangladesh) no jute mill was installed there. There were not even facilities for bailing of jute. Jute mills were located in West (Hindu) Bengal, particularly in Calcutta. While some writers argue that the British being 'utilitarians', were strong supporters of *laissez-faire* and abhorred all kinds of state interference, there is plenty of evidence to suggest that the British rulers were not averse to India's economic development if it increased their markets and economic interests. This indeed made the British record vulnerable to R.C. Dutt's argument about discouraging Indian manufactures to boost the rising manufactures of England, and most importantly, to R. Palme Dutt's charge of continuous 'de-industrialization' of India. See Eric Stokes, *The English Utilitarians and India* (London: Oxford University Press, 1959); R.C. Dutt, *Economic History of India,* 2 Vols. (London: 1963); R.P. Dutt, *India Today* (London: Victor Gollancz, 1940); Maddison, *India and Pakistan since the Moghuls*, 53-4; and W.C. Smith, *Modern Islam in India*, 190. The regions with concentration of modern industry were Calcutta, Bombay and Ahmadabad.

16. See Jagdish Raj, *The Mutiny and British Land Policy in North India, 1856–1868* (Bombay: Asia Publishing House, 1965); B.H. Baden Powell, *A Short Account of the Land Revenue and its Administration in British India, with a Sketch of the Land Tenures* (Oxford: Clarendon Press, 1894); and Kanhia Lal, *British Land Policy and the Economy of the Punjab* (Lahore: New Publishers, 1937).

17. Papanek, *Pakistan's Development*, 1-2. In this sense, many Muslims 'were uncomfortable about the cultural as well as economic consequences of future Hindu rule'. Talbot, *India and Pakistan*, 283.

18. David Page, *Prelude to Partition: The Indian Muslims and the Imperial System of Control, 1920–1932* (Delhi: Oxford University Press, 1982), Ch. 2, 73-140. Also see, Coupland, *Indian Problem*, 75; Judith Brown, *Gandhi and Civil Disobedience*, 10; Francis Robinson, *Separatism Among Indian Muslims: The Politics of the United Province's Muslims, 1860–1923* (Cambridge: Cambridge University Press, 1974), 194; Valentine Chirol, *Indian Unrest* (London: Macmillan, 1910), 128; Hardy, *Muslims of British India*, 152; Aziz Ahmad, *Studies in Islamic Culture*, 269; and Waheed-uz-Zaman, *Towards Pakistan* (Lahore: United Publishers, 1978), 207.

19. Embree, *India's Search for Identity*, 18. As early as 1928, the Muslims made a 'novel suggestion' to the authors of the Nehru Report 'that they should at least dominate in some parts of India'. Cited in Coupland, *Indian Problem*, 89. The point was reiterated in Maulana Mohammed Ali's address to the Fourth Plenary Session of the Round Table Conference on 9 November 1930, in Iqbal's presidential address at the Allahabad session of the League in 1930, and in Jinnah's Fourteen Points. 'A close study of the points', wrote Jamil-ud-Din Ahmad, 'will show that they contained the germs of the eventual evolution of Pakistan in one form or another...'. Jamil-ud-Din Ahmad, *Glimpses of Quaid-i-Azam*, 74; Afzal Iqbal, ed., *Select Writings and Speeches of Maulana Mohamed Ali*, Vol. II (Lahore: Sh. Muhammad Ashraf, 1969), 358; and Sherwani, *Speeches, Writings and Statements of Iqbal*, 19.

20. Jinnah, 18 February 1935. Quoted in R.J. Moore, *The Crisis of Indian Unity, 1917-1940* (Oxford: Clarendon Press, 1974), 292.

21. I.H. Qureshi, *Struggle for Pakistan*, 149.

22. Ibid., 150.

23. Badruddin Tyabji, the only Muslim leader of standing to join the Congress and who was elected its president in 1887, confided to A.O. Hume, the founder-secretary of the Congress that: 'The fact exists and whether we like it or not...an overwhelming majority of Mahomedans are against the movement.... If then the Mussalman community as a whole is against the Congress—rightly or wrongly does not matter—it follows that the movement *ipso facto* ceases to be a general or National Congress'. Cited in Matiur Rahman, *From Consultation to Confrontation* (London: Luzac & Co., 1970), 5. For more on Syed Ahmad Khan's political role see, Shan Muhammad, *Sir Syed Ahmad Khan: A Political Biography* (Lahore: Universal Books, 1976).

24. Embree, *India's Search for National Identity*, 38.

25. See B.N. Pandey, *The Break-up of British India* (London: Macmillan, 1969), 34-5; Embree, *India's Search for National Identity*, 34-5; Valentine Chirol, *Indian Unrest*, 109; Beni Prasad, The *Hindu–Muslim Questions* (London: George Allen & Unwin, 1946), 31; Stanley Wolpert, *Tilak and Gokhale: Revolution and Reform in the making of Modern India* (Los Angeles: University of California Press, 1961), 298; Lajpat Rai, *A History of the Arya Samaj* (Bombay: Orient Longman, 1967), esp., Ch. IV, 49-65, 106, 203; and Kenneth W. Jones, 'Communalism in the Punjab: The Arya Samaj contribution', *The Journal of Asian Studies*, Vol. XXVIII, No. I (Nov. 1968).

26. Chatterjee's *Anandamath* (*The Abbey of Bliss*, 1882) dealing with the period of Muslim decline in Bengal appealed to Hindus to shake off their lethargy and rise in unison to root out the Muslim rule. His approach was uncompromisingly bitter towards the Muslims and dismissed them as merely extraneous to the Indian soil. His song 'Bande Matram' sung in the first chapter became the anthem of Bengali Hindu nationalists. Similarly, Bepin Chandra Pal, a revivalist leader of Bengal in his *The New Spirit* (1907) encouraged Hindu revolt in the promotion of those ideas. Also see, John R. Mclane, *Indian Nationalism and the Early Congress* (Princeton: Princeton University Press, 1977), 337, 362; and Leonard A. Gordon, *Bengal: The Nationalist Movement, 1876–1940* (New York: Columbia University Press, 1974), 79-81.

27. Talbot, *India and Pakistan*, 110.

28. R.P. Dutt, *India Today*, 125. The natural corollary of this 'emphasis' was a 'corresponding note' from the Muslims idealizing 'the Muslim period and its achievements, indeed reviving the romantic version of Islamic/Muslim history, from the early caliphate to Muslim rule in India….' Mujahid, *Ideology of Pakistan*, 41.

29. Hamid, *Muslim Separatism in India*, 57.

30. I.H. Qureshi, *Struggle for Pakistan*, 28.

31. Surrendranath Banerjee, *A Nation in Making* (London: Humphrey Milford, 1925); and Haridas Mukherjee and Uma Mukherjee, *The Growth of Nationalism in India, 1857–1905* (Calcutta: Presidency Library, 1957).

32. Sayeed, *Formative Phase*, 24-2.

33. Ibid., 24.

34. Hardy, *Muslims of British India*, 150.

35. Hasan, *Nationalism and Communal Politics in India*, 52.

36. S.V. Desika Char, ed., *Readings in the Constitutional History of India, 1757–1947* (Delhi: Oxford University Press, 1983), 337-42.

37. Coupland, *Indian Problem*, 48.

38. It was at a later stage that Muslims were to complain that in the Muslim-majority provinces of the Punjab and Bengal the Pact deprived them of their majority. Incidentally, Maulvi A.K. Fazlul Haq was signatory to the Pact. However, the 'catch' was the separate Muslim electorates. They could not have separate electorates in a province where they enjoyed majority status. Still the Muslim position improved considerably all over. The Muslims were to be represented through separate electorates in the following proportions: Punjab 50 per cent of the elected Indian members; United Provinces 30 per cent; Bengal 40 per cent; Bihar 25 per cent; Central Provinces 15 per cent; Madras 15 per cent; Bombay one-third. Char, *Readings in the Constitutional History of India*, 337. Also see, Mujahid, *Studies in Interpretation*, App. 7, 'The Congress–League Scheme of Reform, 1916', 462.

39. Sayeed, *Formative Phase*, 47.

40. Interestingly, Jinnah was not part of the Khilafat–Non-cooperation movement, and the Muslim League, too, did not get directly involved in it either. Instead, it 'helped actively to establish a separate Khilafat Committee'. In this sense, 'we have the strange paradox that, while the Muslim League successfully tried to

keep itself away from Muslim religious issues, the Congress set out to embrace them'. Saleem Ahmad, *All-India Muslim League*, 201.

41. Hamid, *Muslim Separatism in India*, 146. As Gandhi himself put it: 'I have been telling Maulana Shaukat Ali all along that I was helping him to save his cow, i.e. the Khilafat, because I hope to save my cow thereby.' Mohandas Karamchand Gandhi, *The Collected Works of Mahatma Gandhi*, Vol. XXV (New Delhi: Ministry of Information and Broadcasting, 1967), 519. The relationship between the Indian Muslims and the Turks was no less paradoxical. Maulana Mohammed Ali's 'lack of realism in assessing the Turkish aims' was reflected in his belief that the Turks were 'fighting for an ideal *khalifa*, even though the Kemalist revolution was already on its way to achieving success. He believed that once the Turks were free from their 'distractions' they would revive the glories of Ummayad or Abbasid dynasties and the pristine purity of the *Khilafat-i-Rashida*'. Mushirul Hassan, 'My Life: A Fragment, Mohamed Ali's Quest for Identity in Colonial India,' in Hasan, *Islam: Communities and the Nation*, 82.

42. Majumdar, *Jinnah and Gandhi*, 58.

43. *Collected Works of Mahatma Gandhi*, Vol. XXV, 178.

44. Hardy, *Muslims of British India*, 210.

45. See Jinnah's Presidential Address at the Lahore Session of the All-India Muslim League, 1924. M. Rafique Afzal, ed., *Selected Speeches and Statements of the Quaid-i-Azam Mohammad Ali Jinnah, 1911–1934 and 1947-48* (Lahore: Research Society of Pakistan, 1976), 131-6.

46. Ibid., 132.

47. *Collected Works of Mahatma Gandhi*, Vol. XXV, 436.

48. *The Collected Works of Mahatma Gandhi*, Vol. XLIII (New Delhi: Ministry of Information and Broadcasting, 1971), 55. On an another occasion, Gandhi remarked: 'Hindu–Muslim quarrels are in a way unknown to us, a fight for Swaraj. Each party is conscious of its impending coming'. D.G. Tendulkar, *Mahatma: Life of Mohandas Karamchand Gandhi*, Vol. II (New Delhi: Ministry of Information and Broadcasting, 1960), 235.

49. Char, *Readings in the Constitutional History of India*, 535. Also see Afzal, *Selected Speeches and Statements*, 269.

50. Hamid, *Muslim Separatism in India*, 198.

51. Char, *Readings in the Constitutional History of India*, 547.

52. Ibid. For details on the Report see, ibid., 547-9.

53. Ibid., 550.

54. In a letter to Gandhi on 23 August 1929, Jayakar insisted that it was 'not clear on whose behalf Mr Jinnah spoke, and what bulk of the entire Mohamadan community would be placated if his demands were conceded'. B.N. Pandey, ed., *The Indian Nationalist Movement, 1885–1947: Select Documents* (London: Macmillan, 1979), 88.

55. All but two relatively insignificant amendments were lost by a majority. His proposals regarding one-third representation in the Central Legislative Assembly and residuary powers etc, were rejected. Jamshed Nusserwanjee, who listened to Jinnah's speech at Calcutta told Hector Bolitho: 'The first time I saw him weep was after his amendments had been rejected at the Calcutta meeting. About half past eight next morning, Mr Jinnah left Calcutta by train, and I went to see him

off at the railway station. He was standing at the door. He had tears in his eyes as he said, "Jamshed, this is the parting of the ways". 'Bolitho,' *Jinnah: Creator of Pakistan*, 95. However, as the later developments showed, 'the Calcutta experience bitter as it was, left Jinnah in a chastened, not a changed, frame of mind. He did not part company with his old comrades. Nor did he walk out of the nationalist camp'. Hamid, *On Understanding the Quaid-i-Azam*, 23.

56. Text of the draft resolution prepared by Jinnah for the Council of the League meeting held in Delhi on 28 March 1929. Afzal, *Selected Speeches and Statements*, 303. According to Metz, 'The Fourteen Points, then, marked a definite departure from the spirit which motivated Jinnah's political activities up to the All-Parties National Convention'. Metz, 'The Political Career of Mohammad Ali Jinnah', 90-2.

57. Mujahid, *Studies in Interpretation*, 18.

58. Brown, *Gandhi and Civil Disobedience*, 249-389.

59. Ahmad, *Speeches and Writings*, Vol. I., 41.

60. Coupland, *A Re-statement*, 152-3.

61. Sayeed, *Formative Phase*, 83. It captured 711 out of 1585 seats (26 Muslim seats), but not a very convincing number. Ibid.

62. S. Gopal, ed., *The Selected Works of Nehru*, Vol. VIII (New Delhi: Orient Longman, 1976), 52. Paradoxically, the Congress itself sought to form coalition government in a number of provinces and did succeed in its efforts.

63. Jamil-ud-Din Ahmad, 'The Congress in Office (1937–39)', in *A History of the Freedom Movement*, Vol. IV, Parts I & II, (Karachi: Pakistan Historical Society, 1970), 41-2.

64. Prasad, *Hindu–Muslim Questions*, 74.

65. D.G. Tendulkar, *Mahatma: Life of Mohandas Karamchand Gandhi*, Vol. IV (New Delhi: Ministry of Information, 1969), 187.

66. B.R. Tomlinson, *The Indian National Congress and the Raj, 1929–1942* (London: Macmillan Press, 1976), 107.

67. Mujahid, *Studies in Interpretation*, 167-8. The Congress policy was all the more inexplicable in view of the limited importance attached to the formation of governments. As Vijaya Lakshmi Pandit, sister of Jawaharlal Nehru, put it: 'Acceptance of the office, we felt, was but a phase in our freedom struggle. The main objective of the Congress remained to end the present Constitution and to have a Constituent Assembly to frame a new one'. Vijaya Lakshmi Pandit, *The Scope of Happiness: A Personal Memoir* (London: Weidenfeld and Nicolson, 1979), 131-2.

68. Ahmed, *Speeches and Writings*, Vol. I, 195.

69. Ibid., 124. Jinnah was to often reiterate the point both in public and privately. In his meeting with the Cabinet Mission and the Viceroy on 26 June 1946, he went on to claim: 'No Englishman would understand the character of the communal question in India which was quite foreign to anything in English politics'. Mansergh, *Transfer of Power*, Vol. VII, 1061.

70. Ahmad, *Speeches and Writings*, Vol. I. 167-8.

71. Ibid., 170.

72. Cited in Char, *Readings in the Constitutional History of India*, 260

73. Ibid., 267-84.

74. Ibid., 286.
75. Ibid., 286-7.
76. Quoted in Rashiduzzaman, *The Central Legislature in British India, 1921-1947* (Dacca: Mallick Brothers, 1965), 1. For details of Frere's view on legislative reform also see Char, *Readings in the Constitutional History of India*, 404-8.
77. The *Hindoo Patriot* observed 'What we want is not the introduction of a small independent element in the existing council, but an Indian Parliament'. Ibid., 301.
78. Ibid., 307.
79. A.C. Banerjee, ed., *Indian Constitutional Documents*, Vol. II (Calcutta: A. Mukherjee, 1946), 55-6.
80. Ibid., 81-2. This view of life and society was not peculiar to conservative politicians like Curzon. Even to minds as liberal as Mills, there was a 'hideous state of society' in India, thus incapable of receiving representative institutions. Macaulay had alluded to it a generation earlier. See Stokes, *The English Utilitarians and India*, 53; and Char, *Readings in the Constitutional History of India*, 211.
81. Also important were the strategic, financial and commercial arguments. According to Coupland, 'The strategic argument for keeping a firm hold on the defence of India had gained force with the revival of international rivalries in Europe. The idea that Britain should leave the defence of India in Indian hands should have seemed in those days quite fantastic. The financial and commercial arguments for maintaining the stability of the British Raj were also steadily growing stronger'. Coupland, *A Re-statement*, 81.
82. Banerjee, *Indian Constitutional Documents*, 139.
83. Ibid., 158.
84. Ibid., 164.
85. Coupland, *A Re-statement*, 104.
86. Quoted in Coupland, *Indian Problem*, 26.
87. Ramsay MacDonald, *Awakening of India* (London: Hodder & Stoughton, 1910), 168.
88. Coupland, *Indian Problem*, 50.
89. MacDonald, *Awakening of India*, 168.
90. See, in particular, his 'Introduction' in *Papers Relating to the Application of the Principle of Dyarchy* (London: 1920). He wrote: 'That England has granted responsible government to India in strictness should never be said and will never be true. The best she could do was to put India in the way of taking responsible government for herself. That she has done and the rest remains for Indians to do'. Ibid., lx.
91. Later, the register at first general election in the winter of 1920–21 contained over 6 million names, or altogether 2.5 per cent of the male population of British India, still a very small fraction of the whole population. The qualifications of membership of the different legislature varied. Valentine Chirol, *India: Old and New* (London: Macmillan, 1921), 233.
92. Coupland, *A Re-statement*, 113. But, of course, under the watchful eyes of British intelligence. Indeed, according to Patrick French, who made significant use of intelligence material in his study, 'from around the time of the First World War, until the transfer of power in 1947, the British authorities in India operated a

surveillance and intelligence operation of great skill against the forces of nationalism.' Although the Indian leaders were aware of its existence, they had no idea of 'its extent'. Patrick French, *Liberty or Death: India's Journey to Independence and Division* (London: Harper Collins Publishers, 1997), 97.

93. Edwin Montague, Quoted in P.G. Robb, *The Government of India and Reform: Policies towards Politics and the Constitution, 1916-1921* (London: Oxford University Press, 1976), 78. Also see Ch. 2 for some of the detailed discussion on the Act.

94. Waheed Ahmad, *Road to Indian Freedom: The Formation of the Government of India Act 1935* (Lahore: Caravan Book House, 1979), 266-7; and Coupland, *Indian Problem*, Ch. X, 48, 132. Also see Dobbin, *Basic Documents in the Development of Modern India and Pakistan*, 119-21.

95. Hardy, *Muslims of British India*, 222. Although the property qualifications for suffrage were lowered, still the enfranchised electors amounted to a mere 11.0 per cent of the population. A negligible number of women were enfranchised, but the landless labour and peasants were not represented. Brailsford, *Subject India*, 47.

96. Spear, *India,* 389.

97. Nehru charged: 'The Government of India Act of 1935, the new constitution stares at us offensively, this new charter of bondage which has been imposed upon us despite our utter rejection of it.... We go to the Legislatures not to cooperate with the apparatus of British imperialism, but to combat the Act and seek to end it, and to resist in every way British imperialism in its attempt to strengthen its hold on India and its exploitation of the Indian People. That is the basic policy of the Congress and Congressman, no candidate for election, must forget this. Whatever we must do must be within the Four Corners of this policy'. Char, *Readings in the Constitutional History of India*, 599.

98. Spear, *India*, 389.

99. Sir Syed Ahmad, *The Present State of Indian Politics: Speeches and Letters*, introduction by Farman Fatehpuri (Lahore: Sang-e-Meel, 1982), 36.

100. In fact, representative institutions in India, as elsewhere in the world, started off with economic and educational qualifications, such as ownership of land, income-tax, and graduation. For a useful discussion see, Norris Steven Dodge, 'Political Behaviour and Social Change: Causes of the Growth of the Indian Electorate in the Last Half Century', unpublished Ph.D. Thesis, Cornell University, 1971.

101. Syed Ahmed, *The Present State of Indian Politics*, 37.

102. Coupland, *Indian Problem*, 33.

103. Razi Wasti, *Lord Minto and the Indian Nationalist Movement, 1905–1910* (Lahore: People's Publishing House, 1976), 160.

104. It is therefore incorrect to assume that the demand for separate electorates made by the Simla Deputation of 1906 was inspired or engineered by the British Government, as has often been alleged by some critics. As late as 23 February 1909, Morley was informing the House of Lords on the demands made by the Deputation: 'I told them as I now tell your Lordship, I see no chance whatever of meting their views in that way to any extent at all'. Indeed, Morley insisted on 'a mixed or composite electoral college, in which Mahomedans and Hindus pool their votes'. It was, in fact, the consistent Muslim endeavours and particularly

the efforts made by Syed Ameer Ali in London who mobilized considerable parliamentary and public support on the issue that forced the British to yield on separate electorates for the Muslims. Besides it must also be borne in mind that the British, in granting separate electorates to the Muslims were not going against their 'democratic conscience', for, as we have seen above, their plans for constitutional reforms had nothing to do with 'democracy' as such. In conceding the principle of separate electorates, the British Government was doing no more than merely recognizing the peculiar facts of life in India. See Pandey, *Indian Nationalist Movement*, 33; Char, *Reading in the Constitutional History of India*, 430; Wasti, *Lord Minto and the Indian Nationalist Movement*, 176–90. M.Y. Abbasi, 'Syed Ameer Ali: Pioneer of Mulims Politics', *Journal of Pakistan Studies*, Vol. II (1980), 75-7; Robinson, Separatism Among Indian Muslims, 160; Coupland, *Indian Problem*, 34; Coupland, *A Re-Statement*, 106; Hardy, *Muslims of British India*, 160; and Stanley Wolpert, *Morley and India, 1906–10* (Los Angeles: University of California Press, 1967).

105. Ambedkar, *Pakistan or the Partition of India*, 242.

106. Abbasi, 'Syed Ameer Ali', 76.

107. Hardy, *Muslims of British India*, 200.

108. Samad, *A Nation in Turmoil*, 15.

109. Pirzada, *Foundations of Pakistan*, Vol. I, 578.

110. Ibid., Vol. II, 40–68, esp. 60-1.

111. Some of the more prominent leaders supporting the proposal were Sir Mian Mohammad Shafi, Nawab Mohammad Ismail Khan, Sir Abdul Qaiyum, Abdul Aziz and Mohammad Yakkub.

112. Indian dissatisfaction with the Act could be gauged from the fact that within a few years, in 1924, the British Government was forced to appoint a Committee of Inquiry to consider ways and means of improving the 1919 Act (Known as the Muddiman Committee).

113. Quoted in Waheed Ahmad, *Road to Indian Freedom*, 178.

114. Jinnah's letter to British Prime Minister, Ramsay Macdonald. Cited in Saiyid, *A Political Study*, 142.

115. *Proceedings of the Indian Round Table Conference, Third Session, 17 November-24 December 1932* (London: HM's Stationery Office, 1933), 190-1.

116. *Proceedings of the Indian Round Table Conference, Second Session, 7 September-1 December 1931* (London: HM's Stationery Office, 1932), App. I, 'The Congress Scheme for a Communal Settlement (circulated at the request of Mr M.K. Gandhi)', 1391-2. Also see Char, *Readings in the Constitutional History of India*, 556-7.

117. See Ambedkar, *Pakistan or the Partition of India*, 249; Coupland, *Indian Problem*, 126; Brailsford, *Subject India*, 46-7; and Waheed Ahmad, *Road to Indian Freedom*, 200-1.

118. For a detailed criticism of the Act see, Waheed Ahmad, *Road to Indian Freedom*, 267-75. Coupland wondered, 'Is a Federation on the lines of the Act of 1935 practicable'? and went on to argue: 'Evidently not because it clashed with both sides of the Muslim case. The Federation projected in 1935 purported to do what the existing Federation does to combine the principle of local variety and autonomy with the principle of single nationhood. While, therefore, it allotted

a wide field of power to the provinces, it constructed a Centre which was to embody the sense of national unity in all India and to secure and stimulate its further growth'. Coupland, *A Re-Statement*, 267.

119. Ahmad, *Speeches and Writings*, Vol. I, 9. For a full discussion on the subject, see his speech on the *Report of the Joint Parliamentary Committee on Indian Constitutional Reforms* in the Legislative Assembly, on 7 February 1935. Ibid., 2-20.

120. Jamil-ud-Din Ahmad, 'The Congress in Office', in *A History of the Freedom Movement*, Vol. IV, 25.

121. Commenting on the fateful decision, Beni Prasad observed: 'It is obvious that homogenous and coalition cabinets alike offered advantages and disadvantages in the Indian provinces in 1937...[However] a flexible policy would have allowed adequate expression to the forces already in occupation of the political field and facilitated their integration with the public interest. The majority 'principle' is at bottom not an ethical maxim but a rule of expediency and has always to be so interpreted as to communal minority affirmation'. Prasad, *Hindu–Muslim Questions*, 62. Also see, Coupland, *A Re-Statement*, 181-2; and Menon, *Transfer of Power in India*, 56.

122. According to Majumdar, 'The Congress High Command reduced the provincial autonomy and the idea of responsible government in the provinces to a mere sham and consequently healthy development of parliamentary government in the provinces suffered....' Majumdar, *Jinnah and Gandhi*, 167. Also see, R.J. Moore, *Crisis of Indian Unity,* 307.

123. Hodson, *Great Divide*, 75.

124. Gopal, *Selected Works of Jawaharlal Nehru*, Vol. VIII, 22.

125. For instance, except for the NWFP, the Congress could not capture the Muslim vote in 1937. The NWFP was an exception only because of the popularity and strength of the Khudai Kidmatgars led by Abdul Ghaffar Khan who put up their candidates under the Congress umbrella. However, other 'pro-Congress organizations (such as the Jamiat-i-Ulama-i-Hind, Majlis-i-Ahrar, Ittihad-i-Millat, and the Shiah Conference)' refused to do so, and 'put up separate candidates.' Samad, *Nation in Turmoil*, 21.

126. Ahmad, *Speeches and Writings*, Vol. I, 181.

127. Talbot, *India and Pakistan*, 143.

128. The British, as discussed above, were confronted with the problem of developing a system of government suitable to India since the very beginning. For further emphasis see, *Joint Committee on Indian Constitutional Reform Session 1933–34*, Vol. I, part I (London: H.M.'s Stationery Office, 1934). But then, this was not something unique to Indian conditions. There have been problems with self-government and constitutionalism all over the world. For a philosophical perspective on self-government in Europe see, Larry Siedentop, *Democracy in Europe* (London: Allen Lane The Penguin Press, 2000). For an analysis of the controversies and compromises involved in the birth of the American federation see, Christopher Collier and James Lincoln Collier, *Decision at Philadelphia: The Constitutional Convention of 1787* (New York: Ballantine Books, 1993). For a discussion of France's often unsuccessful, yet admirably determined, struggle to achieve liberal democracy see, Pierre Birnbaum, *The Idea of France*, trans. M.B. De Bevoise (New York: Hill and Wang, 2001).

129. Nicholas Mansergh and E.W.R. Lumby, eds., *Constitutional Relations between Britain and India: The Transfer of Power, 1942–7* Vol. IV (London: HM's Stationery Office, 1973), 84. Also see his letter to Linlithgow, again, on 8 September and 15 September 1943, in ibid., 218, 269. Incidentally, Amery had suggested as early as 10 November 1942 to Linlithgow that: 'One or more acknowledged experts in the American federal constitution should be specifically invited to join forces with experts in India in studying the Indian constitutional problem. They and possibly also a Swiss constitutionalist might be co-opted on to the organization that I suggested'. Nicholas Mansergh and E.W.R. Lumby, eds., *Constitutional Relations between Britain and India: The Transfer of Power, 1942–7*, Vol. III (London: HM's Stationery Office, 1971), 229.

130. Mansergh, *Transfer of Power,* Vol. IV, 402.

131. Ibid., 203.

132. Ahmad, *Speeches and Writings*, Vol. I, 95.

133. Ibid., 170. In fact, as B.R. Ambedkar succinctly put it: 'That would not be ending imperialism. It would be creating another imperialism.' Ambedkar, *Pakistan or the Partition of India,* xvii.

134. Thompson and Garratt, *Rise and Fulfilment of British Rule in India,* 466. Subsequently, the Indian army had to undergo radical transformation. The most fundamental change was 'the introduction of an entirely new principle, that of balancing communities inside the army.' Ibid., 466-7.

135. Ibid., particularly Book VII, Ch. 1, 527-40.

136. Michael O' Dwyer, *India As I Knew It,* 1885–1925 (London: Constable, 1925), 298.

137. Chirol, *Indian Unrest,* 98. Between 1906 and 1909, over 550 political cases came up for hearing in the courts of Bengal. The Collector of Nasik was shot dead and an attempt was made on the life of Sir Andrew Frazer, the Lieutenant-Governor of Bengal. In the Punjab, however, disturbances were less clearly violent. See Thompson and Garratt, *Rise and Fulfilment of British Rule in India,* 579-80.

138. Wasti, *Lord Minto and the Indian Nationalist Movement,* 96. For the Bengal Regulation III of 1818 see, *Bengal Code,* 5th ed., Vol. I, 1939, 157-61. Cited in Nicholas Mansergh and E.W.R. Lumby, eds., *Constitutional Relations between Britain and India: The Transfer of Power, 1942–7*, Vol. II (London: HM's Stationery Office, 1971), 452.

139. Annie Besant, *The Future of Indian Politics* (London: Theosophical Society, 1922), 243; and O' Dwyer, *India As I Knew it,* 285-98.

140. Ibid., 243

141. Coupland, *A Re-Statement,* 118. This 'love of arbitrary power' was also clearly evident in British operations against the so-called Indian 'revolutionaries' working from outside India. See, in particular, Soban Singh Josh, *Hindustan Gadar Party: A Short History* (New Delhi: Peoples' Publishing House, 1979); Rafique Afzal, 'A Glimpse of the Life and Thoughts of Maulana Ubaidullah Sindhi,' *Journal of Research Society of Pakistan,* Vol. XII, No. 4, 1975, 1-14; and O' Dwyer, *India As I Knew it,* esp.185-8.

142. O' Dwyer, *India As I Knew It,* 307.

143. See M. Naeem Qureshi, 'Some Reflections on the Mappilla "Rebellion" of 1921–22,' *Journal of the Research Society of Pakistan,* Vol. XVIII, No. 2(1981), 4-5.

144. D.A. Low, 'The Government of India and the first Non-Cooperation Movement, 1920–22,' *Journal of Asian Studies,* XXV, No. 2 (February 1966), 241-59.

145. R.C. Dutt, *India Today and Tomorrow* (London: Lawrence and Vinhart, 1955), 51.

146. See D.A. Low, 'Civilian Martial Law': The Government of India and the Civil Disobedience Movement, 1930–34,' in D.A. Low, ed., *Congress and the Raj: Facets of the Indian Struggle,* 1917–47 (London: Heinemann, 1977), 165–98.

147. Francis G. Hutchins, *India's Revolution: Gandhi and the Quit India Movement* (Cambridge, Massachusetts: Harvard University Press, 1973), 177. Indeed, according to one writer, the treatment meted out to India in 1942 was unprecedented. He wrote: 'In 1857, of course, there had been no planes to bomb or machine gun people from the air, unlike in 1942 when this was done as a legitimate means of crowd control. During and after the Quit India Movement, India was treated not as an ally but as an occupied territory.' Zachariah, *Nehru,* 118.

148. For a detailed discussion on the violence committed and various ordinances promulgated to check violence, especially Revolutionary Movement Ordinance see, Hutchins, *India's Revolution,* 151-79.

149. Jawaharlal Nehru, *An Autobiography,* 435.

150. Ibid., 262.

151. Robert L. Hardgrave, *India: Government and Politics in a Developing Nation* (Harcourt: Brace & World, 1970), 24.

152. Mujahid, *Studies in Interpretations,* 46-7.

153. Afzal, *Selected Speeches and Statements*, 112-13.

154. Coupland, *A Re-Statement,* 11.

155. Mansergh, *Transfer of Power,* Vol. I, 877-9.

156. Cited in R.J. Moore, 'The Problem of Freedom with Unity: London's India Policy, 1917–47,' in Low, *Congress and the Raj,* 390.

157. John Gallagher and Anil Seal, 'The Britain and India Between the Wars,' in Christopher Baker, Gordon Johnson and Anil Seal, eds., *Power, Profit and Politics* (Cambridge: Cambridge University Press, 1981), 413.

158. Ibid., 389.

159. See, in particular, K.F.S. Menon, *Many Worlds: An Autobiography* (London: Oxford University Press, 1965); Leonard Mosley, *The Last Days of the British Raj* (London: Widenfeld & Nicolson, 1961); Moon, *Divide and Quit*; Richard Symonds, *The Making of Pakistan* (London: Faber & Faber, 1950); and Francis Williams, *A Prime Minister Remembers: The War and Post-War Memoirs of Rt. Hon. Earl Attlee* (London: Willliam Heninemann, 1961).

160. Collins and Lapierre, *Mountbatten and the Partition of India,* Vol. I, 14. Besides, the civil servants and the Police in many parts of India were deeply affected with communalism and could no longer be relied upon for firm action against the faltering members of their own communities. Mansergh, *Transfer of Power,* Vol. VIII, 202; and Nicholas Mansergh and Penderel Moon, eds., *Constitutional Relations between Britain and India: The Transfer of Power, 1942–7,* Vol. IX (London: HM's Stationery Office, 1980) 128.

161. In fact, in December 1941, the US President Roosevelt told Churchill, the British Prime Minister, that 'he favoured termination of India's colonial status.' Francis L. Loewenheim, Harold D. Langley, and Manfred Jonas, eds., *Roosevelt and Churchill: Their Secret War Time Correspondence* (New York: E.P. Dutton, 1975), 183. Also see ibid., 231.

162. In his note to Churchill dated 10 March 1942, President Roosevelt suggested 'the setting up of what might be called a temporary government in India….' See ibid., 191. Stalin, too, was worried about India. The first meeting between Roosevelt and Stalin focused on India at great length. See Ibid., 396. Also see Mansergh, *Transfer of Power*, Vol. I, 410.

163. For details of the Plan see, Mansergh, *Transfer of Power,* Vol. VI, 699-701. According to H.M. Close, Wavell was still not prepared 'to promote a plan for partition' of India. He, therefore, opted for the word 'Breakdown'. H.M. Close, *Wavell, Mountbatten and the Transfer of Power* (Islamabad: National Book Foundation, 1997), 85.

164. Mansergh, *Transfer of Power*, Vol. VIII, 455-7.

165. Cited in Brailsford, *Subject India,* 28.

166. Cited in Hutchins, *India's Revolution,* 143.

167. Governor of Bengal, 8 August 1946. Mansergh, *Transfer of Power*, Vol. VIII, 205.

168. Afzal, *Selected Speeches and Statements*, 116.

169. Coupland, *Indian Problem*, 143-6.

170. Brailsford, *Subject India,* 47-8.

171. Ahmad, *Speeches and Writings*, Vol. I, 12-13.

172. *'Essays': The Memoirs of Lawrence, Second Marquess of Zetland* (London: John Murray, 1956), 277. That the British were not reconciled to the loss of India as late as 20 September 1946, was clear from the following note from Pethick-Lawrence, then Secretary of State, to Attlee, the Prime Minister of England: 'The loss of India would greatly weaken the general position and prestige of the British Commonwealth in the world. Our ability to support and assist Australia and New Zealand in the time of need and to maintain our position in Burma, Malaya, and the Far East generally would be substantially weakened.' Mansergh, *Transfer of Power*, Vol. VIII, 551.

173. Page*, Prelude to Partition*, 263.

174. Mansergh, *Transfer of Power*, Vol. I, 81.

175. Page, *Prelude to Partition,* 246.

176. Chirol, *India*, 128, 293. Also see, Coupland, *Indian Problem*, 75.

177. *Report of the Indian Statutory Commission, Simon Commission Report,* Vol. I (London: HM's Stationery Office, 1930), 29-30.

178. Wayne Wilcox, *Pakistan: The Consolidation of a Nation* (New York: Columbia University Press, 1963), 20.

179. Hamid, *Muslim Separatism in India*, 218.

180. C.H. Philips, 'Introduction', in Philips and Wainwright, *Partition of India*, 27.

181. Waheed-uz-Zaman, *Towards Pakistan*, 210.

182. Ahmad, *Speeches and Writings*, Vol. I, 77.

183. Moore, *Crisis of Indian Unity*, 313. In fact, Moore talked of three dualities: 'The first duality was between the Raj and its aspirant successor, the parallel government of the Indian National Congress. The Congress claimed to represent

all India and sought parity of status with the Raj. The accommodation of this duality meant finding a constitution that conceded the essence of the Congress claim whilst the necessary degree of British authority remained. The second duality was between Hindu India and Muslim India. In this case, the accommodation must preserve the separate interests and identity of the Muslim communities within a nation that was bound to be predominately Hindu. The third duality was between British India and the Indian States'. Ibid., 313. Also see P.J. Griffiths, *The British in India* (London: Robert Hale, 1946), 129.

184. Ahmad, *Speeches and Writings*, Vol. I, 155.
185. Rustow, 'Ataturk as Founder of a State', 794.

4 The Muslim Situation: Leadership Crisis

The traditional Muslim political leadership was composed of social elites such as the nobility, titled gentry, and big landowners, provincial leaders of the Muslim-majority provinces, and the *ulama*.[1] The solidarity of each of these groups was derived from the social and political ties among their members that served to promote their special interests. However, they were not 'interests' in the sense relevant to the experience of Western societies and were expressed in informally organized associations. Their purpose was to influence political life to the extent possible through shared attitudes. Thus, it was not surprising to find some of these groups sufficiently flexible to work closely with other groups, indeed reinforcing each other. For instance, some of the provincial leaders were big landowners, and thus could easily be included in the category of social elites. But since many of these provincial leaders, particularly in Bengal, could not be placed in that category, and moreover, enjoyed their power and position independent of their social origins, it is much more useful to treat them at a separate level of analysis. In addition, most provincial leaders did not carry their influence and authority beyond provincial boundaries. It is only because they had their power base in their respective provinces that it is deemed necessary to consider them provincial leaders first and last. The purpose of this classification, therefore, is merely schematic and intended to bring out the essential characteristics of each group.

The Social Elites

The social elites,[2] as represented by the nobility, titled gentry and landowners, were patronized and promoted by the British. The British settlements over the years secured them in a legal position as landlords with inheritable and transferable estates, and enabled them to realize the revenue, and enjoy their possessions.[3] The tax squeeze was considerably less than it was under the Mughals, and thus they could have substantial profit.[4] Except for the Permanent Settlement of Bengal, which adversely affected the Muslim landowning classes,[5] other settlements, particularly in the Punjab, helped the Muslims attain a proprietary right in the land and accumulate wealth, influence, and power. They were also given special representation in councils under various constitutional reforms. The idea, apparently, was to secure a class of 'favoured collaborators',[6] who would support British rule in India much as their social counterparts in Britain supported its parliamentary system during the eighteenth century.[7]

The landowning classes in general, and the Muslim landowners in particular, supported the British rulers for two very important reasons. One, characteristically, being a traditional group, keen on continuity rather than change, they wanted the British to continue to cater to their interests. Thus, they did not want to create any problems for them. Two, their instinctive fear of the developments that crushed their class in Bengal, further suggested to them to look to the British for support and patronage. They stayed away from the agitational politics of the Congress and formulated a separate political platform in defence of particular Muslim interests through concessions and safeguards. This reinforced their dependence on the British Government.

No wonder, the leaders of the nineteenth century Muslim community came from this group. They were the ones who arranged the Simla Deputation of October 1906, signed by nobles, ministers of various states, and great landowners, urging the British Government that their representation in the assemblies should be 'commensurate… [with] the position which they occupied in India a little more than an hundred years ago, and of which the traditions have naturally not faded from their minds'.[8] In December 1906, they founded the All-India Muslim League. The League's manifesto publicly acknowledged that it was led by men of 'prosperity and influence'. Sir Sultan Mohammad Shah, Aga Khan III, who led the Simla Deputation was elected its first 'Permanent President' at the 1907 session of the League held at Karachi.

The Aga Khan was an ideal choice for the position. He was one of the leading members of the commercial and landed classes, having inherited all the 'titles, wealth, and responsibilities, spiritual and temporal'[9] of the Ismailis in 1885, at the tender age of 8, and associated with the Aligarh College and the Muhammadan Educational Conference (founded in 1886). He also had a close association with the British. In 1902, the British Government had nominated him a member of the Imperial Legislative Council. His two-year (1902–4) term in the Legislative Council had convinced him that:

> ...the Congress Party, the only active and responsible political organization in the country, would prove itself incapable—was already proving itself incapable—of representing India's Muslims, or of dealing adequately or justly with the needs and aspirations of the Muslim community.[10]

This faith in the separate Muslim cause inspired confidence among the social elites. They saw it at work in the deliberations of the Simla Deputation. They looked up to him for leadership, especially after the Act of 1909 had granted the right of separate electorates to the Muslims. Indeed, they felt secure and wanted to be involved in political developments in the country.

However, the Aga Khan was not ready for an active role in politics. With the growing strength of the Muslim middle classes in the Muslim League after 1913 (after Jinnah's entry), which demanded 'self-government suitable to India', he felt particularly uncomfortable and resigned from the presidency of the League. He even stopped his financial contribution to the League. In principle, he had nothing against constitutional advance, but if the League, he warned, stood for 'a mere hasty impulse to jump at the apple when only the blossoming stage was over, then the day that witnessed the formulation of the ideal will be a very unfortunate one in the annals of their country'.[11]

While the Lucknow Pact of 1916 showed the increasing presence of the Muslim educated, urban middle classes in politics, the subsequent events leading to the Khilafat–Non-cooperation movement swept aside the influence of both the middle classes and the social elites. While the middle classes could not approve of the extra-constitutional non-cooperation method employed in the service of the Khilafat cause due to their temperament and training, the social elites could scarcely reconcile themselves to a movement in the nature of an anti-British agitation. They were not willing to bring into question, let alone physically challenge, British authority in India. While the Aga Khan personally tried to settle the Khilafat issue amicably,[12] led a mission to British Prime Minister, Lloyd George (1863–1945), at the request of the Legislative Council, and contributed generously to Turkey's war funds, the fact remains that the social elites had little influence over the developments.

The failure of the Khilafat movement to achieve its objectives and the inability of the Muslim middle-classes' leadership of the revived League in 1924 to effect change in the Nehru Report brought the social elites back to the centre of the stage. The Aga Khan came to chair the All-India Muslim Conference of 1929 attracting not only the big landowners, *nawabs* and knights but also the old *Khilafatists* and *ulama* like Maulana Mohammed Ali, Maulana Shaukat Ali, Maulana Hasrat Mohani, Maulana Abdul Qadir Azad Subhani (1873–1957), and Maulana Shafee Daudi. Even some of the middle-class leaders such as Mohammad Yakub, Deputy Leader of Jinnah's Independent Party in the Legislative Assembly, were forced to seek the Conference banner. In the Aga Khan's own estimate, it was clearly 'a vast gathering' representative of all shades of Muslim opinion.[13] After a 'long, full, and frank discussion', the conference adopted a manifesto which, *inter alia*, stressed that:

> ...the only form of government suitable to Indian conditions is a federal system with complete autonomy and residuary powers vested in the constituent states. The right of Muslims to elect their representatives in the various Indian legislatures is now the law of the land, and Muslims cannot be deprived of that right without their consent. In the provinces in which Muslims constitute a majority they shall have a representation in no less than that enjoyed by them under the existing law (a principle known as weightage). It is essential that Muslims shall have their due share in the central and provincial cabinets.[14]

In fact, the Aga Khan was convinced that these demands constituted 'guiding lights' for the Muslims in their search for a safe and secure future in India. The Muslims could not afford to ignore or deviate from these demands.[15] The Aga Khan indeed claimed that it was precisely because of the popularity of these demands among the Muslims that Jinnah decided to play an active part in Muslim politics once again.[16]

While it is difficult to say how much the proceedings of the Muslim Conference influenced his mind and actions in the subsequent years, there is no denying that Jinnah's Fourteen Points carried some of the demands of the Muslim Conference. But then, they also included the Delhi Muslim Proposals of 1927, formulated under his own guidance and leadership. Indeed, according to M.H. Saiyid, the idea of the Fourteen Points was to 'accommodate all the schools of thought' and thus make sure that 'complete harmony would once again prevail within the ranks of the League'.[17]

However, the Muslim Conference itself failed to impress the Muslim masses in the long run, and for a number of reasons. First, the Conference suffered from 'want of leadership....'[18] The Aga Khan could not devote attention and efforts for long. Secondly, the Conference was 'a very mixed bag',[19] purporting to carry the cause of the landowners, the provincial leaders (both from Muslim-majority and Muslim-minority provinces, with all their fine distinctions), the *ulama*, and the middle classes without any mechanism for higher synthesis of their particular interests. At best, it was a ramshackle coalition. Thirdly, the Conference suffered from acute financial problems. Although it had among its sponsors Sir Abdullah Haroon, the Nizam of Hyderabad, the Nawabs of Dacca (Dhaka) and Rampur, the Raja of Salempur, and above all, the Aga Khan himself, nobody contributed regularly and sufficiently. Partly due to these financial problems, the Conference did not have a press to mobilize the Muslim opinion.[20] Finally, and most importantly, the Conference could not free itself from the provincial strategy of Fazl-i-Husain who was chiefly interested in the establishment of the Unionist position in the Punjab,[21] even if it meant compromising on the All-India stance of the Conference. This was in spite of the fact that the Aga Khan and other leaders of the Conference always stressed the need for maintaining an all-India programme and policies.[22]

In the end, the Conference suffered an irreparable loss with the retirement of the Aga Khan from Indian politics. With the termination of the work of the Joint Select Committee on the Government of India Bill in 1934, the Aga Khan ended his connection with local politics,[23] and assumed the international role of representing India at the League of Nations Assembly. Though the Aga Khan's career at the League of Nations was an instant success and he rose to be the only Asian to be elected, in 1937, as President of the League of Nations

Assembly, the Muslim Conference was at a complete loss. As Sir Shafaat Ahmad Khan (1893–1947), one of its active leaders, incisively put it in November 1935: 'The Muslim Conference programme has been exhausted. It is empty of contents. I have been scratching my forehead for the last two years in a vain search for a new programme for Muslim India, but am like a blind man groping in the dark'.[24]

While the decline of the Muslim Conference marked the end of the dominant role of the Muslim social elites on the national scene, it did not kill their instinctive urge for leadership and authority. Some, indeed, concentrated upon regional alliances to safeguard their political interests and to fight the coming elections. Some founded and promoted regional organizations. In the UP, for instance, the Nawab of Chhattari, Sir Mohammad Said Ahmed Khan (1888–1982) organized the National Agriculturist Party. In Sind, Sir Abdullah Haroon formed the Sind United Party. In the North-West Frontier, Sir Sahibzada Abdul Qaiyum (1866–1937) promoted the United Muslims Nationalist Party. The politics of the social elites thus assumed a distinct regional/provincial character.

However, this shift did not take the social elites far. Although some of them could do better than others, their days were numbered. The 1937 elections left them beholden to the Muslim League. Their fear of the Congress's overwhelming strength to influence provincial politics forced them to come to terms with the all-India presence of the League. The Nawab of Chhattari attended the Lucknow session of the League in October 1937. Abdullah Haroon joined the League. Sahibzada Abdul Qaiyum extended cooperation to the League. After his death in December 1937, most of the members of his party formally joined the newly formed Frontier Provincial Muslim League. The highly centralized, authoritarian, and partisan policy of the Congress from 1937 to 1939, helped further limit the options available to the social elites. Most of them moved towards the League. The result was that, in 1942, the landowners, for instance, represented 'the largest single group' in the Muslim League Council. Out of a total membership of 503 members, there were as many as 163 landowners.[25] In addition, there were several knights, *khan bahadurs*, and *nawabs* who were Muslim League members in the Central Legislative Assembly. Although the cause of the Muslim social elites, particularly under the Muslim Conference, was compromised and eventually lost, due to a host of factors, as indicated above, the fact of the matter is that the objective conditions of India in the late 1930s made things all the more difficult for them. Their position had become untenable for a number of reasons. Some of the more important reasons are:

1) The process of the expansion of the electoral franchise began to shift increasingly in favour of the educated, urban middle-classes working in opposition to the *status quo* oriented policies of the social elites. The educated Muslim youth wanted a greater share in the expanding and evolving system of government. They found little comfort in politics in defence of traditional authority.

2) The strongly national character of the educated, urban middle classes, in opposition to the parochial, local, regional character of the social elites, came to appeal more and more to the Muslim masses who were caught up in the heightened Hindu–Muslim communalism of the 1930s. They wanted real long-term solutions. This was, of course, not a development unique to the Indian Muslim case. Most developing societies in their nationalist phase of struggle with colonialism experienced similar shifts in centres of authority.[26]

3) The increasing emphasis on the centre in Indian politics, especially after the promulgation of the Act of 1935, disturbed the traditional base of the social elites and rendered them largely irrelevant to the main concerns of politics. What was at stake was the control of the centre, and the social elites had hardly any idea or programme to offer on that account. All that they could come up with were regional or zonal schemes, such as the one proposed by Sikandar Hayat Khan. But then, the experience of the Congress rule of 1937–39 in the provinces had shown to the Muslim masses how poor and ineffective this option could be. The Muslim mind had, in fact, moved beyond the federal solutions.

4) With the beginning of the Second World War, British authority in India was seriously compromised. The devolution of authority radically reduced the influence of the social elites. Pro-British postures and policies could no longer allay Muslim fears and apprehensions. The social elites could not play the role of

mediators between the British and the Muslim community, especially as India moved closer to freedom.

5) Finally, the re-emergence of Jinnah and the Muslim League as an all-India party of the Muslims in the late 1930s sealed the fate of the social elites in Muslim politics. As a charismatic leader of Muslim India, Jinnah defined the nature and direction of Muslim politics. He reorganized the Muslim League to represent Muslim interests and demands, including its most important demand for a separate homeland for the Muslims. The result was that, in the end, the Muslim League, as the Aga Khan himself admitted,

> ...was an organization whose members were pledged to instant resistance—to the point of death—if Indian independence came about without full and proper safeguards for Muslim individuality or unity, or without due regard for the differences between Islamic culture, society, faith and civilization and their Hindu counterparts.[27]

The Provincial Leaders

The provincial leaders of the Muslim-majority provinces, a product of the system of 'dyarchy' introduced in 1919, were a formidable force. The system of dyarchy had given these leaders the actual handling of administrative powers and a measure of responsibility in the government. The British favoured the devolution of authority to the provinces. The purpose was not only to attract the most influential and practical-minded to the provincial councils, but also to encourage provincial leaders at the expense of the demanding 'nationalist leadership' at the centre.[28] The nationalist leaders 'lacked a strong local electoral power base,' and Jinnah, as Talbot pointed out, became 'the most famous victim of this process,'[29] at least until the initiation of political processes at the centre in the wake of the Second World War.

The provincial leaders came from both the landowning and the middle classes and generally tended to be inclined towards one party or the other, the British, the Congress, or the Muslim League. In the Punjab, leaders such as Mian Mohammad Shafi and Sikandar Hayat Khan were big landowners and represented the so-called 'Anglo-

Mohammedan point of view' in politics.[30] Mian Mohammad Shafi was an important leader of the League. Sikandar Hayat Khan headed the Unionist Government and was favourably disposed towards the League as well. In Bengal, Fazlul Huq was representative of the middle classes and vacillated between pro-British, pro-Congress, and pro-League positions. Khwaja Nazimuddin and Huseyn Shaheed Suhrawardy, rival claimants to provincial leadership, also from the middle-classes, were supporters of the League. In the North-West Frontier Province, Sahibzada Abdul Qaiyum Khan was a pro-British leader, representing the landowners of the province. Dr Khan Sahib (1883–1958), his more successful political rival, was a pro-Congress leader, and relied on the support of the rural middle classes and peasantry. Under the patronage of his more influential brother, Abdul Ghaffar Khan, Dr Khan Sahib was part of the dominant Khudai Khidmatgar movement.[31] In Sindh, the provincial leadership was divided between pro-League and pro-Congress camps. While Abdullah Haroon, Sir Ghulam Hussain Hidayatullah (1879–1948), and Mohammad Ayub Khuhro (1901-80) supported the League, Allah Bukhsh Soomro and some others were allied to the Congress with whose support they were often able to form a coalition government. What further complicated the provincial scene was the ethnic dimension, which often challenged the interests of the Muslim community as a whole, or indeed, Muslim nationalism. In all the Muslim-majority provinces (except for Balochistan, which had a special status and was without provincial autonomy), there were ethnic groups, demands, and stresses on regionalism. However, as this ethnic consciousness was not fully developed, except perhaps for the NWFP, and was also largely expressed through provincial groupings, especially in Sindh, it will be useful to concentrate on the provincial leadership.[32]

While it is not possible in the present study to examine all of these diverse examples of provincial leadership, it is appropriate to discuss one or two provincial leaders in greater depth to highlight the difficulties associated with their roles in the Muslim politics of India. It will be useful to concentrate upon the provincial leadership of the Punjab, a large Muslim-majority province, 'more advanced, prosperous and more influential' than any other Muslim-majority province,[33] and with a more articulate and organized set of provincial leaders. Fazl-i-Husain, whom we have already discussed in the context of Muslim

Conference politics, is an appropriate choice. However, since he passed away when provincial autonomy granted under the Act of 1935 was just beginning to unfold its scope and extent, his case will be complemented with a discussion of the role played by his successors, Sikandar Hayat Khan and Khizar Hayat Khan Tiwana, in provincial politics. References will also be made to other leaders of the province relevant to the analysis.

Fazl-i-Husain was the founder and the undisputed leader of the pro-British Punjab National Unionist Party from 1923 until his death in 1936. Though not a scion of the gentry,[34] Fazl-i-Husain founded the Unionist Party to save the landed interests of the Punjab from the urban *banias* (moneylenders), primarily Hindus, who controlled trade and commerce in the province and were steadily becoming landowners through forfeitures of lands pledged as securities for loans. The gravity of the situation could be gauged from the fact that, according to the 1922–23 survey conducted by Malcolm Darling, 83 per cent of the proprietors of the Punjab were in debt.[35] Sir Chotu Ram, an influential Hindu Jat agriculturalist from Rohtak, and a co-founder of the Unionist Party, writing a few years later, observed: 'In fact, it may be safely presumed that not less than 90 per cent of the agricultural population of the Punjab is in debt at the present time'.[36] Sir Malik Feroz Khan Noon (1893–1970), another stalwart of the Unionist Party then and later a leader of the Muslim League and a Prime Minister of Pakistan in the 1950s, commented that: 'where the Government collected eight million dollars a year by way of land revenue, the moneylender was gathering a harvest of eighty million dollars (rupees forty crores) a year from the same people by way of loans recovered'.[37] It was feared that if the *banias* were not checked, the agricultural economy of the province would sink into the lowest depth of poverty without any hope of recovery except through a rebellion or revolution.[38] The situation was all the more desperate for the Muslims, the bulk of whose population was concentrated in the rural areas.

Fazl-i-Husain sought to meet the difficult situation through the Unionist Party, by forging an alliance with a vigorous agricultural community of the Hindus, the Jats, led by Sir Chotu Ram and the Sikhs, represented by Sir Sunder Singh Majitha. In this endeavour, Fazl-i-Husain was helped by the British authorities. Indeed, according to Talbot, 'the British bent over backwards to make this possible'.[39] The idea was to bring all the landed interests of the Punjab together. The Act of 1919, which was tilted heavily in favour of the rural electorate[40] provided the Unionists the opportunity they needed to transform this alliance into a major political force. In the 1923 elections to the Provincial Legislative Assembly, the Unionist Party secured 45 seats as against 32 of the opposition. They formed the government and the devolution of power to the provinces made it possible for them to consolidate their gains. There was little that the Muslim League, a centralist party, could do other than operate in the small urban areas of the province, which it did. The result was that the Unionist Party dominated the provincial politics, and its leader, Fazl-i-Husain, went on to secure the membership of the Viceroy's Executive Council, on which he served from 1930 to 1935. This latter capacity enabled him to control and guide the Muslim Conference and to influence the membership of the Muslim delegation to the Round Table Conference in London and help draft the Government of India Bill in a way that would further strengthen the Unionist position in the province. Fazl-i-Husain was particularly interested in the separate electorates and in securing statutory majorities in the Punjab (and Bengal). As he wrote to the Nawab of Chhattari on 5 September 1931, 'Muslims very properly demand representation on population basis and are entitled to it....'[41] As to the fate of the Muslim-minority provinces and responsibility at the centre, Fazl-i-Husain was not much interested.

Indeed, it was to check the constitutional advance at the centre that Fazl-i-Husain disapproved of the presence of Jinnah in the Round Table Conference. Jinnah was the only Muslim leader of repute and stature who did not attend the Muslim Conference in 1929. He was still committed to the nationalist cause in politics. As Fazl-i-Husain told Sir Malcolm Hailey, Governor of the Punjab,

> ...I do not like the idea of Jinnah doing all the talking and of there being no one strong-minded enough to make a protest in case Jinnah starts upon expressing his views when those views are not acceptable to Indian Muslims. I want someone who would frankly say that it is not the Indian Muslim view....[42]

Shafaat Ahmad Khan was nominated as a member of the Muslim delegation for this purpose. The inclusion of Fazl-i-Husain's key men in the delegation and the presence of some Muslim leaders accompanying Gandhi at the Second Round Table Conference as his advisors on the communal issue, in fact, prompted Jinnah to comment years later that the attitude of 'toadies and flunkeys on the one hand and traitors in the Congress camp on the other' forced him to quit politics and settle down in London.[43] For the moment, however, Fazl-i-Husain had his way, and through his meticulous exchange of notes and points conveyed through correspondence[44] with the Muslim members of the delegation, particularly the Aga Khan, Shafaat Ahmad Khan, and Sir Zafrullah Khan (1893–1985), managed to secure the Communal Award. His son and biographer, Azim Husain described the Award as 'very much Fazl-i-Husain's creation' that 'put the mind at rest' and reflected 'the labour of Fazl-i-Husain for five years in the Government of India'.[45]

While Azim Husain was right in suggesting that the Communal Award was largely the work of Fazl-i-Husain and his nominees in London, the fact remained that it was far from a satisfactory solution of the Muslim problem. Azim Husain himself admitted that the Muslim demand that residuary power be vested in the provinces was not conceded. The fact that they were to be exercised by the Governor-General in his discretion was a matter of little comfort in the face of increasing demands for responsible self-government at the centre. Azim Husain also conceded that the demand for 33 per cent representation in the cabinet, central and provincial, was not met in the Act. However, Azim Husain was certainly incorrect in suggesting that the Muslims in the Punjab were given a statutory majority.[46] The factual position was that the Muslims were conceded only 49 per cent of the reserved seats, 2 per cent short of a simple majority. More precisely, the Muslims were assigned 86 out of 175 seats.[47] The Muslims, of course, retained separate electorates. The Muslim position in the Muslim-minority provinces did not improve at all. Nothing was promised to them except the retention of separate electorates. The Aga Khan and Shafaat Ahmad Khan tried their utmost to attract the attention of Fazl-i-Husain to the fate of helpless Muslim minorities but to no avail. Fazl-i-Husain could only counter-charge and ridicule, 'Experience is a great thing but it plays hell with illusions'.[48]

Of course, Fazl-i-Husain's real concerns were to strengthen the Unionists in the Punjab and draw benefit from the Communal Award at the provincial level, not the development of Muslim policy on an all-India basis. He hastened to enter into an inter-communal pact with the Hindus and Sikhs in the Punjab, no matter how revolting the whole idea could be to the concept of Muslim unity pursued by his Muslim Conference and promoted by his allies in the Conference in the Muslim-minority provinces. 'I do not see how Punjab Muslims', he bluntly told Shafaat Ahmad Khan in his letter of 19 June 1933, 'can be deprived of the chance of improving their position by accepting this proposal'.[49] However, if 'Punjab Hindus and Sikhs persist in not playing the game', he exclaimed in the privacy of his *Diary*, the Punjab Muslims should not insist, 'but let the Reforms be the establishment of autocracy and make sure that this happens all over India—long live John Bull!'[50] The irony was that while Fazl-i-Husain earned 'a reputation as a strong advocate of Muslim interests' and was 'widely known among Hindus and Sikhs' as a communalist,[51] he lacked the vision to lead Muslim India towards a larger objective. He feared that the articulation of a transcendent vision could create an identification that would undermine 'the structure of rural influence on which he had built the Unionist Party'.[52] The 'Punjab Formula', as Azim Husain put it, was in fact a plan to secure provincial interests in the new constitution and to leave the centre to the British. Things were made easier for Fazl-i-Husain by the reluctance of the Princely States to work for the new Indian centre. Fazl-i-Husain could establish provincial rule unfettered by responsible central control.[53] But then, as fate would have it, Fazl-i-Husain died on 9 July 1936, after a severe attack of bronchitis, well before provincial rule could be realized.

While it is difficult to say what Fazl-i-Hussain would have done if he had lived to witness the operation of the provincial autonomy,[54] his successor in the Unionist Party and the provincial government, Sikandar Hayat Khan had little to gain from the provincial preoccupation of the early years. He had to deal with new realities affecting not only the interests of the Muslims in the Punjab but of Muslims all over India. To begin with, he had to contend with the reality of the Congress ascendancy in the Punjab. In the 1937 elections, the Congress had emerged as the second largest party with 20 seats, after the Unionist party, which won 101 seats. Maulana Abul Kalam Azad, a member of the Congress Parliamentary Board, was actively engaged in the task of pursuing and promoting Congress interests in the Punjab and other Muslim-majority provinces.[55] Sikandar Hayat Khan, along with the provincial leaders of other Muslim-majority areas, Fazlul Huq and Sir Syed Muhammad Saadullah (1885–1955), chief ministers of Bengal and Assam respectively, was left with no option but join the Muslim League at its Lucknow session of October 1937. However, this also meant that Sikandar Hayat Khan had to address the League's demand for Pakistan. This demand, holding the prospect of absolute power to the Muslim-majority areas, was a potential threat to his Unionist stronghold.[56] Indeed, it was a very difficult situation, which demanded strong and imaginative leadership. But Sikandar Hayat Khan was found wanting. He fell for the obvious temptation and chose to sail in two boats. He often spoke in two voices, saying one thing on the League platform and another inside his own province.[57]

However, even this proved a much more difficult exercise than Sikandar Hayat Khan might have originally thought. Old Leaguers in the Punjab, especially Allama Iqbal and Barkat Ali, watched his activities and frequently reported their concerns to Jinnah. They were convinced that he was not sincere to the League. In his letter of 10 November 1937, for instance, Iqbal warned Jinnah:

> After having several talks with Sir Sikandar and his friends, I am now definitely of the opinion that Sir Sikandar wants nothing less than the complete control of the League and Provincial Parliamentary Board.... All this to my mind amounts to capturing of the League and then killing it.[58]

In a similar vein, Barkat Ali wrote in his letter of 4 December 1940 to Jinnah that 'Sir Sikandar's only desire was to capture the organization of the League....'[59] Jinnah, who was carefully following his plan of reorganizing the Muslims under the banner of the League and badly needed support in the Punjab, 'the corner-stone of Pakistan',[60] as he called it, recommended 'patience'. In a letter to Barkat Ali on 20 November 1937, he wrote: '...I assure you that if you people have a little patience these small matters of detail will be adjusted fairly and justly and mainly in the interests of the cause for which we stand'.[61]

The main source of anxiety and uneasiness among the Leaguers in the Punjab was the so-called 'Jinnah-Sikandar Pact' between Jinnah and Sikandar Hayat Khan. They did not quite follow it. Realizing the gravity of the situation, Jinnah decided to explain the pact in the League Council meeting at Delhi on 22 February 1942, and in a letter addressed to a leader of the League on 17 March 1943. He clarified that Sikandar Hayat Khan, along with his followers in the Punjab Assembly, had joined the Muslim League without any reservation. On his part, he had allowed the League to continue their coalition with the Unionist Party or to form any other coalition with any other party that from time to time they may decide. Outside the assembly, the League was free to organize itself in any way it thought fit. There was nothing binding on it.[62] He further elaborated the pact in a public speech on 30 April 1944: 'It was clearly laid down in the so-called pact—if they insist on calling it a pact...that it was open to the League Party to carry on the present coalition or enter into any other new coalition'.[63] Not surprisingly, when Sikandar Hayat Khan's successor in the Unionist Government, Khizar Hayat Khan Tiwana, tried to relegate the League to an inferior status in the provincial politics, Jinnah was furious. He denounced the pact and charged: 'How could there be a pact between a leader and a follower?'[64]

Of course, Jinnah had demonstrated his position and power clearly to Sikandar Hayat Khan in the Defense Council episode of September 1941. Jinnah took the Viceroy to task for inviting a few Muslim leaders including Sikandar Hayat Khan, Fazlul Huq, and Saadullah (not as provincial chief ministers) to join the Council without his approval.[65] Jinnah forced all three of them to resign their seats.[66] Incidentally, this was the first clear instance of Jinnah asserting his charismatic authority over the powerful provincial leaders of the Muslim-majority provinces, with a telling effect. Sikandar Hayat Khan not only resigned his seat, but also assured Jinnah that 'I am willing to abide by the orders of our President [of the Muslim League], whom I have acknowledged as my *Quaid-i-Azam*, and follow his instructions whatever he decides, right or wrong'.[67] In fact, this assurance of loyalty had come after his much publicized and oft-quoted speech on the subject of Pakistan in the Punjab Legislative Assembly in March 1941:

We do not ask for freedom, that there may be Muslim raj here and Hindu raj elsewhere. If that is what Pakistan means I will have nothing to do with it...if you want real freedom for the Punjab, that is to say a Punjab in which every community will have its due share in the economic and administrative fields as partners in a common concern, then Punjab will not be Pakistan, but just *Punjab*, land of the five rivers....[68]

Sikandar Hayat Khan's dilemma was that he wanted to maintain his position both as a member of the League and as head of the Unionist Government, which included Hindus and Sikhs. But that was not easy to reconcile. Chotu Ram and other non-Muslim leaders of the coalition were not happy with Sikandar Hayat Khan's association with the League and the Pakistan demand. Chotu Ram, in fact, warned Sikandar Hayat Khan that if the League wanted Pakistan in the Muslim-majority provinces because they did not have faith in the Hindu community, the Hindus will be forced to make a similar claim on the Punjab. The Punjab, he asserted, had as many as 13 with Hindu or Sikh majorities out of 29 districts. In a meeting of Hindu leaders of the Punjab convened in Lahore on 3 November 1942, Chotu Ram went one step further, and in an emotionally charged speech declared: 'in a matter of loyalty to Hinduism, I yield to none. If anyone were to devour the Hindus, I would not allow him to devour so before I am devoured first'.[69] Such threats and pressures from non-Muslim colleagues in the Unionist Government left Sikandar Hayat Khan in limbo for he could neither serve the cause of the League with enthusiasm nor countenance the disintegration of the mighty coalition that had ruled the Punjab unchallenged and unrivalled since the early 1920s. However, Sikandar Hayat Khan had moved away, steadily but surely, from the head-strong provincial stance taken by Fazl-i-Husain in 1936:

I have asked Ahmad Yar [Daultana] to convey to Jinnah...to strongly press on him the advisability of keeping his fingers out of the Punjab pie. If he meddles, he would only be encouraging fissiparous tendencies already painfully discernable in a section of Punjab Muslims, and might burn his fingers; and in any case we cannot possibly allow provincial autonomy to be tampered with in any sphere, and by anybody be he a nominee of the powers who have given us this autonomy or a President of the Muslim League or any other association or body.[70]

In 1942, the year he died, Sikandar Hayat Khan was a member of the League Working Committee and a self-proclaimed follower of the

Quaid-i-Azam. In his own words, uttered publicly a few weeks before his death: 'People exaggerate petty differences. Although at times, I may differ from the Quaid-i-Azam on an issue, yet I shall never fail to carry out his orders'.[71] This, indeed, was no small measure of change in the attitude of provincial leadership of the Punjab.

Though this change was not clearly reflected in the attitude of his successor, Khizar Hayat Khan, things were quite different by then. For one, Khizar Hayat Khan was not the undisputed leader of the Punjab Unionists in the sense Mian Fazl-i-Husain or Sikandar Hayat Khan were. Many scions of the highest echelons of the Unionist Party, such as the Hayats of Wah, Noons of Sargodha, and Daultanas of Multan district, were up against Khizar Hayat Khan. The most prominent among them were Sardar Shaukat Hayat Khan, the eldest son of Sikandar Hayat Khan, and Mian Mumtaz Muhammad Khan Daultana, son of Mian Ahmad Yar Khan Daultana (1896–1940), former General-Secretary of the Punjab Unionist Party (mentioned in the above passage). Khizar Hayat Khan was thus more of a recalcitrant follower of Jinnah than a political rival, and it became increasingly difficult for him to assert himself. To further add to his woes, the Unionist ministry had become quite unpopular 'because of over-zealous army recruitment and the rationing and requisitioning of grain' during the war years. A large number of the party's 'traditional agriculturalist supporters' had joined 'the Muslim League bandwagon from 1944 onwards'. In addition, the failure of the Simla Conference of 1945 clearly 'signalled to the opportunistic Punjabi landed-elite that future access to high office would be only through the Muslim League' and Jinnah.[72] Khizar Hayat Khan himself appeared 'ready to surrender'.[73] This change in the situation was clearly reflected in the 1945–46 elections, followed by a well-organized civil disobedience movement launched in January 1947, which paved the way for the complete ascendancy of Jinnah and the League over the province.[74]

The fate of the provincial leaders in other Muslim-majority provinces was not much different. Though they were equally keen to maintain their provincial strongholds, in the end they also had to give way to national leadership, which was endowed with the attributes of charisma. The provincial leaders drew their strength and inspiration from the devolution of power to the provinces. However, once the British, in the wake of the Second World War, were forced to enter into crucial negotiations with the Indians, represented by the League and the Congress, the two all-India organizations, to settle the issues of self-government, responsibility and control at the centre, provinces and provincial leaders were readily pushed into the background. This, in fact, explained why Sikandar Hayat Khan proved to be a weaker provincial leader than his predecessor, Fazl-i-Husain. Indeed, the greater the chances of the British system being supplanted by the Congress and the League at the centre, the weaker the influence and authority of the provincial leadership was. That also accounted for the relative weakness and eventual demise of Khizar Hayat Khan in provincial politics. Ultimately, provincial leaders could not even play a decisive role in provincial matters, let alone in the politics of India as a whole, as became evident in the division of the Punjab and Bengal. As Ayesha Jalal observed:

> By grasping too greedily at their provincial fruits, by pursuing monopolies rather than being content with dominant shares, by demanding too high an insurance at the centre for their possessions in the provinces, the inept, short-sighted and above all the faction-ridden and divided Muslim politicians of the Punjab and Bengal lost the chance of keeping their domains undivided.[75]

All-India organizations like the League could interfere in provincial matters, more often than not, at the expense of provincial leaders. Leaders in Bengal and Sindh, in particular, helped the League to expand its power base at the expense of their own provincial leadership.[76] In the end, of course, many provincial leaders in the Muslim-majority provinces became genuinely convinced of the Pakistan cause promoted by the League and thus willingly helped. The remaining leaders could not hold on for long, and were forced to yield to the national political leadership of Jinnah at the centre, which was imbued with 'the sacredness of the nation', and which had acquired charisma in the process. Jinnah had emerged as the charismatic leader of Muslim India.

Ulama

In general, the *ulama* were product of the traditional religious school system and were the custodians of religious learning and values among the Muslims. The substitution of English and vernacular languages for Persian and Arabic for matters of government and professions and the introduction of modern education made it extremely difficult for them to adjust to the new order established by the British in India. In fact, they opposed and condemned it. In 1867, they founded a Dar-ul-Ulum at Deoband (UP) to promote the teaching and practice of traditional Islam.[77]

In 1888, a large number of *ulama* formally entered politics, when Maulana Rashid Ahmad Gangohi, a close associate of Maulana Muhammad Qasim Nanautawi (d. 1880), and a prominent leader of the Dar-ul-Ulum Deoband, along with Maulana Mahmudul Hassan (1851–1920) and about one hundred *ulama* from all over India, issued a *fatwa* (decree) to the effect that, in worldly matters, particularly political matters, alliance with the Hindus was permissible, provided it did not violate any basic tenet of Islam. This *fatwa* was based on the premise that India had become *Dar-al-Harb* (Domain of War) with the coming of the British, and thus help from any quarter to rid India of British rule was desirable and necessary.[78] Indeed, this hostility towards the British proved to be the main source of tension and conflict between the traditionalist Deoband and modernist Aligarh, founded by Syed Ahmad Khan.[79] While Deoband declared a kind of war against the British rulers, Aligarh opted for close cooperation with the British to improve Muslim position under the new dispensation. In 1905, when Maulana Mahmudul Hassan took over the leadership, Deoband adopted a more radical position in politics, and even encouraged Maulana Ubaidullah Sindhi (1872–1944) to launch a revolutionary movement during the First World War to liberate India. The attempt, however, failed[80] and Maulana Mahmudul Hassan and other leaders of the movement were interned before they could make any headway in the implementation of their plans.

The *ulama* of Deoband, however, got their opportunity to participate in the political life of India on a systematic and sustained basis, through the Jamiat-ul-Ulama-i-Hind, established on 22 November 1919,[81] under the guidance of its two most authoritative leaders, Maulana

Hussain Ahmad Madani and Maulana Abul Kalam Azad. Maulana Madani was President of the Jamiat for a number of years, including the critical years of 1940, 1942, and 1945. Maulana Azad was a founder member of the Jamiat and its active leader during the Khilafat campaign. He presided over several conferences of the Jamiat 'in preference to all the senior *ulema*' associated with it.[82] In the 1920s, Maulana Azad became closely associated with the Congress. In 1937, after the death of Mukhtar Ansari, he was elected a member of the Congress Working Committee. In 1940–46, he held the highest office of the President of the Congress.

Maulana Azad was educated through the 'old system of education for Muslims in India',[83] and rose to prominence, at the young age of 24, through his weekly, *Al-Hilal*, which started its publication on 1 June 1912. The weekly, concentrating upon religious and political issues, encouraged cooperation with non-Muslims in the cause of Indian freedom. 'The tenets of Islam', Maulana Azad argued,

> ...under no circumstances, make it permissible for Muslims to enjoy life at the expense of liberty. A true Muslim has either to immolate himself or retain his liberty; no other course is open for him under his religion. Today the Muslims have come to a firm decision that in freeing their country from its slavery they will take their fullest share along with Hindu, Sikh, Parsi and Christian brethren.[84]

The weekly was so well received that within a period of six months its circulation was 11,000—a considerable figure given the fact that it was an Urdu weekly, published from Bengali-speaking Calcutta, and that the bulk of its readers were Muslims. During the First World War the weekly achieved a circulation of 25,000 copies and an all-India readership. However, the government stopped its publication on the charge of spreading 'pro-German sentiment in Calcutta',[85] a serious offence during the war years. Maulana Azad was prohibited from entering the Punjab, the United Provinces, and Madras, and on 7 April 1915, was forced out of Bengal. The Maulana moved to Ranchi, where the Government of India interned him until early 1920. It was during his internment that he wrote the *Tazkira*, a volume of personal memoirs, and two of the three parts of his monumental commentary on the Holy Quran, *Tarjumanul Quran*. 'This work alone', as one writer observed, 'made Abul Kalam's name and fame spread over the entire

Islamic world. This work alone was quite enough to make him immortal'.[86] But then, the problem was the kind of ideas he propounded to promote his political cause.

Maulana Azad asserted that 'the roots—rather the root' of all religion is one. No matter what the country and age, 'all the prophets sent by God taught the same universal truth for the welfare of mankind, viz. faith and good work, i.e. worship of one God and right conduct'.[87] People, however, he lamented,

> ...forgot this teaching, and cut up religion into numerous bits and made several religions out of it, and each group cut itself adrift from another. Diversity instead of unity, separation instead of union became their battle-cry. But, in the end, every one has to return to Him. There everything will be shown up and every group will see where its forgetfulness of the right thing had led to.[88]

These views agitated the Muslims, his main constituency, who saw in them a challenge to their traditional beliefs. In particular, they perceived them as 'an effort to undermine the belief in prophets (*Iman bi-r-rusul*)'.[89] Maulana Azad's association with the Congress made his views all the more anathematic to the Muslims.

Maulana Azad had joined the Congress after serving the Muslim League (1913–1920) and the Khilafat movement. He supported the much maligned Nehru Report claiming that the report protected Muslim rights and indeed was the 'best solution' of the Hindu–Muslim problem.[90] He strongly opposed Jinnah's Fourteen Points. A few years later, when the Muslims, led by Jinnah and the Muslim League, condemned Congress excesses during its rule in the provinces in 1937-39, he proclaimed:

> Every incident which involved communal issue came up before me. From personal knowledge and with a full sense of responsibility, I can therefore say that the charges levelled by Mr Jinnah and the Muslim League with regard to injustice to Muslims and other minorities were absolutely false.[91]

In fact, Maulana Azad, had little regard for the consensus of the community. He claimed that *ijma* 'does not always mean the "majority"'.[92] Indeed, he suggested to the Jamiat-ul-Ulama-i-Hind that an individual should be appointed as *Imam* to conduct the political affairs of the Muslims.[93] Though the Jamiat did not oblige him on that account, and kept postponing the issue, he did succeed in convincing them that Muslim political interests would be better promoted by the Congress. He assured them further that the Muslims in an independent India would constitute an internally autonomous community, and that he would get the Congress to concede the transfer of administration of the Muslim personal law to the *ulama*.[94] The Muslims, he suggested, should demand only such safeguards as they may require for the protection of their personal law and religion. He saw no distinction between the Muslims and Hindus in other aspects of life. He explained:

> The ancestors of most of us were common, and I, for one, do not accept the theory of a superior or inferior race or of different races. Mankind is one race, and we have to live in harmony with one another. Providence brought us together over a thousand years [ago]. We have fought, but so do blood-brothers fight.[95]

Maulana Azad, therefore, could not agree with the aspirations of the Indian Muslims for a separate homeland. First, he refused to accept that the Muslims were an aggrieved and distressed party in India. They were a minority, no doubt. But, he insisted, the Muslim community had the capacity to protect 'itself from the much larger group that surrounds it....'[96] Secondly, he believed that the communal problem would 'disappear' with the dawn of Indian freedom. 'I am one of those', he argued, 'who consider the present chapter of communal bitterness and differences as a transient phase in Indian life. I firmly hold that they will disappear when India assumes the responsibility of her own destiny'.[97] And, finally, he claimed in a statement on 15 April 1946, that his 'formula' for 'the solution of the Indian problem' was far more useful than 'the Pakistan scheme'. In his own words:

> The formula which I have succeeded in making the Congress accept secures whatever merit the Pakistan scheme contains while all its defects and drawbacks are avoided. The basis of Pakistan is the fear of interference by the centre in Muslim majority areas as Hindus will be in a majority in the Centre. The Congress meets this by granting full autonomy to the provincial units and vesting all residuary powers in the provinces. It has

also provided for two lists of Central subjects, one compulsory and one optional, so that if any provincial unit so wants, it can administer all subjects itself except a minimum delegated to the Centre. The Congress scheme therefore ensures that Muslim majority provinces are internally free to develop as they will, but can at the same time influence the Centre on all issues which affect India as a whole.[98]

Not only was this 'formula' regarded by the Muslims in general, and Jinnah in particular, as 'the height of defeatist mentality', to throw them at 'the mercy and good will of others',[99] the Maulana, despite his bold assertion, was not very sure of its success either. In fact, he conceded: 'If a more practical proposal is made, there can be no objection to it'.[100] In the end, however, hard pressed to propose an alternative to the Pakistan demand, he had nothing to offer to the Muslims but the advice to shun 'fears and doubts' and face the future with 'courage and confidence in ourselves'.[101]

Maulana Azad was preoccupied with the British, which meant that he had little time for India minus the British: 'This third power is already entrenched here and has no intention of withdrawing and, if we follow this path of fear, we must need look forward for its continuance'.[102] This estimation pushed the Maulana towards an unconditional Hindu–Muslim alliance and into the Congress camp. Not only did his association with the Congress, especially from 1937 to 1939, not help his political career with the Muslim masses, it also made his position suspect in the eyes of the League leadership. In July 1940, for instance, Jinnah refused to discuss the 'two-nation scheme' with him, saying: 'Can't you realise you are made a Muslim show-boy Congress President to give it colour that it is national and deceive foreign countries. You represent neither Muslims nor Hindus. The Congress is a Hindu body. If you have self-respect, resign at once'.[103]

The fact of the matter was that during the war years, which were also the years of Maulana Azad's Presidency, the Congress was at the beck and call of Gandhi who was openly and 'constantly talking' about the establishment of 'Ram-rajya' in India.[104] Maulana Azad was 'bound to follow the commands of the permanent super-President—Gandhi who, though not even a four-anna member of the party, was the most powerful guiding force behind the Congress machinery'.[105] Maulana Azad could, of course, hardly afford to challenge Gandhi, knowing full well the fate of dissenters like Nariman (Bombay), C.R. Das and

Subhas Chandra Bose (Bengal) and others. The Cripps Mission of 1942 left no doubt about his position in the Congress. The Congress Working Committee passed a major resolution in July 1942, popularly known as the 'open rebellion resolution'. The resolution was emphatic in recognizing 'the leadership of Mahatma Gandhi'. When the Maulana tried to explain to the people that this resolution was not meant to be an ultimatum to the British, Gandhi retorted: 'There is no question of "one more chance". After all this is open rebellion'.[106] In 1946, Maulana Azad was again rebuffed. Though he insisted that the interpretation given by the Cabinet Mission to the 16 May Proposals was correct, indeed, in line with his statement of 15 April,[107] referred to earlier, the Congress did not honour his word. In fact, it announced that it was 'free' to do whatever it liked. On 10 July Jawaharlal Nehru, in a press conference at Bombay, made the 'astonishing statement' that the Congress would enter the Constituent Assembly 'completely unfettered by agreements and free to meet all situations as they arise'.[108] In July 1946, Maulana Azad was duly relieved of the Congress Presidency. The Maulana, of course, saw it as his own voluntary act, and indeed, lamented,

> ...this was perhaps the greatest blunder of my political life. I have regretted no action of mine so much as the decision to withdraw from the Presidentship of the Congress at this critical juncture. It was a mistake which I can describe in Gandhiji's words as one of Himalayan dimension.[109]

Maulana Azad sought the welfare of the Muslims by asking them to merge their political identity with the Hindus. He believed that 'the community would prosper by losing itself; if it did not make conscious efforts to preserve itself, it would invite no hostility and no attack; it had only to let the majority forget that it existed to ensure a continued and unchallenged existence for itself'.[110] But the Muslims in general found little to celebrate in this rather naive optimism. On the contrary, they saw his association with the Hindus in general and the Congress in particular as a 'betrayal of the Muslim cause'. As one writer, in a lengthy newspaper article, put it:

> He wants us to join the Congress and believe that Congress will safeguard the Muslim interests. We trust him for that, but he will have to concede

that Congress is out and out a Hindu body pledged to Purna Swaraj and Akhand Hindustan. It is a pity that the Maulana Saheb, himself being such a big scholar of Urdu literature, could not find one single word to replace the title of 'Rashtrapati' which is so endeared to him. 'Rashtrapati', 'Purna Swaraj', 'Bunde Matarum' and 'Akhand Hindustan' are terms which were chosen by the 'National Congress'. Is there anything national about them? I see everything Hindu about them. Ask the Congress to change one single term, 'Purna Swaraj' into 'Hukoomat-i-Ilahia' and see how many Hindus support it! This shows that the Maulana Saheb wishes us to embrace a die-hard Hindu under the unoffending name of Congressman. We are prepared even to do this, but what are we to do when even in the ordinary routine life, we are hated, betrayed and wronged in every possible manner by the Hindus? …We can make a sacrifice in one thing, two things, three things. But here we have no limit to sacrifices. The Hindus can never be satisfied unless and until we forsake our True Dear Lord, our beloved Prophet and our Cherished Quran. And this shall never be. If the Maulana Saheb finds comfort in Hindu arms, let him. Islam is not a religion of custodians we can sacrifice, and very easily too, Maulana Saheb and their type. We can ignore the difference in the political views of the Maulana, but we cannot forgive betrayal of the Muslim cause.[111]

Maulana Azad sealed his fate with the Muslims[112] through his advocacy of India as 'one nation'. In the process, he also damaged the standing of the Jamiat-ul-Ulama-i-Hind, who found its leader, Maulana Hussain Ahmad Madani, advocating precisely 'similar political views' that the Muslims and the Hindus were members of one Indian nation (*qaum*).[113] Maulana Madani published a treatise under the title of *Mutahhidah Qaumiat aur Islam* in early 1939, stressing the idea of 'composite' Indian nationalism.[114] He referred to the covenant of Medina between the Holy Prophet (peace be upon him) and the inhabitants of Medina, including Jews, concluded in 622. He insisted that this covenant furnished 'the contractual basis of composite Hindu–Muslim nationalism in India.'[115] He, thus, claimed that the Muslims belonged to the 'Hindustani' nation, in spite of religious and cultural differences with other communities of India.[116] In other words, nations were products of territory, not necessarily religion or culture. However, this did not quite resolve the 'controversy' which surrounded 'the question of whether the Muslims of India constituted a separate nation, as argued by the 'modernist'

Muslim leaders who were to lead the movement for Pakistan, or were part of the same nation as the non-Muslim peoples of South Asia.'[117]

First, *ulama* such as Allama Shabbir Ahmad Usmani (1885–1949), a leading light of Deoband himself,[118] were quick to point out that Maulana Madani did not mention a stipulation in the covenant to the effect that the Holy Prophet (peace be upon him) was to be the final arbiter between the Muslims and non-Muslims in case of any dispute or disagreement between the two communities. Could the Maulana, he wondered, guarantee such a position to the Muslims in India?[119] Maulana Zafar Ahmad Usmani (1894–1974) was more emphatic in his rejection of the concept of a 'unified nation' in which the non-Muslims would constitute the majority. He stressed that such a nation would 'signify the destruction of Islam, its laws, and its rituals, and it is therefore forbidden from the viewpoint of the *sharia*'.[120] Secondly, Maulana Madani, and the *ulama* associated with the Jamiat, could not deny that the Muslims were different from the Hindus not only in the religious sense but also culturally and socially, indeed in all aspects of life, as forcefully argued by Jinnah in his presidential address at the Lahore session of the Muslim League in March 1940. Thirdly, Maulana Madani himself was less than confident on the question of 'composite nationality'. He failed, for instance, to tell Allama Iqbal directly and categorically whether he had advised Indian Muslims to accept the thesis that territory, not religion, made nations. Iqbal challenged Maulana Madani on his distinction between '*millat*' or *ummat* (community) and '*qaum*' (nation), and argued that Muslims, as a nation, could not be anything other than what they were as *millat*.[121] In advising the Maulana to seek 'evidence from the Quran' as to the true meaning of the terms '*qaum*' and '*millat*', he went on to ask:

> Is not the '*ummat*' also used in addition to these two words to denote the followers of the Prophet? Are these words so divergent in meaning that because of this difference one single nation can have different aspects, so much so that in matters of religion and law it should observe the divine code, while from the viewpoint of nationality it should follow a system which may be opposed to the religious system? ...So far as I have been able to see, no other word except *ummat* has been used for Muslims in the Holy Quran...*Qaum* means a party of men, and this party can come into being in a thousand places and in a thousand forms upon the basis of tribes, race, colour, language, land and ethical code. *Millat*, on the contrary, will

carve out of the different parties a new and common party. In other words, *millat* or *ummat* embraces nations but cannot be merged in them.[122]

Finally, the history of the Jamiat was no help either in the Maulana's case. The Jamiat had not opposed the League and its point of view until 1937. In fact, it had lent its full support to Jinnah on his proposed amendments to the Nehru Report and had claimed that 'Jinnah's only crime was that he is a Muslim and that he tried to represent the Muslim case, which the Hindus consider a great sin.'[123] A few months later, the Jamiat supported Jinnah's Fourteen Points, and went so far as to suggest that Indian politics would undergo a 'great revolution' should the Indians accept Jinnah's leadership and carry out his political programme.[124] In the 1937 elections, the Jamiat supported the League, issued a *fatwa* in its favour, and its leaders 'barnstormed the countryside in support of League candidates.'[125]

Indeed, one writer claimed that the Jamiat moved along a course parallel to that of the modern, educated, urban middle-class leadership all these years, if not just about the same course. The only difference seemed to be that the Jamiat was more concerned about 'safeguards against interference with the *sharia* and guarantee for its propagation and implementation....'[126] But then, it is difficult to understand how the Jamiat expected to realize its *sharia* in an independent, secular, India. How could the Muslims be expected to live a dual life, one part of it controlled by *sharia*, and the other part governed by a secular state which was certainly not to be run on the basis of *sharia*.[127] There was, of course, no guarantee to the effect that the *sharia* would be given an important place in an independent India. All that Maulana Azad could manage was a letter from Jawaharlal Nehru saying that the Congress was not particularly opposed to the idea. And when the representative of the Jamiat in the Central Legislative Assembly, Muhammad Ahmad Kazmi, took up the matter in the Assembly, it could get only five votes, and thus the bill was rejected. This happened to be first and the last time the matter was raised in the Assembly.[128]

The difficulty with the Jamiat was that its leaders were not trained for public roles, and thus could not really understand the 'potentialities of the modern state—any modern state—in affecting and regulating the lives of its citizens' over a period of time, the 'rise of Hindu nationalism' in India recently being a case in point.[129] They remained obsessed with the British presence in India. They did not see that the departure of the British, especially after the Second World War was 'imminent', and thus the basic obstacle in the way of the resurgence of Islam,[130] as they saw it, would soon be gone. They would be left with the Hindu-majority community. Rather, they committed themselves to 'composite nationalism' without really understanding the long-term implications of such a concept for the Muslims community.[131] This was in spite of the fact that Maulana Madani realized that, after India's freedom, 'the new order will not be entirely based upon an Islamic measure or standard (*Islami mayar*).' He only hoped that 'the education of Muslims will be according to such a measure.'[132] Apparently, the Jamiat considered the 'Muslims' religious freedom to keep their distinctive culture' to be more 'precious than their political freedom'.[133] No wonder, Jinnah, as before in the case of the *Waqf-alal-Aulad* Bill in 1913, was asked to steer the Shariat (Moslem Personal Law Application) Bill through the Legislative Assembly in September 1937.[134] Jinnah went on 'to broaden the bill's support' to the extent possible, and thus made some concessions on the laws of inheritance to help Muslim landed interests save their land-holdings from disintegration.[135] The only point on which Jinnah ruled out any compromise was the name of the bill, for he understood that it was a symbol of Muslim solidarity and his 'identification' with its passage 'left him at the centre of the struggle for Muslim communal unity'.[136]

To conclude, then, the traditional Muslim leadership, as a whole, failed to produce any far-sighted leader who could understand the difficulties confronting the Muslims, rise above sectional concerns, and show them a real way out. The social elites failed to appreciate that the British could not always secure Muslim interests for them, and sank into enervated dependency. The British reciprocated their overtures only to the degree that suited their purposes and interests. Their protection and patronage could not go beyond that point.[137] The provincial leaders remained tied to their provincial rule and authority. They were practically indifferent to the larger Muslim cause. The conduct of Fazl-i-Husain and Sikandar Hayat Khan are clear cases in point. They failed to comprehend that British departure meant that provincial autonomy would not save their rule once the centre, and two-thirds or more of provinces, had come under Congress–Hindu domination. Even a seasoned politician like Sikandar Hayat Khan could not realize that any form of federal zones or provincial autonomy, however perfect on paper, could not serve the Muslim cause in the end. The *ulama* could not suggest any practicable and positive solution to the community's special interests and demands.

It was precisely this failure on the part of the traditional leadership that was to push them off the main stage by the late 1930s and bring Jinnah, who had already fought for Muslim interests in the common cause of Indian self-government for more than three decades, and who was now willing to devote himself fully to the Muslim cause, to the forefront of Muslim politics and sustain him in his new role as the charismatic leader of Muslim India. In the process, Jinnah 'wrested the leadership of the Muslim community from colleagues...and competitors...who had deep roots in the heartland of the Indo-Muslim Civilization and did so with an ease that baffled observers'.[138] Indeed, for all practical purposes, 'the role of charisma as an entirely new kind of leadership' had superceded the hold of the 'traditional loyalties to religious, tribal, feudal and ethnic leaderships'[139] as far as the Muslims were concerned. However, some segments of the traditional groups readily supported Jinnah after they had acquired political consciousness and after the struggle for Pakistan was launched. This was particularly true of some prominent *ulama* from Deoband and other seminaries who, led by Allama Shabbir Ahmad Usmani, Maulana Zafar Ahmad Usmani and others under the aegis of Jamiat-ul-Ulama-i-Islam, went on to mobilize mass support for Jinnah and the Pakistan demand in the crucial 1945–46 elections. Maulana Zafar Ahmad Usmani's 'critique' of composite nationalism became 'a major alternative voice of authority' among the *ulama* 'precisely because it came from them'.[140] But then, collectively, the initiative for leadership had already passed on to the modernist nationalist leadership. Jinnah, 'quite self-consciously a modern man', had emerged as the charismatic leader of Indian Muslims. It was now his task to offer a 'formula' to address their distressful situation. A formula is the crucial test of charismatic leadership. It can make or break a charismatic leader. It may validate his charisma if his formula is approved by his followers. It may hurt his charisma if they do not respond favourably. It may eventually cost him his charisma. In this sense, a leader's charisma is inevitably tied to his formula.

Notes

1. There were some leaders who would not quite fit into any of these categories and represented varied interests. For example, Allama Inayatullah Mashraqi led the Khaksar movement and sought to establish 'Muslim domination' in India through military power. Thus, he was 'very different' from other leaders. See Muhammad Aslam Malik, *Allama Inayatullah Mashraqi: A Political Biography* (Karachi: Oxford University Press, 2000), xiv, 161. There was Syed Attaullah Shah Bokhari, leader of the Majlis-i-Ahrar, a pro-Congress party of Sunni Ulama, and a strong opponent of British rule, who, in 1931, played a major role in the Kashmir Jihad movement, and remained actively involved in the political life of Indian Muslims. See Syed Attaullah Shah Bokhari, *Hayat-i-Amir-i-Shariat* (Urdu) (Lahore: Maktaba Tabsara, 1970); and Shorish Kashmiri, *Syed Attaullah Shah Bokhari: Life and Thoughts* (Urdu) (Lahore: Maktaba Chittan, 1994). For a general overview of all the major Muslim leaders and organizations in India see, K.K. Aziz, ed., *Public life in Muslim India, 1850–1947* (Lahore: Vanguard, 1992).

2. For a comprehensive account of the British policy towards social elites in India in general and the Punjab in particular, and the overall shift in emphasis before and after 1857 see, Andrew Major, *Return to Empire: Punjab under the Sikhs and British in the mid-19th Century* (Karachi: Oxford University Press, 1996). According to Hutchins, 'British officialdom felt the need for a powerful class of natives loyal to British rule because of the stake they would have in its perpetuation. They consequently supported princes and landlords and justified their support by asserting that they were the natural leaders of Indian society.' Francis G. Hutchins, *The Illusion of Permanence: British Imperialism in India* (Princeton: Princeton University Press, 1967), 171.

3. Powell, *A Short Account of the Land Revenue in British India*, 154.

4. Maddison, *India and Pakistan Since the Moghuls*, Ch. 3, esp. 45-53.

5. For some of the details on the plight of Muslim landowning classes in Bengal, see W.W. Hunter, *The Indian Musalmans,* 158-60.

6. Rene Dumont, *Socialisms and Development* (New York: Praeger Publishers, 1973), 233.

7. Barrington Moore, Jr., *Social Origins of Dictatorship and Democracy* (Boston: Beacon Press 1966), 30. For an interesting study of *zamindars* and *taluqdars* and their relations with the British in the nineteenth century in particular see, Thomas R. Metcalf, *Land, Landlords, and the British Raj: Northern India in the Nineteenth Century* (Berkeley: University of California Press, 1979).

8. Desika Char, *Readings in the Constitutional History of India*, 425-26.

9. Aga Khan, *Memoirs*, xi.

10. Ibid., 75.

11. Cited in Noman, *Muslim India*, 135.

12. However, according to one writer, it was a letter from the Aga Khan (and Syed Ameer Ali) sent to Ismat Pasha, Prime Minister of Turkey, defending the cause of Khilafat, that 'influenced and possibly precipitated the decision of the Turkish National Assembly taken on 3 March 1924, to abolish the caliphate....' Aziz Ahmad, *Islamic Modernism,* 138.

13. Aga Khan, *Memoirs*, 209.
14. Ibid.
15. Ibid.
16. Ibid., 210.
17. Saiyid, *A Political Study*, 137-40.
18. Azim Husain, *Fazl-i-Husain: A Political Biography* (Bombay: Longmans, Green & Co., 1946), 247.
19. Page, *Prelude to Partition*, 198. Page discussed at length the affairs of the Muslim Conference. See Ch. 4, 195-258.
20. Ibid., 201-2.
21. Ibid.
22. See, for instance, Aga Khan's letter of 10 May, 1933 to Fazl-i-Husain in Waheed Ahmad, *Letters of Mian Fazl-i-Husain*, 285. For Fazl-i-Husain's response, see his letter of 28 June 1933 to Sir Shafaat Ahmad Khan, a leader of the Conference from the UP, wherein he stated that the minority provinces should not 'stand in the way of Punjab improving its position'. Ibid., 311.
23. Aga Khan, *Memoirs*, 235.
24. Waheed Ahmad, *Letters of Mian Fazl-i-Husain*, 470.
25. For an interesting study of groups and factions in the League see, Sayeed, *Formative Phase*, 206-11.
26. See, in particular, Edward Shils, 'Charisma, Order and Status'; David Apter, 'Nkrumah, Charisma, and the Coup'; and Willners, 'The Rise and Role of Charismatic Leaders', for a comparative study of the subject.
27. Aga Khan, *Memoirs*, 295.
28. Coatman, *Years of Destiny*, 205.
29. Talbot, *India and Pakistan*, 127.
30. See Sir Shafi's letter to Dunlop Smith, dated 8 January 1909, in Mujahid, *Studies in Interpretation*, 389, f.n.4.
31. According to Abdul Ghaffar Khan, the 'mission' of the Khudai Khidmatgars was 'to give comfort to all creatures of God. They are given training and take an oath to this effect. Their object is to rescue the oppressed from the tyrant. They would stand against a tyrant, whether he is a Hindu, a Muslim or an Englishman. If today they are against Englishmen, it is because they are tyrants and we are oppressed'. D.G. Tendulkar, *Abdul Ghaffar Khan: Faith is a Battle* (Bombay: Gandhi Peace Foundation, 1967), 128.
32. For a detailed and informed discussion on the ethnic aspect of provincial politics see, Samad, *A Nation in Turmoil*, especially, 28-46. For the groupings in Sindh, a source of considerable concern for the central leadership see, *Shamsul Hasan Collection*, especially volumes II, III, and IV.
33. Mushirul Hasan, *Nationalism and Communal Politics in India,* 16.
34. But Fazl-i-Husain returned to the Legislative Assembly of the Punjab in 1923–24 by a landowner's constituency. See Madan Gopal, *Sir Chotu Ram: A Political Biography* (Delhi: B.R. Publishing Corp., 1977), 60.
35. Malcolm Lyall Darling, *Punjab Peasant in Prosperity and Debt* (London: Oxford University Press, 1932).
36. Gopal, *Sir Chhotu Ram*, App. 2, 'Indebtedness in the Punjab', 166.
37. Feroz Khan Noon, *From Memory* (Lahore: Ferozsons, 1969), 99.

38. I.H. Qureshi, *Ulema in Politics*, 320.
39. Talbot, *Provincial Politics*, 85.
40. Ayesha Jalal and Anil Seal, 'Alternative to Partition: Muslim Politics Between the Wars', *Modern Asian Studies*, Vol. 15, No. 3 (1981), 424-25.
41. Waheed Ahmad, *Letters of Mian Fazl-i-Husain*, 189.
42. Quoted in Azim Husain, *Fazl-i-Husain*, 251.
43. Ahmad, *Speeches and Writings*, Vol. I, 41.
44. Besides letters given in *Letters of Mian Fazl-i-Husain* see, Waheed Ahmad, ed., *Diary and Notes of Mian Fazl-i-Husain*, (Lahore: Research Society of Pakistan, 1977), especially Part II, 211-349.
45. Azim Husain, *Fazl-i-Husain*, 265.
46. Ibid.
47. In Bengal, the Muslims received 48 per cent, 119 out of 250 seats, short of a majority. Thompson and Garrat, *Rise and Fulfillment of British Rule in India*, App. E, 'Communal Award', 663. The Congress did not accept the Award. As Nehru explained: 'The Congress does not and cannot accept the Communal Award because it is a negation of our fundamental principles of democracy and of a united India. It is incompatible with freedom…the Congress party is to get it altered….' Cited in S.R. Bakhsi, *Congress, Muslim League and Partition of India* (New Delhi: Deep & Deep Publications, 1991), 288.
48. Waheed Ahmad, *Letters of Mian Fazl-i-Husain*, 307.
49. Ibid., 305.
50. Waheed Ahmad, *Diary and Notes of Mian Fazl-i-Husain*, 342.
51. David Gilmartin, *Empire and Islam: Punjab and the Making of Pakistan* (London: I.B. Tauris & Co., 1988), 111-12.
52. Ibid., 112.
53. Page, Prelude to Partition, 229.
54. Waheed Ahmad, *Letters of Mian Fazl-i-Husain*, xxxix.
55. Azad, *India Wins Freedom*, 22.
56. For a detailed discussion of Sikandar Hayat Khan's role in the passage of the Lahore Resolution see, Malik, *Pakistan Resolution*, especially Chapter 4.
57. Ispahani, *Quaid-i-Azam Jinnah As I Knew Him*, 51. H. Craig, Governor Punjab, however, claimed that he 'had always, both in public and in private utterances, opposed any type of Pakistan scheme.' Malik, *Mashraqi*, 131. Penderel Moon was of the opinion that Sikandar Hayat Khan had 'nothing but indignation for the idea of Pakistan'. Moon, *Divide and Quit,* 20.
58. *Letters of Iqbal to Jinnah* (Lahore: Sh. Muhammad Ashraf, 1968, rep.), 31-32. For a more detailed discussion of Iqbal's views see, Ashiq Hussain Batalvi, *Iqbal kay Akhari Do Saal* (Urdu) (Karachi: Iqbal Academy, 1961), 510-12.
59. See, *Quaid-i-Azam Papers*, F/215.
60. Ahmad, *Speeches and Writings*, Vol. I, 494. Conversely, the British were convinced that: 'If the Punjab fell to Jinnah, it would be hard to avoid Pakistan'. Mansergh, *Transfer of Power*, Vol. V, 187.
61. Allana, *Historic Documents*, 167-68.
62. For details see, *Quaid-i-Azam Papers*, F/785, 95-96. Apparently, the Pact was not in writing. It was a verbal agreement between Jinnah and Sikandar Hayat Khan

made on 14 October 1937 at the Muslim League session at Lucknow. *Civil and Military Gazette,* 15 October 1937.

63. Ahmad, *Selected Speeches and Writings,* Vol. II, 45.

64. Ibid., 46. Khizar Hayat Khan addressed Jinnah as 'Quaid-i-Azam'. See, for instance, *Quaid-i-Azam Papers,* F/334. Here one must understand that Khizar Hayat Khan was no Sikandar Hayat Khan, just as Sikandar Hayat Khan was not Fazl-i Hussain. It was, perhaps, more importantly, a difference of situation. Khizar Hayat Khan was in no position to challenge or defy Jinnah. Among other things, the 'participation of the Punjab, breadbasket of India in the war effort' had made the Unionist Party 'very unpopular'. See Jaffrelot, 'Islamic Identity and Ethnic Tensions', 13-14.

65. In this sense, Sugata Bose and Ayesha Jalal were not right in arguing that 'the fundamental flaw in Jinnah's strategy was his lack of effective control over his followers in the Muslim-majority provinces.' Sugata Bose and Ayesha Jalal, *Modern South Asia: History, Culture and Political Economy* (Lahore: Sang-e-Meel, 1998), 193. In fact, Jinnah not only taught these Muslim-majority leaders 'a lesson, but also issued a warning to the viceroy, who preferred to deal with Sikandar rather than with Jinnah'. Herman Kulke and Dietmar Rothermund, *A History of India* (London: Routledge, 1999), 285.

66. Jahan Ara Shahnawaz refused to resign on the plea that the Muslims 'who had been 72 per cent in the army, had already been reduced to 52 per cent and it was essential that at least one should remain there to safeguard their interests in the armed forces.' How naïve and opportunistic this stance was can be gauged by the fact that soon she was forced to concede: 'I did my best to safeguard Muslim interests, but in spite of that, the percentage of Muslims in the army was further reduced to thirty-five and my apprehensions proved correct'. Jahan Ara Shahnawaz, *Father and Daughter,* 163-4. Jahan Ara Shahnawaz was expelled from the League. However, she rejoined it and contributed significantly to the League cause and Pakistan during the crucial 1945–46 elections.

67. *Quaid-i-Azam Papers,* F/353, 38.(Italics for emphasis). Obviously, the result was that Jinnah's 'stock soared in the province and Sikandar became powerless to resist the popularity of the Pakistan slogan.' Samad, *A Nation in Turmoil,* 74. For a perspective on Sikandar Hayat Khan's relations with Jinnah, in spite of his affiliations with the Unionists and the British see, Iftikhar H. Malik, *Sikandar Hayat Khan: A Political Biography* (Islamabad: National Institute of Historical and Cultural Research, 1985).

68. See Punjab Legislative Assembly Debates, 11 March 1941 (25 February to 11 March 1941), Vol. XVI, *Official Report* (Lahore: 1942), 329-362. Cited in Menon, *Transfer of Power in India,* App. I, esp. 454-5 (Italics original).

69. Gopal, *Sir Chotu Ram,* 123.

70. Waheed Ahmad, *Letters of Mian Fazl-i-Husain,* 528.

71. Ikram Ali Malik, ed., *A Book of Readings on the History of the Punjab, 1799–1947* (Lahore: Research Society of Pakistan, 1970), 495.

72. Ian Talbot, 'Jinnah: Role Model for Future Generations of Pakistanis', *South Asian History Academic Paper 1,* University of Leicester, 2001, 5. In May 1944, Khizar Hayat Khan was expelled from the League and was publicly denounced as a 'traitor' and '*Kafir*'. For a detailed discussion of his relations with Jinnah, the

League, and the demand for Pakistan see, Ian Talbot, *Khizr Tiwana: The Punjab Unionist Party and the Partition of India* (Surrey: Curzon Press, 1996), esp. Ch. 7, 'Sailing in Two Boats,' 111-28.

73. Samad, *A Nation in Turmoil*, 75. There were many Unionists who had hastened to join the League. As Craig Baxter explained it: 'Opportunism seems to have vied with conviction as the elections approached, and many who had been elected as Unionists in 1936–37 swtiched their allegiance to the Muslim League at the last moment.' Craig Baxter, 'Union or Partition: Some Aspects of Politics in the Punjab, 1936–45', in Ziring, *Pakistan: The Long View*, 60.

74. In spite of its overwhelming success in the elections, the League could not muster a majority in the assembly, and thus, form a government. Under Section 93, Governor rule was imposed on the province. The League was left with no option but to take the extra-constitutional route of civil disobedience to campaign for its Pakistan demand.

75. Jalal, *Sole Spokesman*, 263.

76. See, for instance, Gordon, *Bengal*, 285; and Shamsul Hasan Collection, Vol. IV. Also see Ispahani's letter to Jinnah in ibid., Vol. III, Bengal, F/33.

77. Barbara Metcalf called them 'the reformist ulama.' Barbara Daly Metcalf, *Islamic Revival in British India: Deoband, 1860–1900* (Princeton: Princeton University Press, 1982), 12. For a detailed discussion of the founding principles of the Dar-ul-Ulum also see, Faruqi, *Deoband School and the Demand for Pakistan*, 25-26. For the rise and role of the Barelvi ulama in politics in general and in the final phase of the Pakistan movement, see, in particular, Mujeeb Ahmad, *Jam'iyyat 'Ulama-i-Pakistan, 1948–1979* (Islamabad: National Institute of Historical and Cultural Research, 1993).

78. Husain Ahmad Madani, *Naqsh-i-Hayat*, Vol. II (Urdu) (Deoband: Maktaba-i-Diniya, 1954), 71; and Muhammad Miyan, *Ulama-i-Haq aur unke Mujahidana Karnamay*, Vols. I and II (Urdu) (Delhi: Delhi Printing Works, 1946).

79. According to Metcalf, Syed Ahmad Khan's 'modernism' was 'not a simple imitation of Western ideas but had its roots in indigenous movements of reform.' Metcalf, *Islamic Revival in British India*, 323.

80. For some details see, I.H. Qureshi, *Ulema in Politics*, 245-56, 310. On Maulana Ubaidullah Sindhi's role in particular see, *Maulana Ubaidullah Sindhi ki Sargarzesht-i-Kabul* (Urdu), ed., Ghulam Mustafa Khan (Islamabad: National Institute of Historical and Cultural Research, 1980). Also see, O'Dwyer, *India as I Knew it*, 178.

81. Muhammad Miyan, *Jamiat-ul-Ulama Kiya Hay?*, Vol. II (Urdu) (Delhi: Jamiat-ul-Ulama, 1946), 16-44. The Ulama of Deoband, and particularly those associated with the Jamiat-ul-Ulama-i-Hind, were the most active group in Indian politics, and hence the present emphasis on their role in Indian Muslim politics. *Ulama* from other institutions like Firangi Mahal and Nadvat-ul-Ulama of Lucknow were active in the Khilafat movement, but subsequently chose to withdraw from active politics. In the 1940s, a section of these *Ulama* became active again and went on to support Jinnah and the demand for Pakistan.

82. In spite of all this deference and respect, the Maulana failed to 'secure the position of the *Imamul Hind* (religious head of the Indian Muslims), which he really sought during this period'. Syeda Saiyidain Hameed, *Islamic Seal on India's*

Independence, Abul Kalam Azad—A Fresh Look (Karachi: Oxford University Press, 1998), 102-3. (Italics added).

83. Azad, *India Wins Freedom*, 2. Interestingly, Maulana Azad was educated at home, and never went to any 'madrasa'. He did not have a university education either. He never got a degree from Al-Azhar. See, ibid., 2-7.

84. Mahadeo Desai, *Maulana Abul Kalam Azad* (Agra: Shivalal Agarwala & Co., 1946), 54-55. The book is essentially a biographical memoir, based on answers given by Maulana Azad himself to a number of questions asked by the author. Also see, Maulana Abul Kalam Azad, *Mazameen-i-Azad* (Urdu) (Lahore: Data Publishers, 1978), 155-56.

85. Desai, *Maulana Abul Kalam Azad*, 35-38.

86. A.B. Rajput, *Maulana Abul Kalam Azad* (Lahore: Lion Press, 1946), 53.

87. Desai, *Maulana Abul Kalam Azad*, 69. Islam, Maulana Azad insisted, 'did not recognize the artificial affiliations of race, country, colour, religion and language. It called men to the one and only relationship of humanism and the natural bonds of brotherhood'. Syeda Hameed, *Islamic Seal*, 142,

88. Desai, *Maulana Abul Kalam Azad*, 74.

89. Mushirul Haq, *Muslim Politics in Modern India, 1857–1947* (Meerut: Meenkshi Prakashan, 1970), 73-76. Also see for a more detailed and critical evaluation of Azad's religious views, Chaudhary Habib Ahmad, *Tehrik-i-Pakistan aur Nationalist Ulama* (Urdu) (Lahore: al Biyan, 1966), 232-37.

90. See Maulana Azad's Presidential Address to the Karachi Session of the Jamiat, 31 March–1 April 1931, in Parveen Rozina, ed., *Jamiat-ul-Ulama-i-Hind: Dastawezat Markazi Ijlasha-i-Aam, 1919–1945*, Vol. II (Urdu) (Islamabad: National Institute of Historical and Cultural Research, 1981), 605. In 1929, Maulana Azad also helped establish the All-India Nationalist Muslim Party to bring all the 'nationalist' Muslims together, but it failed to match 'the charismatic quality of the Muslim League'. Syeda Hameed, *Islamic Seal*, 144.

91. Azad, *India Wins Freedom*, 22.

92. Haq, *Muslim Politics in Modern India*, 94.

93. Maulana Abul Kalam Azad, *Tehrik Nazm-i-Jamaat* (Urdu) (Lahore: Nazir Sons, 1977), 21-22. Also see, Ghulam Rasul Mehr, ed., *Naqsh-i-Azad* (Urdu) (Lahore: Sheikh Ghulam Ali & Sons, 1959), 343-45; Rozina, *Jamiat-ul-Ulama-i-Hind*, Vol. II, 701-72. See the text of proposed duties and obligations assigned by the Jamiat to the *Imam* in Ibid., Vol. I (Islamabad: National Institute of Historical and Cultural Research, 1980), Appendix B, 467-79.

94. Hardy, *Partners in Freedom*, 32; and I.H. Qureshi, *Ulema in Politics*, 328-29.

95. Desai, *Maulana Abul Kalam Azad*, 123.

96. Ibid., 115.

97. Azad, *India Wins Freedom*, 152.

98. Ibid., 150, 152. It was the same old devolution of power to the provinces formula, with little appeal for the Muslim masses after the terrible experience of Congress rule in the provinces from 1937 to 1939. But then, Maulana Azad could not do better. He represented Congress interests, simple and pure, thus could not offer anything new or different.

99. Ahmad, *Speeches and Writings*, Vol. I, 33.

100. Desai, *Maulana Abul Kalam Azad*, 117.

101. Ibid., 115-16.

102. Ibid., 116.

103. Pirzada, *Quaid-i-Azam Jinnah's Correspondence*, 33. Jinnah rejected the Congress criticism against this rebuff to Maulana Azad, and insisted: 'Every word that I have used is absolutely true and the Congress leaders know it. His innocent looking telegram was a pre-meditated move to compel the Muslim League to recognise him and negotiate with him the Hindu–Muslim question…*the Hindu–Muslim question cannot be negotiated between a Muslim and a Muslim….*' Quaid-i-Azam Papers, F/335, 91 (Italics added). Earlier, too, in October 1939, when Maulana Azad expressed his 'wish' to meet him during his stay in Delhi then, Jinnah emphatically told him: '…Cannot talk with you regarding Hindu-Muslim settlement….' *Quaid-i-Azam Papers,* F/17, 33-34. Even the Viceroy, Wavell, who respected Azad as 'an old-fashioned scholar with pleasant manners,' doubted 'if he contributes very much to Congress policy.' He felt that 'his main object is to get even with Jinnah and the League Muslims who despise him as a paid servant of the Congress.' Mansergh, *Transfer of Power,* Vol. V, 1262.

104. Majumdar, *Jinnah and Gandhi,* 169.

105. Rajput, *Maulana Abul Kalam Azad,* 152. Officially, Gandhi resigned his membership of the party in October 1934 session of the Congress held at Bombay.

106. Ibid., 178.

107. In fact, he claimed: 'Basically it was the same as the one sketched in my statement of 15 April.' Azad, *India Wins Freedom,* 156.

108. Ibid., 164.

109. Azad, *India Wins Freedom,* 162. That statement in itself showed how much out of touch Maulana Azad was with the thinking in the Congress and Gandhi in particular. As Gandhi wrote to Nehru about him: 'I do not understand him nor does he understand me. We are drifting apart on the Hindu-Muslim question as well as other questions…we have to face facts. Therefore I suggest that the Maulana should relinquish Presidentship….' Cited in Wolpert, *Gandhi's Passion,* 203. In fact, Maulana Azad was replaced by none other than Nehru. He remained 'little more than the token Congress Muslim that Jinnah had always claimed he was'. French, *Liberty or Death,* 262.

110. I.H. Qureshi, *Ulema in Politics,* 308.

111. Quoted in Rajput, *Abul Kalam Azad,* 201-3. That perhaps explained why Maulana Azad 'endured the garland of shoes flung at him by students at the Aligarh Station in 1947, to express their anger at his stand against demanding a separate homeland for the Muslims'. Syeda Hameed, *Islamic Seal,* 290.

112. Indeed, in the estimate of Syeda Hameed, Maulana Azad 'lost the battle for both principles to which he had dedicated his entire life – Muslim advancement and Hindu–Muslim unity'. Ibid., xxii. In a similar vein, Ian Henderson Douglas wrote, 'Azad has staked his whole political career on the hope of a united India—and lost.' Ian Henderson Douglas, *Abul Kalam Azad: An Intellectual and Religious Biography,* ed., Gail Minault and Christian W. Troll (Delhi: Oxford University Press, 1988), 237.

113. Aziz Ahmad, *Islamic Modernism,* 190.

114. Maulana Hussain Ahmad Madani, *Muttahida Qaumiat aur Islam* (Urdu) (Delhi, n.p., n.d.). Relevant passage were discussed in Habib Ahmad, *Tehrik-i-Pakistan*, 274–344.

115. Aziz Ahmad, *Islamic Modernism*, 192.

116. See the Maulana's Presidential addresses at Jaunpur Session of the Jamiat held on 7–9 June 1940, and at the Suharanpur Session of the Jamiat held on 4–6 May 1945, in Rozina, *Jamiat-ul-Ulama-i-Hind*, Vol. II, 693, 790-1.

117. Muhammad Qasim Zaman, *The Ulama in Contemporary Islam: Custodians of Change* (Princeton: Princeton University Press, 2002), 32.

118. Allama Shabbir Ahmad Usmani broke with the Jamiat-ul-Ulama-i-Hind led by Maulana Madani in late 1945 to form his own political party, the Jamiat-ul-Ulama-i-Islam, which was joined by several prominent ulama. The Allama was a strong votary of Muslim separatism and had always preferred the League over the Congress even in the days when he was formally associated with the Jamiat-ul-Ulama-i-Hind. To dissuade the Allama from supporting the League, a Jamiat delegation led by Maulana Madani met him on 1 December 1945. The Allama 'did not yield,' and instead, advised the delegation to join the League 'and work for the collective betterment of the Indian Muslims.' Sayyid A.S. Pirzada, *The Politics of the Jamiat Ulema-i-Islam, Pakistan, 1971–1977* (Karachi: Oxford University Press, 2000), 11.

119. Anwaral Hassan Sherkoti, comp., *Khutbat-i-Usmani* (Urdu) (Lahore: Nazir Sons, 1972), 75. Allama Shabbir Ahmad Usmani indeed insisted that the very idea of a single community or composite nationalism was against *Shariah*. Ibid., 66.

120. Zaman, *Ulama in Contemporary Islam*, 43. Maulana Zafar Ahmad Usmani was the Vice President of the Jamiat-ul-Ulama-i-Islam.

121. Sherwani, *Speeches, Writings and Statements of Iqbal*, 257.

122. Ibid., 257-59. Maulana Madani denied that he ever meant to advise the Muslims to accept territorial nationalism. Iqbal decided to conclude the debate. See Iqbal and Taloot's letters in *Ihsan* (Lahore), reproduced in Habib Ahmad, *Tehrik-i-Pakistan*, 244-70. Maulana Abul-Ala Maudoodi, an Islamic scholar and the founder of the Jamaat-i-Islami (in 1941) felt that Maulana Madani 'had little understanding of what nationalism meant' or what the Congress meant by it. In fact, he argued that Maulana Madani was 'thinking more in terms of a 'confederation' (*wifaq, tahaluf*) of different autonomous nations in an independent India'. In his opinion, in combining these 'two very different conceptions and, in doing so,' the Maulana was 'pushing the Muslim community along a path of destruction'. See Zaman, *Ulama in Contemporary Islam*, 35.

123. Mujahid, *Studies in Interpretation*, 430-1.

124. Ibid., 431.

125. Ibid. This aspect of the Jamiat–League–Jinnah relationship has been systematically argued in Mujahid's *Studies in Interpretation*, App. I, esp., 430-32. Also see, A.S. Pirzada, *Jamiat Ulema-i-Islam Pakistan*, 3.

126. Hardy, *Partners in Freedom*, 35.

127. Haq, *Muslim Politics in Modern India*, 155.

128. I.H. Qureshi, *Ulema in Politics*, 329-30.

129. Zaman, *Ulama in Contemporary Islam*, 35. The reference is to the rise of Hindu nationalism in the late 1980s and the 1990s. For a critical discussion on the

Hindutva movement, the Ayodha movement, and the 'prejudice against Muslims' see, Christophe Jaffrelot, 'The Rise of Hindu Nationalism and the Marginalisation of Muslims in India Today', in Amita Shastri and A. Jeyaratnam Wilson, eds., *The Post Colonial States of South Asia: Democracy, Identity, Development and Security* (Richmond, Surrey: Curzon Press, 2001).

130. Ishtiaq Hussain Qureshi, *The Muslim Community of Indo-Pakistan Subcontinent, 610–1947* (The Hague: Mouton & Co., 1962), 336.

131. Haq, *Muslim Politics in Modern India*, 116.

132. Hardy, *Partners in Freedom*, 38. According to Samad, this also meant that Maulana Madani, 'who had so vociferously argued against the two-nation theory as divisive and played into the hands of British imperialism', was soon 'modifying his position by proposing an alternative strategy to the strong unitary structure advanced by the Congress'. Samad, *A Nation in Turmoil*, 67.

133. Hardy, *Muslim of British India*, 244. Also see, Mujahid, *Studies in Interpretation*, 399, f/n., for a more detailed comment.

134. See Waheed Ahmed, ed., *Quaid-i-Azam Mohammed Ali Jinnah Speeches: Indian Legislative Assembly, 1935–1947* (Karachi: Quaid-i-Azam Academy, 1991), 285-320. For a useful discussion of the Shariat Act see, Dushka H. Saiyid, *Muslim Women of the British Punjab: From Seclusion to Politics* (London: Macmillan, 1998), 29-35.

135. Gilmartin, *Empire and Islam*, 172.

136. Ibid., 174.

137. Faruqi, *Deoband School and the Demand for Pakistan*, 124.

138. Z.H. Zaidi, ed., *Jinnah Papers*, Vol. I, Part I, xxv-xxvi.

139. Waseem, *Politics and the State in Pakistan*, 85.

140. Zaman, *Ulama in Contemporary Islam*, 47. Pakistan's cause was further helped by the 'scholarly *fatwa*' pronounced by Mufti Muhammad Shafi Deobandi (1897–1976), in which he ruled that Pakistan was 'the only Islamic cause open to the Muslims in the light of the Quran and Sunnah.' Still, the fact remained that although 'a strong group of Deobandis supported the demand for Pakistan...the majority of the school was aligned with the Congress'. A.S. Pirzada, *Jamiat Ulema-i-Islam Pakistan*, 9, 11.

5 The Formula: A Separate Homeland for the Muslims

Although Jinnah had offered several formulas in the past such as the Lucknow Pact of 1916 and the Fourteen Points of 1929, to name the two most important ones, to deal with difficulties faced by the Muslims, the Muslim situation, by the late 1930s, was far more difficult and distressful. Jinnah had to offer something different, radically different. He had to offer a formula that would guarantee the Muslims political power, security, and freedom. This was necessary to ensure their salvation. The formula was also necessary to secure his own leadership. The formula could validate, indeed enhance, his charisma as a charismatic leader of the Muslims.

The way Jinnah's mind was working was indicated in the article he wrote in January 1940 for the *Time and Tide*, which has been earlier discussed claiming that there were 'two nations' in India, but was also discernable in a host of statements after the Lucknow session of the Muslim League in 1937. These statements emphasized a dynamic relationship between religion, culture, society, and politics, as it affected the future of Muslims in the country. For instance, addressing the Calcutta session of the League in April 1939, Jinnah declared:

> Muslims have made it clear more than once that, besides the question of religion, culture, language and personal laws, there is another question, equally of life and death for them, and that their future destiny and fate are dependent upon their securing definitely their political rights, their due share in the national life, the government, and the administration of the country. They will fight for it till the last ditch, and all the dreams and notions of Hindu Raj must be abandoned. They will not be submerged or dominated, and they will not surrender....[1]

This declaration was the very essence of the Muslim separatist political movement in India founded by Syed Ahmad Khan and subsequently challenged and reinstated by Maulana Mohammed Ali and reinforced by Allama Iqbal. Jinnah, after having exhausted all the avenues to Hindu-Muslim unity or settlement eventually adopted this separatist tradition to build the edifice of Muslim nationalism. He went on to propound the 'two-nation' theory.[2]

Historically, the Muslims and Hindus had moved in their separate spheres of life and followed separatist traditions, notwithstanding the efforts of many Muslim rulers and centuries of contact and living together. However, what was implicit in this separatism became more pronounced and clear in Syed Ahmad Khan's formulation aimed at mobilizing the Muslims to the reality of the British rule in India. A scion of the old nobility who had personally witnessed the demise of the Mughal Empire, Syed Ahmad Khan strongly argued that the system of government being introduced by the British in India 'would consign the Muslim minority to permanent domination by the Hindus'.[3] Given the rise and role of the Indian National Congress in his days, Syed Ahmad Khan was further convinced that the political interests of the Muslims were different from the Hindus. It was unlikely that the Hindus would promote Muslim interests in the political life and processes of India. Indeed, he presciently believed that antagonism and conflict would grow as the two communities, especially its educated classes, adjusted to new ground realities. As he told Shakespeare, then Benares's Commissioner (1867): 'The opposition of those people who regard themselves as educated is not yet fierce, but in the future it will increase'.[4] Years later, Syed Ahmad Khan predicted that the Muslims and the Hindus might not even agree to a common government of India:

> Now suppose that all the English…were to leave India…then who would be ruler of India? Is it possible that under these circumstances two nations—the Mohammadan and Hindu—could sit on the same throne and remain equal in power? Most certainly not. It is necessary that one of them should conquer the other and thrust it down. To hope that both could remain equal is to desire the impossible and the inconceivable.[5]

Syed Ahmad Khan thus emerged as a founder of the Muslim separatist political movement in modern India.[6]

Maulana Mohammed Ali followed Syed Ahmad Khan but only after he unsuccessfully explored the vistas of the Hindu–Muslim 'entente cordiale' of the Khilafat–Non-cooperation years.[7] However, Mohammed Ali's shift from the 'separatist' legacy of Syed Ahmad Khan reflected the futility of reliance on the British and indicated that the Congress no longer aroused the kind of hostility that it had done in the past. A new generation of Muslims who had received a modern education similar to their Hindu counterparts had emerged and they were equally keen to find a place for their community in association with others in India. They suspected British intentions and policies. For instance, in the treatment meted out to Turkey and the *Khilafat*, they saw a clear instance of 'Western imperialism' in general, and British imperialism in particular, bent upon 'conquering and destroying' their culture and identity.[8] Thus, they began to appreciate the active, even violent, opposition of the Congress to the British. As Mohammed Ali put it: 'we will not lose by conferring with the Hindus as to the future, but by sitting with folded hands and allowing others to settle the future for us'.[9]

The resultant Khilafat–Non-cooperation movement, however, turned out to be a fiasco. The Muslims and Hindus had little in common except an instant urge to forge a common front against the British. Indeed, one could very clearly discern divergence in the concerns of the two communities that were too pronounced to auger well for the future. Mohammed Ali had joined hands with the Hindus, after a bitter experience at the hands of the British, to save the sole surviving independent Muslim empire, the Ottoman Empire, which represented the temporal greatness of Islam and the Muslim world. For Gandhi, it was essentially the need to mobilize the Muslims in his fight against the British, necessitated by the Amritsar massacre of 1919 and other 'Punjab wrongs'.

The failure of the efforts to save the Khilafat convinced Mohammed Ali and other Muslim leaders that they should, first and foremost, concentrate upon their own survival as a community in the political system. Mohammed Ali's inherent loyalties to the Muslim group surfaced. He swung back in line with the separatist political movement launched by Syed Ahmad Khan. He publicly snapped his ties with the Congress and Gandhi. He strongly criticized the Nehru Report and claimed that it was 'inconsistent with the independent spirit of Islam'.[10] He also appealed to the Muslims not to participate in the Civil Disobedience Movement of 1930. 'We refuse to join Mr Gandhi', he declared, 'because his movement is not a movement for the complete independence of India but for making the seventy millions of Indian Musalmans dependents [sic] of the Hindu Mahasbaha....'[11] But Mohammed Ali was still not in conflict with 'Indian nationalism'. As he gave vent to his feelings at the Fourth Plenary session of the Round Table Conference on 9 November 1930, 'I belong to two circles of equal size, but which are not concentric. One is India and the other the Muslim world.... We belong to these two circles, each of more than 300 millions, and we can leave neither'.[12] It was left to Allama Iqbal, 'the poet of Islamic reawakening in India in the 20th century',[13] as Mohammed Ali himself described him, to reinforce Muslim separatist political movement and thus help formulate the concept of Muslim nationalism, leading to the demand for a separate Muslim state.[14]

Allama Iqbal's formulation was essentially philosophical and intellectual. Iqbal argued that there were no dichotomies in Islam between religion and state, matter and spirit, personal ethics and political life. Islam was an integrated 'religio-political system'.[15] Was it possible, then, he went on to ask in his now famous presidential address at the Allahabad session of the All-India Muslim League in 1930, 'to retain Islam as an ethical ideal and reject it as a polity in favour of national politics in which religious attitude is not permitted to play any part?'[16] The answer was obviously no. In his estimate, 'the religious ideal of Islam...is organically related to the social order, which it has created. The rejection of the one will eventually involve the rejection of the other'. The issue, he emphasized, was all the more relevant in Indian context where the Muslims were a minority, and thus could hardly hope to see Islam as a principle of solidarity in national life. Therefore, he proposed, the only solution of the problem was to allow the Muslims 'full and free development' of their 'own culture and tradition' in those areas where they constituted majorities, especially in the Punjab, the North-West Frontier Province, Sindh and Balochistan.[17] In this sense, there is considerable force in the argument that the demand 'for a separate Muslim homeland was predicated not on Western ideas of nationalism, but rather grounded in the traditional Islamic view that political power was essential to enforce the ethical ideals of the sharia'.[18]

Iqbal elaborated his ideas and concerns further in his letters to Jinnah in 1936–37. In his letter of 28 May 1937, for instance, he told

Jinnah that 'the enforcement and development of the Shariat of Islam[19]...[would be] impossible in this country without a free Muslim state or states'.[20] Again, in his letter of 21 June 1937, he suggested, 'the only way to a peaceful India is a redistribution of the country on the lines of racial, religious and linguistic affinities'.[21] Why, he asked, 'should not the Muslims of North-West India and Bengal be considered as nations entitled to self-determination just as other nations in India and outside India are?'[22] The Act of 1935, with its idea of a 'single Indian federation is completely hopeless'.[23] Therefore, he stressed, 'A separate Federation of Muslim Provinces...is the only course by which we can secure a peaceful India and save Muslims from the domination of non-Muslims'.[24]

Thus, Iqbal emerged as the intellectual guide for the Muslim destiny in India.[25] His ideas influenced Jinnah in particular. They helped Jinnah in his search for a formula to alleviate the distress of the Muslims. However, Iqbal did not live long enough to see the final shape of the formula. He breathed his last on 21 April 1938, after a protracted illness. But Iqbal did identify Jinnah as the man who could show the way out of the difficult situation. In his opinion, Jinnah not only understood the problem very well, especially its constitutional dimension, but was also 'the only Muslim in India today to whom the community has a right to look up for safe guidance through the storm which is coming to North-West India, and perhaps to the whole of India'.[26] Jinnah was, of course, prepared and willing to lead the Muslims through the 'storm'. He had already assumed the mantle of charismatic leadership. However, Jinnah felt that the idea of a separate federation of Muslim provinces was not helpful any more. It was intrinsically tied to Indian Union, and thus not capable of guaranteeing power and security to the Muslims. The distressful situation of Muslim India required a new and radical formula for the salvation of the Muslims, a formula that will not only save them from the stranglehold of Hindu majority rule but will also ensure them a safe and secure future as an independent political community. Thus, on 22 March 1940, Jinnah demanded a separate homeland for the Muslims at the Lahore session of the Muslim League, which was attended by tens of thousands of Muslims from all parts and provinces of India, the largest Muslim gathering to come together so far.[27] On 23 March, a resolution to that effect was moved, and on 24 March it was adopted as the Lahore

Resolution.[28] Jinnah's formula had become the official creed of the Muslim League.

Before we proceed with a detailed analysis of this formula of a separate homeland, a closer examination of the 'timing' will not be out of place here. This is important because of the considerable emphasis laid on this point by Ayesha Jalal in her systematic study of Jinnah and the Lahore Resolution. Jalal offers a number of propositions. First, 'The timing of the Lahore resolution had been dictated by British needs, which in their turn had been made more urgent by Congress's demands [for independence and a constituent assembly]'.[29] Secondly, Linlithgow pressed Jinnah to state the League's 'constructive policy' as a counterweight to the Congress's demand for independence and a constituent assembly.[30] Thirdly, Linlithgow's call to Muslims to produce a 'constructive policy' was an opportunity for Jinnah, the potential spokesman for Muslims at the centre....'[31] Finally, 'This ambassador of Hindu–Muslim unity now seemed the best guarantee the British could find in India against a united political demand'.[32] Apart from the fact that Jalal based her case on immediate causes and did not see the Hindu–Muslim problem in a larger, historical perspective, taking into account the Muslim separatist political movement of Syed Ahmad Khan, Maulana Mohammed Ali and Allama Iqbal, prominent Muslim leaders in British India, or indeed through the distressful situation of Muslim India as argued here, her argument needs careful analysis.

This need for analysis is further augmented by a persistent charge of attributing the demand for a separate homeland, or Pakistan, to the British, especially in the accounts of Indian historians. For instance, Tara Chand, the official historian of the freedom movement from the Indian side has claimed: 'whatever other factors might have contributed to the emergence of the demand for Pakistan, the substantive cause which made it effective was the will of the British rulers'.[33] Ramji Lal asserted that one important factor 'responsible' for the adoption of the Lahore Resolution was 'the role played by the British government....' The government 'was not ready to hand over power to the Indians. In fact, it was bent upon thwarting the issue of independence and deliberately following the policy of the division of India by encouraging disruptive forces, especially the Muslim League and Jinnah'.[34] Similarly, Anita Inder Singh argued that the Lahore Resolution suited the British interests very well. The British were happy to see the Muslim demand as 'the answer to Patna and Ramgarh' sessions that had called for immediate independence, showing 'how deep is the gulf and how little the prospect of these two parties getting together in the present circumstances'.[35] In a similar vein, Uma Kaura noted that: 'Linlithgow was jubilant at the adoption of the Partition Resolution. Obviously he thought that he could use it as a handy tool against the Congress demand for independence'.[36]

In regard to the first assertion, about the timing of the Lahore Resolution being 'dictated by British needs', and the 'Congress's demands', it cannot be denied that the Muslims themselves had more pressing needs than the British at that time. The Congress, in its Ramgarh session of March 1940, had not only demanded 'complete independence' for India but also explicitly stated that a 'permanent solution' of the communal problem shall await the verdict of the Constituent Assembly *after* Indian independence.[37] This was indeed very distressful for the Muslims for they had consistently insisted that the communal problem be resolved prior to independence. Jinnah's numerous statements to this effect, some of which are cited in this study, are self-evident. In his presidential address at the Lahore session of the League in May 1924, for instance, Jinnah declared: 'I am almost inclined to say that India will get Dominion Responsible Government the day the Hindus and the Muhammadans are united. *Swaraj* is an almost interchangeable term with Hindu–Muslim unity'.[38] Two decades later, in 1944, after the Lahore Resolution was adopted and the movement for Pakistan was in full swing, Jinnah still insisted, as he told Gandhi on 11 September 1944:

You say 'the first condition of the exercise of the right of self-determination is achieving Independence by the joint action of all the parties and groups composing India. If such joint action is unfortunately impossible then, too, I must fight with the assistance of such elements as can be brought together'. This in my opinion is, as I have repeatedly said, putting the cart before the horse, and is generally opposed to the policy and declarations of the All-India Muslim League.... In order to achieve the freedom and independence of the people of India, it is essential, in the first instance, that there should be a Hindu–Muslim settlement.[39]

The fact of the matter was that, given his experience of the complexities of politics, especially after 1937–39, Jinnah could not trust the Congress any more, and especially after India attained independence. He had made so many attempts at a Hindu–Muslim settlement, some of them recounted here, but to no avail. He saw no point in pursuing the matter. Indeed, he felt, there was neither the time nor justification for further dealings with the Congress. But, more importantly, he could not agree to the idea of the Constituent Assembly proposed by the Congress for it meant a permanent ratio of,

> three to one, about which the Musalmans say that they will never be able, in that way by the counting of heads, to come to any agreement which will be real agreement from the hearts, which will enable us to work as friends and, therefore, this idea of a Constituent Assembly is objectionable....[40]

Thus, the formulation of a viable alternative to the Congress demand for complete independence and a constituent assembly was essentially the need of the hour for the Muslims. In fact, the League's constitutional and foreign affairs committees were already deliberating upon various schemes to find a way out. As early as 8 April 1939, Jinnah had personally assured the Muslims that the League 'could produce a scheme which would be in the best interest of Muslim India'.[41]

To compound Muslim difficulties, there was Congress threat of 'civil disobedience' in case the British did not concede their demand. On 28 February 1940, at Patna, the Congress Working Committee had passed a resolution demanding independence and threatening to resort to civil disobedience as soon as necessary arrangements for the purpose could be made. The Ramgarh session of the Congress not only approved the Patna resolution with a large majority, but, in fact, encouraged Gandhi to initiate the campaign of individual *satyagarha* or individual civil disobedience. The Muslims got anxious. 'Why all these machinations?', Jinnah wondered, and went on to ask,

> ...why all these methods to coerce the British to overthrow the Musalmans? Why this declaration of non-cooperation? Why this threat of civil disobedience? And why fight for a Constituent Assembly for the sake of ascertaining whether the Musalmans agree or do not agree.[42]

Further complicating the situation was the Muslim fear that the British, bowing to Congress pressure or of their own volition, may once again invite the Congress to form governments in the provinces. As late as January 1940, the British remained eager to revive the 'federal' scheme as given in the 1935 Act, much to the consternation of Jinnah and his Muslim followers. Jinnah had publicly proclaimed on 25 December 1939 that: 'The greatest day of my life was when I heard that the Federation scheme was suspended and a still greater moment will be when it is definitely buried'.[43] However, the British were still hopeful. In spite of his apparently unsuccessful meeting with Congress leadership in early February 1940, Viceroy Lord Linlithgow, 'never appeared to break with Gandhiji, always leaving the impression that he was going to see him again before long and that negotiations would be resumed'.[44] The Muslims naturally feared that 'Congress governments might return to office at any moment'.[45] This was also borne out by the evidence furnished by Maulana Azad and Kanji Dwarkadas, a close associate of Congress leadership. According to Maulana Azad, Gandhi 'seemed convinced that the British Government was ready and willing to recognise India as free if India offered full cooperation in the war effort'.[46] Dawarkadas identified two most prominent leaders of the Congress, Chakravarti Rajagopalachari (1879–1972) and Sardar Vallabhbhai Patel (1875–1950), as particularly desirous of a settlement with the British. Writing of his meeting with Sardar Patel on 11 August 1940, he recalled, 'Sardar Patel then took me aside and told me that it should be brought to the notice of the Viceroy that the Congress, and with it the whole country, would help the British Government to win the war if the British Government satisfied Congress demands'.[47] Patel acknowledged the difficulties: 'Our going back to office does not mean peaceful times for us. It would only mean our getting more abuse from some of our own left-wingers and we shall have a difficult job dealing with problems of internal security as well as of the war effort'.[48] But, he still sought 'a settlement if the [8] August proposals were amended to a certain extent'.[49] The 8 August 1940 proposals conceded the Congress demand for an Indian Constituent Assembly but it was to meet after the war was over. Indeed, Dwarkadas arranged for Patel's meeting with the Viceroy, but was called off at the last moment (by the latter) after it became known that Congress President (Maulana Azad) had refused to put Congress case before the British. Patel was 'disappointed.'[50] Dwarkadas was more disappointed. 'What a great opportunity', he wrote, 'was thus lost for a settlement which foundered on the rocks of pride, prestige and suspicion!'[51]

Indeed, the possibility of the British and the Congress striking a deal was not only alive in the comparatively calm year of 1940, it was also germane in the tense period following the 'Quit India' resolution of 8 August 1942, ironically enough, at the hands of Gandhi, the chief architect and guide of the massive civil disobedience movement itself. In fact, Gandhi was prepared 'to meet to negotiate with the Viceroy after the passing of the 8 August resolution!'[52] However, British strategy of a preemptive attack to shock the Congress into acquiescence foreclosed his options.[53] Thus, Jinnah's call on 23 March 1940, for a separate homeland, was dictated by urgent Muslim needs in a situation where the Muslims found themselves at the losing end.

As to the charge that Linlithgow pressed Jinnah to state the League's 'constructive policy'[54] as a counterweight to the Congress's demand for independence and a constituent assembly, two things need to be understood at the very outset. First, the Congress was far from a serious threat to British rule in March 1940, when the Lahore Resolution was adopted by the Muslim League. Although the young radicals in the Congress, spearheaded by Subhas Chandra Bose, were ready for a confrontation with the British even before the Second World War the majority of Congress leaders were not contemplating a showdown with the authorities for several reasons. The Congress was in disarray, caused by both internal dissensions and external realities. Bose, Congress President in 1938, had stood for re-election and even managed to win the presidential election against a candidate officially endorsed by the Congress Working Committee and personally promoted by Gandhi. The result was factional infighting in the Congress between the 'old Guard' and the radicals. By 1940, the old Guard had managed to re-establish its dominance in the party but they were not in a position to put pressure on the British in India. Thus, between 1937 and 1939, wrote Tomlinson, 'the all-India Congress leaders had been fully occupied by internal problems and had had neither the opportunity nor the power to further the struggle against the British for freedom and independence directly'.[55] Although the war declared by the Viceroy on 3 September 1939 had produced unity within Congress ranks, the Congress was still not ready for a fight with the British. Gandhi understood it very well. 'There is no desire on the part of responsible Congressmen', he wrote to Carl Hearth in London on 13 March 1940, 'to pick a quarrel with the British Government. On the contrary there is keen desire to explore every means of conciliation'.[56] Even after he had taken steps to organize individual civil disobedience, Gandhi was keen to assure the British Government that he did not mean to do any harm to their interests during the war years. 'I protest with all the strength at my command', he wrote in the *Harijan* of 24 April 'that so far as I am concerned I have no desire to embarrass the British, especially at a time when it is a question of life and death with them. All I want Congress to do through civil disobedience is to deny the British Government the moral influence which Congress cooperation would give'.[57] It was only when the 'phoney war in Europe', as an analyst of Congress policy during the war years put it, 'turned into a hot one and when Britain was pushed into a precarious strategic position' that the Congress and the British took a turn away from the 'quietude' into confrontation and clash.[58] But then that was well beyond 23 March 1940, the day the Lahore Resolution was moved.

Secondly, and more importantly, Indian Muslims themselves had been moving towards a separate destiny and goal for a number of years, under the pressure of disquieting events and the growing separatist political movement, especially after the collapse of Khilafat–Non-cooperation movement. The name of 'Pakistan' for the proposed Muslim state was suggested in 1933 by Choudhary Rahmat Ali (1897–1951) and his fellow-students of the Cambridge University. In a pamphlet,[59] *Now or Never: Are we to Live or Perish Forever?*, he explained at length his idea of Pakistan. The Muslims possess 'a separate and distinct nationality from the rest of India, and therefore, they demand the recognition of a separate national status by the grant of a separate Federal Constitution from the rest of India'.[60] In this sense, Rahmat Ali claimed that his demand was different from that of Allama Iqbal, made in his Allahabad address of 1930. As he himself highlighted the difference: 'While he proposed amalgamation of these [Muslim] Provinces into a single state forming a unit of the All-India Federation, we propose that these Provinces should have a separate Federation of their own'.[61]

There were more schemes prepared by Muslim leaders in the subsequent years, and particularly the schemes prepared by Sikandar

Hayat Khan (Premier of the Punjab), Dr Abdul Latif of Hyderabad, Professor Syed Zafar Hasan and Dr Mohammed Afzal Qadri of the Aligarh University, Nawab Sir Shah Nawaz Khan of Mamdot (1883–1942), Abdullah Haroon and Choudhry Khaliquzzaman (1889–1973), received considerable attention.[62] All these schemes provided for a minimal centre, with maximum powers vested in provinces and zones in order to safeguard the separate Muslim interests. Above all these schemes was, of course, Allama Iqbal's idea of a 'Muslim state' within India stated in his Allahabad Address. It was reiterated in his letters to Jinnah during 1936 and 1937, with an emphasis on a separate federation of Muslim provinces, to 'save Muslims from the domination of non-Muslims.' Although at that time Iqbal's ideas failed to move the Muslims to their separate and distinct goal, the intellectual message was always there to inspire and stir them at the right moment. They only had to wait for the Congress rule in 1937–39 to help understand and acclaim the message. The Congress rule had also produced a charismatic leader who could translate this message into action.[63] As M.H. Saiyid described it, 'Iqbal and his followers had tried to place before the Muslims their rightful goal but they could not do it effectively. It required a Jinnah to fulfill the aspirations of a nation and that too at the most psychological moment'.[64]

As regards Linlithgow's 'call to Muslims to produce a 'constructive policy' and hence an 'opportunity for Jinnah', there was all the evidence to suggest that this was more out of contempt than any desire to appease the Muslims or to promote their separatist cause. Linlithgow was responding to Jinnah's severe criticism of the system of government in India in an interview with him on 13 March 1939. Jinnah had told him that he saw 'no solution' to Indian problem and that he was convinced that the system was more a part of the problem than a part of the solution. He lamented that 'he and others who had advocated a reformed system of government' were convinced now 'that the present system would not work and that a mistake had been made in going so far'.[65] But Jinnah did not make any 'positive suggestion for carrying on the government of the country if the present scheme broke down'.[66] Linlithgow chided him to come out with 'constructive policy'. But that did not mean that Linlithgow wanted him to propose the idea of the partition of India. Indeed, when Jinnah, in response to his insistent queries subsequently that if 'he no longer believed in the democratic government for India,' how was India going 'to obtain self-government if not by democracy?' argued that 'the escape from this impasse lay in partition', Linlithgow was not satisfied.[67] He insisted that this was 'not an answer to the question'.[68] But Jinnah remained steadfast and refused to compromise on 'some form of partition of the country' if the British could not offer an acceptable 'solution' of India's 'constitutional' problem.[69]

Linlithgow tried his best to talk Jinnah out of this partition idea. He suggested a few 'possibilities', which included among others that 'there might be some tripartite arrangement by which the presence of His Majesty's Government, in a manner as little out of tune with Indian aspirations as possible, would be needed in India, longer even than some imagined'.[70] However, Jinnah was not convinced and politely but firmly replied,

> ...even here difficulties would arise. He was in favour of a Muslim area run by Muslims.... He was fully aware that this would mean poverty, that the lion's share of the wealth would go to others, but the Muslims would retain their self-respect and their culture and would be able to live their lives in their own way.[71]

Jinnah admitted that his demand might 'be out of tune with the British conception of the future, but it provided the only means of making Muslim existence happy within a particular area....'[72] In the end, Jinnah made it clear to Linlithgow that his views were 'the expression of deep and sincere feeling and that there was no serious division within the Muslim fold with regard to it'.[73] Linlithgow, of course, 'remained non-committal, but he could not dispel the conviction from his mind that the Muslim attitude was undoubtedly hardening'.[74] It is not difficult to judge that Linlithgow's aforementioned comment, at best, as Patrick French suggested, was an instance of 'pragmatic political cynicism'.[75]

How unfounded is the charge of Jinnah's being inspired by Linlithgow is further evidenced by the letter Linlithgow wrote to the Secretary of State Lord Zetland, on 24 March 1940, the day the Lahore Resolution was adopted. 'I do not attach', he wrote, 'too much importance to Jinnah's demand for the carving out of India into an infinite number of so-called 'Dominions''. Indeed, he felt that this 'extreme' and 'preposterous' demand was an attempt on the part of

Jinnah and the Mulim League to free themselves from 'the damaging charge levelled against them that they have no constructive ideas of their own.'[76] Zetland readily agreed: 'I shall be bound to express my dissent from the proposals which have been recently put forward by the All-India Muslim League'.[77] To encourage 'Ulsters in India', he observed, meant 'the wrecking of all that we have been working for a number of years past....'[78] In his speech in the House of Lords on 18 April 1940, he maintained that:

> ...its acceptance would be equivalent to admitting the failure of the devoted efforts of Englishmen and Indians alike over a long period of concentrated striving for those efforts have been based upon the assumption that even in the admitted diversity of India, a measure of political unity could be achieved sufficient to enable India as a whole to take its place as an integral unit in the British Commonwealth of Nations.[79]

Indeed, Zetland was convinced that the partition of India and the creation of a Muslim state were not suited to Britain's long and short-term interests. In his letter to Linlithgow on 18 April, he articulated British perspective of 'the probable destiny of Muslim India' at considerable length:

> I hope that the terms of the reply to Jinnah which I telegraphed to you a few days ago will be sufficient to keep him quiet, though I do not feel by any means sure that this will be so. Indeed the present attitude of the All-India Muslim League seems to me to justify the fear which I expressed last summer, with what I am afraid you must have found somewhat wearisome reiteration, that we should find the Muslims the most formidable obstacle in the way of the Federation which we were then hoping to achieve. I am bound to say that if their present mood persists, I see little chance of our being able to bring them in at any rate on any terms approaching those contemplated by the Act. The diehards over here are secretly delighted at the widening of the gulf between the Muslims and the Hindus; but taking a long view, I should myself doubt very much if a cleavage between the Muslims and the Hindus as fundamental as that contemplated by the present leaders of the All-India Muslim League would prove to be to our advantage. The Hindus have no particular affiliations outside India, whereas the call of Islam transcends the bounds of country. It may have lost some of its force as a result of the abolition of the Caliph[ate] by Mustapha Kemal Pasha; but it still has a very considerable appeal, as witness, for

example, Jinnah's insistence on our giving undertakings that Indian troops should never be employed against any Muslim state, and the solicitude which he has constantly expressed for the Arabs of Palestine....

I cannot help thinking, indeed, if separate Muslim States did come into existence in India, as now contemplated by the All-India Muslim League, the day would come when they might find the temptation to join an Islamic Commonwealth of Nations well-nigh irresistible. More particularly would this be the case with north-west of India which would, in these circumstances, be a Muslim State coterminous with the vast block of territory dominated by Islam, which runs from North Africa and Turkey in the west to Afghanistan in the east. You may think that this is looking unnecessarily far ahead, and that we can but devote our energies to endeavouring to solve our more immediate problems. I dare say that you would be right, yet I feel that one has to keep one's eye on the possible developments of a somewhat distant future if we are to come to right decisions in connection with the problems immediately confronting us.[80]

Leopold Amery, who succeeded Zetland as the Secretary of State for India (May 1940–July 1945), was equally critical of the demand for a separate Muslim state of Pakistan. In a letter to the Viceroy on 25 January 1941, he charged, 'Jinnah and his Pakistanis are beginning to be almost more of a menace [than Congress] and [seem] to have lost all sense of realities....'[81] He wondered:

If there is to be a Pakistan, [sic] Kashmir will obviously have to belong to it and Hyderabad will obviously have to belong to Hindu India and the Nizam would probably have to clear out bag and baggage. The whole future of his state and dynasty, as in the complementary case of Kashmir, depends on India remaining united and on a basis of compromise between Hindu and Muslim.[82]

Linlithgow too was wary of the Pakistan demand and 'remained convinced' that Jinnah could not 'pre-empt the future in that way.' In fact, he warned Jinnah 'that both Britain and the Viceroy were dedicated to the vision of a united India.'[83]

The very idea of Pakistan, as one British writer plainly stated, 'stirred distaste in British governing circles'.[84] They did not approve of it. Though some of the British leaders seemed sympathetic to Muslim leadership, they were not prepared to support Jinnah or his demand for Pakistan. Linlithgow was clearly more favourably inclined towards Sikandar Hayat Khan than Jinnah,[85] as was the case with Zetland.[86]

Lord Wavell, the next Viceroy of India (1943–1947), was relatively sympathetic to the Muslim cause but he was not fond of Jinnah. In the crucial years of his Viceroyalty, he felt 'sorry for the Muslims'.[87] He even suggested that they had 'more honesty, courage and dignity' than their Hindu counterparts but he 'never liked Jinnah' whom he thought 'unyielding' and insistent upon the Pakistan demand.[88] On the contrary, he felt that Khizar Hayat Khan could be 'the best leader of the Muslims in India.'[89] He found it 'odd' that Khizar Hayat Khan 'should be so dominated by a down-country lawyer like Jinnah'.[90] Indeed, he 'tried to hearten him up for his conflict with Jinnah.'[91] Wavell lauded the leadership of Khizar Hayat Khan, for the simple reason that he believed 'Pakistan was nonsense' and that the 'the British ought not to leave' India.[92] Not surprisingly, as late as August 1945, he worked hard to the effect that the 'crudity of Jinnah's ideas ought to be exposed'.[93]

Of course, Wavell was a conservative politician. But the opposition of liberal and socialist British politicians to Pakistan was equally pronounced. Speaking of Sir Stafford Cripps's (1889–1952) role in the Cabinet Mission Plan discussions of 1946, Wavell, ironically, suggested that, 'I should be never surprised to learn that he had already promised Congress some satisfaction' like 'he did in the 1942 negotiations' (the Cripps Proposals).[94] Clement Attlee (1883–1967), even before he became the prime minister after the end of the war in Europe, 'made clear that he was not at all attracted by the theory of Pakistan and that he thought Sikandar a more responsible leader than Jinnah'.[95] Lord Mountbatten's views on Jinnah and Pakistan hardly require elaboration for they have been documented in many narratives.[96] His role in the partition of India has been vividly described by none other than V.P. Menon, the Constitutional Advisor to the Governor-General of India from 1942 to 1947.[97] The British top priority, even when Mountbatten arrived as the last Viceroy of India, was still 'the unity of the subcontinent'.[98] The British wanted to preserve 'a united India' at all costs.[99] Thus, whether there were conservative 'pro-Muslim' politicians or liberal or socialist 'pro-Congress' politicians, they were united in their antipathy to Jinnah and the demand for Pakistan. In the words of Leonard Mosley, 'that their work should end in the division of the country into two separate nations was not something which sincere

British officials in India could contemplate without abhorrence. Liking the Muslim or not, he could not swallow their desire for vivisection',[100] and for obvious reasons. The British had considerable economic, strategic, and political interests in a 'united' India. This was in spite of the fact that during the 1940s, the 'benefits' that Britain obtained from her colony in India were 'badly eroded'.[101] Still, India meant a lot to the British. It was not an 'asset which…the British were happy to abandon'.[102] More importantly, Britain needed a united India for defence and strategic purposes. Britain's whole defence strategy, since the early twentieth century, was 'oriented towards India'.[103]

The British also felt threatened by the Soviet Union—characterized by Professor Harold J. Laski as the biggest threat to peace since the rise of Adolf Hitler. The Soviet Union, indeed, was one of the main preoccupations of British foreign and defence policies in the twentieth century, just as Czarist Russia preoccupied the nineteenth century British statesmen. As a senior British official wrote to the new Secretary of State for India, Lord Pethick-Lawrence (1871–1961), on 1 October 1946:

India would be easily overrun by Russia if we were at war with her, and that Russia would have good reasons for doing this, firstly because it would outflank our position in the Middle East where the oil supplies are essential to us, and secondly because there are important deposits of thorium in Travancore which is at present one of the most important ingredients for the manufacture of atomic bombs.[104]

In addition, the British wanted India to stay united for their own satisfaction. They were convinced that despite difficulties, especially the communal ones, they had succeeded in building the edifice of political 'unity' in the country. They had given India a number of strong, unifying institutions (such as the civil and military bureaucracy and the judiciary). They wanted India to remain united under all circumstances. As the then Secretary of State for India, Amery, declared on 19 November 1941: 'I would say, indeed, that if some sort of Indian unity had not existed it would have to be invented'.[105] The British were not prepared to concede even in theory, let alone encourage in practice, the territorial division of India.

The demand for Pakistan, thus, clearly was the work of the Muslim mind and Muslim leadership of India, particularly Jinnah's, and was dictated in a Muslim situation of 'despair and hope'. It represented the Muslim desire to avert a permanent Hindu majority government in India, with no prospects for the Muslims to be in power. The course of events from the Nehru Report of 1928 to the Congress rule of 1937–39 left no doubt in their minds as to their fate in a polity dominated by the Hindus. On the other hand, the demand for Pakistan opened before them boundless opportunities of life in a separate homeland where they would have power and freedom to shape their destiny in their own way. The immediate and long-range needs of the Muslims were indeed complementary to each other. Jinnah explained the necessary relationship between these needs in a speech delivered at the Muslim University Aligarh on 6 March 1940, some two weeks before the adoption of the Lahore Resolution. He recalled:

> Two years ago at Simla I said that the democratic parliamentary system of government was unsuited to India. I was condemned everywhere in the Congress press. I was told that I was guilty of disservice to Islam because Islam believes in democracy. So far as I have understood Islam, it does not advocate a democracy which would allow the majority of non-Muslims to decide the fate of the Muslims. We cannot accept a system of government in which the non-Muslims merely by numerical majority would rule and dominate us.[106]

This exposition of Muslim interests indeed paved the way for the demand for Pakistan. The Muslims wanted to be free. They wanted to decide their own fate in the light of their own precepts and principles. Even after the creation of Pakistan in August 1947, Jinnah asserted in his major address to government officials on 11 October 1947,

> The idea was that we should have a state in which we could live and breathe as free men, which we could develop according to our own lights and culture and where principles of Islamic social justice could find freeplay.[107]

The Lahore session of the Muslim League on 22–24 March 1940 was the harbinger of this new destiny. After years of exploring formulas meant to help the Muslims, the latest being his Fourteen Points, Jinnah had reached the conclusion that the only way Indian Muslims could survive and 'develop to the fullest' their 'spiritual, cultural, economic, social and political life' was to have their own 'homelands, their territory and their state'.[108] They needed a separate state to get out of their distressful situation. Indeed, this was the crux of the ultimate formula that Jinnah outlined at length in his presidential address to the League session on 22 March 1940, to which we must now turn our attention.

Jinnah opened his presidential address[109] with a survey of developments since the Lucknow session of the League in 1937, and expressed his deep anxieties, and concerns about the future of the Muslims in India. He criticized in particular 'the dangerous scheme of the Central Federal Government embodied in the Government of India Act, 1935'. He condemned the *London Times* report suggesting that the Muslim fear of the Act was largely exaggerated and that, in spite of the differences between the Muslims and the Hindus in the realm of religion, law and culture, 'in the course of time, the superstition will die out and India will be moulded into a single nation'. He asserted that the differences between the two communities were 'fundamental and deep-rooted'. In fact, he charged that the *Times* viewpoint demonstrated 'a flagrant disregard of the past history of the subcontinent of India as well as the fundamental Islamic conception of society vis-à-vis that of Hinduism to characterise them as mere "superstitions".' He claimed that the Muslims and Hindus, 'notwithstanding a thousand years of close contact', were 'nationalities, which are as divergent today as ever'. They 'cannot at any time be expected to transform themselves into one nation merely by means of subjecting them to a democratic constitution and holding them forcibly together by unnatural and artificial methods of British Parliamentary Statute'. He referred to the experience of 'the unitary government of India' and suggested that it was 'inconceivable that the fiat or the writ of a government so constituted can ever command a willing and loyal obedience throughout the subcontinent by various nationalities except by means of armed force behind it'.[110]

Turning to the Congress demand for immediate independence and formation of a Constituent Assembly, Jinnah criticized the Congress rule of 1937–39 and highlighted its relevance and importance for their future in India:

Situated in India as we are, we naturally have our past experiences and particularly by experience of the past 2 1/2 years of provincial constitution in the Congress-governed provinces we have learnt many lessons. We are now, therefore, very apprehensive and can trust nobody...we never thought that the Congress High Command would have acted in the manner which they actually did in the Congress-governed provinces. I never dreamt that they would ever come down so low as that.[111]

This, he pointed out, was in spite the British being still present in India and our crying, 'hoarse, week in and out', reminding them of 'their special responsibilities to us and to other minorities....'[112] As to the Congress claim that the future Constituent Assembly of India would satisfy legitimate minority interests, and if a problem emerged it would be referred to a 'judicial tribunal', Jinnah retorted:

Mr Gandhi says that if the minorities are not satisfied then he is willing that some tribunal of the highest character and most impartial should decide the dispute. Now, apart from the impracticable character of this proposal and quite apart from the fact that it is historically and constitutionally absurd to ask the ruling power to abdicate in favour of a Constituent Assembly—apart from all that, suppose we do not agree as to the franchise according to which the Central Assembly is to be elected, or suppose we, the solid body of Muslim representatives, do not agree with the non-Muslim majority in the Constituent Assembly, what will happen?.... In the event of there being a disagreement between the majority of the Constituent Assembly and the Musalmans, in the first instance, who will appoint the tribunal? And suppose an agreed tribunal is possible and the award is made and the decision given, who will, may I know, be there to see that this award is implemented or carried out in accordance with the terms of that award? And who will see that it is honoured in practice, because we are told, the British will have parted with their power mainly or completely? Then, what will be the sanction behind the award which will enforce it. We come back to the same answer: the Hindu majority would do it.... Besides, can you imagine that a question of this character, of social contract upon which the future constitution of India would be based affecting 90 millions of Musalmans, can be decided by means of a judicial tribunal? Still, that is the proposal of the Congress.[113]

Jinnah declared that he stood 'unequivocally for the freedom of India'.[114] But, he insisted, 'it must be freedom for all India and not freedom of one section, or worse still, of the Congress caucus and slavery of Musalmans and other minorities'.[115] This was all the more necessary because the problem in India, he claimed,

> ...is not of an inter-communal character but manifestly of an international one, and it must be treated as such. So long as this basic and fundamental truth is not realised any constitution that may be built will result in disaster and will prove destructive and harmful not only to the Musalmans but to the British and Hindus also.[116]

Indeed, Jinnah suggested, 'the only course open to us all is to allow the major nations separate homelands by dividing India into 'autonomous national states''.[117] History offered us 'many examples' where 'geographical tracts much smaller than the subcontinent of India' have been eventually 'divided into as many states as there are nations inhabiting them'.[118]

Jinnah argued that 'Musalmans are a nation by any definition'.[119] Like all other free nations, the Muslims had the right to develop to the fullest their 'spiritual, cultural, economic, social and political life in a way that we think best and in consonance with our own ideal and according to the genius of our people'.[120] The trouble with 'our Hindu friends', he lamented, was that they failed to understand 'the real nature of Islam and Hinduism'.[121] Highlighting the 'different and distinct' natures of the two social orders and historical experiences as they impacted upon the present, he explained:

> They are not religions in the strict sense of the word, but are, in fact, different and distinct social orders, and it is a dream that Hindus and Muslims can ever evolve a common nationality, and this misconception of one Indian nation has gone far beyond the limits and is the cause of most of your troubles and will lead India to destruction if we fail to revise our notions in time. The Hindus and Muslims belong to two different religious philosophies, social customs, literatures. They neither intermarry nor interdine together and, indeed, they belong to two different civilizations, which are based mainly on conflicting ideas and conceptions. Their aspects on life and of life are different. It is quite clear that Hindus and Muslamans derive their inspiration from different sources of history. They have different epics, different heroes, and different episodes. Very often the hero of one is a foe of the other and, likewise, their victories and defeats overlap. To yoke together two such nations under a single state, one as a numerical minority

and the other as a majority, must lead to growing discontent and final destruction of any fabric that may be so built up for the government of such a state.[122]

Jinnah was thus convinced that the creation of a Muslim state was the only way out of the difficulties for the Muslims and India as a whole. He stressed that the Muslims 'cannot accept any constitution which must necessarily result in a Hindu majority government'.[123] The Muslims must be invested with power and authority. The Muslims must have their separate homeland. The Muslim League agreed and, on 23 March, fully endorsed Jinnah's formula for the salvation of the Muslims. In a resolution adopted on 24 March, it resolved:

> ...that it is the considered view of this Session of the All-India Muslim League that no constitutional plan would be workable in this country or acceptable to the Muslims unless it is designed on the following basic principles, viz, that geographically contiguous units are demarcated into regions which should be so constituted, with such territorial readjustments as may be necessary, that the areas in which the Muslims are numerically in a majority as in the North-Western and Eastern zones of India, should be grouped to constitute Independent States in which the constituent units shall be autonomous and sovereign.[124]
>
> That adequate, effective and mandatory safeguards should be specifically provided in the constitution for minorities in these units and in the regions for the protection of their religious, cultural, economic, political, administrative and other rights and interests in consultation with them; and in other parts of India where the Musalmans are in a minority, adequate, effective and mandatory safeguards shall be specifically provided in the constitution, for them and other minorities, for the protection of their religious, cultural, economic, political, administrative and other rights and interests in consultation with them.[125]

Jinnah's formula, as stipulated in the Lahore Resolution, which took apart the Old World and envisioned a bold new one, had an irresistible appeal for the Muslims, especially the young, educated urban middle-classes. Facing frustration at the hands of Hindu majority community and Congress leadership, the promise of their own separate homeland, with freedom, provided the Muslims with 'a reassuring anchor in a climate of turbulence and uncertainty'[126] and 'a sense of purpose and worth',[127] both of which they had lost in the face of Hindu majority-rule. In addition, it assured them 'physical protection' and 'political survival' as an independent political community, free to shape its own destiny according to the 'genius' of its people.[128] In this sense, it was a 'positive doctrine'[129] which was neither apologetic nor reactive, but had its own intrinsic value. A separate homeland for the Muslims was not required simply because of the fear of the Hindu majority government, but because it was needed to empower the Muslims to live according to their own faith, religion, culture, traditions and norms.[130] This emphasis on the distinct Muslim way of life was bound to appeal to those who, in Willner's words, 'share the traditions of a given culture', and thus 'earned for Jinnah the deep gratitude of Mussalmans that they never owed to any one ever before'.[131]

While Indian Muslims responded enthusiastically to Jinnah's formula of a separate Muslim homeland and thus validated and enhanced his status as their charismatic leader, the Hindus were offended, and indeed vilified him in their accounts.[132] They strongly opposed the Muslim demand. They could not agree to the demand for a separate homeland. Ironically, an influential section of the Hindus, especially those belonging to the Hindu Mahasbaha, had always considered the Muslims and Hindus to be two separate 'nations'. Lajpat Rai, one of the founders of the Hindu Mahasbaha, insisted that Hindu–Muslim unity was out of the question. In a private letter to C.R. Das in the early 1920s, he explained:

> There is one point more which has been troubling me very much of late and one which I want you to think carefully, and that is the question of Hindu–Mohammedan unity. I have devoted most of my time to the study of Muslims' history and Muslim law and I am inclined to think it is neither *possible* nor *practicable*.... I am also fully prepared to trust the Muslim leaders. But what about the injunctions of the Koran and Hadis? The leaders cannot override them....[133]

V.D. Savarkar (1883–1966), a leading figure of the Mahasbaha, in his presidential address to the Hindu Mahasabha in 1937 declared publicly that there were 'two nations' in India. In his own words: 'India cannot be assumed today to be a unitarian and homogenous nation; but on the contrary, there are two nations in the main, the Hindus and Muslims in India.'[134] Years after the Lahore Resolution was adopted, Savarkar still maintained that he had 'no quarrel with Jinnah's two nations theory', and that the 'Hindus and Muslims are two nations.'[135] What was not acceptable to Savarkar and other Mahasabhites was the 'right and claim to a separate homeland on the Indian territory'.[136] The Muslims, they argued, must 'emigrate' to some other place to found their Muslim State.[137]

In fact, Hindu leaders, whatever their political orientation or position, always considered the territorial integrity of India as the very essence of Hinduism. According to Rajendra Prasad (1884–1963) a prominent Congress leader and first President of India, 'it cannot be denied that irrespective of who rules and what were the administrative or political divisions of the country, Hindus have never conceived of India as comprising anything less than what we regard as India today'.[138] Thus, orthodox Hindus, like the ones represented in the Arya Samaj who held that India *was* Hinduism,[139] and those like Gandhi, who did not share the 'narrow outlook' of the Arya Samaj,[140] were equally adamant that the partition of India was tantamount to 'vivisection'— literally, 'cutting the baby into two halves'.[141] This was in spite of the fact that Gandhi insisted that he had nothing against the Muslim right of self-determination in principle. In his own words: 'The Muslims must have the same right of self-determination as that the rest of India has. We are at present a joint family. Any member can claim a division.'[142]

To further complicate their response to the Lahore Resolution, Hindu leaders failed to appreciate the steady growth and development of Muslim separatism leading into Muslim nationalism. For instance, Gandhi, in his first reaction to the Lahore Resolution argued that the Muslims were Hindus at one time and that 'religion did not change nationality.' The Bengali Muslim, he observed, 'speaks the same tongue as a Bengali Hindu does, eats the same food, has the same amusements as his Hindu neighbour. They dress alike, his (Jinnah's name) name could be that of any Hindu. When I first met him, I did not know he was a Muslim'.[143] However, whatever 'the religious and cultural differences' between the Muslims and the Hindus, he maintained, 'what clash of interests could there be on such matters as revenue, industry, sanitation, or justice? The differences could only be in religious usage and observances, with which a secular state should have no concern.[144] Similarly, Jawaharlal Nehru, in his reaction to the Muslim demand, after conceding religious 'barriers' between the two communities, asserted:

'...Religious barriers are obviously not permanent, as conversions take place from one religion to another, and a person changing his religion does not thereby lose his social background or his cultural and linguistic heritage'.[145] Rajagopalachari went on to remind the Muslims that past Muslim rulers of India, in spite of their religious and cultural differences with their subjects, had never promoted the idea of a division of India. In his estimate,

> ...not even Tippu Sultan or Hyder Ali or Aurangzeb or Akbar, all of whom lived during days when differences seemed more deep-rooted than now, imagined that India was anything but one and indivisible. These great men might have differed from one another in may respects, but they agreed in looking upon this precious land and this great nation as one and essentially indivisible.[146]

These statements suggested a complete lack of understanding of the fundamentals of Islam as they affected political behaviour. Islam demands that 'Church and state' must be 'indivisible'.[147] That is to say, 'the observance of the fundamentals of the faith' must be 'forged in the successful assertion of power' in the state.[148] Thus, an independent political community is the very essence of Islam. Therefore, Indian Muslims, as a community, were not prepared to accept a polity dependent upon the will of the Hindu-majority community. As to Gandhi's charge that the Muslims were Hindus at one time, and could not claim a separate nationality today, Jinnah was astounded:

> They say, supposing an Englishman becomes a Muslim in England, he does not ask for Pakistan...by changing his religion, still remains a member of the same society, with the same culture, same social life and everything remains exactly the same when an Englishman changes his faith? But...a Muslim, when he was converted, granted that he was converted more than a thousand years ago, bulk of them, then according to your Hindu religion and philosophy, he becomes an outcast and he becomes a *malecha* (untouchable) and the Hindus cease to have anything to do with him socially, religiously and culturally or in any other way? He, therefore, belongs to a different order, not only religious but social, and he has lived in that distinctly separate and antagonistic social order, religiously, socially and culturally. It is now more than a thousand years that the bulk of the Muslims have lived in a different world, in a different society, in a different philosophy and a different faith. Can you possibly compare this with that

nonsensical talk that mere change of faith is no ground for a demand for Pakistan? Can't you see the fundamental difference?[149]

Jinnah insisted that India was home to two nations, the Muslims and the Hindus, and he wanted freedom for both. He did not mean to hurt the Hindus or any other community for that matter. He merely wanted the Muslims to live their lives as 'free men' in their own separate homeland. He, therefore, found it 'amazing' that,

...Mr Gandhi and Mr Rajagopalachari should talk about the Lahore Resolution in such terms as 'vivisection of India' and 'cutting the baby into two halves'.... Where is the country which is being divided? Where is the nation, which is denationalized? India is composed of nationalities, to say nothing about the castes and sub-castes. Where is the 'Central National Government' whose authority is being violated? India is held by the British power and that is the hand...that holds and gives the impression of united and the unitary Government.... We propose that the Hindus and Muslims should be provided with their homelands which will enable them to live side by side as two honourable nations, and as good neighbours, and not Hindus as superior and Musalmans as inferior nations, tied artificially together with a Hindu religious majority to dominate and rule over the Muslim India.... Our ideal and our fight is not to harm or injure any other community or interest or block the progress but to defend ourselves. We want to live in this country an honourable life as free men, and we stand for free Islam and free India.[150]

Indeed, the more the Hindus expressed hostility and opposition to his formula of a separate homeland, the more Jinnah pressed for it. He saw no other way out. He made this abundantly clear in his presidential address at the Madras (Chennai) session of the League in April 1941, one year after the Lahore session of the League adopting the Lahore Resolution:

We want the establishment of completely independent states in the North-West and Eastern zones of India, with full control finally of defence, foreign affairs, communications, customs, currency, exchange, etc. We do not want in any circumstances a constitution of an All-India character with one government at the Centre. We will never agree to that. If we once agree to that let me tell you the Muslims will be absolutely wiped out of existence.[151]

Jinnah's formula to alleviate the distress of the Muslims was based on the fundamental premise that the Muslims were a separate nation, and thus a separate homeland was required to secure them political power and freedom. In this sense, it was a simple, straightforward case of the right of self-determination for the Muslims.[152] However, some scholars could not help but notice 'ambiguities' in the Lahore Resolution itself. Indeed, over the years they have endeavoured to interpret these ambiguities in many ways. It will not be inappropriate to examine here some of these ambiguities and try to clarify them in the light of evidence and Jinnah's own pronouncements on the subject.

Three principal ambiguities have been identified. First, critics have observed that it was not clear from the resolution whether the goal it contemplated was 'one sovereign state...or more than one'.[153] If the idea was one state, how could the constituent units be simultaneously 'autonomous and sovereign?'.[154] Secondly, the Lahore Resolution did not suggest 'a connecting link between the two zones'.[155] This meant that the resolution was intended as a 'bargaining counter'. As Ayesha Jalal argued: 'By apparently repudiating the need for any centre, and keeping quiet about its shape, Jinnah calculated that when eventually the time came to discuss an all-India federation, British and Congress alike would be forced to negotiate with organized Muslim opinion, and would be ready to make substantial concessions to create or retain that centre. The Lahore Resolution should therefore be seen as a bargaining counter....'[156] Finally, the resolution failed to define 'areas in which the Muslims are numerically in a majority' particularly in the sense whether 'area' connoted provinces or part of a province.[157]

As to the ambiguity about the number of states in question, it was true that the Lahore Resolution itself was not much help. The key phrase in the resolution was that 'the areas in which the Muslims are numerically in a majority as in the North-Western and Eastern zones of India should be grouped to constitute Independent States....' However, it cannot be denied that, in the final analysis, Jinnah came to interpret it essentially as a demand for one sovereign state. It was at the Muslim League Legislators' Convention at Delhi in April 1946[158] that Jinnah forcefully declared that, 'our formula [sic] is based on the territory of this sub-continent being carved into two sovereign states of Hindustan and Pakistan'.[159] However, there were clear indications all along that what the Muslim League really demanded in the Resolution was one sovereign state and not more. Apart from the fact that Jinnah himself, in his presidential address at the Lahore session, suggested that the 'Musalmans...must have their homelands, their territory and their *state*',[160] many delegates strongly felt that the demand was for a 'a single state'. Abdus Salam Khurshid, one of the delegates thus noted:

> Having been one of the hundreds of delegates to the Lahore session of the All-India Muslim League, I could say without any hesitation that none of my young fellow delegates delved into the wording of the Lahore Resolution and we all had the impression that a single state was aimed at.[161]

This was also true of some of the speeches made by prominent League leaders such as Choudhary Khaliquzzaman and Sardar Aurangzeb Khan who spoke in favour of the resolution. Sardar Aurangzeb Khan, for instance, said: 'We want a home for the Muslim nation, and our home is as indicated in the resolution'.[162]

Significantly, the League, in April 1941, while adopting the Lahore Resolution as one of the fundamental aims and objects of the League, added the word 'together' after the word 'grouped'. The phrase now used was: '...the North-Western and Eastern zones of India, shall be grouped together....'[163] This was the beginning of a process of linkages first within the zones and ultimately between the zones indicated in the resolution. In March 1941, Jinnah had already indicated 'the Punjab as one of the units of Pakistan.'[164] The confusion as to one or more states was laid to rest in Jinnah's historic talks with Gandhi in September 1944. Jinnah plainly told Gandhi that the League sought the establishment of a single Muslim state comprising both the North-Western and the Eastern zones. The two zones 'will form units of Pakistan.'[165] Explaining the whole issue in the broad context of the Muslim rights and demand for 'self-determination', Jinnah exclaimed:

> ...can you not appreciate our point of view that we claim the right of self-determination as a nation and not as a territorial unit, and that we are entitled to exercise our inherent right as a Muslim nation, which is our birth-right? Whereas you are labouring under the wrong idea that 'self-determination' means only that of 'a territorial unit', which, by the way, is

neither demarcated nor defined yet, and there is no union or federal constitution of India in being, functioning as a sovereign Central government. *Ours is a case of division and carving out two independent sovereign states by way of settlement between two major nations, Hindus and Muslims, and not of severance or secession from any existing union, which is non-set in India.* The right of self-determination, which we claim, postulates that we are a nation, and as such it would be the self-determination of the Muslims, and they alone are entitled to exercise that right.[166]

The resolutions or documents of the League never mention the word 'states' in reference to Pakistan after 1944 and the Muslims increasingly came to associate themselves with the ideal of a single state of Pakistan. The polls in 1945–46, which the League swept in the Muslim constituencies except in the NWFP, were a clear verdict on this issue. The Muslim League Legislators' Convention of April 1946, comprising all elected League members of assemblies, national as well as provincial, acknowledged public sentiment on the issue and resolved,

That the zones comprising Bengal and Assam in the North-East and the Punjab, North-West Frontier Province, Sind, Baluchistan in the North-West of India, namely Pakistan zones, where the Muslims are in a dominant majority be constituted into a sovereign independent State....[167]

Apparently, the reason the Lahore Resolution did not clearly suggest one sovereign independent state from the start was tactical. Given the weak position of the Muslim League in 1940 with regard to the British, the Congress and the provincial leaders of the Muslim-majority provinces, who were considerably strengthened by the operation of the provincial part of the 1935 Act, Jinnah found it wise and sensible to stay clear of specifics at that point in time. In the 1937 elections, the League secured only 39 out of 117 and 2 out of 84 seats, respectively in the Muslim-majority Provinces of Bengal and the Punjab. A detailed formula was bound to expose the League demand to attacks from its more powerful adversaries. Jinnah could not afford to provide his opponents, as he told Beverley Nichols, 'in advance, a blue print in which every detail is settled'.[168] The important thing, he explained 'was that the principle of separation was accepted; the rest followed automatically'.[169]

Of course, the 'rest' did not follow 'automatically'. Jinnah had to work very hard to develop his position as a charismatic leader of the Muslims, and to make the Muslim League the 'sole representative body of Muslim India'. The 1945–46 elections helped him establish its representative status by securing an overwhelming majority of Muslim seats in the central and provincial assembly elections. Jinnah's charisma received tremendous boost. Thus, as Jinnah's charisma scaled new heights and the League grew in strength, and the opponents of Pakistan either left the political scene or were weakened, it became possible to explain the Pakistan demand more confidently. One could clearly discern this movement from the adoption of the Lahore Resolution in March 1940 to the League Legislators' Convention held after the League's overwhelming victory in the 1945–46 elections. It was finally announced that 'Pakistan' was a demand for one sovereign state, comprising the North-Western, and Eastern zones of India.

Part of the criticism, however, remains. If the demand was for one state, how could the constituent units be autonomous and sovereign? One explanation is that the word 'units' stood for 'provinces' and as such the provinces were to be autonomous and sovereign.[170] This, according to one writer, 'was the ultimate concession to the Muslims of the provinces where they already enjoyed majorities, to get them to rally around the project of a Pakistani state.'[171] Hence, it was obvious that, in part, the language of the Lahore Resolution was 'loose'. However, as earlier indicated, the ambiguities were deliberate tactical imperatives. Jinnah did not want to offer a formula that would have little appeal for the independent-minded provincial leaders of the Punjab and Bengal in particular. In this sense, he ignored regional interpretations of the Pakistan demand, until a clear verdict emerged in its favour by the Muslim masses in the 1945–46 elections. It did not matter if the provincial leaders thought that the Lahore Resolution called for the establishment of 'autonomous and sovereign' states. British preference for devolution of power to the provinces, rather than the centre, had made these provincial leaders of Muslim-majority provinces a formidable force in politics. Jinnah's relations with Sikandar Hayat Khan were at best 'working relations' at that time. Although Sikandar Hayat Khan had supported the Muslim League at the Lucknow session in 1937, he was quite reluctant to yield to the centre. He sought the cooperation of the League to offset the pressure from the Congress on his province. He did not want the League to interfere with or influence the provincial scene. The same was the case with Fazlul Huq in Bengal. Thus, Jinnah did not want to upset these leaders unnecessarily. He resolved to be patient and conciliatory until he could organize the League in these provinces on a sound footing. Therefore, the Lahore Resolution was deliberately kept vague, subject to favourable interpretations, if these strong provincial leaders so desired. No wonder, as late as March 1941, Sikandar Hayat Khan was claiming that 'Punjab will not be Pakistan but just *Punjab*, land of the five rivers'.[172]

Turning to the second ambiguity about the absence of 'a connecting link between the two zones' and the inference that the Lahore Resolution should 'be seen as a bargaining counter', it needs to be stressed again that the two zones were subsequently 'grouped together' at the Madras session of the League in 1941. It is true that it still did not amount to a union of two zones under a common centre, but it did not mean either in terms of logic or in the light of the available evidence that the idea necessarily was to use the resolution as 'a bargaining counter'. On the contrary, one could argue that the absence of a clear-cut centre in the Lahore Resolution was a conscious, careful decision to forestall this eventuality. Given its past experience, the League feared that any talk about the centre, whether in the context of Muslim India, India as a whole, an Indian federation, or an all-India confederation for that matter, would compromise the very idea of Pakistan. In his presidential address at the Delhi session of the League in April 1943, Jinnah publicly expressed these fears:

There are people who talk of some sort of a loose federation. There are people who talk of giving the widest freedom to the federating units and residuary power resting with the units. But they forget the entire constitutional history of the various parts of the world. Federation, however, described and in whatever terms it is put, must ultimately deprive the federating units of the authority in all vital matters. The units, despite themselves, would be compelled to grant more and more power to the central authority, until in the end a strong central government will have been established by the units themselves and they will be driven to do so by absolute necessity, if the basis of a federal government is accepted.[173]

Illustrating his point with reference to the United States of America, Canada, Australia, South Africa, Germany and other countries of the world, where 'federal or confederal systems have been in existence', he declared:

> We are opposed to any scheme, nor can we agree to any proposal, which has for its basis any conception or idea of a central government—federal or confederal— for it is bound to lead in the long run to the emasculation of the entire Muslim nation, economically, socially, educationally, culturally, or politically and to the establishment of the Hindu majority raj in this sub-continent.[174]

No wonder, the League deliberately avoided discussion of the centre. This was abundantly clear in the evidence of Sikandar Hayat Khan who was involved with the drafting of the Lahore Resolution. 'I have no hesitation in admitting', he declared in 1941 in the Punjab Assembly,

> I was responsible for drafting the original resolution. But let me make it clear that the resolution which I drafted was radically amended by the Working Committee, and there is a wide divergence in the resolution I drafted and the one that was finally passed. The main difference between the two resolutions is that the latter part of my resolution which related to the centre and co-ordination of the activities of the various units, was eliminated.[175]

Thus, the absence of the centre was not due to a desire to use the demand for Pakistan for bargaining purposes. Rather, it was to stem the idea of bargaining altogether. The League did not want to offer any scheme of its own based on the idea of a centre, lest it should become a bargaining counter in the end, either with the British or the Congress. Jinnah himself was aware of this bargaining counter thesis very well. Speaking at the Pakistan session of the Punjab Muslim Students Federation on 2 March 1941, he condemned the whole idea of 'bargaining' in the strongest possible words:

> It is quite obvious that no federal constitution was ever framed or enacted without the agreement and consent of the units entering into the federal scheme of their own free will and accord. The only solution for the Muslims of India, which will stand the test of trial and time, is that India

should be partitioned so that both the communities can develop freely and fully according to their own genius, economically, socially, culturally and politically. The struggle is for the fullest opportunities and for the expression of the Muslim national will. The vital contest in which we are engaged is not only for the material gain but also the very existence of the soul of the Muslim nation. Hence I have said often that it is a matter of life and death to the Musalmans and *is not a counter for bargaining.*[176]

The argument of using the Lahore Resolution and the Pakistan demand as a counter for bargaining is further weakened by the fact that many British and Congress leaders, including Wavell and Mountbatten, and Gandhi and Nehru, respectively, accused Jinnah of intransigence and insistence on Pakistan. Their views are common knowledge and need not be cited here. Many writers held similar viewpoints. For instance, V.P. Menon, writing of the partition of India stressed:

But sadder still is the thought that Jinnah, the hero of my generation, a great nationalist in his time and one who fought many a battle for the freedom of his country, should later have fought so successfully against its freedom, and should eventually, almost single-handed, have brought about its division.[177]

In a similar vein, B.R. Nanda charged:

That communal antagonism should have reached a new peak in the closing years of British rule was perhaps natural; it was, in political terms, a war of succession. However, it is doubtful if the communal problem should have dominated Indian politics in the way it did without Jinnah's impact on it.[178]

Most importantly, Tara Chand, explaining the creation of Pakistan, wrote wryly:

The success was mainly due to the dedication and the single-minded and skilful pertinacity of one man, *viz* Muhammad Ali Jinnah. He had made up his mind in 1937 that the solution of the communal problem lay in the separation of the Muslims in the majority areas from India, hence he played his cards with consummate ability. He persuaded the Muslims of all parts of India—those who would profit by the establishment of Pakistan, as well as those who were bound to suffer from the consequences of partition—to believe that all of them would gain by an independent Muslim State. This speaks volumes for his powers of deluding men to see in a mirage fountains of real water.[179]

Ayesha Jalal, too, in the context of her discussion of Jinnah's feelings about a common Governor-General for India and Pakistan highlighted his devotion and commitment to Pakistan in this manner:

To share a common Governor-General with Hindustan would have given Congress an excuse to use this joint office to make terms separately with the Muslim areas in the event that the Pakistan constituent assembly fell to pieces. It was [sic] to avoid this disaster that Jinnah had to exercise the powers of a Governor-General himself and in the process consolidate the League's authority over the Muslim areas.[180]

Significantly, in her more recent study, *Self and Sovereignty*, Jalal identified Jinnah's 'call to Muslims to observe a Day of Deliverance upon the resignation of Congress Ministries' as the 'fateful parting of the ways' that rendered 'an amicable settlement between the All-India Muslim League and the Indian National Congress...beyond the pale of possibility'.[181] Cleary, if December 1939 is taken as the definite breaking point in Congress–Muslim League relations, then one cannot argue that the Pakistan demand was a mere bargaining counter inspired by the British authorities.

As to the third ambiguity relating to the failure of the Lahore Resolution to define areas in which Muslims constituted numerical majorities, and particularly in the sense 'whether area connoted provinces or part of a province', it appears that the Muslim League had purposefully left this matter 'ambiguous' too in order to help include as many Muslim majority areas as possible, including some in the Muslim-minority provinces. Ashaq Husain Batalvi, who was present in the meetings of the Subject Committee of the League which met on the night of 22 March and the morning of 23 March 1940, recalled that he had recommended that the Muslim demand should clearly restrict itself to Muslim-majority provinces. In fact, he had proposed an amendment to the effect that the word 'provinces' should be substituted for the word 'Muslim majority areas', but the Committee did not agree. Liaquat Ali Khan explained that this 'ambiguity' was 'deliberate', the idea being not to concede any area of the Muslim-majority provinces but to include areas like Delhi and Aligarh in the proposed Muslim state.[182]

It is also pertinent to point out that the Congress leaders were greatly disturbed by the deliberate ambiguity about the 'area' that was to be included in Pakistan. Gandhi repeatedly asked Jinnah about it in his September 1944 talks. He was particularly keen to know how the Muslim areas would be demarcated since they were not clearly specified in the Lahore Resolution. Jinnah, unwilling to reveal his hand, refused to discuss specific details. He knew that the moment he disclosed the areas in mind, the Congress and other parties opposed to the Pakistan demand would do their utmost to rob him of support there. Thus, Jinnah was content to tell Gandhi on 25 September: 'The matter of demarcating and defining the territories can be taken up after the fundamentals…are accepted, and for that purpose machinery may be set up by agreement'.[183] However, he was more precise in his press conference of 30 September 1944. He stated: '…the question of demarcating or defining the boundaries can be taken up later in the same way as a question of boundaries arising between two nations are solved. It will be like one government negotiating with the other and arriving at a settlement'.[184] This, in fact, proved to be the final procedure adopted for the demarcation of areas between India and Pakistan with a Boundary Commission constituted to determine national borders after the partition of India was approved and given effect to.

Although it should be clear from the foregoing discussion that most ambiguities about the Lahore Resolution were more apparent than real, it did not mean that the resolution offered a perfect formula for the Muslims of India. The resolution was mainly concerned with the Muslim-majority areas in the North-Western and Eastern zones of India, where the bulk of Muslim population lived. It could not offer anything more than a promise of 'adequate, effective and mandatory safeguards' to the Muslims of minority provinces. These safeguards were to be arranged on a reciprocal basis. The non-Muslims were to be granted the same safeguards in the Muslim-majority areas. Many Muslims were satisfied with this arrangement. Some saw evidence and support in history. For instance, I.I. Chundrigar, (1897–1960), leader of the Muslim League in the Bombay Assembly, argued,

...a balance of power between Hindustan and Pakistan was the best safeguard for the Muslim minorities. When there was Hindu rule in Deccan, he recalled from the past history of India, the Muslims were oppressed, and similarly when there was Muslim rule there, the Hindus did not always feel happy. But when in the Deccan there was, side by side, a Muslim Nizam and a Marhatta power, neither oppressed its minorities. That is what would happen, he believed, when Pakistan and Hindustan existed side by side as sovereign states, neither would oppress its minorities.[185]

But while Jinnah also insisted that if 'our minorities are ill-treated, Pakistan cannot remain a passive spectator',[186] he was not unmindful of the fact that the Muslims, 'wherever they are in a minority cannot improve their position under a united India or under one central government'.[187] They would 'remain a minority'. By 'coming in the way of the division of India they do not and cannot improve their own position'.[188] Therefore, in his estimate, the 'question for the Muslim minorities' in India was:

Whether the entire Muslim India of 90,000,000 should be subjected to a Hindu majority raj or whether at least 60,000,000 of Musalmans residing in the areas where they form a majority should have their own homeland and thereby have an opportunity to develop their spiritual, cultural, economic and political life in accordance with their own genius and shape their own future destiny....[189]

No wonder, a host of leaders in the Muslim-minority provinces pressed for Pakistan. F.K. Khan Durrani, the author of *The Meaning of Pakistan* (1944), for instance, agreed that there will be Muslims 'left behind in Hindustan after the separate sovereign State of Pakistan has been established'. But, he stressed that, the 'continued residence of these Muslims in Hindustan, even if they are exposed there to undue hardships, is indispensable for the security and well-being of Pakistan....' He did not approve the idea of 'exchange of populations'. He saw it 'harmful not only to Pakistan but also the ultimate purpose of Islam'.[190] In a similar vein, Allama Shabbir Ahmad Usmani argued that the minority Muslims 'should not stand in the way of the welfare and happiness' of the Muslims in Pakistan, or else all the Muslims all over India, 'would have to live under a Hindu Government'.[191]

Jinnah, being a rational charismatic leader, had couched his formula in realistic terms, and only after the alternatives were exhausted and rendered impracticable. He was convinced that Pakistan was 'not only a practicable goal but the only goal' for the Muslims.[192] There was no other way the Muslims could have political power and feel safe and secure. He was confident that the Lahore Resolution was a definite formula for the salvation of the Muslims. In fact, he challenged Gandhi in his talks, in September 1944, to show him 'in what way or respect the Lahore Resolution is indefinite'.[193] He was of course not prepared to give a detailed 'blue-print' of his scheme.[194] Well aware that the Muslims were the weakest of the three major parties in the political struggle in India, he could not afford to offer 'a focus for opposition, either within the Muslim ranks or beyond', that is for the Congress and the British.[195]

But this reluctance to give details was not intended to bargain the Pakistan demand in the final negotiations. While the Congress and British chased a phantom, Jinnah devised a practical and realizable formula that found resonance with the Muslim community and helped him assert his charismatic leadership. There was no question of ever relenting on the fundamentals of the formula. Indeed, as Stanley Wolpert eloquently described it, Jinnah's demand for Pakistan,

...lowered the final curtain on any prospects for a single united independent India. Those who understood him enough to know that once his mind was made up he never reverted to any earlier position realized how momentous a pronouncement their Quaid-i-Azam had just made. The rest of the world would take at least seven years to appreciate that he literally meant every word he had uttered that important afternoon in March. There was no turning back. The ambassador of Hindu–Muslim unity had totally transformed himself into Pakistan's great leader.[196]

All that remained to be seen now was how, Jinnah, this 'great leader', the Quaid-i-Azam, was to bring all the Muslims together on the issue of Pakistan, and to get everybody 'to agree to the formula he had resolved upon'.[197] Of course, Jinnah knew very well that 'you cannot get freedom of independence by mere arguments'.[198] He had to make plans. He had to devise a strategy to mobilize and organize the Muslims for the achievement of Pakistan. In fact, this was to be his next, and most vital, task as the charismatic leader of Muslim India.

Notes

1. Pirzada, *Foundation of Pakistan*, Vol. II, 294.
2. In this sense, Mushirul Hasan was not correct when he claimed that 'the roots of partition or two nations' did not 'lie in the nineteenth century "neo-Muslim" modernist and separatist tradition of Aligarh modernism and its spokesperson Syed Ahmad Khan.' One cannot find the roots in 'the 1930s or early 40s' unless they are traced to Syed Ahmad Khan's thoughts and contributions to Muslim politics in the late nineteenth century. No wonder, Bose and Jalal argued that 'a possible way out of quandary' in the 1930s 'was to invoke Saiyid Ahmad Khan's thinking and asserting that Indian Muslims were...a nation'. See Mushirul Hasan, ed., *Inventing Boundaries: Gender, Politics and the Partition of India* (New Delhi: Oxford University Press, 2000), 4; and Bose and Jalal, *Modern South Asia*, 174.
3. Talbot, *India and Pakistan*, 94.
4. Maulana Altaf Hussain Hali, *Hayat-i-Javed* (Lahore: n.p., 1957, rep.), 194. Syed Ahmad Khan was disappointed with the growing campaign of the Hindu revivalists to replace Urdu with Hindi in the UP. Urdu had become the official language of the provincial government in 1837, replacing Persian.
5. Sir Syed Ahmad Khan, *The Present State of Indian Politics*, ed. Farman Fatehpuri, 61.
6. For a detailed discussion on this aspect of Syed Ahmad Khan's leadership see, Sikandar Hayat, 'Syed Ahmad Khan and the Foundation of Muslim Separatist Political Movement in India', *Pakistan Journal of Social Sciences*, Vol. VIII, No. 1 & 2 (January-July-December 1982).
7. This transformation in Maulana Mohammed Ali's political career is discussed at length in my article, 'Maulana Mohammed Ali and the Growth of Muslim Separatism in India', *Pakistan Journal of History and Culture*, Vol. VI, No. 1 (1985).
8. W.C. Smith, *Modern Islam in India*, 196.
9. Cited in Gail Minault, *The Khilafat Movement: Religious Symbolism and Political Mobilization in India* (New York: Columbia University Press, 1982), 56.
10. Hasan, *Islam, Communities and the Nation*, 84.
11. Address to the All-India Muslim Conference, 1930. Quoted in Coupland, *A Re-statement*, 136.
12. Iqbal, *Selected Writings and Speeches of Maulana Mohamed Ali*, Vol. II, 356-7.
13. Mohamed Ali, *My Life: A Fragment*, ed., Afzal Iqbal (Lahore: Sh. Muhammed Ashraf, 1966), 177. Also see, Mohamed Ali, 'Appreciation of Iqbal', in Syed Rais Ahmad Jafri, ed., *Selections from Maulana Mohammad Ali's Comrade* (Lahore: Mohammad Ali Academy, 1965), 307.
14. In this sense, Iqbal, too, is a founder of Pakistan because 'its political development is not intelligible' without taking into account his contribution and impact. See Embree, *India's Search for Identity*, 100.
15. Muhammad Iqbal, *The Reconstruction of Religious Thought in Islam* (Lahore: Sh. Muhammad Ashraf, 1965), 154.
16. Sherwani, *Speeches, Writings and Statements of Iqbal*, 7.
17. Ibid., 8-9, 22-3.

18. Talbot, *India and Pakistan*, 59.

19. Therein lay the basic difference between Allama Iqbal and the traditional *ulama*. Iqbal believed the *Sharia* to be capable of reinterpretation through *ijtihad*, indeed, 'reconstruction'. The traditionalists did not. See his *Reconstruction of Religious Thought in Islam*, especially Chapters 1 and 2.

20. *Letters of Iqbal to Jinnah*, 18.

21. Ibid., 23.

22. Ibid., 24.

23. Ibid.

24. Ibid. In October 1937, the All-India Muslim League Council in its meeting at Lucknow did discuss the idea of an 'alternative scheme to federation', ironically put forward by Sikandar Hayat Khan, the Unionist Premier of the Punjab, who had recently joined the League. In his opinion: 'Federation meant the ruination of the Muslims of India' as they 'would be under perpetual subjugation of the Hindu *Raj* in the Centre'. He went on to present his own scheme, the so-called 'zonal scheme'. While subsequently, Sikandar Hayat insisted that his scheme had 'animated indirectly from the Muslim League', Jinnah did not agree. He made it absolutely clear that 'the League was not responsible for any of these proposals directly or indirectly', and that its Constitution Subcommittee and later its Working Committee would 'examine the whole question thoroughly.' Malik, *Pakistan Resolution*, 1, 99.

25. In this sense, it is difficult to agree with Jafferlot that the 'intelligentsia' of the Muslim-minority provinces essentially 'shaped an ethnic variety of nationalism based on Islam.' Muslim nationalism was the work of intelligentsia both from the Muslim-minority and Muslim-majority provinces. See Christophe Jafferlot, 'Introduction', in Jafferlot, *Nationalism without a Nation*, 14-15.

26. *Letters of Iqbal to Jinnah*, 20-1.

27. Originally scheduled for December 1939, it was postponed until March 1940 due to the outbreak of the Second World War. Again, in March 1940, the Khaksars and government forces clashed in the Punjab, but Jinnah decided to hold the League session without further delay. For an interesting discussion of the League session against this backdrop, see Iftikhar H. Malik, 'Regionalism or Personality Cult? Allama Mashraqi and the Tehreek-i-Khaksar in pre-1947 Punjab', in Ian Talbot and Gurharpal Singh, eds., *Region and Partition: Bengal, Punjab and the Partition of the Subcontinent* (Karachi: Oxford University Press, 1999), 66-77.

28. It was named as 'Pakistan Resolution' by the Hindu press the next day, and was gladly accepted by the Muslim League leadership and the Muslim masses. The word Pakistan, coined by Chaudary Rahmat Ali in 1933, was neither part of the resolution nor used by anyone in the speeches. Jinnah thanked the press for their 'generosity'. As he explained at the Delhi session of the League on 24 April 1943, '...You will bear me out that when we passed the Lahore Resolution we had not used the word 'Pakistan'. Who gave us this word? (cries of 'Hindus') Let me tell you, it is their fault. They started damning this resolution on the ground that it was Pakistan.... They fathered this word upon us.... Now, our resolution was known for a long time as the Lahore resolution, popularly known as Pakistan. But how long are we to have this long phrase? Now I say to my Hindu and

British friends: We thank you for giving us one word.' Ahmad, *Speeches and Writings*, Vol. 1, 528. Interestingly, Jinnah suggested the observance of 'Pakistan Day' on 23 March (and not 24 March) every year. See his letter to Liaquat Ali Khan, dated 10 February 1941, asking him to take up this issue with the League's Working Committee and the Leagues Council. *Quaid-i-Azam Papers*, F/335.

29. Jalal, *Sole Spokesman*, 60.
30. Ibid., 49.
31. Ibid., 50.
32. Ibid., 46.
33. Chand, *History of the Freedom Movement in India*, Vol. IV., 334.
34. Ramji Lal, *Political India, 1935–42: Anatomy of Indian Politics* (Delhi: Ajanta Publications, 1986), 92-4.
35. Anita Inder Singh, *The Origins of the Partition of India, 1936–47* (Delhi: Oxford University Press, 1987), 57.
36. Uma Kaura, *Muslims and Indian Nationalism* (Lahore: Book Traders, n.d.), 169. Yet another writer, Y.B. Kulkarni, insisted that the Lahore Resolution was 'indeed the natural outcome of the British policy of giving encouragement to separatist politics'. Y.B. Kulkarni, *Pakistan: Its Origin and Relations with India* (Delhi: Sterling Publishers, 1988), 72.
37. Azad, *India Wins Freedom*, 30.
38. Afzal, *Selected Speeches and Statements*, 132.
39. Pirzada, *Quaid-i-Azam Jinnah's Correspondence*, 104. Jinnah asked Kanji Dwarkadas in a private interview the same year, 'Why are your Hindu friends attributing motives to me and calling me a traitor? Why are they forgetting my past record of work? Why are they thinking that I was such a fool as to play into the hands of the British Government and be their tool to keep freedom away from this sub-continent?' Kanji Dwarkadas, *Ten Years to Freedom*, 85-6.
40. Ahmad, *Speeches and Writings*, Vol. 1, 160.
41. Malik, *Pakistan Resolution*, 79. For details on the work of the committees see Chapter 3, 'The Committee Stage', 76-107. Interestingly, apart from Sikandar Hayat Khan, the Aga Khan and Sir Zafrullah Khan had also entered into dialogues with the Congress and even 'prepared a compromise formula' for their acceptance. Jinnah was 'singularly kept out of these talks.' However, they 'soon realized that a settlement without Jinnah was inconceivable'. Ibid., 87.
42. Ahmad, *Speeches and Writings*, Vol. I, 161.
43. The greater 'the pressure for the implementation of the federal scheme...the reaction of the Muslims grew stronger and they eventually rallied around Jinnah'. Malik, *Pakistan Resolution*, 87.
44. Menon, *Transfer of Power in India*, 78. Jinnah himself gave vent to the Muslim feelings in his interview with the Viceroy in early 1940. 'If the Congress ministries returned to office under existing conditions, there would be 'civil war in India'. Ibid. Chaudhary Zafrullah Khan, a member of the Viceroy's Executive Council, was so sure of the Congress returning to office, again, that he advised Choudhary Khaliquzzaman, a League leader from the UP, to bring the League 'to some sort of settlement with the Congress, otherwise you may miss the bus'. Khaliquzzaman, *Pathway to Pakistan*, 323.
45. Menon, *Transfer of Power in India*, 78.

46. Azad, *Indian Wins Freedom*, 36
47. Dwarkadas, *Ten Years to Freedom*, 54.
48. Ibid.
49. Ibid.
50. Ibid., 55.
51. Ibid.
52. Ibid., 78.
53. Hutchins, *India's Revolution*, 168-9.
54. Qalb-i-Abid noted that Viceroy Linlithgow 'kept on using these phrases (constructive plan, constructive scheme, constructive programme, and constructive effort, etc.) before and even after the Lahore Resolution was passed. S. Qalb-i-Abid, *Jinnah,* [The] *Second World War and the Pakistan Movement* (Multan: Nubahar Press, 1999), 135.
55. Tomlinson, *The Indian National Congress and the Raj*, 137.
56. Quoted in Johannes H. Voigt, 'Cooperation or Confrontation? War and Congress Politics, 1939–42', in Low, *Congress and the Raj*, 355.
57. Cited in John Glendevon, *The Viceroy at Bay* (London: Collins, 1971), 169.
58. Voigt, 'Cooperation or Confrontation?' in Low, *Congress and the Raj*, 356.
59. See his *Now or Never: Are we to Live or Perish Forever?*, in K.K. Aziz, ed., *Complete Works of Rahmat Ali* (Islamabad: National Commission on Historical and Cultural Research, 1978), 5-10. In a discussion on Pakistan in the Joint Committee on Indian Constitutional Reform, Muslim delegates to the Round Table Conference characterized it as 'a students' scheme' and 'chimerical and impracticable'. See their statements in K.K. Aziz, ed., *Prelude to Pakistan, 1930–1940: Documents and Readings Illustrating the Growth of the Idea of Pakistan*, Vol. I (Lahore: Vanguard, 1992), 184. Pakistan, or rather 'Pakstan', as Choudhary Rahmat Ali suggested, stood for the five 'northern units' of India, namely, Punjab, the North-West Frontier Province (Afghan Province), Kashmir, Sindh, and Balochistan.
60. Aziz, *Complete Works of Rahmat Ali*, 7.
61. Ibid., 8.
62. See, for instance, Pirzada, *Evolution of Pakistan*; and Mathur, *Growth of Muslim Politics in India*, App. II, 'Plans for the Partition of India', 293-329. Sir Zafrullah Khan also proposed a 'Separation Scheme' weeks before the League's March session at Lahore. This scheme was 'distinctly different' from the League's Lahore Resolution. For details see, Malik, *Pakistan Resolution*, 169, 213-14 (note), and App. G, 239-69. Indeed, according to Syed Sharifuddin Pirzada, Zafrullah Khan's scheme was 'neither the basis of the Pakistan Resolution adopted on 24 March, 1940, nor did Sir Zafrullah have any hand in the drafting of the said Resolution.' Syed Sharifuddin Pirzada, *Quaid-i-Azam Mohammad Ali Jinnah and Pakistan* (Islamabad: Hurmat Publications, 1989), 'Preface', ii.
63. In proposing an interesting typology of political leadership in terms of the 'man of words', and the 'man of action', Hoffer suggested that only when 'disaster' shook the people 'to its foundations' that the 'man of action' emerges to salvage the situation. See Eric Hoffer, *The True Believer* (New York: Harper & Row, Perennial Library, 1966), 104.
64. Saiyid, *A Political Study*, 230.
65. Glendevon, *Viceroy at Bay*, 124.

66. Ibid.
67. Ibid., 138.
68. Ibid.
69. Menon, *Transfer of Power in India*, 81
70. Ibid.
71. Ibid. 81-2.
72. Ibid., 82.
73. Ibid.
74. Ibid.
75. French, *Liberty or Death*, 122.
76. Cited in Waheed-uz-Zaman, *Myth and Reality*, 59.
77. Ibid.
78. Ibid., 59-60.
79. Zetland, Marquess of 'Essayez', *The Memoirs of Lawrence, Second Marquess of Zetland*, 256.
80. Ibid., 291-2.
81. Cited in Glendevon, *Viceroy at Bay*, 198.
82. Ibid., 198-9.
83. Ibid., 199.
84. Ian Stephens, *Pakistan: Old Country, New Nation* (London: Ernest-Benn, 1967), 15.
85. See, for instance, Linlithgow's attitude towards both leaders in the context of the Lahore Resolution and the War effort. Glendevon, *Viceroy at Bay*, 184-98.
86. Comparing him with Jinnah, Zetland described Sikandar Hayat Khan as 'a man of such broad-minded views and so tolerant an outlook....' Zetland, *Memoirs of Lawrence, Second Marquess of Zetland*, 292.
87. Penderel Moon, ed., *The Viceroy's Journal* (Karachi: Oxford University Press, 1974), 368.
88. Ibid.
89. Ibid., 414.
90. Ibid., 81.
91. Ibid., 74.
92. Ibid., 379.
93. Mansergh, *Transfer of Power*, Vol. VI, 29.
94. Moon, *The Viceroy's Journal*, 248.
95. Quoted in Glendevon, *Viceroy at Bay*, 196.
96. See, in particular, Campbell-Johnson, *Mission with Mountbatten*; and Collins and Lapierre, *Freedom at Midnight*. Mountbatten's appointment as Viceroy itself, according to Collins and Lapierre, was masterminded by the Congress leadership. Ibid., 8. Also see, Hodson, *Great Divide*; and Philip Ziegler, *Mountbatten* (New York: Harper & Row Publishers, 1985).
97. See, for instance, Menon, *Transfer of Power in India*, Ch. XV, esp., 357-67. These pages certainly do not, in spite of Menon's claims to the contrary, convey a sense of either Mountbatten's 'even impartiality or the bona fides of His Majesty's Government'. Ibid., 357.
98. John Terraine, *The Life and Time of Lord Mountbatten* (London: Arrow Books, 1970), 192.

99. Ibid.

100. Leonard Mosley, *Last Days of the British Raj,* 17.

101. B.R. Tomlinson, *The Political Economy of the Raj, 1914–1947* (London: Macmillan, 1979), 141.

102. Ibid. The British managed to preserve all their economic assets both in India and Pakistan 'without insisting on any formal recognition of those positions from the successor states.' Gunnar Myrdal, *Asian Drama: An Inquiry into the Poverty of Nations,* Vol. I (New York: Pantheon, 1968), 152, f.n.

103. David Childs, *Britain Since 1945: A Political History* (London: Methuen & Co., 1986), 43.

104. Mansergh, *Transfer of Power,* Vol. VIII, 640-2.

105. Cited in Latif Ahmad Sherwani, ed., *Pakistan Resolution to Pakistan, 1940–47* (Karachi: National Publishing House, 1969), 35. As late as March 1946, British Prime Minister, Clement Attlee, was proclaiming: 'We should be conscious that the British have done a great work in India. We have united India and given her that sense of nationality which she so very largely lacked over the previous centuries' *Quaid-i-Azam Papers,* F/12, 6.

106. Ahmad, *Speeches and Writings,* Vol. I, 147-8.

107. Ahmad, *Speeches and Writings,* Vol. II, 415.

108. Ahmad, *Speeches and Writings,* Vol. I, 171.

109. For the full text of his presidential address see, ibid., 151-72.

110. Ibid., 153, 167-8.

111. Ibid., 155.

112. Ibid.

113. Ibid., 156-8. Though a current issue, the Supreme Court of India has been unable to resolve the dispute between the Muslims and the Hindus over the Babri *Masjid* (mosque) in spite of a lapse of more than a decade. The dispute is a testament to the ineffectiveness of judicial tribunals in settling issues between Muslims and Hindus in modern, 'secular', India.

114. Ahmad, *Speeches and Writings,* Vol. I, 155.

115. Ibid.

116. Ibid., 168.

117. Ibid.

118. Ibid., 169. An Indian Muslim writer felt that the demand for partition led to 'the establishment, ironically, of another majoritarian state.' A.G. Noorani, 'Muslim Identity', in Hasan, ed., *Islam, Communities and the Nation,* 121.

119. Ahmad, *Speeches and Writings,* Vol. I, 164.

120. Ibid., 171.

121. Ibid., 169.

122. Ibid.

123. Ibid., 170.

124. Liaquat Ali Khan, comp., *Resolutions of the All-India Muslim League, from December 1938 to March 1940* (Delhi: All-India Muslim League, n.d.), 47-8. Also cited in Pirzada, *Foundations of Pakistan,* Vol. II, 341. The Resolution was moved by A.K. Fazlul Haq of Bengal, and was seconded by Choudhary Khaliquzzaman (UP) of a Muslim-minority province. Choudhry Khaliquzzaman also seconded the League Legislators' resolution in 1946, demanding 'a sovereign independent

state' of Pakistan. This resolution was moved by Huseyn Shaheed Suhrawardy of Bengal. Fazlul Haq went on to become the Chief Minister and Governor of East Pakistan in the 1950s. Khaliquzzaman became the first President of the Pakistan Muslim League and also served as Governor of East Pakistan, and ambassador to Indonesia and the Philippines. Suhrawardy found the first opposition party, the Awami Muslim League in 1949, and served as Prime Minister of Pakistan from September 1956 to October 1957.

125. Liaquat Ali Khan, *Resolutions of the All-India Muslim League,* 48. In this sense, Aslam Malik is right to conclude that: 'The rights of the minorities thus become *as good a basic principle as the Pakistan demand itself.*' (Italics original). Malik, *Pakistan Resolution,* 151. For the full text of the Resolution see ibid., App. E, 231-32. Also available in the *Muslim League Papers,* Archives of the Freedom Movement, 214, 54-5. On the contrary, it is important to note, as Noorani has very aptly pointed out: 'The Partition Plan of 3 June 1947 did not contain a word about minorities in either countries.' Noorani, 'Muslim Identity', in Hasan, *Islam, Community and the Nation,* 125.

126. Cynthia Enloe, *Ethnic Conflict and Political Development* (Boston: Little Brown & Co. 1973), 15.

127. Hoffer, *The True Believer,* 112. More importantly, as one writer put it: 'What appears to have moved large numbers of younger, urban Muslims, and enabled them to draw into the movement an ever broader mass of Muslims, was the possibility of a Muslim state, at a time when Muslim power was at a low ebb the world over and when few people had considered the possibility of establishing such a modern, Muslim state in the subcontinent.' Gyanandera Pandey, *Remembering Partition* (New Delhi: Foundation Books, 2003), 27.

128. Anthony D. Smith, *Theories of Nationalism* (New York: Harper & Row, 1972), 217.

129. Coupland, *A Re-statement,* 88.

130. They had 'a common set of customs', a 'differentiating' language and religion, and 'a separate political history', constituting all 'the elements of social cohesion' of a separate nation. Smith, *Theories of Nationalism,* 215.

131. Suleri, *My Leader,* 1-2. There were of course some 'nationalist' Muslim groups that met in Delhi in April, under the auspices of the 'Azad Muslim Conference' and did not approve Jinnah's formula. However, as V.P. Menon observed: 'This Conference continued to meet from time to time, but it failed to make any impression on the increasing hold of the League on the Muslim masses'. Menon, *Transfer of Power in India,* 83.

132. See some of the appellations in Suleri, *My Leader,* 1. Indeed, this intense reaction suggested that he had become 'counter-charismatic' for the Hindus.

133. Cited in Ahmad, *Speeches and Writings,* Vol. I., 165-6. (Italics original).

134. Saleem Qureshi, *Jinnah and the Making of a Nation,* 62.

135. Ibid.

136. Ibid., 18-19.

137. Ibid., 19.

138. Rajendra Prasad, *India Divided* (Bombay: Hind Kitab, 1977), 67.

139. This was most clearly set forth in Bhai Parmanand's views expressed in his daily, *The Hindu,* published from Lahore. Also see his *Arya Samaj Aur Hindu Sanghtan*

(1923) and *Aaap-Bitti* (1923). See Hamid, *Muslim Separatism in India*, esp. 175–7, 206.

140. *The Indian Quarterly Register*, 1924, Vol. I, No. 2, 649.

141. Cited in Ahmad, *Speeches and Writings*, Vol. I, 180. Also see Nanda, *Mahatma Gandhi*, 213. But then, the Sikhs, too, were opposed to 'dividing India into two great zones', and thus 'being cut into two....' In the words of one Sikh intellectual, 'the authors of such a scheme would have to face the problem as to where they should shove in the Sikhs.' Indeed, he was convinced that 'the presence of the Sikhs on the border line of the Hindu and Muslim zones would prevent the partition of India'. Professor Sham Singh's lecture at Calcutta, reported in the *Civil and Military Gazette*, 24 April 1940.

142. Quoted in Nanda, *Mahatma Gandhi*, 213.

143. Ibid., 212.

144. Ibid., 213.

145. Jawaharlal Nehru, *The Discovery of India* (London: Meridian Books, 1946), 324. In a speech at Allahabad on 13 April 1940, Nehru, in fact, charged: 'The whole problem has taken a new complexion and there is no question of settlement or negotiation now. The knot that is before us is incapable of being tied by settlement; it needs cutting open. It needs a major operation.' He, thus concluded: 'Without mincing words, I want to say that we will have nothing to do with this mad scheme'. S. Gopal, ed., *Selected Works of Jawaharlal Nehru*, Vol. XI (New Delhi: Orient Longman, 1978), 17.

146. Cited in Ahmad, *Speeches and Writings*, Vol. I, 177–8.

147. Francis Robinson, 'Islam and Muslim Separatism', in David Taylor and Malcolm Yapp, eds., *Political Identity in South Asia* (London: Curzon Press, 1978), 86.

148. Ibid.

149. Ahmad, *Speeches and Writings*, Vol. I, 239–40. (Italics original).

150. Ibid., 180–3.

151. Ahmad, *Speeches and Writings*, Vol. I., 258–9.

152. After all, as Shafer argued, 'Nationalism is what the nationalists have made it...' Boyd C. Shafer, *Nationalism: Myth and Reality* (New York: Harcourt Brace & World, 1955), 7.

153. Chand, *History of the Freedom Movement in India*, Vol. IV., 321.

154. Lal, *Political India*, 100–4.

155. Chand, *History of the Freedom Movement in India*, Vol. IV, 321.

156. Jalal, *Sole Spokesman*, 57.

157. Chand, *History of the Freedom Movement in India*, Vol. IV, 322. Also see Sayeed, *Formative Phase*, 117–18; and Lal, *Political India*, 100–4.

158. The Convention resolved: '1) That the zones comprising Bengal and Assam in the North-East and the Punjab, North-West Frontier Province, Sind and Baluchistan in the North-West India, namely Pakistan zone where the Muslims are in a dominant majority, be constituted into a sovereign independent state...2) that two separate constitution-making bodies be set up by the people of Pakistan and Hindustan for the purpose of framing their respective constitutions....' A.M. Zaidi, *Evolution of Muslim Political Thought*, Vol. VI, 176.

159. Ibid., 170.

160. Ahmad, *Speeches and Writing*, Vol. I, 171.

161. Abdus Salam Khurshid, *History of the Idea of Pakistan* (Lahore: National Book Foundation, 1977), 131. Also see, Waheed Qureshi, *Pakistan ki Nazaryati Bunyadain* (Urdu) (Lahore: Educational Emporium, 1973), 162.

162. Pirzada, *Foundations of Pakistan*, Vol. II, 341-4, esp. 343.

163. Liaquat Ali Khan, comp., *Resolutions of the All-India Muslim League from March 1940 to 1941* (Delhi: All-India Muslim League, n.d.), 35.

164. Ahmad, *Speeches and Writings*, Vol. I, 245.

165. Pirzada, *Quaid-i-Azam Jinnah's Correspondence*, 113.

166. Ibid., 117. (Italics added).

167. A.M. Zaidi, *Evolution of Muslim Political Thought*, Vol. VI, 176. That ended all speculations or references to sovereign independent states including Bengal. Pakistan was to be the one and only state. There has been some consideration as to whether the Delhi Convention was entitled to suggest such a fundamental change in the Lahore Resolution, which was adopted at an annual session of the League. According to M.A.H. Ispahani, the 'objection' was 'merely an irrelevant technicality'. He explained: 'From the practical point of view, the Muslim nation itself was the highest tribunal. The Lahore session could not be considered to be as representative of the Muslim nation as the Delhi Convention which was attended by about [sic] 470 legislators duly and constitutionally elected by the vote of the entire nation. The change effected by the Delhi Convention resolution had the support of the nation; it was not objected to by any Muslim. In fact, the nation from the beginning had looked forward to a united sovereign Pakistan'. Ispahani, *As I Knew Him*, 137.

168. Beverley Nichols, *Verdict on India* (Bombay: Thacker & Co., 1946), 189.

169. Ibid.

170. Malik, *Pakistan Resolution*, 181. However, Malik was of the opinion that the provinces were meant to be 'really *sovereign*'. (Italics original). They were to have powers over defence, external affairs, communications, etc. But then, he suggested that 'powers were to be finally assumed by the respective regions, but with the mutual consent of the provinces opting to join the respective regions.' Ultimately, of course, these regional states '*should in free agreement enter into a joint pact to have a common agency to look after in the name of all component States certain specified subjects delegated to it....*' (Italics orginal). So much for the provinces being 'autonomous and sovereign'. Interestingly, in developing this line of argument, Malik was convinced that: 'Most probably the framers of the Pakistan Resolution had the American model in sight.' Ibid., 183, 186, 187. However, Malik did not provide any evidence to suggest how and why the framers of the Resolution should have an American model before them.

171. Jaffrelot, 'Islamic Identity and Ethnic Tensions', 16.

172. Menon, *Transfer of Power in India*, App. I, esp. 455. As indicated earlier, Sikandar Hayat Khan had his own 'zonal scheme' for India which, in spite of his opposition to the federation, was more like a federal scheme, and was based on Hindu–Muslim cooperation. Thus, according to Aslam Malik, he did not believe in Pakistan and was one of the British 'henchmen' whose job was to force Jinnah to demand 'an aggravated form of the Pakistan scheme.' The explanation was: 'If the Congress behaved reasonably, there was Sikandar's scheme: if, on the other

hand, it adopted a hostile attitude, there was Jinnah's aggravated Pakistan scheme to answer them befittingly.' Malik, *Pakistan Resolution*, 117-23.

173. Ahmad, *Speeches and Writings*, Vol. I, 529-30.

174. Ibid., 530. Indeed, opposition to the centre, in any shape or form, dominated by the Hindu-majority community, was at the root of the demand for Pakistan.

175. Cited in Menon, *Transfer of Power in* India, App. I, 444. In its meeting of February 3-6, 1940, the League Working Committee had already rejected Sikandar Hayat Khan's scheme. However, to secure his 'support' to the Lahore Resolution and also 'for the sake of saving his face', after the Khaksar clash, a brief of his scheme was 'added to the 'outline' of the Working Committee resolution which went on to serve as a preliminary draft' of the Lahore Resolution. See Malik, *Pakistan Resolution*, 138, 141, 147. However, Ashiq Hussain Batalvi argued that Sikandar Hayat Khan had still not lost interest in the final shape of the resolution. According to him, Sikandar Hayat Khan was present on the night of 22 March, when the Lahore Resolution was finally worded by the Muslim League Subject Committee, and was also very keen to see to it that the resolution was correctly translated into Urdu. In fact, he rose from the back seats to come and sit with Maulana Zafar Ali Khan who was doing the translation work to make sure that it was exact. He, thus, claimed that Sikandar Hayat Khan was actively involved in the final drafting of the Resolution. Ashiq Hussain Batalvi, *Chand Yadain, Chand Taasurat* (Urdu) (Lahore: Sang-i-Meel, 1992), 197.

176. Ahmad, *Speeches and Writings*, Vol. I, 246-7. (Italics added). Again, in a speech to the students at Aligarh on 2 November 1941, Jinnah reiterated: 'Pakistan is not a mere slogan or a counter for bargaining. It is a political reality and a practical solution of the most complex problem of India's future constitution. We are not going to budge an inch from our demand.' *Indian Annual Register* (Calcutta: Annual Register Office, 1941), 298. Also note Jinnah's answer at a press conference at Delhi on 13 September 1942: 'Asked if there was any chance of the modification of the Muslim demands, the Quaid-i-Azam declared: if you start asking for sixteen annas in a rupee there is room for bargaining. The Muslim League has never put forward any demand which can, by any reasonable man, be characterized as unreasonable. The Muslim League stands for independence both of the Hindus and of the Musalmans. Hindu India had got three-fourths of India in its pocket according to our proposal, and it is the Hindu India which is bargaining to see if it can get remaining one-fourth also for itself and rid us out of it'. Ibid., 431. Strangely enough, as Tinker pointed out, 'British opinion was almost unanimous in declaring that the "Pakistan demand" was a deliberate over-bid by the League to obtain full consideration for the Muslim point of view in the final reckoning.' Hugh Tinker, *Experiment with Freedom: India and Pakistan, 1947*, 24. This may perhaps explain the emphasis on the 'counter for bargaining' thesis in several accounts subsequently.

177. Menon, *Transfer of Power in India*, 437.

178. Nanda, *Mahatma Gandhi*, 208.

179. Chand, *History of the Freedom Movement in India*, Vol. IV, 541.

180. Jalal, *Sole Spokesman*, 292.

181. Jalal, *Self and Sovereignty*, 386.

182. Batalvi, *Chand Yadain*, 199. This account of Batalvi is also corroborated by another source. See Mohammed Raza Khan, *What Price Freedom?* (Karachi: Indus Publications, 1977), 76.

183. Pirzada, *Quaid-i-Azam Jinnah's Correspondence*, 123.

184. Ahmad, *Speeches and Writings*, Vol. II, 135.

185. A.M. Zaidi, *Evolution of Muslim Political Thought*, Vol. VI, 183.

186. Ibid., 190.

187. Ahmad, *Speeches and Writings*, Vol. I, 174.

188. Ibid.

189. Ibid., 174–5. Indeed, Jinnah ruled out any idea of 'migrations'. In fact, he observed that 'a wrong idea and false propaganda appears to be set in motion in order to frighten the Muslim minorities that they would have to migrate *en bloc* and wholesale'. He maintained: 'I wish to assure my Muslim brethren that there is no justification for this insidious misrepresentation.' Ibid., 174.

190. F.K. Khan Durrani, *The Meaning of Pakistan* (Lahore: Sh. Muhammad Ashraf, 1946), 'Preface', x.

191. Cited in Sayeed, *Formative Phase*, 204.

192. Ahmad, *Speeches and Writings*, Vol. I, 253.

193. Pirzada, *Quaid-i-Azam Jinnah's Correspondence*, 112.

194. Nichols, *Verdict on India*, 189.

195. Hodson, *Great Divide*, 80.

196. Wolpert, *Jinnah of Pakistan*, 182.

197. Ibid.

198. Ahmad, *Speeches and Writings*, Vol. I, 172. Although Jinnah could not secure all the Muslim-majority areas demanded in the Lahore Resolution, as 'he was left with a Pakistan defined by religious distribution district by district', the outcome in August 1947 still lent 'no support to speculation that the Pakistan demand was Jinnah's bargaining counter for power in a united India....' See Moore, 'Jinnah and the Pakistan Demand', 561.

6 The Political Mobilization and Organization of the Muslims

Jinnah based his strategy for political mobilization and organization of the Muslims on a number of systematic, planned moves. In the first instance, he moved to 'expand' the League to accommodate new entrants, particularly those who were inspired by the idea of Pakistan, and were thus more than willing to join the Muslim League and serve its cause. In 1941, in the League session at Madras, Pakistan was made the ultimate goal of the League's programme and policies. However, the problem was that the League, like most political parties in the developing societies, was 'a dispersed, weakly articulated and organized feudalistic traditional system'[1] with little room and scope for new groups and interests. Having gone through the 'expansion' phase, Jinnah sought to bring the newly mobilized and the traditional groups in the League under a single, national authority 'concentrating' power in the hands of the President of the League.[2] If the League was to become 'the sole representative body of Muslim India',[3] it was necessary that his charisma was 'routinized' in the League. It was particularly important given the fact that the Muslim masses were moved, first and foremost, by Jinnah's personal charisma rather than the League itself. In fact, as our discussion will show, Jinnah's charisma went beyond the institutional apparatus of the League. That is why, in addition to securing the support of various groups and interests to the League, Jinnah also planned a mass-mobilization campaign to give the Muslims at large a 'cause' to identify with and influence their attitudes and behaviours as both individuals and as a collectivity, as a community. Finally, Jinnah aimed to take advantage of the favourable situation created by the on-going war, with the Congress not cooperating and thus making many mistakes in the process, to help win the overwhelming support of the Muslims. These moves were not necessarily sequential. They often operated simultaneously. But, in the end, they reinforced and revitalized one another.

Jinnah initiated the expansion of the Muslim League through its structural reorganization. Under the Constitution of 1940,[4] Primary Leagues were established at the grassroots level representing *Mohallahs* (city wards). Primary Leagues were grouped into *Tehsil* and District Muslim Leagues and were entrusted with the League activities within their domains. District Leagues were constituted into Provincial Muslim Leagues, which were given representation at the centre in the Muslim League Working Committee. The Working Committee, in turn, was made responsible to the Council of the All-India Muslim League.[5] It was clearly stipulated in the constitution that all resolutions passed by the Working Committee were subject to approval and ratification by the Council, which was elected by Muslim Provincial Leagues from amongst their members. The President of the All-India Muslim League was elected annually by the Council from a panel of nominees advanced by different branches of the party. Jinnah had refused to become a 'life president' of the Muslim League. As he told the Leaguers: 'Let me come to you at the end of every year and seek your vote and your confidence. Let your President be on his good behaviour. I am definitely opposed to your electing a life president.'[6]

The result of this carefully arranged expansion of the League structure was to open new avenues of association and participation within the organization and attract a host of Muslim groups and interests. The most enthusiastic response, as might be expected, came from the educated, urban middle classes, merchant-industrialists, traders, bankers, professionals, and other newly mobilized groups whose prospects for upward mobility in Hindu-dominated India were limited. Most of them joined the League to avail opportunities in the proposed state of Pakistan. They realized that economic life in India, both in the public and private sectors, offered them very little, and was further going to be dominated by the Hindus.

Their support to the League not only assured 'a greater dispersion' of power within the organization but also afforded Jinnah the much needed strength to balance traditional groupings through 'reciprocal checks and controls'.[7] In the end, heterogeneous groups like the educated urban middle classes, big landowners, and *ulama* went on to support the League. The support of the *ulama* ranged from the Farangi Mahal family to the Barelvis to those *ulama* of Deoband who broke away from the Jamiat-ul-Ulama-i-Hind. Allama Shabbir Ahmad Usmani, for instance, claimed that, 'whatever might be alleged about the landlords, the Nawabs and other titled gentry in the League, there was not a shadow of doubt that Jinnah's integrity was irreproachable'.[8] The support of the *ulama* proved to be a crucial factor in the League victories in the 1945–46 elections, especially in the two Muslim-majority provinces of the Punjab and Sindh, and the 1947 referendums in the NWFP and the district of Sylhet in Assam.

It is true that 'landlords, the Nawabs and other titled gentry' stood firm in their support to the League. Nawab Mohammad Ismail Khan (1886–1958), Chaudhary Khaliquzzaman, Raja Sahib of Mahmudabad, Muhammed Ayub Khuhro, Sardar Aurangzeb Khan, and the Nawabs of Mamdot, Nawab Shah Nawaz Khan and Nawab Iftikhar Hussain Khan (1905–1969), to name a few, extended their whole-hearted support to Jinnah and the demand for Pakistan. Indeed, they did not hesitate to sacrifice their own sectional interests for the sake of the larger cause. Highlighting this metamorphosis in the attitude of the group, Nawab Iftikhar Hussain Khan of Mamdot, a big landowner from the Punjab, claimed in the course of a speech in 1946:

> Whenever the Punjab Muslims showed signs of awakening from their slumber, they were given sleeping doses. This time Sir Bertrand Glancy [Governor] also gave sleeping doses to the Muslims in the form of *murabbas* (squares of land) and *jagirs*. He sometimes gave as many as 20 *murrabba* doses to some Muslims, but he failed.[9]

Jinnah too recognized the importance of the landed interests with their awesome 'control' over 'the traditional channels of political mobilization'.[10] He allowed them to play their legitimate role in the cause of the League and the demand for Pakistan, as was evident from the large number of big landowners serving on the League Working Committee and the Council of the League. He did not approve of their system of 'exploitation' which, he felt, 'is so vicious, which is so wicked and which makes them so selfish that it is difficult to reason with them'.[11] However, he was at pains to assure them that the League had nothing against their interests as long as the demand for Pakistan remained unrealized.[12] Eventually, he acknowledged: 'We shall have time to quarrel among ourselves, and we shall have time when wrongs and injuries will have to be remedied. We shall have time for domestic programme and policies, but first get the Government. This is a nation without any territory'.[13]

The induction of the newly mobilized and politically participant groups in the League, however, ensured that it remained no longer a 'reactionary' organization, under the influence of the landlords and other traditional social groups, as has been often claimed in the past both by the party's supporters and critics.[14] It had also come to represent modern groups—the 'progressive' sections of the Muslim society.[15] The League had transformed itself into a Muslim nationalist organization bringing together the landowners, educated, urban middle classes, and lower classes into a grand synthesis of the traditional and modern groups characteristic of national awakenings in Europe itself. The League tapped into the Muslims' 'new life, and to a consciousness of themselves as a separate people, with a powerful determination and programme of their own'.[16] While this 'new life' encouraged 'complete harmony'[17] at the present, in the long run internecine struggles could defeat the original purpose for which the support of these diverse groups had been successfully obtained, unless, of course, some mechanism was devised to aggregate and articulate their interests.

Although the formula, the demand for Pakistan, was a unifying factor and indeed a rallying point for diverse groups, the difficulty was that each group saw the demand through the prism of its own interests. An institutional framework was desperately needed to provide channels for interest articulation within the League. Jinnah's charisma was already established. But an office was required for the 'routinization' of charisma. The office of the President of the Muslim League, the chief executive of the party, appeared to be ideally suited to the purpose. However, it was necessary to make this office increasingly strong to represent Jinnah's growing status and authority among the Muslims. Thus, successive constitutions of the League in 1941, 1942, and 1944 provided for a steady increase of powers in the hands of the President. The 1944 constitution clearly stipulated that the 'President shall be the principal head of the whole organization, shall exercise all the powers inherent in his office and be responsible to see that all the authorities work in accordance with the constitution and rules of the All-India Muslim League'.[18] The enhanced authority of the office of the president provided Jinnah the organizational basis for his charisma to launch his next move, that is, the 'concentration' of power in his own hands, to control and discipline the diverse social groups and interests, and thus make the League a well-knit and disciplined organization of the Muslims. But for his charisma, there was no other force capable of keeping the Muslims together. It was time for Jinnah to assert his charisma and to help 'routinize' it in the League. The office of the President had already been strengthened for the purpose. But this was not to be an easy task given the fact that Jinnah's charisma was still not accepted by some powerful groups of the Muslim community, particularly the provincial leaders of the Muslim-majority provinces.

In the case of Sindh,[19] for instance, Jinnah found it considerably difficult to discipline the provincial leaders. The 'realities of rural power' coupled with a slender majority of the Muslims,[20] compelled Jinnah 'to work through the existing League leadership much as he would have liked to have dealt with men more loyal to his ideals'.[21] Jinnah also found it difficult to discipline the provincial leaders of the Punjab and Bengal who joined the League in 1937 at Lucknow. They were highly reluctant to yield control to the centre, as evidenced by the attitudes of Sikandar Hayat Khan, the Premier of the Punjab, and Fazlul Huq, the Premier of Bengal. Jinnah understood fully well that without exercising direct and decisive power over these recalcitrant provincial leaders, the League could not claim to be the sole, authoritative and representative organization of the Muslims. He was thus constrained to work to bring these fractious provincial leaders under the authority of the central League, even if it entailed an arduous journey.

Despite Sikandar Hayat Khan's lukewarm support to the League, Jinnah appointed him member of the League Working Committee, and much to the chagrin of the old stalwarts of the League like Allama Iqbal, allowed his followers in the Unionist Party to have a preponderant influence and representation in the League Council. Eventually, the League Council refused the affiliation of the Punjab Provincial Muslim League, represented by the old Leaguers, in its meeting of 3 April 1938. While Jinnah respected and recognized the sentiments of the old Leaguers, he could not ignore the position the Unionists had acquired in the Punjab over the years. He was at pains to ensure that Sikandar

Hayat Khan remained associated with the League, at least until the League could 'take off' and become an effective force in its own right.[22]

This was the 'expansionist' phase in Jinnah's strategy as far as the provincial leaders were concerned. He was content to 'expand' his power for the present without worrying too much about its 'concentration'. However, as the League began to command general respect and recognition in the Punjab and its demand for Pakistan came to inspire a mass following in the province, and Jinnah's own standing as a charismatic leader improved, he could not long postpone the next move.[23] In 1941, he forced Sikandar Hayat Khan to resign from the Viceroy's National Defence Council, which he had joined without the explicit permission and approval of the League President. The result of the League's increased activities in the Punjab was that, by 1942, Sikandar Hayat Khan was not only 'reluctant to break with Jinnah' but more importantly, was 'less inclined even than before to stand up to Jinnah'. In fact, he feared, as he told Penderel Moon, 'that unless he walked warily and kept on the right side of Jinnah he would be swept away by a wave of fanaticism and, wherever he went, would be greeted by the Muslims with black flags'.[24]

But then, Jinnah, as Mirza Abul Hassan Ispahani (1902–1981), a close confidant of Jinnah and important leader of the League in Bengal put it, 'gave a long rope to Sir Sikandar'.[25] The result was that the Muslim public opinion in the Punjab, in spite of Sikandar Hayat Khan's hesitant attitude began to change. By November 1942, the Punjab Muslim League was strong enough to hold a provincial conference at Lyallpur (Faisalabad). Jinnah presided the conference. Sikandar Hayat Khan, 'too, noting the trend of public opinion, appeared at the Conference and made a speech'.[26] So far, 'he had been careful to avoid League meetings inside his province'.[27] Jinnah, in his 'Foreword' to Letters of Iqbal to Jinnah (1942), published when Iqbal was no more, underscored the importance of his approach towards Sikandar Hayat Khan and expressed deep satisfaction at the outcome of his tactical adjustments. 'But unfortunately', he lamented, 'he [Iqbal] has not lived to see that Punjab has all around made a remarkable progress and now it is beyond doubt that Muslims stand solidly behind the Muslim League Organization'.[28]

Jinnah also capitalized on the opportunity furnished by Fazlul Huq's half-hearted, if not involuntary, entry into the League. Fazlul Huq, like Sikandar Hayat Khan, was unwilling to sacrifice his provincial interests at the altar of an all-India body like the League. This was in spite of the fact that he headed a League Coalition Ministry in Bengal. While League leaders, like Ispahani, criticized Fazlul Huq for his 'lip-loyalty to the League',[29] Jinnah, as in the case of Sikandar Hayat Khan, showed patience. He wanted to extend the League's influence and standing in the province through Fazlul Huq's support to the party, no matter how disconcerting it was to the loyal, committed League leaders. As he explained to Ispahani in one of his letters,

> You cannot expect everything to go on the footing of a highly developed standard of public life, as these are only the beginnings that are being made. You must not mix up the aims we have with the achievements. The aims are not achieved immediately when they are laid down. But, I think, on the whole, Bengal has done well and we must be thankful for small mercies. As you go on, of course, with patience and tact, things are bound to develop and improve more and more in accordance with our ideals and aims.[30]

As later events showed, Jinnah's 'patience and tact' helped. The Muslim League emerged as the most powerful organization of the Bengali Muslims and Fazlul Huq was left with no option but to accept the supreme authority of the central League. In 1941, he had shown signs of defiance by protesting over the manner in which the League had asked him to tender his resignation over the issue of the Defence Council, and did not mind deserting the party on that account. But, on 13 November 1942, he was constrained to tell Jinnah that 'you can easily realize I have been longing to meet you and to assure you of my attachment to you and the Muslim League'.[31] Indeed, he was now 'so shaken' by the rising strength of the League and Jinnah among the Muslim masses that he 'was prepared to retire from Bengal politics if a dignified way out, such as a seat on the Viceroy's Executive Council, was offered to him'.[32] This, in fact, he did get, but then he was forced to resign.[33] Jinnah did not want any Muslim leaders on the Council without the consent and approval of the League. On 5 February 1943, Fazlul Huq was prepared to 'liquidate' his 'own' party and resign the office of Prime Minister of Bengal if the League agreed to take him back in its fold. Indeed, he pleaded, 'I hope you will render the barest possible justice by taking me back to the League as soon as your conditions are satisfied'.[34] By then, of course, it was not difficult for Fazlul Huq to see the grim reality on the ground. The League's candidates had achieved overwhelming victories in two by-elections at Natore and Baburghat against the candidates sponsored by the Huq Coalition Ministry. By 1943, Fazlul Huq's Ministry had lost the majority support and Fazlul Huq himself was left with no choice but to 'assure' Jinnah 'that I will abide by the discipline of the party and the instructions of the President of the Muslim League'.[35] He was back in the League in September 1946, exhausted and tamed. Jinnah's rising charisma was well routinized in the office of the President of the League, making it a 'strict disciplinary' organization in the Weberian sense of 'discipline.' The result was that it became exceedingly difficult for 'a Sikandar Hayat or a Fazlul Haq to defy the orders of the Quaid-i-Azam'.[36]

Sikandar Hayat Khan died in 1942, leaving Jinnah at a loss in the Punjab. His successor, Khizar Hayat Khan Tiwana, encouraged by the British Government, defied Jinnah's authority at the centre and tried to break with the League. Not to speak of ordinary British officials, Governor Bertrand Glancy,[37] and Viceroy Lord Wavell did their utmost to encourage Khizar Hayat Khan to resist Jinnah. In fact, Wavell claimed that it was 'right to back up Khizar in the Punjab against Jinnah's attempts to disrupt the Unionist Ministry'.[38] This deliberate effort to support and encourage opposition to Jinnah was not unique to the case of the Punjab, where the British had high stakes, as 'The Punjabi Mussalman was the backbone of the Indian Army'.[39] It was a general manifestation of the British policy of keeping Muslim-majority areas out of Jinnah's reach. Even a Muslim-minority area like the UP was not to be conceded. As early as 1937, Secretary to the Governor of the UP asked, 'what has that fellow Jinnah got to do with UP Muslims: who is he in the UP any way?'[40]

Though Jinnah was keen to retain Khizar Hayat Khan's association with the League, he was not willing to accept him as an 'ally', as he had accepted Sikandar Hayat Khan early in his regime. Aware of the phenomenal growth in the popularity of the League in the Punjab in recent years, and the need for discipline in the party in this critical phase of the struggle for Pakistan, Jinnah was inclined to treat Khizar

Hayat Khan more as a follower. Jinnah thus demanded that Khizar Hayat Khan subject himself to the discipline of the central League. In fact, he personally came to Lahore in April 1944 to discuss the issue with him at length.[41] However, Khizar Hayat Khan refused to submit to his authority, encouraged by the British on the one hand, and his Unionist colleagues, particularly Sir Chotu Ram, on the other. Subsequent events indicated that this was the beginning of the end for Khizar Hayat Khan's political fortunes. Jinnah effectively blocked his manoeuvres at the centre in the Simla Conference of 1945,[42] and challenged his authority in his home province. The Conference itself was doomed 'by Jinnah's refusal' to allow non-League Muslims to 'serve on a new Viceroy's Council', including the Unionists.[43] Mobilizing masses in the Punjab over the issue of Pakistan, the Muslim League routed the Unionist Party in the 1945–46 elections[44] and forced Khizar Hayat Khan, through a massive agitation launched in January 1947, mainly in the urban areas of the province, to resign his office and the ministry. On 3 March Khizar Hayat Khan publicly agreed 'to leave the field clear for the Muslim League...in the best interests of the Muslims and the province'.[45]

Interestingly, while Jinnah was prone to 'expand' and 'concentrate' power in his own hands to bring the Muslims under the authority of the League President, he was not hesitant to delegate powers to senior party leaders. In December 1943, he set up a 'Committee of Action' under the chairmanship of Nawab Ismail Khan, with the authority to act on his behalf whenever necessary. As he explained at the Karachi session of the League on 24 December 1943,

> ...now the work of the Muslim League Organization has gone beyond the physical capacity of any single man. If you were to know what I have to attend to all alone, you will be astonished. All over India, today this happening in Patna, tomorrow that thing happening in Bengal; the day after tomorrow this thing happening in NWFP; the day after that this thing happening in Madras. All sorts of questions arise from day to day and from week to week. Now it is not possible for one single man to do justice to all this....[46]

This delegation of authority also revealed that Jinnah, like a true 'modernizing' leader, had decided to move from a phase marked by the expansion and concentration of power to the 'dispersion of power'.[47] He wanted to 'disperse' power. But here, too, he followed a path peculiar to modernizing leaders. Power had to be dispersed within the League and not outside it. It was to be 'a single-party system',[48] as Jinnah made abundantly clear on a number of occasions. There must be no Muslim 'show-boy' of the Congress as he told Maulana Abdul Kalam Azad in July 1940, nor a possible Muslim 'Quisling', like Khizar Hayat Khan, as he informed Lord Wavell at the 1945 Simla Conference. Indian Muslims belonged to one party, and that was the All-India Muslim League.[49] In his message to the Muslims of the NWFP on 27 November 1945, he plainly stated, '...support the League candidate even though he may be a lamp-post....'[50] Jinnah insisted that the League was 'the sole representative body of Muslim India'. He challenged any opponent to 'let him convince him and the League that the League policy was detrimental to the interests of the Muslims'.[51] Indeed, he equated the support for the League with the support for Pakistan. 'Every vote in favour of Muslim League candidates', he contended in the course of a speech in the 1945-46 elections, 'means Pakistan. Every vote against Muslim League candidates means Hindu Raj'.[52] The League's integral relationship with Pakistan was an important part of Jinnah's charismatic appeal.

Analytically speaking, Jinnah's charismatic appeal had two components, the 'normative' and the 'structural'. The normative appeal, in turn, had two elements. The first represented the special interests of the Muslims and involved opposition to both the existing British Raj and the imminent threat of Hindu rule once the former left India. The parliamentary system of government, resting on the majority principle and its application by the Congress from 1937 to 1939 clearly demonstrated that formal constitutional guarantees, such as separate electorates, were woefully inadequate safeguards for Muslim interests. 'Muslim India, therefore', Jinnah asserted, 'cannot accept any constitution which must necessarily result in a Hindu majority government. Hindus and Muslims brought together under a democratic system forced upon the minorities can only mean Hindu Raj'.[53] Jinnah also made it clear that the Muslims were 'not a minority as it is commonly known and understood'.[54] The Muslims and Hindus were two separate and distinct nations and that the Muslim nation was 'a nation according to any definition of a nation, and they must have their homelands, their territory and their state'.[55] Muslims, Jinnah elaborated,

> ...are a nation of a hundred million, and, what is more, we are a nation with our own distinctive culture and civilization, language and literature, art and architecture, names and nomenclature, sense of value and proportion, legal laws and moral codes, customs and calendar, history and traditions, aptitudes and ambitions—in short, we have our own distinctive outlook on life and of life. By all canons of international law, we are a nation.[56]

The second, and arguably the more important, component of Jinnah's normative appeal was his emphasis on Islam as an ideal, a system of life, indeed as an ideology. He wanted the Muslims to 'develop to the fullest our spiritual, cultural, economic, social and political life in a way that we think best and in consonance with our own ideal....'[57] Islam, he pointed out, 'regulates' a Muslim's 'life and his conduct...,'[58] and includes,

> ...everything from the ceremonies of religion to those of daily life; from the salvation of the soul to the health of the body; from the rights of all to those of each individual, from morality to crime, from punishment here to that in the life to come.... It is complete code regulating the whole Muslim society, every department of life, collectively and individually.[59]

In this sense, Jinnah's appeal was a blend of both modern and traditional norms. He promoted the modern concept of nationalism based on the nationalist attributes of Indian Muslims on the one hand, and stressed the ideological, traditional character of Islam on the other. The reconciliation of the two, that is nationalism and Islam, in the demand for Pakistan, served as the basis for Muslim nationalism in India. That is why it developed into such a formidable force. But then, this was not a unique development. Many nationalist leaders have employed the concept of nationalism and religious traditions towards political advance, especially in the Muslim world.[60] In fact, as Wilfred Cantwell Smith insisted, nationalism, for Muslims, has always been a 'Muslim nationalism.' As he elaborated:

> ...the driving force of nationalism has become more and more religious the more the movement has penetrated the masses. Even where the leaders

and the form and the ideas of the movement have been nationalist on a more or less western pattern, the followers and the substance and the emotions were significantly Islamic.[61]

Muslim nationalism in India followed an identical route. The more it spread and gained strength among the masses, the more the Islamic content became pronounced and dominant. It was not long before Jinnah himself exhorted the Muslims to come forward not only for their own 'emancipation in the form of a separate independent State' of Pakistan but for the sake of 'Islamic renaissance'. As he explained at some length to Sardar Shaukat Hayat Khan, one of his ardent followers, early in 1943:

> The Muslims ruled India for well-nigh a thousand years. But what is the position now? You can go round Delhi and see the descendants of Moghul Princes earning a miserable living by carrying earth-loads on their heads. The Muslims have been going down and down due to Hindu machination and discrimination under British rule. What will be the Muslim's lot in an independent United India with Hindus in absolute power? They will be just another class of pariahs occupying a status lower than even that of the Scheduled Castes. That is the economic aspect of the situation which makes it essential and indispensable for Muslims to seek their emancipation in the form of a separate independent State in regions of their majority. But that is not the whole object of the Pakistan movement. The other and higher aspect of Pakistan is that it would be a base where we will be able to train and bring up Muslim intellectuals, educationists, economists, scientists, doctors, engineers, technicians, etc. who will work to bring about Islamic renaissance.[62]

In the end, of course, the strength of Muslim nationalism and the demand for Pakistan rested on Jinnah's personal charisma having been 'routinized' in the Muslim League. The League represented and symbolized his charismatic authority, having matured through the three phases of expansion, concentration and dispersion of power. But then, as Max Weber suggested, charisma resides essentially in the *personality* of the charismatic leader and is not fully transferred to the organization no matter how much it is routinized at a particular point in time. Jinnah's case was no exception. All of Jinnah's charisma could not be transferred to the League. It transcended the League's organizational framework and indeed its capacity. A large number of Muslims owed their allegiance and loyalty to Jinnah and Jinnah alone. They were not interested in party politics or affiliation with a political party. They believed in Jinnah and his demand for Pakistan. They were ready and willing to support the League without being formally associated with the party. In this sense, it will not be inappropriate to argue that the League was a charismatic movement rather than a political party in the conventional sense. That explained why the League, in spite of the criticism that it was a 'weak' and 'disorganized' party, became a dominant force by the mid-1940s, and secured overwhelming Muslim support for Pakistan in the crucial elections of 1945–46. Jinnah's charisma made all the difference. Although routinized in the League, and thus synonymous with the League, his charisma was not limited to the League as such. It had its roots in the vast array of masses. The masses recognized and responded to his personal charisma. This confirms the charisma hypothesis that, in the end, it is the leader's personality and not the organization itself, which ensures the success of a political party in the elections.

However, like any charismatic leader, Jinnah had the support of some enthusiastic followers who saw the demand for Pakistan as primarily their own call to duty, and thus were prepared to contribute crucially to its realization. Most of these followers came from three social groups: 1) the students; 2) the *ulama*, *pirs* and *sajjadanashins*; and 3) the women.[63] They were the ones who felt, more than others, the irresistible appeal of Jinnah and his Pakistan demand and thus served the cause of the League with enthusiasm, determination and dedication.[64] As their efforts were of critical importance for the success of the League's mass-mobilization campaign, it will not be out of place to discuss them in some detail.[65]

1. The Students. Educated, informed and aware of constitutional and communal developments in India, the Muslim students were enraptured by Jinnah's charisma and the Pakistan demand.[66] They already lagged behind the Hindus in government jobs and professions, and the future seemed bleak to them. They found it increasingly difficult to compete with the Hindus and get employment commensurate with their education and aspirations. They were convinced that this had much to do with their 'minority' status in a united India, made all the more distressful by the inadequate system of government and the indifferent, if not hostile, attitude of the Hindu-majority. Of course, this difficulty was not peculiar to the students as most social groups and classes confronted a similar state of affairs. However, the frustrations of youth added a further impetus to their agony. They 'needed a political outlet'.[67] The Pakistan demand provided a natural outlet for their suppressed energies and denied opportunities. This was amply demonstrated by their aggressive zeal and enthusiasm in the struggle for the creation of Pakistan.

While Indian students had been active on the political scene since the partition of Bengal (1905–11), Jinnah, in particular, advised the students to shun active politics and confine their interest to studies and cultivation of political awareness. He was, for the most part, content to urge the students to stay out of the political arena. It was only when he realized that the Muslims were confronted with an extraordinarily difficult situation that he blessed, in 1937, the formation of the All-India Muslim Students Federation to organize the Muslim students on a political platform.[68] However, he still did not countenance an active political role for the students. He wanted the students 'to study and think and realise your responsibility'.[69] But then Jinnah could not for long deny that the students had a role to play in the political developments, and an active one at that, especially in mobilizing support for Pakistan among the masses. In a message to the UP branch of the Muslim Students Federation in late 1944, he urged:

> ...it is up to you now—Muslim students and Muslim young men—to take up this nation-wide task in its right perspective and in the spirit of voluntary service in the cause of Islam and the Millat. It is the young men who can make the great contribution to mould the destinies of a nation. It is the youth who fight, toil and struggle for the freedom of a nation. I hope this grim reality is not lost upon you.[70]

The 'grim reality' was not lost upon the Muslim students. They organized and launched an active campaign to make sure that the struggle for Pakistan was not lost for want of efforts. Indeed, moved by the 'twin objects of their adoration of the Quaid and Pakistan',[71] the students toured different parts of the country, especially the Muslim-majority provinces, to make personal contacts with the masses and to explain to them the rationale and need for Pakistan. In particular, they made it a point to visit the far-flung rural areas of the Punjab, the stronghold of the Unionists. Students of Aligarh University, in particular, travelled extensively in the rural areas of the Punjab and Sindh to enlist support for the Muslim League and Pakistan. In addition, the students also brought out a number of journals and magazines devoted to the 'Pakistan' cause. Journals like *Awakening*, a quarterly published by the Aligarh Muslim Students Federation, played a distinct role in the propaganda work.[72] In this effort, the students were greatly helped by the administration and staff of Aligarh University. In fact, the Vice-Chancellor of the university, Dr Ziauddin Ahmad (1878–1947), his colleagues, such as A.B.A. Haleem (the first Vice-Chancellor of the University of Karachi, after the creation of Pakistan) and Obaidur Rahman Sherwani, and faculty members such as Jamil-ud-Din Ahmad (the editor of Jinnah's *Speeches and Writings* frequently cited here), M.B. Mirza and Mohammad Afzal Husain Qadri helped convert Aligarh into 'a League stronghold'. It is no exaggeration to claim that 'Aligarh's support for the Pakistan movement was crucial for winning over the Muslim intelligentsia throughout India and putting them in the forefront of the movement'.[73]

The Muslim students not only helped Jinnah with the political aspect of the campaign for Pakistan but also played an important role in the social and economic uplift of the masses. Indeed, they pressed forward 'an active mass campaign for social and economic mass issues, winning mass support among poor Moslems'.[74] Hailing predominantly from a middle-class background, they saw the plight of the Muslim masses from an angle different to that of big landowners dominating for the most part the Provincial Leagues, especially in the Punjab and Sindh. Their approach was bound to pay dividends in the short-term as well. By the end of 1944, the Punjab and Sindh Leagues claimed a following of nearly 200,000 and 300,000 members respectively.[75] The result was an overwhelming victory for the League in the two key provinces in the 1945–46 elections. Jamil-ud-Din Ahmad claimed that: 'I can say without fear of contradiction that the League's cent-per-cent success in the second general election held in Sind towards the end of 1946 was due, in a large measure, to the thorough and systematic work done by Aligarh men'.[76]

The students were not simply keen to mobilize support for the League among the pro-Pakistan Muslim masses. They were also determined to take on the recalcitrant provincial leaders. This was convincingly demonstrated in the Punjab, where the Punjab Muslim

Students Federation, led by Mian Bashir Ahmad, Hameed Nizami, Zahoor Alam Shaheed, and others, not only bore 'the brunt of the entire opposition' to the Pakistan idea but also took it upon themselves to launch a mass movement against Khizar Hayat Khan's ministry, the most powerful organized opposition to the League in the province.[77] The ouster of Khizar Hayat Khan was the turning point in the fortunes of the League and the demand for Pakistan. Jinnah was elated. 'Perhaps the students do not know' he exclaimed, 'that by organizing this successful movement, they have changed the course of [the] history of India'.[78]

2. The *Ulama, Pirs* and *Sajjadanashins*. Those *ulama*, *pirs* and *sajjadanashins* who came to foster, in the years following the demand for Pakistan in 1940, a fervent hope of Islamic order in the proposed Muslim State responded enthusiastically to Jinnah's call. They issued *fatwas* in favour of the Muslim League[79] and pledged all-out support. While some contributed individually, many leading *ulama*, *pirs* and *sajjadanashins* launched collective efforts under the auspices of the Jamiat-ul-Ulama-i-Islam, established in October 1945. Led by Allama Shabbir Ahmad Usmani and his associates from Deoband who disapproved of the Jamiat-ul-Ulama-i-Hind's pro-Congress stance of 'composite' nationalism, they promoted the League's cause and whole-heartedly defended Jinnah's leadership from attacks by the dissenting *ulama*. Allama Usmani highlighted the fact that Jinnah was honest and 'incorruptible'. He was also convinced, like Allama Iqbal before him, that Jinnah was the only Muslim leader who fully understood the intricacies of modern-day politics in India.[80] He had, thus, nothing but contempt and ridicule for those *ulama* who dubbed him the '*Kafir-i-Azam*, or great infidel', and thus challenged his leadership.[81] The Allama and his associates' faith in Jinnah's leadership was fully vindicated in the 1945–46 elections, and the 1947 referendums in the North-West Frontier Province and Sylhet.[82]

The *ulama*, *pirs* and *sajjadanashins* toured the length and breadth of the country,[83] particularly, the Punjab, Sindh, and the NWFP, and exhorted the Muslims to vote for the League. Their support 'helped to neutralize the religious opposition to Pakistan' from the *ulama* associated with Jamiat-ul-Ulama-i-Hind, and indeed, conveyed a distinct sense of 'the religious foundations of the Pakistan demand'.[84] More importantly, their efforts helped Jinnah build support among the religiously conscious Muslim masses of the rural areas.[85] They voted overwhelmingly in favour of the Muslim League candidates in the 1945–46 elections. In the NWFP, where the League failed to do well,[86] the religious leaders had to wage another campaign in early 1947 to secure the support of the province for Pakistan in the referendum scheduled in July 1947. Led by the Pir of Manki Sharif, Mohammad Aminul Hasanat (1923–1960), Allama Shabbir Ahmad Usmani, Pir Jamaat Ali Shah, and Maulana Abdus Sattar Khan Niazi, they toured different parts of the province. They insited that, 'A Pathan is a Muslim first and a Muslim last', and thus the Pathans must support Pakistan in the referendum.[87] They claimed that Islamic *Shariat* would be enforced in Pakistan after it came into being. In this way, they managed to arouse their Muslim consciousness over and above their Pakhtun ethnicity. In addition, the *pirs* and *sajjadanashins* took full advantage of their *piri-muridi* networks to woo reluctant voters in the province, particularly in the Pakhtun areas traditionally aligned with Abdul Ghaffar Khan's Khudai Khidmatgars. The Pir of Manki Sharif was particularly helpful as he had a large following in the province, which he mobilized for the crucial referendum. He travelled all over the province, even to the remotest corners, to warn the Muslims that they will become 'slaves' of the Hindus in a united India if they did not vote for Pakistan.[88] The result of all these efforts was that the League won the July referendum convincingly, securing 289,244 votes for Pakistan as against 2,874 votes for India, or 99.02 per cent of the total votes cast, or 50.49 per cent of the total electorate entitled to vote, with the Khudai Khidmatgars and the Congress having boycotted.[89] Led by Maulana Zafar Ahmad Usmani, the *ulama* also helped the League secure Sylhet's merger with Pakistan. The district voted overwhelmingly in favour of Pakistan with 239,619 in favour, and 184,014 against.[90]

3. Women. Although Muslim women[91] had been associated with the Muslim League's activities since 1938,[92] they acquired a new sense of purpose and direction in Jinnah's call for Pakistan, which offered them immense opportunities for a change in their social conditions. As Jinnah highlighted the issue in the course of a speech on 10 March 1944:

Another very important matter which I wish to impress on you is that no nation can rise to the height of glory unless your women are side by side with you. We are victims of evil customs. It is a crime against humanity that our women are shut up in the four walls of the houses as prisoners. I do not mean that we should imitate the evils of western life. But let us try to raise the status of our women according to our Islamic ideas and standards. There is no sanction anywhere for the deplorable conditions in which our women have to live.[93]

Jinnah understood 'the need to have women participate' in the League's 'struggle'. In fact, he was convinced that the League would not succeed unless and until 'men and women...struggle together for the achievement of its goals'.[94]

Increasingly large numbers of Muslim women responded to Jinnah's efforts to involve them in the political struggle. Not only did they get involved, they also launched a campaign 'to mobilize girls in schools and colleges by holding functions' on their campuses.[95] Many women leaders associated with other organizations such as the Unionists[96] and the pro-Congress All-India Women's Conference[97] joined the League. Even Begum Jahan Ara Shahnawaz (1896–1979), who was expelled from the League in 1941 over the Defence Council issue, requested Jinnah in 1945 to allow her to re-enter the League and serve its cause.[98]

The Muslim women made the most of the opportunity provided by the 1945–46 elections to mobilize the Muslim masses behind the League, especially in the Punjab and the NWFP, the two provinces Jinnah needed to win for Pakistan.[99] They organized themselves into several groups and canvassed for the League candidates in their respective constituencies. Prominent women's leaders like Begum Salma Tassadduque Hussain, Begum Jahan Ara Shahnawaz, and Begum Bashir Ahmad, personally visited electoral constituencies in many areas, particularly in Lahore, and appealed to the Muslim masses to vote for the League. In areas that the women's leaders could not personally visit, they assigned the task to the Punjab Girls Students' Federation and the Women's National Guards, two auxiliary organizations attached to the League. In order to ensure that the popular response to their strenuous efforts was not wasted, they saw to it that the maximum possible number of Muslim women were enrolled as voters for the forthcoming elections. Besides, they also took upon themselves the responsibility for the transportation of women to polling stations and back, to secure maximum electoral participation in favour of the League.[100] The results were very encouraging. The League captured an overwhelming majority of the Muslim seats in the Punjab legislature and two of its women candidates managed to get elected with huge margins. In the NWFP, of course, things proved a little disappointing, in spite of the best efforts of the women's leaders in the province and a helping hand extended by their counterparts from the Punjab. While they toured the province under the leadership of Lady Abdullah Haroon, the League could not secure a majority in the provincial assembly. However, women leaders maintained pressure until Dr Khan Sahib's Ministry was put on the defensive and the province finally voted for the League and Pakistan in the July 1947 referendum. In the Punjab, too, they were called upon to launch a campaign against the provincial government after the Governor invited Khizar Hayat Khan to form another Ministry in coalition with non-Muslim members of the provincial assembly, in spite of the fact that the Unionists had badly lost the elections in the province.

In a meeting held at Lahore on 8 March 1946 the Punjab Provincial Muslim League Women's Sub-Committee condemned the 'unconstitutional and unjust' position in the province,[101] and launched a province-wide mass agitation. The agitation started slowly but gathered momentum and force when the provincial government, on 24 January 1947, declared the League National Guards, an auxiliary body of the Muslim Youth, an unlawful organization. The women's leaders brought out huge processions throughout the Punjab, particularly in the urban areas. In the process, 'not only had they shed the seclusion of their homes, but they also were courting arrest', thus demonstrating 'remarkable militancy and organizational abilities', as the movement progressed.[102] The more arrests were made, the more other women activists came forward to join the agitation to press for the release of their colleagues and to reiterate their demand that the Unionist Ministry must be dismissed. Soon, the civil administration found it difficult to cope with the deteriorating law and order situation. Toward the end of February 1947, some women activists succeeded in removing the Union Jack from the Civil Secretariat Lahore and hoisting the League flag in its place. This proved to be a turning point in the fortunes of the Unionist Ministry, which now found it impossible to govern. In exasperation, the provincial government released all the imprisoned leaders and workers of the League. On 28 February, the orders declaring the Muslim National Guards unlawful were withdrawn.[103] On 3 March, the Unionist Ministry was constrained to submit its resignation.

In the NWFP, the Muslim women's leaders launched their mass-movement in February 1947. The political situation in the province which was already tense in the wake of the 1945–46 elections, and was further complicated through a highly unpopular intervention of the provincial government in January 1947 to hand over a Sikh woman (Basanti) who had embraced Islam, to her Sikh relatives, helped the women in their campaign against the government.[104] They accused the government of pursuing an 'anti-Muslim' policy, aimed at compromising Muslim interests for the sake of Hindu and Sikh allies in the Congress. The government responded with repressive orders, imposed Section 144 of the Criminal Procedure Code, and banned political meetings, processions, and demonstrations throughout the province. Hundreds of League workers, and prominent leaders such as Abdul Qayyum Khan (1901–1981), Samin Jan, and the Pir of Manki Sharif, were arrested, but the women refused to yield. Demanding the immediate resignation of Dr Khan Sahib, they continued to arrange processions and demonstrations in Peshawar almost every day in front of government buildings. In line with the practice in the Punjab, they even attempted to hoist League flags on some of these buildings. In a society where it was highly improper for elite women to come out on the streets in processions, 'Ladies of upper-middle class families more than once scaled ladders propped up against the walls of the jails which housed political prisoners, and brandished League flags aloft'.[105] The climax was reached on 3 April when a big, noisy procession picketed Dr Khan Sahib's residence and raised the League flag there. Towards the end of April 1947, Viceroy Mountbatten and his entourage were surprised to find an 'immense Muslim League demonstration' organized on their arrival in Peshawar, which included 'a surprisingly large number of women and children in its midst'.[106] The tireless efforts of women leaders like Begum Zari Sarfraz, Begum Mumtaz Jamal, and Begum Shirin Wahab against Dr Khan Sahib's ministry in the NWFP[107] indeed convinced Mountbatten that a referendum must be held in the province to ascertain the wishes of its people.[108]

On 4 June 1947, the women ceased agitation and began preparation for the referendum, responding to Jinnah's call to 'withdraw the movement of peaceful civil disobedience…and…to organize our people to face this referendum with hope and courage'.[109] Public meetings were held, processions arranged, and the masses exhorted to vote for Pakistan. The intensity of their campaign could be gauged from the fact that soon Dr Khan Sahib was forced to approach the Acting Governor of the province to help find a way to deal with the situation.[110] A long, strenuous, and difficult struggle by the women[111] finally contributed to a positive vote in favour of Pakistan in the referendum. Their 'remarkable' efforts had been successful.[112] They vindicated the trust Jinnah reposed in them.

The active and sustained support of the Muslims students, *ulama, pirs* and *sajjadanashins* and women must have clearly shown to Jinnah the normative strength of his charismatic appeal as it had come to build up a political momentum in favour of the Muslim League and the demand for Pakistan. But Jinnah wanted this momentum to be reinforced with concrete, tangible solutions to the problems faced by the Muslims. He, therefore, moved to extend the scope of his appeal by offering the depressed and deprived sections of the Muslim community a new mode of political participation and behaviour. He sought to influence and shape, in particular, the conduct of the industrial and commercial classes, labourers and farmers, and the general mass of the Muslim youth. This, in fact, constituted the second, 'structural' component of his charismatic appeal.[113]

In the case of Muslim industrial and commercial classes, it hardly needs emphasis that most of the industries, internal trade, and financial services, ranging from money-lending to the production and sale of economic goods—raw and finished—were in the hands of Hindus. The Muslims were largely producers of jute, cotton, and food grains, which were purchased from them at 'exploitation rates' by the Hindu industrialists and traders leaving them a meagre margin. In the case of jute, for instance, out of 111 mills in India on the eve of partition in 1947, comprising about 69,000 looms, only two mills belonged to the Muslims, one of 500 looms and the other of 150 looms. All these mills were located in and around Calcutta. There was not a single jute mill installed in the East Bengal area. As for cotton, there were two textile mills in the western, and three or four small mills in the eastern regions of Pakistan, all of them owned by the Hindus. The vast majority of textiles mills, about 400 in all, were located in Hindu-majority areas.

The tea industry, which was another big source of earnings, presented a similar dismal picture. Except for a handful of inconsequential Muslim garden-owners, the entire industry, worth 561,740,000 lbs in 1947, was in the hands of the Hindus (and the British). In other industries, such as mining, engineering, cement, etc., the position of the Muslims was 'even more pathetic'.[114]

Commerce and financial services offered no solace either. The Muslims were generally traders, mostly retailers, such as Memons, Khojas, and Bohras, who were dependent upon the supply of goods from Hindu wholesalers. The nature of their relationship was so precarious that the Muslims were afraid to publicly acknowledge their financial contributions to the League's campaigns, especially the election funds, lest it should offend their Hindu 'benefactors'. Besides, the commercial system was biased in favour of the Hindus. The Muslims had only one bank—the Habib Bank (the Muslim Commercial Bank was founded on 9 July 1947), which was no match for several large Hindu and British banks in India. There were, however, three Muslim-owned insurance companies in operation—The Eastern Federal Union Insurance Co., the Habib Insurance Co., and the Muslim Insurance Co. But they were small companies and much 'smaller than the smallest non-Muslim companies, and their field of operation was very limited'.[115]

Jinnah was thus greatly moved by the plight of the industrial and commercial classes, especially as he saw them in relation to the Hindu community. He lamented, for instance, that: 'We claim that we are a nation one hundred million strong and yet we have just one bank (Habib Bank)...out of the scores which operate in India'.[116] Again, he felt sorry that in spite of 'many rich merchants' he could 'hardly think of any one who was running a heavy industry. Great and heavy industries formed the backbone of a nation'.[117] Jinnah saw the usefulness of the industry and commerce not only for their own sake but also for the benefit of the community as a whole. As he advised the Muslim entrepreneurial classes:

> you must have your own commerce and your own industry in which you will be able to give employment not only to thousands of workers and labourers, but also to the educated youth, who have infinitely better

prospects and will be in a position to do better work in these lines than Government services.[118]

Jinnah did not hesitate to prod the commercial classes into action. Despite his very demanding schedule of political activities in the 1940s, he repeatedly urged them to organize themselves under the umbrella of an All-India Federation of Muslim Chamber of Commerce, and fast. In fact, he gave Ispahani, a leading Muslim businessman himself, 'a full charge blast' on 15 April 1945:

Have you been sleeping over the Federation of Muslim Chamber of Commerce, and is it merely to remain a paper scheme? I am very much disappointed indeed that so much delay has been caused in holding even your first meeting…. Every week that passes is now not only creating a sense of frustration and despair amongst those who have worked and are willing and ready to work, but in the rapid developments that are taking place…the business and commercial Muslim India will suffer very seriously.[119]

Although the first meeting took place soon thereafter, Jinnah was still not satisfied, and pressed forward. 'I hope', he wrote to Ispahani, 'that our people realise the urgency and the importance of Muslim India making every effort to make up the leeway. What we now want is selfless workers and deeds and not mere words and thoughts and speeches'.[120]

Thus, Jinnah, not only helped create the All-India Federation of Muslim Chamber of Commerce, 'one more instrument of unity and commercial and industrial strength which was so necessary for achieving independence',[121] but also took personal interest in the establishment of a number of industrial and commercial concerns under its auspices. In particular, he encouraged the formation of the Muslim Commercial Bank, which was eventually founded in July 1947, Muhammady Steamship Company, and Orient Airways, a Muslim owned and operated airline. 'It is all very well', he told Ispahani, in June 1946,

to talk of Muslims as a nation and to demand a separate homeland for them, a homeland in which they can live according to their own light and shape their own destiny, but do you realise that such a State would be useless if we did not have the men, the material and the wherewithal to run it? Do you realize that in India there is not a single airline which is owned and operated by Muslims? ...Do you know how many Muslim pilots and mechanics we have in the country? How can we do anything with this inadequacy of material—material which every nation must have in ample supply?[122]

Jinnah himself purchased shares in the proposed airline 'to prove that he backed his idea with financial participation'.[123] Had it not been for this airline, which operated from its new base at Karachi in 1947 without a day's break until it was absorbed by the new corporation, Pakistan International Airlines (PIA), 'there would not have been an air-link between East Bengal and West Pakistan for a long time after the partition.'[124] Such was the importance of this airline to the future development of the new state.

Jinnah, in fact, appeared to be planning all along to cater to the needs of the new state. He personally persuaded the Ispahani family, Habib brothers, Adamjee, and a number of other prominent Muslim businessmen to invest in industries and invited a number of Muslim entrepreneurs from outside India to help. As early as 1944, he was looking for 'suitable and qualified' men to staff the Planning Committee to be 'ready before the occasion arises to make the fullest use of the potentialities of Pakistan areas'.[125] By early 1947, he was working on the formation of five 'expert committees to advise in connection with the various subjects affecting the future of Pakistan', which included committees on Finance, Currency, Assets, Communications, Post and Telegraph, Civil Aviation, Meteorology, and Industry.[126] In the long run, their recommendations made noteworthy contributions to the development of Pakistan's economy. However, in the short run they helped Jinnah win the support of the industrial, commercial classes who themselves could not remain oblivious to the benefits which would accrue to them in a separate Muslim state once they had established their own business concerns.

Jinnah's interest in economy constituted only one 'pillar' in his scheme of things. In his opinion, there was no real progress unless it was supported by the two equally important pillars of education and social uplift. Only 'when the Muslims had built up those three pillars', he argued, 'they would be strong enough to put up the political pillar without difficulty.'[127] All four of them, he insisted, were 'interwoven.'

As he told the Memon Chamber of Commerce on 1 October 1943, at Bombay:

> ...it was impossible to separate politics from economics and the social and educational life of a nation. One was so closely interwoven with the other, that every Muslim, man and woman, should take the keenest interest in politics.

He said he knew of no nation that had built up its economic, social and educational life without political power and authority vested in the hands of the people.[128]

Jinnah was convinced that, 'Educationally, the condition of the Mussalmans today was hopelessly bad'.[129] He realized that the Muslims could not go any further with their national struggle unless they committed themselves to education. The extent of this faith in the primacy of education could be gauged from the fact that when the Balochistan Muslim League presented him 'a historic sword' in its meeting on 4 July 1943, he was not impressed. He told them:

> It will rise only in defence. But for the present the most important thing is education. Knowledge is a greater force than sword. Go and acquire it.... When you have done it successfully then comes sword which we have been wielding for the last thirteen centuries.[130]

In 1944, Jinnah appointed an Education Committee to 'examine the system of education in vogue in India', taking into consideration the present and future 'problems', and to make necessary 'recommendations' for 'the preservation, fostering and promotion of Islamic traditions, culture and ideals; and general well-being of the Muslims; and to suggest ways and means for implementing the recommendations....'[131] The Committee appointed sub-committees on 'different aspects of education' including primary, secondary, higher, and scientific education. These committees made contacts with eminent educationists and submitted a number of proposals for the promotion and improvement of education among the Muslims.[132] On 25 November 1945, Jinnah claimed that the Muslim League had not only 'awakened the Musalmans politically but had organised them economically as well as educationally too because without money there is starvation and without education darkness'.[133]

Some concrete steps for social uplift of the Muslims were suggested in the Karachi session of the League held on 24-26 December 1943, especially the reform of the land-tenure system, stabilization of rent, security of land tenure, improvement in the condition of labour and agriculture, and control of money lending.[134] Jinnah sought in particular a deal based on 'rule of justice and fairplay' for the Muslim labourers and farmers, the two most depressed sections of Muslim society.[135] He was not prepared to allow any 'undue advantage to other interests at the cost of farmers'. He wanted 'a fair deal to all interests'.[136] But given the weak position of the farmers, he did not hesitate to publicly condemn and censure the 'exploitative' landowning classes in one of his major speeches, in April 1943:

> The exploitation of the masses have gone into their blood. They have forgotten the lessons of Islam. Greed and selfishness have made these people subordinate the interests of others in order to fatten themselves.... You go anywhere to the countryside.... There are millions and millions of our people who hardly get one meal a day. Is this civilization? Is this the aim of Pakistan? (Cries of No, no) Do you visualize that millions have been exploited and cannot get one meal a day! If that is the idea of Pakistan I would not have it. (Cheers) If they are wise they will have to adjust themselves to the new modern conditions of life.[137]

Jinnah's public censure forced the League leaders to take stock of the 'poverty and social inequalities that stared them in the face whenever they went in the countryside'.[138] They began to highlight the need for agrarian and social reforms in their political campaigns. The result was that poor Muslim farmers and labourers saw the League in a new light and thus joined it by the thousands. They could no longer remain indifferent to the League and its concern for their welfare. In Bengal, the provincial Muslim League, in its annual report submitted in 1944, claimed that the League had become a 'revolutionary' and 'mass movement'. It had 'penetrated into rural Bengal', with 550,000 members enrolled, a figure that 'exceeded the number ever scored by any organization in the province not excluding Congress'. This, the report insisted, was 'apart from the vast allegiance of the large Muslim population to the League'.[139] The Punjab and Bengal Provincial Leagues' manifestos, issued before the 1945-46 elections, reiterated the League's commitment to the poor masses.[140] The masses of course responded with an overwhelming support to the League in these two exceedingly important Muslim-majority provinces for Pakistan.

Jinnah finally made the most of his efforts to consolidate Muslim India under the banner of the League by taking full advantage of the wartime situation. The Congress provided him the first and the most momentous opportunity by resigning its ministries in reaction to the decision of the British Government in 1939 to declare war on behalf of India, and thus leaving 'the field entirely to the Muslim League....'[141] Jinnah called for a day of 'Deliverance' and hastened to install League ministries in its place, especially in the provinces of Assam, Sindh, Bengal, and the NWFP[142] The only province that remained outside the League's purview was the Punjab. But then, in the Punjab, the League still had some sort of 'alliance' with the Unionists under the aegis of the so-called 'Jinnah–Sikandar Pact'. Thus, Jinnah had come to have League ministries in virtually all the Muslim-majority provinces included in his Pakistan formula. This had important implications for the League. First, it provided the provincial League leadership a direct stake in the organization's fortunes, encouraging them to work more actively and devotedly for its growth and development. Secondly, it helped Jinnah control and direct, for the first time, Muslim-majority provinces from the centre, and impress upon all the concerned actors in Indian political drama, including the wavering Muslims that the League was a power to reckon with. Finally, and related to the foregoing, was the all-important message conveyed to the British and the Congress leaders that the League's demand for a separate Muslim homeland was not simply a creation of the centre but an equally popular demand of the Muslim-majority provinces comprising that homeland. The Congress, in particular, saw clearly that it could no longer 'overwhelm the Muslim majority areas, except by wading through a bloody civil war in order to impose unity by its own strength'.[143]

As if the resignation of ministries was not enough, the Congress, after failing to come to terms with the British, launched a Civil Disobedience Movement on 8 August 1942 to press the British to 'Quit India'. The manner and mode of this movement led the Muslims to the 'firm conclusion' that in fighting the British, the Congress was 'fighting the Muslims by proxy'.[144] Jinnah himself gave vent to these feelings in unambiguous terms: 'Under the facade of nationalism the

Congress demand, in short, from the British is to hand over to it power to establish Hindudom in this country'.[145]

In fact, the Muslim reaction to the Quit India movement was akin to the reaction during the 1937–1939 years, when the Congress rule in the provinces aroused Muslim feelings and fears. The Muslims saw the movement 'not merely [as] a declaration of war against the British and the Government, but...[also] a war against the Muslim League, which means Muslim India....'[146] The result was that any illusions that the Muslims may still have had about the Congress were shattered. Maulana Abul Kalam Azad conceded, in subsequent years, that the 'Muslims who stood on Congress or any other ticket had great difficulty in even securing a hearing from the people'.[147] Indeed, a large majority of the Muslims aligned with the Congress began trickling into the League.[148] There was no turning away from the League and Jinnah's leadership. As W.C. Smith put it, the League emerged as 'a mass movement of the Indian Muslims, virtually unanimous'.[149]

Apart from the Congress's acts of omission and commission during the war years, the war itself provided Jinnah an ideal opportunity to mobilize support for the League. The British were left with no choice but to woo the non-Congress parties and leaders in the country, especially Jinnah,[150] and his League, for two very important reasons. Jinnah was the leader of a party which was second only to the Congress at the all-India level, and as a leader of Indian Muslims, he had a special clout. Although the Muslims were a 'minority' in India, they contributed as much to the army as the Hindus, a fact known to responsible British authorities both in Britain and in India.[151] They contributed 37.65 per cent soldiers against 37.50 per cent contributed by the Hindus.[152] Jinnah was mindful of this critical value of the Muslims to the armed forces. On 13 September 1942, he told a British correspondent who wanted to know what effect League's decision to hamper the war effort would have on the army and the Muslims in the Middle East:

...the League campaign if launched, will affect a large body of the army and besides the entire Frontier would be ablaze...and the various Muslim countries (such as Afghanistan, Iran, Iraq, Turkey and Egypt)...were bound to be influenced if there was a conflict between the Muslims and the British Government...we can give five hundred times more trouble....[153]

There was no denying the fact that 'the strategic importance of the north-west frontier of India had increased manifold due to its comparative nearness to the theatres of war'. More than 50 per cent of the armed forces were 'deployed in the areas now constituting Pakistan'.[154]

Jinnah perceived very early and very clearly that the League had a ready opportunity in the war and that the British urgently needed their support. As he explained to his followers about the invitation from the Viceroy to meet him in the days immediately following the declaration of war:

> After the war was declared, the Viceroy naturally wanted help from the Muslim League. It was only then that he realized that the Muslim League was a power. For it will be remembered that up to the time of the declaration of war, the Viceroy never thought of me but of Gandhi and Gandhi alone. I have been the leader of an important Party in the Legislature for a considerable time, larger than the one I have the honour to lead at present, the Muslim League Party in the Central Legislature. Yet the Viceroy never thought of me before. Therefore, when I got this invitation from the Viceroy along with Mr Gandhi, I wondered within myself why I was suddenly promoted....[155]

The fact was that unlike Gandhi and other Congress leaders, Jinnah had correctly judged the war situation and its value and importance to the British authorities. The war had to be won at all costs. The British would do everything possible to keep India behind the war effort. With the Congress in non-cooperation mode, the League was their only chance. Not only was the League a major national organization like the Congress, but it also represented the Muslims more than any other political party in the country.

This, of course, did not mean that Jinnah was willing to participate unconditionally in the war effort. He would have nothing to do with it unless the British, in turn, were prepared to offer the Muslims, 'their real voice and share in the government of the country'.[156] On 8 August 1940, the British were obliged to state publicly that they,

> could not contemplate the transfer of their present responsibilities for the peace and welfare of India to any system of government whose authority is directly denied by large and powerful elements in India's national life.

Nor could they be parties to the coercion of such elements into submission to such a government.[157]

This, according to Khalid bin Sayeed, was 'perhaps one of the greatest triumphs that Jinnah had achieved through his brilliant strategy'.[158] Though Jinnah did not accept the August offer as it did not ensure the League its 'real voice and share' in the government, and the British also did not intend a substantive transfer of authority at the centre, as the later events demonstrated, the die was cast. Henceforth, no move could be made at the centre without the League influencing the course of events. In fact, there was no denying that there was,

a marked difference between the Muslim struggle for independence before and after World War II. The military considerations, particularly the Muslim potential for contribution to the war effort had, on the one hand, made the British more susceptible to the Indian public opinion and, on the other hand, altered the relative importance of the Muslim community vis-à-vis the Hindus.[159]

Indeed, in 1940, the Viceroy 'could see no prospect of getting any Muslim League leader' to join his proposed, expanded Executive Council and a War Advisory Council who would be 'prepared to disregard the League's mandate.'[160] Subsequent moves at the centre in 1942 (the Cripps Mission), 1945 (the Simla Conference), and 1946 (the Cabinet Mission), merely confirmed the importance of the League,[161] which was *the* party as far as the Muslims were concerned. By the end of 1946, in fact, it stood as the 'sole representative body of Muslim India'. Jinnah's 'charismatic appeal' had 'defeated other loyalties of the Muslims all over India'.[162] In the Central Legislative Assembly, the League won all thirty Muslim seats. The so-called 'nationalist' Muslims lost all their seats. They forfeited their security deposits in many constituencies. In the provincial assemblies, the League secured an overwhelming majority of Muslim seats. Its most spectacular success was in the Punjab where it won 75 out of 86 Muslim seats.[163] The League failed to secure the North–West Frontier Province where the Congress, in alliance with the Khudai Khidmatgars of Abdul Ghaffar Khan, won a clear majority of 30 out of 50 seats[164] and formed the ministry under Dr Khan Sahib. Still, the League bagged 17 seats, 15 Muslim and 2 landholder seats. In 1937, the League was not able to find a single candidate to fight the elections let alone win any seats. In this sense, the League had done exceedingly well in the province. Indeed, there was no comparison between the League's performance in 1937 and 1945–46 elections all over India. In 1937, the League had polled a paltry 4.4 per cent of the Muslim vote.[165] 'If one remembers', wrote Z.H. Zaidi, 'the weak, disorganized League of 1935, with its small membership and extremely limited appeal, one is filled with wonder at the revolution in Muslim politics which the party had brought about in a decade'.[166] The 1945–46 elections clearly and convincingly demonstrated the success of Jinnah's well-thought out and planned strategy employed in the political mobilization and organization of the Muslims for the cause of Pakistan. As Ian Talbot noted: 'Their votes for the League in the 1946 Indian elections represented a crucial landmark in the emergence of Pakistan.'[167]

This electoral victory, though immensely 'crucial', represented, for all practical purposes, the halfway mark on the road to Pakistan. Jinnah had also to make the British concede the demand for Pakistan. He had to employ his extraordinary negotiating skills,[168] which, among other qualities, had made him a charismatic leader of Muslim India in the first place. This was not going to be an easy task. The Pakistan demand, as already discussed, was emphatically rejected by the British and the Congress. The British did not find it useful for either their long or short-term interests. The Congress could not countenance what it considered the 'vivisection' of India. However, Jinnah had to furnish proof of his charismatic power. He had to deliver. He had to make the most of his leadership abilities and skills to work for the creation of Pakistan.

Notes

1. Huntington, *Political Order in Changing Societies,* 146. For a detailed analysis of the League, especially its foundation and subsequent developments till 1919 see, Saleem Ahmed, *All India Muslim League.* For the subsequent period see, Sharif al Mujahid, 'The Re-emergence of the All-India Muslim League', in *A History of the Freedom Movement,* Vol. III, Part II (Karachi: Pakistan Historical Society, 1963); Sayeed, *Formative Phase,* 176-219; and Z.H. Zaidi, 'Aspects of the Development of the of the Muslim League Policy', in Philips and Wainwright, *Partition of India.*
2. Jinnah himself was President of the League.

3. Ahmad, *Speeches and Writings*, Vol. II, 217.

4. *The Constitution and Rules of the All-India Muslim League*, published by Liaquat Ali Khan, Honorary Secretary, All-India Muslim League (Delhi: All-India Muslim League, April 1940).

5. By the mid-1940s, through successive amendments to the constitution of the League, the Working Committee had become 'the principal executive body of the League by assuming new powers that allowed it to control, direct and regulate all activities and to suspend, dissolve, or disaffiliate any Provincial League or to take disciplinary action against any member'. If fact, it became 'the instrument of domination that was used to discipline independent-minded provincial leaders such as, Sikandar Hayat, and to expel Fazlul Haq and G.M. Syed.' Samad, *A Nation in Turmoil*, 61. In the process, of course, the provincial Leagues became amenable to the decisions made at the centre.

6. Ravoof, *Meet Mr Jinnah*, 167.

7. For a discussion of this aspect of political leadership see, Huntington, *Political Order in Changing Societies*, 146.

8. Sayeed, *Formative Phase*, 203.

9. A.M. Zaidi, *Evolution of Muslim Political Thought*, Vol. VI, 182-3.

10. Talbot, *Provincial Politics*, 112.

11. Ahmad, *Speeches and Writings*, Vol. I, 526.

12. Ahmad, *Speeches and Writings* Vol. II, 46.

13. Ibid., 199.

14. Even an ardent supporter like Iqbal was not sparing. Commenting upon the moribund state of the League in the late 1930s, Iqbal advised Jinnah 'to decide finally whether it will remain a body representing the upper classes of Indian Muslims or Muslim masses who have so far, with good reason, shown no interest in it'. *Letters of Iqbal to Jinnah*, 16-17. For Nehru's critical and indeed hostile views on the League see, Ram Gopal, *The Indian Muslims: A Political History* (Bombay: Asia Publishing House, 1959), 251.

15. Z.H. Zaidi, 'Aspects of Development of Muslim League Policy', in Philips and Wainwright, *Partition of India*, 267.

16. W.C. Smith, *Modern Islam in India*, 269.

17. Ahmad, *Speeches and Writings*, Vol. I, 260.

18. *The Constitution and Rules of the All-India Muslim League*, published by Liaquat Ali Khan, Honorary Secretary, All-India Muslim League (Delhi: All-India Muslim League, 1944), 17. This enhanced authority of the President was further augmented by the steady increase in power of the Working Committee, a creation of the President himself, vis-à-vis the League Council. Whereas, in 1940, the League Council was invested with powers 'to control, direct and regulate all the activities' of the party, in the 1944 constitution the scales were heavily tilted in favour of the Working Committee. The Working Committee was all-powerful, required only to place its decisions before the League Council for 'information'. The say of the Working Committee in the affairs of the League was reinforced by the powers given to it to frame the rules and regulations of the Central Parliamentary Board and help the President to appoint its members. This was clearly the case on the eve of 1945–46 elections. The Council was a huge body. Not only did it comprise hundreds of nominees from various provinces but it

also included the ex-officio members of the Indian Legislative Assembly, the Council of the State, the President and Secretaries of the various provincial Muslim League and some nominees of the President.

19. Sindh presented Jinnah with difficulties in the form of a bitter feud between G.M. Syed, President of the Provincial League, and Sir Ghulam Hussain Hidayatullah, leader of the League parliamentary party in the provincial assembly. Jinnah did his utmost, through public appeals, correspondence, and personal visits to Sindh, to settle the differences between the two, but to no avail. In the end, Syed was expelled from the League. Syed challenged the League in the 1945–46 elections, but he could not do well. He managed to secure only four seats as against 28 won by the League. For some of the details regarding Jinnah's efforts to placate Syed see, in particular, Muhammad Qasim Soomro, 'Muslim Politics in Sindh, 1938-1947', unpublished M. Phil. Thesis, Quaid-i-Azam University, Islamabad, 1985, 92-4. For a larger perspective on the provincial politics at this point in time and particulary in the context of Ayub Khuhro's efforts to ensure Muslim candidates' success in Sindh in spite of Syed's expulsion see, Hamida Khuhro, *Mohammed Ayub Khuhro: A Life of Courage in Politics* (Karachi: Ferozsons, 1998), esp. Ch. 15, 'Working for Freedom', 269-304.

20. They had 34 out of 60 seats even though they constituted about 70 per cent of the population.

21. Talbot, *Provincial Politics*, 43.

22. But it did not take long. After the adoption of the Lahore Resolution in 1940, Sikandar Hayat Khan was 'powerless to resist the popularization of the Pakistan slogan,' and thus the emergence of the League in the Punjab. Samad, *A Nation in Turmoil*, 74.

23. Jinnah indeed appeared so concerned with the Punjab that there were indications of Jinnah's 'taking up permanent residence in Lahore....' For, as Jinnah told a public meeting in Lahore on 2 April 1944, 'the League was fighting for the establishment of Pakistan not in Bombay but in the Punjab which was the key-stone of the proposed Pakistan State'. Ahmad, *Speeches and Writings*, Vol. II, 31-2.

24. Moon, *Divide and Quit*, 38.

25. Ispahani, *As I knew Him*, 49.

26. Ibid.

27. Ibid.

28. *Letters of Iqbal to Jinnah*, 5-6.

29. Ispahani, *As I knew Him*, 43.

30. Ibid., 143.

31. Pirzada, *Quaid-i-Azam Jinnah's Correspondence*, 78.

32. Samad, *A Nation in Turmoil*, 70.

33. Ibid.

34. Pirzada, *Quaid-i-Azam Jinnah's Correspondence,* 80.

35. Ibid., 81.

36. Sayeed, *Formative Phase*, 94.

37. Glancy continued with his support of Khizar Hayat Khan even after his Unionist Ministry was routed in the 1945–46 elections. He allowed Khizar Hayat Khan to form a ministry and thus deny transfer of power to the League. Penderel

Moon, who was closely associated with the Punjab Administration, observed that this ministry, 'a combination of Congress banias, Khizar and the Sikhs', was 'designed with the connivance of the British Governor, simply to keep them from power'. In this sense, he maintained, 'It was an example of just the thing that Jinnah always feared and that had prompted the demand for Pakistan. In a United India, the wily Hindus would always succeed in this manner in attaching to themselves a section of the Muslims and using them to defeat the larger interests of the community'. Moon, *Divide and Quit*, 71-2.

38. Moon, *Wavell's Journal*, 107.

39. Charles Chenevix Trench, *The Indian Army and the King's Enemies 1900–47* (London: Thames and Hudson, 1988), 28.

40. Quoted in C.S. Vekatachar, '1937-47 in Retrospect: A Civil Servant's View', in Philips and Wainwright, *Partition of India*, 469.

41. Jinnah declared at Lahore: 'I want to make it clear that there is no question of our being bound by any commitment to any one which stands in our way, nor are we under any obligation to any other party in the present coalition, which in any way constitutes any bar or precludes us from taking any decision or decisions we think proper, consistently with our creed, policy and programme'. Ahmad, *Speeches and Writings*, Vol. II, 34-35. Khizar Hayat Khan was 'prepared to agree that he himself and the Muslim members of the party should owe direct allegiance to the Muslim League alone, and should in this sense cease to be Unionists....' However, Glancy, Governor of the Punjab had different ideas: '...the dissolution of the Unionist Ministry and the substitution for it of a Muslim League Ministry, such as Jinnah wants, would be a disaster'. As he informed Wavell on 14 April 1944, 'I can only tell him as a friend what I would do in his place and it is my considered opinion that he will have no peace hereafter, nor will he be serving the interests of the Province or of India or of Muslims of the Empire if he gives way to Jinnah and places himself in his power'. Mansergh, *Transfer of Power*, Vol. IV, 881-2, 923.

42. Jinnah was determined to make clear to all Muslim leaders, and especially Khizar Hayat Khan, that they could not get their nominees in the Viceroy's expanded Executive Council over and above the head of the League President. In a letter to L.S. Amery, Secretary of State for India, Wavell, thus wrote on 27 June 1945: 'We have arrived at the critical point of the Conference and the main stumbling block is the attitude of Jinnah, i.e. his claim to nominate all Muslim members.... The most difficult problem will be to provide for the inclusion of a Punjab Muslim'. Mansergh, *Transfer of Power*, Vol. V, 1166. While Amery felt that the 'rejection of a Punjabi Unionist would surely put him in a position of grave discredit with much of Muslim public opinion', Jinnah's position improved, ironically enough, not only in the Punjab where many Unionist leaders, including Feroz Khan Noon, a close relative of Khizar Hayat Khan, rushed to join him but also in a Khudai Khidmatgar Congress-dominated province like the NWFP. Khan Abdul Qayyum Khan, Deputy Leader of the Congress Parliamentary Party, was moved to offer his services to Jinnah and the League. On 16 August 1945, he wrote to Jinnah: 'I have decided to join the Muslim League. I believe that the stand taken by you is absolutely correct and that any Muslim who opposes you is betraying the cause of Islam in India.' George

Cunningham, Governor NWFP's letter to Wavell, dated 24 July 1945. Ibid., 1228,1293; *Shamsul Hasan Collection*, Vol. II; and Pirzada, *Quaid-i-Azam Jinnah's Correspondence*, 301.

43. French, *Liberty or Death*, 199-200.
44. The party manifesto 'stressed economic achievement, provincial autonomy, complete independence and free education' but, it had no answer to 'the magnetic Pakistan slogan', which offered 'something for everyone' in the province, and thus, 'the resistance of the Unionists collapsed.' The League secured all the urban seats and many rural seats, leaving only twenty to the Unionists. Samad, *A Nation in Turmoil*, 110.
45. Quoted in Moon, *Divide and Quit*, 76-77.
46. Ahmad, *Speech and Writings*, Vol. I, 576.
47. Huntington, *Political Order in Changing Societies*, 146.
48. It was extremely rare that modernizing leaders had gone for more 'competitive two-party or multiparty systems' for expansion and assimilation of groups. Ibid., 146.
49. In this sense, of course, the League appeared more of 'a nationalist movement' to a perceptive observer. For instance, W.C. Smith described it as 'the organ of a surging nationalism', Muslim nationalism, rather than a political party. W.C. Smith, *Modern Islam in India*, 275.
50. Ahmad, *Speeches and Writings*, Vol. II, 247.
51. Ibid., 212. Jinnah, thus, asserted in a meeting in Delhi on 23 March 1942: 'We cannot tolerate Muslims in the camp of the enemy. Non-League Muslims are traitors in the enemy camp'. Mansergh, *Transfer of Power*, Vol. I, 468.
52. Ahmad, *Speeches and Writings*, Vol. II, 247.
53. Ahmad, *Speeches and Writings*, Vol. I, 170. There is considerable merit in Waseem's argument that 'the Two-Nation theory emerged as an ideological manifestation of a tangible move to establish a constitutional majority of Muslims in a separate homeland.' Waseem, *Politics and the State in Pakistan*, 81.
54. Ahmad, *Speeches and Writings*, Vol. I, 171.
55. Ibid.
56. Pirzada, *Quaid-i-Azam Jinnah's Correspondence*, 113.
57. Ahmad, *Speeches and Writings*, Vol. I, 171.
58. Afzal, *Selected Speeches and Statements*, 456.
59. Ahmad, *Speeches and Writings*, Vol. II, 208-9.
60. Jamal-ad-Din Al-Afghani offers the most striking example. Echoes of his rhetoric were heard in the speeches of modern 'nationalists' like Muhammad Musaddiq in Iran and Gamal Abdul Nasir in Egypt.
61. Wilfred Cantwell Smith, *Islam in Modern History* (Princeton: Princeton University Press, 1957), 75. Very often leaders have been 'surprised to discover the degree to which they have let loose an Islamic upsurge' among the masses. Ibid. In a similar vein, Anwar Syed, argued: 'Muslim nationalism is preeminently ideological in all actual or potential confrontations with the non-Muslims'. Anwar Syed, *Pakistan: Islam, Politics, and National Solidarity* (Lahore: Vanguard, 1984), 58.
62. Jamil-ud-Din Ahmad, *Quaid-i-Azam as Seen by His Contemporaries*, 43.
63. According to Huntington, 'In theory' the most effective support 'should come from groups which are not so directly identified with particular ethnic or

economic strata. In some measure, students, religious leaders…may fall into this category'. Huntington, *Political Order in Changing Societies*, 239. In this context, it must be pointed out that the students constitute an important segment of the educated, urban middle class. Indeed, this class was the mainstay of the Pakistan movement, and included intelligentsia, lawyers, journalists, professionals, etc. All of them made significant contributions to the cause of Pakistan and have been documented. But since the students were the most active and the most vocal and mobile, a special emphasis is being placed on their role here.

64. The students and the *ulama* helped in particular with the ideological content of Muslim nationalism, and thus helped overcome some of the organizational weaknesses of the League. In particular, they were very successful in spreading the message of Pakistan to the rural areas of all the Muslim-majority provinces, over and above the heads of provincial/regional leaders.

65. In fact, these groups constituted the 'nucleus' of Jinnah's charismatic following.

66. For a detailed view of the students role in the struggle for Pakistan see, Mukhtar Zaman, *Students Role in Pakistan Movement* (Karachi: Quaid-i-Azam Academy, 1978); Sarfraz Hussain Mirza, ed., *The Punjab Muslim Students Federation: An Annotated Documentary Survey, 1937–47* (Lahore: Research Society of Pakistan, 1978) and *The Punjab Muslim Students Federation, 1937–1947* (Islamabad: National Institute of Historical and Cultural Research, 1991); and Mujahid, *Studies in Interpretation*, App. 2, 'Jinnah and Muslim Students', 437-51.

67. C.H. Philips, 'Introduction', in Philips and Wainwright, *Partition of India*, 27.

68. Yet, Jinnah was careful to point out to the organizers of the All-India Muslim Students Federation in its very first Conference held at Calcutta on 29 December 1937, 'You are in no way auxiliary to the Muslim League although you may have sympathy with it'. Cited in Mukhtar Zaman, *Students Role*, 28. Again, in a letter to a student leader, dated 22 May 1944, Jinnah told the students that 'politics should not be a part of their studies so that when they emerge from their colleges they will be all the better qualified to play their part in the actual struggle of life that is awaiting them'. *Shamsul Hasan Collection*, Vol. I.

69. Ahmad, *Speeches and Writings*, Vol. I, 40.

70. Shamsul Hasan Collection, 'Students', Vol. II, 129.

71. Mukhtar Zaman, *Student's Role*, 38.

72. Here it would not be inappropriate to mention the important role played by the Muslim press in general. Urdu and English dailies and weeklies like *Dawn* (Delhi), *Manshoor* (Delhi), *Anjam* (Delhi), *Jang* (Delhi), *Inqilab* (Lahore), *Nawa-i-Waqt* (Lahore), *Paisa Akhbar* (Lahore), *Zamindar* (Lahore), *The Eastern Times* (Lahore) *Asr-e-Jadid* (Calcutta), and *Star of India* (Calcutta), worked particularly hard to propagate and promote the cause of the League and Pakistan. The League was conscious of the need for a Muslim press for quite some time. Liaquat Ali Khan wrote to Jinnah on 11 December 1939: '…I think we should consider the question of having a sort of press because it is needed most at this time so that people…may come to understand our point of view'. *Quaid-i-Azam Papers*, F/335, 58. In order to help the cause of Pakistan further, the League went on to constitute a committee of Muslim writers to highlight various aspects of the Pakistan demand for the benefit of an average, educated Muslim. Most important contribution made by this committee was in the form of the *Pakistan Literature*

Series and *Home Study Series*. That material helped a great deal in widening and sustaining political consciousness on Pakistan demand. See M. Rafique Afzal, ed., *Case for Pakistan* (Islamabad: National Commission on Historical and Cultural Research, 1979).

73. Samad, *A Nation in Turmoil*, 63.
74. R.P. Dutt, *India Today and Tomorrow*, 235.
75. Z.H. Zaidi, 'Aspects of the Development of Muslim League Policy', in Philips and Wainwright, *Partition of India*, 268; and W.C. Smith, *Modern Islam in India*, 274.
76. Jamil-ud-Din Ahmad, 'A Disciple Remembers', in Jamil-ud-Din Ahmad, *Quaid-i-Azam as Seen by His Contemporaries*, 216.
77. Mukhtar Zaman, *Students Role*, 59. Khizar Hayat Khan and his Unionist Party were in power in the Punjab in spite of the fact that the League secured 75 out of 86 Muslims seats in the Assembly. However, as Ayesha Jalal argued, 'denial of office to the Punjab Muslim League after a good electoral showing did much to strengthen support for Pakistan.' Ayesha Jalal, *Self and Sovereignty*, 473.
78. Quoted in Mirza, *Punjab Muslim Students Federation*, ciii.
79. The most important *fatwa* was issued by Mufti Muhammad Shafi, the Grand Mufti of Dar-ul-Uloom Deoband. See Hazrat Maulana Muhammad Shafi Deobandi, *Congress aur Muslim League kay mutalliq Shari Faisalah* (Urdu) (Deoband: n.p., 1946), 1-3. The *pirs* and *sajjadanashins* were particularly helpful in the rural areas, as they could successfully 'influence the combination of *biraderi* and *sufi* networks in the countryside', in favour of the League. Samad, *A Nation in Turmoil*, 109.
80. Sherkoti, *Khutbat-i-Usmani*, 77. Also see, A.S. Pirzada, *Jamiat Ulama-i-Islam Pakistan*, 10.
81. Ibid., 10-11.
82. The 3 June Partition Plan suggested a referendum in the NWFP to determine if its people wished to join either Pakistan or India. Basically, Nehru had insisted on a referendum rather than an election. Indeed, he warned the British authorities that if they tried 'to force through an election merely as a result of pressure from the Muslim League civil disobedience movement, Congress will refuse to take part in the election as a strong gesture of their disapproval....' Mountbatten readily agreed, saying: 'I am sure that it [referendum] is the fairest and best way...of making sure that decision whether the NWFP goes to Pakistan or Hindustan is in accordance with the will of the people.' Saleemullah Khan, comp., *The Referendum in [The] NWFP, 1947* (Islamabad: National Documentation Center, 1996), 21, 51.
83. A special *Mashaikh* committee was appointed by the League in 1946 to lend further support to the efforts made by the Jamait-ul-Ulama-i-Islam, comprising eminent religious leaders like Pir Sahib of Manki Sharif, Pir Jamaat Ali Shah, Khawaja Nazimuddin of Taunsa Sharif and Makhdum Raza Shah of Multan. In addition, the League was also able to utilize the support of the *sajjadanashins* of the highly prestigious shrines in the Punjab such as, Pakpattan (Sahiwal), Sial (Sargodha), Jalalpur (Jhelum) and Golra (Rawalpindi/Islamabad).
84. Gilmartin, *Empire and Islam*, 215.

85. In a letter to Amery, the Secretary of State for India, Wavell described the Unionist predicament in the Punjab. 'According to Khizar', he wrote, 'Jinnah is importing into the Punjab a number of Maulvis, religious leaders from the United Provinces to agitate against the Unionist Government on religiousness'. Mansergh, *Transfer of Power*, Vol. IV, 1035. Also see a letter reiterating: 'Muslim Leaguers have been exhibiting an increased tendency to make use of mosques for propaganda purposes'. Ibid., 1148.

86. This was in spite of the fact that the League was able to secure 'a slightly larger percentage (41–39 per cent) of the rural Muslim votes cast' in the province. Talbot, *Provincial Politics and the Pakistan Movement*, 20. Also, out of 347,632 Muslim votes polled, the League did 'slightly' better than the Congress. 145,510 votes went to the League; 143,571 to the Congress. The remainder went to others. See Sayed Wiqar Ali Shah, *Ethnicity, Islam and Nationalism: Muslim Politics in the North-West Frontier Province, 1937-47* (Karachi: Oxford University Press, 1999), 166.

87. *Dawn* (Delhi) 2 July 1947. Also see, A. Sattar Khan, 'The Role of Ulama and Mashaikh in the Pakistan Movement', *Journal of the Research Society of Pakistan*, Vol. XXXVI, No. 2 (1999).

88. Syed Wiqar Ali Shah, *Pir Saheb Manki Sharif, Syed Aminul Hasnat and his Political Struggle* (Islamabad: National Institute of Historical and Cultural Research, 1990), 89. Earlier, in a letter of 18 November 1945, Jinnah had personally asked Pir Sahib to 'work and serve the cause which is a matter of life and death for 100 million Muslims of India….' Ibid., 144. (App. 4).

89. Quaid-i-Azam Papers, F/2, 239; and Burke and Quraishi, *The British Raj in India*, 514. This data was provided by Brigadier R.J. Booth, Referendum Commissioner, NWFP. The referendum was held under the supervision of army officers, with Lt. General Lockhart as Acting Governor (Olaf Caroe was sent on leave). However, as reported in the press, Brigadier Booth acknowledged that in the course of the referendum, 'the main difficulties encountered by the military supervising staff have been dissemination of the exaggerated reports of intimidation and occasional absence of the party agents and in some case their unreasonable attitudes.' See Khan, *The Referendum in* [The] *NWFP, 1947*, 197-8. Abdul Ghaffar Khan, leader of the Khudai Khidmatgars, advised his supporters to boycott the referendum since it did not allow them the option of an independent 'Pakhtunistan'. However, as Lockhart explained: 'There is no provision in the plan for any province to declare itself independent.' Ibid., 136.

90. Menon, *Transfer of Power in India*, 388. Also see, S.A.S. Pirzada, *Jamiat Ulama-i-Islam Pakistan*, 11.

91. For an informative discussion on the role of women in Indian Muslim politics in general, and the Pakistan movement in particular, see, Sarfraz Hussain Mirza, *Muslim Women's Role in the Pakistan Movement* (Lahore: Research Society of Pakistan, 1969); Jahan Ara Shahnawaz Begum, and others, eds., *Quaid-i-Azam and Muslim Women* (Karachi: National Book Foundation, 1976); and Dushka Saiyid, *Muslim Women of the British Punjab*.

92. In its annual session held at Patna in December 1938, the League resolved that 'an All-India Muslim Women's Sub Committee be formed…with the following objects in view: (a) to organize provincial and district women's sub-committees

under the Provincial and District Muslim Leagues; (b) to enlist large numbers of women to the membership of the Muslim League; (c) to carry out an intensive propaganda amongst the Muslim women throughout India in order to create in them a sense of the greatest political consciousness, and (d) to advise and guide them in all such matters as mainly rest on them for the uplift of Muslim society'. Pirzada, *Foundations of Pakistan,* Vol. II, 318.

93. Ahmad, *Speeches and Writings,* Vol. II, 17–18.
94. Dushka Saiyid, *Muslim Women of the British Punjab,* 91.
95. Ibid., 91.
96. For instance, Baji Rashida Latif resigned from the Unionist Party to join the League in October 1945. *Inqilab,* 11 October 1945.
97. The most prominent woman to leave the All-India Women's Congress was the provincial head of its Punjab branch, Begum Mian Iftikhar-ud-Din. She also joined the League in October 1945. Ibid., 13 October 1945.
98. Ibid., 21 October 1945.
99. Punjab, in particular, Jinnah told them is 'the soul of Pakistan, and it is a pity that it is slumbering'. *The Eastern Times,* 18 January 1946.
100. For a more detailed discussion of some of these aspects of women's activities see Mirza, *Muslim Women's Role,* 74–9.
101. *Eastern Times,* 9 March 1946.
102. Dushka Saiyid, *Muslim Women of the British Punjab,* 98–9.
103. Mirza, *Muslim Women's Role,* 89–93.
104. For some of the details on the case see, Erland Jansson, *India, Pakistan or Pakhtunistan?* (Uppsala: Acta Universitaties Upsaliensis, 1981), 191. Also see, Shah, *Ethnicity, Islam and Nationalism,* 194–5. However, Jinnah made it absolutely clear to the leaders of the movement that: 'In no circumstances the movement should be allowed to take a communal turn. Our fight is not against the Hindus or the Sikhs; we are fighting for a verdict of the people to be obtained by fair and free methods'. *Quaid-i-Azam Papers,* F/4, 26.
105. Stephens, *Pakistan,* 186.
106. Campbell-Johnson, *Mission With Mountbatten,* 74.
107. For the important role of the women wing of the League in Peshawar in particular see, Muhammad Anwar Khan, *The Role of NWFP in the Freedom Struggle* (Lahore: Research Society of Pakistan, 2000), 231.
108. In fact, he visited the province for two days, 28–29 April 1947. No wonder, in a meeting with him at Peshawar, on 28 April, Mountbatten told Dr Khan Sahib that he felt he had to ascertain the wishes of the people before moving any further with the idea of the partition of India. Campbell-Johnson, *Mission with Mountbatten,* 75.
109. Ahmad, *Speeches and Writings,* Vol., II, 396.
110. On 14 July 1947, Dr Khan Sahib and Abdul Ghaffar Khan met the Acting Governor, Sir Eric Mieville, and told him that they were prepared to open negotiations with Jinnah. However, Jinnah informed Mieville on 25 July 1947, 'I have carefully considered the matter and I regret to say that it is not possible for me to meet Abdul Ghaffar Khan and discuss an agreement on the basis reported to you by the governor of the NWFP. I am sure you will see that all these matters can only be dealt with by the Constituent Assembly of Pakistan

which will frame the constitution of the Pakistan Federation. It is obvious that I cannot negotiate with any section or party over the head of the Constituent Assembly. Besides, I have no power to commit the Constituent Assembly in advance or anticipate their final decisions'. *Quaid-i-Azam Papers*, F/2, 253–54.

111. At times, women were *lathi*-charged, tear-gassed, and beaten severely, as happened during a peaceful demonstration in Dera Ismail Khan. *Inqilab*, 18 April 1947.

112. Duskha Saiyid, *Muslim Women of the British Punjab*, 99.

113. Samad described it as a case of 'economic nationalism.' As he put it: 'An important factor that widened the League's arena of influence was the increased significance of economic nationalism. It opened channels of communication between the elites and the masses, drew in groups previously unaffected by Muslim nationalism and gathered them around the banner of Pakistan.' Samad, *A Nation in Turmoil*, 117.

114. See M.A.H. Ispahani, 'Factors leading to the Partition of British India', in Philips and Wainwright, *Partition of India*, 356–8. In fact, as Rafique Afzal pointed out, of all the 14,677 'registered factories', Pakistan got only 1,414, less than one-tenth, out of which a very large number comprised 'small-scale establishments'. M. Rafique Afzal, *Pakistan's History and Politics, 1947–1971* (Karachi: Oxford University Press, 2001), 15.

115. Ispahani, 'Factors Leading to the Partition of British India', in Philips and Wainwright, *Partition of India*, 359.

116. Ispahani, *As I Knew Him*, 125.

117. Ahmad, *Speeches and Writings*, Vol. II, 552.

118. Ibid., 7.

119. Ispahani, *As I Knew Him*, 120.

120. Ibid., 121.

121. Ibid., 123.

122. Ibid.

123. Ibid., 124.

124. Ibid., 125.

125. Ahmad, *Speeches and Writings*, Vol., II, 7. Jinnah was happy to declare, on 25 November 1945: 'The Muslim League Planning Committee was at work and was making useful schemes'. Ibid., 246.

126. Nawab of Bhopal to Jinnah, 9 June 1947. *Quaid-i-Azam Papers*, F/10, 61. In fact, Jinnah was receiving proposals and plans from Muslims all over India as to how to help improve economic development of Muslim areas. For instance, see an article submitted by an engineer, Abdur Rahman Khan, for the economic development of NWFP and the tribal areas and the one by Mohammad Akram Khan (from Calcutta) titled, 'The Construction of the State of Eastern Pakistan'. *Quaid-i-Azam Papers*, F/11, 1–8; and F/337.

127. Ahmad, *Speeches and Writings*, Vol. I, 599.

128. Ibid., 551.

129. Ibid., 599

130. Ibid., 541–2.

131. Z.H. Zaidi, 'Aspects of the Development of Muslim League Policy', in Philips and Wainwright, *Partition of India*, 271.

132. Ibid.

133. Ahmad, *Speeches and Writings*, Vol. II, 246.
134. Pirzada, *Foundations of Pakistan*, Vol. II, 468.
135. Jinnah told the League workers at Calcutta on 1 March 1946, 'I have seen the abject poverty of the people. Some of them did not get food, even once a day...my heart goes out to them....' Ahmad, *Speeches and Writings*, Vol. II, 272.
136. Pirzada, *Foundations of Pakistan*, Vol. II, 454.
137. Ahmad, *Speeches and Writings*, Vol. I, 526-7.
138. Sayeed, *Formative Phase*, 209.
139. Z.H. Zaidi, 'Aspects of the Development of Muslim League Policy', in Philips and Wainwright, *Partition of India*, 268.
140. These manifestoes were greatly influenced by the 'leftist', socialist leaders like Danyal Latifi in the Punjab and Abul Hashim in Bengal.
141. Menon, *Transfer of Power in India*, 438.
142. These ministries were installed in August 1942, October 1942, March 1943, and May 1943, respectively. As a Memorandum by the Secretary of State for India, in April 1944, noted, Jinnah 'has seized the opportunity of the Congress eclipse to strengthen the position of the League, with great success...his party is in the ascendant and growing in power', Mansergh, *Transfer of Power*, Vol. IV, 962.
143. Venkatacher, '1937–47 in Retrospect', in Philips and Wainwright, *Partition of India*, 474.
144. Ibid., 473.
145. Ahmad, *Speeches and Writings*, Vol.I, 428.
146. Ibid.
147. Azad, *India Wins Freedom*, 132.
148. The most important defection was that of Mian Iftikhar-ud-Din, President of the Punjab Congress, who resigned his office to join the League in September 1945. See Wavell's letter to Pethick-Lawrence on the subject, dated 1 October 1945, in Mansergh, *Transfer of Power*, Vol. VI, 306. Also see Cunningham's letter to Wavell, Ibid., 318.
149. W.C. Smith, *Modern Islam in India*, 271.
150. This, insisted Humayun Kabir, a long-time Indian nationalist Muslim, was in spite of the fact the British 'did not like Jinnah who often criticized the British in sharper language than any used by the Congress.' Humayun Kabir, 'Muslim Politics 1942–47', in Philips and Wainwright, *Partition of India*, 391. But then, as Wavell put it plainly to Amery: 'The more vociferous the Congress demands and the more intransigent their claims, the more essential it is that Government should have at its back the support of the Muslim League....' Wavell insisted, 'This is a consideration which should not be overlooked when dealing with a triangular contest in which one of the parties refuses to play and, by so doing, hopes to disqualify the other two from taking part in the game'. Mansergh, *Transfer of Power*, Vol. IV, 888, 892.
151. See, for instance, Francis Tuker, *While Memory Serves* (London: Cassell, 1950), 653. Also see, Linlithgow to Sir G.S. Bajpai, 21 July 1942. Mansergh, *Transfer of Power*, Vol. II, 423. The British Prime Minister, Winston Churchill, warned President Roosevelt of the United States on 31 July 1942 that the 'loyalty' of the Army, 'would be gravely impaired by handing over the Government of India to Congress Control.' Ibid., 553.

152. Noor-ul-Haq, *Making of Pakistan: The Military Perspective* (Islamabad: National Institute of Historical and Cultural Research, 1993), 38. For further details and information on other communities contributing to the Indian army see, Appendices, 6 and 7, in ibid., 209-10.
153. Ahmad, *Speeches and Writings*, Vol. I, 434.
154. Noor-ul-Haq, *Making of Pakistan*, 38.
155. Ahmad, *Speeches and Writings*, Vol. I, 154.
156. Ibid., 433. Apart from the pro-British Muslim leaders such as, Sikandar Hayat Khan, there were some like Inayatullah Mashraqi, the Khaksar leader, who 'not only offered 50,000 men to help the British in their war effort, but also assured the Viceroy...to counteract the impending Congress civil disobedience movement.' Malik, *Mashraqi*, 91.
157. Mansergh, *Transfer of Power*, Vol. I, App. 1, 878.
158. Sayeed, 'The Personality of Jinnah and his Political Strategy', in Philips, *Partition of India*, 287.
159. Noor-ul-Haq, *Making of Pakistan*, 40.
160. Menon, *Transfer of Power in India*, 102.
161. Wavell informed Amery on 22 July 1945: 'The most important parties in India now are the Congress and the Muslim League, and I do not see how you can disregard either or both of them any more than you could disregard the Conservative and Labour Parties at home'. Mansergh, *Transfer of Power*, Vol. V, 1291. However, it needs to be pointed out that once the war was over, the British attitude towards Jinnah, the League, and the demand for Pakistan, changed radically, as evidenced by negotiations leading to the Cabinet Mission Plan and subsequent developments until the partition of India in 1947. There was a clear and considered shift towards the Congress.
162. Waseem, *Politics and the State in Pakistan*, 82.
163. The League's spectacular success was all the more creditable in view of the fact that there were in some areas reports of official support to the opponents of the League. One such area was the Punjab, where the Unionists were in power since the early 1920s. In a letter to Wavell on 12 October 1945, Pethick-Lawrence thus explained: 'officials in the Punjab were not being impartial as regards the conduct of the elections. I quite agree that we have to accept a fundamental difference from western conditions.' Mansergh, *Transfer of Power*, Vol. VI, 335.
164. However, the Congress won nineteen Muslim (out of twenty-seven contested) and eleven minority seats. One minority seat was won by the Akali Dal in Peshawar. See Shah, *Ethnicity, Islam and Nationalism*, 165. According to Muhammad Anwar Khan, it was 'anamolous' that non–Muslims, comprising less 'than 9% population [according to 1941 census] were given around 25% (12 seats) accommodation under weightage system in the provincial assembly.' Anwar Khan, *Role of NWFP in the Freedom Struggle*, 212.
165. Incidentally, the Congress secured 4.4 per cent of the Muslim vote this time, a tremendous reversal of fortunes for the two organizations as far as their claims to be representative of the Muslims were concerned. Waheed Ahmad, 'The General Elections of 1945–46: Quaid-i-Azam's Springboard to Pakistan', *Pakistan Journal of History and Culture*, Vol. XXII, No. 2 (July–December 2001), 135.

166. Z.H. Zaidi, 'Aspects of the Development of the Muslim League Policy', in Philips and Wainwright, *Partition of India*, 274-5. Jinnah himself recalled in late 1945, 'how in 1936 when Pandit Nehru thundered that there were only two parties in India, namely, the British government and the Congress, he, like a lamb, bleated that there was a third party!' Ahmad, *Speeches and Writings*, Vol. II, 254.

167. Talbot, *Freedom's Cry*, 10.

168. Especially now 'that events, as they finally took shape, had much more to do with elite negotiations, and with Muhammad Ali Jinnah's negotiating skills in particular....' Zachariah, *Nehru*, 138.

7 The Creation of Pakistan

Jinnah's demand for Pakistan was a major issue in Indian politics since its adoption in March 1940. This was in spite of the opposition of the many forces ranged against him and his Pakistan. The British, the Congress, and the 'nationalist' Muslims,[1] including the *ulama* associated with the Jamiat-ul-Ulama-i-Hind, all opposed his demand for Pakistan. However, the more his opponents attacked Pakistan and created difficulties in its realization, the higher his stock rose among the Muslims. The more he succeeded in forcing them to concede Pakistan, the more his charismatic power was enhanced and extended. The ranks of his disciples and followers swelled. These followers secured him a massive victory in the 1945-46 elections. But then, like all charismatic leaders, Jinnah had to show to his followers that the 'recognition' and 'complete personal devotion' accorded to him were fully justified. He had to prove his charisma, indeed, produce a 'miracle', in the Weberian sense of the term. He had to create Pakistan.

Jinnah launched his campaign to create Pakistan emphasizing in particular the following aims and objectives: l) Pakistan was the only solution to the Hindu–Muslim problem in India; 2) the Muslim League was the sole representative body of Indian Muslims; 3) the League would enter into negotiations on constitutional advance only after the recognition of the Pakistan demand; and 4) the League would enter into an interim government at the centre only if it was given 'parity' with the Congress.[2]

Jinnah found the war conditions,[3] especially in the early years with the British on the retreat in Singapore, Malaya, and Burma, and the Congress in a political wilderness following the resignation of its provincial ministries and the subsequent 'Quit India' movement of 1942, ideally suited to the success of his mission. Between the two of his political adversaries, that is the British and the Congress, Jinnah realized that the British were more vulnerable. At loggerheads with the Congress, they could not afford to antagonize the Muslims in general and the Muslim League in particular. To ignore or offend the League at this point would have meant that virtually all of India was opposed to the British. The need of the hour was to conciliate the non-Congress parties, especially the League, which was the second largest political party in the country and the most organized body of Indian Muslims. The support of the League was important to the British militarily, too, for facilitating recruitment of the Muslims in the army and their eventual deployment in the Middle East, Africa, and South-East Asia during the war years. On the other hand, the Congress had aroused Muslim anxieties and fears in their 'Quit India' movement. The Muslims were convinced that the Congress was out to stifle the Pakistan demand before it could gather any force. 'Their only object', declared Jinnah, 'is by hook or by crook to bring about a situation which will destroy the Pakistan scheme'.[4] However, Jinnah was convinced that the Pakistan demand ought to be aimed at the British, the sovereign power in India, and not the Congress or the Hindus who, like the Muslims were just another party to the dispute. As he put it: 'It was the British who took India from the Musalmans. So, we are not asking the Hindus to give us anything. Our demand is made to the British, who are in possession. It is utter nonsense to say that Hindustan belongs to the Hindus'.[5]

Jinnah's wartime strategy was thus primarily aimed at bringing pressure on the British to concede the Pakistan demand. In order to make sure that this pressure worked, and worked effectively, he was careful not to hurt British sensitivities during the war. He was a realist, and thus knew fully well how much this war meant to the British, who sought cooperation, not opposition. In addition, Jinnah understood his own strengths and weaknesses. For instance, he knew how strong the League was at this point in time. Therefore, he decided to cooperate, but with qualifications. He adopted a policy of selective cooperation. He refused to extend full cooperation unless the British conceded the Pakistan demand at the centre. In the provinces, especially in the Muslim-majority provinces like the Punjab and Bengal, where he needed the Muslim League ministries to mobilize support for the Pakistan demand, he approved their cooperation with the war effort, lest deliberate obstruction prompt the British to dismiss them. However, even these ministries, as Liaquat Ali Khan informed a local League leader, were supposed to help the British 'as ministers and not as members of the Muslim League'.[6] But then, as ministers, as heads of government departments and with all the 'spoils' of office at their disposal, they helped the League attract a larger following at a very critical point in its struggle. In fact, they helped contribute to the growth of the League as a truly national party of the Muslims with support in all the Muslim-majority provinces of Pakistan.

The British, of course, saw this development quite clearly as 'a further example of Jinnah's skill in consolidating his position'.[7] However, under the circumstances, with the Congress up in arms, they had little choice but to accommodate Jinnah. Though they recognized that he was going to stand 'no nonsense'[8] from them, they did not fully gauge the impact of his wartime strategy upon the future politics of India. In particular, they failed to realize how Jinnah was going to transform his demand for Pakistan into a clarion call of Muslim India. They simply assumed 'that there is going to be nothing doing with either the Congress or the Muslim League while the war lasts....'[9]

Jinnah challenged this assumption on 27 June 1940, demanding that: 'No pronouncement should be made by His Majesty's Government which would in any way militate against, or prejudice, the 'two nations' position which had become the universal faith of Muslim India'.[10] He also sought a 'definite assurance' to the effect that 'no interim or final scheme of constitution would be adopted by the British Government without the previous approval and consent of Muslim India'.[11] In addition, he insisted, the Muslims would be accorded 'an equal share in the authority and control of the governments, central and provincial', and the Muslim representatives would be 'chosen by the Muslim League.'[12] Indeed, Jinnah made it absolutely clear that unless these 'essential' demands were met, the League could not support the war effort.[13]

Although the British put up a tough stand, telling Jinnah that there were other parties in India, apart from the League and the Congress, which might fairly claim their consideration, they could not ignore him or his demands. Of course, they did not fear the League and did not think of it as a highly organized body of Muslim public opinion at this point in time. But, these were the early difficult years of the war, and the Congress, by opting for non-cooperation and defiance, had created a dangerous situation for the British. Upsetting Jinnah would not only have led to the League's opposition to the war effort but to a possible alliance between the League and the Congress against the British. After all, Rajagopalachari,[14] and more importantly, Tej Bahadur Sapru, as late as May 1941, were in touch with Jinnah, seeking 'rapprochement' between the League and the Congress.[15]

Thus, the British had no option but to conciliate Jinnah and the League in the given circumstances. They found it difficult 'to stand still',[16] in spite of their self-professed resolve, and readily responded to Jinnah's demands in the form of the so-called 'August Offer'. This Offer assured the Muslims that the British Government could not impose its system of government upon unwilling 'minorities'. This assurance was the first major victory for Jinnah as a charismatic leader of Muslim India. He had made a major gain over the issue of Pakistan. The League Working Committee, in its meeting of 1 September 1940, noted 'with satisfaction that His Majesty's Government had, on the whole, practically met the demand of the Muslim League for a clear assurance to the effect that no future constitution, interim or final, should be adopted by the British Government without their approval and consent'.[17] However, the Working Committee, went on to 'record' its disapproval of some of the comments made by the Viceroy and the Secretary of the State with regard to the 'unity of national life' in India, characterizing them as 'historically inaccurate and self-contradictory'.[18] Indeed, the Committee emphasized that, 'the Muslim League again makes its position clear that Muslims of India are a nation by themselves and will exercise their right of self-determination and that they alone are the final judges and arbiters of their own destiny'.[19]

The August Offer, nonetheless, committed the British publicly to some sort of understanding of Muslim apprehensions as to their future in India. Their views were to be taken into account in the future scheme of things. Jinnah felt that the British could concede more on Pakistan, given more pressure and opportune circumstances. His keen 'practical sense' told him that this was just the beginning and not the end of the matter.[20] Rather than taking a rigid stand on his Pakistan demand, and thereby frightening the British out of the implicit recognition contained in the Offer, he had the League reject the offer on grounds related to the details of the League's association with the Government. He rejected the offer on the following grounds: 1) no 'real and substantial share' was given to the League in the authority of the Government at the centre; 2) no clear-cut indication was given as to what would be the 'position' of the League representatives in the Executive Council in the event of any other party (namely Congress) deciding to join in; 3) there was no guarantee of a 'real and effective' role for the League in the administration of the provinces; and 4) no precise 'information' on the proposed War Advisory Council was made available.[21] It may not be out of place to mention that the Congress had already rejected the offer, making it easier for Jinnah to reject it without any risk of being outmanoeuvred in the process. Jinnah seemed determined at this point in time not to commit to any British move unless it had prior approval of the Congress for he was convinced that the British and the Congress were still engaged. As he told Liaquat Ali Khan, on 3 August 1940, the British 'have not yet definitely made up their mind to displease the Congress as there is still lingering hope on their part and much more so with His Majesty's Government in England that the Congress will still fall in line with them'.[22]

The veracity of Jinnah's statement became evident during the visit of Sir Stafford Cripps (1889–1952) to India, in March 1942, as the British War Cabinet's representative, to get in touch with the Congress leaders to press them to support the British war effort. The westwards advance of Japan and the precarious situation developing in India forced the British to launch a fresh political initiative. However, the choice of Cripps was very suggestive. He was not only 'reported to be a personal friend of Nehru',[23] but also reputed to be a great supporter of the Congress cause. Cripps's identification with the Congress was so well known among the ruling circles that the Secretary of State for India, Amery, thought it necessary to advise Viceroy Linlithgow to keep Jinnah 'quiet' until his arrival. He wrote:

> I am afraid of the immediate reaction of his being the emissary on Moslems who will think we are selling out to Congress, and you may find it necessary to convey beforehand some sort of assurance to Jinnah (which indeed will, I think, be clearly implied in the Prime Minister's statement) to keep him quiet till Cripps arrives.[24]

Linlithgow, more in touch with the realities on the ground in India, went one step further and told Cripps on his arrival that: 'An early word to emphasize your complete open-mindedness would, I think, be of great value'.[25] Cripps was no novice in politics either. He understood these things. He moved to calm Jinnah's apprehensions in his very first meeting with him. He told Jinnah:

I have changed my opinion in the last eighteen months, particularly during the last six months. I do not hold my old views. The Cabinet of Britain too wholly holds my view. We appreciate the Muslim case. I give you the assurance that I recognize that so far as the Musalmans are concerned, I recognize no body and no party among them other than the League and its President.[26]

Whether or not Cripps created a favourable impression on Jinnah in this meeting is unknown. What is certain is that he was not interested in Jinnah, the League, and 'the Muslim case' as such. He had come to India to solicit the support of the Congress for the war period with the promise that the British would help create 'a new Indian Union' after the war, a 'Dominion', like other British Dominions, 'in no way subordinate in any aspect of its domestic or external affairs.' Cripps, however, found it expedient to state that if any province of British India refused to accept the 'new constitution' or 'present constitutional position', the British Government would have no choice but to grant such 'non-acceding Provinces' the same status as that of the Indian Union.[27] In the meanwhile, he stressed, the Government would 'invite the immediate and effective participation' of the Indian leaders in the 'counsels of their country'.[28] However, he made it clear that 'the defence of India,' during the war years and until the new constitution is framed, will remain the 'responsibility' of the British Government.[29] Cripps, indeed, warned that his 'proposals are definite and precise' and if they were 'rejected' now, 'there would be neither the time nor the opportunity to reconsider this matter till after the war....'[30]

One measure of Cripps' indifference and lack of attention to Jinnah and his concerns was his failure to discuss with him the present, where details 'were more important than the principles themselves'.[31] 'No discussion', Jinnah complained, 'took place between me and Sir Stafford Cripps regarding the present period except that details would be worked out and settled by the Viceroy with the parties concerned'.[32] Jinnah was, of course, more disappointed to learn through 'the maze of correspondence and statements' issued by Congress leaders that he 'was discussing with them alternative proposals of theirs',[33] without taking the League into confidence. Highlighting the devastating nature of those proposals, Jinnah charged,

> ...if the alternative proposals of the Congress were accepted—immediate freedom and independence of India, cabinet to be nominated...with the Viceroy to act as constitutional Governor-General...irremovable and responsible to nobody but the majority, which would be at the command of the Congress in the Cabinet. If such an adjustment had been arrived at, then, it would have been a 'Fascist Grand Council' and the Muslims and other minorities would have been entirely at the mercy of the Congress raj. Then to say that the future would be considered after the war is to my mind absurd, because there would be nothing left of the future to discuss, except details.[34]

But then, of course, the Congress and the British could not agree amongst themselves. Although according to the British authorities at home, Cripps went 'very near giving the whole case away',[35] the Congress did not oblige. The most important consideration that weighed heavily on their minds was the timing of the proposals. In the light of military setbacks suffered by the British at that time, the Congress saw the proposals as a confession of weakness. Gandhi, in fact, described them as 'a post-dated cheque', advising Cripps to take the 'first plane home....'[36] In the event of a Japanese advance, the Congress had even planned to 'step in and take over the control of the country'.[37] Congress leadership was particularly upset with the 'non-accession' clause. They felt it was an invitation to the Muslims to 'insist' on their demand for Pakistan.[38] 'The acceptance beforehand of the novel principle of non-accession for a Province', claimed the Congress Working Committee, 'is also a severe blow to the conception of Indian unity and an apple of discord likely to generate growing trouble....'[39]

The 'non-accession' clause in the proposals was no more than an attempt to check Jinnah until the British and the Congress could settle things based on 'a United India between themselves'. As Cripps explained to Gandhi, 'the document was primarily based on the conception of a United India, and that it was only if Congress failed to come to an agreement with the Muslims in the constitution-making body that the danger of non-accession would arise'.[40] Cripps, in fact, believed that such an agreement was 'more likely if the Muslim Provinces had the option of not coming into a constitution framed by a Constituent Assembly'.[41] But, more importantly, the Cripps proposals 'did not provide for the right of option to be exercised by vote of Muslim population alone'.[42] In case of the vote of the whole province, comprising Muslim and non-Muslim populations, the British knew very well that the 'situation proposed in Cripps offer practically amounts to rejecting the Pakistan claim, since the League could not obtain necessary majorities in Bengal and Punjab'.[43]

This point was certainly not lost on Jinnah. Addressing the Allahabad session of the League on 4 April 1942, Jinnah warned:

> ...the alleged power of the minority in the matter of secession suggested in the document is illusory, as Hindu India will dominate the decision in favour of one All-India Union in all the provinces, and the Muslims in Bengal and the Punjab will be at the mercy of the Hindu minority in those provinces who will exert themselves to the fullest extent and length for keeping the Musalmans tied to the chariot wheel of Hindudom. Thus the Musalmans will be doomed to subjection in all the provinces.[44]

Jinnah, thus, rejected the Cripps proposals. 'So far as the Pakistan demand is not agreed to', he asserted, 'we cannot agree to any present adjustment which will in any way militate against or prejudice the Pakistan demand'.[45] Though he conceded that some 'recognition' of the 'principle of partition'[46] was there in the proposals, he was convinced that Pakistan was 'treated as a remote possibility and there is a definite preference for a new Indian Union which is the main objective....'[47] Under the circumstances, therefore, he felt, it was not wise to 'play the game with loaded dice'.[48]

But there was no denying that the Cripps proposals represented considerable improvement on the August Offer,[49] in spite of the fact they did not concede the Pakistan demand 'unequivocally' and the 'right of self-determination', for the Muslims.[50] Things could never be the same henceforth. The British had tacitly recognized the case for Pakistan. Jinnah had made an important advance in pursing the goal of Pakistan. Indeed, the proposals offered Jinnah 'a hole in the dyke' which he was determined to widen[51] as more opportunities came his way in the course of time.

The 'Quit India' movement launched by the Congress, in August 1942, to force the British to withdraw immediately, and declare India independent was one such opportunity. The movement rallied the anxiety-ridden Muslims further behind Jinnah and the League, convinced that it was primarily directed against them. Jinnah called the movement a 'declaration of war', not only against the British Government but also 'a war against the Muslim League' and 'Muslim India'.[52] He warned the Congress 'not to molest or harass the Muslims in order to compel them to carry out their orders'.[53] He even appealed to the 'Hindu public to stop this internecine civil war before it is too late'.[54] In the end, of course, the British came down heavily on the Quit India movement and crushed the 'open rebellion'. The League got a major impetus out of the widening chasm between the British and the Congress growing into 'a power unto itself'.[55] The British found it increasingly difficult to ignore Jinnah and his demand for Pakistan in the following years.

This did not mean that the British were prepared to recognize and concede his demand for Pakistan. Viceroy Linlithgow had nothing but disdain for Pakistan. On 8 January 1942, Linlithgow wrote to Amery saying: 'Jinnah has been at pains not to define exactly what he means by the blessed word [Pakistan] and all we should get would be something woolly and general'.[56] On 6 November, the Governor of Bengal, Richard Casey, in a letter to the new Viceroy, Wavell, insisted that Pakistan was 'nonsense'.[57] But what was significant in this trifling process was the fact that the British had also come to reckon that Pakistan was 'the first and foremost issue' in Indian politics,[58] and that attempts had to be made to 'clear up' the issue.[59] Indeed, in the estimate of some responsible British officials, 'a considerable amount of work will have to be done on the Muslims if they are to be weaned away from the Pakistan idea'.[60]

The British, as later developments showed, proposed to do it in two ways. First, they hoped to 'attack the Pakistan issue'[61] frontally by projecting and promoting practical difficulties in the way. For instance, British Under-Secretary of State for India questioned the ability of Pakistan to meet its defence requirements. In a note to the new Secretary of State for India, Pethick-Lawrence, on 5 February 1946, he pointed out: '...Eastern Pakistan would be incapable of coping with its defence problems except to the limited extent that it might raise and maintain locally the five battalions of Assam Rifles required for the control of tribal areas....'[62] Pethick-Lawrence readily agreed, and went one step further suggesting that finance and economic management would pose serious difficulties. Emphasizing the economic aspects, in particular, he claimed: 'No doubt the weight of the economic arguments against Pakistan, if they are realised by those concerned, will cause them to turn their minds to some form of federal arrangement with Hindu India'.[63]

Secondly and more importantly, the British planned to generate opposition to the Pakistan demand from within the community by encouraging ethnicity or what was then described as 'local patriotisms' among the Muslims, especially the old Punjab Strategy of Fazl-i-Husain and Sikandar Hayat Khan's days. In a letter to Casey on 1 January 1945, Wavell stated: 'In the Punjab, Sikandar Hayat Khan, and I am told, Fazl-i-Husain before him, saw that something could be made of local patriotism and national feeling that exists in a province with a common language and a way of life of its own. The answer may be to exploit this local patriotism....'[64] Wavell indeed took special pains 'in speaking to anyone from the Punjab that their slogan should be, 'we are the united Punjab and care nothing for Congress or League and have no intention of letting them interfere in our affairs''.[65]

In spite of these attempts to make short work of the Pakistan demand, the British could not postpone a serious discussion of the issue for long. They were, in fact, forced to face 'the inevitable issue of Pakistan'[66] at the Simla Conference of June–July 1945,[67] the first organized political conference of leaders of all the major political parties of India[68] after the end of war in Europe. Jinnah made it absolutely clear to them at the outset that he sought a 'declaration' by the British Government 'guaranteeing the right of self-determination of Muslims and pledging that after the war, or as soon as it may be possible, the British Government would establish Pakistan having regard to the basic principles laid down in the Lahore resolution of the Muslim League passed in March 1940.'[69] Although the Conference, in the end, concerned itself primarily with the short-term proposals of the Viceroy's expanded Executive Council for the war's duration, with Jinnah demanding parity with the Congress and an exclusive right to nominate its Muslim members, the long-term and short-term proposals were intertwined. Thus, in spite of an assurance that the plan to expand the Viceroy's Executive Council was 'without prejudice to any future constitution or constitutions of India', especially without prejudice to the Pakistan issue, Jinnah could not help but draw the conclusion:

>...that if we accept this arrangement the Pakistan issue will be shelved and put in the cold storage indefinitely whereas the Congress will have secured under this arrangement what they want, namely, a clear road for their advance towards securing Hindu national independence of India, because the future Executive will work as a unitary Government of India and we know that this interim or provisional arrangement will have a way of settling down for an unlimited period and all the forces in the proposed Executive plus the known policy of the British Government and Lord Wavell's strong inclination for a united India, would completely jeopardize us....[70]

In this sense, Jinnah's stand at the Simla Conference was not a question of a few seats on the Executive Council. Nor was Jinnah aiming to secure the exclusive right to nominate Muslim members on the Executive Council simply to keep the Unionist and the Congress Muslims[71] out of office, lest it should affect 'his claim to be the sole spokesman of all Muslims', as has been suggested by Ayesha Jalal in her account of the proceedings.[72] At stake was the fundamental principle of Pakistan. Jinnah could not agree to compromise the principle for the sake of a doubtful advantage in a 'provisional arrangement.' This was precisely what Jinnah had emphasized in his talks with Gandhi in September 1944 (9-27 September) by asking him to 'accept the fundamentals of the Lahore resolution' first and then 'proceed to settle details?'[73] By then, Gandhi had 'realized' that a settlement of the Indian problem 'could not be accomplished by disregarding Jinnah'.[74] He himself had proposed to Jinnah that the two 'life servants of the nation' should meet to solve the 'communal tangle which had hitherto defied solution'.[75] Jinnah agreed, and the talks were held at his residence in Bombay.

The talks,[76] in fact, brought into sharp focus Jinnah's position on the Pakistan demand and the strategy to achieve it. Jinnah insisted that no interim arrangement would be agreed to unless this demand was conceded first. He wanted a recognition of Pakistan first. He would not agree to the idea of a 'separate State' after 'India was free'.[77] He would 'not trust a Congress-ruled India to implement a Pakistan promise'.[78] This also explained why Jinnah blasted the so-called 'Desai–

Liaquat Pact' supposedly reached between Liaquat Ali Khan and Bhulabhai Desai, leader of the Congress Party in the Legislative Assembly, in early 1945[79] in the wake of the failure of the Jinnah–Gandhi talks. The pact stipulated, *inter alia*, the formation of an interim government at the centre (on the basis of parity between the League and the Congress!) prior to the settlement of the long-term Pakistan issue.[80] Wavell indeed tried to emulate this pact at Simla, without, of course, conceding the League parity at the centre, and the right to nominate all Muslims to the Executive Council. Wavell, somehow, felt that the political 'deadlock' could be 'broken only by a *demarche* by the third party'.[81] Hence, he organized the Simla Conference. But Jinnah refused to compromise on principles.

However, there was no denying that the Simla Conference marked a breakwater in the political history of India. Pakistan emerged as the main issue at the highest levels. This was publicly acknowledged by the Congress as well as the British leaders. For example, the Congress President, Maulana Abul Kalam Azad, admitted that the Conference represented 'not merely a question of seats, but one affecting a fundamental principle'.[82] Viceroy Wavell, who accused Jinnah of 'intransigence', and ultimate breakdown of the negotiations, grudgingly conceded that Jinnah's attitude at the Conference represented 'the real distrust of the Muslims...for the Congress and the Hindus'.[83] Wavell, in fact, saw little hope of reconciliation between the League and the Congress precisely for that reason. Indeed, he went on to suggest to the authorities at home a 'Breakdown Plan' in case, 'as, is quite likely, the Congress and the Muslim League are unable to come to any agreement on the Pakistan issue'.[84]

Although Wavell reckoned that it was 'most unlikely that Jinnah would now enter into discussions without a previous guarantee of acceptance, in principle, of Pakistan',[85] he was still not willing to make any concessions on the issue. In fact, he appeared to be more critical of the demand for Pakistan. In line with recommendations of the Governors Conference of 1 and 2 August 1945,[86] he informed the Secretary of State of his own feelings and that of his governors in these words:

There was strong feeling that Jinnah's attitude was obstructive, that dangers and disadvantages of Pakistan both from a political and economic point of view should be exposed, and that in particular H.M.G's Government should make it clear that they are unable to agree to partition of India on purely Muslim vote.[87]

The Governor of the Punjab was particularly harsh on the Pakistan demand. He believed that 'the main issue for his province was Pakistan.' He suggested that the proposed 1945–46 elections should be postponed 'until a determined attempt had been made to clear up the Pakistan issue'.[88] He insisted that 'the hollowness of Pakistan in its crude form should be exposed before provincial elections were held'.[89] Indeed, he warned: 'If Jinnah won the elections, the Muslims would regard themselves as committed to Pakistan....'[90] Though Wavell readily accepted the 'significance' of the point, he felt, 'It is easy to say that the Muslims cannot be allowed to hold up the settlement; but they are too large a population to be by-passed or coerced without danger'.[91] Assessing the hold of Jinnah on the Muslim community at this point in time, Wavell wrote home:

> While it was possible to over-estimate the importance of any individual political leader, his own judgement was that Jinnah spoke for 99 per cent of the Muslim population of India in their apprehensions of Hindu domination...that fear might or might not be well-founded but of its existence and reality there could be no question.[92]

The fact of the matter was that by now both Jinnah and his Pakistan demand were a 'reality.' The British had to deal with them, whether they liked it or not. The failure of the Simla Conference phenomenally raised Jinnah's standing and status as the charismatic leader of Muslim India. Earlier, the Jinnah–Gandhi talks in September 1944 had boosted Jinnah's status as a charismatic leader. The talks had established the 'equality' of Jinnah's status with Gandhi, 'the holy hero of the Congress'.[93] The failure of the Simla Conference enhanced his charisma manifold, making it clear to his friends and foes; followers and detractors, indeed, all parties involved in the political processes in India, that Jinnah was *the* leader of the Muslims. He was the man who settled matters with the Government. No deal could be offered or brokered with the British Government without his consent and approval. This message had been conveyed during the National Defence Council episode in 1941 also. But it was never so emphatic and telling as this time. Muslim leaders 'were not likely to get any prize offices by remaining outside the Muslim League, they would all have to flock to the Muslim League'.[94] They would have to follow Jinnah.

The result was that a large number of Muslim leaders from all parts of India, including the Punjab and the NWFP, two most difficult provinces for the League, moved to join Jinnah and the League. In the Punjab, leaders such as Sir Muhammad Feroz Khan Noon (1893–1970), Sayed Amjad Ali and Khizar Hayat Khan's own clansmen 'forsook old loyalties' and joined the League. Indeed, big landowners in the Punjab such as the Noons, Daultanas, Hayats, and Dastis parted company with the Unionists 'realizing that...the future lay with the Muslim League'.[95] In many ways, this was the beginning of the end of the Unionist domination in the Punjab. The 1945–46 elections merely confirmed this downward trend. Similarly, in the NWFP, prominent leaders such as the Pir of Manki Sharif, Abdul Qayyum Khan, former Deputy Leader of the Congress in the Central Legislative Assembly, Arbab Abdul Ghafoor, former Congress member of the Legislative Assembly, Ghulam Mohammad Khan Lundkhawar, former President of the Frontier Congress, and M. Abbas Khan, a former minister in the Congress ministry, joined the League and thus 'gave an impetus to the League organization in the NWFP'.[96]

In this changed scenario, Wavell and the British Government realized that it was useless to pursue provisional arrangements until problems of a long-term settlement were seriously addressed. In fact, there was a perceptible effort now on the part of the British Government to lessen and eradicate, if possible, this 'psychological' fear on the part of the Muslims by offering them not 'Jinnah's crude Pakistan'[97] but a 'modified' concept of Pakistan, a concept resting essentially on 'federal' principles,[98] and 'more likely to lead to a unified India'.[99]

The argument for a 'modified' concept of Pakistan was both familiar and old, and was essentially based on three premises. First, 'the dynamic behind the demand for Pakistan is in its essence the demand that they shall not be subjected to Hindu Raj'.[100] Secondly, the Pakistan demand, as promoted and pursued by Jinnah, was beset with 'practical difficulties',[101] and was not a 'practicable scheme whereby the Muslim majority areas can be brought together to form an independent Sovereign State wholly separated from the rest of India'.[102] Finally,

'Pakistan represents a very powerful, tenacious body of conviction that cannot easily be placated....'[103]

The foundations of the modified concept of Pakistan were succinctly articulated in a draft entitled, *Proposals for a Provisional Constitution: Synopsis*, prepared by the India Office in March 1946 on the eve of the Cabinet Mission's visit to India. These proposals sought to resolve India's constitutional problem with the help of Indians themselves. The main argument was as follows:

> The foundations of a provisional constitution for India must lie in the Act of 1935. Such a constitution must continue to provide a unitary framework but within it means of satisfying, to the greatest degree compatible with presentation of India as a single State, the aspirations of Indian Moslems for self-rule.... To effect these changes the Act of 1935 would require amendments to serve two main purposes (a) to enable the Provinces and the States to become federated, for such matters only as are essential to maintain Indian status and authority in the United Nations. That is to say, defence, external affairs and their means of execution (b) to give the provinces the fullest measure of self-government compatible with (a). Further, to provide for a stable provincial executive elected by the legislatures so as to reflect their communal proportions and thus qualified to appoint delegates to the centre who, with those of Indian States, could form a federal legislature and elect a ministry to transact the business of the Agency centre.[104]

It was precisely as a result of this line of argument that the Cabinet Mission, comprising Pethick-Lawrence, Stafford Cripps, and A.V. Alexander arrived in India on 24 March 1946, to force Jinnah to choose between his concept of a sovereign Pakistan, restricted to Muslim-majority areas,[105] and 'a larger Pakistan which would come into a central federal nexus....'[106] Cripps, in particular, minced no words in telling Jinnah 'that we could not press Congress to accept anything more than what we might call a smaller Pakistan'. Pakistan, he insisted, could only mean Balochistan, Sindh, the NWFP, and West Punjab in the Northwest, and Eastern Bengal minus Calcutta, plus Sylhet, in the East. There was no way 'larger areas within Pakistan including essentially all the Punjab and Bengal' could be secured. 'It is not possible to get agreement with the Hindus or the Sikhs upon such an area....'[107] Cripps was looking out for 'old friends in Congress'.[108]

He had started 'mending his fences with the Congress' since January 1946. He had befriended Nehru, and had 'special access to Congress'.[109] But then, he was not the only one who was fond of the Congress and its leadership. Pethick-Lawrence did not lag behind. He 'effusively admired' Gandhi's 'idealism'.[110]

Members of the Mission and Viceroy Wavell had no doubt in their mind that the idea of a 'smaller,' though 'sovereign Pakistan', would have no appeal for Jinnah and thus he would eventually come around to accept the second alternative, that is, of a 'larger Pakistan', federated with India. However, for the moment they were convinced that the preliminary statement to be issued by the Mission 'should not say that the full claim of Pakistan could not be supported by us. It was felt that at this stage the Delegation should maintain an attitude of impartiality....'[111] But not for long.

Soon the Mission took it upon itself to press Jinnah to concede his demand for a larger and sovereign Pakistan in spite of the fact that he 'made a fairly good case for Pakistan on cultural and religious grounds....'[112] On 16 April, the Mission plainly asked Jinnah 'whether he would prefer the matter to be considered on the basis of sovereignty and the small area or a Union and a larger area.'[113] The Mission had already 'come to the conclusion' that:

> ...the full and complete demand for Pakistan in the form in which Mr Jinnah had put forward had little chance of acceptance...Mr Jinnah could not reasonably hope to receive both the whole of the territory, much of it inhabited by non-Muslims, which he claimed and the full measure of sovereignty which he said was essential. If the full territories were insisted upon then some elements of sovereignty must be relinquished if there were to be a reasonable prospect of agreement. If, on the other hand, full sovereignty is desired, then the claims to the [non-] Muslim territories could not be conceded.[114]

Jinnah, who could not agree to the partition of the Muslim-majority provinces, was left with no option but to signal his readiness to accept the idea of Indian 'Union'. However, he demanded that the six Muslim-majority provinces (Punjab, North-West Frontier Province, Balochistan, Sindh, Bengal, and Assam) must constitute a 'Pakistan Group', and that there must be 'a separate Constitution-making body', to frame constitutions for this Group and the provinces in the Group.

After these constitutions are 'finally framed by the constitution-making body, it will be open to any Province of the Group to decide to opt out of its Group, provided the wishes of the people of that Province are ascertained by a referendum to opt out or not.'[115] Since these demands were not acceptable to the Congress leaders, who sought, among other things, one all-India 'Constituent Assembly', and for groups later to frame the provincial constitutions for their group, if so desired by the provinces concerned,[116] the Mission saw no point in further deliberations with the League and the Congress, and thus ended on 12 May the Second Simla Conference with much the same outcome as the first. The Mission 'thanked both parties for the efforts they had made and were sorry it had not been possible to agree.'[117] The Mission announced their own plan, a curious blend of the positions taken by the League and the Congress during the Conference as expressed in the Statement of 16 May supplemented by the Statement of (25 May and) 16 June, popularly referred to as the Cabinet Mission Plan as a whole.

The main thrust of the Cabinet Mission Plan was to offer India a three-tiered constitutional structure in which provinces were grouped to form 'sections' which, in turn, would determine themselves what subjects would be under the jurisdiction of their respective sectional government. Section A comprised Madras, Bombay, United Provinces, Bihar, the Central Provinces, and Orissa. Section B included the Punjab, the North–West Frontier Province and Sindh (with the addition of a representative of British Balochistan). Section C consisted of Bengal and Assam. The three sections of the Constituent Assembly had to come together along with representatives of the Indian States, to settle the Union Constitution after the provincial constitutions had been formed. Once the Union Constitution had come into force, the provinces could 'opt out' of their assigned groups/sections. This, the Mission contended, was a 'solution', largely 'just to the essential claims of all parties, and would at the same time be most likely to bring about a stable and practicable form of constitution for All-India'. The Mission was emphatic that 'neither a larger nor a smaller sovereign state of Pakistan would provide an acceptable solution of the communal problem'. Besides the long-term proposals, the statement of 16 May also suggested a short-term proposal relating to the formation of an interim government. 'While the constitution-making proceeds', the

Mission argued, 'the administration of India had to be carried on. We attach the greatest importance to the setting up at once of an interim government....'[118] The 16 June statement reinforced and refined the idea further. The two sets of proposals, that is the long-term proposals and the short-term proposals were integral to the Mission Plan to be accepted or rejected as a whole. The Plan, however, conceded that: 'The constitutions of the Union and of the Groups should contain a provision whereby any Province could, by a majority vote of its legislative Assembly, call for a reconsideration of the terms of the constitution after an initial period of 10 years and at 10 year intervals thereafter'.[119]

While the Mission Plan pleased the Congress leaders for passing a 'sentence of death on Mr Jinnah's Pakistan',[120] it left Jinnah distressed and disappointed 'that the Mission should have thought fit to advance commonplace and exploded arguments against Pakistan...calculated to hurt the feelings of Muslim India'.[121] It appeared, Jinnah charged, 'that this was done by the Mission simply to appease and placate the Congress....'[122] Jinnah identified as many as nine areas in which the Plan violated the fundamental Muslim interests, identified by the League during the Second Simla Conference. He was particularly critical of the fact that the Plan did not accept: I) 'two constitution-making bodies', and 2) 'our proposal that the Pakistan Group should have a right to secede from the Union after an initial period of ten years'.[123]

In spite of all this criticism, it was not easy for Jinnah to reject the Cabinet Mission Plan as it was. Jinnah had to be realistic about the whole thing. He had to employ his logic and reason to assess the situation. First, the World War was over, and it was no longer easy to reject British offers offhand. The British were under no pressure to woo the League any more. In fact, they were free, once again, to take charge of political developments, and the Congress was back in mainstream politics as the largest political party of the country. In the three-party contest, the loss of one party was bound to be the gain of the others. In the context of the conciliatory nature of the relationship between the Congress and the Labour Government of Prime Minister Attlee, the loss of the League, the weakest of the three parties, could also have been a loss beyond redemption. This context, in fact, constituted the necessary framework of politics for Jinnah in the crucial post-War years, and Jinnah understood it well. Jinnah, indeed, like many of his followers, was:

> ...given the option of accepting what the Mission offered, in which we were clearly told no change of a major nature could be made, or of rejecting their proposals in toto and thereby drawing upon ourselves the responsibility of the failure of the Mission and with it the consequences which might follow.[124]

To make things more difficult for Jinnah, the League Working Committee, in session almost daily during the stay of the Cabinet Mission in India, had decided to leave the matter of acceptance or rejection of the Cabinet Mission Plan entirely to Jinnah's discretion. He was the charismatic leader of Muslim India, and it was his call. But Jinnah was not worried about the long-term proposals alone. He also had to contend with the short-term proposals leading to the formation of an interim government, and their impact upon his demand for Pakistan. To add to his difficulties, the statement of 16 May was far from definite. He was not sure as to what the British would do in case one party accepted the offer while the other rejected it. How then would the interim government be formed? Since the long-term proposals were essentially linked with the short-term proposals, Jinnah, in fact, saw no sense in considering the statement even on its face value unless doubts about the short-term proposals were removed. Indeed, he approached the Viceroy, Wavell, as early as 3 June to clarify the issue. Wavell's response was quite positive and encouraging. He told Jinnah that, although the Cabinet Mission

> cannot give you a written assurance of what its action will be in the event of the breakdown of the present negotiations; but can give you, on behalf of the Delegation, my *personal assurance* that we do not propose to make any discrimination in the treatment of either party; and that *we shall go ahead with the plan* laid down in our statement as far as circumstances permit; *if either party accepts*....[125]

This 'assurance' from the Viceroy was 'one of the most important considerations' with the League Working Committee in their acceptance of the statement of 16 May.[126] The subsequent approval of the League Council was also precisely the result of this assurance. As

Jinnah informed Wavell: 'I may further inform you that similarly I had to repeat the assurance to the Council before they finally gave their approval'.[127] There were quite a few prominent leaders, including Maulana Hasrat Mohani, who opposed the statement of 16 May. However, after lengthy deliberations, on 6 June 1946, a large majority of the members of the League Council approved the Cabinet Mission Plan.[128] On 16 June, the Cabinet Mission in a declaration of their final proposals went on to proclaim:

> In the event of the two major parties or either of them proving unwilling to join the setting up of a coalition government…it is the intention of the Viceroy to proceed with the formation of an interim government which will be as representative as possible of those willing to accept the Statement of 16 May.[129]

But then, one wonders, what more, besides the crucial 'assurance' of the Viceroy on the formation of the interim government, may have influenced Jinnah's mind. After all, he had been so successfully able to mobilize the Muslims around his own sovereign concept of Pakistan, reflected in the massive League victory in the 1945–46 elections. That it was not an easy and straightforward decision was clear from Jinnah's own reflections the day after he had communicated the decision of the League to the Viceroy. As he told Ispahani:

> Naturally, I have slept very little during the last week. My brain worked incessantly. I have tossed in bed from one side to the other, thinking and worrying about what we should do. The responsibility has been so heavy that it has taken much out of me. I have thought much…and have prayed for guidance, because the decision I was called upon to make would mar or make the destiny of our nation.[130]

Not only did some of his followers question the wisdom of his decision,[131] Jinnah himself wondered, and rightly so, if 'the decision to accept was the right one'.[132] The fate of his charisma and charismatic leadership, which had increasingly grown over the years, apart from the fate of Muslim India, hinged on this one crucial decision.

While Ayesha Jalal argued that Jinnah accepted the Cabinet Mission Plan because it 'offered him the substance of what he was really after', i.e. two federations representing Muslim provinces (Pakistan), and

Hindu provinces (Hindustan), coordinated by 'a British Crown Representative', with equal status and few union subjects,[133] the facts of the case hardly support the argument. The Misson Plan represented the British concept of Pakistan rather than Jinnah's concept of a separate, sovereign Pakistan. Jinnah had demanded a sovereign state of Pakistan since 1940, and in discussions with the Cabinet Mission, he had insisted on two constitution-making bodies and the right for the 'Pakistan Group' to secede from the Union after an initial period of ten years. In this sense, the Cabinet Mission Plan did not give him 'what he was really after,' so to speak. So, the question remains, why did Jinnah accept the Cabinet Mission Plan? The only plausible explanation seems to be that, as an astute strategist that he was, he accepted the Plan more out of tactical considerations than any compromise on the fundamental principle of Pakistan. He was aware of his limitations, especially after the end of the war. He realized that he could not dictate terms. He had to act with a 'sense of responsibility and proportion'. He had to consider the whole situation carefully. Some of the important considerations that must have helped him decide in favour of the acceptance are suggested here.

First, Jinnah was convinced that 'the foundation and the basis of Pakistan are there in their own scheme'.[134] Sections B and C, comprising essentially the Muslim-majority areas, ensured that the Muslims could 'reach our goal and establish Pakistan'.[135] In addition, the Cabinet Mission Plan provided for 'reconsideration' after an initial period of ten years. Indeed, the League's resolution of 6 June accepting the Mission Plan, clearly stated that: 'it will keep in view the opportunity and the right to secession of provinces or groups from the Union, which have been provided in the Mission's Plan by implication.'[136] In fact, this 'right to secession' was Jinnah's best opportunity to secure Pakistan in the end, if the Plan did not work. Secondly, being a constitutionalist, and a very good one at that, Jinnah, in fact, knew that the Plan was 'cryptic with several lacunas',[137] out of touch with the realities of Hindu–Muslim politics, and thus unworkable. This was amply borne out by his sharp criticism of the various aspects of the Plan in his statement of 23 May 1946. A few instances of his critical judgment will illustrate the point.

Taking the case of three subjects given to the Union, that is, foreign affairs, defense, and communications, for instance, Jinnah noted: 'There is no indication at all that the communications would be restricted to what is necessary for defence. Nor is there any indication as to how this Union will be empowered to raise finances required for these three subjects....'[138] In this context, Jinnah referred to the 'Advisory Committee on the rights of citizens, minorities, and tribal and excluded areas,' and explained how in effect its recommendations 'will destroy the very basic principle that the Union is to be strictly confined to three subjects.'[139] His argument was that if it was 'left to the Union Constituent Assembly to decide these matters by a majority vote whether any of the recommendations of the Advisory Committee should be incorporated in the Union Constitution, then it will open a door to more subjects being vested in the Union Government.'[140] This will be the end of the Union.[141] With regard to particular Muslim interests, Jinnah also highlighted the role of the Executive and the Legislature on the questions of a communal nature, stipulating that 'a major communal issue in the Legislature should require for its decision a majority of the representatives present and voting of each of the two major communities as well as a majority of all the members present and voting', and wondered: 'who will decide and how as to what is a major communal issue and as to what is a purely non-communal issue?'[142] Thus, Jinnah had no doubt whatsoever that the constitutional package had serious problems and thus was not workable. Woodrow Wyatt, Private Secretary to Cripps, during his stay in India, too, was convinced that 'the scheme contained in the Cabinet Mission's Statement was impracticable and could not work.'[143]

Thirdly, Jinnah did not want the Congress to have a free hand in the formation of the interim government. A Congress government could badly hurt his efforts to create Pakistan. Jinnah knew that the Congress was keen to form a government at the centre for a long time now. As early as 1940, an emergency meeting of the Congress Working Committee held in Delhi had called for the formation of 'a provisional national government' at the centre to 'enable the Congress to throw its full weight into the efforts for the effective organization of the defence of the country.'[144] Again, the main burden of the Congress negotiations with Cripps in 1942 rested on its demand for the formation of a 'national government'. Indeed, the most important reason for the failure of the negotiations was the question whether the 'Executive Council' which the Congress appeared willing to join for the war period could 'function like a cabinet'.[145] In a similar vein, it was the desire to form the government at the centre that brought the Congress to the Simla Conference of 1945. In fact, the Conference failed on the issue of nominations to the Executive Council. Even during the talks with the Cabinet Mission this time, the formation of the government at the centre seemed to be the main concern of the Congress. Wavell stressed the point in his *Journal* after his meeting with the Congress leaders on 16 May. 'Nehru', he wrote, 'disclosed almost nakedly the real Congress objective—immediate control of the Centre, so that they can deal with Muslims and Princes and then make at leisure a Constitution to suit themselves'.[146]

However, this preoccupation with the formation of the government at the centre without a prior settlement of long-term issues, especially that of Pakistan, was not something unique to the Congress. The British were equally keen about it. Their policy, since the start of the Second World War, rested principally on the formation of a government at the centre, whether through the medium of Viceroy's expanded Executive Council or through the establishment of an interim government, as the Statement of 16 June clearly suggested. This also explained why, Pethick-Lawrence, in his negotiations with the Congress leaders, gave 'further assurances to the Congress' over the powers of the interim government.[147] This commonality of interest between the British and the Congress was a great source of anxiety to Jinnah who realized fully well that a Congress government had the potential to damage the cause of Pakistan irreparably. That is why Jinnah made strenuous efforts to seek an 'assurance' from the Viceroy and the Cabinet Mission on the formation of the interim government before announcing his response to its Plan. Indeed, it was particularly because of this assurance that the League eventually approved the Plan.

Finally, Jinnah reckoned that some proposals in the Cabinet Mission Plan were not, and could not, be acceptable to the Congress under any circumstances. The Congress would 'sabotage' the Plan sooner or later.[148] For instance, Jinnah knew that the grouping clause, which formed the 'crux' of the long-term proposals[149] as far as he was concerned, was not acceptable to the Congress. Not only had the Congress claimed during talks at Simla that 'the previous consent of the province is not necessary for joining the group', it insisted presently that the 'matter should be left to the Provinces and if they wish to function as a group they are at liberty to do so and to frame their own constitution for the purpose'.[150] The main problem was that Gandhi was 'frontally opposed to Assam and NWFP being placed, without their prior approval, in the 'Pakistan' area....'[151] Gandhi, in fact, called upon the provincial government of Assam 'to offer *satyagraha*'.[152] Jinnah, thus, like some of his ardent followers, hoped that the Congress 'would either reject the proposal or ask for such amendments or put such interpretations on it as would vitiate their acceptance of it'.[153] In the process, naturally, 'the blame would...fall upon the Congress, and the Muslim League would be able to extricate itself from a difficult situation'.[154] That this was not a forlorn hope was evident in less than 24 hours, and interestingly enough, provided by a man no other than Gandhi whose prior 'full approval' of the Plan had been claimed by Cripps only a few days back.[155]

In an article in the *Harijan*, on 17 May Gandhi asserted:

> *There was no 'take it or leave it' business about their recommendations. If there were restrictions, the Constituent Assembly would not be a sovereign body free to frame a constitution of independence for India.* Thus the Mission had suggested for the Centre certain subjects. It was open to the Assembly, the majority vote of Muslims and non-Muslims separately, to add them or even reduce them.... *Similarly about grouping. The provinces were free to reject the very idea of grouping. No province could be forced against its will to belong to a group even if the idea of grouping was accepted.*[156]

Two days later, Gandhi reiterated the point in a letter to Pethick-Lawrence, making an issue not of 'the legal position' but 'the honourableness of opposition to grouping'.[157] The Congress Working Committee in its meeting on 20 May followed the lead, and passed a resolution putting 'its own interpretation on the grouping of Provinces'.[158]

On 25 May, the Mission and the Viceroy were constrained to publicly declare:

> The interpretation put by the Congress...to the effect that Provinces can in the first instance make the choice whether or not to belong to the sections in which they are placed do not accord with the Delegation's intentions. The reasons for the grouping of the Provinces are well known

and this is an essential feature of the scheme and can only be modified by agreement between the parties.[159]

However, the Congress kept on insisting that it was not necessary for a province to enter the Sections and Groups in which it had been placed, even after its so-called acceptance of the long-term proposals,[160] communicated to the Viceroy on 25 June. On 10 July, in a press conference, Jawaharlal Nehru delivered the fatal blow to the Mission Plan, declaring:

> ...the big probability is that from any approach to the question, there will be no grouping. Obviously Section A will decide against grouping'. Speaking in betting language, he further maintained, 'there was a four-to-one chance of the North-West Frontier Province deciding against partition. Then Group B collapses. It is highly likely that Assam will decide against grouping with Bengal...I can say, with every assurance and conviction there is going to be, finally, no grouping there, because Assam will not tolerate it under any circumstances whatever. Thus this grouping business approached from any point of view does not get on at all.[161]

Interestingly, Maulana Abul Kalam Azad characterized Nehru's statement as a 'bombshell' for Jinnah and the League, and indeed accused Nehru of doing 'immense harm to the national cause,' like 'an almost equal blunder in 1937' (of rejecting the League's offer of cooperation in the formation of ministries in the UP).[162] The Maulana conveniently forgot that he himself was present in Nehru's meeting with the Cabinet Mission on 10 June (a month before the fateful statement) when Nehru declared that '*the Congress was going to work for a strong centre and to break the Group system and they would succeed.*'[163] But he failed to disagree or challenge him. He also heard Nehru say that: 'They did not think that Mr Jinnah had any real place in the country,' and again, he remained quiet.[164] The fact of the matter was that Nehru was representing Congress leadership, including Maulana Azad. More importantly, he was representing Gandhi who, as discussed above, was deadly opposed to the grouping provision in the Cabinet Mission Plan. After all, he was the 'Western face' of Gandhi,[165] and the newly elected Congress President entrusted the all-important task of leading India to independence.

What was surprising, however, was the Cabinet Mission's acceptance of the Congress interpretation. While Jinnah was reminding them repeatedly that 'the Sections and Groups were an essential feature of the scheme which the Congress wanted to smash', and that these were 'the one thing for which the Muslim League had made concessions one after another' in accepting the Plan,[166] the Mission remained unmoved. They insisted that the Congress had accepted the Plan, though 'with reservations'. But then, they maintained, the League too had accepted the Plan with 'reservations'. As Pethick-Lawrence told Jinnah on 25 June 1946,

...the Delegation was satisfied that the Congress letter constituted an acceptance. The Muslim League in accepting the statement had also adhered to their own point of view and had made statements about maintaining their goal of complete sovereign Pakistan and others which went quite as far as any reservations made by the Congress.[167]

What Pethick-Lawrence and other members of the Mission were perhaps unable to appreciate was the difference in the nature of these reservations. While the Congress had reservations pertaining both to the short-term and long-term proposals, particularly the long-term proposals, so crucial to the working of the Plan, the League's reservations were essentially about its future obligations, beyond the initial period of 10 years. The League was committed to the present long-term proposals. As Jinnah explained:

...the Muslim League had reiterated that sovereign Pakistan was their goal but they had accepted the Delegation's plan and put no interpretation on its provisions. In the first place the Muslim League did not dispute that a Union constitution should be formed on the basis laid down in the Statement. They did not dispute that the constitution should continue for 10 years....[168]

That the Mission did not understand the point seems all the more difficult to believe in view of the fact that Wavell, in a subsequent interview with Nehru, recognized that the League's reservations were based 'on a possible Pakistan a number of years ahead; whereas the Congress reservations were short-term ones and affected the immediate issue'.[169] Thus, there was a fundamental difference between the two reservations, even if one were to make an issue of the League's 'reservations' on the Plan.

Whatever logic the Mission may have employed for their satisfaction with the Congress acceptance of the Cabinet Mission Plan, one cannot escape the conclusion that the Mission went out of its way to accomodate the Congress. Even the Viceroy, Wavell admitted that the Mission was 'living in the pocket of Congress' while negotiating their proposals.[170] In fact, he blamed Cripps, 'an old friend of several Congress leaders', especially Nehru, for his 'hole-and-corner private negotiations' with the Congress, promising them more 'satisfaction' than was there in the Plan. He even suspected that Cripps might have 'instigated' the Congress to 'accept' the Statement of 16 May by pointing out 'the tactical advantage they would gain as regards the Interim Government'.[171] But then, Wavell also acknowledged that the Mission, as a whole, was 'unable to remain really impartial'.[172] Pethick-Lawrence, for instance, made extraordinary efforts to devise a 'formula', an 'agreement', aimed at helping to set the Congress 'fears definitely at rest'.[173] As he explained it to Wavell at some length:

> ...in this agreement Congress would I suggest accept the proposition that the Sections would meet and decide *whether there should be groups and if so the nature of Group Constitution*. It would be agreed that the decision as to the procedure of the Section Constituent Assembly would all be taken by majority vote of the Sections meeting. On the other hand it would be agreed that a majority of the representatives of the individual Provinces concerned would be required for all decisions relating to the Constitution of a Province except in so far as those provisions necessarily follow from the character of the Group constitution. This would give some concession to the Congress in Assam and North-West Frontier where there is natural dislike of the idea that provincial constitutions should be determined by the votes from another province.[174]

While Wavell did not hesitate to term this agreement 'both dishonest and cowardly',[175] he himself could do no better than tell Pethick-Lawrence 'to avoid pressing the grouping question to a final issue before the Interim Government takes over and has a period of office'.[176] In this sense, there was hardly any difference between the two, except that Wavell seemed to be more opportunistic in his dealings over the issue than the Cabinet Mission.

As the Muslim League had accepted both the long-term and short-term proposals, the latter on 25 June, and the Congress had serious reservations, Jinnah naturally expected that the British would invite the League to form the government at the centre.[177] Jinnah's expectation was based on the Mission's Statement of 16 June and the 'personal assurance' given by Wavell in the event of 'either party' accepting the Plan.[178] Jinnah thus asked Wavell to 'go ahead with the formation of the Interim Government.'[179] But Wavell was not interested. He could not contemplate let alone actually hand over the government to the League. He denied that there ever was any 'assurance' given to Jinnah or the League. But then, this somersault exposed the real objective of the Mission and the British Government, that is, to entrust the government to the Congress, with or without the League. As Wavell himself confided in his note to the Secretary of State on 25 June:

Relying on a letter from Congress that the acceptance of the Statement of 16 May and the Interim Government hang together, and an assurance that there was no possibility of the Congress rejecting an Interim Government and accepting the Statement of 16 May we committed ourselves, in paragraph 8 of the Statement of 16 June to forming an Interim Government with *anyone* who had accepted the Statement of 16 May.[180]

Wavell acknowledged that, due to Congress machinations, the 'assurances given to Mr Jinnah have disappeared'. He conceded that, 'we have been outmaneuvered by the Congress…mainly due to their continuous contacts with the Mission, especially since the Statement of 16 June….'[181] In a note of 29 June, the day the Cabinet Mission left India postponing the question of the formation of the interim government, Wavell even admitted that: '…the negotiations have undoubtedly alienated the Muslim League and have aroused their deep suspicion; and there is no doubt whatever that the League feels that it has not had fair treatment.'[182]

The difficulty with the British was that they wanted both the Cabinet Mission Plan and the Congress, and for several reasons.[183] The most important reason was that they were keen to preserve the unity of India, which they considered a singular British achievement, and which secured both their short-term and long-term interests. No wonder, even while they prepared their 'modified' concept of Pakistan to allay Muslim apprehensions, they were at pains to develop it within the framework of a united India. The Congress was equally keen to save India from 'vivisection'. This congruence of interests encouraged the British to help the Congress enter the Constituent Assembly, form the interim government and eventually thwart Jinnah's efforts to create an independent, sovereign Pakistan. As Attlee told Kanji Dwarkadas in December 1946, '…once Jinnah came into a Constituent Assembly, it would be easier to deal with him.'[184]

But Jinnah could not be duped. He understood both the British and the Congress very well. He was sure that the 'Congress had accepted their proposals conditionally, and the Cabinet Mission and the Viceroy had committed a flagrant breach of faith'.[185] He convened a meeting of the League Council on 27 July 1946 to review the developments arising out of the British–Congress duplicity. He explained to the Council at length how the British had 'gone back on their plighted word and abandoned what was announced as their final proposals embodied in their Statement of 16 June'.[186] He derided the fact that, in spite of Congress 'reservation and interpretation' especially relating to the grouping and the functions of the Constituent Assembly, the Mission had 'treated this conditional acceptance of the Congress as genuine acceptance'.[187] The idea behind this 'dishonest interpretation', he stressed, was to throw the League at the mercy of the Congress, which 'had had a brute majority in the whole Constituent Assembly', and thus could take 'any decision it liked' by 'ignoring, nullifying and repudiating every term of the scheme', indeed, which is 'ultra vires' of the functions of that body.'[188] He was therefore convinced that: 1) 'the only solution of India's problem is Pakistan…we have learnt a bitter lesson—the bitterest I think so far. Now there is no room left for compromise'; and 2) 'It is no use looking at any other source for help or assistance. There is no tribunal to which we can go. The only tribunal is the Muslim Nation'.[189] The League Council could not agree more. On 29 July, the League rejected the Cabinet Mission Plan, and resolved that, 'now the time has come for the Muslim nation to resort to Direct Action to achieve Pakistan….'[190] Jinnah who had already moved the Working Committee to withdraw the League's acceptance of the Plan, called it 'a most historic decision'. 'Never before in the whole life-history of the Muslim League', he declared,

...did we do anything except by constitutional methods and constitutional talks. We are today forced into this position by a move in which both the Congress and Britain have participated. We have been attacked on two fronts—the British front and the Hindu front. Today we have said good-bye to constitutions and constitutional methods. Throughout the painful negotiations, the two parties with whom we bargained held a pistol at us; one with power and machine-guns behind it, and the other with non-cooperation and threat to launch mass civil disobedience. This situation must be met. We also have a pistol. We have taken this decision with full responsibility and all the deliberations possible for a human being, and we mean it.[191]

Jinnah's rejection of the Cabinet Mission Plan, and a decision to resort to 'Direct Action' heralded the end for united India in the ensuing struggle for transfer of power. The 'modified' concept of Pakistan was buried forever. The Muslims rallied around Jinnah whose charisma was now truly at its peak. They were ready and willing to follow him to the bitter end. They realized that he was the man who had the passion, confidence, authority, and the determination necessary to create Pakistan.

While the Muslims pinned their faith on Jinnah, the British and the Congress failed to truly appraise his perseverance and commitment to the goal of Pakistan. Their underestimation of Jinnah's faith in himself and his cause was abundantly clear in their attitude towards the formation of the interim government. For instance, Wavell suggested to Jinnah that, 'if they [Congress] make a reasonable offer to you of a coalition, I can rely on you for a ready response'.[192] Jinnah was shocked. He needed no more proof and provocation to say that 'the Viceroy has now completed the prearranged conspiracy with the Congress and finally by-passed the Muslim League'.[193]

But then, Nehru, who had already annoyed Jinnah with his 'harmful and tactless' statements in the past,[194] in a letter on 13 August 1946, went ahead and asked him to join 'in the formation of a coalition provisional government. It is naturally our desire to have as representative a government as possible'. Jinnah was enraged. He not only rejected the offer but also went on to remind Nehru that the Congress itself was a party to the political dispute in India. It was not a paramount power. However, he did not mind meeting with him 'to settle the Hindu–Muslim question and resolve the serious deadlock.'[195]

But Nehru was not interested in any settlement. He did no more than reiterate that 'perhaps, on fuller consideration of the position you would be agreeable to reconsider your decision'.[196] He was the future prime minister of India, tipped to head the interim government soon.

As already decided by the League Council, Jinnah called for the observance of 'Direct Action Day' on 16 August, and asked the Muslims to 'conduct themselves in a peaceful manner.'[197] But, in spite of that word of caution, the Direct Action Day was not fated to be a peaceful day, particularly in Calcutta. In what has come to be known as the 'Great Calcutta Killing', Calcutta suffered 4,400 dead, 16,000 injured and 100,000 homeless, with casualties in the end equally shared between the Muslims and the Hindus.[198] According to Percival Spear, 'No communal riot in British Indian history had ever reached such dimensions'.[199]

Calcutta, however, was just the beginning. More was to follow in the two Hindu-majority provinces of Bihar, UP and other parts of India. It was 'the beginning of civil war in an odious and horrible form', spread all over eastern and northern India.[200] Wavell did not hesitate to acknowledge that these riots were, 'on the scale of numbers and degree of brutality, far beyond anything that I think has yet happened in India since British rule began.'[201] He was convinced that they were 'undoubtedly organized, and organized very thoroughly, by supporters of Congress....'[202] Eventually, the riots affected the princely states, too, generally outside the scope of British Indian politics. The Muslim rulers got alarmed at the increasingly volatile situation. The Nawab of Bhopal, in particular, in a letter to Wavell on 17 August warned:

If no settlement is reached soon between the Moslem League and the Congress, and the Congress alone forms the Interim Government, the situation will become extremely tense, and most difficult. The fate of the Moslems will hang in the balance, and they will be facing a situation which will require supreme effort of every Musalman if they are to be saved from annihilation. No true Moslem worth the name can remain a silent spectator to events which follow in the wake of the formation of a Govt. by the Congress (the Hindus) alone.[203]

The Nawab threatened to resign from his position of Chancellor and Ruler and place his services 'unreservedly at the disposal of my Moslem countrymen'.[204]

Wavell himself viewed the rapidly deteriorating situation with dismay and shock, indeed, as a 'tragic ending of rule in India'.[205] He decided to act. However, in spite of the Congress's reservations on the Cabinet Mission Plan, and the bloodbath in a number of places subsequently, he chose to invite the Congress to form a government at the centre. He admitted that it would be 'manifestly unfair to the Muslim League', but, then, he claimed, he had no choice in the matter. Cripps had threatened him 'that he would resign if this was not done'.[206] The Congress formed the interim government on 24 August and the Cabinet was sworn in on 2 September 1946.

Although an interim government was installed at the centre in utter disregard of the League, its formation was hardly the solution of the problem in the highly charged communal atmosphere. The day the government took office there was a murderous assault on the life of one of its members, Shafaat Ahmad Khan of the Round Table Conference fame, and a dreadful spread of communal violence in Bombay and Ahmedabad. There was a general feeling of apprehension in the country. Gandhi gave vent to this feeling by stating that, 'we are not yet in the midst of civil war but we are nearing it'.[207] Wavell was compelled to tell Pethick-Lawrence, the Secretary of State, on 27 August 1946: 'I am afraid we are in for a very great deal more violence all over India unless I can find some means of changing the present attitude of Jinnah and the League'.[208] But then, the problem was not the League. The problem was the Congress which was keen 'to consolidate itself in power, to use British assistance in putting down riots from day-to-day, and perhaps if necessary to buy off the Muslims at a lower price when we finally go'.[209]

But realizing the gravity of the situation, Wavell entered into negotiations with Jinnah to persuade him to join the government. He had to contend with two difficulties in particular. First, there was not much encouragement from the British Government. Pethick-Lawrence was inclined to give the Congress government 'some time' to deal with the League on its own.[210] Secondly, Jinnah wanted the British to concede to the League the sole right to nominate all the Muslim members of the interim government, and that too on the basis of parity with the Congress. This was a demand that he had insisted upon since it was first made on 27 June 1940, and which ultimately led to the failure of the Simla Conference of 1945. While Wavell now assured Jinnah that he was prepared to honour the demand for parity (though in a modified form: six members, including one Scheduled Caste representative, nominated by the Congress, five members nominated by the League, and three representatives of other minorities, nominated by the Viceroy), he could not guarantee that the Congress list of nominees would not include a Muslim. In fact, he explained to Jinnah that there was no way he could force the Congress to renounce their right to nominate anyone that they liked to represent them. Jinnah, as later development showed, had his own ideas, and thus did not press the issue further. Instead, he thought it proper to concentrate upon some broad issues concerned with the formation of the government itself, and presented a 'nine point' formula for the purpose. In this formula, he made it a point to stress, in clear emphatic terms that: 'The question of the settlement of the long-term plan should stand over until a better and more conducive atmosphere is created and an agreement has been reached...and after the interim Government has been re-formed and finally set up'.[211] Wavell agreed with most of Jinnah's demands, including the crucial one regarding the long-term plan, hoping 'that the League Council will meet at a very early date to reconsider its Bombay resolution'.[212] He was convinced that peace in India depended on 'settlement at the centre', and the sooner the better.[213] On 14 October, Jinnah sent Wavell the names of Liaquat Ali Khan, I.I. Chundrigar, Sardar Abdur Rab Nishtar (1899–1958), Raja Ghazanfar Ali Khan (1895–1963), and Jogendra Nath Mandal, to represent the League at the centre.[214] On 15 October, an official press release was issued to the effect that the League had joined the interim government.

Though the League's decision to join the interim government was received with relief all over the country, there was little doubt from the outset that it was more of a tactical than a conciliatory move. As Jinnah explained on 13 October, they found it 'fatal to leave the entire field of administration of the Central Government in the hands of the Congress'.[215] That they had come to assert their own interests rather than strengthen the interim government itself was further clear from the choice of Mandal, a member of the Scheduled Castes, as a counterblast to the Congress claim to nominate a Muslim on their quota. Nehru was, of course, quick to grasp the point, and wrote to Wavell on 15 October complaining that Jinnah's choice of Mandal represented 'a desire to have conflict than to work in cooperation'.[216] He also expressed his reservations on some other nominees, and charged that 'the standard of the Cabinet will be much lowered by their association'.[217] Wavell agreed, and remarked: 'I was to a certain extent disappointed with the names that he [Jinnah] had put forward. I had hoped that he would come in himself, and I also regretted the absence of...leading members of the Muslim League of whom I had formed high opinions from contact with them....'[218] Nehru and Wavell did not understand that Jinnah had asked the League to join the government not to come up to their expectations but only to guard its fundamental interests till the demand for Pakistan was finally realized. He had achieved this position without 'rescinding the League Council's resolution rejecting the Cabinet Mission Plan.'[219] But there was little that the British or the Congress could do about it in the given situation. There were disturbances and communal riots all over India, in places as widely separated as Chapra, Ahmednagar, Ahmedabad and Bihar.[220]

Jinnah explained his stance on the interim government publicly in a press conference at Delhi on 15 November, attended largely by foreign correspondents. He declared that the League ministers had joined the government, 'as sentinels who would watch Muslim interests in the day-to-day administration of Government'.[221] They would 'resist every attempt which would directly or indirectly militate or prejudice our demand of Pakistan'.[222] Jinnah refused to accept the interim government as a 'cabinet' or a 'coalition', insisting, as a constitutionalist and lawyer that he was, that it was essentially the Executive Council of the Governor-General, formed under the Government of India Act of 1919 (the federal part of the Act was not operative).[223]

That the interim government did not work on the principle of 'cabinet' was soon demonstrated in the preparation and presentation of the annual budget on 28 February 1947. The Minister of Finance, Liaquat Ali Khan proposed measures against 'tax-evaders' which, as Maulana Azad observed, took the Congress 'by complete surprise'.[224] Some of their leaders charged that his 'main motive was to harm the members of the business community as the majority of them were

Hindus'.[225] However, Azad maintained, they conveniently forgot that the measures were 'in conformity with declared Congress objectives'.[226] The interim government, thus, in actual practice, merely helped to accentuate the bitterness between the Muslims and the Hindus and caused further distrust and suspicion between the League and the Congress. It represented, in Wavell's words, 'the two blocks in the Cabinet'.[227] Given Jinnah's considered attitude towards the whole issue, it was futile even to expect otherwise.

Jinnah not only refused to accept the interim government as a legitimate source of authority, but also went on to reject the bona fides of the Constituent Assembly, insisting that since the Cabinet Mission Plan had failed to win the support and approval of the two major political parties, the Assembly could not come into existence. He insisted 'that the Congress has not and never had accepted the long-term plan embodied in the statement of the Cabinet Mission Plan of 16th May, and clarified by the statement of 25 May'.[228] Thus, he refused to attend the session of the Constituent Assembly on 9 December. He did not change his mind after the British government's announcement of 6 December which, after detailed discussion with the representatives of both the League and the Congress in London, had endorsed the League's stand regarding the grouping of provinces.[229] He was sure that there was no chance of Congress making mends. The Congress Working Committee resolution of 5 January 1947, which stated that the Congress could not accept any 'compulsion' on a Province[230] proved his point beyond any shadow of doubt. On 31 January, thus, a long resolution of the League Working Committee reiterated the League position that the Cabinet Mission Plan had absolutely failed, and described the 6 December clarification as a 'dishonest trick',[231] and that the proceedings and decision of the Constituent Assembly were 'ultra vires'.[232] On 3 February, Jinnah again refused to attend the session of the Constituent Assembly.

Jinnah's refusal to attend the Constituent Assembly affected the future of the constitution-making body in India in the long run and the interim government in the short run. The two, as the Cabinet Mission and the Viceroy had emphasized all along, were parts of a single package. If Jinnah was not prepared to enter the Constituent Assembly, the question was how far it was fair and 'legitimate' to allow the League to continue to hold ministries in the interim government.

The question, of course, was not so important to Wavell, who was convinced that the ouster of the League from the government at this stage would lead to bloody civil war in the country.[233] The issue was primarily the work of the British Government in London,[234] sitting at a safe distance from India, and the Congress, which was determined to oust the League from the government and assume full control of the centre. The Congress members of government, in their memorandum of 5 February were unanimous in demanding that the 'League must either get out of the interim Government or change its Karachi decision' (i.e. demand for dissolution of the Constituent Assembly and refusal to reconsider the decision of July 1946). Otherwise, they threatened, the Congress would quit the government.[235] This was a grave situation. 'To ask for the resignation of the League representatives from the Interim Government', as V.P. Menon argued,

> ...would have serious repercussions in India and in the Muslim countries of the world. To allow the Congress to resign would lead to even more disastrous consequences. His Majesty's Government had already committed itself to hand over power to Indian hands.... In further communal disorders, it was doubtful if the loyalty of the Army and the Services could be relied upon.[236]

Wavell was already convinced that in case of 'a general deterioration of the communal situation on an even wider scale than we have seen in recent weeks and a refusal of the two major parties to be responsible for dealing with it...the only alternative in the circumstances...is withdrawal'.[237] He was also realistic enough to concede that 'the machinery on which our control of India has depended is rapidly running down'.[238] 'The recent troubles, he pointed out, had clearly shown that:

> ...police in many parts of India were affected with communalism and were no longer to be relied on for firm action against their own community. The same applied to a certain degree to the officials also. Even where officials and police would have been prepared to carry out their duties loyally, their morale had been so shaken by the campaign carried on against them in the past year or two that they no longer took the prompt and firm action that they would previously have done. Only the army had so far escaped any taint of communalism and was carrying out its duties in loyalty

to the orders of its officers. But this would not last indefinitely, if troops continued to be employed in the suppression of civil disturbances....[239]

The situation in the provinces was particularly precarious. In some provinces, the 'loyalty' of the police was certainly 'doubtful'. They were 'tinged with communalism'.[240] The number of British officers, civil and military, had dropped significantly, with the result that the 'depleted personnel' hardly seemed sufficient for the 'unusually exacting task on hand'.[241] To make matters worse, a majority of the provinces were being governed by 'ordinance or decree, empowering them arbitrarily to ban meetings and processions and to inflict drastic punishments'.[242]

On 20 February 1947, Prime Minister Attlee was constrained to announce in the British Parliament that the 'present state of uncertainty is fraught with danger and cannot be indefinitely prolonged', and thus 'His Majesty's Government wish to make it clear that it is their definite intention to take the necessary steps to effect the transference of power to responsible Indian hands by a date not later than June 1948'.[243] In order to make sure that the transfer of power happened 'in a manner that will best ensure the future happiness and prosperity of India' the prime minister also announced the appointment of a new viceroy, 'Admiral the Viscount Mountbatten'.[244]

A number of explanations have been offered in the years to explain this change, at the top,[245] including the one by Wavell himself, as he complained to Attlee, 'I cannot continue to be responsible for affairs in India if some members of your Government are keeping in touch with the Congress through an independent agent behind my back', namely Sudhir Gosh.[246] However, the significance of the move did not lie so much in getting rid of Wavell as in the appointment of Mountbatten, believed by some to have been done on Nehru's recommendation.[247] Nehru and Mountbatten had known each other since their first contact in Singapore in March 1946, where Mountbatten was serving as the Supreme Allied Commander of the South-East Asian Command. The two had developed an instant liking for each other.[248] But then, as later events were to show, it was not to be simply a case of sharing likes but also one of sharing dislikes. Both intensely disliked Jinnah and his demand for Pakistan. Nehru's views on Jinnah were well known and he did not hesitate to express them to Mountbatten in his meeting with him on 24 March 1947,[249] the day he assumed the viceroyship. No wonder, Mountbatten found Jinnah 'frigid, haughty and disdainful'[250] in his first encounter and it was not long before he called him an 'evil genius...a psychopathic case...hell bent on his Pakistan'.[251] These likes and dislikes were to bring Nehru so close to Mountbatten in the following years, especially after Gandhi's death on 30 January 1948, that Mountbatten would claim: 'The very funny thing was that...he always came and cried on my shoulder. He wanted someone to go back to. I had a sort of funny feeling that Nehru actually required a presence in order to be able to function, and after Gandhi it was me'.[252]

The Mountbatten–Nehru relationship[253] was to make Jinnah's task exceedingly difficult. Mountbatten and Nehru operated 'on the same wavelength'.[254] They created a host of problems for Jinnah in spite of the fact, that for all practical purposes, the partition of India was a settled issue by the time Mountbatten arrived on the scene. Only the details relating to 'the time, manner and extent of partition'[255] remained to be worked out. Attlee's statement of 20 February clearly stipulated that if an agreed constitution could not be worked out before June 1948:

> His Majesty's Government will have to consider to whom the power of the central Government in British India should be handed over, on the due date, whether as a whole to some form of central Government for British India, or in some areas to the existing provincial Governments, or in such other ways as may seem most reasonable and in the best interests of the Indian people.[256]

Nehru himself, in a public speech on 20 April, conceded that: 'The Muslim League can have Pakistan if they wish to have it....'[257] On 28 April, Rajendra Prasad, President of the Constituent Assembly stated in unambiguous terms that: '...no constitution will be forced upon any unwilling part of it'. However, he ominously went on to add a rider by insisting: 'This means not only the division of India, but also a division of some provinces. For this we must be prepared and the Assembly may have to draw up a constitution based on such a division'.[258]

Clearly the Congress leaders were contemplating not only the partition of India but also 'a division of some provinces', namely the

Punjab, Bengal and Assam.[259] The 'concern for the practical details of partition' brought the question of provinces into the open.[260] That is where Mountbatten was to extend his full support to the Congress to exploit the situation to force Jinnah to accept the Cabinet Mission Plan or settle for 'a truncated, moth-eaten Pakistan' that he had forcefully ruled out in September 1944 and in May 1946 in his talks with Gandhi and the Cabinet Mission, respectively. In the process, of course, Mountbatten was to lose the confidence of Jinnah and the Muslim League, and the governor-generalship of Pakistan. But then, in his estimate, it was no small gain to win the 'trust' and 'friendship' of the Congress leaders, the leaders of independent India. As he told his television series audience in the 1970s, 'Pandit Nehru…was already a friend, of course…. With Nehru the trust that I was trying to build with the [Indian] leaders was already there—and more than trust—friendship'.[261]

Jinnah did his best to explain to Mountbatten that the division of the Punjab and Bengal would destroy the administrative and economic structure of these provinces, and thus would make his Pakistan 'economically very difficult if not impossible to function'.[262] In fact, he charged that the whole idea of division was born out of 'bitterness and spitefulness'[263] and constituted no more than 'a red herring'[264] to frighten him out of the demand for Pakistan. The Congress wanted 'to convince the Muslims that they could only get a truncated and moth-eaten Pakistan which would not be worthwhile'.[265] Jinnah suggested to Mountbatten that the best course to follow would be to arrange a 'referendum' to ascertain the wishes of the people of these provinces.[266] This idea of a referendum did not appeal to the British Government, and was summarily rejected, saying that it would 'achieve no useful purpose and would merely result in delays'.[267]

The problem was that the British were as opposed to Jinnah's concept of a sovereign Pakistan of all the six Muslim-majority provinces, that is, the Punjab, NWFP, Sindh, Balochistan, Bengal, and Assam in 1947, as they were in March 1946, when a 'modified' concept of Pakistan was given concrete shape in the Cabinet Mission Plan. They were keen to preserve the unity of India. They wanted to deny Jinnah these provinces to force him to come round to the Cabinet Mission Plan. Attlee's letter of instruction to Mountbatten on 18 March clearly stated, 'It is the definite objective of His Majesty's Government to obtain a unitary Government of British India and the Indian States, if possible within the British Commonwealth, through the medium of a Constituent Assembly, set up and run in accordance with the Cabinet Mission Plan'. Even when the British finally agreed to the partition of India and the demand for an independent, sovereign Pakistan, the 3 June Statement still insisted: 'The Cabinet Mission Plan...offers the best basis for solving the Indian problem.... But, as Indian leaders have finally failed to agree on a plan for a united India, partition becomes the inevitable alternative....'[268] The British had the full backing of the Congress to force Jinnah to accept the Cabinet Mission Plan, subject of course to their own interpretations. Indeed, Nehru repeatedly urged the British Government, since the formation of the interim government, to ask Jinnah to accept the Cabinet Mission Plan or else, 'the division of Bengal and Punjab becomes inevitable'.[269]

There was no way Jinnah could accept the Cabinet Mission Plan at this stage. In May 1946, he told Mountbatten, 'there had been some prospect that this atmosphere could be created. Now, nearly a year later, the atmosphere so far from improving had taken a serious turn for the worse, and it was clear that in no circumstances did Congress intend to work the plan either in accordance with the spirit or the letter'.[270] The Congress was interpreting the Union subjects to suit its own purposes. The Union Powers Committee of the Constituent Assembly in its report, presented on 28 April, interpreted the three common subjects assigned to the Union Centre 'into something very different from what the Mission had intended'.[271] Defence, for instance, was to include 'nearly all the basic industries.' Foreign Affairs included areas such as 'implementing the decisions of international conferences and treaties or agreements made with other countries; naturalization and aliens; trade and commerce with foreign countries; import and export across custom frontiers as defined by the Union Government, and, most important of all, foreign loans.' Communications were 'broadly defined as involving the control and regulation of airways, certain highways and waterways, posts and telegraphs, all telephones and broadcasting, maritime shipping, major ports, Union railways and even some minor railways.' As opposed to 'the League's insistence that the Union centre should be financed by contributions from the groups, the report specified fourteen areas where the Union centre could expect to raise revenues.'[272] The result was that even Mountbatten, notwithstanding his bias, could not deny that the Congress had 'no intention of working the Mission's plan 'fairly'', and that Jinnah's fear as to the future role of the Congress had 'some foundations'.[273]

However, Mountbatten was not prepared to tell the Congress that if it was not interested in implementing the Cabinet Mission Plan as proposed by the Cabinet Mission it should not insist on the division of the two provinces of the Punjab and Bengal to the detriment of Jinnah's demand for a full, sovereign Pakistan. On the contrary, Mountbatten himself went on to invent a new argument to show to Jinnah the 'inwardness' of his demand for a sovereign Pakistan. What was good for the Muslim 'minority' in the country was good also for the non-Muslim minority in the Muslim-majority provinces. 'I simply could not visualise', he told Jinnah, 'being so inconsistent as to agree to the partition of India without also agreeing to partition within any Province in which the same problem arose'.[274]

Mountbatten, however, could not force the division of the Punjab and Bengal on Jinnah that easily. There were forces in the Punjab and Bengal who opposed the division of their provinces and among them were groups who were willing to join or support the Pakistan state.[275] In the Punjab, Giani Kartar Singh, President Shiromani Akali Dal, for instance, had 'a private emissary' sent to Jinnah 'suggesting that they should hold discussions about the Sikh state [Khalistan] joining Pakistan after partition'.[276] Jinnah himself encouraged the Sikhs to stay within Pakistan. He assured them that they were 'an important community in the Punjab', and thus, will 'play a very big part in the affairs of the province....'[277] Indeed, he warned them that it would be 'a great mistake' to support the division of the Punjab. He explained:

> There were $3\frac{1}{2}$ millions of them and if the province was divided, there would be 2 million or so in one part and $1\frac{1}{2}$ million in the other. It would be far better that they should all stay together in Pakistan, where they could expect to be well-treated.... If they were divided, they could not play the part they might hope to do if they stayed together—in Pakistan.[278]

The movement to prevent the division of Bengal was led by Huseyn Shaheed Suhrawardy, an important leader of the Muslim League in the province.[279] He was in contact with Kiron Shanker Roy and Sarat Chandra Bose (1889–1950) to keep Bengal united and independent.[280]

Bose, in particular, was quite enthusiastic about the prospects of a 'United Independent Bengal,' and developed some 'concrete proposals' for discussion with the League leaders, which were also publicly announced in May 1947. Jinnah and Gandhi were approached to seek their support. But before any significant 'conversations' with Jinnah could be held, the Congress High Command 'turned down' Bose's proposals, with Gandhi announcing in one of his prayer meetings that he 'had been taken to task for supporting Sarat Babu's move'.[281] Jinnah saw independent Bengal as 'a sort of subsidiary Pakistan'.[282] However, he remained noncommittal, leaving it to the Congress Hindus of Bengal to inform Mountbatten that if 'India is to be divided on communal consideration, partition of Bengal becomes an immediate necessity.... Sovereign undivided Bengal will be a virtual Pakistan...we are not prepared to make any compromise on this issue on any consideration whatsoever'.[283]

Jinnah's efforts to save the division of the Punjab and Bengal unnerved the Congress leadership. They feared that the longer Jinnah argued against the division of the provinces the stronger the possibility that they would lose the support of the Sikhs in the Punjab and the Hindus in Bengal. Similarly, Mountbatten, in spite of his vehement opposition to Jinnah's demand for undivided Punjab and Bengal found it increasingly difficult to dismiss it out of hand. In a shrewd move, he decided to pass on the burden of the demand to the provinces themselves, by preparing a partition plan, suggesting transfer of power to the Indians on a provincial basis rather than to two Dominions. 'The more we look at the problem in India' he wrote on 1 May 1947:

> ...the more we realise that all this partition business is sheer madness and is going to reduce the economic efficiency of the whole country immeasurably.... The most we can do...is to put responsibility for any of these mad decisions fairly and squarely on the Indian shoulders in the eyes of the world....[284]

On 10 May, Mountbatten received the approval of the British Government for the Partition Plan. On 11 May, he proposed a conference of Indian leaders to discuss the plan. However, he could not resist the temptation of showing the plan to his friend, Nehru, first, 'as an act of friendship and on the understanding that he would not utilize his prior knowledge or mention it to his colleagues that he had seen it'.[285] But the plan 'produced a devastating effect' upon Nehru.[286] He saw it as 'a picture of fragmentation and conflict and disorder'.[287] In a letter sent to Mountbatten the same day, Nehru charged: 'It appears to me that the inevitable and obvious consequences of the proposals and the approach in them are...to invite the Balkanization of India...to create many 'Ulsters' in India'.[288] While his aides could 'only be thankful that we did not wait until meeting of leaders to find out his attitude',[289] Mountbatten rushed to 'redraft' the plan in the light of Nehru's objections. In fact, he asked Nehru's (and also Sardar Patel's) confidant, and the Constitutional Advisor to the Government of India, V.P. Menon, to prepare a draft 'Head of Agreement' to be shown to prominent Indian leaders before he personally took it to London to seek the assent.[290] Though he appeared determined 'not to talk to Jinnah about it until after the announcement of the plan',[291] he did show the Second Plan to Jinnah to seek his 'agreement to avoid bloodshed....'[292] There were reports to the effect that 'the Muslim League would resort to arms if Pakistan in some form was not conceded'.[293]

The Second Plan, of course, did not satisfy Jinnah, who immediately noticed the proposal for the division of the Punjab and Bengal. The division, he emphasized, once again,

> ...cannot be justified historically, economically, geographically, politically or morally. These provinces have built up their respective lives for nearly a century...and the only ground which is put forward for partition is that the areas where the Hindus and Sikhs are in a majority should be separated from the rest of the provinces...the results will be disastrous for the life of these two provinces and all the communities concerned...if you take this decision—which in my opinion will be a fateful one—....[294]

Mountbatten, nonetheless, went to London, armed with the Congress support for the Second Plan. The British Government approved this plan 'without the alteration of a comma'. However, under the advice of their allies and supporters in the Congress, the Government also agreed to advance the date of British withdrawal to August 1947. Krishna Menon, Nehru's confidant in London, told Mountbatten on 21 May that Nehru and Sardar Patel (Gandhi seemingly out of the picture as India approached independence) were 'ready to accept' the new plan if it were to be implemented in 1947. He explained this at some length in a letter written to Mountbatten the same day, and added: 'If Mr Jinnah wants a total separation, and that straight away, and if we agree to it for the sake of peace and dismember our country, we want to be rid of him, so far as the affairs of what is left to us of our country are concerned. I feel sure you will appreciate this, and also that it is not a matter of detail, but is fundamental'.[295] On 31 May, Mountbatten, with the full support of the British Government[296] returned to India, and on 2 June called representative Indian leaders, Jinnah, Liaquat Ali Khan, Abdur Rab Nishtar (Muslim League), Nehru, Patel, Acharya J.B. Kirpalani (1888–1982) (Congress), and Sardar Baldev Singh (Sikhs) to a conference to finalize the discussion on the approved Partition Plan leading to a formal announcement by British Prime Minister, Attlee, on 3 June.[297]

Jinnah was, of course, not happy with the Partition Plan. He was being 'forced to accept the minimum territorial extent for Pakistan'.[298] He, therefore, refused to commit himself readily, except that he assured Mountbatten he would endeavour 'to get the All-India Muslim League Council to accept', and that in the meanwhile he 'would be justified in advising the Prime Minister to go ahead and make the announcement'.[299] Mountbatten had no problems with the Congress. It was more of a 'Gandhi Plan' already.[300] However, taking refuge behind the Congress allegation that he always 'waited until the Congress Party had made a firm decision about some plan, and then left himself the right to make whatever decision suited the Moslem League', Mountbatten decided to bully Jinnah: '...If that is your attitude, then leaders of the Congress Party and Sikhs will refuse final acceptance at the meeting in the morning; chaos will follow, and you will lose your Pakistan, probably for good'.[301] But Jinnah was not to be intimidated: 'What must be, must be', was his only reaction, as he shrugged his shoulders.[302] He knew his Pakistan, no matter how much 'smaller', was there. It could no longer be denied. It had been created and secured. True to his quality of an organization man, and given the importance and sensitivity of the issue, he wanted to operate through the League. He wanted to take the League into confidence first. However, this bullying tactic and a host of other subsequent developments clearly showed that Mountbatten 'departed widely from the duty of the Viceroy to hold the scales even'[303] between the Muslims and other communities, between the Muslim League and the Congress, and between Jinnah, Nehru, and other Indian leaders. 'In his graphic words', noted Seervai, 'Congress was to be given a building, the Muslim League could only be given a tent and no more'.[304]

On 3 June 1947, the Partition Plan was formally announced with a statement from Prime Minister Attlee calling it 'the inevitable alternative' to the Cabinet Mission Plan. The same day, Jinnah went on the air, exhorting his followers to give it 'our most earnest consideration'. Though he did not wish to 'prejudice' the decision of the League Council, due to meet on 9 June as 'the final decision' can only be taken by the League Council 'according to our Constitution, precedents and practice', he could not help suggest that,

> the Plan does not meet in some important respects our point of view and we cannot say or feel that we are satisfied or that we agree with some of the matters dealt with in the plan. It is for us now to consider whether the plan as presented to us by His Majesty's Government should be accepted by us as a compromise or a settlement.[305]

The implication obviously was that it was a 'compromise'. As a truly charismatic leader, who was sober and rational, as Weber defined 'genuine' charismatic leaders, Jinnah had reckoned that 'all prospects of negotiations and bargaining had been exhausted'.[306] It was time to decide. Taking its cue from Jinnah, the League Council, in its meeting of 10 June accepted the plan as a 'compromise', and resolved to,

> give full authority to the President of the All-India Muslim League, Quaid-i-Azam M.A. Jinnah, to accept the fundamental principles of the Plan as a compromise, and to leave it to him, with full authority, to work out all the details of the Plan in an equitable and just manner with regard to carrying out the complete division of India on the basis and fundamental principles embodied in H.M.G's Plan....[307]

Mountbatten had already announced, in his press conference on 4 June that the partition of India would take place on 15 August 1947,[308] and the Congress leaders were quite happy about it. In fact, according to Sarat Chandra Bose, 'they had already begun to talk in the Churchillian strain about Co-operative Commonwealth'.[309]

On 20 June, the members of the Bengal Legislative Assembly met and decided by 126 votes to 90 that the province, if it remained united, should join the new Constituent Assembly of Pakistan (based on these numbers, it is not difficult to see why Mountbatten refused Jinnah's plea for a referendum in the province). However, members from the non-Muslim majority areas of West Bengal met the same day and decided by 58 votes to 21 that the province should be divided and that West Bengal should join the existing Indian Constituent Assembly. A meeting of the members of the East Bengal Legislative Assembly decided by 106 votes to 35 that the province should not be divided, and by 107 to 34 that East Bengal should join the new Constituent Assembly should the division take place. It was also decided, by 105 votes to 34, that in the event of the division of the province, Sylhet should be merged with East Bengal.[310]

The Punjab Legislative Assembly, meeting in a joint session on 23 June decided by 91 votes to 77 to join a new, separate Constituent Assembly if the province remained united.[311] The members from the non-Muslim majority areas of East Punjab, a few moments later, meeting in a separate session, rejected by 50 votes to 22, a motion by the Provincial President of the League that the province should not be divided. Under the plan, this decided the division issue, although West Punjab members rejected a division motion by 69 votes to [2]7.[312] The Sindh Legislative Assembly at its special meeting on 26 June decided by 33 votes to 22 that Sindh should join the new Pakistan Constituent Assembly.[313]

There was some difficulty in settling the procedure for ascertaining the wishes of the people of Balochistan. The province had a special status, and thus there was dispute about the mode of representation. The Viceroy, Mountbatten, finally resolved that the members of *Shahi Jirga* (excluding Sardars nominated by Kalat State) and non-official members of the Quetta Municipality should decide the future of the province. Fifty-four members of these bodies met and unanimously decided to join the new Constituent Assembly of Pakistan. The eight non-Muslim members did not attend the meeting. [314]

The NWFP, as discussed earlier, voted in favour of joining Pakistan in the referendum held during 6–17 July 1947. Helped by the Khudai Khidmatgar and Congress boycott, it was virtually a 'walk-over' for the League.[315] The government made all the necessary preparations to make the referendum peaceful, fair, and above all, to the satisfaction of Dr Khan Sahib, the Chief Minister of the province. As demanded by

Dr Khan Sahib and his colleagues in the provincial government, Mountbatten also removed Sir Olaf Caroe from the Governorship of the province.[316] In addition, Mountbatten made sure that British officers of the Indian army were appointed to 'run the referendum', not the regular ICS officers.[317] Still in spite of their boycott of the referendum, some 'Congress representatives', according to a Peshawar police confidential diary of the week ending 18 July did visit 'polling stations for checking bogus voters'.[318] The referendum in Sylhet, held on 7 July 1947, as indicated earlier, was won by the League by a huge margin.

This completed the difficult and complex process of East Bengal, West Punjab, Sindh, Balochistan, NWFP, and Sylhet, all joining Pakistan. 'We can now look upon the creation of Pakistan on 15 August as legally decided upon', reported Viceroy Mountbatten.[319] The League had already conveyed to the Viceroy (on 4 July) Jinnah's nomination for the office of the first Governor-General of Pakistan. Though this nomination hurt the 'pride'[320] and vanity of Mountbatten, who perhaps thought of 'the history books of the future in which he would be named, not only as the man who discovered how to give India independence, but also as the one who taught the two infant Dominions how to walk and talk',[321] the League could hardly afford to entrust Pakistan's destiny to a man friendly to Congress leadership and sympathetic to its cause and concerns. But, more importantly, there was an inherent reason for Jinnah's nomination. Jinnah was the charismatic leader of the Muslims and it had to be his singular burden and responsibility to lead them through the difficult situation arising out of partition and the creation of Pakistan. It was his formula of Pakistan that had shown the Muslims a way out of their distressful situation. He had mobilized and led them towards the goal of Pakistan. He had made Pakistan possible against all odds. He was the only man capable of leading them into the 'unknown', the new State of Pakistan. The Muslims recognized and followed him and nobody else. Thus, the whole discussion about the nomination of Mountbatten or anybody else for that matter as the first Governor-General of Pakistan was merely academic.[322] It had no relationship with the realities on the ground. Jinnah had to be the Governor-General because he alone possessed the charisma and charismatic authority to assume the responsibility of leading the new nation-state of Pakistan, whether he wanted to or not.[323]

In this context, one must also bear in mind that the Congress leaders had agreed to the partition of India with deep reservations, and some, like Sardar Patel, were 'convinced that the new State of Pakistan was not viable and could not last'.[324] In fact, Patel thought 'the acceptance of Pakistan would teach the Muslim League a bitter lesson. Pakistan would collapse in a short time'.[325] Gandhi, in one of his prayer meetings shortly after the partition was announced, went one step further, and hoped: 'The Moslem League will ask to come back to Hindustan. They will ask Jawaharlal (Nehru) to come back, and he will take them back'.[326] Nehru himself could not suppress his inner feelings and told Josef Korbel, a member of the United Nations Commission for India and Pakistan '...one day integration will inevitably come. If it will be in four, five, ten years—I do not know'.[327] Above all, there was the Congress Committee resolution on the Partition Plan which stated: 'The AICC earnestly trusts that when the present passions have subsided, India's problems will be viewed in their proper perspective and *the false doctrine of two nations in India will be discredited and discarded by all*'.[328] Jinnah was fully aware of these fond hopes of the Congress leadership. As he told a Reuters correspondent on 25 October 1947,

I want to make it quite clear that Pakistan will never surrender and never agree in any shape or form to any constitutional union between the two sovereign states with one common centre. Pakistan has come to stay and will stay...we must try to stop any effort or attempt which is intended to bring about a forced union of the two Dominions.[329]

Indeed, in accepting the office of the Governor-General at a moment when he was 'very weak, exhausted' and 'sick'[330] as it was eventually to be known to the world, [331] Jinnah made 'a final sacrifice of all real prospects of recovering his health to the cause with which he had identified himself....' [332] But then, he had no regrets. He was convinced that no 'suffering and sacrifice' was too much for the cause he had espoused for so long, as he told a mammoth rally at the Punjab University ground on 30 October 1947: 'There is no better salvation for a Muslim than the death of a martyr for a righteous cause'.[333] Some writers argue that Jinnah committed a grave error of judgement by refusing to accept Mountbatten as common Governor-General of Pakistan and India. The transfer of power in general and the task of the Pakistan Council in particular would have been much easier, ensuring 'a smooth partition' between India and Pakistan.[334] The fact of the matter is that the inevitable mechanism for an unfair and injudicious decision on the division of the provinces and the demarcation of their boundaries was implicit in the Partition Plan of 3 June in the form of 'other factors',[335] much before Jinnah's nomination as Governor-General. It was also evident in the various statements of Wavell, Mountbatten, Cripps, and indeed in the Statement of 16 May 1946.[336] Thus, there was ample evidence to suggest that 'these one-sided verdicts were more political' than most people realized.[337]

On 7 August, Jinnah left Delhi for Karachi where thousands of people awaited his arrival at the airport in the afternoon 'in white clothes—a snow-field of the Muslims he had freed—on the edge of the desert'. They cried Pakistan 'Zindabad!', Pakistan 'Zindabad!' (Long Live Pakistan) as the plane landed. They 'pressed forward, close, hot and frenzied, extending their hands so that they might be as near as possible to their deliverer'.[338] On 11 August, Jinnah was elected President of the Constituent Assembly of Pakistan. In his address, he assured his eager, enthusiastic audience of legislators that the partition of India and the creation of Pakistan on the basis of his formula of 1940, was the only solution to the problem in India. 'I know', he claimed,

> ...there are sections of people who may not agree with it, who may not like it, but in my judgement there was no other solution and I am sure future history will record its verdict in favour of it. And what is more it will be proved by actual experience as we go on that that was the only solution of India's constitutional problem. Any idea of a United India could never have worked and in my judgement it would have led us to terrific disaster.[339]

On 14 August, Mountbatten came to Karachi, announced the transfer of power, and welcomed Pakistan into the British Commonwealth. On 15 August, Jinnah took the oath of office as the first Governor-General of Pakistan. The new Pakistani Cabinet headed by Liaquat Ali Khan was also sworn in. 'It was the first time', reported Flight Lieutenant Ata Rabbani, Jinnah's ADC, 'I had ever seen a look of happiness on his face'.[340] Understandably so. This was no mean achievement for a man who had made a cause his own and who prevailed against the combined might of British Empire and Congress leadership. In fact, in the opinion of a distinguished British writer, Hugh Tinker, 'He had the unenviable task of confronting the British and the Congress leaders eyeball to eyeball. And he did not flicker or flinch'.[341] He created Pakistan. He realized his formula for the salvation of Indian Muslims, and thus, among all the contemporary charismatic leaders of India, Gandhi and Nehru included, he was the only leader who had successfully accomplished his mission. His political life and career was 'capped by a lasting achievement, namely the creation of Pakistan.'[342]

Notes

1. As Mushirul Hasan noted, these nationalist Muslims 'mainly depended on the support of the leading Congressmen who encouraged them to counter the activities of anti-Congress Muslims and patronized them in order to give credence to their claims of representing all Indians.' Mushirul Hasan, ed., *Muslims and the Congress* (Lahore: Book Traders, 1980), xxxiii.
2. According to Seervai, parity between the League and the Congress was a 'solution to the Hindu–Muslim problem' and of 'preserving the unity of India' in the end. It could help allay 'the fears of the Muslims.' But, the Congress was opposed to parity all along. In his opinion, 'grouping provisions of the Plan, and the claim to parity led the Congress in effect to reject the Cabinet Mission Plan.' See H.M. Seervai, *Partition of India: Legend and Reality* (Rawalpindi: Service Book Club, 1991), 34–5, 97.
3. Viceroy Linlithgow had declared India at war with Germany on 3 September 1939, through an official proclamation.
4. Mansergh, *Transfer of Power*, Vol. II, 251.
5. Ahmad, *Speeches and Writings*, Vol., II, 239.
6. *Quaid-i-Azam Papers*, F/392, 20.
7. Mansergh, *Transfer of Power*, Vol. II, 872.
8. Ibid., 257.
9. Ibid., 811.
10. Menon, *Transfer of Power in India*, 90.
11. Ibid.
12. Ibid.
13. Ibid., 89–90.
14. Rajagopalacharia did indeed make a 'sporting offer' of the premiership to Jinnah. Though Jinnah did not take any notice of it, the offer was repeated a number of times. Gandhi made the offer in 1946, and again in April 1947, asking

Mountbatten to appoint Jinnah the Prime Minister of India. Ibid., 95; Campbell-Johnson, *Mission with Mountbatten*, 52, and Mansergh, *Transfer of Power*, Vol. X, 69.

15. Dwarkadas, *Ten Years to Freedom*, 57–8.
16. Menon, *Transfer of Power in India*, 78.
17. *Quaid-i-Azam Papers*, F/18, 28.
18. Ibid., 29.
19. Ibid., 30.
20. Griffiths, *British in India*, 160.
21. Menon, *Transfer of Power in India*, 99.
22. *Quaid-i-Azam Papers*, F/335, 130.
23. Menon, *Transfer of Power in India*, 121.
24. Mansergh, *Transfer of Power*, Vol. I, 396.
25. Ibid., 450.
26. Cited in Ispahani, *As I Knew him*, 53.
27. Mansergh, *Transfer of Power*, Vol. I, 565.
28. Ibid., 567.
29. Ibid.
30. Ibid., 570.
31. Ahmad, *Speeches and Writings*, Vol. I, 395.
32. Ibid.
33. Ibid., 395–6.
34. Ibid., 396.
35. Mansergh, *Transfer of Power*, Vol. I, 756.
36. D.G. Tendulkar, *Mahatma: Life of Mohandas Karamchand Gandhi*, Vol. VI (Delhi: Ministry of Information and Broadcasting, 1969), 72.
37. Azad, *India Wins Freedom*, 74. Forced by Gandhi to resign as President of Congress in 1939, and having fled from his detention in Calcutta first to Germany and then Japan, Subhas Chandra Bose had already waged a military struggle for Indian independence through the Indian National Army (INA). In October 1943, he publicly declared the setting up of the 'Provisional' Government of India. For an interesting account of Bose's flight from India see, Sayed Wiqar Ali Shah, 'Escape of Subhas Chandra Bose—Myth and Reality', *Oracle*, July–October 1996 (Netaji Research Bureau, Calcutta).
38. Colin Cooke, *The Life of Richard Stafford Cripps* (London: Hodder & Stoughton, 1957), 288.
39. Mansergh, *Transfer of Power*, Vol. I, 746.
40. Cripps also availed this opportunity to remind the Congress that they had always claimed that, if the British Government stepped aside, there would be 'no difficulty' in reaching an 'agreement' with the Muslims. Cooke, *Stafford Cripps*, 288.
41. Mansergh, *Transfer of Power*, Vol. II, 323.
42. Ibid., Vol. VI, 464.
43. Ibid., 938.
44. Ahmad, *Speeches and Writings*, Vol. I, 391.
45. Ibid., 397.
46. Ibid., 395.

47. Ibid., 392.
48. Ibid., 393.
49. In Jinnah's own words: 'The recognition given to the principle of partition, however, was very much appreciated by Muslim India', Ahmad, *Speeches and Writings*, Vol. I, 395.
50. Ibid.
51. Hodson, *Great Divide*, 105.
52. Ahmad, *Speeches and Writings*, Vol. I, 428.
53. Ibid., 422.
54. Ibid.
55. Hutchins, *India's Revolution,* 278.
56. Mansergh, *Transfer of Power*, Vol. I, 46,
57. Mansergh, *Transfer of Power*, Vol. V, 182.
58. Ibid., 811.
59. Mansergh, *Transfer of Power*, Vol. VI. 5-6.
60. Mansergh, *Transfer of Power*, Vol. V, 309.
61. Mansergh, *Transfer of Power*, Vol. VI, 117.
62. Ibid., 882.
63. Ibid., 955-63.
64. Mansergh, *Transfer of Power*, Vol. V, 345. Casey once asked Richard Symonds, who was involved in the relief operations in Bengal, whether he 'preferred the Hindus or the Muslims, which seemed an improper question to put even to a temporary government official'. Richard Symonds, *In the Margin of Independence: A Relief Worker in India and Pakistan, 1942–1949* (Karachi: Oxford University Press, 2001), 27.
65. Mansergh, *Transfer of Power*, Vol. V, 528.
66. Mansergh, *Transfer of Power*, Vol. VI, 208. But it was still more to stifle rather than address the issue. As Wavell succinctly put it: 'Since I took charge as Viceroy it has been quite clear that on the Pakistan issue the Muslims and other communities are at present irreconcilable. The object of the Simla proposals was to by-pass the Pakistan issue and to get the parties working together in the Central Government in the hope that after some inside experience they would take a more realistic view. As things are now we cannot evade the issue.' Mansergh, *Transfer of Power*, Vol. VI, 113.
67. Wavell announced his decision to convene the Conference on 14 June 1945. Earlier, Amery, Secretary of State for India, had broached the subject in the House of Commons. It was after much hesitation that the British Government finally agreed. In order to secure their participation in the conference on 25 June Wavell released several Congress leaders including Maulana Abul Kalam Azad and Jawaharlal Nehru, who had been in jail since 8 August 1942, after the launching of the 'Quit India' movement.
68. Gandhi did not accept the invitation to attend the conference, insisting on the 'fiction that he is not the member of Congress and cannot represent them'. Nanda, *Mahatma Gandhi*, 239. However, by all accounts, Gandhi remained active behind the scenes at Simla. The Congress leadership was in touch with him all the time. Indeed, according to Stanley Wolpert, 'Gandhi was back in harness as

the force behind the Congress, despite his repeated disclaimers of power or influence'. Wolpert, *Gandhi's Passion*, 213–14.

69. Ahmad, *Speeches and Writings*, Vol. II, 186.

70. Ibid., 186–7.

71. As Wavell himself described it: 'He seemed to think that I was thinking of nomination of Muslims by the Congress. I said that I had also in mind the nomination by the Unionist Party of the Punjab of a Muslim'. Wavell, *Viceroy's Journal*, 146. In fact, it is plausible to argue that, among other things, it was Wavell's insistence over 'the inclusion of a Punjab Muslim' that wrecked the conference. Mansergh, *Transfer of Power*, Vol. V, 1166.

72. Jalal, *Sole Spokesman*, 130. However, it needs to be remembered that, as Jinnah told the Viceroy, the League 'had always been successful' in the by-elections of the last two years. Wavell, *Viceroy's Journal*, 146. In this sense, Jinnah had already established himself as 'the sole spokesman of all the Muslims'.

73. Ahmad, *Speeches and Writings*, Vol. II, 124. In a way, this was Jinnah's response to Rajagopalacharia 'formula' which called for a joint League–Congress government at the centre, with the right of secession after independence conceded to 'contiguous Muslim-majority districts', with arrangements for common defence, communications, etc. See Rajmohan Gandhi, *Eight Lives*, 160. For details of the formula see, C.H. Philips, *The Evolution of India and Pakistan, 1858–1947: Select Documents* (London: The English Language Book Society and Oxford University Press, 1965), 355–6.

74. Hutchins, *India's Revolution*, 278.

75. Tendulkar, *Mahatma*, Vol. VI, 268.

76. According to Burke and Quraishi, the talks were also 'a tacit admission on Gandhi's part that it was the Muslim League that really represented the Muslims and that Jinnah was as much a personification of the League as he himself was of Congress.' Burke and Quraishi, *British Raj in India*, 409.

77. Menon, *Transfer of Power in India*, 165. Gandhi acknowledged that 'the breakdown took place because we could not come to agreement on the two nations theory of Quaid-i-Azam's.... He wanted two independent sovereign (states) with no connection between them, except by treaty.' Mansergh, *Transfer of Power*, Vol. V, 758–9.

78. Rajmohan Gandhi, *Eight Lives,* 161.

79. The British were not only aware of this development but also made efforts to encourage the pact. Indeed, Wavell went on to suggest to the Secretary of State that not only Bhulabhai Desai's plan 'accorded' with his own thinking on the subject, but 'it had the advantage of being put forward by an Indian'. Menon, *Transfer of Power in India*, 177.

80. Ibid., 176–7. Subsequently, Liaquat Ali Khan denied that there was any such 'pact'. According to John Colville, Governor of Bombay, 'Jinnah was emphatic that any impression that there had been authorized discussion between Desai and Liaquat is entirely false. Liaquat had no authority to negotiate and he has rightly issued a denial.' Mansergh, *Transfer of Power*, Vol. V, 607.

81. Hodson, *Great Divide*, 115.

82. Azad, *India Wins Freedom*, 123.

83. Mansergh, *Transfer of Power*, Vol. V, 1263.

84. Mansergh, *Transfer of Power*, Vol. VI, 699.

85. Ibid., 174.

86. Wavell had also received feedback from the governors on the issue of the formation of an Executive Council without the League. But most of the governors, including Bertrand Glancy, Governor of the Punjab, felt that it would further contribute to Jinnah's popularity, making him an 'Islamic hero'. Mansergh, *Transfer of Power*, Vol. V, 1195-6.

87. Mansergh, *Transfer of Power*, Vol. VI, 37.

88. Ibid., 6.

89. Ibid., 22.

90. Ibid.

91. Ibid., 106.

92. Ibid., 174. That really explained why, much to the chagrin of Jinnah's critics, 'Wavell hesitated to call Jinnah's bluff and finally agreed…that it would be unwise to go ahead with the plans for an interim government without the League.' Samad, *A Nation in Turmoil*, 82. Ayesha Jalal claimed that Wavell's 'attitude was still dominated by an exaggerated sense of the importance of Jinnah's role, which he had inherited from his predecessor [Linlithgow].' Jalal, *Sole Spokesman*, 125. Apparently, Ayesha Jalal did not take into account the huge surge in the popularity of Jinnah during the war years. However, she acknowledged in a later study that these years 'witnessed a spectacular jump in the popularity graph of a "Pakistan" amongst most Muslims, whether in the majority or minority provinces.' Bose and Jalal, *Modern South Asia*, 178.

93. Hodson, *Great Divide*, 113.

94. Sayeed, *Formative Phase*, 131.

95. Samad, *A Nation in Turmoil*, 93, 108. Governor of the Punjab, Bertrand Glancy, was most upset. As he told Wavell: 'Since Jinnah succeeded by his intransigence in wrecking the Simla Conference his stock has been standing very high with his followers and with a large section of the Muslim population. He has been hailed as the champion of Islam. He has openly given out that the elections will show an overwhelming verdict in favour of Pakistan.' Mansergh, *Transfer of Power*, Vol. VI, 71.

96. Shah, *Ethnicity, Islam and Nationalism*, 149-50.

97. Mansergh, *Transfer of Power*, Vol. VI, 936.

98. Ibid., 463. While the main thrust of British argument was devoted to 'federal' schemes, there were also suggestions to consider the 'confederation' option. See, Ibid., 1060.

99. Ibid., 936.

100. Ibid., 151.

101. Ibid., 787. Also see Mansergh, *Transfer of Power*, Vol. VII, 305.

102. Ibid.

103. Mansergh, *Transfer of Power*, Vol. VI, 1181.

104. Ibid., 1213.

105. As early as 7 February Wavell wrote to Pethick-Lawrence: 'If compelled to indicate demarcation of genuinely Muslim areas I recommend that we should include: (a) Sindh, North West Frontier Province, British Balochistan, and Rawalpindi, Multan and Lahore divisions of Punjab less Amritsar and Gurdaspur

(b) In Bengal, the Chittagong and Dacca divisions, the Rajshahi division (less Jalpaiguri and Darjeeling), the Nadia Murshidabad and Jessore districts of Presidency division; and in Assam the Sylhet district. In the Punjab the only Muslim majority district that would not go into Pakistan under this demarcation is Gurdaspur (51 per cent Muslim). Gurdaspur must go with Amritsar for geographical reasons and Amritsar being the sacred city of the Sikhs, must stay out of Pakistan. But for this case based on the importance of Amritsar, demarcation in the Punjab could have been on divisional boundaries....' Ibid., 912.

106. Mansergh, *Transfer of Power*, Vol. VII, 210.
107. Ibid., 233-4.
108. Peter Clarke, *The Cripps Version: The Life of Sir Stafford Cripps* (London: Allen Lane, the Penguin Press, 2002), 393.
109. Ibid., 399.
110. Ibid., 397.
111. Mansergh, *Transfer of Power*, Vol. VII, 251.
112. Ibid., 277.
113. Ibid., 284.
114. Ibid., 281.
115. Ibid., 516-17. For a detailed summary of Jinnah's position see, *Quaid-i-Azam Papers*, F/12, 131-7.
116. Ibid., 518-19.
117. Ibid., 526.
118. Ibid., 582-91. Following quotations on the statement of 16 May are from Ibid.
119. Ibid.
120. *National Herald*, quoted in I.H. Qureshi, *Struggle for Pakistan*, 259.
121. Ahmad, *Speeches and Writings*, Vol. II, 293.
122. Ibid.
123. Ibid., 295-6.
124. Ispahani, *As I knew him*, 200.
125. Mansergh, *Transfer of Power*, Vol. VII, 785. (Italics added).
126. Ibid., 841.
127. Ibid.
128. Earlier, highlighting 'the gravity of the situation' facing the Muslims, Jinnah told the Council: 'I want, therefore, every member to feel that he is free and he is not tied down or fettered by any step that we have taken which prevents him in any way from expressing his opinion or taking his final decision, whatever it may be. It is now up to you as the Parliament of the Muslim Nation to take your decision'. Ahmad, *Speeches and Writings*, Vol. II, 299.
129. Mansergh, *Transfer of Power*, Vol. VII, 954-5.
130. Ispahani, *As I Knew him*, 200. This is not to suggest that there was no feedback from the League leadership or prominent Muslim intellectuals. See, for instance, Professor A.B.A. Haleem's note on the Cabinet Mission Plan. *Quaid-i-Azam Papers*, F/12, 96-9. Also see, Ibid., 109-19, 146-7.
131. In fact, Jinnah had known as early as 18 May that 'the reaction of the Muslims against the statement is very strong....' Mansergh, *Transfer of Power*, Vol. VII, 619.

132. Ispahani, *As I Knew Him*, 200. According to I.H. Qureshi, 'Jinnah's acceptance of the plan was not received well by the rank and file of the Muslim League or the Muslim community in general, except in those circles which were opposed to Pakistan. It speaks volumes for Jinnah's influence that Muslim discontent did not result in a revolt.' I.H. Qureshi, *Struggle for Pakistan*, 262.

133. Based on a Note by George Abell on a conversation between Major Wyatt and Jinnah on 5 February 1946. The fact of the matter was that Major Rankin, an important functionary of the British administration, in his Note on the same conversation prepared the day the conversation took place between the two, that is 8 January as reported to him by Wyatt himself, stated that: '1. Jinnah will not take part in any interim Government without (a) a prior declaration accepting the *principle* of Pakistan.... (b) Parity of the Muslim League in the Government with all other parties, i.e. out of 14 portfolios 7 must be Muslim League. This, he said, follows from the acceptance of the principle of Pakistan....Jinnah will insist on 2 C.M.B.s [Constitution Making Bodies] ....Any attempt to impose a unified constitution or to accept a majority decision by a single C.M.B. would be resisted, if necessary, by force....Relations with Hindustan would be purely diplomatic: there would be no common currency, transportation system, army, etc.' All this was said in a very definite fashion; and Wyatt received the impression (no doubt as he was intended to) that Jinnah would not budge from this position. Jinnah thought that the Hindus would accept it as it would give them three-quarters of India 'which is more than they have ever had before'. The foregoing is hardly a case for further negotiations on an all-India set-up. Clearly, Jinnah wanted *his* Pakistan. Indeed, as Patrick French observed: 'Wyatt realized that Pakistan was more than a fantasy in Jinnah's mind; it was a serious proposition with support from many Indian Muslims.' See Jalal, *Sole Spokesman*, 174-5, 186; Mansergh, *Transfer of Power* Vol. VI, 798-9; and French, *Liberty or Death*, 219.

134. Ahmad, *Speeches and Writings*, Vol. II, 300.
135. Ibid., 301.
136. Mansergh, *Transfer of Power*, Vol. VII, 838.
137. Ahmad, *Speeches and Writings*, Vol. II, 292.
138. Ibid., 294.
139. Ibid., 297.
140. Ibid.
141. Ibid.
142. Ibid., 295.
143. Mansergh, *Transfer of Power*, Vol. VII, 687.
144. Menon, *Transfer of Power in India*, 91-2.
145. Azad, *India Wins Freedom*, 53.
146. Moon, *Viceroy's Journal*, 271.
147. Mansergh, *Transfer of Power*, Vol. VII, 786-7.
148. Majumdar, *Jinnah and Gandhi*, 238.
149. Ahmad, *Speeches and Writings*, Vol. II, 291.
150. Mansergh, *Transfer of Power*, Vol. VII, 519.
151. Rajmohan Gandhi, *Eight Lives*, 176.
152. Majumdar, *Jinnah and Gandhi*, 238.
153. Ispahani, *As I Knew Him*, 200.

154. Ibid., 201.
155. Moon, *Viceroy's Journal*, 260.
156. Mansergh, *Transfer of Power*, Vol. VII, 614. (Italics added for emphasis). Gandhi, according to Rajmohan Ganhdi, was not in favour of accepting the Plan, but, then, 'ministerial office was beckoning,' and therefore, the Congress 'rejected his advice.' Rajmohan Gandhi, *Eight Lives*, 168.
157. Mansergh, *Transfer of Power*, Vol. VII, 622.
158. Full text in ibid., 679–82.
159. Ibid., 689.
160. The Working Committee resolution stated that the Congress could not agree to 'a veto of a communal group' and the Congress 'should join the proposed Constituent Assembly 'with a view to framing the constitution of a free, united, and democratic India" Menon, *Transfer of Power in India*, 277.
161. Mansergh, *Transfer of Power*, Vol. VIII, 26. (Italics added).
162. Azad, India Wins Freedom, 165–70.
163. Mansergh, *Transfer of Power*, Vol. VII, 855. (Italics added).
164. Ibid.
165. Campbell Johnson, *Mission with Mountbatten*, 55. According to Stanley Wolpert, thus, Vallahbbhai Patel was deprived of 'his rightful inheritance as Gandhi's true heir to leadership over the Congress and the nation'. Wolpert, *Gandhi's Passion*, 203.
166. Mansergh, *Transfer of Power*, Vol. VII, 1045. French noted that the Congress wanted 'to break up the two nascent autonomous Pakistans [Sections B and C] before they were even created.' French, *Liberty or Death*, 243.
167. Mansergh, *Transfer of Power*, Vol. VII, 1044–46.
168. Ibid., 1044–45. For the League's position also see, *Quaid-i-Azam Papers*, F/13, 70. Maulana Azad, too, was convinced that: 'The Muslim League had accepted the Cabinet Mission Plan regarding both its long term and short term arrangements.' Azad, *India Wins Freedom*, 183.
169. Mansergh, *Transfer of Power*, Vol. VIII, 144. Strangely enough, Wavell did not mention its reservations on the long-term plan, which was the main problem and which ultimately led to a tripartite meeting between the League, the Congress and British Government in London on 9 December 1946.
170. Moon, *Viceroy's Journal*, 324.
171. Ibid., 251, 305.
172. Ibid., 287.
173. Mansergh, *Transfer of Power*, Vol. VIII, 431.
174. Ibid., 333. (Italics added).
175. Ibid., 439.
176. Ibid., 382.
177. Even Maulana Azad agreed. In his opinion, 'Mr Jinnah had perhaps thought that since the Congress rejected the proposals of the interim Government while the League had accepted both, he would be invited to form the Government.' Azad, *India Wins Freedom*, 183–84.
178. No wonder, Wavell had requested Jinnah to take 'as much care as possible to see that it [assurance] did not become public.' *Quaid-i-Azam Papers*, F/13, 61, 67.
179. Mansergh, *Transfer of Power*, Vol. VII, 1058.

180. Ibid., 1038.

181. Ibid., 1039.

182. Ibid., 1085. Maulana Azad lamented: 'The Congress was neither wise nor right in raising doubts. It should have accepted the Plan unequivocally if it stood for the unity of India.' Azad, *India Wins Freedom*, 185.

183. For one, the Congress was the largest single political party in India and the British wanted to seek its favour, especially now that they were planning to transfer political power to the Indians. A friendly and cooperative Congress was the key to better relations with Britain in the post-colonial period. The British were also keen to retain India in the Commonwealth.

184. Dwarkadas, *Ten Years to Freedom*, 196.

185. Ahmad, *Speeches and Writings*, Vol. II, 315.

186. Ibid., 305.

187. Ibid., 304-5.

188. Ibid., 305-11.

189. Ibid., 308-16.

190. Pirzada, *Foundation of Pakistan*, Vol. II, 558.

191. Ibid., 560-1. Jinnah, notwithstanding the fact that he was a constitutionalist by training and temperament, like most nationalist leaders in British colonial societies, had opted for constitutionalism and constitutional methods for the simple reason that they provided the only natural outlet in the 'imperial system of control.' Jinnah had 'no instrument for physically seizing power' and thus had to make his efforts to rid India of colonial rule 'within the limits' set by its rulers. Moreover, the constitutional methods worked. These methods forced the British to make one concession after the other, and thus facilitate the process of devolution of authority in India. But now that Jinnah was convinced that the colonial system of government which had so far determined the relations between the British and the Indians was on decline and perhaps irrelevant as the British were on their way out, he found no harm in adding extra-constitutional means to his constitutional methods to achieve his goals. For some details on Jinnah's constitutional approach see, David Page, 'The Development of Mr Jinnah's Constitutional Ideas', in Dani, *World Scholars*, 272-9. Also see for a theoretical discussion, Benda, 'Non-western Intelligentsia as Political Elite', *The Australian Journal of Politics and History*, Vol. VI, No.2, 1960, 245.

192. Mansergh, *Transfer of Power*, Vol. VIII, 203.

193. Ahmad, *Speeches and Writings*, Vol. II, 323.

194. Dwarkadas, *Ten Years to Freedom*, 202. See his statements on the 'coalition' government in 1937, and on the grouping clause in July 1946.

195. Ahmad, *Speeches and Writings*, Vol. II, 334.

196. Ibid., 335.

197. Ibid. 323.

198. Mansergh, *Transfer of Power*, Vol. VIII, 323. By 31 August, Wavell revised his estimates upwards and claimed 20,000 casualties (3000 dead and 17,000 injured), with more Muslims than Hindus killed. But, more importantly, he realized that 'a one party Government at the Centre was likely to cause fierce disorders everywhere.' Ibid.

199. Spear, *India*, 415-16.

200. Ibid., 416.
201. Mansergh, *Transfer of Power*, Vol. IX, 139-40.
202. Ibid., 140.
203. Mansergh, *Transfer of Power*, Vol. VIII, 247.
204. Ibid., 248.
205. Mansergh, *Transfer of Power*, Vol. IX, 141.
206. Moon, *Viceroy's Journal*, 299. Of course, Wavell did not agree to an interim government without the League at the Simla Conference in 1945, when the League was not as representative of the Muslim opinion as it was now, after the 1945-46 elections. Was it a further proof of the increasing British bias towards the Congress as India approached freedom? The League did not matter any more.
207. Menon, *Transfer of Power in India*, 305-6.
208. Mansergh, *Transfer of Power*, Vol. VIII, 311.
209. Ibid., 482. Little did the Congress realize that the communal riots were helping the cause of the League and Pakistan more than they could ever imagine. It helped the League even in a province like the NWFP, the only Muslim-majority province dominated by the Congress. As Shah observed, the riots 'provided the League with its best weapon for winning over the sympathies of a large segment of the Muslims. It achieved within months success which otherwise it could not have thought of achieving in years. Public opinion changed in favour of the League, and its demand for a separate homeland for the Muslims.' Shah, *Ethnicity, Islam and Nationalism*, 174-5.
210. Menon, *Transfer of Power in India*, 307.
211. Ibid., 312, and Ahmad, *Speeches and Writings*, Vol. II, 353-4.
212. Ibid., 355.
213. Mansergh, *Transfer of Power*, Vol. VIII, 311.
214. According to Ayesha Jalal, Mandal's appointment 'also was the first hint of Jinnah's ultimate intentions of extending the League's umbrella of protection to the Scheduled Castes, certainly in Bengal, and other non-Congress elements.' Jalal, *Sole Spokesman*, 225. The Scheduled Castes have had a rough deal at the hands of the Congress in spite of Dr B.R. Ambedkar, its leaders' best efforts and the 'Poona Pact' of 1932.
215. Mansergh, *Transfer of Power*, Vol. VIII, 709.
216. Ibid., 735.
217. Ibid.
218. Ibid., 745. It was amazingly naïve on part of Wavell to expect that Jinnah himself would join a government headed by Nehru. Apparently, Wavell still did not have a full measure of Jinnah's status and standing with the Muslim masses. He was their charismatic leader. How could he possibly work under Nehru? Wavell should have known better.
219. Menon, *Transfer of Power in India*, 319. Mansergh, *Transfer of Power*, Vol. VIII, 321. The Governor of the Punjab, Evan Jenkins, had already indicated as early as 31 August 1946, that: 'we have here the material for a vast communal upheaval'. Ibid., 372.
220. Ibid., 321.
221. Ahmad, *Speeches and Writings*, Vol. II, 363.

222. Ibid.

223. Ibid., 364.

224. Azad, *India Wins Freedom*, 189. But then, as Burke and Quraishi pointed out, 'it was also alleged that Liaquat had tried to drive a wedge between the right and left wings of the Congress party (led respectively by Patel and Nehru).' Burke and Quraishi, *British Raj in India*, 483-4. For the important concluding part of Liaquat Ali Khan's budget speech see, Roger D. Long, ed., *Dear Mr Jinnah: Selected Correspondence and Speeches of Liaquat Ali Khan* (Karachi: Oxford University Press, 2004), 296-304.

225. Azad, *India Wins Freedom*, 189-90.

226. Ibid., 190.

227. Mansergh, *Transfer of Power*, Vol. VIII, 842. The Muslim 'block' worked under Liaquat Ali Khan. The Congress 'block' was led by Nehru. There were some Muslim Leaders who demanded that 'the premiership in the Interim Government should alternate between Muslim and Congressmen each term'. *Quaid-i-Azam Papers*, F/196.

228. Ahmad, *Speeches and Writings*, Vol. II, 372.

229. Interestingly, before the Conference could be called in London, the Lord Chancellor, in response to a 'secret reference' on the legal aspect of the controversy, had already given his verdict in favour of the League. Mansergh, *Transfer of Power*, Vol. IX, 220-4, 238-40. Also see ibid., 155, 69.

230. Ibid., 462.

231. 'Consul Speaks to Secretary of State Marshall', Karachi, 1 February 1947. *Foreign Relations of the United States, 1947*, Vol. III, *The British Commonwealth; Europe* (Washington: United States Government Printing Office, 1972), 140. This volume shadows the *Transfer of Power Volumes* for the 1946-1947 period.

232. Mansergh, *Transfer of Power*, Vol. IX, 586.

233. Menon, *Transfer of Power in India*, 337.

234. Pethick-Lawrence was worried about the possibility of Congress resigning on the issue. Mansergh, *Transfer of Power*, Vol. IX, 646.

235. Menon, *Transfer of Power in India*, 337.

236. Ibid., 337-8. The American Embassy in India (New Delhi) too hoped that the British Government 'will endeavour to avoid if possible instructing Viceroy to dismiss League members'. Indeed, the embassy was assured by Ian Scott, Assistant Private Secretary to the Viceroy that 'while Viceroy had as yet received no clear indication of what His Majesty's Governments' decision would be it seemed unlikely that League members would be dismissed immediately'. Scott, in fact, opined that the 'wisest approach would be to endeavour to persuade Congress to alter 6 June AICC resolution sufficiently to enable Viceroy to tell League Congress had accepted 6 December statement unconditionally and League would have to join CA or withdraw from interim govt.' The Chargé in India (George R. Merrell) to the Secretary of State on 14 February 1947. *Foreign Relations of the United States, 1947*, Vol. III, 142.

237. Mansergh, *Transfer of Power*, Vol. IX, 65.

238. Mansergh, *Transfer of Power*, Vol. VIII, 456.

239. Mansergh, *Transfer of Power*, Vol. IX, 128. Already in February 1946, 'mutinies' of the sailors in the Royal Indian Navy in Bombay and Karachi harbours, calling

themselves INN (Indian National Navy), after Bose's INA, had exposed the discipline of the armed forces. This was the first instance of its kind since the British takeover of India.

240. Wavell, *Viceroy's Journal*, 402.
241. Stephens, *Pakistan*, 125.
242. Ibid., 149.
243. Ibid.
244. Full text was available in Menon, *Transfer of Power in India*, App. IX, 506-9.
245. For instance, see Hodson, *Great Divide*, 190-1; and Mosley, *Last Days of the British Raj*, 41-8. According to Attlee, 'Wavell was frankly pretty defeatist by then... I came to the conclusion that Wavell had shot his bolt, and that I must find somebody else'. Williams, *War and Post-War Memoirs of Rt. Hon. Earl Attlee*, 209.
246. Mansergh, *Transfer of Power*, Vol. VIII, 328.
247. According to Charles Smith, Mountbatten's valet and butler, 'who shared his master's fortunes, triumphs and agonies for nearly fifteen years', Mountbatten was appointed Viceroy on Nehru's recommendation. Sharif al Mujahid, 'Introductory', in S. Hashim Raza, ed., *Mountbatten and Pakistan* (Karachi: Quaid-i-Azam Academy, 1982), 19. The name of Mountbatten was also suggested by Lady Willington to Pethick-Lawrence. Mansergh, *Transfer of Power*, Vol. VI, 872. For other views on the subject including the roles of Cripps and Krishna Menon see, Collins and Lapierre, *Freedom at Midnight*, 8.
248. Collins and Lapierre wrote: 'To the horror of his staff Mountbatten even rode through Singapore's streets in his open car with Nehru at his side. His action, his advisers had warned, would only dignify an anti-British political rebel. "Dignify him?" Mountbatten had retorted. 'It is he who will dignify me. One day this man will be Prime Minister of India.' Collins and Lapierre, *Freedom at Midnight*, 98.
249. Campbell-Johnson, *Mission with Mountbatten*, 44.
250. Mansergh, *Transfer of Power*, Vol. X, 137.
251. Uncirculated record. Ibid., 190.
252. Collins and Lapierre, *Mountbatten and the Partition of India*, Vol. 1, 59.
253. In addition, there soon was to be an Edwina-Nehru relationship complicating matters further. According to Akbar S. Ahmad, 'whether the friendship was sexual or platonic barely matters. What is most significant is the impact of this close relationship.' Akbar S. Ahmed, *Jinnah, Pakistan and Islamic Identity: The Search for Saladin* (Karachi: Oxford University Press, 1997), 143-58. Also see, Stanley Wolpert, *Nehru: A Tryst With Destiny* (London: Oxford University Press, 1997), 360-1, 435-6.
254. Masarrat Hussain Zubairi, *Voyage Through History*, Vol. II (Karachi: Hamdard Foundation Press, 1984), 7.
255. Chaudhri Muhammad Ali, *The Emergence of Pakistan* (Lahore: Research Society of Pakistan, 1973), 122.
256. Menon, *Transfer of Power in India*, 507-8.
257. Ibid., 354.
258. Ibid., 355.
259. Ibid., 354-5.

260. Golant, *Long Afternoon*, 239.

261. Cited in Mujahid, 'Introductory', in Hashim Raza, *Mountbatten and Pakistan*, 20.

262. Mansergh, *Transfer of Power*, Vol. X, 187.

263. Ibid., 380.

264. Ibid., 280.

265. Ibid.

266. Ibid., 921.

267. Ibid., 922.

268. Ibid., 108.

269. Ibid., 897.

270. Mansergh, *Transfer of Power*, Vol. X, 149.

271. Cited in Jalal, *Sole Spokesman*, 261.

272. Ibid.

273. Mansergh, *Transfer of Power*, Vol. X, 507-8.

274. Ibid., 163-4.

275. And these forces included the Muslims. For instance, Jamiat-ul-Ulama-i-Hind and the Majlis-i-Ahrar, in particular, "trashed Congress' for its *volte face* on the principles of a single nation by adopting the Mahasabha's demand for the partition of the Punjab.' Jalal, *Self and Sovereignty*, 516.

276. 'Record of Interview' between Jinnah and Mountbattn, 26 April 1947. Z.H. Zaidi, *Jinnah Papers, Vol. I, Part II*, 667. Also see, Mansergh, *Transfer of Power*, Vol. XI, 38. But then the Sikhs, under Master Tara Singh and Sardar Baldev Singh, were insistent on the division of the Punjab. Sardar Baldev Singh, who was a member of the interim government, and who represented Sikhs in the crucial talks on partition, told Mountbatten: 'I would reiterate with all the emphasis I command that as the division of India is being planned at Mr Jinnah's insistence, he cannot be allowed to impose his will on the minorities. The partition of the Punjab is necessitated by the Sikh case. The Sikhs cannot and will not be dominated by the Muslims and no partition will meet the ends of justice if it does not exclude from the Muslim area as large a percentage of Sikh population as possible.' Mansergh, *Transfer of Power*, Vol. X, 521. Samad is of the opinion that perhaps things may have been different if the Muslim League had offered a hand of friendship to the Sikhs immediately after their overwhelming victory in the Punjab in the 1945–46 elections. The League leadership remained adamant that 'the Muslims were entitled to rule the province on their own, and urged their supporters to maintain the agitation.' Samad, *A Nation in Turmoil*, 95. However, it needs to be borne in mind that the Hindus, too, were 'bent on partition' of the Punjab. Some Hindu members of the Central Legislative Assembly from the Punjab wrote to Jawaharlal Nehru to inform the interim government that 'We have come to the conclusion that the only way out of the present deadlock is to partition the Punjab into two provinces. That and that alone, in our view, can cease the tension in the province which may increase at any moment.' Amarjit Singh, *Punjab Divided: Politics of the Muslim League and Partition, 1935-1947* (New Delhi: Kanishka Publishers, 2001), 194.

277. Ahmad, *Speeches and Writings*, Vol. I, 245.

278. Mansergh, *Transfer of Power*, Vol. X, 280. For a critical analysis of 'the Sikh Standpoint' on the issue of Pakistan see, Javed Hassan, *India: A Study in Profile* (Rawalpindi: Services Book Club, 1990), 40-1.

279. In a letter to Liaquat Ali Khan on 5 May 1947, Suhrawardy explained: 'If Bengal is divided both sections will be weak and negligible. More so, our section, which although it has got a large enough population, is so deficient in food grains, that no amount of intensive cultivation will be able to produce a sufficiency. I am also unable to realize how a weak Eastern Bengal can be of any assistance to the Muslim cause or be any strength to the Muslims or help the Muslims in the minority areas'. *Shamsul Hasan Collection*, Vol. III, F/33. An additional concern with the Muslim leaders was to 'avoid the loss to Pakistan of Calcutta—a loss they dreaded more than anything else, and which seemed inevitable.' France Bhattacharya, 'East Bengal: Between Islam and a Regional Identity,' in Jafferlot, *A History of Pakistan*, 42. In fact, a Calcutta District Muslim League Memorandum of 31 May 1947 claimed that: '[Nawab] Serajuddaula lost Bengal because he lost Calcutta.' *Quaid-i-Azam Papers*, F/10, 25.

280. Unlike the Punjab, Bengal's case offered a unique opportunity. As Gurharpal Singh described it: 'In Bengal, though there was no parallel to the Unionist Party as an inter-communal coalition, a sense of regional cultural unity did appear to transcend religious divisions. The provincial "quasi regime" was indeed buffeted by all-India developments but (unlike the Punjab) when the possibility of state contraction reached the regime threshold in 1946, it was able to generate a counter proposal to the regime collapsing, by proposing a united independent Bengal.' Gurharpal Singh, 'The Partition of India in a Comparative Perspective: A Long-term View', in Talbot and Singh, *Region and Partition*, 104.

281. Sisir Kumar Bose, ed., *I Warned my Countrymen: Works of Sarat Chandra Bose, 1945-50* (Calcutta: Netaji Research Bureau, 1996), esp., 'United Independent Bengal, Sarat Bose Formula', 156-65. In a speech on 13 April 1948, much after the partition of India and the division of Bengal, Bose claimed: 'I have not the slightest doubt myself that if the Congress leadership had displayed a certain amount of statesmanship, the partition of Bengal could have been prevented.' Ibid.

282. Mansergh, *Transfer of Power*, Vol. X, 898.

283. Ibid., 555-7. It is of interest to note that as early as 1928, the Nehru Report had suggested that both Bengal and the Punjab had 'definite zones of Hindu or Muslim population.' Mujahid, 'Jinnah and Separate Electorates', 27.

284. Mansergh, *Transfer of Power*, Vol. X, 540.

285. Ibid., 776.

286. Ibid., 756. Ironically, Nehru had already approved the plan before it was sent to London. Thus, Waheed-uz-Zaman found it 'difficult to understand the logic behind Nehru's protests when he had himself approved of the draft plan which has subsequently received the consent of the British Government'. For some of the useful discussion on this aspect see, Waheed-uz-Zaman, *Myth and Reality*, 95-6.

287. Mansergh, *Transfer of Power*, Vol. X, 756.

288. Ibid., 768.

289. Ibid., 780.

290. Menon, *Transfer of Power in India*, 366-7.
291. Mansergh, *Transfer of Power*, Vol. X, 775.
292. Ibid., 825.
293. Ibid., 896.
294. Ibid., 852-3. For the full text of Jinnah's reaction to the plan see Ibid., 851-3.
295. Ibid., 940.
296. And also the support of the conservative opposition leader in the House, Winston Churchill, with a threat to Jinnah: 'This is a matter of life and death for Pakistan, if you do not accept this offer with both hands'. Ibid., 945-6.
297. While some writers claimed that there was not much difference between the two plans, the fact of the matter was that the second plan was a complete *volte face*. Power was to be devolved at the centre, to the existing Constituent Assembly, and not to the provinces, as originally conceived. Provinces, if they did not desire to remain part of the Constituent Assembly, could secede under specific conditions stipulated in the plan. The plan, thus, according to Waheed-uz-Zaman, was 'a clear concession to India. While the six Hindu majority provinces remained intact and automatically became the constituent parts of the Indian Union the Muslim Provinces were not made over to Pakistan as such but were only given the option to decide their future. They alone were 'to face the "ifs" and "buts" of a hazardous journey to statehood'. The prospect of 'Balkanization' of India which Nehru apprehended in the first partition plan now stared the Muslim majority provinces in the face'. Waheed-uz-Zaman, *Myth and Reality*, 99.
298. Talbot, *India and Pakistan*, 143.
299. Mansergh, *Transfer of Power*, Vol. X, 945-6.
300. As Mountbatten described his meeting with Gandhi on 4 June 1947, 'I told him that although many newspapers had christened it "The Mountbatten Plan", they should really have christened it "The Gandhi Plan", since all the salient ingredients were suggested to me by him. I enumerated these as follows:....' Mansergh, *Transfer of Power*, Vol. XI, 132.
301. Campbell Johnson, *Mission With Mountbatten*, 102.
302. Ibid., 103.
303. Seervai, *Partition of India*, 99, 159. In fact, there is one whole section devoted to this subject entitled, 'The Viceroyalty of Mountbatten in Retrospect', 152-61.
304. Ibid., 159.
305. Ahmad, *Speeches and Writing*, Vol. II, 394-5. Also see, *Quaid-i-Azam Papers*, F/10, 37. There could be little doubt that Jinnah himself saw the whole thing more as a 'compromise' than a 'settlement'. A sovereign Pakistan, comprising Muslim-majority provinces as they were, undivided, was not conceded. A number of reasons can be deduced for this 'compromise'. The first and the foremost was the increasingly intense communal conflict and violence in the country, especially in the Punjab, the 'cornerstone' of Jinnah's Pakistan, which saw by mid-April, in little less than a month of communal rioting, more than 3,500 dead. Indeed, the communal riots in the Punjab were the most important reason for Jinnah's compromise on the plan. The Sikhs, in particular, under the leadership of Master Tara Singh and Sardar Baldev Singh, had made it exceedingly difficult for Jinnah to press any longer for the unity of the Punjab and its inclusion in Pakistan.

Secondly, Jinnah could not be expected, realist that he was, 'to throw away the chance of getting a limited Pakistan in an attempt to get the whole'. He had come to the conclusion, as he eventually told Mountbatten: 'I do not care how little you give me so long as you give it to me completely'. Finally, as he explained to an Egyptian delegation, he accepted the 3 June Plan 'as a compromise...because we want peace and be able to get rid of British domination as soon as possible'. Mansergh, *Transfer of Power*, Vol. IX, 109; Mansergh, *Transfer of Power*, Vol. X, 991; and *Quaid-i-Azam Papers*, F/10, 83.

306. Hugh Tinker, 'Jinnah and the British Government, August 1945–August 1947: The Attainment of Agreement by the Assertion of Difference', in Dani, *World Scholars*, 281.

307. Pirzada, *Foundations of Pakistan*, Vol. II, 568.

308. Why August 15? Apparently, there is no definite answer except what Mountbatten told Collins and Lapierre: 'I thought it had to be about August or September and I then went to the 15th of August. Why? Because it was the second anniversary of Japan's surrender.' Collins and Lapierre, *Mountbatten and the Partition of India*, Vol. I, 72. Mountbatten served as Supreme Commander for South-East Asia during the Second World War.

309. Bose, *I Warned my Countrymen*, 168.

310. Mansergh, *Transfer of Power*, Vol. XI, 681.

311. Among those voting for the new separate Constituent Assembly was Khizar Hayat Khan, the former Unionist Chief Minister of the Punjab. He voted for Pakistan. However, that was not much help at this late stage. As Talbot aptly described it: 'Khizer's public career ended in abject failure. He could never protect his loyal Hindu and Sikh workers at Kalra [his estate]. Instead, he scuttled to a self-imposed exile in Britain when India finally achieved self-rule 'at the midnight hour''. Talbot, *Khizr Tiwana*, 179. In all, eight Muslim Unionists voted for the new Constituent Assembly of Pakistan. Mansergh, *Transfer of Power*, Vol. XI, 567.

312. Ibid., 566.

313. Ibid., 681.

314. Ibid., 535, 896. For more details see, Inam ul Haq Kausar, *Pakistan Movement and Balochistan* (Quetta: United Printers, 1999), 55–79.

315. Mansergh, *Transfer of Power*, Vol. XI, 686. However, Shah was of the opinion that the 'Khudai Khidmatgars were perturbed by the "treachery" of the Congress who in agreeing to the partition plan, had sacrificed their allies in the Frontier who were forced to join Pakistan against their will.' Shah, *Ethnicity, Islam, and Nationalism*, 227.

316. However, Jansson suggested there was no 'convincing evidence of partiality against the Congress on his part.' In fact, he insisted, 'an analysis of his reports and standpoint shows that his views and aims were basically the contrary to what he had been accused of. He was not in favour of Pakistan; he was opposed to partition. Moreover, he preferred the Khan brothers to the Muslim League leaders.' Jansson, *India, Pakistan or Pakhtunistan?*, 215.

317. Mansergh, *Transfer of Power*, Vol. XI, 150. As Mountbatten explained: 'Dr Khan Saheb had previously told me that he would not trust ICS officers to run the referendum...he "preferred military people".' Ibid.

318. *Quaid-i-Azam Papers*, F/4, 58.
319. Mansergh, *Transfer of Power*, Vol. XI, 139.
320. Ian Stephens, *Horned Moon* (London: Chatto & Windus, 1954), 112-13. On 10 July, the British Prime Minister, Attlee, announced that Jinnah had been recommended as the Governor-General of Pakistan.
321. Mosley, *Last Days of the British Raj*, 151. Defence may also have been an important consideration with Mountbatten in seeking the office of the common Governor-General for both India and Pakistan. This was evident from his 'efforts to obtain the acceptance of the Indian leaders for an Anglo-Indian military alliance which was designed to have a centrally controlled administration to supervise the division of the armed forces, retain British military officers for a few years for reorganizing the forces of the new Dominions and obtain a continuity in defence arrangements with the Commonwealth countries'. Clearly the British government 'wished to maintain an all-British chain of command for as long as possible,' thus jeopardizing 'the sovereign status of Pakistan.' Noor-ul-Haq, *Making of Pakistan*, 182, 195.
322. For some of the more important discussions on the subject, nonetheless, see, Sayeed, *Formative Phase*, 223-32; Waheed-uz-Zaman, *Myth and Reality*, 87-127, esp., 99-115; S.M. Burke, 'Quaid-i-Azam Jinnah's Decision to become Pakistan's First Governor-General', in Dani, *World Scholars*, 318-28; M. Rafique Afzal, 'The Governor Generalship Issue and the Quaid-i-Azam: Mountbatten's Version and the Real Story', *South Asia* (January 1986); and Mussarat Abid, 'Quaid-i-Azam and Mountbatten: Nature of Relationship', *Journal of Research Society of Pakistan*, Vol. XXXVI, No. 2 (1999), esp., 11-14.
323. In a meeting of the Council of the Muslim League on 9 June held to formally approve the 3 June Plan, Jinnah stressed that he had 'done his job,' indicating that he could opt out of future responsibilities. Sayeed, *Formative Phase*, 228.
324. Azad, *India Wins Freedom*, 207.
325. Ibid.
326. Cited in Latif Ahmad Sherwani, 'The Objectives of Pakistan's Foreign Policy', in M.A. Ahsan Chaudhri, et al., *Foreign Policy of Pakistan: An Analysis* (Karachi: Pakistan Institute of International Affairs, 1964), 11-12.
327. Josef Korbel, *Danger in Kashmir* (Princeton: Princeton University Press, 1954), 128.
328. Cited in Burke and Quraishi, *British Raj in India*, 512. (Italics added).
329. Afzal, *Selected Speeches and Statements*, 439.
330. Fatima Jinnah, *My Brother*, 7-10. For more on Jinnah's health all along, see Ch. 1, 'A Nation is Orphaned', in ibid., 1-42.
331. Mountbatten, when he came to know of it in 1975, years later, lamented, 'it is a horrifying thought that we were never told (about his illness)...'that I was not told was almost criminal' since, as long as, he was alive, nothing could be done'...because he was the only, I repeat, the only, stumbling block'. Collins and Lapierre, *Mountbatten and the Partition of India*, Vol. I, 40-44.
332. L.F. Rushbrook Williams, *The State of Pakistan* (London: Faber & Faber, 1962), 29-30.
333. Ahmad, *Speeches and Writings*, Vol. II, 425.

334. For instance, see Hodson, *Great Divide*, 541; and Menon, *Transfer of Power in India*, 394-5.

335. For a more detailed discussion see, in particular, Justice Din Muhammad on Radcliffe's Boundary Award in Latif Ahmed Sherwani, ed., *Pakistan Resolution to Pakistan, 1940–1947, A Selection of Documents Presenting the Case of Pakistan* (Karachi: National Publishing House, 1969), 276-8; Chaudhri Muhammad Ali, *Emergence of Pakistan*, 218-19; Muhammad Munir, 'Days to Remember', *Pakistan Times*, 24 June 1964; and Waheed-uz-Zaman, *Myth and Reality*, 115-27. For Mountbatten's version see, in particular, Hodson, *Great Divide*, 346-55.

336. See, for instance, Mansergh, *Transfer of Power*, Vol. VII, 582-5. Also see Wavell's prophetic 'demarcation of genuinely Muslim areas.' Mansergh, *Transfer of Power*, Vol. VI, 912.

337. Bolitho, *Jinnah: Creator of Pakistan*, 179-80. The result of one of these 'one sided verdicts', as reflected in the Radcliffe Award was communal rioting and the movement of millions of Muslim refugees into the Punjab in particular, forcing the Government of Pakistan to establish a full-fledged Ministry of Refugees (in Karachi) in the second week of September 1947. In order to better cope with these refugees from the Punjab, the headquarters of the ministry were transferred to Lahore by the end of October. For very useful information on the refugees from the Punjab and other parts of India see, Saleemullah Khan, comp., *The Journey to Pakistan: A Documentation on [the] Refugees of 1947* (Islamabad: National Documentation Centre, 1993). One good explanation for this huge influx of refugees and the explosive problem of the accession of princely states could be that in 1946–47, 'too much concentration' was placed 'on the competition for power rather than on the mechanics of the transfer of power and the way in which the transfer was achieved.' Richard Bonney, 'Three Giants of South Asia: Gandhi, Ambedkar, and Jinnah on Self-Determination,' *South Asia History Academic Paper 5*, University of Leicester, 2002, 140. And then, the British Government failed to prevent or deal with the riots in spite of a so-called 'complete assurance'. In response to Maulana Azad's concerns about the 'rivers of blood flowing in different parts of the country' as the 'likely consequences of the partition,' Mountbatten had bravely declared: 'At least on this question I shall give you complete assurance. I shall see to it that there is no bloodshed and riot. I am a soldier, not a civilian. Once partition is accepted in principle, I shall issue orders to see that there are no communal disturbances anywhere in the country. If there should be the slightest agitation, I shall adopt measures to nip the trouble in the bud. I shall not use even the armed police. I shall order the Army and the Air Force to act and use tanks and aeroplanes to suppress anybody who wants to create trouble.' Azad, *India Wins Freedom*, 207. Also see the British Prime Minister Attlee's remarks in the Cabinet Committee meeting of 23 May 1947, along the same lines. Mansergh, *Transfer of Power*, Vol. X, 967. For a documentary record of the princely states relevant to Pakistan in particular see, Z.H. Zaidi, ed., *Quaid-i-Azam Mohammad Ali Jinnah Papers: The States, Historical and Policy Perspectives and Accession to Pakistan*, Vol. VIII (Islamabad: Quaid-i-Azam Papers Project, National Archives of Pakistan, 2003).

338. Bolitho, *Jinnah: Creator of Pakistan*, 193-5.

339. Ahmad, *Speeches and Writings*, Vol. II, 402. In the light of an interesting typology of 'Indus and India', it has been argued that 'the impulse of [the] Indus towards separatism was natural and primordial, and that because it was itself based on foundations that lay in remote antiquity that history was turning full circle. [The] Indus was reverting to its primordial status.' Aitzaz Ahsan, *The Indus Saga and the Making of Pakistan* (Karachi: Oxford University Press, 1996), 335.

340. Bolitho, *Jinnah: Creator of Pakistan*, 198. For more of Rabbani's personal reflections on Jinnah see, Mian Ata Rabbani, *I was the Quaid's ADC* (Karachi: Oxford University Press, 1996).

341. Hugh Tinker, 'Jinnah and the British Government', in Dani, *World Scholars*, 284. As James Cameron described it: 'On the one side were arrayed these figures [Gandhi, Patel, Nehru...], all apparently larger than life, on the other side stood one man: the implacable breakwater against united India...Mahommed Ali Jinnah. It was Mr Jinnah and nobody else who invented Pakistan.' James Cameron, 'A Place of Politics', in *India*, eds., Frank Moraes and Edward Howe (New York: McGraw Hill, 1974), 65. In this sense, there was no merit in the criticism that Jinnah 'achieved only a "moth-eaten" Pakistan, the real wonder is that he achieved any Pakistan at all. No freedom fighter in history was ever faced with such awesome odds as he was'. S.M. Burke and Salim al-Din Quraishi, *Quaid-i-Azam Mohammed Ali Jinnah: His Personality and his Politics* (Karachi: Oxford University Press, 1997), 375.

342. Ian Copland, 'Quaid-i-Azam and the Nawab Chancellor: Literary Paradigms in the Historical Construction of Indian Muslim Identity', in Hasan, *Islam, Communities and the Nation*, 118.

Conclusion

The creation of Pakistan was essentially the work of Quaid-i-Azam Mohammad Ali Jinnah's charisma and charismatic leadership. In the late 1930s, Jinnah rose to lead Indian Muslims at a time when the state of Muslim politics in India was distressful, and insecurity and helplessness prevailed. The Muslims were anxious about their future in a system of government where the Hindus, being the majority community, would always be in power. To compound their difficulties, the Congress, insisting on its claim to represent 'Indian nation', remained indifferent to the peculiar conditions of India where a Muslim 'minority' of about 70 million was distributed in a manner that the Muslims formed majorities in certain provinces of India. It was not willing to accommodate their special interests and demands, let alone give them a palpable share of power. The Muslim traditional political leadership, attached to the present, and for the most part indifferent about the future, offered little to the Muslims as India advanced towards self-government and freedom and their fears of being submerged under the weight of Hindu-majority rule became profound and real. In the end, of course, it became clear to the provincial leaders of the Muslim-majority provinces, the most organized and powerful group of the traditional leaders, that they, too were not 'secure' in a system dominated by the Hindu centre.

Muslim apprehensions about the system of government had their roots in the long history of Hindu–Muslim relations in India. The Muslims and Hindus could not really call any historical ruler their 'national ruler'. All the rulers were either 'heroes or despots', depending upon the religion of the rulers and the ruled.[1] It was this sentiment, developed over the centuries, which found a new shape and pattern in British India. While the Hindu community, given the inexorable logic of majority rule in the system of government introduced by the British in India, could safely grow and prosper under the inspiring ideal of 'Indian nationalism', the Muslims had to find ways and means to secure their special interests. Syed Ahmad Khan, Maulana Mohammed

Ali, and Allama Iqbal, in particular, helped them emerge as a unified and separate political community worthy of a separate destiny. Allama Iqbal saw the 'Muslims of India…[as] the only people who can fitly be described as a nation in the modern sense of the word', for Islam, he argued, was an 'ethical ideal plus a certain kind of polity….'[2] But that did not mean that Iqbal and other Muslim leaders did not make efforts to settle the Hindu–Muslim problem within the framework of one, united India first. They did their utmost until they were convinced that the Muslims would never be secure politically in the emerging system of self-government in India. However, what ultimately worried them the most, as Iqbal stressed in particular, was the fact that they would not be able to develop their 'own culture and tradition' fully and freely in India.[3]

Although Jinnah inherited this separatist legacy from the past, he himself did not hesitate to make conscious and consistent efforts to persuade the Hindus in general and the Congress in particular to adopt a fair and conciliatory attitude towards the Muslims and to accomodate their interests and demands for the greater cause of India and its freedom. He also tried his best to impress upon the British the need to contemplate a system of government under which the Muslims could live without the fear of being subjected to Hindu-majority rule. The British and the Congress, however, could not offer anything more than a unitary state, with the central government having supremacy over the whole political system. In the end, of course, the British leaders, such as Secretary of State for India, Leopold Amery, were of the opinion that, 'the one type of government to which there is not the slightest hope of ever reaching agreement in United India is the British type…'[4] but the die had been cast. The Muslims had concluded that the system of representative government in India would certainly mean 'the domination and supremacy of the majority communal rule over the minorities'.[5] Jinnah, in particular, became convinced that the only way out of this distressful situation was the partition of India and the creation of a separate homeland for the Muslims.

Jinnah's 'formula' for the salvation of the Muslims represented the 'final and, perhaps, the most important contribution to the historical process towards Muslim separatism' in India.[6] It was based on the premise that Islam, as a system of individual and collective life, could work only if it was a political power as well. 'So far as I have understood

Islam', claimed Jinnah, 'it does not advocate a democracy which would allow the majority of non-Muslims, to decide the fate of the Muslims. We cannot accept a system of government in which the non-Muslims, merely by numerical majority, would rule and dominate us'.[7] Jinnah, therefore, went on to insist that the Muslims were a 'self-determining political community, a nation in the modern sense of the term'.[8] They were justified in demanding a separate homeland (Pakistan) to free themselves not only from the stranglehold of a permanent Hindu-majority government but also live according to their own, spiritual, cultural, economic, social and political ideals.

Jinnah's demand for Pakistan generated instant hope and expectations and revived the Muslims. It brought almost all social groups and classes of Muslim society, both traditional and modern, including the landlords, the educated, urban middle classes, merchant-industrialists, traders, bankers, professionals, students, women, and even *ulama*, together in a joint struggle for freedom and Pakistan.

Although the demand for Pakistan was to a large extent based on a normative appeal, promoting both nationalism and Islamic ideology, Jinnah also made concerted efforts to secure it in a more tangible shape by offering the educated urban middle classes, industrial and commercial classes, and the general mass of the idle Muslim youth, a structural alternative and a stake in the new state. The days of the old 'traditional' politics were gone, and the cry for Pakistan turned into a clarion 'call' of both traditional and modern groups.

Jinnah proceeded to transform this call into a charismatic movement[9] under the banner of the Muslim League. Insisting that the League alone represented the Muslims, Jinnah demanded the unity of the Muslim 'nation', and moved to 'expand' the League in a way that it could make room for all the newly mobilized groups and classes as well as the old traditional groups, like the landlords, *nawabs*, and titled gentry, already represented in the League. He followed up by concentrating power in the office of the President, and thus facilitated the 'routinization' of his personal charisma in the League. The League came to represent his charisma and his charismatic authority. The result was that the old recalcitrant provincial leadership of the Muslim-majority provinces found it difficult to defy the League. In the process, the League emerged as a single, national authority of the Muslims. The Muslim masses readily identified with the League and its cause. They worked for Pakistan with devotion. In addition, Jinnah took full advantage of the opportunities provided by the on-going Second World War to further promote the cause of Pakistan. Indeed, he made sure that the Muslims all over India were ready and willing to embrace Pakistan. The overwhelming victory of the League in the central and provincial assembly elections of 1945–46, over the issue of Pakistan, vindicated his claim that Pakistan was indeed the demand of Muslim India. It could not be denied, however, that even though the League came to be 'synonymous with Jinnah' in the 1940s,[10] the fact remained that 'the very name' of Jinnah worked 'miracles among the masses'.[11] He was their charismatic leader. The Muslims followed him whether or not they belonged to the League. They owed personal allegiance to him. They were convinced that he was the only man capable of realizing their demand for Pakistan.

The demand for Pakistan did not find favour with the British. The very idea of Pakistan violated the British claim of political unity in India, and thus inculcated 'a sense of defeat' in their minds.[12] Thus, Jinnah, had to tread a wary and difficult path in his negotiations with the British, especially after the war when they were free to concentrate their attention upon political developments in India, under the influence of the Labour Cabinet. Prime Minister Attlee and his colleagues were favourably inclined towards the Congress and seemed determined, with its support and cooperation, to preserve the unity of India. The Congress was already opposed to the 'vivisection' of India. The Cabinet Mission Plan, with its 'All-India Union', was one clear manifestation of this determination confronting Jinnah with the most difficult decision of his political life. This was a decision that could, in his own words, 'mar or make' their destiny.[13] Jinnah's extraordinary ability to grasp the realities of a given situation, and acting rationally ensured that he made the right decision by accepting the Cabinet Mission Plan rather than rejecting it offhand. But then, the British Government, in its eagerness to 'placate' the Congress, allowed the Congress leadership, including Gandhi and Nehru, to interpret and misinterpret the Plan at will. In particular, it allowed the Congress leadership to break the Group system, and thus wreck the Plan from within. The result was that Jinnah's demand for Pakistan emerged as the only viable alternative to the British–Congress concept of the future constitution of India. But it was not without long and strenuous efforts that Jinnah could make the British and the Congress ultimately concede his demand for Pakistan. The two, however, managed to deny him the entire provinces of the Punjab and Bengal, the two large Muslim-majority provinces. They had to be divided. Jinnah was not satisfied with the 'smaller' Pakistan, but, as a rational leader, he understood fully well that this was all he could get under the circumstances. He accepted the 3 June Plan as a 'compromise', and went on to complete his mission of Pakistan accordingly.

Jinnah succeeded in his mission because he offered a despaired people, at a particularly difficult and distressful hour in their history, a charismatic leadership, with an abiding faith in himself as well as the cause that he espoused. The various stages in the struggle for Pakistan clearly demonstrated 'the really decisive role that Jinnah played at various junctures and in its emergence'.[14] Indeed, if it were not for Jinnah, and his charismatic leadership, the struggle for Pakistan could well have been lost. But for him 'there was no Muslim leader who could have done it or even attempted it'.[15] And even if one were to assume for the sake of argument that it would have been attempted without Jinnah, it is still possible to conceive that a deal on the principle of Pakistan would have been made long before 1947, and an independent, sovereign Pakistan 'would never have come into being'.[16] Pakistan came into being because of the charisma and charismatic leadership of Jinnah.

Jinnah emerged as the charismatic leader of Indian Muslims in the crisis-ridden decade of 1937–47, when the traditional pattern of authority in Muslim India was no more. This was partly due to the efforts of the British to introduce Western representative institutions into India and partly due to the role of Syed Ahmad Khan, Maulana Mohammed Ali, and Allama Iqbal in reconciling the Muslims to the realities of 'the new order'.[17] However, soon the new system of government, with all the so-called safeguards, such as separate electorates, could not satisfy the Muslims. They felt inadequate, insecure and anxious. There was also a decline in the power and will of the British to maintain their rule in India by coercion in part due to the upsetting effects of the Second World War and the increasing loss of legitimacy in the eyes of Indian people. The process of devolution of British authority in India caused further apprehensions and fears among the Muslims as to their fate in a Hindu-dominated India. Thus, the necessary conditions that help to explain the emergence of a charismatic leader were present.

Jinnah was present too, endowed with all the 'extraordinary' personal qualities necessary in a charismatic leader, and willing and ready to lead the Muslims. Indeed, he was 'prepared to assume the role destiny had again thrust in his path'.[18] He was a sober, rational, and realistic person. He possessed in abundance the adeptness and flair for 'saying it like it really is', and finding viable formulas to deal with difficult situations. He had demonstrated this, again and again, through the Lucknow Pact, Delhi Muslim Proposals, and the Fourteen Points which represented the main Muslim interests at different points in time. In this sense, when he stepped into the distressful situation of Muslim India and offered the ultimate formula of a separate Muslim homeland in 1940, it was in the nature of 'an extension, perhaps a logical corollary, of his erstwhile role'[19] as a leader of the Muslims for more than three decades. One very significant reason why his opponents failed to 'match' his charisma was that they could not offer an alternative formula to his Pakistan. Coupled with his exceptional ability to develop new and better formulas was, of course, Jinnah's immense faith in himself and in his cause. However, in spite of all these charismatic qualities he had to wait until the difficult and daunting crises shook the Muslims, and made their lives untenable.

Jinnah's case indeed proved that charismatic leadership is a relationship, not an isolated phenomenon. Unless the conditions necessary for the emergence of a charismatic leader are ripe, the 'potential' leader, no matter how 'gifted', and how 'potent' his 'cause', remains 'without a following'.[20] There must be 'an eagerness to follow and obey' and strong 'dissatisfaction' with the present state of affairs before a charismatic leader can make his 'appearance'.[21] This also proves that charisma lies in the 'perceptions' of the followers.[22] The charismatic leader is a creation of his followers and his power to command allegiance and authority lies in the eyes of the followers he leads. The 'response' of the followers is 'the crucial test' of charisma.[23]

There is no doubt that Jinnah was able to inspire as well as to win the response of the Muslims as no one else had done before. The Muslims withdrew their allegiance from the present system of government in his favour, as was abundantly clear from the increasing support he received from them after asserting his demand for Pakistan.

He emerged as their *authority*, their system, their link between the discredited present and the yet uncertain future. The Muslims were convinced that he alone could lead them out of their predicament. Hence, they not only followed him enthusiastically, but also 'surrounded him with that spontaneous cult of personality' which is one of the 'symptomatic marks' of charismatic leadership.[24] They called him their *Quaid-i-Azam* (Great Leader).

This did not mean, of course, that all of them followed Jinnah or that he always received the 'absolute obedience' of his followers. There were quite a few who did not follow him, and they have been discussed at some length in the main narrative. The 'nationalist' Muslims were a prime example. Even among the followers, there were those who disagreed with his policies at times. The most prominent were the provincial leaders of the Muslim-majority provinces. But that was understandable and expected. As charismatic leaders tend very often 'to break with established ways of thinking and acting', there are bound to be occasions where their positions 'diverge' from those of their followers and consequently raise 'disturbing' questions in their minds.[25] What is 'specific' to the charismatic response is simply the fact that by virtue of his exceptional powers and qualities, the charismatic leader exercises a 'kind of domination' over his followers.[26] In this sense, one important manifestation of charisma seems to be 'the inspired way in which he conquers dissent by the sheer power of his political discourse'.[27] Jinnah's acceptance of the Cabinet Mission Plan proved the point.

Jinnah's case also proves that a charismatic leader tends to communicate to his followers a sense of being connected with 'their legendary heroes and their missions'.[28] Jinnah, along with Syed Ahmad Khan, Maulana Mohammed Ali and Allama Iqbal represented 'a watershed between the past and the present, and *the* bridge between them as well'.[29] This continuity of purpose and 'traditions' made it possible for the Muslims to respond to Jinnah's appeal as strongly and as massively as they did.[30] It also made possible that Jinnah's charismatic authority rested on a secure foundation.

In the growth of Jinnah's charismatic authority over his followers, one could clearly discern a steady pattern. From 1937 to 1940, Jinnah marshalled all available support in the cause of Muslim unity, offered his leadership to Muslim India, and indeed emerged as a charismatic leader. From March 1940, after the adoption of the Lahore Resolution, his 'formula' for the salvation of Indian Muslims, until the Simla Conference of June–July 1945, his charisma was validated and increasingly enhanced. His charisma reached new and unprecedented heights after the failure of the Simla Conference and particularly after the rejection of the Cabinet Mission Plan of 1946, the last opportunity to keep India united. The Muslims flocked to Jinnah like never before. They demanded Pakistan. In August 1947, with the creation of Pakistan eventually, Jinnah's charisma was at its 'zenith'. Indeed, in the opinion of one writer who in a way summed up Jinnah's charismatic power, the 'great mystery' was not that Jinnah possessed 'so much power', but that he 'had not been corrupted by such excessive power'.[31]

Before we conclude our evaluation of the concept of charisma and its application to the case of Jinnah, it would not be inappropriate here to compare Jinnah with some other charismatic leaders that have been studied systematically. It will help develop a comparative perspective for a better understanding of the concept of charisma and charismatic leadership.

Jinnah seems to be quite close to Mustafa Kemal Ataturk in many ways.[32] Jinnah, like Ataturk, was primarily an 'elitist' who eventually went on to arouse a 'popular response' in his later career.[33] One reason why Jinnah could not win the following of Muslim India in his early political career, in spite of 'his earnestness, devotion and statesmanship',[34] was his involvement with the elitist politics of India. But after he switched to a popular role, he showed 'remarkable qualities of mass leadership'.[35] It surprised both his friends and foes. Jinnah, like Ataturk, was committed to 'legality'[36] and to building a consensus that was inclusive in nature. Like Ataturk, who mobilized the Anatolian *ulama*,[37] Jinnah sought the support of Indian *ulama* and other traditional groups while building up an inclusive Muslim solidarity. Jinnah remained devoted to constitutional and legal methods throughout his political career to make the most of what the constitutional reforms in India had to offer, while demanding more and more reforms, except from 1946 to 1947, when he was left with no option but to encourage 'civil disobedience' movements in the Punjab and the NWFP. However, even then, Jinnah did not mean to do away with his constitutional struggle. The idea was merely to supplement it with extra-constitutional means to help push the cause of Pakistan in the final, crucial years.

Jinnah, like Ataturk, remained 'notably diffident about the personal, charismatic basis of his power'.[38] In spite of the fact that a vast majority of the Muslims regarded him as their saviour and followed him faithfully, Jinnah always endeavoured that the opinion of the Muslim League Working Committee or the League Council, if it related to a more important issue, was ascertained before he could make up his own mind.[39] He remained scrupulously committed to this practice throughout the charismatic period,[40] especially from the day he demanded Pakistan in March 1940 to its creation in August 1947. This explained why Jinnah rejected the offer of the life-Presidentship of the League, and insisted on seeking a vote of confidence from members of the League every year during this period. This also explained why Jinnah, much to the chagrin of Viceroy Mountbatten, refused to commit to the 3 June 1947 Partition Plan without the agreement of the League Council.

Jinnah, like Ataturk, showed that his 'tactical instinct continued to be unerring'.[41] He defined his goal in a way that it would 'veil its novelty and preserve his freedom of action' in seeking its realization.[42] He only fixed the long-range goal of 'Pakistan', but to secure it in concrete form he dealt firmly with every situation as it developed, and indeed, showed an extraordinary capacity to seize every 'unprecedented' situation.[43]

Jinnah shared with Kwame Nkrumah, another charismatic leader, his skill as a brilliant legislator but also the 'immediate political context' of his rise to power.[44] Representative system of government in India, as in the case of Nkrumah in Ghana, provided Jinnah the means to create Pakistan. However, whereas Nkrumah was also committed to the system of government itself, with Jinnah, it was 'not an ideal but only an instrument' through which he was trying to achieve his 'major objective'.[45] The British system of government introduced into India was inherently biased in favour of Hindu majority community. It was not able to respond to and satisfy the Muslim interests, and thus, had little appeal for Jinnah.

Jinnah, like Nkrumah, also touched upon 'a wide range of grievances' of his followers.[46] The result was that the Muslim League, like the Convention People's Party of Nkrumah, appeared to be 'a "movement" rather than an effectively organized party'.[47] It showed a 'loose and diverse following' comprising almost all groups of the Muslim society joined with 'a charismatic nucleus' of devoted followers.[48]

Jinnah, like Vladimir Lenin,[49] another charismatic leader of a very different type, possessed the element of being 'a party man', of being 'sustained by, and developed within, the party'.[50] Whether it was the Congress, the Muslim League, or the Home Rule League for a while, Jinnah was always a member of a political organization. In his scheme of things, 'politics without the party' was not conceivable.[51] Jinnah, like Lenin, also had tremendous faith in his own exceptional powers, and thus like Lenin 'forced' in no small way 'the flow of events'[52] to change the political destiny of Indian Muslims. Had Jinnah been assassinated in 1943 (attempt on his life), or died in 1944 or 1946, when he was reportedly seriously ill, the probability of Muslim Leaguers opting for a coalition government with the Congress or conceding the Pakistan demand cannot be ruled out.[53] Jinnah alone could force the goal of Pakistan. He was 'Gandhi, Nehru, Patel and V.P. Menon rolled into one man'.[54] He possessed 'the iron will, daring and vision',[55] along with the rare ability to exploit to his own benefit the 'lack of purpose and coordination between his antagonists'.[56]

However, what made Jinnah's task difficult was the fact that he had to deal with his antagonists all at the same time. He had to contend with Congress leadership, which was bent upon denying the Muslims 'the spoils of the real power'.[57] He had to challenge the nationalist Muslims, who were opposed to the demand for Pakistan. He had to confront the British rulers, who always had 'innate, traditional disapproval of recalcitrant minorities',[58] and disapproved his Pakistan. To make things more difficult for him, there was no Muslim 'nation', to begin with. He had to create a Muslim nation before he could create the nation-state of Pakistan.

In the end, Jinnah was not only a founder of a state like Ataturk or an architect of a political movement like Nkrumah or a proponent of change like Lenin, but he was also the maker of a nation, the Muslim nation of India (and Pakistan). This Muslim nation recognized him as a charismatic leader, revered him as the *Quaid-i-Azam*, and indeed nominated him to the highest office of the Governor-General of Pakistan. He remained the Governor-General from 15 August 1947 to 11 September 1948, the day he breathed his last. How his personal charisma influenced and affected the institutional office of the Governor-General is an interesting subject for exploration. It is interesting not only for its own sake but also for a greater understanding of the problems of 'routinization' of charisma, an often ignored area of research in political leadership. But then, it is beyond the scope of the present study.

Notes

1. Waheed-uz-Zaman, *Towards Pakistan*, 206.
2. Sherwani, *Speeches, Writings and Statements*, 3, 23.
3. Ibid., 25.
4. Mansergh, *Transfer of Power*, Vol. IV, 203.
5. Ahmad, *Speeches and Writings*, Vol. I, 95.
6. Mujahid, *Studies in Interpretation*, 328-9.
7. Ahmad, *Speeches and Writings*, Vol. I, 147-8. Thus, Jinnah's formula of Pakistan 'formulated the tradition of succeeding generations of Indo-Muslim resistance to the concentration of power in non-Muslim hands.' Aziz Ahmad, *Studies in Islamic Culture*, 208.
8. Paul Brass, 'Elite Groups, Symbol Manipulation and Ethnic Identity among the Muslims of South Asia', in David Taylor and Malcolm Yapp, eds., *Political Identity in South Asia* (London: Curzon Press, 1979), 61.
9. Peter Hardy described it as a 'chiliastic movement'. Hardy, *Muslims of British India*, 239.
10. Saleem Qureshi, 'The Consolidation of Leadership in Last Phase of the Politics of the All-India Muslim League', 298.
11. Ravoof, *Meet Mr Jinnah*, 170.
12. Brailsford, *Subject India*, 111.
13. Ispahani, *As I Knew Him*, 200.
14. Mujahid, *Studies in Interpretation*, 371.
15. Penderel Moon, 'Jinnah's Changing Attitude to the Idea of Pakistan', in Dani, *World Scholars*, 289.
16. Altaf Hussain, 'Memories of the Quaid-i-Azam', in Jamil-ud-Din Ahmad, *Quaid-i-Azam as Seen by His Contemporaries*, 73.
17. Hamid, *On Understanding the Quaid-i-Azam*, 71.
18. Lawrence Ziring, *Pakistan: At the Crosscurrents of History* (Lahore: Vanguard, 2004), 16.
19. Mujahid, *Studies in Interpretation*, 39.
20. Hoffer, *True Believer*, 103.
21. Ibid.
22. Willners, 'The Rise and Role of Charismatic Leaders', 79.
23. Tucker, 'The Theory of Charismatic Leadership', 737.
24. Ibid., 747.
25. Ibid., 736.
26. Ibid.
27. Ibid. Jinnah allowed 'free and full discussion' in the League meetings and indeed 'respected' those who held their views honestly and responsibly. In the end, however, they, more or less always, accepted his viewpoint. This even included those leaders of the League who held administrative positions, and hence power and prestige associated with their positions. The case of Muslim premiers of Muslim-majority provinces illustrates the point.
28. Willners, 'The Rise and Role of Charismatic Leaders', 83.
29. Mujahid, *Studies in Interpretation*, 359. (Italics original).

30. According to Willners, a charismatic leader's appeal was 'limited to those who share the traditions of a given culture.' Willners, 'The Rise and Role of Charismatic Leaders', 84.

31. Sayeed, *Formative Phase*, 196.

32. Bolitho, his biographer, in his account of one morning in November 1932, took note of his reading of H.C. Armstrong's *Grey Wolf* and wondered how much Ataturk might have inspired Jinnah in his political life. This happened to be the time that Jinnah was in self-imposed exile in London and pondering over the situation of Muslim India. Bolitho, *Jinnah: Creator of Pakistan*, 102-3. It needs to be stressed, however, that Armstrong's account was highly controversial. Although he 'grudgingly acknowledges Mustafa Kamal's' manifold qualities he goes too far in parading the Turk's personal shortcomings.' For details see, M. Naeem Qureshi, 'Ataturk and Armstrong's *Grey Wolf: Myth and Reality.' The Fifth International Congress on Ataturk*, 8-12 December 2003, Ankara, Vol. II (2005), 985.

33. Rustow, 'Ataturk as Founder of a State', 807.

34. A leader of the Muslim League. Cited in Sayeed, *Formative Phase*, 178.

35. Mujahid, *Studies in Interpretation*, 41.

36. Rustow, 'Ataturk as Founder of a State', 810.

37. For details see Kinross, *Ataturk*, esp., 231-40, 330-40, and 354-64.

38. Rustow, 'Ataturk as Founder of a State', 796.

39. Mujahid, *Studies in Interpretation*, 122.

40. Ibid., 124-5.

41. Rustow, 'Ataturk as Founder of a State', 813.

42. Ibid., 803.

43. Tucker, 'Personality and Political Leadership', 386

44. Apter, 'Nkrumah, Charisma, and the Coup', 758.

45. Sayeed, *Formative Phase*, 212.

46. Apter, 'Nkrumah, Charisma, and the Coup', 767.

47. Ibid., 768.

48. Ibid.

49. For more on Russian and Soviet history with reference to Lenin see, Nicholas V. Riasanovsky, *A History of Russia* (New York: Oxford University Press, 1977), 515–44.

50. Mujahid, *Studies in Interpretation*, 375.

51. Ibid.

52. Hoffer, *True Believer*, 104. According to A.N. Potresov, 'only Lenin represented that rare phenomena, especially rare in Russia, of a man of iron will and indomitable energy who combines fanatical faith in the movement, the cause, with no less faith in himself'. Cited in Tucker, 'The Theory of Charismatic Leadership', 742.

53. Mujahid, *Studies in Interpretation*, 403.

54. Z.H. Zaidi, *Jinnah Papers*, Vol. I, Part I, xxviii.

55. Hoffer, *True Believer*, 104.

56. Rustow, 'Ataturk as Founder of a State', 796. Stephen Cohen, in a recent study, described Jinnah as a 'brilliant political strategist and speaker, he was Pakistan's Tom Paine and George Washington'. Stephen Philip Cohen, *The Idea of Pakistan* (Lahore: Vanguard, 2005), 28.

57. Wolpert, *India*, 147.

58. K.K. Aziz, *Britain and Muslim India* (London: William Heinmann, 1963), 21.

Bibliography

PRIMARY SOURCES

Unpublished

National Archives of Pakistan, Islamabad

Quaid-i-Azam Papers. Papers of (Quaid-i-Azam) Mohammad Ali Jinnah.
Syed Shamsul Hasan Collection. Papers of Mohammad Ali Jinnah and the All-India Muslim League (AIML) maintained by Syed Shamsul Hasan, Asst. Secretary, AIML.
Lakha Collection. Newspaper and periodical clippings maintained by Ahmed Hamid Lakha.

Archives of the Freedom Movement, Karachi/Islamabad
Records of the AIML, including records of meetings, resolutions, official pronouncements, policy decisions and important correspondence.

Published

Official Publications

British Government

United Kingdom. *Report of the Indian Statutory Commission, Simon Commission Report*, Vols. 1–2. London: HM's Stationery Office, 1930.
United Kingdom. Proceedings of the Indian Round Table Conference, First Session, 12 November–19 January 1931. London: HM's Stationery Office, 1931.
————. Second Session, 7 September 1931–1 December 1931. London: HM's Stationery Office, 1932.
————. Third Session, 17 November–24 December 1932. London: HM's Stationery Office, 1933.
*Joint Committee on Indian Constitutional Reform, Session 1933-34,*Vol. 1, Part I. London: HM's Stationery Office, 1934.
Mansergh, N., and Lumbey, E.W.R./Penderel Moon, eds. *Constitutional Relations Between Britain and India: The Transfer of Power 1942-47.* Vols. I–XII. London: HM's Stationery Office, 1970–83.

Government of Pakistan

Khan, Saleemullah, comp. *The Journey to Pakistan: A Documentation on [the] Refugees of 1947.* Islamabad: National Documentation Centre, 1993.

————, comp. *The Referendum in [the] NWFP, 1947*. Islamabad: National Documentation Centre, 1996.

Zaidi, Z.H., ed. *Quaid-i-Azam Mohammad Ali Jinnah Papers*. Vols. I-XII. Islamabad: National Archives of Pakistan, 1993-2005.

Government of India

M.K. Gandhi, *The Collected Works of Mahatma Gandhi*. Vols. I-LXXXIX. New Delhi: The Publications Division, Ministry of Information and Broadcasting, Government of India, 1964-1983.

Government of the United States of America

US Department of State. *Foreign Relations of the United States, 1947*, Vol. III, *The British Commonwealth; Europe*. Washington: United States Government Printing Office, 1972.

All-India Muslim League

The Constitution and Rules of the All-India Muslim League. Published by Liaquat Ali Khan, Honorary Secretary, All-India Muslim League. Delhi: All-India Muslim League, April 1940

The Constitution and Rules of the All-India Muslim League. Published by Liaquat Ali Khan, Honorary Secretary. All-India Muslim League. Delhi: All-India Muslim League, 1944.

Khan, Liaquat Ali, comp. *Resolutions of the All-India Muslim League from May 1924 to December 1936*. Delhi: All-India Muslim League, n.d.

————, comp. *Resolutions of the All-India Muslim League from October 1937 to December 1938*. Delhi: All-India Muslim League, n.d.

————, comp. *Resolutions of the All-India Muslim League from December 1938 to March 1940*. Delhi: All-India Muslim League, n.d.

————, comp. *Resolutions of the All-India Muslim League from December 1940 to March 1941*. Delhi: All-India Muslim League, n.d.

————, comp. *Resolutions of the All-India Muslim League from April 1942 to May [December] 1943*. Delhi: All-India Muslim League, n.d.

————, comp. *Resolutions of the All-India Muslim League from January 1944 to December 1946*. Delhi: All-India Muslim League, n.d.

Indian National Congress

Sitaramayya, B. Pattabhi. *The History of the Indian National Congress, 1885-1935*. Madras: Working Committee of the Congress, 1935.

Documents, Letters, Speeches and Statements

Afzal, M. Rafique, ed. The *Case for Pakistan*. Islamabad: National Commission on Historical and Cultural Research, 1979.

————, ed. *Guftar-i-Iqbal*. Lahore: Research Society of Pakistan, 1969.

_____, ed. *Selected Speeches and Statements of the Quaid-i-Azam Mohammad Ali Jinnah, 1911-34 and 1947-48.* Lahore: Research Society of Pakistan, 1976.

Ahmad, Jamil-ud-Din, ed. *Speeches and Writings of Mr Jinnah.* 2 Vols. Lahore: Sh. Muhammad Ashraf, 1968, 1976.

Ahmad, Rizwan, ed. *The Quaid-i-Azam Papers, 1940.* Karachi: East and West Publishing Co., 1976.

Ahmad, Waheed, ed. *Jinnah-Irwin Correspondence, 1927-30.* Lahore: Research Society of Pakistan, 1969.

_____, ed. *Letters of Mian Fazl-i-Husain.* Lahore: Research Society of Pakistan, 1976.

_____, ed. *The Nation's Voice.* Vols. I-VII. Karachi: Quaid-i-Azam Academy, 1992-2003.

_____, ed. *Quaid-i-Azam Mohammad Ali Jinnah Speeches: Indian Legislative Assembly, 1935-1947.* Karachi: Quaid-i-Azam Academy, 1991.

Allana, G., ed. *Pakistan Movement: Historic Documents.* Lahore: Islamic Book Service, 1977.

Azad, Abul Kalam. *Mazameen-i-Azad.* (Urdu). Lahore: Daata Publishers, 1978.

Aziz, K.K., ed. *The All-India Muslim Conference, 1928-1935: A Documentary Record.* Karachi: National Publishing House, 1972.

_____, ed. *Complete Works of Rahmat Ali.* Islamabad: National Commission on Historical and Cultural Research, 1978.

_____, ed. *The Indian Khilafat Movement, 1915-1933: A Documentary Record.* Karachi: National Publishing House, 1972.

_____, ed. *Muslims Under Congress Rule, 1937-39: A Documentary Record*, Vol. I. Islamabad: National Commission on Historical and Cultural Research, 1978.

_____, ed. *Prelude to Pakistan, 1930-1940: Documents and Readings Illustrating the Growth of the Idea of Pakistan*, Vol. I. Lahore: Vanguard, 1992.

Banerjee, A.C., ed. *Indian Constitutional Documents.* Calcutta: A. Mukherjee, 1946.

de Barry, William Theodore, ed. *Sources of Indian Tradition.* New York: Columbia University Press, 1958.

Bose, Sisir Kumar, ed. *I warned my Countrymen: Works of Sarat Chandra Bose, 1945-50.* Calcutta: Netaji Research Bureau, 1996.

Char, S.V. Desika, ed. *Readings in the Constitutional History of India, 1757-1947.* Delhi: Oxford University Press, 1983.

Dobbin, Christine, ed. *Basic Documents in the Development of Modern India and Pakistan.* London: Van Nostrand Reinhold Co., 1970.

Gopal S., ed. *Selected Works of Nehru.* Vols. VII-XI. New Delhi: Orient Longman, 1976-78.

Gwyer, Maurice and Appadorai, A., eds. *Speeches and Documents on the Indian Constitution, 1921-1947,* Vol. II. Bombay: Oxford University Press, 1957.

Hasan, Mushirul, ed. *Mohamed Ali in Indian Politics: Selected Writings.* Delhi: Atlantic Publishers, 1982.

Iqbal, Afzal, ed. *Selected Writings and Speeches of Maulana Mohamed Ali.* 2 Vols. Lahore: Sh. Muhammad Ashraf, 1969.

Jafar, Malik Muhammad, ed. *Jinnah as a Parliamentarian.* Lahore: Afzar Publications, 1977.

Jafri, S. Qasim Hussain, ed. *Quaid-i-Azam's Correspondence with Punjab Muslim Leaders.* Lahore: Aziz Publishers, 1977.

Jafari, Syed Rais Ahmad, ed. *Nigarishat – Mohammad Ali.* (Urdu). Hyderabad Deccan: Razzaqui Machine Press, 1944.

———. ed. *Selections from Maulana Mohammad Ali's Comrade.* Lahore: Mohammad Ali Academy, 1965.

Khan, Syed Ahmad. *The Present State of Indian Politics: Speeches and Letters.* Edited by Farman Fatehpuri. Lahore: Sang-e-Meel Publications, 1982.

Letters of Iqbal to Jinnah. Lahore: Sh. Muhammad Ashraf, 1968. Preface by M.A. Jinnah.

Loewenheim, Francis L., Harold D. Langley, and Manfred Jonas, eds. *Roosevelt and Churchill: Their Secret Wartime Correspondence.* New York: E.P. Dutton, 1975.

Long, Roger D., ed. *Dear Mr Jinnah: Selected Correspondence and Speeches of Liaquat Ali Khan.* Karachi: Oxford University Press, 2004.

Madani, Husain Ahmad. *Maktubat-i-Sheikh-ul-Islam.* (Urdu). Deoband: Maktaba-e-Diniya, 1956.

Malik, Hafeez, ed. *Political Profile of Sayyid Ahmad Khan: A Documentary Record.* Islamabad: National Institute of Historical and Cultural Research, 1982.

Mirza, Sarfraz Hussain, ed. *The Punjab Muslim Students Federation: An Annotated Documentary Survey, 1937-47.* Lahore: Research Society of Pakistan, 1978.

Nizami, Khalique Ahmad, ed. *Shah Waliullah Kay Siyasi Maktubat.* (Urdu). Aligarh: Muslim University Press, 1950.

Pandey, B.N., ed. *The Indian Nationalist Movement 1885-1947: Select Documents.* London: Macmillan, 1979.

Panipati, Muhammad Ismail, ed. *Maqalat-i-Sir Syed.* (Urdu). Lahore: Majlis-i-tarraqi-i-Adab, 1962.

Philips, C.H., ed. *The Evolution of India and Pakistan, 1858-1947: Select Documents.* London: The English Language Book Society and Oxford University Press, 1965.

Pirzada, Syed Sharifuddin, ed. *Foundations of Pakistan: All India Muslim League Documents: 1906-1947.* 2 Vols. Karachi: National Publishing House, 1969, 1970.

———, ed. *Quaid-i-Azam Jinnah's Correspondence.* Karachi: East and West Publishing Company, 1977.

———, ed. *The Collected Works of Quaid-i-Azam Mohammad Ali Jinnah.* Karachi: East and West Publishing Co., 1984.

Rozina, Parveen, ed. *Jamiat-ul-Ulama-i-Hind: Dastawezat Markazi Ijlasha-i-Aam, 1919-1945,* Vol. II. (Urdu). Islamabad: National Institute of Historical and Cultural Research, 1981.

Sherwani, Latif Ahmad, ed. *Pakistan Resolution to Pakistan, 1940-1947: A Selection of Documents Presenting the Case for Pakistan.* Karachi: National Publishing House, 1969.

———, ed. *Speeches, Writings and Statements of Iqbal.* Lahore: Iqbal Academy, 1977.

Usmani, Allama Shabbir Ahmad. *Khutbat-i-Usmani.* (Urdu). Compiled by Mohammad Anwar Hasan Sherkoti. Lahore: Nazir Sons, 1972.

Zaidi, A.M., ed. *Evolution of Muslim Political Thought.* Vols. I-VI. Delhi: S. Chand & Co., 1975-79.

Autobiographies, Memoirs and Diaries

Ahmad, Jamil-ud-Din. 'A Disciple Remembers'. In Jamil-ud-Din Ahmad, ed., *Quaid-i-Azam As Seen by His Contemporaries*. Lahore: Publishers United, 1976.

——. *Glimpses of Quaid-i-Azam*. Karachi: Educational Press, 1960.

Ahmad, Waheed, ed. *Diary and Notes of Mian Fazl-i-Hussain*. Lahore: Research Society of Pakistan 1977.

Ali, Choudhri Muhammad. *The Emergence of Pakistan*. Lahore: Research Society of Pakistan, 1973.

Ali, Mohamed. *My Life: A Fragment*. Edited by Afzal Iqbal. Lahore: Sh. Muhammad Ashraf, 1966.

Azad, Abul Kalam. *India Wins Freedom*. New Delhi: Orient Longmans, 1988.

——. *Tehrik Nazm-i-Jamaat*. (Urdu). Lahore: Nazir Sons, 1977.

Bakhsh, Ilahi. *With the Quaid-i-Azam During His Last Days*. Karachi: Quaid-i-Azam Academy, 1978. Reprint.

Batalvi, A.H., ed. *The Forgotten Years: Memoirs of Sir Muhammad Zafrullah Khan*. Lahore: Vanguard, 1991.

Birla, G.D. *In the Shadow of the Mahatma: A Personal Memoir*. Bombay: Orient Longmans, 1955.

Cambell-Johnson, Alan. *Mission with Mountbatten*. London: Robert Hale, 1951.

Choudhuri, Nirad C. *The Autobiography of an Unknown Indian*. London: Macmillan, 1951.

Fraser, Andrew. *Among Indian Rajas and Ryots*. Philadelphia: J.B. Lippincott, 1912.

Fuller, Bamfylde. *Some Personal Experiences*. London: John Murray, 1930.

Gandhi, Mohandas Karamchand. *An Autobiography or the Story of my Experiment with Truth*. Ahmedabad: Navajivan Publishing House, 1945.

Hussain, Altaf. 'Memories of the Quaid-i-Azam.' In Jamil-ud-Din Ahmad, ed., *Quaid-i-Azam as seen by his Contemporaries*.

Ismay, Lord. *The Memoirs of General the Lord Ismay*. London: Heinemann, 1960.

Ispahani, M.A.H. *Quaid-i-Azam Jinnah As I knew Him*. Karachi: Forward Publications Trust, 1966.

Jayakar, M.R. *The Story of My Life, 1873-1922*. Bombay: Asia Publishing House, 1958.

Jinnah, Fatima. *My Brother*. Karachi: Quaid-i-Azam Academy, 1987.

Khaliquzzaman, Chaudhary. *Pathway to Pakistan*. Lahore: Longman, 1961.

Khan, Aga. *The Memoirs of Aga Khan: World Enough and Time*. New York: Cassel and Co., 1954.

Khan, Syed Ahmad. *The Causes of the Indian Revolt*. Translated by his two European Friends. Lahore: n.p., n.d., reprint.

Madani, Husain Ahmad. *Naqsh-i-Hayat*. 2 Vols. (Urdu). Deoband: Maktaba-i-Diniya, 1954.

Mary, Countess of Minto. *India: Minto and Morley, 1905-10*. London: Macmillan, 1934.

Menon, K.F.S. *Many Worlds: An Autobiography*. London: Oxford University Press, 1965.

Montague, Edwin S. *An Indian Diary*. London: William Heinemann, 1930.

Moraes, Frank. *Witness to an Era: India 1920 to the Present Day.* London: Weidenfeld & Nicolson, 1973.

Nehru, Jawaharlal. *An Autobiography.* London: Bodley Head, 1958.

Noon, Feroz Khan. *From Memory.* Lahore: Feroz Sons, 1969.

O'Dwyer, Michael. *India As I Knew It, 1885-1925.* London: Constable, 1925.

Pandit, Vijay Lakshami. *The Scope of Happiness: A Personal Memoir.* London: Weidenfeld and Nicolson, 1979.

Prasad, Rajendra. *India Divided.* Bombay: Hind Kitab, 1977.

Rabbani, Mian Ata. *I was the Quaid's ADC.* Karachi: Oxford University Press, 1996.

Shahnawaz, Jahan Ara. *Father and Daughter.* Karachi: Oxford University Press, 2002, Lahore: Nigarishat, 1971.

Sindhi, Maulana Ubaidullah. *Maulana Ubaidullah Sindhi ki Sargarzesht-i-Kabul.* (Urdu). Edited by Ghulam Mustafa Khan. Islamabad: National Institute of Historical and Cultural Research, 1980.

Tucker, Francis. *While Memory Serves.* London: Cassell, 1950

Wavell, Archibald. *Wavell: The Viceroy's Journal.* Edited by Penderel Moon. Karachi: Oxford University Press, 1974.

Williams, Francis. *A Prime Minister Remembers: The War and the Post War Memoirs of the Rt. Hon. Earl Attlee.* London' William Henineman, 1961.

Zetland, Marquess of. 'Essayez.' *The Memoirs of Lawrence, Second Marquess of Zetland.* London: John Murray, 1956.

SECONDARY SOURCES

Biographies, Books, Chapters and Articles

Abbasi, M. Yusuf. 'Syed Ameer Ali: Pioneer of Muslim Politics', *Journal of Pakistan Studies,* Vol. II (1980).

———. 'Quaid-i-Azam's Rapport with Common Man'. In Ahmad Hasan Dani, ed., *Quaid-i-Azam and Pakistan.* Islamabad: Quaid-i-Azam University, 1981.

———. 'Sir Syed Ahmad Khan and the Re-awakening of the Muslims', *Journal of Pakistan Studies,* Vol. II (1980).

Abid, Mussarat. 'Quaid-i-Azam and Mountbatten: Nature of Relationship,' *Journal of the Research Society of Pakistan,* Vol. XXXVI. No. 2 (1999).

Abid, S. Qalb-i. *Jinnah,* [The] *Second World War and the Pakistan Movement.* Multan: Nubahar Press, 1999.

Afzal, M. Rafique. 'A Glimpse of the Life and Thoughts of Maulana Ubaidullah Sindhi,' *Journal of Research Society of Pakistan,* Vol. XII, No. 4 (1975).

———. 'The Governor Generalship Issue and the Quaid-i-Azam: Mountbatten's Version and the Real Story,' *South Asia* (January 1986).

———. *Pakistan's History and Politics, 1947-1971.* Karachi: Oxford University Press, 2001.

———. 'Quaid-i-Azam Muhammad Ali Jinnah and the Home Rule Movement,' *Journal of Research Society of Pakistan,* Vol. XX, No. 1 (1983).

Ahmad, Aziz. *Islamic Modernism in India and Pakistan.* London: Oxford University Press, 1967.

————. *Studies in Islamic Culture in the Indian Environment.* Oxford: Clarendon Press, 1964.

Ahmad, Chaudhary Habib. *Tehrik-i-Pakistan aur Nationalist Ulama.* (Urdu). Lahore: al Biyan, 1966.

Ahmad, Jamil-ud-Din. *Creation of Pakistan.* Lahore: Publishers United, 1976.

————. 'The Congress in Office (1937-39)'. *In A History of the Freedom Movement,* Vol. IV. Parts I & II. Karachi: Pakistan Historical Society, 1970.

Ahmad, Muhammad Saleem. *The All-India Muslim League: A History of the Growth and Consolidation of Political Organization.* Bhawalpur: Ilham Publishers, 1988.

————. 'Iqbal and Politics - Part I', *Pakistan Studies,* Vol. II, No.3 (Winter 1983/84)

————. 'Iqbal and Politics - Part 2' *Pakistan Studies,* Vol. II, No. 4 (Summer 1984).

Ahmad, Mujeeb. *Jam'iyyat 'Ulema-i-Pakistan, 1948-1979.* Islamabad: National Institute of Historical and Cultural Research, 1993.

Ahmad, Riaz, ed. *Pakistani Scholars on Quaid-i-Azam Mohammad Ali Jinnah.* Islamabad: National Institute of Historical and Cultural Research, 1999.

————. *Quaid-i-Azam Mohammad Ali Jinnah: The Formative years, 1892-1920.* Islamabad: National Institute of Historical and Cultural Research, 1986.

Ahmad, Rizwan. *Quaid-i-Azam: Ibtidai Tees Saal.* (Urdu). Karachi: n.p., 1977.

Ahmad, Saeed. 'Iqbal's Concept of an Islamic State'. In Mohammad Maruf, ed., *Contributions to Iqbal's Thought.* Lahore: Islamic Book Service, 1977.

Ahmad, Waheed. 'The General Elections of 1945-1946: Quaid-i-Azam's Springboard to Pakistan,' *Pakistan Journal of History and Culture,* Vol. XXII, No. 2 (July-December 2001).

————. *Road to Indian Freedom: The Formation of the Government of India Act 1935.* Lahore: Caravan Book House, 1979.

Ahmad, Zaiuddin, ed. *Mohammad Ali Jinnah: Founder of Pakistan.* Karachi: Ministry of Information and Broadcasting, 1967.

Ahmed, Akbar S. *Jinnah, Pakistan and Islamic Identity: The Search for Saladin.* Karachi: Oxford University Press, 1997.

Ahsan, Aitzaz. *The Indus Saga and the Making of Pakistan.* Karachi: Oxford University Press, 1996.

Ali, Mahmud. *Quaid-i-Azam As a Constitutionalist.* Islamabad: National Committee for Birth Centenary Celebrations of Quaid-i-Azam Mohammad Ali Jinnah, 1986.

Ali, Parveen Shaukat. *The Political Philosophy of Iqbal.* Lahore: Publishers United, 1978.

Allana, G. *Quaid-i-Azam Jinnah: The Story of a Nation.* Lahore: Ferozsons, 1967.

Ambedkar, B.R. *Pakistan or the Partition of India.* Bombay: Thacker & Co., 1946.

Apter, David E. 'Nkrumah, Charisma, and the Coup', *Daedalus,* Vol. 97, No. 3 (1969).

Aziz, Javed. *Quaid-i-Azam Aur Sarhad.* (Urdu). Peshawar: Idara-i-Tehqiq-o-Tasneef, 1977.

Aziz, K.K. *Britain and Muslim India.* London: William Heinmann, 1963.

————. *The Making of Pakistan.* London: Chatto & Windus, 1967.

————. *Public Life in Muslim India, 1850-1947.* Lahore: Vanguard, 1992.

Bahadur, Lal. *The Muslim League History.* Lahore: Book Traders, 1979.

Baker, Christopher, Gordon Johnson, and Anil Seal, eds. *Power, Profit and Politics.* Cambridge: Cambridge University Press, 1981.

Bakhsi, S.R. *Congress, Muslim League and Partition of India*. New Delhi: Deep & Deep Publications, 1991.

Banerjee, Surendernath. *A Nation in Making*. London: Humphrey Milford, 1925.

Batalvi, Ashiq Hussain. *Chand Yadain, Chand Taasurat*. (Urdu). Lahore: Sang-i-Meel, 1992.

_____. *Hamari Qaumi Jidd-o-Juhd*. (Urdu). Lahore: Altaf Husain, 1968.

_____. *Iqbal kay Akhri Do Saal*. (Urdu). Karachi: Iqbal Academy, 1961.

Baxter, Craig. 'Union or Partition: Some Aspects of Politics in the Punjab, 1936-45'. In Lawrence Ziring, Ralph Braibanti, and W. Howard Wriggins, eds., *Pakistan: The Long View*. Durham: Duke University Press, 1977.

Bayly, C.A. *The Birth of the Modern World: 1780-1914*. Oxford: Blackwell Publishing, 2004.

Beg, Aziz. *Jinnah and His Times*. Islamabad: Babur and Amer Publishers, 1986.

_____. *Quaid-i-Azam Centenary Bouquet*. Islamabad: Baber and Amer Publications, 1977.

Benda, Harry J. 'Non-Western Intelligentsia as Political Elites', *Australian Journal of Politics and History*, Vol. VI, No. 2 (1960).

Bendix, Reinhard. *Max Weber: An Intellectual Portrait*. New York: Doubleday & Co. 1960.

Berger, Morroe, ed. *Freedom and Control in Modern Society*. New York: D. van Nostrand, 1954.

Besant, Annie. *The Future of Indian Politics*. London: Theosophical Publishing House, 1922.

_____. *How India Fought for Freedom: The Story of the National Congress told from Official Records*. Madras: Theosophical Publishing House, 1915.

Bhatnagar, S.K. *History of the M.A.O. College, Aligarh*. Lahore: n.p., n.d., reprint.

Bhattacharya, France. 'East Bengal: Between Islam and a Regional Identity'. In Christophe Jaffrelot, ed., *A History of Pakistan and its Origins*. London: Anthem Press, 2002.

Birnbaum, Pierre. *The Idea of France*. Translated by M.B. DeBevoise. New York: Hill and Wang, 2001.

Bloomfield, Maurice. *The Religion of the Veda*. New York: Putnam's, 1908.

Bokhari, Syed Attaullah Shah. *Hayat-i-Amir-i-Shariat*. (Urdu). Lahore: Maktaba Tabsara, 1970.

Bolitho, Hector. *Jinnah: Creator of Pakistan*. Karachi: Oxford University Press, 1964.

Bonney, Richard. 'Three Giants of South Asia: Gandhi, Ambedkar, and Jinnah on Self-Determination', South Asia History Academic Paper 5. Leicester: University of Leicester, 2002.

Bose, Sugata and Ayesha Jalal. *Modern South Asia: History, Culture and Political Economy*. Lahore: Sang-e-Meel, 1998.

Brailsford, H.N. *Subject India*. Bombay: Vora & Co., 1946.

Brass, Paul R. 'Elite Groups, Symbol Manipulation and Ethnic Identity among the Muslims of South Asia'. In David Taylor and Malcom Yapp, eds., *Political Identity in South Asia*. London: Curzon Press, 1979.

_____. *Language, Religion and Politics in North India*. Cambridge: Cambridge University Press, 1974.

Brecher, Michael. *Nehru: A Political Biography*. Boston: Beacon Press, abridged edn., 1962.

Brown, Judith M. *Gandhi and Civil Disobedience: The Mahatma in Indian Politics, 1928-34*. Cambridge: Cambridge University Press, 1977.

Brown, Norman. *The United States and India, Pakistan Bangladesh*. Cambridge, Massachusetts: Harvard University Press, 1972.

Burke, S.M. *Landmarks of the Pakistan Movement*. Lahore: Research Society of Pakistan, 2001.

————. *Mainsprings of Indian and Pakistani Foreign Policies*. Minneapolis: University of Minnesota Press, 1974.

————. 'Quaid-i-Azam Jinnah's Decision to become Pakistan's First Governor-General'. In Ahmad Hasan Dani, ed., *World Scholars on Quaid-i-Azam Mohammad Ali Jinnah*. Islamabad: Quaid-i-Azam University, 1979.

Burke, S.M. and Salim Al-Din Quraishi. *The British Raj in India*. Karachi: Oxford University Press, 1995.

————. *Quaid-i-Azam Mohammad Ali Jinnah: His Personality and his Politics*. Karachi: Oxford University Press, 1997.

Callard, Keith. *Pakistan: A Political Study*. London: George Allen & Unwin, 1968.

Cameron, James. 'A Place of Politics'. In Frank Moraes and Edward Howe, eds., *India*. New York: McGraw Hill, 1974.

Chada, Yogesh. *Rediscovering Gandhi*. London: Century, 1997.

Chamberlain, M.E. *Britain and India*. Newton Abbot: David and Charles, 1974.

Chand, Duni. *The Ulster of India*. Lahore: Navajiwan Press, 1936.

Chand, Tara. *History of the Freedom Movement in India,* Vol. 4. Lahore: Book Traders, 1972.

Child, Davids. *Britain since 1945: A Political History*. London: Methuen & Co., 1986.

Chirol, Valentine. *India: Old and New*. London: Macmillan, 1921.

————. *Indian Unrest*. London: Macmillan, 1910.

Chughtai, Mohammad Abdullah. *Iqbal ki Suhbat Mein*. (Urdu). Lahore: Majlis-i-Taraqi-i- Adab, 1971.

Clarke, Peter. *The Cripps Version: The Life of Sir Stafford Cripps*. London: Allen Lane the Penguin Press, 2002.

Coatman, J. *Years of Destiny: India, 1926-32*. London: Jonathan Cape, 1932.

Cohen, D.L. 'The Concept of Charisma and the Analysis of Leadership', *Political Studies*, Vol. XX, No. 3 (1972).

Cohen, Stephen Philip. *The Idea of Pakistan*. Lahore: Vanguard, 2005.

Cohn, Bernard. *India: The Social Anthropology of a Civilization*. New Jersey: Englewood Cliffs, Prentice-Hall, 1971.

Close, H.M. *Wavell, Mountbatten and the Transfer of Power*. Islamabad: National Book Foundation, 1997.

Collier, Christopher and James Lincoln Collier. *Decision at Philadelphia: The Constitutional Convention of 1787*. New York: Ballantine Books, 1993.

Collins, Larry and Dominique Lapierre. *Freedom at Midnight*. New York: Simon and Schuster, 1975.

————. *Mountbatten and the Partition of India,* Vol. I. Delhi: Vikas, 1982.

Cooke, Colin. *The Life of Sir Stafford Cripps*. London: Hodder & Stoughton, 1957.

Copland, Ian. 'Quaid-i-Azam and the Nawab Chancellor: Literary Paradigms in the Historical Construction of Indian Muslim Identity'. In Mushirul Hasan, ed. *Islam, Communities and the Nation*. Delhi: Manohar, 1998.

Coupland, Reginald. *India: A Re-Statement*. London: Oxford University Press, 1945.

_____. *Report on the Constitutional Problem in India, Part I, The Indian Problem, 1833-1935*. London: Oxford University Press, 1968.

Cragg, Kenneth. *Counsels in Contemporary Islam: Islamic Surveys 3*. Edinburgh: University Press, 1965.

Cumming, John, ed. *Political India, 1832-1932*. London: Oxford University Press, 1932.

Dani, Ahmad Hasan, ed. *Quaid-i-Azam and Pakistan*. Islamabad: Quaid-i-Azam University, 1981.

_____, ed. *World Scholars on Quaid-i-Azam Mohammad Ali Jinnah*. Islamabad: Quaid-i-Azam University, 1979.

Darling, Malcolm Lyall. *Punjab Peasant in Prosperity and Debt*. London: Oxford University Press, 1932.

Desai, Mahadeo. *Maulana Abul Kalam Azad*. Agra: Shivalal Agarwala & Co., 1946.

Dilks, David. *Curzon in India: Frustrations*, Vol. II. New York: Taplinger Publishing Co., 1970.

Dion, Leon. 'The Concept of Political Leadership,' *The Canadian Journal of Political Science and History*, Vol. VI, No. 2 (1960).

Douglas, Ian Henderson. *Abul Kalam Azad: An Intellectual and Religious Biography*. Edited by Gail Minault and Christian W. Troll. Delhi: Oxford University Press, 1988.

Dumont, Rene. *Socialisms and Development*. New York: Praeger Publishers, 1973.

Dunbar, George. *A History of India*. London: Nicholson and Watson, 1943.

Durrani, F.K. Khan. *The Meaning of Pakistan*. Lahore: Sh. Muhammad Ashraf, 1946.

Dutt, R.P. *India Today and Tomorrow*. London: Lawrence Vinhart, 1955.

_____. *India Today*. London: Victor Gollancz, 1940.

Dwarkadas, Kanji. *India's Fight for Freedom, 1913-1937*. Bombay: Popular Prakashan, 1966.

_____. *Ten Years to Freedom*. Bombay: Popular Prakashan, 1968.

Edwards, Michael. *Nehru: A Political Biography*. Harmondworth: Penguin Books, 1973.

Eisenstadt, S.M. *Max Weber: On Charisma and Institution Building*. Chicago: University of Chicago Press. 1980.

Embree, Ainslie T. *India's Search for National Identity*. New York: Alfred A Knopf, 1972.

Enloe, Cynthia H. *Ethnic Conflict and Political Development*. Boston: Little Brown & Co. 1973.

Fagen, Richard R. 'Charismatic Authority and the Leadership of Fidel Castro,' *The Western Political Science Quarterly*, Vol. XVIII, No. 2, part I (1965).

Farquhar, J.N. *A Primer of Hinduism*. London: Oxford University Press, 1912.

Faruqui, Zia-ul-Hasan. *The Deoband School and the Demand for Pakistan*. Bombay: Asia Publishing House, 1963.

Fatimi, S. Qudratullah. 'Quaid-i-Azam and Lord Morley'. In Dani, ed., *World Scholars on Quaid-i-Azam Mohammad Ali Jinnah*.

French, Patrick. *Liberty or Death: India's Journey to Independence and Division*. London: Harper Collins Publishers, 1997.

Friedrich, Carl J. 'Political Leadership and the Problem of Charismatic Power', *Journal of Politics*, Vol. 23, No. 1 (1961).

Gandhi, Rajmohan. *Eight Lives: A Study of the Hindu Muslim Encounter*. Albany: State University of New York Press, 1986.

Gallagher, John, and Anil Seal. 'British India between the Wars'. In Christopher Baker, Gordon Johnson and Anil Seal, eds., *Power, Profit and Politics*. Cambridge: Cambridge University Press, 1981.

Gauba, K.L. *Passive Voices: A Penetrating Study of Muslims in India*. Lahore: Student Services, 1975.

Gilmartin, David. *Empire and Islam: Punjab and the Making of Pakistan*. London: I.B. Tauris & Co., 1988.

Glendevon, John. *The Viceroy at Bay*. London: Collins, 1971.

Golant, William. *The Long Afternoon: The British India, 1601-1947*. London: Hamish Hamilton, 1975

Gopal, Madan. *Sir Chhotu Ram: A Political Biography*. Delhi: B.R. Publishing Corporation, 1977.

Gopal, Ram. *British Rule in India: An Assessment*. London: Asia Publishing House, 1963.

————. *The Indian Muslims: A Political History*. Bombay: Asia Publishing House, 1959.

Gordon, Leonard A. *Bengal: The Nationalist Movement, 1876-1940*. New York: Columbia University Press, 1974.

Graham, G.F.I. *The Life and Work of Sir Sayyid Ahmed Khan*. Karachi: Oxford University Press, 1974.

Griffiths, P.J. *The British in India*. London: Robert Hale, 1946.

Hali, Altaf Husain, *Hayat-i-Javed*. (Urdu). Lahore: n.p., 1957.

Hameed, Syeda Saiyidain. *Islamic Seal on India's Independence, Abul Kalam Azad – A Fresh Look*. Karachi: Oxford University Press, 1998.

Hamid, Abdul. *Muslim Separatism in India*. Lahore: Oxford University Press, 1967.

————. *On Understanding the Quaid-i-Azam*. Islamabad: National Committee for Birth Centenary Celebrations of Quaid-i-Azam Mohammad Ali Jinnah, 1977.

————. 'Quaid-i-Azam and the Pakistan Demand', *Journal of Pakistan Studies*, Vol. II (1980).

Hamilton, Peter. *Knowledge and Social Structure*. London: Routledge & Kegan Paul, 1974.

Hanna, Willard, A. *Eight Nation Makers: Southeast Asia's Charismatic Statesmen*. New York: St. Martin's, 1964.

Haq, Mushirul, *Muslim Politics in Modern India, 1857-1947*. Meerut: Meenkshi Parakashan, 1970.

Haq, Noor-ul. *Making of Pakistan: The Military Perspective*. Islamabad: National Institute of Historical and Cultural Research, 1993.

Hardgrave, Robert L. *India: Government and Politics in a Developing Nation*. Harcourt. Brace & World, Inc., 1970.

Hardy, Peter. *Partners in Freedom – and True Muslims: The Political Thought of Some Muslim Scholars in British India, 1912-1947*. Lund: Student Literature Scandanavian Institute of Asian Studies, 1971.

————. *The Muslims of British India*. Cambridge: Cambridge University Press, 1972.

Hasan, Khalid, ed. *Quaid-i-Azam Mohammad Ali Jinnah: A Centenary Tribute, 1876-1976*. London: Information Division, Embassy of Pakistan, 1976.

Hasan, Mushirul, ed. *India Partitioned: The Other Face of Freedom*, Vol. 1. New Delhi: Roli Books, 1997.

————, ed. *Inventing Boundaries: Gender, Politics and the Partition of India*. New Delhi: Oxford University Press, 2000.

————, ed. *Islam, Communities and the Nation*. Delhi: Manohar, 1998.

————, ed. *Muslims and the Congress*. Lahore: Book Traders, 1980.

————. *Nationalism and Communal Politics in India, 1916-1928*. Delhi: Manohar, 1979.

Hasan, Syed Shamsul. *Plain Mr Jinnah*. Karachi: Royal Book Co., 1976.

Hassan, Javed. *India: A Study in Profile*. Rawalpindi: Services Book Club, 1990.

Hayat, Sikandar. 'Maulana Mohamed Ali and the Growth of Muslim Separatism in India,' *Pakistan Journal of History and Culture*, Vol. VI, No. 1 (1985).

————. 'Syed Ahmad Khan and the Foundation of Muslim Separatist Political Movement in India,' *Pakistan Journal of Social Sciences*, Vol. VIII, No. I-II (January-July-December 1982).

Hodson, H.V. *The Great Divide*. London: Hutchinson, 1969.

————. 'Quaid-i-Azam and the British'. In Dani, ed., *World Scholars on Quaid-i-Azam Mohammad Ali Jinnah*.

Hoffer, Eric. *The True Believer*. New York: Harper and Row, Perennial Library, 1966.

Hough, Richard. *Mountbatten: Hero of our Time*. London: Pan Books, 1980.

Huntington, Samuel P. *Political Order in Changing Societies*. New Haven: Yale University Press, 1968.

Hunt, Roland, and John Harrison. *The District Officer in India, 1930-1947*. London: Scholar Press, 1980.

Hunter, W.W. *The Indian Musalmans*. Calcutta: Comrade Publishers, 1945.

Husain, Azim. *Fazl-i-Husain: A Political Biography*. Bombay: Longmans, Green & Co., 1946.

Hutchins, Francis G. *The Illusion of Permanence: British Imperialism in India*. Princeton: Princeton University Press, 1967.

————. *India's Revolution: Gandhi and the Quit India Movement*. Cambridge: Massachusetts; Harvard University Press, 1973.

Ikram, Sheikh Muhammad. *Modern Muslim India and the Birth of Pakistan*. Lahore: Sh. Muhammad Ashraf, 1970.

————. *Raud-i-Kausar*. (Urdu). Lahore: Ferozsons, 1958.

Iqbal, Afzal. *Life and Times of Mohamed Ali*. Lahore: Institute of Islamic Culture, 1974.

Iqbal, Muhammad. *The Reconstruction of Religious Thought in Islam*. Lahore: Sh. Muhammad Ashraf, 1965.

Ispahani, M.A.H. 'Factors Leading to the Partition of British India'. In C.H. Philips and Mary Doreen Wainwright, eds., *The Partition of India: Policies and Perspectives, 1935-1947*. London: George Allen & Unwin, 1970.

Jackson, Stanley. *The Aga Khan: Prince, Prophet and Sportsman*. London: Odham Press, 1952.

Jafari, Syed Rais Ahmad. *Quaid-i-Azam Aur Unka Ehad*. (Urdu). Lahore: Maqbool Academy, 1962.

Jaffrelot, Christophe, ed. *A History of Pakistan and its Origins*. London: Anthem Press, 2002.

_____, ed. *Pakistan: Nationalism without a Nation*. London: Zed Books, 2000.

_____. 'The Rise of Hindu Nationalism and the Marginalisation of Muslims in India Today'. In Amita Shastri and A. Jeyaratnam Wilson, eds. *The Post Colonial States of South Asia: Democracy, Identity, Development and Security*. Richmond: Surrey, Curzon Press, 2001.

Jain, M.S. *The Aligarh Movement: Its Origins and Developments, 1858-1906*. Agra: Sri Ram Mehra, 1965.

Jalal, Ayesha. *Self and Sovereignty: Individual and Community in South Asian Islam since 1850*. Lahore: Sange-e-Meel, 2001.

_____. *The Sole Spokesman: Jinnah, the Muslim League and the Demand for Pakistan*. Cambridge: Cambridge University Press, 1985.

Jalal, Ayesha and Anil Seal. 'Alternative to Partition: Muslim Politics between the Wars', *Modern Asian Studies*, Vol. 15, No. 3 (1981).

Jones, Allen H. 'Mr Jinnah's Leadership and the Evolution of the Pakistan Idea: The Case of the Sind Provincial Muslim Conference, 1938'. In Dani, ed., *World Scholars on Quaid-i-Azam Mohammad Ali Jinnah*.

Jones, Kenneth W. 'Communalism in the Punjab: The Arya Samaj Contribution,' *Journal of Asian Studies*, Vol. XXVIII, No. 1 (November 1968).

Jonsson, Erland. *India, Pakistan or Pakhtunistan?* Uppala: Acta Universitaties Upsaliensis, 1981.

Josh, Soban Singh. *Hindustan Ghadar Party: A Short History*. New Delhi: People's Publishing House, 1979.

Kashmiri, Shorish. *Syed Attaulah Shah Bokhari*. (Urdu). Lahore: Maktaba Chittan, 1994.

Kaura, Uma. *Muslims and Indian Nationalism*. Lahore: Book Traders, n.d. reprint.

Kausar, Inam ul Haq. *Pakistan Movement and Balochistan*. Quetta: United Publishers, 1999.

Kazimi, Muhammad Reza. *Liaquat Ali Khan: His Life and Work*. Karachi: Oxford University Press, 2003.

_____. ed., *M.A. Jinnah: Views and Reviews*. Karachi: Oxford University Press, 2005.

Khairi, Saad R. *Jinnah Reinterpreted*. Karachi: Oxford University Press, 1996.

Khan, A. Sattar. 'The Role of Ulama and the Mashaikh in the Pakistan Movement,' *Journal of Research Society of Pakistan*, Vol. XXXVI, No. 2 (1999).

Khan, Abdul Waheed. *India Wins Freedom: The Other Side*. Karachi: Pakistan Educational Publishers, 1961.

Khan, Mohammad Ahmad. *Iqbal ka Siyasi Karnamah*. (Urdu). Lahore: Iqbal Academy, 1977.

Khan, Mohammed Raza. *What Price Freedom?* Karachi: Indus Publications, 1977.

Khan, Mohammad Yusuf. *The Glory of Quaid-i-Azam*. Multan: Carvan Book Centre, 1976.

Khan, Muhammad Anwar. *The Role of NWFP in the Freedom Struggle.* Lahore: Research Society of Pakistan, 2000.

Khan, Shafique Ali. *Mr Jinnah as a Political Thinker.* Karachi: Royal Book Co., 1974.

Khuhro, Hamida. *Mohammad Ayub Khuhro: A Life of Courage in Politics.* Karachi: Ferozsons, 1998.

Khursheed, Abdus Salam. *History of the Idea of Pakistan.* Lahore: National Book Foundation, 1977.

————. *Quaid-i-Azam aur Pakistan.* (Urdu). Karachi: National Book Foundation, 1976.

————. *Sarguzashat-i-Iqbal.* (Urdu). Lahore: Iqbal Acdemy, 1977.

Korbel, Josef. *Danger in Kashmir.* Princeton: Princeton University Press, 1954.

Kulkarni, Y.B. *Pakistan: Its Origin and Relations with India.* Delhi: Sterling Publishers, 1988.

Kulke, Herman and Dietmar Rothermund. *A History of India.* London: Routledge, 1999.

Lal, Kanhia. *British Land Policy and the Economy of the Punjab.* Lahore: New Publishers, 1937.

Lal, Ramji. *Political India, 1935-1942: Anatomy of Indian Politics.* Delhi: Ajanta Publishers, 1986.

Lasswell, Harold D., and Abraham Kaplan. *Power and Society: A Framework for Political Inquiry.* New Haven: Yale University Press, 1965.

Lateef, S.A. *The Great Leader.* Lahore: Lion Press, 1947.

Lewis, Bernard. *The Emergence of Modern Turkey.* Oxford University Press, 1967.

Lewin, Ronald. *The Chief: Field Marshal Lord Wavell, Commander-in-Chief and Viceroy, 1939-1947.* New York: Farrar, 1980.

Low, D.A. "Civilian Martial Law': The Government of India and the Civil Disobedience Movement, 1930-34'. In D.A. Low, ed., *Congress and the Raj: Facets of the Indian Struggle, 1917-1947.* London: Heinemann, 1977.

————, ed. *Congress and the Raj: Facets of the Indian Struggle, 1917-1947.* London: Heinemann, 1977.

————. 'The Government of India, and the first Non–cooperative Movement, 1920-22', *Journal of Asian Studies,* Vol. XXV. No.2 (February 1966).

————, ed. *The Indian National Congress: Centenary Hindsights.* Delhi: Oxford University Press, 1988.

Lumby, E.W.R. *The Transfer of Power in India, 1945-1947.* London: Allen and Unwin, 1954.

Lyall, Alfred. *Asiatic Studies: Religious and Social.* London: 1884.

Macdonald, Ramsay. *The Awakening of India.* London: Hodder & Stoughton, 1910.

Madani, Husain Ahmad. *Muttahida Qaumiat aur Islam.* (Urdu). Delhi: n.d.

Maddison Angus. *Class Structure and Economic Growth: India and Pakistan since the Moghuls.* New York: W.W. Nortorn, 1971.

Major, Andrew. *Return to Empire: Punjab under Sikhs and British in the mid-19th Century.* Karachi: Oxford University Press, 1996.

Majumdar, S.K. *Jinnah and Gandhi: Their Role in India's Quest for Freedom.* Lahore: Peoples Publishing House, 1976.

Malik, Hafeez. *Iqbal: the Poet-Philosopher of Pakistan.* New York: Columbia University, 1971.

_____. *Moslem Nationalism in India and Pakistan*. Washington D.C.: Public Affairs Press, 1963.

_____. *Sir Saiyyid Ahmed Khan and Muslim Modernization in India and Pakistan*. Karachi: Royal Book Co., 1988.

Malik, Iftikhar Haider. 'Regionalism or Personality Cult? Allama Mashraqi and the Tehreek-i-Khaksar in pre-1947 Punjab'. In Ian Talbot and Gurharpal Singh, eds. *Region and Partition: Bengal, Punjab and the Partition of the Subcontinent*. Karachi: Oxford University Press, 1999.

_____. *Sikandar Hayat Khan: A Political Biography*. Islamabad: National Institute of Historical and Cultural Research, 1985.

Malik, Ikram Ali, ed. *A Book of Readings on the History of the Punjab, 1799-1947*. Lahore: Research Society of Pakistan, 1970.

Malik, Muhammad Aslam. *Allama Inayatullah Mashraqi: A Political Biography*. Karachi: Oxford University Press, 2000.

_____. *The Making of the Pakistan Resolution*. Karachi: Oxford University Press, 2001.

Manglori, Tufail Ahmad. *Musalmanon ka Roshan Mustaqbil*. (Urdu). Delhi: Ilmi Delhi, 1945.

Maruf, Mohammad, ed. *Contributions to Iqbal's Thought*. Lahore: Islamic Book Service, 1977.

Mathur, Y.B. *Growth of Muslim Politics in India*. Lahore: Book Traders, 1980.

McDonough, Sheila, ed. *Mohammad Ali Jinnah: Maker of Modern Pakistan*. Lexington, Massachusetts: D.C. Heath & Co., 1970.

Mclane, John R. *Indian Nationalism and the Early Congress*. Princeton: Princeton University Press, 1977.

Mehr, Ghulam Rasul, ed. *Naqsh-i-Azad*. (Urdu). Lahore: Sheikh Ghulam Ali & Sons, 1959.

Menon, V.P. *The Transfer of Power in India*. Princeton: University Press, 1957.

Merchant, Liaquat H., comp. and ed. *The Jinnah Anthology*. Karachi: Oxford University Press, 1999.

Metcalf, Barbara Daly. *Islamic Revival in British India: Deoband, 1860-1900*. Princeton: Princeton University Press, 1982.

Metcalf, Thomas R. *The Aftermath of Revolt*. Princeton: Princeton University Press, 1964.

_____. *Land, Landlords, and the British Raj: Northern India in the Nineteenth Century*. Berkeley: University of California Press, 1979.

_____, ed. *Modern India: An Interpretative Anthology*. London: Macmillan Co., 1971.

Minault, Gail. *The Khilafat Movement: Religious Symbolism and Political Mobilization in India*. New York: Columbia University Press, 1982.

Mirza, Sarfraz Hussain. *Muslim Women's Role in the Pakistan Movement*. Lahore: Research Society of Pakistan, 1969.

_____. *The Punjab Muslim Student Federation, 1937-1947*. Islamabad: National Institute of Historical and Cultural Research, 1991.

Mitzman, Arthur. *The Iron Cage: An Historical Interpretation of Max Weber*. New York: Alfred A. Knopf, 1970.

Miyan, Muhammad. *Jamiat-ul-Ulama Kiya Hay?* (Urdu). 2 Vols. Delhi: Jamiat-ul-Ulama, 1946.

————. *Ulama-i-Haq aur unkay Mujahidana Karnamay* (Urdu). Delhi: Delhi Printing Works, 1946.

Moin Mumtaz. *The Aligarh Movement.* Karachi: Salman Academy, 1976.

Moon, Penderel. *Divide and Quit.* London: Chatto & Windus, 1961.

————. 'Jinnah's Changing Attitude to the Idea of Pakistan'. In Dani, ed., *World Scholars on Quaid-i-Azam Mohammad Ali Jinnah.*

————. *Strangers in India.* London: Faber & Faber, 1944.

Moore, Barrington, Jr. *Social Origins of Dictatorship and Democracy.* Boston: Beacon Press, 1966.

Moore, R.J. *The Crisis of Indian Unity, 1917-1940.* Oxford: Clarendon Press, 1974.

————. 'Jinnah and the Pakistan Demand', *Modern Asian Studies,* Vol. 17, No. 4 (1983).

————. 'The Problem of Freedom with Unity: London's India Policy, 1917-47'. In Low, ed., *Congress and the Raj: Facets of the Indian Struggle.*

Mosley, Leonard. *The Last Days of the British Raj.* London: Weidenfeld & Nicolson, 1961.

Muhammad, Shan. *Sir Syed Ahmad Khan: A Political Biography.* Lahore: Universal Books, 1976.

Mujahid Sharif al. 'Communal Riots'. In *A History of Freedom Movement,* Vol. IV Part II. Karachi: Pakistan Historical Society, 1963.

————. *Founder of Pakistan: Quaid-i-Azam Mohammad Ali Jinnah, 1876-1948.* Islamabad: National committee for Birth Centenary Celebrations of Quaid-i-Azam Mohammad Ali Jinnah, 1976.

————. *Ideology of Pakistan.* Islamabad: International Islamic University, 2001.

————. *Indian Secularism.* Karachi: University of Karachi, 1970.

————. 'Introductory'. In S. Hashim Raza, ed., *Mountbatten and Pakistan.* Karachi: Quaid-i-Azam Academy, 1982.

————. 'Jinnah's Place in History', *Journal of Pakistan Historical Society* (April 1966).

————. 'Jinnah's Entry into Mainstream Muslim Politics: A Reappraisal'. In Riaz Ahmad, ed. *Pakistani Scholars on Quaid-i-Azam Mohammad Ali Jinnah.* Islamabad: National Institute of Historical and Cultural Research, 1999.

————. 'Jinnah and the Congress Party'. In D.A. Low, ed. *The Indian National Congress: Centenary Hindsights.* Delhi: Oxford University Press, 1988.

————. 'Jinnah and Separate Electorates', *Pakistan Perspectives,* Vol. 6, No. 2 (July-December 2001).

————. 'The Khilafat Movement'. In S. Moinul Haq, comp., *Mohamed Ali: Life and Work.* Karachi: Pakistan Historical Society, 1978.

————. *Quaid-i-Azam Jinnah: Studies in Interpretation.* Karachi: Quaid-i-Azam Academy, 1981.

————. 'The Re-emergence of the All India Muslim League.' In *A History of Freedom Movement,* Vol. III, Part 2. Karachi: Pakistan Historical Society, 1963.

Mujeeb, M. *The Indian Muslims.* London: George Allen & Unwin, 1967.

Mujtaba, Fathullah. *Aspects of Hindu-Muslim Cultural Relations.* New Delhi: National Book Bureau, 1978.

Mukherjee, Ramkrishna. *The Rise and Fall of the East India Company.* Lahore: Book Traders, 1976.

Mukherjee, Uma and Haridas Mukherjee. *The Growth of Nationalism in India, 1857-1905*. Calcutta: Presidency Library, 1957.

Myrdal, Gunnar. *Asian Drama: An Inquiry into the Poverty of Nations*, Vol. 1. New York: Pantheon, 1968.

Naidu, Sarojini, ed. *Muhammad Ali Jinnah: An Ambassador of Unity*. Lahore: Atishfishan Publications, 1989.

Nanda, B.R. *Mahatma Gandhi: A Biography*. London: Unwin Books, 1965.

Nehru, Jawaharlal. *The Discovery of India*. London: Meridian Books, 1946.

Niazi, Syed Nazir. *Iqbal kay Hazoor*. (Urdu). Karachi: Iqbal Acdemy, 1971.

Nichols, Beverley. *Verdict on India*. Bombay: Thacker & Co., 1946.

Noman, Muhammad. *Muslim India: Rise and Growth of the All India Muslims League*. Allahabad: Kitabistan, 1942.

Noorani, A.G. 'Muslim Identity: Self-Image and Political Aspirations'. In Hasan, ed., *Islam, Communities and the Nation*.

Page, David. "The Development of Jinnah's Constitutional Ideas". In Dani, ed., *World Scholars on Quaid-i-Azam Mohammad Ali Jinnah*.

————. 'Mohammad Ali Jinnah and the System of Imperil Control in India, 1909-1930: A Case Study in Political Leadership and Constitutional Innovation'. In B.N. Pandey, ed., *Leadership in South Asia*. New Delhi: Vikas, 1977.

————. *Prelude to Partition: The Indian Muslims and the Imperial System of Control, 1920-1932*. Delhi: Oxford University Press, 1982.

Paige, Glenn D. *The Scientific Study of Political Leadership*. New York: Free Press, 1977.

Pandey, B.N. *The Break-up of British India*. London: Macmillan, 1969.

————, ed. *Leadership in South Asia*. New Delhi: Vikas, 1977.

Pandey, Deepak, 'Congress–Muslim League Relations, 1937-39', *Modern Asian Studies*, Vol. 12, part 4 (1978).

Pandey, Gyanandera. *Remembering Partition*. New Delhi: Foundation Books, 2003.

Pandit, Vijaya Lakshmi. *The Scope of Happiness: A Personal Memoir*. London: Weidenfeld and Nicolson, 1979.

Panikkar, K.M. *Asia and Western Dominance*. New York: Collier, 1969.

Papanek, Gustav F. *Pakistan's Development: Social Goals and Private Incentives*. Cambridge, Massachusetts: Harvard University Press, 1967.

Philips, C.H. 'Introduction'. In C.H. Philips and Mary Doreen Wainright, eds., *The Partition of India: Policies and Perspectives, 1935-1947*. London: George Allen & Unwin, 1970.

————. *The Partition of India*. Leeds: University Press, 1967.

Philips, C.H. and Mary Doreen Wainright, eds. *The Partition of India: Policies and Perspectives, 1935-1947*. London: George Allen & Unwin, 1970.

Pirzada, Syed Sharifuddin. *Evolution of Pakistan*. Lahore: All-Pakistan Legal Decisions, 1963.

————. *Quaid-i-Azam Mohammad Ali Jinnah and Pakistan*. Islamabad: Hurmat Publications, 1989.

————. *Some Aspects of Quaid-i-Azam's Life*. Islamabad: National Commission on Historical and cultural Research, 1978.

Pirzada, Sayyid A.S. *The Politics of the Jamiat Ulama-i-Islam Pakistan, 1971-1977*. Karachi: Oxford University Press, 2000.

Powell, B.H. Baden. *A Short Account of the Land Revenue and Its Administration in British India; with a Sketch of the Land Tenures.* Oxford: Clarendon Press, 1894.

Prasad, Beni. *The Hindu-Muslim Questions.* London: George Allen & Unwin, 1946.

Prasad, Bimal. *Pathway to India's Partition,* Vol. II, *A Nation Within a Nation:1877-1937.* New Delhi: Manohar Publishers, 2000.

Prawdin, Michael. *The Builders of the Mughul Empire.* London: George Allen and Unwin, 1963.

Qureshi, Ishtiaq Husain. *The Administration of the Sultanate of Delhi.* Karachi: Pakistan Historical Society, 1958.

———. 'Hindu communal Movements'. In *A History of the Freedom Movement,* Vol. III, Part, I. Karachi: Pakistan Historical Society, 1961.

———. 'Mohammad Ali Jinnah: But for his leadership there would have been no Pakistan'. *Impact International* (London), Vol. 9, No. 24 (28 December 1979- 10 January 1980).

———. *The Muslim Community of the Indo-Pak Sub-continent, 610-1947.* The Hague: Mouton & Co., 1962.

———. *The Struggle for Pakistan.* Karachi: University of Karachi, 1969.

———. *Ulema in Politics.* Karachi: Ma'aref, 1977.

Qureshi, M. Naeem. 'Ataturk and Armstrong's *Grey Wolf:* Myth and Reality.' *Proceedings of the Fifth International Congress on Ataturk, Dec. 8-12, 2003,* Ankara, Vol. VI (2005).

———. 'Jinnah and the Khilafat Movement, 1918-24'. In Dani, ed., *World Scholars on Quaid-i-Azam Mohammad Ali Jinnah.*

———. 'Jinnah and the Khilafat Movement (1918-1924)', *Journal of South Asian and Middle Eastern Studies,* Vol. I, No. 2 Iqbal Centennial Issue (December 1977).

———. *Pan-Islam in British Indian Politics: A Study of the Khilafat Movement, 1918-1924.* Leiden: Brill, 1999.

———. 'Some Reflections on the Mappilla 'Rebellion' of 1921-22,' *Journal of Research Society of Pakistan,* Vol. XVIII, No. 2 (1981).

Quershi, Salim, comp. *Jinnah: Founder of Pakistan.* Karachi: Oxford University Press, 1998.

Qureshi, Saleem M.M. 'The Consolidation of Leadership in the Last Phase of the Politics of the All-India Muslim League', *Asian Profile,* Vol. 1, No. 2 (October 1973).

———. *Jinnah and the Making of a Nation.* Karachi: Council for Pakistan Studies, 1969.

———. 'Mohammad Ali Jinnah: A Personality Assessment by His Contemporaries'. In Dani, ed., *Quaid-i-Azam and Pakistan.*

Qureshi, Waheed. *Pakistan ki Nazaryati Bunyadain.* (Urdu). Lahore: Educational Emporium, 1973.

———. *Iqbal aur Pakistani Qaumiyat.* (Urdu). Lahore: Muktaba Aliya, 1977.

Rahman, Matiur. *From Consultation to Confrontation.* London: Luzac & Co., 1970.

Rai, Lajpat. *A History of the Arya Samaj.* Bombay: Orient Longman, 1967.

Raj Jagdish. *The Mutiny and British Land Policy in North India, 1856-1868.* Bombay: Asia Publishing House, 1965.

Rajput, A.B. *Maulana Abul Kalam Azad.* Lahore: Lion Press, 1946.

———. *Muslim League Yesterday and Today.* Lahore: Sh. Muhammad Ashraf, 1948.

Rashiduzzaman, *The Central Legislature in British India, 1921-1947*. Dacca: Mallick Brothers, 1965.

Ratnam, K.J. 'Charisma and Political Leadership', *Political Studies,* Vol. XII, No. 3 (October 1964).

Ravoof, A.A. *Meet Mr Jinnah.* Lahore: Sh. Muhammad Ashraf, 1955.

Raza, Syed Hashim. 'Charisma of Quaid-i-Azam'. In Dani, ed., *Quaid-i-Azam and Pakistan.*

————, ed. *Mountbatten and Pakistan.* Karachi: Quaid-i-Azam Academy, 1982.

Riasanovsky, Nicholas V. *A History of Russia.* New York: Oxford University Press, 1977.

Rigby, T.H. 'Totalitarianism and Changes in Communist System', *Comparative Politics* (1972).

Rizwan-ul-Islam. 'Iqbal's Concept of Muslim Nationalism (Millat)'. In Maruf, ed., *Contribution to Iqbal's Thought.*

Robb, P.G. *The Government of India and Reform: Policies Towards Politics and the Constitution, 1916-1921.* London: Oxford University Press, 1976.

Robinson, Francis. 'Islam and Muslim Separatism'. In David Taylor and Malcolm Yapp, eds., *Political Identity in South Asia.* London: Curzon Press, 1978.

————. *Separatism Among Indian Muslims: The Politics of the United Province's Muslims, 1860-1923.* Cambridge: Cambridge University Press, 1974.

Rosen, George. *Democracy and Economic Change in India.* Berkeley: University of California Press, 1967.

Runciman, W.G. *Social Science and Political Theory.* Cambridge: Cambridge University Press, 1967.

Rustow, Dankwart, A. 'Ataturk as Founder of a State', *Daedalus,* Vol. 97, No. 3 (1968).

Sachau, Edward C. *Alberuni's India,* Vol. 1. London: Kegan-Paul & Co., 1914.

Saeed, Ahmad. *Iqbal aur Quaid-i-Azam.* (Urdu). Lahore: Iqbal Academy, 1977.

Saiyid, Matlub-ul-Hasan. *Muhammad Ali Jinnah: A Political Study.* Karachi: Elite Publishers, 1970.

Salik, Abdul Majid. *Zikr-i-Iqbal.* (Urdu). Lahore: Bazm-i-Iqbal, 1955.

Samad, Yunus. *A Nation in Turmoil: Nationalism and Ethnicity in Pakistan, 1937-1958.* New Delhi: Sage Publications, 1995.

Sayeed, Khalid bin. 'The Creative Process of Founding a State'. In Dani, ed., *World Scholars on Quaid-i-Azam Mohammad Ali Jinnah.*

————. *Pakistan: The Formative Phase, 1858-1947.* London: Oxford University Press, 1968.

————. 'The Personality of Jinnah and his Political Strategy'. In Philips, ed., *The Partition of India: Policies and Perspectives.*

————. 'Political Leadership and Institution Building under Jinnah, Ayub and Bhutto'. In Ziring, ed., *Pakistan: The Long View.*

————. *The Political System of Pakistan.* Boston: Houghton Mifflin Company, 1967.

Saiyid, Dushka H. *Muslim Women of the British Punjab: From Seclusion to Politics.* Foreword by Ainslee T. Embree. London: MacMillan Press Ltd., 1998.

Sen, Shila. *Muslim Politics in Bengal, 1937-47.* New Delhi: Impex India, 1976.

Seervai, H.M. *Partition of India: Legend and Reality.* Rawalpindi: Service Book Club, 1991.

Shafer, Boyd C. *Nationalism: Myth and Reality.* New York: Harcourt Grace & World, 1955.

Shafi, Alhaj Mian Ahmad. *Haji Sir Abdullah Haroon: A Biography.* Karachi: Begum Daulat Anwar Hidayatuah, n.d.

Shah, Sayed Wiqar Ali. 'Escape of Subhas Chandra Bose – Myth and Reality', *Oracle* (July–October 1996).

————. *Ethnicity, Islam, and Nationalism: Muslim Politics in the North-West Frontier Province, 1937-1947.* Karachi: Oxford University Press, 1999.

————. *Pir Saheb Manki Sharif, Syed Aminul Hasnat and his Political Struggle.* Islamabad: National Institute of Historical and Cultural Research, 1990.

Shahnawaz, Jahan Ara, and others, eds. *Quaid-i-Azam and Muslim Women.* Karachi: National Book Foundation, 1976.

Shahid, Mohammad Hanif. *Allama Iqbal aur Quaid-i-Azam kay Siyasi Nazariat.* (Urdu). Lahore: Sang-e-Meel Publications, 1975.

Shastri, Amita and A. Jeyaratnam Wilson, eds. *The Post Colonial States of South Asia: Democracy, Identity, Development and Security.* Richmond: Surrey, Curzon Press, 2001.

Sheikh, Atique Zafar, and Malik Mohammad Riaz, eds. *Quaid-i-Azam and the Muslim World.* Karachi: Royal Book Co., 1978.

Sherwani, Latif Ahmad. 'The Objective of Pakistan's Foreign Policy'. In M.A. Ahsan Chaudhri, et al., *Foreign Policy of Pakistan: An Analysis.* Karachi: Pakistan Institute of International Affairs, 1964.

Shils, Edwards A. 'Charisma, Order and Status', *American Sociological Review,* Vol. 30, No. 2 (1965).

————. 'The Concentration and Dispersion of Charisma', *World Politics,* Vol. XI, No. I (1958).

Siddiqui, M.H. and T.K. Gilani., eds. *Essays on Quaid-i-Azam.* Lahore: Shahzad Publishers, 1976.

Siedentop, Larry. *Democracy in Europe.* London: Allen Lane, the Penguin Press, 2000.

Singh, Amarjit. *Punjab Divided: Politics of the Muslim League and Partition, 1935-1947.* New Delhi: Kanishka Publishers, 2001.

Singh, Anita Inder. *The Origins of the Partition of India, 1936-47.* Delhi: Oxford University Press, 1987.

Smith, Anthony D. *Theories of Nationalism.* New York: Harper & Row, 1972.

Smith, Wilfred Cantwell. *Islam in Modern History.* Princeton: Princeton University Press, 1957.

————. *Modern Islam in India: A Social Analysis.* London: Victor Gollacz, 1946.

Spear, Percival. *India: A Modern History.* Ann Arbor: University of Michigan Press, 1961.

————. *India, Pakistan and the West.* New York: Oxford University Press, 1967.

————. *Twilight of the Moghuls: Studies in Late Moghul Delhi.* Karachi: Oxford University Press, 1980.

Srinivas, M.N. *Social Change in Modern India.* Berkeley: University of California Press, 1973.

Stepaniants, Marietta. 'Development of the Concept of Nationalism: The Case of Muslims in the India Subcontinent', *Muslim World,* Vol. LXIX, No. 1 (January 1979).

Stephens, Ian. *Horned Moon*. London: Chatto & Windus, 1954.

————. *Pakistan: Old Country, New Nation*. London: Ernest Benn, 1967.

Stokes, Eric. *The English Utilitarians and India*. London: Oxford University Press, 1959.

Suleri, Z.A. *My Leader.* Lahore: Nawa-i-Waqat Press, 1973.

Syed, Anwar. *Pakistan: Islam, Politics, and National Solidarity.* Lahore: Vanguard, 1984.

Symonds, Richard. *In the Margins of Independence: A Relief Worker in India and Pakistan, 1942-1949.* Karachi: Oxford University Press, 2001.

————. *The Making of Pakistan*. London: Faber & Feber, 1950.

Talbot, Ian. *Freedom's Cry: The Popular Dimension in the Pakistan Movement and Partition Experience in North-West India*. Karachi: Oxford University Press, 1996.

————. *India and Pakistan: Inventing the Nation*. London: Arnold, 2000.

————. *Khizr Tiwana: The Punjab Unionist Party and the Partition of India*. Surrey: Curzon Press, 1996.

————. *Provincial Politics and the Pakistan Movement*. Karachi: Oxford University Press, 1990.

Talbot, Ian and Gurharpal Singh, eds. *Region and Partition: Bengal, Punjab and the Partition*. Karachi: Oxford University Press, 1999.

Taylor, David. 'Jinnah's Political Apprenticeship, 1906-24'. In Dani, ed., *World Scholar on Quaid-i-Azam Mohammad Ali Jinnah.*

Tendulkar D.G. *Abdul Ghaffar Khan: Faith is a Battle*. Bombay: Gandhi Peace Foundation, 1967.

————. *Mahatma: Life of Mohandas Karamchand Gandhi*, Vol. II. Delhi: Ministry of Information and Broadcasting, 1960.

Terraine, John. *The Life and Times of Lord Mountbatten*. London: Arrow Books, 1970.

Thomas, F.W. *The History and Prospects of British Education in India.* Cambridge: 1891.

Thompson, Edward, and G.T. Garratt. *Rise and Fulfillment of British Rule in India*. Allahabad: Central Book Depot, 1962.

Tiger, L. 'Bureaucracy and Charisma in Ghana', *Journal of Asian and African Studies*, No. 1 (1965).

Tinker, Hugh. *Experiment with Freedom: India and Pakistan, 1947*. London: Oxford University Press, 1967.

————. 'Jinnah and the British Government, August 1945–August 1947: The Attainment of Agreement by the Assertion of Difference'. In Dani, ed., *World Scholars on Quaid-i-Azam Mohammad Ali Jinnah.*

————. *Re-Orientation*. London: Pall Mall, 1966.

————. *South Asia: A Short History*. New York: 1966.

Tomlinson, B.R. *The Indian National Congress and the Raj, 1929-1942*. London: Macmillan, 1976.

————. *The Political Economy of the Raj, 1914-1947*. London: Macmillan, 1979.

Trench, Charles Chenevix. *The Indian Army and the King's Enemies, 1900-47*. London: Thames and Hudson, 1988.

Tucker, Robert C. 'The Theory of Charismatic Political Leadership', *Daedalus*, Vol. 97, No. 3 (1968).

Vahid, Abdul. *Studies in Iqbal*. Lahore: Sh. Muhammad Ashraf, 1976.

Vekatachar, C.S. '1937-47 in Retrospect: A Civil Servant's View'. In Philips, ed., The *Partition of India: Policies and Perspectives*.

Voigt, Johannes H. 'Cooperation or Confrontation? War and Congress Politics, 1939-1942'. In Low, ed., *Congress and the Raj: Facets of the Indian Struggle*.

Waheed-uz-Zaman. *Quaid-i-Azam Mohammad Ali Jinnah: Myth and Reality*. Islamabad: National Institute of Historical and Cultural Research, 1985.

————. 'Quaid-i-Azam-Mountbatten Clash: The Question of Joint Governor-Generalship for India and Pakistan', *Journal of Pakistan Historical Society*, Vol. XXIV, Part III-IV (July-October 1976).

————. 'Quaid-i-Azam's Vision of Pakistan'. In Dani, ed., *Quaid-i-Azam and Pakistan*.

————. *Towards Pakistan*. Lahore: United Publishers, 1978.

————. 'Why the Quaid Left the Congress'. In Dani, ed., *World Scholars on Quaid-i-Azam Mohammad Ali Jinnah*.

Waseem, Mohammad. *Politics and the State in Pakistan*. Lahore: Progressive, 1989.

Wasti, Razi. *Lord Minto and the Indian Nationalist Movement 1905-1910*. Lahore: People's Publishing House, 1976.

Weber, Max. *From Weber: Essays in Sociology*. Translated, edited and with an introduction by H.H. Gerth and C. Wright Mills. New York: Oxford University Press, 1958

————. *The Theory of Social and Economic Organization*. Translated and edited by A.R. Henderson and Talbot Parsons. New York: Free Press, 1947.

————. *On the Methodology of Social Sciences*. Translated and edited by Edward A. Shils and Henry A Finch. Glencoe: Free Press, 1949.

Wilcox, Wayne. *Pakistan: The Consolidation of a Nation*. New York: Columbia University Press, 1963.

————. 'Wellsprings of Pakistan'. In Ziring, ed., *Pakistan: The Long View*.

Williams, Rushbrook. *The State of Pakistan*. London: Faber & Faber, 1962.

Wilner, Ann Ruth. 'Charismatic Political Leadership: A Theory.' Monograph. Princeton University Center of International Studies, 1968.

————. *The Spellbinders: Charismatic Political Leadership*. New Haven: Yale University Press, 1984.

Wilner, Ann Ruth and Dorothy Wilner. 'The Rise and Role of Charismatic Leaders', *The Annals of The Academy of Political and Social Sciences,* Vol. 358 (1965).

Wolpert, Stanley. 'Congress Leadership in Transition: Jinnah to Gandhi, 1914-1920'. In B.N. Pandey, ed., *Leadership in South Asia*.

————. *Gandhi's Passion*. New York: Oxford University Press, 2002.

————. *India*. Englewood Cliffs: Prentice-Hall, 1965.

————. *Jinnah of Pakistan*. New York: Oxford University Press, 1984.

————. *Morley and India, 1906-10*. Los Angeles: University of California Press, 1967.

————. *Nehru: A Tryst with Destiny*. London: Oxford University Press, 1997.

————. *Tilak and Gokhale: Revolution and Reform in the Making of Modern India*. Los Angeles: University of California Press, 1961.

Woodruff, Philip. *The Men Who Ruled India*. 2 Vols. London: Jonathan Cape, 1953 - 1954.

Wriggins, Howard, ed. *Pakistan in Transition*. Islamabad: University of Islamabad Press, 1975.

Yajnik, Indulal K. *Gandhi As I Knew Him*. Delhi: Danish Mahal, 1943.

Zachariah, Benjamin. *Nehru*. London: Routledge, 2004.

Zaidi, Z.H. 'Aspect of the Development of Muslim League Policy, 1937-47'. In Philips, ed., *The Partition of India: Policies and Perspectives*.

———. 'M.A. Jinnah: The Man, His Glimpses through Personal Correspondence'. In Dani, ed., *World Scholars on Quaid-i-Azam Mohammad Ali Jinnah*.

Zaman, Muhammad Qasim. *The Ulema in Contemporary Islam: Custodians of Change*. Princeton: Princeton University Press, 2002.

Zaman, Mukhtar. *Students' Role in the Pakistan Movement*. Karachi: Quaid-i-Azam Academy, 1978.

Ziegler, Philip. *Mountbatten*. New York: Harper & Row, 1985.

Ziring, Lawrence, 'Jinnah: The Burden of Leadership'. In Dani, ed., *World Scholars on Quaid-i-Azam Mohammad Ali Jinnah*.

———. *Pakistan: At the Crosscurrents of History*. Lahore: Vanguard, 2004.

Ziring, Lawrence, Ralph Braibanti, and W. Howard Wriggins, eds. *Pakistan: The Long View*. Durham: Duke University Press, 1977.

Zubairi, Masarrat Hussain. *Voyage Through History*, Vol. II. Karachi: Hamdard Foundation Press, 1984.

Zuberi, Muhmmad Amin. *Siyasat-i-Milliayah*. (Urdu). Agra: n.p., 1941.

Dissertations

Dodge, Norris Steven. 'Political Behavior and Social Change: Causes of the Growth of the Indian Electorate in the Last Half Century'. Unpublished Ph.D. Dissertation. Cornell University, 1971.

Lateef, Abdul. 'From Community to Nation: The Development of the Idea of Pakistan'. Unpublished Ph.D. Dissertation, Southern Illinois University, 1965.

Metz, William. 'The Political Career of Mohammad Ali Jinnah'. Unpublished Ph.D. Dissertation in South Asia Regional Studies, University of Pennsylvania, 1952.

Soomro, Muhammad Qasim. 'Muslim Politics in Sind, 1938-47'. Unpublished M.Phil Thesis, Quaid-i-Azam University, Islamabad, 1985.

Newspapers

Civil and Military Gazette (Lahore)
Dawn (Delhi)
Eastern Times (Lahore)
Inqilab (Lahore)
Nawa-i-Waqat (Lahore)
Pakistan Times (Lahore)

Journals

American Sociological Review
Annals of the Academy of Political and Social Sciences
Asian Profile (Hong Kong)
Australian Journal of Politics and History
Comparative Politics
Daedalus
Impact International (London)

Journal of Asian Studies
Journal of Asian and African Studies
Journal of Research Society of Pakistan (Lahore)
Journal of Pakistan Studies (Islamabad)
Journal of Pakistan Historical Society (Karachi)
Journal of South Asian and Middle Eastern Studies
Modern Asian Studies
Muslim World
Oracle (Calcutta)
Pakistan Journal of History and Culture (Islamabad)
Pakistan Journal of Social Sciences (Islamabad)
Pakistan Studies (London)
Political Studies
Western Political Science Quarterly
World Politics

Index

105, 109, 112-14, 118, 125, 127, 130, 132, 138, 140, 141, 144, 146, 151, 156, 158, 159, 160, 161, 162, 165, 170, 173, 174, 179, 182-86, 191, 192, 194, 196, 197, 198, 200, 203, 205, 207, 208, 209, 210-11, 213, 216, 218, 222, 225, 234, 241, 244, 251-55, 258, 265, 266-69, 270, 271-79, 282-85, 289, 290-99, 300-03, 305-08, 310-11, 314-15, 317, 319, 320, 324-27, 329, 332, 336-37, 339, 340, 345; Patna session 183-84; Ramgarh session 183-84; government 86, 102, 185, 289, 290; Ahmedabad session 45

Congress-League Pact, 97, 109

Constituent Assembly, 4, 29, 70, 162, 184, 195, 196, 291, 296, 302, 307, 324

Constitutional autocracy, 107

Constitutional government, 104-5

Convention People's Party, 344

Council of India Bill, 40

Coupland, Reginald, 97, 107

Craig, H., 170

Cripps Mission (1942), 7, 162, 254

Cripps Proposals, 3, 7, 192, 275

Cripps, Sir Stafford, 192, 272, 273-74, 282, 289, 291, 284, 299, 316, 328

Croft, Sir Fredrick, 37

Cunnigham, George, 258-9

Curtis, Lionel, 107

Curzon, Lord, 96, 105, 131

Czarist Russia, 193 *see also* Russia; Soviet Union

D

Dacca (Dhaka), Nawab of, 143

Dacca, 322

Daily *Aman,* 27

Dal, Shiromani Akali, 308

Dalmias, 93

Daoodi, Mohammad Shafee, 83, 142

Dar-al-Harb (Domain of War), 157

Darling, Malcolm Lyall, 148

Dar-ul-Ulum Deoband, 157, 261

Das, C.R., 161, 199

Dastis, 281

Daultana, Mian Ahmad Yar Khan, 154, 155

Daultana, Mian Mumtaz Muhammad Khan, 155

Daultanas, 155, 281

Day of Deliverance, 64, 67, 210, 251

Dayanand, Swami, 95

Defence of India Act of 1915, 116

Delhi Convention, 222

Delhi Durnest, 60

Delhi Muslim Proposals (1927), 30, 48, 50, 69, 83, 143, 341

Delhi, 47, 48, 50, 56, 82, 111, 130, 153, 174, 203, 211, 220, 236, 259, 301, 316; coronation ceremony 97; assembly 82

Deoband, 157, 164, 167, 172, 227, 261; Ulama of, 172

Deobandi, Mufti Muhammad Shafi, 176, 261

Dera Ismail Khan, 264

Desai, Bhulabhai, 279, 320

Desai-Liaquat Pact, 278-79

Devolution, 46, 94, 115, 121-24, 145-46, 149, 155, 173, 206, 325, 340

Din, Begum Mian Iftikhar-ud-, 263

Din, Khalifa Shuja-ud-, 59

Din, Mian Iftikhar-ud-, 265

Direct Action, 296-98

Dominion Status, 118-19, 120, 189, 273, 309, 314-15

Douglas Graham and Company, 37

Dufferin, Lord, 105

Durrani, F.K. Khan, 212, 224

Dutt, R.P., 96

Dwarkadas, Kanji, 82, 84, 185, 216-17, 296

Dyarchy system, 107, 146

E

East Bengal, 248, 283, 313-14, 330; Legislative Assembly 313

East Pakistan, 220

East Punjab, 313

Eastern Federal Union Insurance C., 246

Eastern zones, 198, 202-05, 211, 245

Education Committee, 249
Egypt, 252, 259
Elections of 1912, 109
Elections of 1937, 27, 58-60, 151, 205
Elections of 1945-46, 4, 171, 206, 227, 237, 240, 241, 244, 250, 255-56, 268, 280, 281, 287, 326, 329, 339
Ellenborough, Lord, 104
Elphinstone, Lord, 104
England, 79, 105, 106, 131, 272
English, 14, 157
Europe, 40, 131, 134, 187, 192, 277

F

Fazlul Huq Report, 64
Firangi Mahal, 172, 227
First World War, 13, 15, 17, 23, 131, 157, 158
Fourteen Points (1929), 5, 30, 50, 51, 69, 83, 84, 85, 127, 130, 143, 159, 165, 177, 194, 341
French, Patrick, 189
Frere, Sir Bartle, 105
Frontier Provincial Muslim League, 144

G

Gallagher, John, 118
Gandhi, M.K., 1, 6, 8, 9, 10, 11, 22, 28, 30, 32, 43, 44, 45, 48, 50, 51, 52, 53, 55, 60, 65, 66, 67, 68, 71, 74, 78, 81, 84, 87, 96, 98, 101, 102, 112, 114, 126, 129, 133, 150, 161, 162, 174, 179, 183, 184, 185, 186, 187, 196, 200-02, 204, 209, 211, 253, 274, 278, 280, 283, 291-92, 299, 305, 306, 309, 310-11, 315, 317-19, 320, 331, 334-35, 339, 345
Gandhi, Rajmohan, 60
Gandhi-Jinnah talks (1944), 7, 279, 280
Gangohi, Maulana Rashid Ahmad, 157
George, King, V, 97
George, Llyod, 142
German-Soviet Pact, 67
Germany, 15, 17, 34, 208, 317-18
Ghafoor, Arbab Abdul, 281
Ghana, 21, 344

Glancy, Sir Bertrand, 227, 232, 257, 258, 321
Gokhale, Gopal Krishna, 39, 40, 42, 73, 79, 82
Golra (Rawalpindi/Islamabad), 261
Gondal, 37
Gosh, Sudhir, 304
Government of British India, 307
Government of India Bill of 1934, 143
Government of India, 117-18, 120, 158, 265, 310
Gurdaspur, 321, 322

H

Habib Bank, 246
Habib brothers, 248
Habib Insurance Co., 246
Hailey, Sir Malcolm, 149
Haleem, A.B.A., 239
Haq, Maulvi Abul Kasem Fazlul, 59, 114, 128, 147, 152, 153, 207, 219, 220, 229, 231, 232, 256; headed League Coalition Ministry 231-32
Haque, Mazhar-ul-, 40
Harijan, 187, 291
Haroon, Lady Abdullah, 243
Haroon, Sir Abdullah, 26, 55, 143, 144, 147, 188
Hasan, Maulana Mahmudul, 157
Hasan, Professor Syed Zafar, 26, 188
Hayats, 155
Hearth, Carl, 187
Hidayatullah, Begum Daulat Anwar, 26
Hidayatullah, Sir Ghulam Hussain, 147, 257
Hindu Mahasabha, 47, 48, 49, 53, 54, 58, 82, 101, 180, 199, 329
Hindu raj, 39, 102, 153, 177, 208, 212, 215, 234, 281; rule 91, 95, 113, 123, 212, 234
Hinduism, 91, 96, 103, 106, 124, 125, 154, 195, 197, 200
Hindu-Muslim problem, 60-1, 68, 70, 159, 182, 268, 317, 337
Hindu-Muslim riots, 92, 98, 123

Resignation from Imperial Legislative Council 43; as Champion of Islam 321

Jinnah, Ruttie (Rattanbai), 83

Jinnah's formula, 198-99, 314, 317, 346

Jinnah-Sikandar Pact, 152, 170, 251

Joint Parliamentary Committee, 57, 121

K

Kabir, Humayun, 265

Kafir-i-Azam, 240

Kalat State, 313

Kali cult, 96

Kaplan, Abraham, 13

Karachi, 37, 79, 140, 247, 316, 327; Conference 66

Kashmir, 191, 217

Kathiawar, 37

Khaksar movement, 168, 215, 223, 266

Khaliquzzaman, Chaudhary, 26, 188, 204, 216, 219, 220, 227

Khalistan, 308

Khan III, Sir Sultan Mohammad Shah Aga, 6, 11, 27, 53, 83, 84, 85, 140, 141, 142, 143, 146, 150, 168, 169, 216; as President of the League of Nations Assembly 143-4

Khan, Abdul Ghaffar, 59, 134, 147, 169, 241, 254, 262, 263

Khan, Abdul Qaiyum, 244, 258, 281

Khan, Abdur Rahman, 264

Khan, Hakim Ajmal, 11

Khan, M. Abbas, 281

Khan, Maulana Zafar Ali, 87, 223

Khan, Nawab Iftikhar Hussain, 227

Khan, Nawabzada Liaquat Ali, 59, 85, 210, 216, 219, 220, 222, 256, 260, 269, 272, 279, 300-01, 311, 316, 320, 327, 330

Khan, Raja Ghazanfar Ali, 83, 300

Khan, Sardar Aurangzeb, 204, 227

Khan, Sardar Shaukat Hayat, 155, 236

Khan, Sir Mohammad Ismail, 83, 133, 227, 233

Khan, Sir Mohammad Said Ahmed, 144

Khan, Sir Muhammad Shah Nawaz, 26, 188

Khan, Sir Shafaat Ahmed, 144, 149, 150, 151, 169, 299

Khan, Sir Sikandar Hayat, 26, 59, 62, 145, 146-7, 148, 151, 152, 153, 154, 155, 156, 166, 170, 171, 187-8, 192, 206, 207, 208, 214, 215, 216, 218, 222, 223, 229-32, 256, 257, 266, 277; Scheme 222-23

Khan, Sir Syed Ahmad, 93, 95, 108, 109, 127, 132, 157, 172, 177, 178, 179, 182, 214, 336, 340, 342

Khan, Sir Zafrullah, 150, 216, 217

Khilafat (Caliphate), 43, 99, 129, 141, 142, 158, 159, 172, 179

Khilafat-Non-cooperation movement, 43, 44, 45, 46, 74, 98, 99, 116, 128, 141, 179, 187

Khomeini, Ayatollah, 22

Khudai Khidmatgars, 59, 86, 134, 147, 169, 241, 254, 258, 262, 313, 332

Khuhro, Mohammad Ayub, 147, 227, 257

Khurshid, Abdus Salam, 204

Kirpalani, Acharya J.B., 311

Kitchlew, Dr Saifuddin, 46

Korbel, Josef, 315

Krishak Praja Party, 59

L

Lahore Resolution, 73, 170, 182, 183, 186, 187, 189, 194, 198, 199, 200, 202-09, 210, 211, 213, 215, 216, 217, 218, 222-24, 257, 277, 278, 343

Lahore, 46, 51, 55, 154, 233, 242, 243, 321, 334

Laski, Professor Harold J., 193

Lasswell, Harold, 13

Lateef, Dr S.A., 26

Latif, Baji Rashida, 263

Latif, Dr Abdul, 188

Latin America, 21, 28

Lausanne, Treaty of, 45

Lawrence, Lord Pethick-, 29, 137, 193, 265, 266, 276, 282, 283, 290, 291, 293, 299, 327-28

League of Nations Assembly, 143

Lenin, Vladimir, 345, 347
Letters of Iqbal to Jinnah, 230
Lincoln's Inn, 37
Linlithgow, Lord, 74, 113, 135, 182, 183, 185, 186, 188, 189, 190, 191, 217, 265, 272, 276, 317
Lockhart, Lt. General, 262
London Times, 195
London, 1, 8, 30, 37, 38, 39, 40, 43, 51, 52, 54, 55, 56, 68, 74, 84, 101, 111, 133, 149, 302–03, 327, 330
Lucknow Pact (1916), 5, 41, 46, 49, 57, 58, 69, 97, 99, 123, 141, 177, 341
Lucknow Pact (1937), 61, 69, 101
Lucknow, 30, 41, 65, 172; Railway Station 63
Lundkhawar, Ghulam Mohammad Khan, 281
Lyallpur (Faisalabad), 80, 230

M

Macaulay, 107, 131
Macdonald, Ramsay, 51, 52, 53, 112
MacPherson, John Molesworth, 37
Madani, Maulana Hussain Ahmad, 10, 158, 163, 164, 166, 175
Maddison, Angus, 126, 168
Madras (Chennai), 128, 158, 233, 284
Mahmud, Syed, 86
Mahmudabad, Raja Mohammad Amir Ahmed Khan of, 55
Mahmudabad, Raja Muhammad Ali Muhammad Khan of, 29
Mahmudabad, Raja Sahib of, 29, 83, 227 *see also* Mahmudabad, Raja Mohammad Amir Ahmed Khan of 55
Majitha, Sir Sunder Singh, 148
Majlis-i-Ahrar, 134, 168, 329
Malaviya, Madan Mohan, 48, 50, 53
Malcolm, John, 104
Mamdot, Nawab of 26, 188, 227 *see also* Khan, Sir Mohammad Shah Nawaz
Mandal, Jogendra Nath, 300–01, 326
Manki Sharif, Pir of, Mohammad Aminul Hasanat, 241, 244, 261, 281
Mappillas, 116

Marhatta, 212
Mashaikh committee, 261
Mashraqi, Allama Inayatullah, 168, 215, 266
Maudoodi, Maulana Abul-Ala, 175
Maugham, W. Somerset, 27
Medina, 163
Mehta, Sir Pherozeshah, 39, 42, 73, 79
Memon Chamber of Commerce, 249
Memons, 93, 246
Memorandum of the Nineteen, 41
Menon, Krishna, 136, 310, 328
Menon, V.P., 30, 209, 303, 310, 345
Merrell, George R., 327
Middle East, 252, 269
Ministry of Refugees, 334
Mirza, M.B., 239
Mohammadan Anglo-Oriental Defence Association, 95
Mohani, Maulana Hasrat, 45, 142, 287
Mohatta Palace, 90
Montague, Edwin Samuel, 74
Moon, Penderel, 230
Moore, R.J., 5, 8, 9, 13
Moplah uprising, 45
Morley, Lord, 106, 132
Mosley, Leonard, 192
Mountbatten, Lord, 4, 32, 75, 90, 119, 192, 209, 244, 261, 263, 304–09, 310–14, 316, 318, 328–29, 331–34, 344
Mountbatten-Nehru relationship, 305
Muddiman Committee Report, 82
Mughal Empire, 93, 178
Muhammadan Education Conference (1886), 141
Muhammady Steamship Company, 247
Mujahid, Sharif al, 5, 6, 7, 102
Multan, 155, 261, 321
Munir, Muhammad, 334
Muslim Commercial Bank, 246, 247
Muslim India, 4, 6, 8, 10, 11, 12, 13, 26, 28, 181, 190, 234, 247, 252, 254, 255, 339, 341–43
Muslim Insurance C., 246
Muslim League Council, 40, 50, 55, 130, 144, 153, 226, 227, 286, 287, 296, 298, 300–01, 311–12, 322, 333, 344

258, 259, 261, 264, 281-84, 291-92, 306, 313-14, 321, 326, 343

North-Western Zone, 198, 202-05, 211, 245

Now or Never: Are we to Live or Perish forever?, 187

Nusserwanjee, Jamshed, 129, 130

NWFP, *see also* North-West Frontier Province

O

Old Boys Association of the Osmania University, 67

Old Vic Theater, 37

Orient Airways, 247

Osmania University, 67

Ottoman Empire, 23, 43, 45, 97, 98, 179

P

Page, David, 122

Pakistan Day, 216

Pakistan Federation, 264

Pakistan International Airlines (PIA), 248

Pakistan Movement, 7, 86, 172, 183, 236, 260, 262

Pakistan Resolution, 215, 222

Pakistan, 3, 4, 6, 7, 8, 9, 10, 13, 54, 73, 75, 77, 93, 102, 125, 152, 161, 164, 167, 170-2, 182, 187, 191, 194, 201-09, 210-13, 215, 217, 220, 221, 222, 223, 225, 226, 227, 230, 233, 234, 235, 236, 238, 239, 240-43, 245, 247, 250, 251, 253, 255, 259, 260, 261, 268, 269, 270, 275-79, 280-82, 284-86, 288-89, 290, 293, 296, 297, 305-08, 310-11, 314-17, 319, 321, 323, 330, 332-34, 336, 338-39, 343-45; economy 247

Pakistan, Constituent Assembly of, 4, 210, 263, 313, 316

Pal, Bepin Chandra, 39, 128

Pandit, Vijaya Lakshmi, 130

Papanek, Gustov F., 93

Parmanand, Bhai, 220

Parsis, 93, 158

Partition Plan (3 June 1947), 309, 311-12, 315-16, 344

Partition Resolution, 183

Pasha, Ismat, 168

Patel, Sardar Vallabhbhai, 29, 185, 310-11, 315, 324, 327, 335, 345

Persian, 157, 214

Peshawar, 244, 263, 266, 314

Petit, Sir Dinshaw, 83

Pirpur report, 64

Pirs, 237, 240, 241, 245, 261

Politik als Beruf (Politics as a Vocation), 14

Poonjah, Jinnahbhai, 37

Prasad, Rajendra, 200, 305

Pro-Congress Muslim, 73

Proposal for a Provisional Constitution: Synopsis, 282

Provincial Congress Committee, 102

Provincial Legislative Assembly, 149

Punjab Girls Students' Federation, 242

Punjab Muslim Students Federation, 208, 239-40

Punjab National Unionist Party, 148

Punjab Provincial Muslim League Women's Sub-Committee, 243

Punjab Provincial Muslim League, 229, 230, 250; President 313

Punjab Unionist Party, 155, 258 *see also* Unionist Party

Punjab University, 315

Punjab, 43, 46, 48, 49, 52, 56, 59, 62, 81-3, 93, 94, 95, 98, 99, 100, 109, 110, 111, 112, 116, 128, 135, 140, 143, 146, 147, 148, 149, 152, 154, 155, 156, 158, 169, 171, 179, 180, 204, 205, 206, 207, 215, 217, 227, 229, 230, 232, 233, 238, 239, 240, 242, 243, 244, 250-51, 254, 257, 261, 262, 263, 265, 266, 269, 277, 280-81, 283-84, 306-09, 310, 320-22, 329, 330-31, 334, 340, 343; Legislative Assembly 153, 169, 171, 208, 243, 313

Purna Swaraj, 61, 84, 99, 129, 163, 183

United Provinces (UP), 41, 50, 59, 60, 63, 64, 86, 113, 128, 144, 157, 158, 169, 214, 216, 232, 284, 292, 298
United States of America, 119, 208, 265
University of Karachi, 239
Urdu, 158, 163, 214, 223, 260
Usmani, Allama Shabbir Ahmad, 164, 167, 175, 212, 227, 240, 241
Usmani, Maulana Zafar Ahmad, 164, 167, 175, 241

V

Viceroy's Executive Council, 149, 231, 233, 254, 272, 277, 278, 279, 290, 301, 321
Viceroy's National Defence Council, 230-31, 242, 280
Vidyamandir scheme, 102

W

Wahab, Begum Shirin, 244
Waqf-alal-Aulad, 4-5, 38, 39, 166
War Advisory Council, 254, 272
Wardha scheme, 64, 67
Wavell Plan, 4
Wavell, Lord, 114, 119, 137, 174, 192, 209, 232, 234, 258, 259, 262, 265, 266, 276, 277, 278, 279, 280, 283, 286, 287, 290, 293-95, 297-99, 300-03, 316, 319, 320-21, 324, 326-27, 334

Wavell's Journal, 290
Weber, Max, 5, 13, 14, 15, 16, 17, 18, 19, 20, 24, 72, 236, 312
West Bengal, 126, 313
West Pakistan, 245, 248
West Punjab, 282, 313-14
Westminster, 108
White Paper, 55
Wilhelm, Kaiser, II, 15, 17
Willingdon, Lord Freeman-Thomas, 42-43
Willington, Lady, 328
Willners, Ann Ruth, 5, 20, 21, 22, 199
Willners, Dorothy, 5, 20, 21, 22, 199
Wolpert, Stanley, 5, 9, 10, 13, 213
Women's National Guard, 242
Wood, Sir Charles, 105
Wyatt, Major, 323
Wyatt, Woodrow, 289

Y

Yakub, Sir Mohammad, 55, 83, 142
Young India, 50

Z

Zaidi, Z.H., 255
Zaman, Waheed-uz-, 5, 6, 13
Zetland, Lord, 26, 53, 121, 189, 190, 191, 192, 218
Ziarat, 90